Professional Responsibility

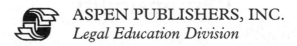

Professional Responsibility

Problems of Practice and the Profession

Second Edition

Nathan M. Crystal
Class of 1969 Professor of
Professional Responsibility
University of South Carolina

ASPEN LAW & BUSINESS
Aspen Publshers, Inc.
Gaithersburg   New York

Permissions
Aspen Law & Business
1185 Avenue of the Americas
New York, NY 10036

Printed in the United States of America

ISBN 0-7355-1207-8

2 3 4 5 6 7 8 9 0

Library of Congress Cataloging-in-Publication Data

Crystal, Nathan M.
    Professional responsibility : problems of practice and the profession / Nathan M. Crystal.—[2nd ed.].
        p. cm.
    ISBN 0-7355-1207-8
    1. Legal ethics—United States. 2. Legal ethics—United States—Cases. I. Title.

KF306.C79 2000
174'.3'0973—dc21

                                            00-020258

To Monroe Freedman, who has so often led the way

Summary of Contents

Contents

─────────── **Chapter 1** ───────────

Introduction to Professional
Responsibility   1

─────────── PROBLEM 1-1 ───────────
INTEGRATING PERSONAL VALUES AND
PROFESSIONAL LIVES: PROFESSIONAL HEROES
AND VILLAINS   8

─────────── **Chapter 2** ───────────

Defense and Prosecution of Criminal Cases   67

—————————— Chapter 4 ——————————
Ethical Issues in Civil Litigation: Limitations on Zealous Representation, Alternative Dispute Resolution, and Delivery of Legal Services   357

──────────── Chapter 5 ────────────

Ethical Issues in Office Practice   487

——————— Chapter 7 ———————
Special Ethical Problems of Law Firms

Preface

The fundamental theme of this book is the necessity for lawyers to develop a philosphy of lawyering. Chapter 1 outlines three interrelated aspects of a philosophy of lawyering. At the personal level, a philosophy of lawyering deals with the relationship between lawyers' personal lives and values and their professional roles. At the practice level, a philosophy of lawyering provides guidance for lawyers on how to resolve uncertain issues of professional ethics. At the institutional level, a philosophy of lawyering involves a critical examination of the fundamental values of the legal system, such as the adversary system of dispute resolution, methods of regulating lawyers, and mechanisms for delivering legal services. Chapter 1 also provides an overview of various rules and standards of professional conduct and the regulatory structure governing lawyers.

Chapters 2 through 6, the core of the book, present difficult problems of professional responsibility in various areas of practice — criminal defense and prosecution, civil litigation, office practice, government, public interest, and the judiciary. These chapters focus on both the practice and the institutional dimensions of a theory of lawyering. The problems do not have easy answers and will require you to learn to exercise personal and professional judgment within a framework of rules of ethics.

The book is organized first by area of practice (chapters) and then by ethical concept within area of practice (chapter divisions). Thus, problems of the client-lawyer relationship, confidentiality, conflicts of interest, limitations on zealous representation, and delivery of legal services appear in several chapters. I have chosen this organization for several reasons. First, context matters; for example, confidentiality problems in the criminal defense area differ from those in office practice. The book includes frequent cross-references so that you can compare confidentiality or conflict of

interest problems as they appear in different practice fields. I hope
that review and comparision of problems in various types of practice will deepen your understanding of ethical problems. Second,
choice of area of practice is an important aspect of a person's philosophy of lawyering. Organization by area of practice should help
you to obtain a feel for what it would be like to be, for example, a
criminal defense lawyer, a prosecutor, a civil litigator, or a business
attorney. The book contains references to the literature on various
areas of practice for those of you who would like to delve further
into these issues.

Instructors who used the first edition will notice three major
changes in this edition. I have moved the material dealing with the
adversary system and moral values from chapter 8 to chapter 1,
both to emphasize this material and to integrate it with the concept
of a philosophy of lawyering. Similarly, the material on delivery of
legal services, found in chapter 7 of the first edition, is now integrated into each of the chapters on areas of practice. It seemed to
me that a long chapter on delivery of legal services at the end of
the course was a large dose to take. In addition, incorporating the
material on delivery of legal services into each of the substantive
chapters gives a more complete picture of that area of practice,
one of the principal reasons for this method of organization. Because delivery of legal services material is the last section in chapters 2, 4, and 5, instructors who wish to treat this material at one
time can easily do so by assigning this material in a block. Finally,
this edition includes a new chapter 7 that focuses on ethical problems flowing from practice in law firms: supervision of lawyers and
nonlawyers, firm organization and breakups, practice with nonlawyers, and quality of life in law firms.

Please note that this book contains extensive references to the
Restatement (Third) of the Law Governing Lawyers. When the
book was being written, the Restatement was available only in two
proposed final drafts and one tentative draft. Publication of the
Restatement is expected in Spring 2000. In its final version, the
sections of the Restatement will be numbered from the sections
cited in the book. A Restatement Section Conversion Table has
been added to this book and can be found on page xxxvii. The
conversion table can be used to convert from draft to final section.

A number of instructors who used the first edition offered
comments to help me with the second edition. My thanks especially go to Anita Bernstein (Emory), Jennifer Brown (Quinni-

piac), David Cummins (Texas Tech), Marjorie Girth (Georgia State), Vincent Johnson (St. Mary's), and Lena Velasquez (California Western). Colleagues at South Carolina — Gregory Adams, Jane Aiken, Ladson Boyle, James Flanagan, John Freeman, Alan Medlin, Dennis Nolan, Eldon Wedlock, and Robert Wilcox — reviewed portions of the manuscript and made invaluable suggestions. As always, my wife, Nancy McCormick, provided terrific support and assistance.

Writing and revising this book has been both educational and pleasurable (at least, most of the time). I hope that students and instructors who use the book have a similar experience. Needless to say, I would appreciate receiving your comments on the book.

Nathan Crystal

January 2000

Acknowledgments

I would like to thank the following authors and copyright holders for permission to reprint portions of their work:

American Academy of Matrimonial Lawyers, Bounds of Advocacy, Standards 2.21 and 2.27, with comments. Excerpts reprinted with consent of the American Academy of Matrimonial Lawyers.

American Bar Association, Canons of Professional Ethics, Canons 33 and 35. Copyright 1967. Reprinted with permission of the American Bar Association.[1]

American Bar Association, Commission on Evaluation of Professional Standards (Kutak Commission), Discussion Draft of the Model Rules of Professional Conduct (Jan. 30, 1980), Rule 3.1. Copyright 1980. Reprinted with permission of the American Bar Association.

American Bar Association, Commission on Evaluation of Professional Standards (Kutak Commission), Proposed Final Draft of the Model Rules of Professional Conduct (May 30, 1981), Proposed Rule 1.6. Copyright 1981. Reprinted with permission of the American Bar Association.

American Bar Association, Commission on Multidisciplinary Practice, Proposed Rule 5.8. Copyright 1999. Reprinted with permission of the American Bar Association.

American Bar Association, Committee on Ethics and Professional Responsibility, the following Formal and Informal Opinions: Formal Op. 266 (1945), at 1-2; Formal Op. 280 (1949), at 1; Formal Op. 288 (1954), at 1; Formal Op. 335 (1974), at 3; Formal Op. 337 (1974), at 3; Formal Op. 339 (1975), at 3;

---

1. Copies of ABA publications are available from Service Center, American Bar Association, 750 North Lake Shore Drive, Chicago, IL 60611-4497. Telephone: 800-285-2221.

Formal Op. 346 (1982), at 9; Formal Op. 85-352, at 4; Formal Op. 87-355, at 2; Formal Op. 91-359, at 6; Formal Op. 91-361, at 4-5; Formal Op. 92-362, at 5; Formal Op. 92-363, at 4-5; Formal Op. 92-364, at 1-2; Formal Op. 92-366, at 12; Formal Op. 92-368, at 1-2; Formal Op. 93-372, at 2; Formal Op. 94-389, at 8-9; Formal Op. 95-396, at 21; Formal Op. 99-413, at 11; Informal Op. 89-1530, at 3. Reprinted with permission of the American Bar Association.

American Bar Association, Criminal Justice Mental Health Standard, §7-4.2, at 179-180 (1989). Copyright 1989. Reprinted with permission of the American Bar Association.

American Bar Association, Ethics 2000 Commission, Proposed Model Rule 1.6. Copyright 1999. Reprinted with permission of the American Bar Association.

American Bar Association, Model Code of Judicial Conduct (1990), Canon 3(E)(1)(d). Copyright 1990. Reprinted with permission of the American Bar Association.

American Bar Association, Model Code of Professional Responsibility, the following Disciplinary Rules and Ethical Considerations: DR 5-102, 7-102, 7-108(D); EC 5-9, 7-14, 7-21. Copyright 1983. Reprinted with permission of the American Bar Association.

American Bar Association, Model Rules of Professional Conduct and Comments as follows: Preamble, paragraph 8; Scope, cmt. 4; definition of knowingly; 1.2 cmts. 5, 7; 1.4 cmt. 1; 1.2(d); 1.5(b); 1.5(e); 1.6 cmts. 14, 15; 1.7 cmts. 7, 9, and 13; 1.8(c); 1.8(d); 1.13(b) (partial quote); 2.2(a)(2); 2.2 cmt. 2; 2.3 cmt. 4; 3.3(a)(4); 3.4(c); 3.4(e); 3.5; 3.6; 3.7(b); 3.8(d); 3.8(g); 4.2; 4.2 cmt. 2 (partial quote) and 4; 4.3; 4.4; 5.7; 6.1 (provision in effect from 1983-1993). Reprinted with permission of the American Bar Association.

American Bar Association, Real Property, Probate and Trust Section, Special Study Committee on Professional Responsibility, Comments and Recommendations on the Lawyer's Duties in Representing Husband and Wife, 28 Real Prop. Prob. & Trust J. 765, 796-797 (1994). Copyright 1994. Reprinted with permission of the American Bar Association.

American Bar Association, Real Property, Probate and Trust Section, Special Study Committee on Professional Responsibility, Counseling the Fiduciary, 28 Real Prop. Prob. & Trust J. 825, 852 (1994). Copyright 1994. Reprinted with permission of the American Bar Association.

American Bar Association, Real Property, Probate and Trust Section, Special Study Committee on Professional Responsibility, Preparation of Wills and Trusts That Name Drafting Lawyer as Fiduciary, 28 Real Prop. Prob. & Trust J. 803, 818-820 (1994). Copyright 1994. Reprinted with permission of the American Bar Association.

American Bar Association, Special Committee on Evaluation of Disciplinary Enforcement (Clark Committee), Problems and Recommendations in Disciplinary Enforcement 1-2 (1970). Copyright 1970. Reprinted with permission of the American Bar Association.

American Bar Association, Standards for Criminal Justice, Defense Function Standards 4-3.5 and 4-5.2 (3d ed. 1993). Copyright 1993. Reprinted with permission of the American Bar Association.

American Bar Association, Standards for Criminal Justice, Proposed Revised Defense Function Standard 7.7 (1979). Copyright 1979. Reprinted with permission of the American Bar Association.

American Bar Association, Standards for Criminal Justice, Prosecution Function Standard 3-5.7 (3d ed. 1993). Copyright 1993. Reprinted with permission of the American Bar Association.

American Bar Association, Standards for Criminal Justice, Providing Defense Services, Standards 5-1.2 and accompanying comments (3d ed. 1992). Copyright 1992. Reprinted with permission of the American Bar Association.

American Bar Association, Standards of Practice for Lawyer Mediators in Family Disputes, Black Letter Standards I through VI and special considerations for Standard I. Copyright 1984. Reprinted with permission of the American Bar Association.

American Bar Association, Young Lawyers Division, The State of the Legal Profession 1990 (1991), at 81. Copyright 1991. Reprinted with permission of the American Bar Association.

American Law Institute, Restatement (Third) of the Law Governing Lawyers §§12 cmt. f; 26; 30 cmt. c; 48 (Preliminary Draft #11, May 18, 1995); 117B; 118; 132; 159; 176 cmt. b; 179; 202(2)(b) and cmt. g(iii); 209 cmt. f; 211 illus. 5; 213 cmt. d(iii). Permission includes the above-listed material as renumbered in the final publication of the Restatement. Copyright by The American Law Institute. Reprinted with the permission of The American Law Institute. Quoted sections are from proposed final drafts Nos. 1 and 2 and tentative draft No. 8. Drafts are tentative until the Restatement is published in final form by the Institute.

American Law Institute, Restatement (Second) of Torts §§674 & 682 and comment d to §674. Copyright 1977 by The Amercian Law Institute. Reprinted with the permission of The American Law Institute.

Robert M. Bastress & Joseph D. Harbaugh, Interviewing, Counseling, and Negotiating, 391 and 402 (1990). Reprinted with permission of Little, Brown & Co. and the authors.

Hugo Adam Bedau & Michael L. Radelet, Miscarriages of Justice in Potentially Capital Cases, 40 Stan. L. Rev. 21, 49 and 57 (1987). Reprinted with permission of the authors.

Nicole T. Chapin, Note, Regulation of Public Interest Law Firms By the IRS and the Bar: Making It Hard to Serve the Public Good, 7 Geo. J. Legal Ethics 437, 439-440 (1993). Reprinted with permission of the Georgetown University Journal of Legal Ethics. Copyright 1993.

Nathan M. Crystal, Ethical Problems in Marital Practice, 30 S.C. L. Rev. 323, 328-332 (1979). Reprinted with permission of the South Carolina Law Review.

Nathan M. Crystal, The Lawyer's Duty to Disclose Material Facts in Contract or Settlement Negotiations, 87 Ky. L.J. 1055, 1097 (1998-1999). Reprinted with permission of the author.

Nathan M. Crystal, Unrelated Matter Conflicts of Interest, 4 Geo. J. Leg. Ethics 273, 308-309 (1990). Reprinted with permission of the Georgetown University Journal of Legal Ethics. Copyright 1990.

Charles P. Curtis, The Ethics of Advocacy, 4 Stan. L. Rev. 3, 14-18 (1951). Copyright 1951 by the Board of Trustees of the Leland Stanford Junior University. Reprinted with permission of the Stanford Law Review and Fred B. Rothman & Co.

Developments in the Law — Conflicts of Interest in the Legal Profession, 94 Harv. L. Rev. 1244, 1428-1433 (1981). Copyright 1981 by the Harvard Law Review Association. Reprinted with permission.

Arnold N. Enker, The Rationale of the Rule That Forbids a Lawyer to Be Advocate and Witness in the Same Case, 1977 Am. Bar Found. Res. J. 455, 457 and 463. Copyright 1977. Reprinted with permission of the University of Chicago Press.

Bruce Fein, Time to Rein in the Prosecution, 80 A.B.A. J. 96 (July

1994). Copyright 1994. Reprinted with permission of the ABA Journal.

William H. Fortune et al., Modern Litigation and Professional Responsibility Handbook §4.5, at 169-170 and §14.3.1, at 461-462 (1996). Copyright 1996. Reprinted with permission of Aspen Law & Business.

Monroe H. Freedman, Must You Be the Devil's Advocate? Legal Times of Washington (Aug. 23, 1993). Reprinted with permission of the Legal Times. Copyright 1993.

Monroe H. Freedman, The Morality of Lawyering, Legal Times of Washington (Sept. 20, 1993). Reprinted with permission of the Legal Times. Copyright 1993.

Monroe H. Freedman, Understanding Lawyers' Ethics, 13-14 and 155 (1990). Copyright 1990. Reprinted with permission of Matthew Bender & Co. and the author.

Stephen B. Goldberg et al., Litigation, Arbitration or Mediation: A Dialogue, 75 A.B.A. J., 70-72 (June 1989). Copyright 1989. Reprinted with permission of the ABA Journal.

Geoffrey C. Hazard, Jr. & W. William Hodes, The Law of Lawyering, (vol. 1), 537 and 588 (2d ed. 1994). Copyright 1994. Reprinted with permission of Aspen Law & Business.

Robert C. Heist, The Tripartite Relationship and the Insurer's Duty to Defend Contrasted with Its Desire to Manage and Control Litigation Through the Introduction of the Legal Audit, 602 PLI/Lit 221, 230-233 (1999). Reprinted with permission of Robert C. Heist.

Michael Horowitz, Making Ethics Real, Making Ethics Work: A Proposal for Contingency Fee Reform, 44 Emory L.J. 173, 175-176 (1995). Reprinted with permission of the Emory Law Journal and the author.

Oliver A. Houck, With Charity for All, 93 Yale L.J. 1415, 1439-1443 (1984). Reprinted with permission of The Yale Law Journal Company, Fred B. Rothman & Company, and the author.

Catherine J. Lanctot, The Duty of Zealous Advocacy and the Ethics of the Federal Government Lawyer: The Three Hardest Questions, 64 S. Cal. L. Rev. 951, 955-957 (1991). Reprinted with permission of the Southern California Law Review.

David Luban, Lawyers and Justice: An Ethical Study, 84 (1988). Copyright 1988 by Princeton University Press. Reprinted with permission of Princeton University Press.

Gerald E. Lynch, The Lawyer as Informer, 1986 Duke L.J. 491, 537. Reprinted with permission of the Duke Law Journal.

Ronald E. Mallen & Jeffrey M. Smith, Legal Malpractice, (vol. 4) §30.6, at 20 (4th ed. 1996). Reprinted with permission of West Group.

Sara Mathias, Electing Justice: A Handbook of Judicial Election Reforms, 5 (1990). Reprinted with permission of the American Judicature Society.

Geoffrey P. Miller, Government Lawyers' Ethics in a System of Checks and Balances, 54 U. Chi. L. Rev. 1293, 1294-1295 (1987). Reprinted with permission of the University of Chicago Law Review.

Leslie A. Minkus, The Sale of a Law Practice: Toward a Professionally Responsible Approach, 12 Golden Gate U.L. Rev. 353, 356-357 (1982). Reprinted with permission of the Golden Gate University Law Review and Leslie A. Minkus.

John B. Mitchell, The Ethics of the Criminal Defense Attorney — New Answers to Old Questions, 32 Stan. L. Rev. 293, 296-303, 321-323, 326-331 (1980). Copyright 1980 by the Board of Trustees of the Leland Stanford Junior University. Reprinted with permission of the Stanford Law Review and Fred B. Rothman & Co.

National Association of Criminal Defense Lawyers, Adv. Op. 92-2, The Champion, at 26 (Mar. 1993). Reprinted with permission of the National Association of Criminal Defense Lawyers.

New Jersey Supreme Court Ethics Advisory Committee, Adv. Op. 454, 1980 WL 78467. Reprinted with permission of Westlaw.

Lee A. Pizzimenti, Prohibiting Lawyers from Assisting in Unconscionable Transactions: Using an Overt Tool, 72 Marq. L. Rev. 151, 174 (1989). Reprinted with permission of the Marquette Law Review.

Ted Schneyer, Moral Philosophy's Standard Misconception of Legal Ethics, 1984 Wis. L. Rev. 1529, 1532-1533. Reprinted with permission of the author.

E. Wayne Thode, Reporter's Notes to the Code of Judicial Conduct, 84-85 (1974). Copyright 1974. Reprinted with permission of the American Bar Association.

Michael Tigar, Setting the Record Straight on the Defense of John Demjanjuk, Legal Times of Washington (Sept. 6, 1993). Reprinted with permission of the Legal Times. Copyright 1993.

United States Department of Justice, U.S. Attorneys' Manual titles 9-105.600 and 9-119.200 (1997). Reprinted with permission of the United States Department of Justice.

Rodney J. Uphoff, The Role of the Criminal Defense Lawyer in Representing the Mentally Impaired Defendant: Zealous Advocate or Officer of the Court? 1988 Wis. L. Rev. 65, 99. Reprinted with permission of the Wisconsin Law Review.

Lyle Warrick, Judicial Selection in the United States: A Compendium of Provisions, 1993, page v. Reprinted with permission of the American Judicature Society.

James J. White, Machiavelli and the Bar: Ethical Limitations on Lying in Negotiation, 1980 Am. B. Found. Res. J. 926, 927-928. Copyright 1980. Reprinted with permission of the University of Chicago Press.

Wigmore on Evidence (Vol. 8) §2292, at 554 (McNaughton ed. 1961). Reprinted with permission of Little, Brown & Co.

Charles W. Wolfram, Modern Legal Ethics §13.5.8, at 724 (1986). Reprinted with permission of the West Publishing Corporation. Copyright 1986.

Restatement Section
Conversion Table

This book contains extensive references to the Restatement (Third) of the Law Governing Lawyers. When the book was being written, the Restatement was available only in two proposed final drafts and one tentative draft. Publication of the Restatement is expected in spring 2000. In its final version, the sections of the Restatement will be renumbered from the sections cited in the book. The following table can be used to convert from draft to final section. In addition, the final version of the Restatement has some editorial revisions from the drafts.

Restatement Draft Section	Restatement Final Section	Restatement Draft Section	Restatement Final Section
1	1	28	16
2	2	29	17
3	3	29A	18
4	4	30	19
5	5	31	20
6	6	32	21
7	7	33	22
8	8	34	23
No 9		35	24
10	9	No 36	
11	10	37	25
12	11	38	26
13	12	39	27
14	13	40	28
26	14	41	29
27	15	42	30

Restatement Draft Section	Restatement Final Section	Restatement Draft Section	Restatement Final Section
43	31	118	68
44	32	119	69
45	33	120	70
46	34	121	71
47	35	122	72
48	36	123	73
49	37	124	74
50	38	125	75
51	39	126	76
52	40	127	77
53	41	128	78
54	42	129	79
55	43	130	80
56	44	131	81
57	45	132	82
58	46	133	83
59	47	134A	84
71	48	134B	85
No section in		135	86
tentative draft	49	136	87
72	50	137	88
73	51	138	89
74	52	139	90
75	53	140	91
76	54	141	92
76A	55	142	93
77	56	151	94
78	57	152	95
79	58	No 153	
111	59	No 154	
112	60	155	96
113	61	156	97
114	62	157	98
115	63	158	99
116	64	159	100
117	65	No 160	
117A	66	161	101
117B	67	162	102

Restatement Draft Section	Restatement Final Section	Restatement Draft Section	Restatement Final Section
163	103	180	120
164	104	201	121
165	105	202	122
166	106	203	123
167	107	204	124
168	108	No 205	
169	109	206	125
170	110	207	126
171	111	208	127
172	112	209	128
173	113	210	129
174	114	211	130
175	115	212	131
176	116	213	132
177	117	214	133
178	118	215	134
179	119	216	135

Professional
Responsibility

Chapter 1

Introduction to Professional Responsibility

A. The Foundations of Professional Responsibility and the Concept of a Philosophy of Lawyering

Issues of professional responsibility pose some of the most difficult problems that lawyers face in practice. The perplexing nature of these problems usually flows from the fact that troubling issues of professional ethics involve tensions or conflicts among three ideas that are central to the lawyer's role: the lawyer as fiduciary, the lawyer as an officer of the court functioning in an adversarial system, and the lawyer as an individual with personal values and interests. As the Preamble to the American Bar Association's Model Rules of Professional Conduct says:

> Virtually all difficult ethical problems arise from conflict between a lawyer's responsibilities to clients, to the legal system and to the lawyer's own interest in remaining an upright person while earning a satisfactory living.

Model Rules, Preamble, ¶8.

1

1. The Lawyer as Fiduciary

Courts, disciplinary bodies, and scholars often state that lawyers owe fiduciary obligations to their clients. As we will see, many of the rules of professional ethics can be understood as expressing fiduciary duties of attorneys. In addition, the law of agency, which governs the client-lawyer relationship, also defines the nature of fiduciary obligations. Indeed, one leading scholar of professional ethics, Professor Charles Wolfram, has referred to lawyers as "fiduciary agents."[1]

What does it mean to say that a lawyer is a fiduciary? A fiduciary relationship is different from an arm's-length business relationship. In an arm's-length transaction the parties do not have obligations to protect the interests of the other party, although they do owe each other certain obligations, such as the duty not to engage in fraud. Instead, parties to an ordinary business transaction have the responsibility to protect their own interests. By contrast, fiduciaries have special obligations to care for and to protect the interests of their beneficiaries or clients.[2] While fiduciary relationships may have contractual aspects (for example, fee agreements between lawyers and clients), the contractual aspects of fiduciary relationships are secondary to the duties that fiduciaries owe to their clients. What are these fiduciary duties?

The fiduciary obligations that lawyers owe their clients include three specific duties: First, attorneys owe their clients a *duty of competence*, a duty expressed in American Bar Association (ABA) Model Rule 1.1. See also Model Rule 1.3 (duty to handle matter with reasonable diligence and promptness).[3] Section B below discusses the method of adoption of rules of professional conduct and the ABA's role in the process. Note that the duty of competence expressed in Model Rule 1.1 goes beyond simple knowledge of the law to encompass both skills and character. Lawyers who violate

---

1. Charles W. Wolfram, Modern Legal Ethics 145 (1986) [hereinafter Wolfram, Modern Legal Ethics]. On the relationship between agency law and professional responsibility see Deborah A. DeMott, The Lawyer as Agent, 67 Fordham L. Rev. 301 (1998).

2. See Restatement (Second) of Agency §13, cmt. *a* (1958).

3. See also id. §379(1) (agent subject to duty to principal to act with standard care and with the skill that is standard in locality for kind of work that agent is employed to perform and, in addition, to exercise any special skill that agent has).

the duty of competence not only commit an ethical transgression but also can be held liable to their clients for damages.[4] Indeed, courts are increasingly willing to hold attorneys liable even to third parties who are not clients.[5]

Second, attorneys owe their clients a *duty of loyalty*. The ethical rules dealing with conflicts of interest express this concept of loyalty. Conflicts of interest can arise in various forms: between current clients in a single matter or in unrelated matters (Model Rule 1.7), between a current client and a former client (Model Rule 1.9), conflicts between the interest of a client and a lawyer's personal or financial interest (Model Rule 1.8(a)).[6]

The rules dealing with conflicts of interest are rarely absolute. For example, a lawyer is not necessarily precluded under Model Rule 1.9 from undertaking representation against a former client. The lawyer may do so, even without the former client's consent, if the current and former matters are not "substantially related."[7] The fact that the rules do not adopt a per se prohibition on representation against a former client shows that the issue involves interests in addition to those of the former client. When we discuss former client conflicts of interest, we will examine those interests in more detail.

Third, attorneys owe their clients a *duty of confidentiality*. While closely related to the duty of loyalty, the obligation of confidentiality is important enough to warrant separate treatment. Attorneys have an ethical obligation to maintain confidentiality of information. Model Rule 1.6 broadly expresses this duty as follows: "A lawyer shall not reveal information relating to representation of a client unless the client consents after consultation. . . ."[8] Like the rules dealing with conflicts of interest, the duty

4. See generally Ronald E. Mallen & Jeffrey M. Smith, Legal Malpractice (4th ed. 1996) [hereinafter Mallen & Smith, Legal Malpractice]; Manuel R. Ramos, Legal Malpractice: The Profession's Dirty Little Secret, 47 Vand. L. Rev. 1657 (1994).
5. E.g., Lucas v. Hamm, 364 P.2d 685 (Cal. 1961) (attorney who negligently drafted will liable to beneficiaries who were deprived of bequest); Bohn v. Cody, 832 P.2d 71 (Wash. 1992) (en banc) (attorney may be liable to parents of his client for negligent misrepresentation in transaction involving refinancing of client's home).
6. See also Restatement (Second) of Agency §387 (1958).
7. See id. §396 (after termination of relationship agent "has no duty not to compete with the principal").
8. See also id. §395.

of confidentiality is not absolute. Rule 1.6 provides a number of exceptions to the duty, exceptions that express interests thought to be sufficiently important to override the general duty of confidentiality.[9]

The scope and limitations of the duty of confidentiality have been among the most controversial issues facing the profession in recent years. Debate continues to rage over issues such as whether lawyers should be required to reveal perjury committed by criminal defendants and whether lawyers must reveal information showing that clients have committed fraud in business transactions.

2.   *The Lawyer as an Officer of the Court Functioning in an Adversarial System of Justice*

Professional obligations would be difficult enough if lawyers simply owed fiduciary obligations to their clients. However, lawyers serve not only as fiduciaries but also as officers of the court functioning in an adversarial system of justice.

What is meant by an *adversarial system of justice*? In broad terms an adversarial system is characterized by (1) a neutral decisionmaker, (2) competent advocates zealously presenting the positions of each of the interested parties, and (3) rules of procedure fairly designed to allow the presentation of relevant evidence to the decisionmaker.[10] A number of rules of professional conduct that we will study are designed to preserve the integrity and proper functioning of the adversarial system. For example, lawyers may not make false statements of law or fact to tribunals (Model Rule 3.3); try to influence judges, jurors, or other officials by improper means (Rule 3.5); or engage in trial publicity that has a substantial likelihood of materially prejudicing a proceeding (Rule 3.6).

Like other rules of professional conduct, the rules dealing with the maintenance of the adversarial system are subject to ex-

---

9. Similarly, agency law recognizes exceptions to the duty of confidentiality. The Restatement of Agency provides that an agent is privileged to reveal confidential information to protect the superior interest of the agent or of a third person, including information that the principal is committing or about to commit a crime. Id. §395, cmt. *f.*

10. Charles W. Sorenson, Jr., Disclosure Under Federal Rule of Civil Procedure 26(a) — "Much Ado about Nothing?" 46 Hastings L.J. 679, 764 (1995).

ceptions and qualifications. For example, consider the possibility of what could be called a "pure" adversarial system. Under such a system, lawyers would have no obligation to evaluate the merits of their clients' cases. If a client wished to bring a case in court, the lawyer could do so. Indeed, we might even go further, viewing lawyers as, in essence, common carriers, required to bring an action in court if clients wanted to employ their services. The prevailing conception of the adversarial system is not, however, this pure version. Under the standard view of the adversarial system, the lawyer may not bring an action, indeed may not file any document in court, when the claim would be frivolous. See Model Rule 3.1 and Federal Rule of Civil Procedure 11. We will consider these limitations in Problem 4-1.

Many lawyers function in capacities that do not involve litigation. A growing body of law and commentary is focusing on the lawyer's role as what might be called "an officer of the regulatory system." For example, lawyers who engage in securities transactions may not continue to represent a client if the lawyer knows that the client is perpetrating a fraud on investors. At a minimum, the lawyer would be required to withdraw from representation. We will consider the issue of lawyers' disclosure obligations in connection with business transactions in Problem 5-2.[11]

3. The Lawyer as a Person with Personal and Financial Interests

Our lives have many dimensions: work, family, religion, community. As a professional occupation law is or will soon be an important part of your lives, but most of us hope that the law will not become our entire life. Personal interests and professional obligations interact in various and complex ways. Since the practice of law is both a profession and a livelihood for most lawyers, the relationship between the business and professional aspects of practice is significant. The practice of law has become much more competitive in recent years. Solo practitioners, small to medium-sized firms, and mega-firms practicing throughout the country and

---

11. See generally Developments in the Law — Lawyers' Responsibilities and Lawyers' Responses, 107 Harv. L. Rev. 1547, 1556 (1994) (exploring the "diverse and sometimes conflicting responsibilities of the modern-day lawyer").

the world face growing economic pressures. In part, the pressure flows from changes in the market for legal services, including increased advertising and solicitation by lawyers and greater scrutiny of fees by clients such as insurance companies.

The rules of professional conduct deal to a limited degree with the business aspects of legal practice. The rules contain some regulation of fee agreements and business transactions between lawyers and clients (Model Rules 1.5 and 1.8(a)), limitations on advertising and solicitation (Model Rules 7.1–7.5), and prohibitions on unauthorized practice of law (Model Rule 5.5). But the formal rules only touch the ways in which business considerations shape a whole range of issues of professional ethics, such as conflicts of interest, establishment of legal fees, and marketing of legal services. Moreover, the rules barely hint at the relationship between the business pressure of practice and the personal lives of lawyers.

Professional obligations can involve personal values and interests at a level deeper than financial. For example, a lawyer who is opposed to abortion may be appointed to represent a minor who is seeking the right to have an abortion. A lawyer who strongly supports the rights of gays and lesbians may represent a testator who has decided to disinherit his gay son. Problem 5-4 considers issues involved in counseling clients in estate planning.

4.   *The Concept of a Philosophy of Lawyering*

The tensions among these central aspects of a lawyer's role generate the need for what can be called a "philosophy of lawyering," a general approach to dealing with conflicts among these fundamental ideas. A philosophy of lawyering operates at three interrelated levels: the personal, the practice, and the institutional.

At the personal level a philosophy of lawyering focuses on how lawyers integrate their personal and professional lives. For example, consider the dilemma facing lawyers who wish to advance their professional careers without sacrificing the needs of their families in the process. Or think about the problem facing lawyers who may be asked by clients or senior lawyers to engage in conduct that they find personally distasteful although not illegal.

Lawyers choose how they integrate their personal and professional lives. These choices can be made intelligently, based on thoughtful analysis of the relevant considerations, or they can be made haphazardly, by default, or even by others on the lawyer's behalf. An important aspect of how you decide to integrate the personal and the professional is your choice of type of practice. Different types of practice will make distinctive demands on your time and energies and will provide disparate forms of rewards. In addition, the nature of the ethical problems and the tensions you face will vary depending on the type of practice you choose. For example, in private business or commercial practice you will usually not encounter problems of pretrial publicity, but you will certainly face issues of conflicts of interest, and you may face difficult questions of how to deal with client fraud. You cannot avoid difficult ethical problems regardless of your choice of type of practice, but you can shape the nature of the problems you face. Thus, as you begin to develop a philosophy of lawyering, you will want to consider a number of questions:

1. What type of practice do I see myself going into: plaintiff's litigation, corporate law, prosecution or defense, legal services? Large or small organization? What area of the country or the world?

2. What types of ethical problems am I likely to encounter in this type of practice?

3. What level of income do I aspire to have? Will the practice that I plan to undertake meet this goal?

4. What kind of personal life do I wish to have? Will the demands of the type of practice that I envision allow me to have the kind of personal life I desire?

5. Do I have enough information about the type of practice that I envision to answer these questions? If not, how am I going to get this information? If the type of practice that I contemplate will not allow me to meet either my income or personal desires, are there alternatives that I should consider?

In the chapters that follow we will examine a variety of problems of professional responsibility arising in several areas of practice: criminal defense and prosecution, civil litigation, office practice, and government and public interest practice. As you study these chapters, you may find it useful to sample some of the literature dealing with various areas of practice. The bibliography at the end of this chapter provides some suggestions for your reading. To further stimulate your thinking about the personal dimension of a philosophy of lawyering, consider the following problem. (We will return to the second and third components of a philosophy of lawyering — the practice and the institutional — in the last two sections of this chapter.)

——————————— **Problem 1-1** ———————————

Integrating Personal Values and Professional Lives: Professional Heroes and Villains

a.   One way to begin thinking about the myriad questions involved in integrating professional and private life is to look for role models. What lawyers do you admire? They may be family members, friends, or outstanding lawyers whose biographies you have read or plan to read. What is it you admire about these lawyers? How did they integrate their private and professional lives? The bibliography at the end of this chapter includes biographies of a number of lawyers from which you may wish to sample.

b.   As one example of how a lawyer integrated the personal and the professional, consider the life of Atticus Finch, the hero of Harper Lee's Pulitzer Prize–winning novel, *To Kill a Mockingbird*. In class be prepared to discuss Finch's professional values and in particular the way in which he integrates professional life and private values. (You may either read the book or view the video.)[12]

c.   Another way to think about the issue of public and private life is to consider lawyers whose careers have gone awry. In class we will see excerpts from a videotape

_____

12. For different perspectives on Atticus Finch, *compare* Thomas L. Shaffer, The Moral Theology of Atticus Finch, 42 U. Pitt. L. Rev. 181 (1991) *with* Monroe H. Freedman, Atticus Finch — Right and Wrong, 45 Ala. L. Rev. 473 (1994). The Freedman article is part of a symposium issue on *To Kill a Mockingbird*.

of lawyers who have been disciplined. As you view this tape ask yourself what lessons can be learned from their stories.

B. Sources of Lawyers' Obligations

Lawyers' obligations flow principally from two sources: professional standards and general legal principles. It is important to recognize that professional responsibility is a body of law, the violation of which can expose lawyers to substantial sanctions — money damages and loss of professional license, not to mention the anguish caused by being charged with unprofessional conduct. Professional responsibility or legal ethics, like other fields of law, is a latticework of court rules, judicial decisions, statutes, and other authorities. The following research tools are particularly useful in this field:

- ABA, Annotated Model Rules of Professional Conduct (3d ed. 1996)
- Lawyers' Manual on Professional Conduct (ABA/BNA), a comprehensive research service covering reported decisions, ethics opinions, and current developments
- American Law Institute, Restatement (Third) of the Law Governing Lawyers[13]
- William H. Fortune, Richard H. Underwood & Edward J. Imwinkelried, Modern Litigation and Professional Responsibility Handbook (1996) [hereinafter Fortune et al., Modern Litigation and Professional Responsibility Handbook], treatise focusing on ethical problems arising at various stages of litigation
- Monroe H. Freedman, Understanding Lawyers' Ethics

---

13. The Restatement was approved by the ALI in 1999; publication of the full text of the Restatement is expected in 2000. Currently, the provisions of the Restatement can be found in three documents: Proposed Final Draft No.1, March 29, 1996; Proposed Final Draft No.2, April 6, 1998; and Tentative Draft No.8, March 21, 1997. These drafts are available on Westlaw. In final version, sections will be renumbered. A conversation table from draft to final section is on page xxxvii.

(1990) [hereinafter Freedman, Understanding Lawyers' Ethics], a critical view of the Model Rules, particularly in the context of criminal defense and prosecution

- Geoffey C. Hazard, Jr. & W. William Hodes, The Law of Lawyering (2d ed. 1990) [hereinafter Hazard & Hodes, The Law of Lawyering], textual discussion with illustrations of the Model Rules containing citations to significant decisions and scholarship
- Ronald E. Mallen & Jeffrey M. Smith, Legal Malpractice (4th ed. 1996) [hereinafter "Mallen & Smith, Legal Malpractice"], the leading treatise on legal malpractice.
- Charles W. Wolfram, Modern Legal Ethics (1986) [hereinafter, "Wolfram, Modern Legal Ethics"], a comprehensive handbook

The status of a third source of lawyers' obligations — general principles of ethics or morality — is more uncertain and controversial. It is clear that the field of professional responsibility is not identical to conventional ethics or morality. Many rules of professional conduct, such as the rules on advertising and solicitation, have nothing to do with morality. It would be a mistake, however, to conclude that moral principles are irrelevant to professional responsibility. The profession often debates what the rules of professional conduct should be, and moral principles are germane to many aspects of this debate. In addition, within the framework of existing rules, principles of ethics or morality play a role when lawyers decide how to act, although as we shall see the nature and scope of that role is controversial.

1. *Professional Standards: ABA Codes of Ethics, Ethics Advisory Opinions, Specialized Codes, and Practice Norms*

In almost all states, authority to regulate the practice of law in the state courts rests with the highest court in the state. New York is a notable exception. In New York, section 90 of the Judiciary Law authorizes the four appellate divisions of the New York Supreme Court to issue rules of conduct for lawyers in the state. Each federal court has its own rules of admission and practice, but these rules often follow those of the state in which the federal court sits.[14]

Pursuant to their authority to regulate the practice of law, courts issue a number of rules. The primary focus of this book is on the rules of professional conduct. Rather than writing their own rules of professional conduct, most state and federal courts base their rules of professional conduct on the American Bar Association's Model Rules of Professional Conduct, adopted in 1983.

While the ABA has no legal authority over the practice of law, it does wield considerable influence in the area of professional responsibility. The Model Rules of Professional Conduct is the third in a series of ABA standards of lawyers' ethics. The immediate predecessor to the Model Rules was the ABA's Model Code of Professional Responsibility, adopted in 1969. The 1969 Code succeeded the ABA's Canons of Ethics, issued in 1908 and amended on a number of occasions until replaced by the Code.

Even though the Code of Professional Responsibility is no longer in effect in most jurisdictions, some familiarity with the Code is useful because many provisions of the Model Rules are based on provisions of the Code and because a number of important court decisions under the Code continue to be relevant under the Model Rules. This book refers to significant provisions of the Code when relevant.

The format of the Code differs significantly from that of the Model Rules. The Code has a three-part structure: canons, disciplinary rules (DRs), and ethical considerations (ECs). The drafters intended for the canons to serve as axioms of lawyers' obligations. For example, Canon 4 states: "A lawyer should preserve the confidences and secrets of a client." The disciplinary rules are more detailed black-letter statements of minimum standards, the violation of which could be the basis of professional discipline. By contrast, the ethical considerations serve as both commentary on the disciplinary rules and aspirational norms that lawyers should strive to achieve, but the violation of which would not be the basis of discipline.[15]

---

14. See Bruce A. Green, Whose Rules of Professional Conduct Should Govern Lawyers in Federal Court and How Should the Rules be Created? 64 Geo. Wash. L. Rev. 460 (1996).

15. See ABA, Model Code of Professional Responsibility, Preliminary Statement.

Soon after its adoption, the Code of Professional Responsibility was criticized on two grounds. First, the division into canons, ethical considerations, and disciplinary rules was complex and confusing.[16] Second, the Code concentrated on the role of lawyers as advocates, largely ignoring representation as counselors or transactional attorneys. In 1977, only eight years after adopting the Code, the ABA appointed a Commission on Evaluation of Professional Standards (the Kutak Commission) to recommend revisions to the Code. The Kutak Commission instead proposed replacement of the Code, and in 1983 the ABA adopted the Model Rules of Professional Conduct.

The Model Rules abandoned the structure of the Code and adopted a simpler framework of black-letter rules followed by comments, much like the Restatements. The Model Rules are grouped under eight sections:

1. client-lawyer relationship
2. counselor
3. advocate
4. transactions with persons other than clients
5. law firms and associations
6. public service
7. information about legal services
8. maintaining the integrity of the profession

Some of the rules, such as Rule 1.8 dealing with prohibited transactions, are quite specific; others, such as Rule 1.7 dealing with conflicts of interest, set forth general standards. Some provisions of the Model Rules are not rules at all because they give lawyers discretion as to how to act. For example, Rule 1.6(b) and comments 12 and 13 state that lawyers have professional discretion to reveal confidential information in some situations. Other provisions are aspirational, as illustrated by Model Rule 6.1, which states that lawyers "should aspire" to render at least 50 hours of pro bono service per year. As to the authority of the comments, the Scope states: "The Comments are intended as guides to interpretation, but the text of each Rule is authoritative."

At this writing, more than 40 states have adopted the Model

---

16. Geoffrey C. Hazard, Jr., Address, Legal Ethics: Legal Rules and Professional Aspirations, 30 Clev. St. L. Rev. 571 (1981).

Rules, although most states have approved some variations from the ABA's Model Rules.[17] New York has a Code of Professional Responsibility that in form is based on the ABA's 1969 Code but actually is a medley of the Code, the Model Rules, and provisions unique to New York.[18] California has adopted its own Rules of Professional Conduct that vary considerably from the ABA's Model Rules. Other jurisdictions with significant deviations from the Model Rules include the District of Columbia, Illinois, North Carolina, Oregon, and Virginia.

In 1997 the president of the ABA appointed an Ethics 2000 Commission to consider changes in the Model Rules.[19] The Commission has decided against fundamental restructuring of the Model Rules. Instead, it will propose modest revisions in an effort to improve the current rules.[20]

The ABA has also been influential in the area of judicial ethics. In 1972 the ABA adopted a Model Code of Judicial Conduct that has since been adopted in most states. In 1990 the ABA revised the Code of Judicial Conduct. While the 1990 Code carries forward many of the provisions of the 1972 Code, it includes important changes, particularly with regard to racial bias and sexual discrimination. Chapter 6 examines ethical issues facing judges.

Some scholars of the legal profession have been extremely critical of the bar's efforts to write rules of professional conduct. They have argued that the purpose of these rules is not to control the conduct of lawyers but to serve the interests of lawyers, principally by enhancing professional prestige, controlling competition, and maintaining independence from outside regulation.[21]

17. For a listing of the states that have adopted the Model Rules, the dates of their adoption, and a summary of variations from the ABA's Model Rules, see Laws. Man. on Prof. Conduct (ABA/BNA) 01:3 et seq. For an argument in support of federalization of legal ethics, see Fred C. Zacharias, Federalizing Legal Ethics, 73 Tex. L. Rev. 335 (1994).

18. See N.Y. Sup. Ct. App. Div. R. 1200 et seq.

19. See Laws. Man. on Prof. Conduct (ABA/BNA), 13 Current Rep. 140, 168 (1997).

20. Current drafts and other materials are available at the Commission's Web site, ⟨http://www.abanet.org/cpr⟩.

21. See Richard L. Abel, Why Does the ABA Promulgate Ethical Rules? 59 Tex. L. Rev. 639 (1981); Stephen Gillers, What We Talked About When We Talked About Ethics: A Critical View of the Model Rules, 46 Ohio St. L.J. 243 (1985); Susan P. Koniak, The Law Between the Bar and the State, 70 N.C. L. Rev. 1389 (1992); Deborah L. Rhode, Why the ABA Bothers: A Functional

Any set of rules raises issues of interpretation. National, state, and local bar associations have established committees to offer interpretations of the Code of Professional Responsibility and the Model Rules; one of the most influential of these committees is the ABA Standing Committee on Ethics and Professional Responsibility.[22] The ABA committee issues both formal and informal opinions on issues of professional ethics. Formal opinions are those that the committee considers to be of widespread interest or unusual importance. All other opinions are informal.[23] Bar association ethics advisory opinions are not binding on courts, but good faith reliance on an opinion could be used in defense of a disciplinary or perhaps even a malpractice case. Professors Finman and Schneyer have evaluated the ethics opinions issued by the ABA committee. While finding the committee's work to be of substantial influence, they also conclude that "these opinions are seriously flawed, so much so that their overall influence may well be unfortunate."[24]

While the Rules of Professional Conduct set forth general standards of behavior, the practice of law is highly specialized. Because of this gap between general professional standards and specific problems that lawyers encounter in practice, various bodies, including associations of lawyers and bar-appointed study commissions, have prepared standards or codes of conduct focusing on ethical problems in particular areas of practice. Although these standards or codes are of no legal effect unless adopted by a court or legislature, they may provide guidance to practitioners in

---

Perspective on Professional Codes, 59 Tex. L. Rev. 689 (1981). See also Charles W. Wolfram, Parts and Wholes: The Integrity of the Model Rules, 6 Geo. J. Legal Ethics 861 (1993) (criticizing Model Rules for failure to "interconnect well and clearly with each other").

22. ABA committee opinions are published in the ABA Journal, the ABA/BNA Lawyers' Manual on Professional Conduct, and in computerized research services. Opinions from state and local bar associations are available in the ABA/BNA Lawyers' Manual and computerized research services.

23. See ABA Comm. on Ethics and Prof. Resp., Rules of Procedure, Rule 3.

24. Ted Finman & Theodore Schneyer, The Role of Bar Association Ethics Opinions in Regulating Lawyer Conduct: A Critique of the Work of the ABA Committee on Ethics and Professional Responsibility, 29 UCLA L. Rev. 67, 72 (1981). See also Lawrence K. Hellman, When "Ethics Rules" Don't Mean What They Say: The Implications of Strained ABA Ethics Opinions, 10 Geo. J. Legal Ethics 317 (1997).

those fields, be used as evidence of the appropriate standard of conduct in a malpractice case, and help support a good faith defense if a lawyer faces disciplinary charges. Some of the more important standards are the following:

- *arbitration and mediation:* Code of Ethics of the American Arbitration Association for Arbitrators in Commercial Disputes and Standards of Conduct for Mediators[25]
- *criminal defense and prosecution:* American Bar Association, Standards for Criminal Justice: The Prosecution Function and the Defense Function
- *matrimonial practice:* American Academy of Matrimonial Lawyers, The Bounds of Advocacy[26]
- *professionalism in general:* American Bar Association, "Lawyer's Creed of Professionalism";[27] many state bar associations have also adopted standards of professionalism
- *trust and estate practice:* American College of Trust and Estate Counsel, Commentaries on the Model Rules of Professional Conduct[28]

Norms of conduct or mores of the legal institutions in which lawyers practice are also an important source of lawyers' obligations. For example, issues of professional responsibility arise in a wide range of day-to-day settings in which lawyers practice: small firms in rural communities, mega-firms practicing throughout the world, boutique firms with highly specialized practices, offices of prosecutors or public defenders, legal services programs, private corporations, and federal or state agencies, to name just a few. Every practice context will have its own norms of behavior — ways in which the lawyers in that organization handle professional problems that they encounter.[29] These norms of behavior will, of

---

25. Howard M. Holtzmann, The First Code of Ethics for Arbitrators in Commercial Disputes, 33 Bus. Law. 309 (1977); 50 Disp. Resol. J. 78 (January 1995) (text of agreement on Standards of Conduct for Mediators between American Arbitration Association, American Bar Association, and Society of Professionals in Dispute Resolution).

26. 9 J. Am. Acad. Matrimonial Law. 1 (Fall 1992).

27. Laws. Man. on Prof. Conduct (ABA/BNA) 01:401.

28. 28 Real Prop. Prob. & Tr. J. 865 (1994).

29. *Compare* John P. Heinz & Edward O. Laumann, Chicago Lawyers: The Social Structure of the Bar (rev. ed. 1994) *with* Donald D. Landon, Country Lawyers: The Impact of Context on Professional Practice (1990).

course, be heavily influenced by formal professional standards, but some institutions may develop norms that conflict with established professional standards. One of your tasks as you move into the practice of law should be to judge critically the norms of behavior of the various practices with which you come into contact: What norms of behavior has this particular practice developed? Do these norms conflict with formal professional norms? If so, what is my reaction to this conflict? If the norms are within the "range of discretion" allowed by formal rules of the profession, do I agree with how discretion is being exercised? If not, what if anything can I do to change these practice norms?

2.   Law Governing Lawyers

When adopted by a court with authority to regulate the practice of law, rules of professional conduct become law, and lawyers who violate these rules are subject to professional discipline. The rules of professional conduct are not, however, the only source of law applicable to lawyers. Court decisions, statutory law, administrative rules and regulations, and procedural rules all apply to lawyers.[30]

Court decisions are an important source of standards of professional conduct. In the field of professional responsibility, courts have rendered decisions in five major categories of cases: disciplinary, malpractice, disqualification, sanctions, and criminal. Disciplinary cases are proceedings brought against lawyers charging them with violation of the rules of professional conduct or other forms of misconduct. The ultimate punishment in a disciplinary proceeding is disbarment from the practice of law; lesser sanctions include suspensions and reprimands. Section C(2) of this chapter examines the disciplinary system in more detail. Malpractice actions are civil lawsuits brought by clients or third parties seeking damages from lawyers. Malpractice claims may be based on a variety of legal theories, including negligence, fraud, and breach of fiduciary duty. Disqualification motions are not separate proceedings but motions filed as part of civil or criminal actions. The essence of the disqualification motion is that the attorney representing the opposing party should be disqualified from representing

---

30. See generally Hazard & Hodes, The Law of Lawyering.

that party because of some ethical violation, typically a conflict of interest. Like disqualification motions, claims for sanctions are part of an underlying case rather than separate proceedings. Such motions typically seek a monetary punishment against a party or that party's lawyer for some form of litigation misconduct, such as discovery abuse. Lawyers have been prosecuted criminally or held in contempt of court for various types of misconduct.

Statutory law is somewhat less significant in the area of law-yers' obligations than in many other fields of law because the regulation of lawyers and judges is largely the constitutional province of courts. Indeed, courts have declared some legislation dealing with the practice of law unconstitutional as a violation of the doctrine of separation of powers.[31] A number of federal and state statutes, however, may be applicable to lawyers. At the federal level, statutes govern the conduct of lawyers (and nonlawyers) entering or leaving government service.[32] Federal statutes also govern the disqualification and discipline (short of removal) of federal judges.[33] Various statutes and rules also apply to lawyers acting in other capacities, such as members of Congress or lobbyists.

Statutory regulation of lawyers varies widely from state to state. Both California and New York have fairly extensive schemes of statutory regulation; most other states do not.[34] For example, a California statute provides that sexual relations between a lawyer and a client may subject the attorney to discipline under some circumstances.[35] California also has a statutory provision limiting the percentage of fees that attorneys may charge in contingent fee cases against health care providers.[36] Most states have ethics-in-government statutes regulating the activities of governmental of-

31. Wolfram, Modern Legal Ethics §2.2.3, at 27-31.

32. E.g., Restrictions on Former Officers, Employees, and Elected Officials of the Executive and Legislative Branches, 18 U.S.C. §207; Acts Affecting a Personal Financial Interest, 18 U.S.C. §208; Disclosure of Confidential Information Generally, 18 U.S.C. §1905.

33. Disqualification of Justice, Judge, or Magistrate, 28 U.S.C. §455; Retirement for Disability; Substitute Judge on Failure to Retire; Judicial Discipline, 28 U.S.C. §372(c). Note, however, that federal judges may be removed from office only through impeachment under U.S. Const. art. II, §4.

34. Cal. Bus. & Prof. Code, Attorneys, §§6000 et seq.; N.Y. Jud. Law, Attorneys and Counselors, §§460 et seq.

35. Cal. Bus. & Prof. Code §6106.9.

36. Id. §6146.

ficials, governmental employees, and lobbyists, many of whom are lawyers.

Many lawyers practice before federal and state agencies, such as the Internal Revenue Service (IRS), the Securities and Exchange Commission (SEC), the Patent and Trademark Office (PTO), workers' compensation boards, and zoning commissions. These agencies, particularly federal agencies, may have *administrative rules and regulations* governing admission of practitioners and rules of conduct for practitioners before such agencies.[37] (It should be noted that many administrative agencies like the IRS allow nonlawyers as well as lawyers to practice before the agency.) Agency rules often provide standards similar to the Rules of Professional Conduct, but they may specify different or additional obligations. For example, the IRS has adopted standards of conduct with respect to matters such as preparing tax returns and issuing tax shelter opinions.[38] Problem 5-5 considers ethical obligations of attorneys who specialize in tax. Administrative agencies can also render decisions that determine standards of conduct for lawyers. For example, In re Carter & Johnson[39] (discussed in connection with Problem 5-2) was a disciplinary proceeding brought against two lawyers, claiming that they violated SEC Rule of Practice (2)(e)(1)(ii), which prohibits a practitioner from engaging in "unethical or improper professional conduct." The case established duties for attorneys admitted to practice before the SEC who learn their clients are engaged in fraud.

In court proceedings lawyers have a duty to comply with applicable *court rules*. Indeed, the Rules of Professional Conduct incorporate by reference procedural rules as standards of conduct. Model Rule 3.4(c) states that a lawyer shall not "knowingly disobey an obligation under the rules of a tribunal except for an open refusal based on an assertion that no valid obligation exists." Lawyers who violate court rules, such as Rule 11 of the Federal Rules of Civil Procedure, may be subject to monetary sanctions.

In an effort to bring some order to the body of law dealing with lawyers' obligations, the American Law Institute has com-

37. E.g., SEC, 17 C.F.R. pt. 201; IRS, 31 C.F.R. pt. 10.
38. 31 C. F. R. §§10.33, 10.34.
39. Fed. Sec. L. Rep. (CCH) ¶82,847 (SEC 1981). See generally Simon M. Lorne & W. Hardy Callcott, Administrative Actions Against Lawyers Before the SEC, 50 Bus. Law. 1293 (1995).

pleted the preparation of the *Restatement (Third) of the Law Governing Lawyers.*[40] The relationship between the Restatement and the Model Rules is complex. To some extent the two documents deal with different topics. For example, the Restatement contains extensive treatment of lawyer civil liability; such liability is outside the scope of the Model Rules. Often, however, the Restatement and the Model Rules both deal with the same issue. When the Restatement and the Model Rules treat the same topic, conflicts can arise. For example, both the Model Rules and the Restatement deal with the scope of the lawyer's duty of confidentiality, but they adopt different positions on exceptions to the duty. *Compare* Model Rule 1.6 *with* Restatement (Third) of the Law Governing Lawyers sections 117A and 117B. Since the Restatement does not constitute law, while rules of professional conduct adopted by a court are legally binding, lawyers must follow applicable rules rather than the Restatement. When the Restatement differs from rules of professional conduct, however, it may serve as the basis for revision of the rules. The Ethics 2000 Commission is considering provisions of the Restatement as it works on its recommendations for revision of the Model Rules.

3. *Moral Principles: Developing the Practice Component of a Philosophy of Lawyering*

In some situations rules of professional conduct will provide clear answers to questions of how a lawyer should act. For example, a lawyer may not ethically prepare a will for a client if the lawyer would be a beneficiary under the will unless the lawyer is related to the client. Model Rule 1.8(c). Contingent fee agreements with clients must be in writing. Model Rule 1.5(c). The difficult questions of professional responsibility, however, do not admit of such black-and-white answers. Lawyers often must make difficult judgments governed only by general standards in a context that involves the lawyer personally: Should I agree to handle this multimillion dollar case against a company that my firm did some work for three years ago? How much pro bono work should I assume as an associate, when my firm doesn't have any clear

---

40. See generally Symposium, Restatement of the Law Governing Lawyers, 10 Geo. J. Legal Ethics 541 (1997).

rules, when I want to make partner, and when I have a two-year-old at home? Should I accept this malpractice case against one of my classmates when I think the case has merit, when the client has not been able to find another lawyer to take the case, and when the statute of limitations is about to run? How should I respond to a request for production of documents in discovery when I know what the other side wants, but the request is worded in such a way that I could, arguably, deny the existence of what was requested?

Resolving hard questions of professional responsibility requires close attention to the rules of ethics and other standards of professional behavior, but it also demands more: It means that lawyers must develop an approach to handling such issues. This approach is the practice component of your philosophy of lawyering.

You probably already have some ideas about how you would deal with such questions. Your thinking will develop as you consider issues raised in this course and as you face a myriad of ethical problems in practice. To begin developing your philosophy of lawyering, you may find it useful to think about the various approaches that have been debated by scholars of the legal profession.

One approach could be labeled a *client-centered philosophy*. In articles written in 1978 and 1983, Professor Murray Schwartz set forth two principles that he argued accurately described the essence of client-centered lawyering. First, lawyers act as zealous partisans on behalf of their clients, doing everything possible to enable their clients to prevail in litigation or to obtain their clients' objectives in nonlitigation matters, except to the extent that clear rules of professional conduct or legal principles prohibit the lawyer from acting. Under a client-centered philosophy, if doubt exists about the propriety of an action, the lawyer is justified in proceeding. Only clear violations of law or rules of ethics, such as bribing witnesses, are prohibited. Schwartz referred to this idea as the "principle of professionalism." Second, when acting in this professional role, lawyers are not legally or morally accountable for their actions. Schwartz called this concept the "principle of non-accountability."[41] Similarly, Professor William Simon has re-

41. Murray L. Schwartz, The Zeal of the Civil Advocate, 1983 Am. Bar Found. Res. J. 543; Murray L. Schwartz, The Professionalism and Account-

ferred to two principles of conduct — neutrality and partisanship — as forming the core of what he called the "ideology of advocacy."[42] Following Simon, many writers now use the term "neutral partisanship" to refer to the standard conception of the lawyer's role. A more colloquial way of putting these ideas is that lawyers are "hired guns."

Critics of neutral partisanship have argued that the client-centered philosophy is morally unsound[43] because it requires lawyers in the course of representation of clients to engage in conduct that violates conventional morality:

> [The critics] claim that lawyers routinely do things for clients that harm third parties and would therefore be immoral, even in the lawyers' eyes, if done for themselves or for non-clients. Such actions constitute "role-differentiated behavior" in the sense that the actors, if asked to justify themselves, would claim that their role as a lawyer required them to "put to one side [moral] considerations . . . that would otherwise be relevant if not decisive." A lawyer's role-differentiated behavior could involve helping a client pursue a morally objectionable aim, or using a hurtful or unfair tactic to give a client an advantage. Specific examples might include invoking the statute of frauds to help a client avoid paying a debt he really owes, attacking an honest person's veracity in order to discredit him as a witness, taking advantage of an opponent's misunderstanding of the applicable law in settlement negotiations, or suggesting that a corporate client lay off some of its workers until the Justice Department comes to see the merits of the company's merger proposal. Off duty, lawyers would presumably not think it appropriate to avoid repaying a debt, impugn a truthful person's honesty, take advantage of

---

ability of Lawyers, 66 Cal. L. Rev. 669 (1978). See also David Luban, Lawyers and Justice 7 (1988) (relying on Schwartz's principles as the basis for a normative evaluation of the adversary system).

42. William H. Simon, The Ideology of Advocacy: Procedural Justice and Professional Ethics, 1978 Wis. L. Rev. 29, 34-39.

43. Another thread of the critique of client-centered lawyering is that this philosophy ignores the importance of truthful resolution of legal disputes. In 1975, federal Judge Marvin Frankel noted that the litigator "is not primarily crusading after truth, but seeking to win." Marvin E. Frankel, The Search for Truth: An Umpireal View, 123 U. Pa. L. Rev. 1031, 1039 (1975). See also Marvin E. Frankel, Partisan Justice (1980). Judge Frankel went on to propose a rule of professional ethics designed to force lawyers to give greater weight to the truth. 123 U. Pa. L. Rev. at 1057-1058. For a critique of Judge Frankel's views see Freedman, Understanding Lawyers' Ethics 26-33.

another's mistake, or exploit workers. On duty, the philosophers say, lawyers routinely do such things for their clients.[44]

The critics of neutral partisanship have offered an alternative philosophy that could be called a *philosophy of morality*.[45] Under this philosophy, lawyers are morally accountable for the actions that they take on behalf of their clients and must be prepared to defend the morality of what they do. Adoption of a philosophy of morality has a number of practical lawyering consequences. Lawyers would decline representation in more cases than under a client-centered philosophy, turning down cases in which the lawyer concluded that the representation was morally indefensible. Lawyers would withdraw from representation more frequently, for example in cases in which clients demanded that lawyers pursue goals or tactics that the lawyer found to be morally unsound. Lawyers would take a broader view of their obligations as counselors, at a minimum raising moral issues with their clients and often trying to convince their clients to take what the lawyer considered to be the morally correct action. In situations in which lawyers had professional discretion about how to act or in which the rules were unclear, a lawyer acting under a philosophy of morality would take

44. Ted Schneyer, Moral Philosophy's Standard Misconception of Legal Ethics, 1984 Wis. L. Rev. 1529, 1532-1533. The moral critique of the role of neutral partisanship is developed in Alan H. Goldman, The Moral Foundations of Professional Ethics 90-155 (1980); David Luban, Lawyers and Justice (1988); Gerald J. Postema, Moral Responsibility in Professional Ethics, 55 N.Y.U. L. Rev. 63 (1980); William H. Simon, The Ideology of Advocacy: Procedural Justice and Professional Ethics, 1978 Wis. L. Rev. 29; and Richard Wasserstrom, Lawyers as Professionals: Some Moral Issues, 5 Human Rights 1 (1975).

45. Probably the most comprehensive development of a philosophy of morality can be found in David Luban, Lawyers and Justice (1988). A number of other scholars have also offered their views on how moral values can be incorporated into the lawyer's role. See generally Thomas L. Shaffer & Robert F. Cochran, Jr., Lawyers, Clients, and Moral Responsibility (1994). See also Alan H. Goldman, The Moral Foundations of Professional Ethics 138 (1980) (lawyers should only aid clients in exercising their moral rights); Leslie Griffin, The Lawyer's Dirty Hands, 8 Geo. J. Legal Ethics 219 (1995) (calls for lawyers' conduct to be judged by common morality). Professor Serena Stier contends that the standard conception of the lawyer's role, in which professional conduct and morality are separate spheres, is fundamentally flawed. She argues for an "integrity thesis," in which professional conduct and morality are integrated rather than distinct. Serena Stier, Legal Ethics: The Integrity Thesis, 52 Ohio St. L.J. 551 (1991).

the action that the lawyer believed to be indicated by principles of morality, even if this action was not necessarily in the client's interest.[46]

Other critics of the client-centered philosophy have sought to develop approaches based on social values or norms rather than principles of morality. The major advantage of a *philosophy of social value* is that it is grounded in norms expressed in social institutions. Such values are likely to be seen as more objective and justified than moral values, which are often viewed as individual, subjective, and controversial. It should be noted that the philosophies of morality and social value are not inconsistent because social values often embody moral principles. For example, Professor Robert Gordon advocates a vision of law as a public profession and describes ways in which lawyers could implement that ideal in the conditions of modern practice.[47] Professor Bradley Wendel strives to develop a set of public values of lawyering derived from the "social function of lawyers and from the traditions and practices of the legal profession."[48] Professor Timothy Terrell and Mr. James Wildman examine the factors that have caused a crisis of professionalism for lawyers.[49] They argue that the true foundation of professionalism must be found in a commitment to the rule of law.[50] Terrell and Wildman identify six values that they believe lie at the core of professionalism:

- an ethic of excellence
- an ethic of integrity: a responsibility to say "no"
- a respect for the system and rule of law: a responsibility to say "why"
- a respect for other lawyers and their work
- a commitment to accountability
- a responsibility for adequate distribution of legal services[51]

46. Luban, Lawyers and Justice at 160, 173-174.
47. Robert W. Gordon, Corporate Law Practice as a Public Calling, 49 U. Md. L. Rev. 255 (1990).
48. W. Bradley Wendel, Public Values and Professional Responsibility, 75 Notre Dame L. Rev. 1, 7 (1999).
49. Rethinking "Professionalism," 41 Emory L.J. 403 (1992).
50. Id. at 423.
51. Id. at 424-431. For other perspectives on the issue of professionalism, see other essays in 41 Emory L.J. no. 2 (1992).

The most comprehensive statement of a philosophy of lawyering based on social values is found in Professor Simon's work.
He argues for the following basic principle: "[T]he lawyer should
take such actions as, considering the relevant circumstances of the
particular case, seem likely to promote justice."[52] Simon uses the
term "justice" not in some abstract or philosophical sense, but
rather as equivalent with "legal merit" of the case.[53] In deciding
the legal merit of the case, the lawyer must exercise contextual or
discretionary decisionmaking.[54] Simon identifies two dimensions
to this approach. First, in deciding whether to represent a client a
lawyer should assess the "relative merit" of the client's claims and
goals in relation to other clients that the lawyer might serve. Simon
recognizes that financial considerations play a significant role in
lawyers' decisions to represent clients, but he calls on lawyers to
take into account relative merit in addition to financial considerations.[55] Second, in the course of representation, Simon calls on
lawyers to assess the "internal merit" of their clients' claims.
Simon rejects the view that lawyers should assume responsibility
for determining the outcome of cases: "Responsibility to justice is
not incompatible with deference to the general pronouncements
or enactments of authoritative institutions such as legislatures and
courts. On the contrary, justice often, perhaps usually, requires
such deference."[56] When procedural defects exist, however, the
lawyer's obligation to do justice requires the lawyer to assume responsibility for promoting the substantively just outcome: "[T]he
more reliable the relevant procedures and institutions, the less direct responsibility the lawyer need assume for the substantive justice of the resolution; the less reliable the procedures and
institutions, the more direct responsibility she needs to assume for
substantive justice."[57]

These criticisms and suggestions for modification of the role
of neutral partisanship have generated a number of responses.

52. William H. Simon, The Practice of Justice 9 (1998).
53. Id. at 10.
54. See id. ch. 6.
55. William H. Simon, Ethical Discretion in Lawyering, 101 Harv. L. Rev.
1083, 1092-1093 (1988).
56. Simon, The Practice of Justice at 138. See also Simon, Ethical Discretion in Lawyering, 101 Harv. L. Rev. at 1096-1097.
57. Simon, The Practice of Justice at 140. See also Simon, Ethical Discretion in Lawyering, 101 Harv. L. Rev. at 1098.

Some scholars have challenged the claim that neutral partisanship accurately describes the behavior of most lawyers.[58] Professors Stephen Ellmann and Ted Schneyer have made at least three major objections to the empirical validity of the concept of neutral partisanship. First, the rules of ethics already grant lawyers considerable discretion to take into account moral considerations in their representation: "Lawyers have considerable freedom to reject cases, to limit their representation so as to exclude repugnant objectives or tactics, and to urge their own moral views upon clients whether or not the clients have requested such enlightenment."[59] In particular, Model Rule 2.1 states that, in giving advice to their clients, lawyers "may refer not only to law but to other considerations such as moral, economic, social and political factors," and Rule 1.16(b)(3) allows lawyers to withdraw when "a client insists upon pursuing an objective that the lawyer considers repugnant or imprudent."

Second, some empirical studies of the behavior of criminal defense lawyers, lawyers in small communities, lawyers in nonlitigation activities, and lawyers in large law firms, although limited in number and scope, cast doubt on the claim that neutral partisanship accurately describes the behavior of most lawyers. Indeed, some of these studies suggest that the problem of the role of lawyers is the opposite of neutral partisanship: lawyers are not sufficiently zealous in representing their clients because they are concerned about protecting their reputations; preserving relationships with other lawyers, judges, or officials; or advancing their own interests.[60]

58. See Stephen Ellmann, Lawyering for Justice in a Flawed Democracy, 90 Colum. L. Rev. 116 (1990) [reviewing Luban, Lawyers and Justice]; Ted Schneyer, Moral Philosophy's Standard Misconception of Legal Ethics, 1984 Wis. L. Rev. 1529.

59. Ellmann, Lawyering for Justice in a Flawed Democracy, 90 Colum. L. Rev. at 121. See also Schneyer, Moral Philosophy's Standard Misconception of Legal Ethics, 1984 Wis. L. Rev. at 1564-1566. Professor Fred Zacharias agrees that the Code and the Model Rules authorize lawyers to incorporate moral factors in their representation of clients, but he argues that the ethos of the practice has developed to limit the exercise of objective judgment. He proposes a number of institutional changes that can help reintroduce objectivity into the lawyer's role. Fred C. Zacharias, Reconciling Professionalism and Client Interests, 36 Wm. & Mary L. Rev. 1303 (1995).

60. Schneyer, Moral Philosophy's Standard Misconception of Legal Ethics, 1984 Wis. L. Rev. at 1544-1550. For a response to the criticism that

Third, lawyers are not necessarily acting as neutral partisans simply because they agree to represent or continue representation of clients even though they believe that the client's goals are morally repugnant. Lawyers may find such representation morally justified because the representation advances some higher principle — freedom of speech or due process of law, for example. An ACLU lawyer who defends the Nazi Party's right to march in a Jewish neighborhood may do so, not because he is acting as a neutral partisan, but because he considers protecting the principle of free speech more important than restricting dissemination of their immoral views.[61] Further, many lawyers find moral value to the preservation of the client-lawyer relationship. Professor Stephen Pepper argues that the lawyer's amoral role is morally justified because the role assists clients in exercising autonomy. For lawyers to exercise moral control over their clients would undermine that autonomy.[62]

Problem 1-2

The Moral Accountability of Lawyers

Write a letter to the editor commenting on the following exchange between Professor Monroe Freedman and Professor Michael Tigar regarding the moral accountability of lawyers.

---

neutral partisanship does not accurately describe lawyer behavior, see Luban, Lawyers and Justice at 393-403.

61. Ellmann, Lawyering for Justice in a Flawed Democracy, 90 Colum. L. Rev. at 126; Schneyer, Moral Philosophy's Standard Misconception of Legal Ethics, 1984 Wis. L. Rev. at 1562-1564.

62. See Stephen L. Pepper, The Lawyer's Amoral Ethical Role: A Defense, A Problem, and Some Possibilities, 1986 Am. Bar Found. Res. J. 613. For criticisms of this view and Professor Pepper's response, see Symposium on the Lawyer's Amoral Ethical Role, 1986 Am. Bar Found. Res. J. 613. See also Charles Fried, The Lawyer as Friend: The Moral Foundations of the Lawyer-Client Relation, 85 Yale L.J. 1060 (1976).

Monroe Freedman, Must You Be the Devil's Advocate?

Legal Times, August 23, 1993

Item. A lawyer at New York's Sullivan & Cromwell recently turned down a court appointment to represent Mahmoud Abou-Halima, who is charged with involvement in the car-bombing of the World Trade Center. A Sullivan & Cromwell partner explained to *The Wall Street Journal* that the firm did not want to dedicate its resources to the case, because the bombing was "such a heinous crime" and because the defendant is "so personally objectionable." The partner added that Abou-Halima is "anti-Semitic in the most dangerous way." And the firm was also concerned about adverse reactions from some of its current clients.

Item. Michael Tigar, a professor at Texas Law School, recently argued in a federal appeals court that John Demjanjuk should be allowed to return to the United States when he leaves Israel. The Israeli Supreme Court has reversed Demjanjuk's conviction for participating in the mass murder of Jews in the gas chambers of Treblinka. The court was won over by compelling evidence that Demjanjuk has an alibi. Because he had been engaged in the mass murder of Jews at other Nazi camps, Demjanjuk couldn't possibly have been a guard at Treblinka.

Was Sullivan & Cromwell right to refuse to defend Abou-Halima? Was Tigar right to represent Demjanjuk? And what do the rules of ethics say about it?

. . . Under the traditional view, a lawyer is bound to represent a client zealously, using all reasonable means to achieve the client's lawful objectives. . . .

That does not mean that lawyers should disregard moral concerns in representing clients. On the contrary, if a lawyer believes that what the client proposes is immoral or even simply imprudent, the client is entitled to the lawyer's judgment and counsel. But "[in] the final analysis . . . the lawyer should always remember that the decision whether to forgo legally available objectives or methods because of non-legal factors is ultimately for the client and not for himself." American Bar Association Model Code of Professional Responsibility, EC 7-8. [See Model Rules 1.2(a) and 2.1.]

Thus, a lawyer's decision to represent a client may commit that lawyer to zealously furthering the interests of one whom the lawyer or others in the community believe to be morally repugnant. For that reason, the question of whether to represent a particular client can present the lawyer with an important moral decision — a decision for which the lawyer can properly be held morally accountable, in the sense of being under a burden of public justification.

FREE TO CHOOSE

[Freedman then pointed out that ethically a lawyer may generally refuse to represent a client whose character or cause the lawyer finds repugnant. Model Rule 6.2, cmt. 1]

Thus, Sullivan & Cromwell violated no ethical rule in declining to defend Mahmoud Abou-Halima. Indeed, on the facts as reported, the firm would have acted unethically if it had taken the case. Under Disciplinary Rule 5-101 of the ABA Model Code, which is controlling in New York, a lawyer has a conflict of interest if the exercise of her professional judgment on behalf of her client "reasonably may be affected" by her own personal or business interests. [See Model Rule 1.7(b).]

And that is precisely the position of the lawyers at Sullivan & Cromwell who find the potential client so personally objectionable that they don't think the partnership should put its resources into the case, who find the crime so heinous that they don't want to be associated with its defense, and who are worried about how other clients and potential clients will view the representation. Certainly those powerful concerns may reasonably be expected to affect the zeal with which those lawyers would represent that client.

What then about Michael Tigar's representation of John Demjanjuk?

[Freedman then stated that at one time he did not believe that lawyers were morally accountable for their decisions to represent clients, but he changed his mind after a debate with Michael Tigar.]

And so I now ask my victorious opponent in that long-ago debate: Mike Tigar, is John Demjanjuk the kind of client to whom you want to dedicate your training, your knowledge, and your extraordinary skills as a lawyer? Did you go to law school to help a client who has committed mass murder of other human beings with poisonous gases? Of course, someone should, and will, represent him. But why you, old friend?

Michael Tigar, Setting the Record Straight on the Defense of John Demjanjuk

Legal Times, September 6, 1993

All of Monroe Freedman's statements about me in this newspaper are wrong, except two: We are — or were — old friends. And I do represent John Demjanjuk. . . .

Professor Freedman is wrong about the Israeli Supreme Court decision and about the American judicial decisions that caused Demjanjuk to linger in a death cell for years, for a crime he did not commit.

John Demjanjuk was extradited to Israel to stand trial as "Ivan the Terrible" of Treblinka, one of the worst mass murderers of the Holocaust. It turned out that crucial exculpatory evidence — that someone named Ivan Marchenko, not Demjanjuk, was Ivan the Terrible — was withheld from the defense. That evidence was not an "alibi"; it had to do with tragically mistaken identification and the U.S. government's failure to live up to its obligations of candor to its adversary and to the courts.

Freedman is wrong about what the Israeli Supreme Court did once it found doubt that Demjanjuk was Ivan. That court did not, as Freedman asserts, hold that Demjanjuk was guilty of other crimes. The Israeli court did consider whether Demjanjuk should be convicted as having served at other Nazi death camps, but found that Demjanjuk never had a fair opportunity to rebut evidence of service at other camps.

In 1981, a U.S. district judge found that Demjanjuk should be denaturalized. The judge found that Demjanjuk was Ivan the Terrible, a decision that is now universally conceded to have been wrong. There is powerful evidence that government lawyers suppressed evidence that would have shown that decision to have been wrong when made.

The U.S. judge also considered the question of whether Demjanjuk served at other camps. The judge found that, since Demjanjuk was Ivan and denied being Ivan, he probably should not be believed when he denied other culpable conduct at other camps. Thus, the judge's decision, now argued by the government as barring judicial review of Demjanjuk's right to enter the United States, was taken in the shadow of these now-discredited allegations.

Those are the facts. I represent Mr. Demjanjuk pro bono, along with the federal public defender, in an American judicial proceeding. The proceeding will, we hope, vacate earlier judgments against Demjanjuk and leave the government free — if it wishes — to bring and try fairly its allegations that John Demjanjuk served at death camps.[63] If, as Professor Freedman says, there is evidence of such service, which Mr. Demjanjuk has denied, my client is entitled to a fair trial where that evidence can be tested. . . .

We must remember the Holocaust, and we should pursue and punish its perpetrators. We dishonor that memory and besmirch the pursuit if we fail to accord those accused of Holocaust crimes the same measure of legality and due process that we would give to anyone accused of wrongdoing. Precisely because a charge of culpable participation in the Holocaust is so damning, the method of judging whether such a charge is true should be above reproach.

STANDING UP

So much for the factual difficulties in which Professor Freedman finds himself. Let us turn to his analysis of the ethical issues.

Professor Freedman begins by lauding a major law firm for refusing a court appointment to represent an unpopular indigent defendant. The firm doesn't like the client, doesn't like the fact that he is accused of a "heinous crime," and is afraid that its other clients will object. OK, says Freedman, those are good reasons for the law firm to refuse.

Let us all hurry to the library, and rewrite *To Kill a Mockingbird.* Atticus Finch is not a hero after all. He should have thought more of maintaining his law practice and refused to represent

---

63. The Sixth Circuit subsequently upheld Demjanjuk's appeal. Demjanjuk v. Petrovsky, 10 F.3d 338 (6th Cir. 1993), *cert. denied,* 513 U.S. 914 (1994). — ED.

someone charged with a heinous — and possibly racially motivated — crime. Clarence Darrow should have stayed with the railroad, instead of taking on those Commie unionists as clients. The lawyers who lost their licenses for daring to represent the colonial newspaper editor John Peter Zenger for the heinous crime of seditious libel were chumps. And John Hancock, that notorious tax evader, had no right to have John Adams as his counsel.

Maybe Sullivan & Cromwell has the right to refuse a court appointment, and maybe it should have that right. I have represented plenty of unpopular folks in my 25 years at the bar and have always stood up to the task of telling my paying clients that they just have to understand a lawyer's responsibility in such matters, or they should take their business elsewhere.

ONE MAN'S CONSCIENCE

From praise of Sullivan & Cromwell, Professor Freedman then makes a giant leap. He invents a new rule of legal ethics. Based on the supposed right to refuse a court appointment, we are told that every lawyer must bear "a burden of public justification" for representing someone accused of odious crimes. There is no rule of professional responsibility that so provides, and several rules cut directly against his assertions.

If Atticus Finch decides to represent an indigent defendant, Freedman will require him not only to incur the obloquy of his friends and clients, but to undertake a public defense of his ethical right to accept the case.

To put lawyers under such a burden of public justification undermines the right to representation of unpopular defendants. It invites the kind of demagoguery that we are now seeing in the attacks on lawyers for defendants in capital cases. It even invites the kinds of unwarranted attacks on zealous advocacy that have often been directed — and quite unjustly — at Professor Freedman.

I undertook the pro bono representation of John Demjanjuk in the 6th Circuit after a thorough review of the facts and law. I can no more be under a duty to make a public accounting of why I took this case than I can be under a duty to open up the files of all my cases to public view.

AN INSULTING QUESTION

[Tigar went on to argue that lawyers were morally accountable to their own consciences for the clients they choose to represent and the positions they advance.]

I have answered that question for myself, and it is insulting for Professor Freedman to suggest that I am faithless to my principles. When the most powerful country on earth gangs up on an individual citizen, falsely accuses him of being the most heinous mass murderer of the Holocaust, and systematically withholds evidence that would prove him guiltless of that charge, there is something dramatically wrong. When that man is held in the most degrading conditions in a death cell based on those false accusations, the wrong is intensified. When the government that did wrong denies all accountability, the judicial branch should provide a remedy. I have spent a good many years of my professional life litigating such issues. I am proud to be doing so again.

Monroe Freedman, The Morality of Lawyering

Legal Times, September 20, 1993

. . . My question to Tigar relates to one of the most fundamental issues of lawyers' ethics and the nature of the lawyer's role. That issue is frequently posed by asking whether one can be a good person and a good lawyer at the same time. Or whether the lawyer forfeits her conscience when she represents a client. Or whether the lawyer is nothing more than a hired gun. Essentially, these questions ask whether the lawyer, in her role as a lawyer, is a moral being. There are three answers to that question:

• *The amoral lawyer.* One answer has been dubbed "the standard conception." It holds that the lawyer has no moral responsibility whatsoever for representing a particular client or for the lawful means used or the ends achieved for the client. Critics have accurately pointed out that under the standard conception, the lawyer's role is at best an amoral one and is sometimes flat-out immoral.

• *Moral control of the client.* A second answer insists that the lawyer's role is indeed a moral one. It begins by agreeing with the standard conception that the lawyer's choice of client is not subject to moral scrutiny. But it holds that the lawyer can impose his moral views on the client by controlling both the goals pursued and the means used during the representation.

According to this view, the lawyer can properly stop the client from using lawful means to achieve lawful goals. For example, the lawyer, having taken the case and having induced the client to rely upon her, can later threaten to withdraw from the representation — even where this would cause material harm to the client — if the client does not submit to what the lawyer deems to be the moral or prudent course. . . .

• *Choice of client as a moral decision.* The third answer also insists that the lawyer's role is a moral one. It begins by agreeing with the standard conception that the client is entitled to make the important decisions about the client's goals and the lawful means used to pursue those goals. But this answer recognizes that the lawyer has the broadest power — ethically and in practice — to decide which clients to represent. And it insists that the lawyer's decision to accept or to reject a particular client is a moral decision. Moreover, that decision is one for which the lawyer can properly be held morally accountable.

Although critics have erroneously, and repeatedly, identified me with the standard conception, I have consistently advocated the third answer for 17 years. It is refreshing, therefore, to be criticized at last for what I believe, rather than for what I don't believe.

A JUDGMENT OF ONE'S OWN

Some of the responses to my column suggest that a lawyer can't "know" that a potential client or cause is morally repugnant until there has been a trial by jury that has determined guilt or innocence. But this confuses a legal adjudication of guilt with the lawyer's personal decision about what is true or false and what is right or wrong based upon the available evidence.

And we make that kind of personal decision all the time. . . .

One letter in response to my column said that the question was "impertinent." No lawyer, the writer said, should be under a burden of public moral accountability. That, indeed, is the standard conception. As I have indicated, one reason I reject that view is that I believe that the lawyer's role is neither an immoral nor an amoral one.

Moreover, we are a profession that exists for the purpose of serving the public, and we hold a government-granted monopoly to do so. As the U.S. Supreme Court has repeatedly held, lawyers are an essential part — a constitutionally required part — of the administration of justice. It is therefore contrary to democratic principles for lawyers to contend that we owe the public no explanation of what we do and why we do it. Further, I believe that a major reason for lawyer-bashing (which is not a new phenomenon) is that our profession has failed to explain and to justify the true nature and importance of the lawyer's role in American society. . . .

A MORAL DEFENSE

It is no surprise that Tigar, in response to my question, has come through with a powerful, persuasive explanation — a moral explanation — of his decision to represent John Demjanjuk. . . .

First, he notes that the memory of the Holocaust should not be dishonored by denying even its perpetrators the fullest measure of legality. One lesson of the Holocaust is that the vast powers of government must constantly be subjected to the most exacting scrutiny in order to guard against their abuse.

Further, Tigar refers to "powerful evidence" that lawyers in the Department of Justice suppressed evidence that would have shown that Demjanjuk should not have been extradited on charges of being Ivan the Terrible. (Note that these government lawyers have not been found guilty after trial by jury, but that Tigar nevertheless — and properly — finds enough evidence of their guilt to justify his personal moral decision.) This kind of corruption of justice is an intolerable threat to American ideals, regardless of one's opinion of the accused.

And Tigar concludes: "When the government that did wrong denies all accountability, the judicial branch should provide a remedy. I have spent a good many years of my professional life litigating such issues. I am proud to be doing so again."

Thus, Tigar's moral response to my question illuminates a crucial issue of enormous public importance about what lawyers do and why they do it. And it illustrates why I am proud to call Mike Tigar my friend.

C. Methods of Regulating Attorney Conduct

2 controls
1) Admission
2) Discipline

Formal regulation of attorney conduct has traditionally occurred in two ways: admission of lawyers to practice and discipline of lawyers admitted to practice for misconduct. While the courts have ultimate authority over both the admission and disciplinary systems, in fact the legal profession has exercised substantial control over both systems. A major theme in the history of the American legal profession has been the question of whether the legal profession can be trusted to regulate its members in the public interest or whether the profession will exercise this power for the benefit of its members.[64]

As a result of criticism of the profession's ability to regulate its members in the public interest, in recent years courts and to some extent legislatures have made a number of inroads into the self-regulatory power of the legal profession. Court decisions imposing civil liability or criminal punishment on attorneys and establishing constitutional rights of attorneys have been particularly significant developments. Some state legislatures are assuming a more active role in regulation of the legal profession. The likelihood is that these pressures on the self-regulatory authority of the profession will continue and even intensify. This section provides an overview of the traditional methods of attorney regulation — admission and discipline — along with these emerging methods of control. Professor David Wilkins has written a comprehensive analysis of the various mechanisms for regulating lawyer conduct.[65] Professor Wilkins argues against a unitary system of en-

---

64. See Symposium, Ethical Codes and the Legal Profession, 59 Tex. L. Rev. 639 (1981).

65. David B. Wilkins, Who Should Regulate Lawyers? 105 Harv. L. Rev. 799 (1992). See Special Issue, Institutional Choices in the Regulation of Lawyers, 65 Fordham L. Rev. No. 1 (1996) (symposium examining and developing Professor Wilkins's approach to lawyer regulation).

forcement and in favor of a multifaceted system in which enforcement methods are matched with problems.

1.   *Admission to Practice*

To practice law before a court, a lawyer must be admitted to the bar of that court. In state court this is normally done by admission to practice before the highest court in the state. This admission typically carries with it the right to practice law before all lower courts in that state. To practice before a federal court — whether the Supreme Court, the courts of appeal, or the district courts — an attorney must be admitted to practice by that court. The federal courts, however, normally rely heavily on the state court admission process. Federal administrative agencies have the power to establish their own rules of practice, including rules that allow nonlawyers to practice before the agency. Under the Supremacy Clause of the United States Constitution, art. VI, cl. 2, states may not prohibit nonlawyers admitted by federal agencies from practicing before those agencies pursuant to agency rules.[66]

The rules for admission to practice vary from state to state. Typically, states have three requirements for admission. First, applicants must have graduated from law school. Most states require applicants to have graduated from a law school accredited by the ABA, but some states, including California, allow applicants to graduate from unaccredited law schools. The requirement of ABA accreditation obviously gives the ABA a powerful voice in the control of legal education and of the practice of law. In a critical study of the ABA's role in raising bar educational requirements, Professor Jerold Auerbach argues that increased educational requirements were part of an overall effort by the organized bar to reduce the impact of the rising tide of immigrants on the profession.[67] Second, most states require applicants to pass the state's bar examination. In a few states applicants who graduate from a law school within the state have a "diploma privilege" for admission

[handwritten margin notes: 1) Grad from Law School - usually must be accredited; 2) Pass Bar exam]

---

66. Sperry v. Florida ex rel. Florida Bar, 373 U.S. 379 (1963) (Florida could not prevent nonlawyer admitted to practice before United States Patent Office from representing clients pursuant to Patent Office Rules on the ground that he was engaged in the unauthorized practice of law).

67. Jerold S. Auerbach, Unequal Justice (1976).

3) Good moral char.

to the bar without having to sit for the bar examination.[68] Third, applicants must be of "good moral character."[69]

Good moral character is a universal requirement for admission to the bar, but its precise meaning is unclear. The Supreme Court has characterized the term as "unusually ambiguous," but has indicated that the inquiry should focus on whether a "reasonable man could fairly find that there were substantial doubts about [the applicant's] 'honesty, fairness and respect for the rights of others and for the laws of the state and nation.' "[70]

honest fair respect for others

In a series of cases beginning in the 1950s the Supreme Court considered constitutional limitations on inquiry by bar officials into political beliefs and activities of applicants for admission to the bar. The Court held that states could not deny bar admission simply because of past membership in organizations like the Communist Party when the applicants introduced substantial evidence of good moral character.[71] Later cases dealt with the extent to which bar officials could inquire into applicants' political affiliations in application questions. The Court ruled that most such inquiries were unconstitutional.[72] In Law Students Civil Rights Research Council, Inc. v. Wadmond,[73] however, the Court in a 5-4 opinion upheld several questions on the New York bar application that inquired into the applicant's *knowing* membership in organizations that advocated the violent overthrow of the government with *specific intent* to foster the aims of such organization.

Since the trilogy of 1971 cases the Supreme Court has not dealt with the constitutionality of the moral character requirement, but the issue of moral character has been before the state courts on a number of occasions. One issue of interest is the extent to

68. E.g., Wis. Sup. Ct. R. 40.03.

69. For a state-by-state comparison of bar admission requirements, see Comprehensive Guide to Bar Admission Requirements, published annually by the American Bar Association Section of Legal Education and Admissions to the Bar and the National Conference of Bar Examiners.

70. Konigsberg v. State Bar of California, 353 U.S. 252, 263-264 (1957) (*Konigsberg I*).

71. Schware v. Board of Bar Examiners, 353 U.S. 232 (1957); *Konigsberg I*, 353 U.S. at 267-268.

72. Konigsberg v. State Bar of California, 366 U.S. 36 (1960) (*Konigsberg II*); In re Anastaplo, 366 U.S. 82 (1960); In re Stolar, 401 U.S. 23 (1971); Baird v. State Bar of Arizona, 401 U.S. 1 (1971).

73. 401 U.S. 154 (1971).

which sexual conduct amounts to lack of moral character. In Cord v. Gibb,[74] the Virginia Supreme Court reversed a lower court decision holding that an applicant to the bar lacked good moral character because she resided and owned a home with a man to whom she was not married. The court found no rational connection between her conduct and fitness to practice law. Similarly, in Florida Board of Bar Examiners re N.R.S.,[75] the Florida Supreme Court held that there was no rational connection between an applicant's acknowledged homosexuality and his fitness to practice law. By contrast, the Oklahoma Supreme Court, in Vaughn v. Board of Bar Examiners,[76] denied admission to an applicant because of sexual involvement with two 14-year-old girls while he was their teacher, even though charges were later dismissed.

problems

In a comprehensive study of the history and implementation of the moral character requirement, Professor Deborah Rhode questions the wisdom of having this condition for bar admission. Among the criticisms she makes are the following: First, bar admission officials do not have the resources for adequate investigation into moral character, and the inquiries they do conduct are only minimally helpful in determining the moral character of applicants. Second, because of the vagueness of the moral character concept, the admission process is left to the subjective judgment of bar officials. Her study indicates a lack of consensus among these officials as to the types of conduct that warrant investigation or denial of admission. Third, review of character has First Amendment implications, inhibiting freedom of expression by some individuals and deterring others from applying for bar admission. Wide-ranging inquiry into the activities of applicants also raises privacy issues. Professor Rhode concludes that the bar would be better off abandoning the moral character requirement for bar admission and instead using its limited resources in disciplining lawyers for actual misconduct.[77]

1) cannot investigate good morals

2) it is vague and hard to apply

3) Freedom of speech implications

Historically, states have also included some form of residency

74. 254 S.E.2d 71 (Va. 1979).
75. 403 So. 2d 1315 (Fla. 1981).
76. 759 P.2d 1026 (Okla. 1988).
77. Deborah L. Rhode, Moral Character as a Professional Credential, 94 Yale L.J. 491 (1985). See also Michael K. McChrystal, A Structural Analysis of the Good Moral Character Requirement for Bar Admission, 60 Notre Dame L. Rev. 67 (1984).

in the state as a requirement for bar admission.[78] A lawyer who is admitted in one state and who represents a client in a matter that arises in another state can obtain a temporary or "pro hac vice" admission for the purpose of handling that matter.[79] Pro hac vice admission typically requires association of local counsel and is not available for a lawyer who regularly engages in practice in the state.[80] Many lawyers and law firms have developed a regular national practice. In addition, law departments of large corporations must deal with both national and international legal problems. This reality has produced some pressure for change in the traditional residency requirements. At the same time, local lawyers may be resistant to change, in part out of fear of increased competition.[81] In a series of decisions the Supreme Court has held invalid various residency requirements under the Privileges and Immunities Clause of the United States Constitution, art. IV, §2.[82]

[handwritten margin notes: temp. exemption to practice out of state — Associate w/ in state counsel; S.C. has not recognized residency restrictions yet]

2. The Disciplinary System

━━━━━━━━ Problem 1-3 ━━━━━━━━

Reporting Misconduct by Another Lawyer

You are the only associate recently hired by a solo practitioner, Norman Wilson. You were hired about a year

---

78. Citizenship as a requirement for bar admission is unconstitutional. See In re Griffiths, 413 U.S. 717 (1973) (state failed to satisfy heavy burden of proof required to use suspect category of status as alien).

79. See Leis v. Flynt, 439 U.S. 438 (1979) (no due process right to hearing on denial of pro hac vice admission).

80. See South Carolina Medical Malpractice Joint Underwriting Assn. v. Froelich, 377 S.E.2d 306 (S.C. 1989) (out-of-state attorney could not continue to use pro hac vice admission and would be enjoined from engaging in the unauthorized practice of law). See generally Stephen E. Kalish, Pro Hac Vice Admissions: A Proposal, 1979 S. Ill. U.L. J. 367.

81. See generally Samuel J. Brakel & Wallace D. Loh, Regulating the Multistate Practice of Law, 50 Wash. L. Rev. 699 (1975).

82. See Supreme Court of N.H. v. Piper, 470 U.S. 274 (1985); Supreme Court of Virginia v. Friedman, 487 U.S. 59 (1988); Barnard v. Thorstenn, 489 U.S. 546 (1989). Cf. Frazier v. Heebe, 482 U.S. 641 (1987) (invalidating Louisiana federal district court residency rule under Court's supervisory power).

ago after a lengthy job search. You feel extremely fortunate to have the job because the market for lawyers in your area has been very tight; a number of your classmates still do not have a position.

One of the matters on which you have worked is Sylvia v. United Truck Lines, an automobile accident case in which the firm represented the plaintiff, Sylvia. The case settled about a month ago for $250,000, and the file was closed. You did some legal research on the case and met with the client on several occasions regarding discovery issues. You did not participate in settlement negotiations or in disbursement of settlement funds.

Recently, you came across a research memo that you did in Sylvia v. United Truck Lines that was misfiled. You pulled the file of the *Sylvia* case from the firm's closed files. As you were putting the research memo into the file, you happened to notice the closing statement in the case. The statement signed by the client showed a structured settlement in which $100,000 was paid immediately and $25,000 payable over each of the next six years. The statement also showed that the firm's one-third attorney fee was paid fully out of the initial payment. Thus, the client only received about $17,000 now. The closing statement struck you as strange because you were sure that the case had been settled for a lump sum. As you thumbed through the file, you found a letter from the insurance company stating that it was enclosing its draft in the amount of $250,000 as lump sum settlement of the case, along with its standard form general release. You are mystified about this and unsure how to proceed. What should you do?

Read Model Rules 1.6, 5.2, 8.3, and comments.

Duty to report misconduct by another lawyer

Disciplinary Rule 1-103(A) of the Code of Professional Responsibility required lawyers to report unprivileged knowledge of violations of any disciplinary rule by other lawyers. The language of the rule imposed a reporting obligation regardless of the seriousness of the violation. Thus, under the rule lawyers were equally obligated to report violations of the advertising rules and theft of client money. It was clear, however, that in fact lawyers did not comply with this broad duty of disclosure. A 1978 study conducted by the Arizona Law Review found that where the conduct involved serious harm to a client or obstruction of justice, the vast majority of attorneys would report the misconduct: 89 percent of the respondents would report misappropriation of client funds to a disciplinary body and 79 percent would report the destruction of evidence. If the conduct did not involve serious harm to a client or obstruction of justice, however, attorneys were generally unwilling to report even serious criminal conduct. More than 50 percent of the respondents would take no action on learning that another attorney had willfully evaded income tax. Similarly, 65 percent would not report improper solicitation of business.[83]

Recognizing this reluctance to report misconduct, the drafters of the Model Rules imposed a more limited but realistic obligation to report misconduct. Rule 8.3(a) of the Model Rules of Professional Conduct provides that a lawyer having knowledge of misconduct by another lawyer "that raises a substantial question as to that lawyer's honesty, trustworthiness or fitness as a lawyer in other respects, shall inform the appropriate professional authority." Section (b) imposes a similar obligation on lawyers to report misconduct by judges.

A leading case dealing with the lawyer's obligation to report misconduct by another lawyer is Wieder v. Skala.[84] The plaintiff, Wieder, was a litigation associate in the defendant law firm. Wieder asked the law firm to represent him in the purchase of a condominium apartment. The firm agreed to do so, and assigned a fellow associate (L.L.) to handle the matter. L.L. neglected the matter and made fraudulent misrepresentations to Wieder to conceal his neglect. Wieder learned from two senior associates that the firm knew that L.L. was a "pathological liar" and that he had

---

83. David R. Ramage-White, Note, The Lawyer's Duty to Report Professional Misconduct, 20 Ariz. L. Rev. 509, 516-517 (1978). See also David O. Burbank & Robert S. Duboff, Ethics and the Legal Profession: A Survey of Boston Lawyers, 9 Suffolk L. Rev. 66, 100 (1974) (few respondents would contact the bar association when they learned of serious criminal conduct by a member of their firm).

84. 609 N.E.2d 105 (N.Y. 1992).

previously lied to other members of the firm about pending matters. When Wieder discovered the fraud, he informed the partners in the firm and asked them to report L.L.'s misconduct as required by DR 1-103(A) of the New York Code of Professional Responsibility. The partners refused to do so. In an effort to dissuade Wieder from reporting L.L.'s misconduct, the firm agreed to reimburse Wieder for his losses. In addition, the firm threatened to fire Wieder if he reported L.L.'s misconduct. Ultimately, however, at Wieder's insistence, the firm reported L.L.'s misfeasance. The firm continued to employ Wieder for several months because he was working on an important litigation matter, but two partners in the firm berated him for forcing them to report L.L. Finally, the firm fired Wieder.

Wieder brought suit for breach of contract and in tort for abusive discharge. The lower courts dismissed both causes of action, relying on prior decisions of the New York Court of Appeals holding that an at-will employee could be discharged regardless of cause, unless the employer had expressly agreed in manuals or otherwise to limit its right of discharge. The court of appeals affirmed the dismissal of the tort claim, holding that while the plaintiff's arguments were persuasive and the circumstances compelling, recognition of a tort cause of action was best left to the legislature.[85] The court, however, reversed as to the breach of contract cause of action. While reaffirming the rules that it had established in prior employment cases, the court of appeals held that the employment relationship between lawyers and their firms was fundamentally different from the relationship between employees and commercial enterprises:

> We agree with plaintiff that in any hiring of an attorney as an associate to practice law with a firm there is implied an understanding so fundamental to the relationship and essential to its purpose as to require no expression: that both the associate and the firm in conducting the practice will do so in accordance with the ethical standards of the profession. Erecting or countenancing disincentives to compliance with the applicable rules of professional conduct, plaintiff contends, would subvert the central professional purpose of his relationship with the firm — the lawful and ethical practice of law. . . .
>
> Moreover, as plaintiff points out, failure to comply with the

85. Id. at 110.

reporting requirement may result in suspension or disbarment. . . . Thus, by insisting that plaintiff disregard DR 1-103(A) defendants were not only making it impossible for plaintiff to fulfill his professional obligations but placing him in the position of having to choose between continued employment and his own potential suspension and disbarment. We agree with plaintiff that these unique characteristics of the legal profession in respect to this core Disciplinary Rule make the relationship of an associate to a law firm employer intrinsically different from that of the financial managers to . . . corporate employers. . . . [86]

In Bohatch v. Butler & Binion,[87] the Texas Supreme Court decided as a matter of law a firm could not be held liable for damages to a partner who the firm expelled for alleging in good faith that another partner had violated ethical rules. The court was sensitive to the argument that its decision discouraged lawyers from reporting misconduct, but it concluded that the firm's action nonetheless did not subject it to liability because allegations of misconduct, whether true or not, undermine the trust that is essential to the partnership relationship.[88] While the majority did not mention *Wieder*, concurring Justice Hecht distinguished the case because *Wieder* did not involve a partnership relationship and because the misconduct in *Wieder* was clear.[89] Two justices dissented and would have held the firm liable for retaliating against a partner who made a good faith effort to alert other members of the firm to possible overbilling of a client.[90]

Exceptions to the duty to report misconduct by another lawyer

The duty to report misconduct by another lawyer is subject to several limitations and exceptions. First, the duty applies only if the lawyer has "knowledge" of misconduct. When does a lawyer "know" of misconduct? The terminology section of the Model Rules draws a distinction between "know" and "reasonably

86. Id. at 108-109.
87. 977 S.W.2d 543 (Tex. 1998).
88. Id. at 546-547.
89. Id. at 557.
90. Id. at 561.

objectiue not reasonable standard

should know." The former requires actual knowledge while the latter is an objective standard based on what a reasonably prudent and competent lawyer would know. It should be noted, however, that since it is impossible to penetrate into a person's mind, actual knowledge can be inferred from the circumstances.[91] Relevant also is a well-established body of criminal law involving lawyers and other professionals holding that a person has knowledge of a fact if the person's conduct shows conscious avoidance or deliberate ignorance of facts.[92]

Additionally IT tell if objectively knew

Second, an attorney's duty to report misconduct under Rule 8.3(c) is subject to the attorney's duty of confidentiality to the client: "This rule does not require disclosure of information otherwise protected by Rule 1.6. . . ." Rule 1.6 states: "A lawyer shall not reveal information relating to representation of a client unless the client consents after consultation . . . [subject to certain exceptions]."[93]

2) subject to attn'y's duty to confidentiality

In In re Himmel,[94] the Illinois Supreme Court held that the attorney-client privilege did not excuse an attorney from the duty to report misappropriation of funds by the client's former attorney. In *Himmel*, however, the client had not asked the lawyer to maintain confidentiality, and the lawyer thought that the client had reported the matter. In addition, *Himmel* was decided under DR 1-103(A) of the Code of Professional Responsibility, which states that the lawyer has a duty to report "unprivileged" knowledge of misconduct by another lawyer. The use of the word "privilege" seems to refer to the attorney-client evidentiary privilege. In fact, the Illinois Supreme Court in *Himmel* found that the attorney-client privilege did not prevent Himmel from being required to report the former lawyer's misconduct because Himmel had not received the information about the former lawyer's misconduct in a communication from his client that was protected by the evidentiary attorney-client privilege. A communication is subject to the attorney-client privilege only if the communication is made in

---

91. See generally 1 Hazard & Hodes, The Law of Lawyering §402.

92. See generally John P. Freeman & Nathan M. Crystal, Scienter in Professional Liability Cases, 42 S.C. L. Rev. 783, 833-838 (1991).

93. State Bar of Mich., Comm. on Prof. and Jud. Ethics, Op. RI-220 (1994) (no duty to report under Rule 8.3 when information is covered by Rule 1.6).

94. 533 N.E.2d 790 (Ill. 1988).

confidence; if a third party, who is not the agent of either the lawyer or the client, is present when the communication is made, the communication usually is not in confidence.[95] When the client told Himmel of the former lawyer's misconduct, a third party was present; Himmel also obtained information about the lawyer's misappropriation from an insurance company.[96] By contrast, under the Model Rules the duty to report does not apply to information "relating to representation of a client," regardless of whether it is subject to the evidentiary attorney-client privilege.[97] Later problems in these materials explore in more detail the relationship between the ethical duty of confidentiality and the evidentiary attorney-client privilege.

Confidential / privilege - later

Wisdom of the reporting requirement as a matter of policy

Should the rules of professional conduct impose a duty to report misconduct by another lawyer at all? Our society does not impose an obligation on citizens to report crimes of which they have knowledge.[98] Professor Gerald Lynch argues that the absence of such a general duty is justified because the decision whether to inform is a complex moral choice that requires weighing the harm to relationships that may result from informing with the harm to be avoided by reporting.[99] He goes on to argue that the ethical obligation to report that is imposed on lawyers is also unjustified:

> It is difficult to imagine that the special circumstances of the lawyer's position in society alter the balance in every case to the point that the complexity of the moral calculation disappears. In other words, it is not clear, even for lawyers, that the moral basis of informing will be so clear in so many cases that a generalized obligation to inform should be imposed.[100]

95. Restatement (Third) of the Law Governing Lawyers §120 (definition of "privileged persons").

96. 533 N.E.2d at 794.

97. See In re Ethics Advisory Panel Op. No. 92-1, 627 A.2d 317 (R.I. 1993) (distinguishing *Himmel* and holding that the duty to report under Rule 8.3 is subordinate to the duty of confidentiality under Rule 1.6).

98. See Gerald E. Lynch, The Lawyer as Informer, 1986 Duke L.J. 491, 517-521.

99. Id. at 521-535.

100. Id. at 537.

Some states, notably California, do not include an obligation to report misconduct by another lawyer.[101]

--- **Problem 1-4** ---

Evaluation of Your State's System of Lawyer Discipline

    a.   How does your state's system of lawyer discipline compare with ABA recommendations as discussed in the reading material that follows? Consider the following topics.

1. authority to discipline: bar or court?
2. confidentiality
3. disciplinary effect of conviction of a crime
4. scope of public protection: To what extent does your state have the following in addition to a system of lawyer discipline?
   a. client protection fund
   b. mandatory arbitration of fee disputes
   c. voluntary arbitration of lawyer malpractice claims and other disputes
   d. mediation
   e. lawyer practice assistance
   f. lawyer substance abuse counseling
5. provisions for minor misconduct
6. degree of lay participation
7. complainants' rights
8. random audit of trust accounts

    b.   Your instructor will invite to class one or more individuals involved in your state's disciplinary system to speak on the current operation of the system, problems that they see with the system, and their recommendations for change. Be prepared to ask them questions about the operation of the system. Consider the areas set forth in part *a* above.

---

101. See Laws. Man. on Prof. Conduct (ABA/BNA) ¶101:201.

The system of lawyer discipline received little attention until 1967,[102] when the ABA appointed a special committee chaired by Justice Tom C. Clark of the United States Supreme Court to study the system and to make recommendations. In 1970 the committee issued its report finding the "existence of a scandalous situation that requires the immediate attention of the profession."[103] Among the problems found by the committee were the following:

> The Committee has found that in some instances disbarred attorneys are able to continue to practice in another locale; that lawyers convicted of federal income tax violations are not disciplined; that lawyers convicted of serious crimes are not disciplined until after appeals from their convictions have been concluded, often a matter of three or four years, so that even lawyers convicted of serious crimes, such as bribery of a governmental agency employee, are able to continue to practice before the very agency whose representative they have corrupted; that even after disbarment lawyers are reinstated as a matter of course; that lawyers fail to report violations of the Code of Professional Responsibility committed by their brethren, much less conduct that violates the criminal law; that lawyers will not appear or cooperate in proceedings against other lawyers but instead will exert their influence to stymie the proceedings; that in communities with a limited attorney population disciplinary agencies will not proceed against prominent lawyers or law firms and that, even when they do, no disciplinary action is taken, because the members of the disciplinary agency simply will not make findings against those with whom they are professionally and socially well acquainted; and that, finally, state disciplinary agencies are undermanned and underfinanced, many having no staff whatever for the investigation or prosecution of complaints.[104]

The report identified 36 major problems with the disciplinary system nationwide and made specific recommendations for change.

As a result of the Clark Committee's report, the ABA appointed a standing Committee on Professional Discipline. The

---

102. See generally Mary M. Devlin, The Development of Lawyer Disciplinary Procedures in the United States, 7 Geo. J. Legal Ethics 911 (1994).

103. ABA, Special Comm. on Evaluation of Disciplinary Enforcement, Problems and Recommendations in Disciplinary Enforcement 1 (1970) [hereinafter the Clark Committee].

104. Id. at 1-2.

committee prepared Standards for Lawyer Discipline, adopted by the ABA in 1979, which followed many of the recommendations made by the Clark Committee. In 1989 the ABA adopted Model Rules for Lawyer Disciplinary Enforcement to replace the 1979 standards; it revised these model rules on several occasions since then. The description of the disciplinary process that follows is based on the ABA's model rules, but it is important to note that the procedures for lawyer discipline, like those for admission to the bar, vary from state to state, so lawyers should consult their local rules of court to determine the procedures in effect in that state.

The ABA Model Rules for Lawyer Disciplinary Enforcement call for the creation of a statewide board to administer the lawyer discipline and disability system. Rule 2(A). The board is appointed by "the court with the requisite authority and responsibility to administer the lawyer discipline and disability system." Rule 2(B). Typically, this will be the state supreme court. The board appoints hearing committees and the court appoints disciplinary counsel. Rules 3 and 4. When a charge of misconduct is filed against an attorney, disciplinary counsel has the responsibility of conducting an investigation. Rule 11. At the conclusion of the investigation, disciplinary counsel may (a) dismiss, (b) in a matter involving minor misconduct, refer respondent to the Alternatives to Discipline Program, or (c) recommend probation, admonition, the filing of formal charges, the petitioning for transfer to disability inactive status, or a stay. Rule 11(B)(1). The complainant may ask for review by the chair of the hearing committee of the disciplinary counsel's decision to dismiss the matter. Rule 11(B)(3). If the disciplinary counsel recommends either admonition or probation, the accused lawyer may request formal proceedings. If the lawyer does not request formal proceeding, the lawyer is deemed to have consented to the sanction recommended by disciplinary counsel. Rule 11(C).

If formal charges are instituted against an attorney, disciplinary counsel gives the attorney written notice of the charges, the attorney files an answer to the charges, and certain discovery is conducted. When the case involves material issues of fact, or when the attorney wishes to present evidence in mitigation, the hearing committee will hold an evidentiary hearing where the accused lawyer may be represented by counsel, present evidence, and cross-examine witnesses. Rule 11(D). The hearing committee then prepares a report to the board that includes its findings of fact, conclusions of law, and recommendations. Rule 3(D). The board reviews the report of the hearing committee and issues its own report and decision, subject to review by the court. Rule 11(E), (F).

The ABA Model Rules for Lawyer Disciplinary Enforcement specify grounds for discipline, which include violation of the state's rules of professional conduct. Rule 9(A). Under the Model Rules of Professional Conduct, a lawyer engages in misconduct when a lawyer commits a criminal act that "reflects adversely on the lawyer's honesty, trustworthiness or fitness as a lawyer in other respects." Model Rule 8.4(b). Thus, criminal conduct is also a basis for professional discipline. Indeed, the Model Rules for Lawyer Disciplinary Enforcement provide for automatic suspension of a lawyer who has been convicted of a serious crime. Rule 19. The Model Rules of Professional Conduct also apply to lawyers even when they are acting in a nonlegal capacity. As a result, a lawyer could be disciplined for "improper conduct in connection with business activities, individual or personal activities, and activities as a judicial, governmental or public official."[105] A lawyer may also be disciplined for willful failure to cooperate with disciplinary authorities. Rule 9(A)(3). See also Model Rule 8.1 (prohibiting misrepresentation, nondisclosure, and noncooperation in connection with admissions and disciplinary matters). If a lawyer is found guilty of misconduct, sanctions include the following: disbarment, suspension for a fixed period not to exceed three years, probation not in excess of two years, reprimand, admonition, restitution to persons financially injured by the attorney, costs of the disciplinary proceeding, and limitations on the attorney's future practice. Rule 10. The sanctions of disbarment, suspension, probation, and reprimand are made public. Rule 10(D). An admonition, which is in effect a warning to the attorney, can be issued only in cases of minor misconduct. Rule 10(A)(5).

What is the nature of the disciplinary process and to what extent are lawyers entitled to constitutional protections? The ABA Model Rules for Lawyer Disciplinary Enforcement refer to the disciplinary process as sui generis. Rule 18(A). The Supreme Court, however, has characterized the disciplinary process as "quasi criminal" and has held that certain (but not all) due process requirements apply, including the requirement of fair notice of the

105. ABA Comm. on Ethics and Prof. Resp., Formal Op. 336, at 2 (1974).

charges.[106] Similarly, the Court held in Spevack v. Klein,[107] that a lawyer could not be disciplined for invoking the privilege against self-incrimination in responding to a subpoena duces tecum in a disciplinary proceeding. The *Spevack* decision, however, provides lawyers only a limited degree of protection because the Supreme Court subsequently limited the scope of the privilege. The privilege against self-incrimination generally does not prevent lawyers from being required to produce documents and records; it does not preclude a state from disciplining lawyers for noncooperation in disciplinary cases that do not involve criminal misconduct; and it would allow a state to compel lawyers to testify in disciplinary cases that involved possible criminal liability so long as the lawyers received use immunity against any criminal prosecution resulting from their testimony.[108]

The burden of proof required to find a lawyer guilty of misconduct reflects the unique character of disciplinary proceedings. In most states, a finding of misconduct must be supported by "clear and convincing evidence," a standard higher than the civil standard of a preponderance of the evidence but lower than the criminal standard of proof beyond a reasonable doubt. See ABA Model Rules for Lawyer Disciplinary Enforcement, Rule 18(C).

Since the issuance of the Clark Committee's report in 1970, the disciplinary process has been the subject of considerable debate.[109] The overriding question in the discussion has been whether the process deals effectively with lawyer misconduct. Critics argue that a system controlled by lawyers can never properly regulate lawyers. Opponents of the present system have sought a process subject to public control. Defenders of self-regulation argue that issues of professional responsibility are too complex to be left to laypeople, that the bar has done a generally credible job in dealing with misconduct, that public control would undermine the independence of lawyers, and that defects in the system can be remedied by greater openness and some public participation in the system rather than scrapping the system in its entirety.

106. See In re Ruffalo, 390 U.S. 544 (1968).

107. 385 U.S. 511 (1967).

108. See generally Geoffrey C. Hazard, Jr. & Cameron Beard, A Lawyer's Privilege Against Self-Incrimination in Professional Disciplinary Proceedings, 96 Yale L.J. 1060 (1987).

109. See Eric H. Steele & Raymond T. Nimmer, Lawyers, Clients, and Professional Regulation, 1976 Am. Bar Found. Res. J. 917.

The ABA Model Rules for Lawyer Disciplinary Enforcement, while obviously preserving the principle of professional self-regulation, do include some modest reforms in the disciplinary system. The rules place the system under the control of the judiciary rather than the bar and call for lay membership on both the board and hearing committees, but lay membership is a minority of both of these bodies. See Rules 2(B) and 3 (three of nine members of board and one of three members of hearing committees are public members). The rules provide that proceedings are generally confidential until formal proceedings begin, at which time the proceedings become public. Rule 16. Admonitions of attorneys remain private. Rule 10(A)(5).

In 1989 the ABA appointed another commission to study the disciplinary system and to make recommendations to the ABA. In 1991 the ABA Commission on Evaluation of Disciplinary Enforcement (the McKay Commission) issued its report. The commission found "revolutionary changes" since the Clark Committee's report.[110] The commission also found that "times have changed" and that further improvements and modifications of disciplinary systems were required.[111] The commission's report outlined 21 recommendations for improvement of the disciplinary process. At its February 1992 meeting the ABA House of Delegates adopted the McKay Commission's report and its recommendations, with some modifications. As adopted by the ABA, the recommendations include the following:

- Professional conduct should be regulated by the judiciary rather than the bar. Recommendations 1-2.
- The scope of public protection should be expanded to include the following component agencies:
  - (a) lawyer discipline
  - (b) client protection fund
  - (c) mandatory arbitration of fee disputes
  - (d) voluntary arbitration of lawyer malpractice claims and other disputes
  - (e) mediation
  - (f) lawyer practice assistance

---

110. ABA Commn. on Evaluation of Disciplinary Enforcement, Lawyer Regulation for a New Century xiv (1992).
111. Id. at xv.

- (g) lawyer substance abuse counseling. Recommendations 3-4.
- Courts should appoint disciplinary officials and disciplinary counsel to assure independence from the bar. Recommendations 5-6.
- All disciplinary proceedings should be made public after a determination has been made that probable cause exists. Recommendation 7.
- Complainants should be entitled to greater involvement in disciplinary proceedings. Recommendation 8.
- The disciplinary process should include procedures for cases involving minor misconduct. Recommendations 9-10.
- Disciplinary systems should be adequately funded. Recommendations 13-15.
- Lawyers' trust accounts should be subject to random audit. Recommendation 16.
- Improvements should be made in the National Discipline Data Bank and in interstate coordination. Recommendations 20-21.

Probably the most significant change made by the ABA to the commission's recommendations dealt with confidentiality of the disciplinary process. The commission had recommended that the disciplinary process be public from the time of the complainant's initial communication with the disciplinary agency. The ABA House of Delegates changed this proposal to make the process public after a determination has been made that probable cause exists.[112]

While the disciplinary process has traditionally focused on the conduct of individual lawyers, some studies have argued that the process should be applied to law firms.[113] In 1996 New

112. On the need for more public information about disciplined lawyers, see Sandra L. DeGraw & Bruce W. Burton, Lawyer Discipline and "Disclosure Advertising": Toward a New Ethos, 72 N.C. L. Rev. 351 (1994).

113. Ted Schneyer, Professional Discipline for Law Firms? 77 Cornell L. Rev. 1 (1991). See also Comm. on Prof. Resp., Assn. of Bar of the City of New York, Discipline of Law Firms, 48 The Record 628 (1993); Irwin D. Miller, Preventing Misconduct by Promoting the Ethics of Attorneys' Supervisory Duties, 70 Notre Dame L. Rev. 259 (1994).

York became the first state to adopt rules for discipline of law firms.[114]

3. Civil Liability (Malpractice, Disqualification, and Monetary Sanctions) and Criminal Punishment

Three forms of civil remedies now occupy a central place in regulation of lawyer conduct: legal malpractice, disqualification, and monetary sanctions. The term *legal malpractice* is often used to refer to lawyers' civil liability, but the term is a misnomer because the law does not recognize a single cause of action for legal malpractice. Legal malpractice is a catch-all phrase that refers to a group of causes of action by which clients, and in some cases third parties, can recover damages from lawyers (or their malpractice insurers) for some form of lawyer misconduct.[115] When a client claims that a lawyer mishandled a legal matter, the client's cause of action will typically be for negligence. The duty of care that lawyers owe their clients requires them to "exercise the competence and diligence normally exercised by lawyers in similar circumstances."[116] Lawyers who practice in a specialized field, such as securities or tax, are held to the standard of care normally exercised by specialists.[117] If a lawyer in the course of representation intentionally violates a fiduciary obligation to the client — for example, by representing conflicting interests — then the client may have a cause of action

114. See Laws. Man. on Prof. Conduct (ABA/BNA), 12 Current Rep. 191 (1996). DR 1-102 of the New York Code of Professional Responsibility defines misconduct to include conduct by a lawyer or a law firm.
115. See generally Mallen & Smith, Legal Malpractice. See also Restatement (Third) of the Law Governing Lawyers, ch. 4.
116. Restatement (Third) of the Law Governing Lawyers §74(1).
117. See Horne v. Peckham, 158 Cal. Rptr. 714 (Ct. App. 1979); Restatement (Third) of the Law Governing Lawyers §74, cmt. *d*. See generally Buddy O. Herring, Liability of Board Certified Specialists in a Legal Malpractice Action: Is There a Higher Standard? 12 Geo. J. Legal Ethics 67 (1998) (board certification will not increase attorneys' malpractice liability because attorneys who qualify will already be subject to higher standard of care applicable to specialists).

for breach of fiduciary duty.[118] In some cases, clients have alleged that their lawyers misrepresented facts to them or failed to disclose material information giving rise to causes of action for fraud, misrepresentation, or nondisclosure.[119]

Causes of action by nonclients against lawyers have traditionally been much more difficult to sustain than causes of action by clients because of the "privity" rule. Under this rule, lawyers generally have not been liable to persons other than their clients. The privity rule has been justified for two reasons: First, liability to nonclients would create conflicts of interest between lawyers' duties to their clients and their duties to third persons. Second, liability to nonclients would expose lawyers to potentially vast damages of uncertain amount and scope. Despite these policies, the privity rule has been eroded in recent years, and lawyers are increasingly being held liable to third parties.[120]

What is the relationship between the rules of professional responsibility and malpractice liability?[121] Both the Code of Professional Responsibility and the Model Rules impose an obligation of competence on lawyers. See DR 6-101 and Model Rule 1.1. See also Model Rule 1.3 (diligence). Both the Code (Preliminary Statement) and the Model Rules (Scope, par. 6), however, state that violation of the rules is not a basis for malpractice liability. Thus, merely because a lawyer has violated the rules of professional conduct does not per se produce malpractice liability. To establish malpractice liability for negligence, it is necessary to show that the attorney's conduct fell below generally accepted standards of conduct in the profession. This standard typically requires expert testimony.[122] Most courts will allow experts to consider

118. Restatement (Third) of the Law Governing Lawyers §76A. See, e.g., Moguls of Aspen, Inc. v. Faegre & Benson, 956 P.2d 618 (Colo. Ct. App. 1997) (negligence does not equal breach of fiduciary duty).

119. Restatement (Third) of the Law Governing Lawyers §77.

120. See 1 Mallen & Smith, Legal Malpractice ch. 7; Restatement (Third) of the Law Governing Lawyers §§73 (duty of care to certain nonclients), 77 (liability to client or nonclient under general law). See generally Symposium, The Lawyer's Duties and Liabilities to Third Parties, 37 S. Tex. L. Rev. 957 (1996).

121. See generally John Leubsdorf, Legal Malpractice and Professional Responsibility, 48 Rutgers L. Rev. 101 (1995).

122. See Vandermay v. Clayton, 984 P.2d 272 (Or. 1999) (en banc) (while expert testimony is generally required in legal malpractice cases, court may determine whether jury is capable of deciding lawyer's negligence without expert testimony).

rules of ethics in deciding whether the attorney's conduct did not meet generally accepted standards of the profession.[123] In addition, to establish malpractice liability a plaintiff must also prove that the attorney's breach of duty caused damages to the plaintiff.[124] Potential malpractice liability can be a powerful force affecting the conduct of lawyers, just as it has been for doctors. These materials include discussion of significant malpractice cases.

Modern litigation has seen an explosive growth of *disqualification motions* — motions filed by one party seeking a court order that the other party's lawyer may not continue to represent that party because of some violation of the rules of professional responsibility, typically a conflict of interest.[125] Disqualification motions are not separate proceedings but are filed as part of civil or criminal actions. Originally, disqualification motions were used in cases in which the party filing the motion was a former client and was seeking disqualification to prevent that former lawyer from now using confidential information on behalf of a new client against the former client. This situation continues to be a major area in which disqualification motions have come before the courts. See Problem 3-5. Disqualification motions, however, are now being filed in many other situations, for example if the opposing lawyer might be called as a witness in the case or if the lawyer had used some improper investigative technique, such as contacting the employees of the moving party. Courts have begun to register some skepticism about disqualification motions because they deprive clients of the right to counsel of their choice, because they can interfere with the efficient processing of cases, and because they can be used for strategic purposes. We will consider the use of disqualification motions in a number of problems in these materials.

---

123. See, e.g., Allen v. Lefkoff, Duncan, Grimes & Dermer, P.C., 453 S.E.2d 719 (Ga. 1995) (ethics rules relevant on standard of care in legal malpractice case); Smith v. Haynsworth, Marion, McKay & Geurard, 472 S.E.2d 612 (S.C. 1996) (expert witness may rely on violation of rule of ethics as evidence of violation of standard of care). See generally Note, The Evidentiary Use of the Ethics Codes in Legal Malpractice: Erasing a Double Standard, 109 Harv. L. Rev. 1102 (1996).

124. See Restatement (Third) of the Law Governing Lawyers §75.

125. See generally Kenneth L. Penegar, The Loss of Innocence: A Brief History of Law Firm Disqualification in the Courts, 8 Geo. J. Legal Ethics 831 (1995).

Monetary sanctions for litigation abuse is another form of civil liability that in recent years has come to have an increasingly important impact on lawyer conduct. The principal source of this body of law is Rule 11 of the Federal Rules of Civil Procedure. Under this rule, if a lawyer files a motion or other paper in court, the lawyer certifies that the document is not "frivolous" either in law or in fact. During the past 20 years, courts have rendered a vast body of decisional law establishing obligations of lawyers regarding frivolous lawsuits and motions under Rule 11. Courts have ordered lawyers who have violated this rule to pay monetary sanctions, such as attorney fees of the opposing party. Rule 11 applies only to actions in federal court, but many states have rules of civil procedure modeled on federal Rule 11. Problem 4-1 examines Rule 11 and other limitations on frivolous litigation conduct.

The *criminal law* plays an increasingly important role in the regulation of lawyers, both directly when lawyers engage in conduct that violates the criminal law and indirectly when criminal standards influence disciplinary standards.[126] Lawyers can also be held in *contempt of court* for violation of court orders or court rules. Contempt orders can be either criminal or civil.[127] When an order is intended to punish misconduct, vindicate the court's authority, or deter future conduct, it is criminal in nature, and various due process safeguards are necessary.[128] If the contempt order is intended to coerce compliance with a court's order rather than punish for violation, it amounts to civil contempt.[129] Thus, if a court orders a person incarcerated until the person complies with the court's order, the sanction amounts to civil contempt so long as it is still reasonably possible for the person to comply with the order.[130] Regardless of whether the contempt is criminal or civil, a

126. See Bruce A. Green, The Criminal Regulation of Lawyers, 67 Fordham L. Rev. 327 (1998). Professor Green discusses the tensions that can arise between criminal and ethical standards and argues that the criminal law and prosecutors should sometimes show greater deference to lawyers' ethical obligations.

127. For a discussion of the distinction between civil and criminal contempt, see United States v. Lippitt, 180 F.3d 873 (7th Cir.), *cert. denied*, 120 S. Ct. 389 (1999)).

128. See In re Air Crash at Charlotte, N.C. on July 2, 1994, 982 F. Supp. 1092 (D.S.C. 1997) (lawyer subject to criminal contempt for providing daily transcript to fact witness and for improper use of subpoena).

129. See United States v. Lippitt, 180 F.3d at 876-877.

130. Id.

hearing is generally required before issuance of an order, but when the contempt occurs in the presence of the court and immediate action is necessary to vindicate the court's authority, courts have the power to order summary contempt.[131]

4. Legislation

As mentioned earlier, legislatures have not been a major force in the regulation of the legal profession because courts have been aggressive in asserting their constitutional prerogative to supervise attorneys. Courts have often struck down on separation of powers grounds legislative attempts to regulate the profession.[132]

In recent years legislatures have become somewhat more active in efforts to control the profession. Several states have statutes limiting contingent fee agreements. A few states have authorized nonlawyers to provide legal services. We will consider some of these provisions in connection with problems later in these materials. Increased legislative regulation of the profession is likely eventually to produce confrontation with the courts.

The concept of a philosophy of lawyering, outlined in the first section of this chapter, has three dimensions: the personal, the practice, and the institutional. The last of these, the institutional, refers to issues facing the profession as a whole rather than the individual lawyer.[133] As this section shows, the effectiveness of the attorney disciplinary system has been a significant issue for the profession for a number of years. Increasingly, the profession's effort to preserve the principle of self-regulation has come under attack from various quarters.[134] At several places in these materials we will consider a number of other issues facing the profession as a whole: the adequacy of our system for delivery of legal services

131. See Pounders v. Watson, 521 U.S. 982 (1997) (no need to show pattern of repeated violations by attorney for court to exercise power of summary contempt when necessary to vindicate court's authority).

132. Wolfram, Modern Legal Ethics §2.2.3, at 27-31.

133. See Deborah L. Rhode, Ethical Perspectives on Legal Practice, 37 Stan. L. Rev. 589 (1985).

134. See Deborah L. Rhode, The Rhetoric of Professional Reform, 45 Md. L. Rev. 274 (1986).

to indigents and people of moderate means, criticisms of the adversarial system of dispute resolution, and the problem of discrimination within the profession. Lawyers seeking to develop a comprehensive philosophy of lawyering will strive to be knowledgeable about institutional issues facing the profession and prepare to work for institutional reform where appropriate.[135]

────────── Problem 1-5 ──────────
Developing a Philosophy of Lawyering

   a. Write an essay describing and either defending or critiquing the philosophy of lawyering of some lawyer that you know well personally, or who has been the subject of a biography, or who has been depicted in literature or film. See the list of biographies contained in the bibliography at the end of this chapter.

   b. Write an essay describing and defending your own philosophy of lawyering. Your essay should include discussion of the personal, the practice, and the institutional dimensions of a philosophy of lawyering. It should discuss a broad range of specific issues, such as the following:

1. choosing a type of practice
2. deciding to take or decline cases
3. counseling a client regarding exercise of the client's legal rights

    135. On the topic of reform of the legal profession, see John S. Dzienkowski, The Regulation of the American Legal Profession and Its Reform, 68 Tex. L. Rev. 451 (1989) (reviewing Richard L. Abel, American Lawyers (1989)); John Leubsdorf, Three Models of Professional Reform, 67 Cornell L. Rev. 1021 (1982); Deborah L. Rhode, Institutionalizing Ethics, 44 Case W. Res. L. Rev. 665 (1994); David B. Wilkins, Legal Realism for Lawyers, 104 Harv. L. Rev. 468 (1990). For a skeptical view of the possibilities for reform from the perspective of the sociology of the legal profession, see Mark J. Osiel, Lawyers as Monopolists, Aristocrats, and Entrepreneurs, 103 Harv. L. Rev. 2009 (1990) (reviewing Richard L. Abel & Philip S. C. Lewis, Lawyers in Society, 3 vols. (1988-1989)). See also Robert W. Gordon, The Independence of Lawyers, 68 B.U. L. Rev. 1 (1988) (examining conditions under which lawyers can be independent from their clients and analyzing criticisms of value of independence).

4. exercising professional discretion on behalf of a client (e.g., deciding whether to cross-examine a witness)
5. withdrawing from representation because the lawyer concludes that the client is acting immorally
6. preventing the client from doing harm to others (e.g., disclosing the client's intention to commit a wrongful act)
7. acting on behalf of a client in ways that will harm others
8. participating in pro bono, law reform, and other professional activities to improve the law

Your essay is due the last day of class unless otherwise instructed.

Bibliography on the Practice of Law and Selected Biographies of Lawyers

Generally

Richard L. Abel, American Lawyers (1989).

Jerold S. Auerbach, Unequal Justice: Lawyers and Social Change in Modern America (1976).

Gary Bellow & Martha Minow eds., Law Stories (1996).

Mary Ann Glendon, A Nation Under Lawyers: How the Crisis in the Legal Profession is Transforming American Society (1994).

John P. Heinz & Edward O. Laumann, Chicago Lawyers: The Social Structure of the Bar (rev. ed. 1994).

Philip B. Heymann & Lance Liebman, The Social Responsibilities of Lawyers (1988).

Michael J. Kelly, Lives of Lawyers: Journeys in the Organizations of Practice (1994).

Anthony T. Kronman, The Lost Lawyer: Failing Ideals of the Legal Profession (1993).

Sol M. Linowitz with Martin Mayer, The Betrayed Profession: Lawyering at the End of the Twentieth Century (1994).

Mark C. Miller, The High Priests of American Politics: The Role of Lawyers in American Political Institutions (1995).

Robert L. Nelson, David M. Trubek & Rayman L. Solomon, Lawyers' Ideals/Lawyers' Practices: Transformations in the American Legal System (1992).

Rodent (Attorney), Explaining the Inexplicable: The Rodent's Guide to Lawyers (1995).

Two periodicals, The American Lawyer and the National Law Journal, contain extensive coverage of various aspects of professional life.

Biographies

Clark M. Clifford, Counsel to the President: A Memoir (1991).

Johnnie L. Cochran with Tim Rutten, Journey to Justice (1996).

Morris Dees with Steve Fiffer, A Season for Justice: The Life and Times of Civil Rights Lawyer Morris Dees (1991).

William Henry Harbaugh, Lawyer's Lawyer: The Life of John W. Davis (1973).

Laura Kalman, Abe Fortas (1990).

William M. Kuntsler with Sheila Eisenberg, A Man of the Sixties: My Life as a Radical Lawyer (1994).

Arthur L. Liman with Peter Israel, Lawyer: A Life of Counsel and Controversy (1998).

Alpheus Thomas Mason, Brandeis, A Free Man's Life (1946).

Louis Nizer, Reflections Without Mirrors: An Autobiography of the Mind (1978).

Victor Rabinowitz, Unrepentant Leftist (1996).

Mary Beth Rogers, Barbara Jordan: American Hero (1998).

Gerry Spence, The Making of a Country Lawyer (1996).

Evan Thomas, The Man to See: Edward Bennett Williams (1991).

Kevin Tierney, Darrow, A Biography (1979).

Juan Williams, Thurgood Marshall: American Revolutionary (1998).

Career Choice

American Bar Association, Careers in Law Series, includes publications on admiralty and maritime law, civil litigation, entertainment law, family law, government practice, intellectual property, international law, labor law, natural resources and environmental law, nonlegal careers, public interest law, and sports law. The ABA Journal also runs a monthly column on Law Practice.

Deborah L. Arron, What Can You Do with a Law Degree? A Lawyer's Guide to Career Alternatives Inside, Outside & Around the Law (3d ed. 1997).

Susan J. Bell, Full Disclosure: Do You *Really* Want to be a Lawyer? (1989).

Jay G. Foonberg, How to Start & Build a Law Practice (4th ed. 1999).

Hillary Jane Mantis, Alternative Careers for Lawyers (1997).

Suzanne B. O'Neill & Catherine Gerhauser Sparkman, From Law School to Law Practice: The New Associate's Guide (1989).

Civil Rights (See also *Public Interest* and *Legal Services)*

Jack Greenberg, Crusaders in the Courts: How a Dedicated Band of Lawyers Fought for the Civil Rights Revolution (1994).

Richard Kluger, Simple Justice: The History of Brown v. Board of Education and Black America's Struggle for Equality (1975).

Mark V. Tushnet, Making Civil Rights Law: Thurgood Marshall and the Supreme Court, 1936-1961 (1994).

Corporate Counsel

Symposium, The Role of General Counsel, 46 Emory L.J. 1005 (1997).

Criminal Practice (See also *Prosecutors)*

Abraham S. Blumberg, The Practice of Law as a Confidence Game: Organizational Cooption of a Profession, 1 Law & Socy. Rev. 15 (1967).

Alan M. Dershowitz, The Best Defense (1982).

James S. Kunen, "How Can You Defend Those People?": The Making of a Criminal Lawyer (1983).

Kenneth Mann, Defending White-Collar Crime: A Portrait of Attorneys at Work (1985).

Lisa J. McIntyre, The Public Defender: The Practice of Law in the Shadows of Repute (1987).

Seymour Wishman, Confessions of a Criminal Lawyer (1981).

Labor Law

Thomas Geoghegan, Which Side Are You On? Trying to Be For Labor When It's Flat on Its Back (1991).

Law Firms (See Separate Entry for *Washington Lawyers)*

Lincoln Caplan, Skadden: Power, Money, and the Rise of a Legal Empire (1993).

Marc Galanter & Thomas Palay, Tournament of Lawyers: The Transformation of the Big Law Firm (1991).

Robert W. Gordon, Corporate Law Practice as a Public Calling, 49 Md. L. Rev. 255 (1990).

Deborah Holmes, Structural Causes of Dissatisfaction Among Large-Firm Attorneys: A Feminist Perspective (1988).

William R. Keates, Proceed with Caution: A Diary of the First Year at One of America's Largest, Most Prestigous Law Firms (1997).

Ralph Nader & Wesley J. Smith, No Contest: Corporate Lawyers and the Perversion of Justice in America (1996).

James B. Stewart, The Partners: Inside America's Most Powerful Law Firms (1983).

Legal Services

Gary Bellow, Turning Solutions into Problems: The Legal Aid Experience, 34 Natl. Legal Aid Defender Assn. Briefcase 106 (1977).

Douglas J. Besharov, Legal Services for the Poor: Time for Reform (1990).

Melissa Fay Greene, Praying for Sheetrock (1991).

Stephen Wexler, Practicing Law for Poor People, 79 Yale L.J. 1049 (1970).

Litigation

F. Lee Bailey, To Be a Trial Lawyer (2d ed. 1994).

Jonathan Harr, A Civil Action (1995).

John A. Jenkins, The Litigators: Inside the Powerful World of America's High-Stakes Trial Lawyers (1989).

Douglas E. Rosenthal, Lawyer and Client: Who's in Charge? (1974).

Stuart M. Speiser, Lawsuit (1980).

Matrimonial Practice

Richard Ross, A Day in Part 15: Law and Order in Family Court (1997).

Austin Sarat & William L. F. Felstiner, Divorce Lawyers and Their Clients: Power and Meaning in the Legal Process (1995).

Prosecutors

Mark Baker, D.A.: Prosecutors in Their Own Words (1999).

David Heilbroner, Rough Justice: Days and Nights of a Young D.A. (1990).

James B. Stewart, The Prosecutors: Inside the Offices of the Government's Most Powerful Lawyers (1987).

Public Interest

Nan Aron, Liberty and Justice for All: Public Interest Law in the 1980s and Beyond (1989).

Ann Fagan Ginger, The Relevant Lawyers (1972).

Gerald P. Lopez, Rebellious Lawyering: One Chicano's Vision of Progressive Law Practice (1992).

Roger V. Stover, Making It and Breaking It: The Fate of Public Interest Commitment During Law School (1989).

Small Firm/Small Town

Jerome E. Carlin, Lawyers on Their Own: The Solo Practitioner in an Urban Setting (1994).

Donald D. Landon, Country Lawyers: The Impact of Context on Professional Practice (1990). See also articles by the same author at 1985 Am. Bar Found. Res. J. 81 and at 1982 Am. Bar Found. Res. J. 459.

Philip C. Williams, From Metropolis to Mayberry: A Lawyer's Guide to Small Town Law Practice (1996).

Washington Lawyers

Joseph C. Goulden, The Super-Lawyers: The Small and Powerful World of the Great Washington Law Firms (1972).

Mark J. Green, The Other Government: The Unseen Power of Washington Lawyers (rev. ed. 1978).

Robert L. Nelson et al., Private Representation in Washington: Surveying the Structure of Influence, 1987 Am. Bar Found. Res. J. 141.

Women and Minorities

ABA Commn. on Women in the Profession, Various Reports on the Status of Women in the Profession.

Virginia G. Drachman, Sisters in Law: Women Lawyers in Modern American History (1998).

Cynthia Fuchs Epstein, Women in Law (2d ed. 1993).

John Hagan & Fiona Kay, Gender in Practice: A Study of Lawyers' Lives (1995).

Mona Harrington, Women Lawyers: Rewriting the Rules (1994).

Suzanne Nossel and Elizabeth Westfall, Presumed Equal: What America's Top Women Lawyers Really Think About Their Firms (1998).

Jennifer L. Pierce, Gender Trials: Emotional Lives in Contemporary Law Firms (1995).

J. Clay Smith, Jr. ed., Rebels in Law: Voices in History of Black Women Lawyers (1998).

Symposium, First Women: The Contribution of American Women to the Law, 28 Val. U. L. Rev. No.4 (1994).

Chapter 2

Defense and Prosecution of Criminal Cases

No doubt many more students will engage in civil litigation or office practice than in representation of clients in criminal cases. These materials begin with the field of criminal practice, however, because this area presents a wide range of fundamental issues of professional responsibility in a setting that illuminates the difficult decisions that lawyers often must make. Lawyers who represent criminal defendants can face gut-wrenching problems of confidentiality, zealous representation, and obligations to the system of justice. In an era of increasing public concern about criminality, prosecutors may face enormous pressures to publicize their activities and obtain rapid convictions. Examining tensions among the values that are at the core of professional responsibility helps to build a foundation for study of these values in other settings.[1]

Section A considers the client-lawyer relationship in criminal defense practice, focusing on justifications for defending guilty clients, the duty of competency, and payment of legal fees. The scope and limitations of the duty of confidentiality form the topics of section B. The materials examine the lawyer's duty of confiden-

---

1. See generally ABA Criminal Justice Section, Ethical Problems Facing the Criminal Defense Lawyer (Rodney J. Uphoff ed., 1995); John Wesley Hall, Jr., Professional Responsibility of the Criminal Lawyer (2d ed. 1996).

tiality when the lawyer learns that the client intends to commit a crime, when the lawyer discovers incriminating material, and when the lawyer knows that the client either has or intends to commit perjury. Section C considers conflicts of interest that can arise in criminal defense practice, while section D focuses on limitations on defense and prosecutorial conduct. Delivery of legal services to indigent criminal defendants is the topic of section E.

A. The Client-Lawyer Relationship

———————————— **Problem 2-1** ————————————

Justifications for Defending the Guilty

You have been asked to speak to a local community group on the topic, "How can lawyers defend clients they know are guilty?" What would you say? What questions would you expect to receive and how would you respond?

Read Model Rules 1.2(d), 3.1, and comments.

Charles P. Curtis, The Ethics of Advocacy

4 Stan. L. Rev. 3, 14-18 (1951)

The classical solution to a lawyer taking a case he knows is bad is Dr. Johnson's. It is perfectly simple and quite specious. . . .

"What do you think," said Boswell, "of supporting a cause which you know to be bad?"

Johnson answered, "Sir, you do not know it to be good or bad till the Judge determines it. I have said that you are to state facts fairly; so that your thinking, or what you call knowing, a cause to be bad, must be from reasoning, must be from your supposing your arguments to be weak and inconclusive. But, Sir, that is not enough. An argument which does not convince yourself, may convince the Judge to whom you urge it: and if it does convince him, why, then, Sir, you are wrong, and he is right."

Dr. Johnson ignored the fact that it is the lawyer's job to know how good or how bad his case is. It is his peculiar function to find out. Dr. Johnson's answer is sound only in cases where the problem does not arise.

A lawyer knows very well whether his client is guilty. It is not the lawyer, but the law, that does not know whether his case is good or bad. The law does not know, because it is trying to find out, and so the law wants everyone defended and every debatable case tried. Therefore the law makes it easy for a lawyer to take a case, whether or not he thinks it bad and whether or not he thinks other people think it bad. It is particularly important that it be made as easy as possible for a lawyer to take a case that other people regard as bad. Otherwise, to take a current example, people who are now being charged with being Communists, who heaven knows need a lawyer, what with the capering of congressional committees, will find it hard to get counsel. . . .

No, there is nothing unethical in taking a bad case or defending the guilty or advocating what you don't believe in. It is ethically neutral. It's a free choice. There is a Daumier drawing of a lawyer arguing, a very demure young woman sitting near him, and a small boy beside her sucking a lollypop. The caption says, "He defends the widow and the orphan, unless he is attacking the orphan and the widow." And for every lawyer whose conscience may be pricked, there is another whose virtue is tickled. Every case has two sides, and for every lawyer on the wrong side, there's another on the right side.

I am not being cynical. We are not dealing with the morals which govern a man acting for himself, but with the ethics of advocacy. We are talking about the special moral code which governs a man who is acting for another. Lawyers in their practice — how they behave elsewhere does not concern us — put off more and more of our common morals the farther they go in a profession which treats right and wrong, vice and virtue, on such equal terms. Some lawyers find nothing to take its place. There are others who put on new and shining raiment.

I will give you as good an example as I know that a lawyer can make a case as noble as a cause. I want to tell you how Arthur D. Hill came into the *Sacco-Vanzetti Case*. It was through Felix Frankfurter, and it is his story. Frankfurter wrote some of it in the newspapers shortly after Arthur's death, and he told it to me in more detail just after the funeral.

When the conviction of Sacco and Vanzetti had been sustained by the Supreme Judicial Court of Massachusetts, there was left an all but hopeless appeal to the federal courts, that is, to the Supreme Court. "It was at this stage," Felix Frankfurter said, "that I was asked if I would try to enlist Arthur Hill's legal services to undertake a final effort, hopeless as it seemed, by appeal to the Federal Law."

Frankfurter called Arthur Hill up and said that he had a very serious matter to discuss with him. "In that case," said Arthur Hill, "we had better have a good lunch first. I will meet you at the Somerset Club for lunch and afterwards you will tell me about it." They lunched together at the Somerset Club, and after lunch they crossed Beacon Street and they sat on the bench in Boston Common overlooking the Frog Pond. And Frankfurter asked Arthur Hill if he would undertake this final appeal of the *Sacco-Vanzetti Case* to the Supreme Court.

Arthur Hill said, "If the president of the biggest bank in Boston came to me and said that his wife had been convicted of murder, but he wanted me to see if there was any possible relief in the Supreme Court of the United States and offered me a fee of $50,000 to make such an effort, of course I would take the retainer, as would, I suppose, everybody else at the bar. It would be a perfectly honorable thing to see whether there was anything in the record which laid a basis for an appeal to the Federal Court.

"I do not see how I can decline a similar effort on behalf of Sacco and Vanzetti simply because they are poor devils against whom the feeling of the community is strong and they have no money with which to hire me. I don't particularly enjoy the proceedings that will follow, but I don't see how I can possibly refuse to make the effort."

. . . Arthur Hill was hired. He did get a fee. Arthur Hill took it as a law case. To him it was a case, not a cause. He was not the partisan, he was the advocate. . . .

I have talked perhaps too lovingly about the practice of the law. I have spoken unsparingly, as I would to another lawyer. In a way the practice of the law is like free speech. It defends what we hate as well as what we most love. . . .

**Monroe H. Freedman, Understanding Lawyers'
Ethics**

13-14 (1990)

THE ADVERSARY SYSTEM

In its simplest terms, an adversary system is one in which disputes are resolved by having the parties present their conflicting views of fact and law before an impartial and relatively passive judge and/or jury, who decides which side wins what. In the United States, however, the phrase "adversary system" is synonymous with the American system for the administration of justice, as that system has been incorporated into the constitution and elaborated by the Supreme Court for two centuries. Thus, the adversary system represents far more than a simple model for resolving disputes. Rather, it consists of a core of basic rights that recognize and protect the dignity of the individual in a free society.

The rights that comprise the adversary system include personal autonomy, the effective assistance of counsel, equal protection of the laws, trial by jury, the rights to call and to confront witnesses, and the right to require the government to prove guilt beyond a reasonable doubt and without the use of compelled self-incrimination. These rights, and others, are also included in the broad and fundamental concept that no person may be deprived of life, liberty, or property without due process of law — a concept which itself has been substantially equated with the adversary system.

An essential function of the adversary system, therefore, is to maintain a free society in which individual rights are central. In that sense the right to counsel is "the most pervasive" of rights, because it affects the client's ability to assert all other rights. As Professor Geoffrey Hazard has written, the adversary system "stands with freedom of speech and the right of assembly as a pillar of our constitutional system." It follows that the professional responsibilities of the lawyer within such a system must be determined, in major part, by the same civil libertarian values that are embodied in the Constitution.

John B. Mitchell, The Ethics of the Criminal Defense
Attorney — New Answers to Old Questions

32 Stan. L. Rev. 293, 296-303, 321-323, 326-331 (1980)

I.   *"MAKING THE SCREENS WORK": THE ROLE OF THE CRIMINAL DEFENSE ATTORNEY*

By providing a rigorous defense for a person the attorney knows is factually guilty, an attorney fulfills two significant functions. First, the attorney ensures that the guilty defendant — entitled to the full benefit of our legal process regardless of guilt or innocence — is treated fairly and humanely while in that legal process. I will discuss this function in some detail later when I explore why I personally defend the guilty. Second, and as I will discuss in this part, the attorney performs a function which protects all members of society; I will call this function "making the screens work." . . .

Our criminal justice system is more appropriately defined as a screening system than as a truth-seeking one. This screening process is directed at accurately sorting out those whose deviancy has gone beyond what society considers tolerable and has passed into the area that substantive law labels criminal. The ultimate objective of this screening is to determine who are the proper subjects of the criminal sanction. The process goes on continually at every level of society. We all make judgments about someone's unusual behavior, a window that looks pried open, a suspicious-looking stranger. Neighbor talks to neighbor, and information filters to the police. The police comb the streets gathering information to find those whose behavior warrants special attention. Finally, prosecutors, courts, and juries constantly sift through those selected by the police to make final determinations about who is to be subjected to the criminal sanction.

In performing this screening process, however, the criminal justice system does not operate primarily as a truth-seeking process in the scientific sense. It is weighted at trial in favor of protecting the innocent, even at the cost of acquitting the guilty. It is weighted on the streets in favor of protecting the individual from intrusion by the state, at the cost of the more efficient methods of crime control that would result if police could stop, question, and search anyone they desired. In so doing, our process protects two inter-related and overlapping values (or perhaps, more accurately, two aspects of the same value, human freedom) — dignity and auton-omy.

The "weighting" of the system to avoid conviction of the innocent reflects the paramount value this society places upon the dignity of the individual, as well as our concern for the value of human autonomy, a concern which makes us reticent to allow government to enter our daily lives either to restrict our freedom or to intrude into our privacy. The "weighting" against police in-trusion similarly reflects these two interrelated values.

The criminal justice system is itself composed of a series of "screens," of which trial is but one. By keeping innocents out of the process and, at the same time, limiting the intrusion of the state into people's lives, each of these screens functions to protect the values of human dignity and autonomy while enforcing our criminal laws. Further, to ensure that the intrusion of the state into the individual's life will be halted at the soonest possible junc-ture, our system provides a separate screen at each of the several stages of the criminal process. Thus, at any screen, the individual may be taken out of the criminal process and returned to the so-ciety with as little disruption of his or her life as possible. . . .

[T]he ingenuity of our criminal justice system goes beyond the screens themselves, for the quality of the screens is no better than the performance of those who make them work. The system has built-in checks on those in charge of the various screens, and . . . the defense attorney who insists on defending the innocence of a guilty defendant plays an important role in making sure that these built-in checks operate effectively. . . .

II.   WHY I DEFEND THE GUILTY

A.   Lessons Better Not Learned

The criminal justice system provides an institution through which we as a society can demonstrate that we are just and can teach that there is a better way to live than the predatory life of crime. But somehow the noble purpose of our criminal courts, our "schools for justice," has gone awry. Our courts are not just, and they are most frequently unjust when dealing with the most powerless defendants, the poor and the minorities.

Many judges in large urban court systems, interested only in clearing their dockets, and often given to a martinet's temperament, shuttle the 20 or so new faces represented by the same public defender each day from arraignment through guilty plea. Police often lie, while prosecutors suppress evidence favorable to the defense. This governmental lawbreaking passes without the slightest notice. Under the umbrella of almost limitless discretion, judges are often guided only by their inclinations. From my experience, many of them consistently rule in favor of the prosecution and hide their biases while prejudicing any jury over which they are presiding. It is my belief that written motions filed by the defense attorney are frequently not read, while they are routinely denied with no more cogent opposition from the district attorney than the single word "submitted." If it seems that the process is rigged, it is because it is meant to appear that way. Defendants are not there to file motions, have hearings, and go to trial; they are there to plead guilty. As such, the courts have not ceased to be teachers of lessons. It is only that the lessons have changed — and they have changed in a way that approves the normative system of the criminal defendant. . . .

Our criminal courts must teach better lessons. It is to this end that I defend the guilty, for they, above all, must be taught the right lesson. It is not that I naively believe that most convicted defendants would thank a judge for being "fair" while sending them to prison. From my experience, however, the prevalent injustice in the current process does do harm by further lessening respect for the law, not just in the criminal defendants, but also in friends, family, witnesses, and spectators. The lessons are communicated to all of those who are touched by the process.

The defense of the guilty teaches new lessons. The act of defense itself teaches that the indigent defendant is not alone and worthless without money. The slow process of a rigorous defense may anger the judge by delaying the court's schedule, but it also forces the court to view the defendant as a person rather than a file. On some deeper level, the attorney's ardent defense itself communicates to the judge a sense of the defendant's human worth, and to the extent that a sincere, competent advocate earns the grudging respect of the court, some of that respect transfers to the defendant. As a result of this respect — and the knowledge that every ruling adverse to the defense will be contested — the judge rules more favorably for the defendant in order to avoid complications. Finally, police and prosecutors, aware that a defense attorney is carefully questioning and reviewing all their actions, begin to hesitate to engage with such broad abandon in illegality and misconduct for fear of getting caught. Power will thus begin to conform more to law than the other way around.

B. THE RAVAGES OF CONVICTION

1. *The Prisons*

A lengthy exposition on the nightmarish conditions in our jails and prisons would cover little new ground. Literature and reports documenting the horrors are extensive. These horrors are not isolated to some crazed southern jail or labor camp, or to a 20th century Bastille in upstate New York called Attica — they exist even in our most affluent state, California. I have seen many of California's prisons and jails and witnessed the ravages of boredom and the constant fear of violent assault. Over the past 7 years, I have seen inmates who were assaulted and tormented by guards, and others who were beaten by members of prison gangs. I have listened to a terrified young man who, sentenced to 45 days in county jail for vehicular manslaughter, sat awake his first night to the sounds of the inmate in the cell to the left of him being sexually assaulted and the old man in the cage to his right having his head slammed against the floor by some younger ones; while the guards just ignored both and busied themselves with paperwork and cups of coffee. I have seen the anger and bitterness build in some, and I have seen the total mental degeneration of others. Worst of all, I have seen the inhuman degradation of their spirit.

I will not dwell on this. Those guilty of serious crimes merit the wrath of our society. But almost no one deserves the hell holes that we call jails and prisons. There is almost no case I would not defend if that meant keeping a human being, as condemnable as he or she may be, from suffering the total, brutal inhumanity of our jails and prisons. . . .

2. *The Revolving Door*

The entire criminal system, at least for minority defendants, seems to operate like a great revolving door from which they cannot exit once they have been caught up in its momentum. . . .

Long periods of incarceration in prison mean extreme dislocation from family, friends, and work. On release, assimilation is difficult. This time the defendant is an ex-con on parole, not probation. It makes little difference. Before he can reestablish his personal or work lives, one of the dozens of prying eyes now looking at him detect something and he is returned to the system. This cycle continues.

The earlier this cycle is broken by a defense attorney's acquittal or dismissal for the defendant, the better the chances that he can get his life in order. . . .

Hugo Adam Bedau & Michael L. Radelet, Miscarriages of Justice in Potentially Capital Cases

40 Stan. L. Rev. 21 (1987)

[In an effort to contribute to the debate on the wisdom of continuing to have the death penalty, Professors Bedau and Radelet identified 350 cases in which defendants were convicted of capital or potentially capital crimes and were later found to have been innocent.[2]

Table 5 in their article summarizes the evidence on which the authors based their conclusions of innocence. Table 6 summarizes the causes of erroneous convictions.]

---

2. 40 Stan. L. Rev. 21, 23-24 (1987). An article in the ABA Journal reports on the growing number of cases in which individuals who have been convicted of capital or other serious crimes have been exonerated. In many of these cases, DNA evidence has been instrumental in establishing the defendant's innocence. See Terry Carter, Numbers Tell the Story, 83-Oct A.B.A. J. 20 (1997). See also Michael A. Mello, Dead Wrong: A Death Row Lawyer Speaks Out Against Capital Punishment (1997). For a dramatic account of one such case, see Edward Humes, Mean Justice (1999). The ABA has recommended a moratorium on the death penalty until steps are taken to reduce the risk of sentencing innocent persons to death. ABA, Resolution 107 (1997).

TABLE 5[3]

PRIMARY EVIDENCE FOR JUDGMENT OF ERROR
(N = 350)*

		Number of Cases	
I. State decisions indicating error			309
A. Legislative indemnity		20	
B. Executive		129	
1. Pardon	64		
2. Other action	65		
C. Judicial		160	
1. Indemnity	9		
2. Reversal (by trial or appellate court)	151		
a. No retrial; conviction set aside or *nolle prosequi* entered	113		
b. Acquitted by retrial or directed verdict	38		
II. Other (unofficial) actions indicating error			41
A. Confession of another person		13	
B. Another person implicated		7	
C. Opinion of state official		6	
D. Subsequent scholarly judgment		15	

*Note: Each case is counted only once even though in many cases, there is more than one type of evidence.

TABLE 6[4]

CAUSES OF ERRONEOUS CONVICTION

Type of Error		*Number of Cases*
I. Police error		82
A. Coerced or other false confession	49	
B. Negligence	11	
C. Other overzealous police work	22	
II. Prosecutor error		50
A. Suppression of exculpatory evidence	35	
B. Other overzealous prosecution	15	
III. Witness error		193
A. Mistaken eyewitness identification	56	

3. 40 Stan. L. Rev. at 49.
4. Id. at 57.

TABLE 6 (continued)

	Type of Error	Number of Cases	
B.	Perjury by prosecution witness	117	
C.	Unreliable or erroneous prosecution testimony	20	
IV.	Other error		209
A.	Misleading circumstantial evidence	30	
B.	Incompetence of defense counsel	10	
C.	Judicial denial of admissibility of exculpatory evidence	7	
D.	Inadequate consideration of alibi evidence	45	
E.	Erroneous judgment on cause of death	16	
F.	Fraudulent alibi or false guilty plea made by defendant	17	
G.	Conviction demanded by community outrage	70	
H.	Unknown	14	

Number of cases counted once: 198 (including all "unknown" cases)
Number of cases counted twice: 120
Number of cases counted three times: 32

———————— **Problem 2-2** ————————

Competency of Defense Counsel and Legal Fees in Criminal Cases

Armed Robbery   *a.*   You have been appointed to represent Edward Donald to seek postconviction relief from his conviction in state court for armed robbery of a check-cashing service. Attorney Thomas Long represented Donald at trial. Donald first met Long a week before trial for about an hour. Donald told Long that he was innocent of the charges and that he was at a bar with a friend when the robbery occurred. Donald also asked Long about the possibility of a plea bargain. Long said he would try to locate the friend and to discuss a plea with the prosecutor. At trial the next week, Long told Donald that he had been unable to locate the friend. Long also advised Donald that the prosecutor refused to plea bargain because of Donald's criminal history. (Donald has a long record, beginning with minor crimes as a juvenile and now including burglary, assault, and drug offenses.)

At trial the prosecution called the owner of the service as its only witness; the owner testified about the robbery and identified Donald as the perpetrator of the crime. Long did not ask the owner any questions. Donald was particularly upset about this because the owner was old and wore glasses. Donald told Long that he wanted to testify to refute the owner's testimony and to establish his alibi, but Long said that he could not call him as a witness because of his criminal record. The defense rested without calling any witnesses. Long gave a brief closing argument in which he pointed out that the case rested on the store owner's identification, that the store owner was elderly and wore glasses, and that under these circumstances the state had not proven its case beyond a reasonable doubt. The jury convicted Donald, the trial judge sentenced him to twenty years in prison (the maximum allowed by statute), and the conviction and sentence were affirmed by the state supreme court. Be prepared to argue in support of and in opposition to a motion to set aside Donald's conviction because of ineffective assistance of counsel.

b.   You are an associate in a private law firm that specializes in criminal defense work. The firm would like your opinion of the propriety of the following provision in its standard engagement agreement:

Client agrees to pay the Firm a fee of _____ . This fee covers the Firm's representation of Client through the trial of this case. The fee does not cover subsequent proceedings, such as appeals, or retrials of the case should that be necessary. The Firm does not agree to represent Client in any subsequent proceedings unless Client and the Firm enter into a written engagement agreement covering such a proceeding. The fee for any subsequent proceeding shall be subject to negotiation by Client and the Firm. **THE CLIENT UNDERSTANDS AND AGREES THAT THE FEE SET FORTH ABOVE IS NONREFUNDABLE REGARDLESS OF WHEN THIS MATTER IS CONCLUDED.**
This fee does not cover expenses, such as the cost of expert witnesses, travel expenses, transcription

costs, and other out-of-pocket expenses incurred by the Firm. The Client has paid _____ as an advance against expenses. If this advance is exhausted, the Firm will bill Client for actual expenses incurred on a monthly basis. The Client agrees to pay such expenses within 15 days.

c.　The firm has been asked to represent the defendant in a highly publicized prosecution for homicide. The state contends that the defendant murdered two infants in a day care center by brutally shaking them. The defendant and her family have only limited funds. Your partner tells you that the firm is willing to handle the case pro bono if necessary, but the possibility exists that the defendant or her family might receive revenue as a result of the publicity surrounding the case, such as fees for appearances on television shows and royalties from books, television, or movies. The partner wants to know whether the firm could take a security interest in any revenues that the defendant might receive from such sources to secure payment of its fees. What advice would you give?

Read Model Rules 1.1, 1.5(a) and (d), 1.8(d), 1.15, and comments.

The ethical duty of competency, ineffective assistance of counsel, and malpractice liability of defense counsel

Under the Model Rules of Professional Conduct, lawyers have an ethical duty to provide competent representation. The duty of competency is multidimensional, including knowledge of the law, skill, and preparation. See Model Rule 1.1. Despite this obligation in criminal cases, the level of representation provided by appointed counsel is often shockingly low, even in death penalty cases. Examples of recent cases in which lawyers have slept through substantial portions of the trial[5] or have been under the influence of

---

5. See Tippins v. Walker, 77 F.3d 682 (2d Cir. 1996) (defendant's constitutional rights violated when counsel was repeatedly unconscious at trial for periods of time in which significant testimony was taking place).

alcohol or drugs[6] are easy to find. One reason for the low level of representation by appointed counsel is that the compensation paid to such counsel is woefully inadequate in most states. See Zarabia v. Bradshaw, 912 P.2d 5 (Ariz. 1996) (en banc) (county system for appointment of counsel in criminal cases violated defendants' constitutional right to effective assistance of counsel because, among other reasons, system provided compensation for defense counsel at amount that was significantly less than their overhead expenses with no compensation for their time). We will return to the topic of delivery of legal services to indigents in criminal cases in Problem 2-12.

Lawyers who fail to adhere to their duty to provide competent representation may be subject to professional discipline.[7] For example, in Florida Bar v. Sandstrom[8] the respondent represented the defendant in a prosecution for the murder of his wife, who died after the defendant struck her during an altercation. The defendant was convicted, but his conviction was set aside because of ineffective assistance of counsel. The Florida Supreme Court imposed a 60-day suspension on defense counsel based on the following findings of fact by the referee in the case about defense counsel's ineffective assistance at trial:

> Sandstrom failed to take any pretrial depositions; failed to conduct a proper investigation as related to evidence available to establish that the proximate cause of the wife's death was medical malpractice; failed to timely challenge the admission of evidence relating to a search of Arner's car trunk; failed to discover that a fence, surrounding the scene of the alleged crime and injurious to Arner's defense, was not erected until over a year after the alleged crime; failed to present a tape recording to impeach a prosecution witness; and failed to become familiar with or know the physical evidence in the case.[9]

While disciplinary proceedings charging lawyers with incompetent representation in criminal cases are not uncommon, the

6. Payne v. United States, 697 A.2d 1229 (D.C. 1997) (drug use by defense counsel known by trial judge).
7. Debra T. Landis, Annotation, Negligence, Inattention, or Professional Incompetence of Attorney in Handling Client's Affairs in Criminal Matters as Ground for Disciplinary Action — Modern Cases, 69 A.L.R.4th 410 (1989).
8. 609 So. 2d 583 (Fla. 1992).
9. Id.

number of such cases is tiny compared to the frequency of proceedings in which defendants seek postconviction relief based on
charges of ineffective assistance of counsel. In Strickland v. Washington[10] the Court established a two-part test for determining
when ineffective representation required reversal of a conviction:
First, the defendant must show that counsel's performance fell
below an objective standard of "reasonably effective assistance."[11]
In making this judgment, a court should consider all facts and
circumstances, including prevailing norms of the profession. The
Court warned that judicial scrutiny should be "highly deferential"
and should engage in a "strong presumption" that counsel's conduct was reasonable.[12] Second, "any deficiencies in counsel's performance must be prejudicial to the defense in order to constitute
ineffective assistance under the Constitution."[13] In defining prejudice, the Court rejected a test that would have required the defendant to show that the attorney's ineffective assistance was
"outcome determinative." Instead, the Court stated: "The defendant must show that there is a reasonable probability that, but for
counsel's unprofessional errors, the result of the proceeding would
have been different. A reasonable probability is a probability sufficient to undermine confidence in the outcome."[14]

In thousands of cases federal and state courts have applied
the Strickland standard to determine whether to grant postconviction relief.[15] Cases in which defendants are successful are rare. A
typical example is Wilson v. Henry,[16] a prosecution for murder.
The Ninth Circuit outlined Wilson's claims of ineffective assistance of counsel as follows:

> Wilson raises six claims of ineffective assistance by trial coun-
> sel La Rue Grim ("Grim"), who had represented him in previous
> matters. According to Wilson, Grim met with him for about an hour

10. 466 U.S. 668 (1984).
11. Id. at 687.
12. Id. at 689.
13. Id. at 692.
14. Id. at 694.
15. In 1996 Congress passed the Antiterrorism and Effective Death Penalty Act of 1996, Pub. L. No. 104-132, 110 Stat. 1214. The Act included amendments to the federal postconviction relief statute, 28 U.S.C. §2254, which limit
the authority of federal courts to grant postconviction relief.
16. 185 F.3d 986 (9th Cir. 1999).

before trial and spoke with him for fifteen minutes each day of trial. Grim informed Wilson that he would be asked about his prior convictions, but did not review them with him. While in jail awaiting trial, Wilson told Grim that Jacqueline James ("James") had seen Henry in her home near the site of the shooting immediately before the shooting, with a shotgun under his coat. Grim did not call James as a witness and, following trial, did not move for a new trial based on James' written declaration.[17]

The court denied relief, finding no merit to Wilson's contentions, because Grim's conduct did not fall below the standard of reasonably effective assistance and, even if it did, because Wilson had failed to establish prejudice from Grim's ineffective assistance.

As *Wilson* demonstrates, the *Strickland* requirement that the defendant show prejudice to obtain postconviction relief is often an insurmountable barrier, either because the other evidence of guilt is overwhelming or because it is difficult to show a reasonable probability that the outcome would have been different except for the attorney's ineffective assistance. In a few limited types of cases, however, the courts will presume that the defendant has suffered prejudice. As we shall see in connection with Problem 2-7, when defense counsel has an actual conflict of interest in connection with the representation, prejudice is presumed. In addition, some cases of ineffective assistance involve structural errors that go to the accuracy and reliability of the trial process. In these cases prejudice is presumed. Examples of structural errors include defense counsel's failure to inform the defendant of the right to a jury trial[18] or the right to appeal.[19] Finally, in some cases defense counsel's representation is so deficient that the trial did not constitute a true adversary proceeding. Rickman v. Bell[20] is an example of such a situation. In *Rickman* defense counsel in effect abandoned his role as advocate for the defendant. In a later decision the Sixth Circuit summarized the situation in *Rickman* as follows:

Rickman was a capital murder case before us on federal habeas review in which we concluded that trial counsel had not only failed to investigate the case or prepare for the guilt phase of the trial,

17. Id. at 987-988.
18. McGurk v. Stenberg, 163 F.3d 470 (8th Cir. 1998).
19. White v. Johnson, 180 F.3d 648 (5th Cir. 1999).
20. 131 F.3d 1150 (6th Cir. 1997), *cert. denied*, 118 S. Ct. 1827 (1998).

failed to consider the possibility of an insanity defense, and failed
to construct any rational theory of defense, but, in the guise of
attempting to portray Rickman as sick and abnormal, had "convey[ed] to the jurors an unmistakable personal antagonism toward
Rickman, characterized both by attacks on Rickman and by repeatedly eliciting information detrimental to Rickman's interests,"
. . . particularly during the guilt phase of the trial. This information
included detailed testimony that Rickman had carefully planned
every aspect of the murder at issue and that he had threatened to
commit unrelated crimes, including bombings. Finally, and perhaps most importantly, counsel, while not claiming that Rickman
was insane, went to great lengths to portray Rickman as crazed and
dangerous, and to soliloquize to the jury about his shame that Rickman's victim had suffered horribly and his knowledge that as Rickman's counsel, he himself would suffer guilt by association. The
issue, we said, was whether Rickman's counsel's performance fell
within the narrow exception to the *Strickland* requirement of proving prejudice carved out by *Strickland*'s companion case, United
States v. Cronic, 466 U.S. 468 (1984). The *Cronic* exception includes the circumstance in which counsel "entirely fails to subject
the prosecution's case to meaningful adversarial testing. . . ."
Cronic, 466 U.S. at 659. Rickman's counsel, we noted, had done
just that; he had "succeeded in presenting a terrifying image of
Rickman, and thereby aligned himself with the prosecution against
his own client."[21]

Defendants can assert ineffective assistance of counsel claims
not only as a basis for setting aside convictions but also in actions
for damages for legal malpractice against defense counsel.[22] These
claims are likely to be difficult to sustain, however. Most courts
require such defendants to show that they were innocent of the
crimes with which they were charged.[23] Further, courts typically

21. Khalife v. United States, 1999 WL 357802 (6th Cir. 1999) (unpub-
lished opinion).
22. On the malpractice liability of criminal defense counsel, see generally
3 Mallen & Smith, Legal Malpractice ch. 25 and Gregory G. Sarno, Annotation, Legal Malpractice in Defense of Criminal Prosecution, 4 A.L.R.5th 273
(1993).
23. *Compare* Wiley v. County of San Diego, 966 P.2d 983 (Cal. 1998);
Glenn v. Aiken, 569 N.E.2d 783 (Mass. 1991); Carmel v. Lunney, 511 N.E.2d
1126 (N.Y. 1987); and Peeler v. Hughes & Luce, 909 S.W.2d 494 (Tex. 1995)
(proof of innocence required) *with* Fischer v. Longest, 637 A.2d 517 (Md. Ct.
Spec. App.), *cert. denied*, 644 A.2d 488 (Md. 1994) and Krahn v. Kinney, 538
N.E.2d 1058 (Ohio 1989) (proof of innocence not required).

require defendants to seek postconviction relief before filing malpractice actions.[24] Most courts have ruled that defendants who are
unsuccessful in obtaining postconviction relief are collaterally estopped from bringing actions for legal malpractice against defense
counsel.[25] States are divided on whether public defenders and appointed counsel should be entitled to immunity from malpractice
liability.[26] Actions against federal public defenders must be
brought against the United States under the Federal Tort Claims
Act rather than against the individual attorney.[27] Professor Susan
Koniak has criticized the cases that have erected barriers to malpractice actions against defense counsel. She argues that a proper
assessment of the values at stake would impose greater obligations
on criminal defense counsel than those imposed on counsel in civil
cases.[28]

Ethical issues regarding fees in criminal cases

Model Rule 1.5 establishes ethical standards for legal fees. Under
Rule 1.5(a) fees must be reasonable. We will consider the general
reasonableness standard in connection with fees in civil cases in
Problem 3-1.

In criminal cases private defense lawyers often require clients
to make substantial payments before undertaking representation.
The ethical propriety of such fee arrangements depends on the
type of payment received. Lawyers often refer to such advance
payments as "retainers." It is important to distinguish, however,
among general retainers, special retainers, flat fees, and expense
deposits. A general retainer is a payment to the lawyer for agreeing

24. See Shaw v. State, 816 P.2d 1358 (Alaska 1991).

25. Steele v. Kehoe, 1999 WL 343071 (Fla. 1999); Knoblauch v. Kenyon,
415 N.W.2d 286 (Mich. Ct. App. 1987); Adkins v. Dixon, 482 S.E.2d 797 (Va.),
cert. denied, 118 S. Ct. 348 (1997).

26. Compare Dziubak v. Mott, 503 N.W.2d 771 (Minn. 1993) (public
defenders immune) with Ferri v. Ackerman, 411 A.2d 213 (Pa. 1980) (appointed
counsel not immune). See also Coyazo v. State, 897 P.2d 234 (N.M. Ct. App.
1995) (statutory immunity for public defenders and private attorneys providing
defense services under contract).

27. See Sullivan v. United States, 21 F.3d 198 (7th Cir.), cert. denied, 513
U.S. 1060 (1994).

28. Susan P. Koniak, Through the Looking Glass of Ethics and the Wrong
With Rights We Find There, 9 Geo. J. Legal Ethics 1, 5 (1995).

to take the case, or for agreeing to be available to handle legal matters for the client during a specified period of time. A special retainer (or advanced fee), as the name indicates, is an advanced payment by the client of fees for services to be rendered in the future.[29] A flat fee is a payment of a fixed amount for specific services. An expense deposit is an amount paid to the firm to be applied to future expenses in the client's case.

Gen/specific

·Gen is
part of
revenue

·specific is
not

General retainers differ from special retainers in two significant respects. First, the lawyer earns a general retainer when it is received, so it is part of the firm's general revenue and should not be deposited in the firm's trust account. By contrast, the firm does not earn the special retainer when received. It should be deposited in the firm's trust account, and the firm should then charge against this amount periodically as it performs services for the client. See Model Rule 1.15 on lawyers' obligations regarding trust accounts, discussed more fully below. Second, since the purpose of the general retainer is to assure the availability of the firm rather than to serve as payment for specific services rendered, the retainer is nonrefundable. By contrast, since the special retainer is an advanced fee payment, if the fee for those services is less than the advance payment, the lawyer must refund to the client any excess of the advance fee over the fee for services rendered.[30]

A flat fee differs from a special retainer in one crucial respect: Under a flat fee a lawyer cannot contractually charge the client any additional amounts for the services rendered, regardless of how long it takes to perform those services. Because a special retainer is simply an advance fee, however, the lawyer is not contractually limited to the amount of the retainer. The lawyer may charge the client additional amounts for services rendered if the special retainer is exhausted.

In Iowa Supreme Court Board of Professional Ethics & Conduct v. Apland,[31] the Iowa Supreme Court held that nonrefundable special retainers in criminal cases were unethical and void. The court stated:

29. On the distinction between special and general retainers, see Iowa Supreme Court Bd. of Professional Ethics & Conduct v. Apland, 577 N.W.2d 50 (Iowa 1998).
30. See Wolfram, Modern Legal Ethics §9.2.2, at 505-506.
31. 577 N.W.2d 50 (Iowa 1998).

such agreements (1) interfere with client's right to discharge an attorney, (2) attempt to limit attorney's duty to refund promptly, upon discharge, all those fees not yet earned . . . and (3) result in an excessive fee to the extent the fee is not earned. . . . [32]

Other courts agree that nonrefundable special retainers are improper.[33]

The courts that have voided nonrefundable retainers have not, however, discussed whether the decisions apply to flat fees. In contrast to a nonrefundable retainer, a flat fee offers an advantage to the client because it imposes a limit on the amount the client must pay for the lawyer's services. In fact, the flat fee has advantages and disadvantages to both the lawyer and the client. A flat fee provides certainty to both the lawyer and client regarding the amount of the fee. In exchange for this certainty, however, both the client and the lawyer make concessions. The client gives up the right to a refund if the time value of the lawyer's services is less than the amount of the flat fee (for example, if the case is dismissed or the client pleads guilty before the case goes to trial). The lawyer gives up the right to seek additional compensation if the time value of the lawyer's services exceeds the amount of the flat fee (for example, if the case goes to trial and the trial takes substantially longer than the lawyer anticipates). Ethics opinions in North Carolina and Ohio have advised that lawyers may charge clients flat fees provided the amount of the fee is reasonable. The opinions ruled that lawyers may consider flat fees like general retainers, treating the flat fee payment as earned income to be deposited in the firm's business account rather than in its trust account. The opinions warned lawyers that the amount of the flat fee must be reasonable and cautioned lawyers against characterizing flat fees as nonrefundable.[34]

32. Id. at 57.

33. E.g., In re Thonert, 682 N.E.2d 522 (Ind. 1997) (unethical to demand nonrefundable fee in criminal case when no evidence of any value received by the client or detriment incurred by the attorney in return for the nonrefundable provision); In re Cooperman, 633 N.E.2d 1069 (N.Y. 1994) (divorce case). See generally Lester Brickman & Lawrence A. Cunningham, Nonrefundable Retainers Revisited, 72 N.C.L. Rev. 1 (1993) (supporting the decision in *Cooperman* finding that nonrefundable retainers result in excessive fees).

34. N.C. St. Bar Op. 4 (1998) (Nonrefundable Fees), 1998 WL 716663; Ohio Bd. Com. Griev. Disp., Adv. Op. 96-4, 1996 WL 362465.

In addition to the prohibition on nonrefundable special retainers, fees in criminal cases are subject to several other specific restrictions. Model Rule 1.5(d) prohibits contingent fees in criminal cases,[35] although it is difficult to offer a sound rationale for the rule.[36] Indeed, the comments to Rule 1.5 offer no justification.[37] It has been argued that the purpose of the rule is to prevent corruption of justice by criminal defense counsel who would have a financial interest in the outcome through a contingent fee, but the same argument could be made against contingent fees in civil cases.[38] Some commentators have suggested that the prohibition of contingent fees in criminal cases exists to avoid a conflict of interest: If the contingent fee were earned only by an acquittal, defense counsel would have a conflict of interest because counsel would have a financial disincentive against plea bargaining.[39] This problem could be handled, however, by requiring a sliding scale of contingent fees depending on the outcome, much like the sliding scale typically used in personal injury cases.

Another rule that restricts legal fees in criminal cases is Model Rule 1.8(d), which provides as follows:

> Prior to the conclusion of representation of a client, a lawyer shall not make or negotiate an agreement giving the lawyer literary or media rights to a portrayal or account based in substantial part on information relating to the representation.

While the rule is not strictly limited to criminal cases, it comes up more frequently in criminal cases because they are more likely to

---

35. See Winkler v. Keane, 7 F.3d 304 (2d Cir. 1993), *cert. denied*, 511 U.S. 1022 (1994) (fee agreement in which defense counsel was to receive additional $25,000 if defendant was found not guilty constituted an unethical contingency fee, but court refused to set aside conviction because defendant failed to prove that trial counsel's representation was adversely affected).

36. See Thomas D. Morgan, The Evolving Concept of Professional Responsibility, 90 Harv. L. Rev. 702, 734 (1977) (arguing that prohibition on contingent fees in criminal cases protects defense bar's practice of charging up-front fixed fees by suppressing competition through contingent fees).

37. For a criticism of the traditional justifications of the rule and an argument that contingent fees should be allowed in criminal cases in some limited circumstances, see Pamela S. Karlan, Contingent Fees and Criminal Cases, 93 Colum. L. Rev. 595 (1993).

38. Wolfram, Modern Legal Ethics §9.4.3, at 535-536.

39. 1 Hazard & Hodes, The Law of Lawyering §1.5:501.

be sensational than are civil cases. The rationale for the rule is to prevent lawyers from having a financial interest that would interfere with their independent professional judgment. For example, if a lawyer who is representing a client in a criminal case has acquired literary or media rights based on the representation, the lawyer might be inclined to forgo plea bargaining in order to sensationalize the case and thereby increase the value of the lawyer's interest in media or literary rights. Note that the rule applies only to agreements made "[p]rior to the conclusion of representation of a client." Presumably this means that a lawyer in a criminal case, after the conclusion of the criminal matter, could agree to represent the client in connection with literary or media rights growing out of the case, with the lawyer receiving an interest in such rights as payment for the lawyer's services.[40]

The California Supreme Court has held that in order to be able to retain counsel a criminal defendant may consent to a fee agreement in which the lawyer has an interest in literary or media rights.[41] The California Rules of Professional Conduct, however, do not have a provision like Model Rule 1.8(d). It appears that the drafters of the Model Rules intended to prohibit such fee agreements even with client consent because the drafters concluded that such fee agreements inherently involved a conflict of interest.[42]

It is also interesting to note that a number of states and the federal government have enacted statutes to prevent criminal defendants from profiting from commercial exploitation of their crimes.[43] (Such statutes are often referred to as "Son of Sam" laws, after the New York serial killer David Berkowitz.) These statutes typically require convicted criminals to pay any funds received from commercial portrayals of their crimes to a fund for victims of their crimes. In Simon & Schuster, Inc. v. Members of

---

40. Even after the conclusion of a criminal case, a lawyer could not acquire an interest in literary or media rights that were the subject of litigation. See Model Rule 1.8(j). The lawyer could, however, have an interest in such rights and represent the client in negotiating contracts regarding those rights without violating Rule 1.8(j), provided the lawyer also complied with the requirements of Rule 1.8(a) dealing with business transactions between lawyer and client.

41. Maxwell v. Superior Court, 639 P.2d 248 (Cal. 1982) (en banc).

42. See 1 Hazard & Hodes, The Law of Lawyering §1.8:501, at 271 n.1.

43. See 18 U.S.C. §§3681-3682 (special forfeiture of collateral profits of crime).

the New York State Crime Victims Board,[44] the Supreme Court held the New York statute invalid under the First Amendment. In 1992 the New York legislature passed a revised law.[45]

Trust accounts and client property

Lawyers often come into possession of client money or property, or money or property belonging to a third person. In criminal cases lawyers often receive special retainers, flat fees, or expense advances. In personal injury matters lawyers obtain and disburse settlement proceeds. In real estate matters lawyers hold payments for property. See Problem 5-3. In business transactions lawyers receive and disburse funds in corporate acquisitions. Model Rule 1.15,[46] dealing with lawyers' obligations regarding money and property belonging to clients and third parties, imposes several obligations:

1.   *The duty not to commingle.* Lawyers must keep money and property belonging to clients and third persons separate from their personal and firm funds.

The rule against commingling acts as a prophylactic against lawyer misuse of client funds and protects such funds from being subject to the claims of lawyers' creditors.[47] Lawyers have been disciplined for commingling even when clients have not suffered any financial harm and even when the lawyer acted innocently.[48] The standard method used to prevent commingling is establishment of escrow or trust accounts, separate from lawyers' general accounts, into which money belonging to a client or third party is

---

44. 502 U.S. 105 (1991).

45. See N.Y. Exec. Law §632-a. For an analysis of the Supreme Court's decision in *Simon & Schuster* and of the revised law, see Amr F. Amer, Comment, Play It Again Sam: New York's Renewed Effort to Enact a "Son of Sam" Law that Passes Constitutional Muster, 14 Loy. L.A. Ent. L.J. 115 (1993).

46. Restatement (Third) of the Law Governing Lawyers §§56 and 57 impose similar duties.

47. Id. §56, cmt. *b.*

48. See State ex rel. Oklahoma Bar Assn. v. Watson, 897 P.2d 246 (Okla. 1994).

deposited. It is unnecessary for lawyers to have a separate account for each client or third party. Client and third-party funds may be combined with the funds of other clients and third parties in one account, so long as lawyers' records identify the share of each client or third party and so long as the account is separate from the lawyer's funds.[49] Since funds in trust accounts belong to the clients, lawyers may not receive interest on the account. If the account bears interest, the interest must be allocated to the clients. In many states, court rules allow lawyers to participate in IOLTA (interest on lawyer trust account) programs, in which interest on trust accounts is paid to a special fund to be used for a public purpose, typically delivery of legal services to indigents.[50] As noted previously, lawyers must deposit special retainers and expense advances in their trust accounts, while general retainers and flat fees are earned income deposited in the firm's business account. When fees are earned or expenses incurred, lawyers must withdraw these funds from their trust accounts, so long as there is no dispute about the lawyer's right to receive these funds.[51]

2. *The duty to maintain records.* Lawyers must keep careful records of client money and property that comes into their possession. Model Rule 1.15(a) provides that records shall be kept for a period of five years after termination of representation, but prudent lawyers will keep important records indefinitely.

3. *The duty to notify promptly* clients or third parties when lawyers receive money or property in which clients or third parties have an interest.

4. *The duty to deliver promptly* to clients or third parties any funds or other property in which such person has an interest.

---

49. Restatement (Third) of the Law Governing Lawyers §56, cmt. *d.*

50. In Phillips v. Washington Legal Found., 524 U.S. 156 (1998), the Supreme Court held that clients had a constitutionally protected property interest in the interest income generated by their funds held in trust under the Texas IOLTA program. The Court remanded for further proceedings to determine whether the client's property had been "taken" constitutionally, and if so, the amount of just compensation. The impact of *Phillips* on IOLTA programs is unclear.

51. Restatement (Third) of the Law Governing Lawyers §56, cmt. *f.*

5. On request, *the duty to render a full accounting* regarding such money and property.

B. Confidentiality

────────── **Problem 2-3** ──────────

Information About Unsolved or Contemplated Crimes

You are an attorney with the office of the public defender. You have been appointed to represent Albert Simmons, who has been accused of a series of burglaries in the community.

For several months the police have been investigating the disappearance of a teenager. The family and friends of the teenager have organized a massive public campaign in an effort to obtain information about their daughter, but with no success. According to the local newspaper, the investigation is at a dead end, without any leads.

During the course of one of your interviews with Simmons, he begins crying uncontrollably and tells you that he has a terrible secret that he can't keep to himself any longer: He killed the girl that the police have been looking for. Simmons also tells you that he left her body in an abandoned mine several miles from the city. Simmons goes on to tell you that he is sure the police will find her body and that they'll trace it to him because he left "some other stuff there." Simmons says he's got to get out of jail to get the stuff and to hide the body. He asks you what his chances are of getting out on bail. What would you tell him? Be prepared to analyze your ethical obligations and to explain how you would proceed.

Suppose you tell Simmons that he doesn't qualify for bail. He tells you that "I'm dead if they find the body, but I know I can break out of here. I've got a friend who will get me a gun." What would you do? Why?

Read Model Rules 1.2, 1.6, 1.16, 4.3, and comments.

The ethical duty of confidentiality, the attorney-client privilege, and the work product doctrine

In understanding the principle of confidentiality, it is important to distinguish among three related but distinct concepts: the *ethical duty of confidentiality*, the evidentiary *attorney-client privilege*, and the *work product doctrine.* Model Rule 1.6 expresses the ethical duty of confidentiality. Subject to certain exceptions that we will discuss later, the rule requires lawyers to maintain the confidentiality of information "relating to representation," under all circumstances, whether in connection with court proceedings or otherwise.

R 1.6

By contrast, the attorney-client privilege is a rule of evidence that deals with the question when a lawyer may be compelled in court or other official proceedings or investigations to reveal information received in confidence from a client. Although the scope of the attorney-client privilege depends on the rules of evidence applicable in each jurisdiction, a frequently cited formulation is the one offered by Professor Wigmore:

∆ Ct situations

> (1) Where legal advice of any kind is sought (2) from a professional legal adviser in his capacity as such, (3) the communications relating to that purpose, (4) made in confidence (5) by the client, (6) are at his instance permanently protected (7) from disclosure by himself or by the legal adviser, (8) except the protection be waived.[52]

Def. of privilege

An excellent case dealing with the distinction between the ethical duty and the evidentiary privilege is Purcell v. District At-

---

52. 8 Wigmore on Evidence §2292, at 554 (McNaughton ed. 1961). See also Unif. R. Evid. 502, 13A U.L.A. 518 (1994). Comment 5 to Model Rule 1.6 summarizes the distinction between the evidentiary privilege and the ethical duty of confidentiality. See generally Geoffrey C. Hazard, Jr., An Historical Perspective on the Attorney-Client Privilege, 66 Cal. L. Rev. 1061 (1978).

torney for the Suffolk District.[53] In *Purcell* a lawyer represented a client who had received a court order to vacate his apartment. The client made a threat, which the attorney took seriously, to burn down the apartment building. The attorney warned the police of the client's threat, leading to the client's arrest and prosecution for attempted arson. The prosecution subpoenaed the lawyer to testify at trial about the client's threat, and the lawyer moved to quash the subpoena. The Massachusetts Supreme Judicial court held that the lawyer had acted properly under DR 4-101(C)(3) of the Code of Professional Responsibility (compare Model Rule 1.6(b)(1)) in revealing the client's threat to commit a crime, but the court held that the admissibility of the lawyer's testimony was a different issue.[54]

The court considered the application of the attorney-client privilege and the crime-fraud exception to the privilege. Because the trial court based its refusal to quash the subpoena on the crime-fraud exception to the attorney-client privilege, the Supreme Judicial Court addressed that issue first. The exception provides that a communication is not privileged "[i]f the services of the lawyer were sought or obtained to enable or aid anyone to commit or plan to commit what the client knew or reasonably should have known to be a crime or fraud."[55] The court found that the record would not support application of the exception because the client had "reflectively made a disclosure," rather than seeking advice to further criminal conduct.[56] The court went on to discuss the prosecution's argument that the privilege did not apply at all because the client's communication was not for the purpose of "facilitating the rendition of legal services," an essential requirement for the privilege to exist.[57] Rejecting this argument, the court stated: "Unless the crime-fraud exception applies, the attorney-client privilege should apply to communications concerning possible future, as well as past, criminal conduct, because an informed lawyer may be able to dissuade the client from improper future conduct and, if not, under the ethical rules may elect in

53. 676 N.E.2d 436 (Mass. 1997).
54. Id. at 438.
55. Id. at 439.
56. Id. at 440.
57. Id.

the public interest to make a limited disclosure of the client's threatened conduct."[58]

The work product doctrine, a discovery rule recognized by the Supreme Court in the leading case of Hickman v. Taylor,[59] prevents discovery of materials prepared "in anticipation of litigation" unless the party seeking discovery makes a special showing that the party has "substantial need" for the materials and cannot obtain equivalent materials without "undue hardship."[60] Although client confidences may be embodied in attorney work product, the work product doctrine is designed to preserve the proper functioning of the adversarial system — to allow attorneys to prepare their cases without fear that material prepared in anticipation of litigation will be available to the opposing side.[61] In criminal cases, where discovery is limited, the work product doctrine has little application.[62]

The duty of confidentiality, the attorney client privilege, and the work product doctrine are all subject to exceptions that we will discuss in these materials. We will examine the scope of the evidentiary attorney-client privilege in more detail in connection with Problems 2-11 and 3-3.

Exceptions to the duty of confidentiality: consent, prevention of harm, and past wrongful conduct

Rule 1.6(a) provides that a lawyer may reveal confidential information if the "client consents after consultation." Rule 1.6 is practically identical to DR 4-101(C)(1) of the Code of Professional Responsibility, which provides that a lawyer may reveal "[c]onfidences or secrets with the consent of the client or clients affected, but only after a full disclosure to them."

An interesting example of the application of the consent exception is People v. Lopez.[63] *Lopez* was an attorney disciplinary

---

58. Id. at 441.
59. 329 U.S. 495 (1947).
60. See Fed. R. Civ. P. 26(b)(3).
61. See 1 McCormick on Evidence §96 (5th ed. 1999). See generally Edna S. Epstein, The Attorney-Client Privilege and the Work Product Doctrine (3d ed. 1997).
62. See 1 McCormick on Evidence §97.
63. 845 P.2d 1153 (Colo. 1993) (en banc).

proceeding growing out of a criminal case. The defendant had retained Lopez to defend him against felony charges arising from a kidnapping and shooting. At Lopez's request, the defendant prepared an eight-page summary of his version of the events. The document contained various damaging admissions. In connection with plea negotiations, Lopez gave the document to the prosecutor without the defendant's knowledge or express consent. The prosecutor retained the document but did not use it at trial. The defendant was convicted, but later obtained a new trial. Lopez claimed that he had informed his client that he planned to deliver the document to the prosecutor in an effort to obtain a favorable plea bargain and that his client had not objected to this plan. In rejecting this argument the Colorado Supreme Court held that a lawyer may reveal confidential information only after full disclosure and express consent:

Not implied consent

> This provision [DR 4-101(C)(1)] does not encompass "implied" consent, even if the facts warranted a finding that [the defendant] by his conduct impliedly consented to the respondent's conduct.[64]

One of the most hotly debated issues in the profession over the past 20 years has been the extent to which the duty of confidentiality should be limited when disclosure would either *prevent* the client from committing a wrongful act or would *rectify* the consequences of a wrongful act that the client has committed.[65] DR 4-101(C)(3) of the Code of Professional Responsibility provided that a lawyer "may reveal . . . [t]he intention of his client to commit a crime and the information necessary to prevent the crime." Under the Code, disclosure of confidential information to rectify past criminal or fraudulent conduct by a client was improper, but a lawyer had discretion to reveal confidential information to prevent any future crime.

Model Rule 1.6 continues the Code's prohibition with regard to past wrongful conduct, but narrows lawyers' discretion to reveal confidential information to prevent wrongful conduct. Under Model Rule 1.6(b)(1) a lawyer may reveal confidential information only to prevent a client from committing a criminal act that in-

---

64. Id. at 1155.
65. See Nathan M. Crystal, Confidentiality Under the Model Rules of Professional Conduct, 30 Kan. L. Rev. 215 (1982).

revelation is limited to stop imm. death + sub. bodily harm.

volves imminent death or substantial bodily harm. Lawyers may not reveal confidential information to prevent criminal or fraudulent conduct that would damage the property or financial interests of third parties. Under both the Code and the Model Rules, lawyers may not reveal confidential information to prevent a horrible injustice, such as execution of an innocent person.[66]

While the ABA has historically taken a strong stand in favor of confidentiality, the issue remains controversial. A number of states that have generally adopted the Model Rules, have nonetheless refused to follow the ABA's position on confidentiality. Some states have simply returned to the formulation found in the Code of Professional Responsibility, giving lawyers discretion to reveal confidential information to prevent clients from committing crimes. Other states have broadened the exceptions to confidentiality.[67] We will encounter the debate again in connection with the issue of a lawyer's obligation regarding fraud by clients in business transactions. See Problem 5-2.

The California Rules of Professional Conduct do not contain a provision on confidentiality. The California Supreme Court rejected a proposed rule that would have allowed a lawyer to disclose confidential information to prevent a client from committing a "criminal act that the member believes is likely to result in death or substantial bodily harm."[68] California statutory law, however,

66. Symposium, Executing the Wrong Person: The Professionals' Ethical Dilemmas, 28 Loy. L.A.L. Rev. 1543 (1996). Of course, even if a lawyer could ethically reveal confidential information to prevent an unjust conviction or incarceration, the attorney-client privilege might prevent the attorney from testifying about such communications. See State v. Macumber, 544 P.2d 1084 (Ariz. 1976) (en banc) (attorneys were properly prevented, on grounds of attorney-client privilege, from testifying that person other than defendant, which person had since died, had confessed to them of committing crime for which defendant was being tried); State v. Macumber, 582 P.2d 162 (Ariz. 1978) (en banc) (after waiver by mother of deceased son's attorney-client privilege, trial judge properly excluded testimony of former attorneys that their client had confessed to crime for which defendant was charged because testimony lacked sufficient circumstantial probability of trustworthiness). See also Purcell v. District Attorney for the Suffolk Dist., 676 N.E.2d 436 (Mass. 1997), discussed above.

67. For a state-by-state discussion of variations from the ABA's Model Rules, see Laws. Man. on Prof. Conduct (ABA/BNA) 01:3 et seq. For a comparison of various state rules of ethics on the duty of confidentiality, see Restatement (Third) of the Law Governing Lawyers §117B, Reporter's Note (chart showing different approaches taken by states on scope of duty of confidentiality).

68. Prop. Cal. R. Prof. Conduct 3-100(C)(2) (1993).

provides a broad duty of confidentiality. Cal. Bus. & Prof. Code §6068(e) states that an attorney has the duty "[t]o maintain inviolate the confidence, and at every peril to himself or herself to preserve the secrets, of his or her client." One bar association has interpreted this provision to mean that a lawyer cannot reveal confidential information even to prevent murder.[69]

The debate over the scope of the ethical duty of confidentiality continues with the work of the ABA's Ethics 2000 Commission. The Commission has proposed revisions of Model Rule 1.6 to allow disclosure of confidential information to prevent or to rectify the consequences of certain serious harms:

(a) A lawyer shall not reveal information relating to the representation of a client or a former client unless the client gives informed consent, the disclosure is impliedly authorized in order to carry out the representation, or the disclosure is permitted by paragraph (b) or required by paragraph (c).

(b) A lawyer may reveal information relating to the representation of a client or a former client to the extent the lawyer reasonably believes necessary:

(1) to prevent reasonably certain death or substantial bodily harm;

(2) to prevent the client from committing a crime or fraud that is likely to result in substantial injury to the financial interests or property of another and in furtherance of which the client has used or is using the lawyer's services;

(3) to rectify or mitigate substantial injury to the financial interests or property of another resulting from the client's commission of a crime or fraud in furtherance of which the client has used the lawyer's services;

(4) to secure legal advice about the lawyer's compliance with these Rules; or

(5) to establish a claim or defense on behalf of the lawyer in a controversy between the lawyer and the client, to establish a defense to a criminal charge or civil claim against the lawyer based upon conduct in which the client was involved, or to respond to allegations in any proceeding concerning the lawyer's representation of the client.

(c) A lawyer shall reveal information relating to the represen-

69. San Diego County Bar Assn., Legal Ethics & Unlawful Practice Comm., Op. 1990-1, Laws. Man. on Prof. Conduct (ABA/BNA) 901:1803.

tation of a client or a former client to the extent required by law or
court order or when necessary to comply with these Rules.

Tort or criminal liability for failure to disclose confidential information to prevent or rectify wrongful conduct

The rules of professional conduct are not the only guidelines for
determining whether a lawyer is authorized or required to disclose
confidential information to prevent or rectify wrongful conduct.
An additional question must be addressed: What does "other law"
require? In particular, does either tort or statutory law require disclosure of what would otherwise be confidential information?

The Code of Professional Responsibility specifically incorporated "other law" into the duty of confidentiality. DR 4-
101(C)(2) provided that a lawyer could reveal confidential
information when "required by law or court order." While the
Model Rules have omitted this provision, Professors Hazard and
Hodes argue that a "required by law" exception must be read into
Rule 1.6 for the rule to make any sense.[70] The omission of the
"required by law" exception from the Model Rules is a good example of Professor Susan Koniak's thesis that the bar through its
ethics codes attempts to establish its own norms of conduct, norms
that often vary from a competing vision of proper conduct held by
the state.[71]

Assuming that a required-by-law exception is part of Rule
1.6, when if ever does tort or statutory law provide for a duty of
disclosure? In Tarasoff v. Regents of the University of California,[72]
a patient confided to a psychotherapist employed by the University
of California his intention to kill a young woman who had rejected
his advances. The doctor concluded that his patient should be
committed and notified the police, who arrested the patient but
released him when he appeared to be rational. The doctor did not
notify the young woman or her family of the threat to her life. The
patient subsequently carried out his threat and killed the young

70. 1 Hazard & Hodes, The Law of Lawyering §1.6:112.
71. Susan P. Koniak, The Law Between the Bar and the State, 70 N.C.L.
Rev. 1389 (1992).
72. 551 P.2d 334 (Cal. 1976) (en banc).

woman. The California Supreme Court held that her parents stated a cause of action against the defendants for negligent failure to warn the young woman of the threat to her life. The court held that the special relationship between doctor and patient was sufficient to create a duty of care to third parties foreseeably injured by the patient.[73] Defendants argued that liability should not be imposed because psychotherapists cannot accurately predict dangerousness. The court rejected this blanket argument, noting that doctors were required only to exercise reasonable care, and in any event the argument did not apply to the case before the court since the doctor had accurately concluded that the patient was dangerous but had failed to warn the potential victim.[74] Defendants also argued that the imposition of liability interfered with "free and open communication . . . essential to psychotherapy." While recognizing that there was a public policy in favor of confidentiality between psychotherapist and patient, the court concluded that this policy must yield to the public policy in favor of preventing harm to others: "The protective privilege ends where the public peril begins."[75]

Subsequent California cases, however, have limited *Tarasoff* to situations in which the patient threatens an "identifiable" victim rather than simply posing a danger to the community as a whole.[76] Failure-to-warn claims have also been brought in other jurisdictions, but recovery has been rare.[77]

Could attorneys be held liable in tort for failure to warn third parties of threats by their clients?[78] Hawkins v. King

73. Id. at 344.
74. Id. at 345.
75. Id. at 346-347.
76. See, e.g., Thompson v. County of Alameda, 614 P.2d 728 (Cal. 1980). But see Reisner v. Regents of the University of California, 37 Cal. Rptr. 2d 518 (Ct. App.), *review denied* (1995) (doctor who learned that patient was HIV-infected during operation had duty to warn because it was reasonably foreseeable that patient would have intimate relationships in the future, even though doctor did not know identity of future partners).
77. Cases are collected in John C. Williams, Annotation, Liability of One Treating Mentally Afflicted Patient for Failure to Warn or Protect Third Persons Threatened by Patient, 83 A.L.R.3d 1201 (1978).
78. See generally Vanessa Merton, Confidentiality and the "Dangerous" Patient: Implications of *Tarasoff* for Psychiatrists and Lawyers, 31 Emory L.J. 263 (1982). See also Laurie S. Kohn, Note, Infecting Attorney-Client Confidentiality: The Ethics of HIV Disclosure, 9 Geo. J. Legal Ethics 547 (1996) (arguing

County[79] appears to be the only case that has dealt directly with the issue. In *Hawkins* the court appointed an attorney to represent Hawkins, who was accused of possession of marijuana. The attorney learned from another lawyer employed by his client's mother that his client was mentally ill and dangerous. A psychiatrist advised the attorney that his client was dangerous to himself and to others and should not be released from custody. The attorney represented the client at a bail hearing and obtained his release on a personal surety bond. The attorney did not inform the court of the information about his client's dangerousness. Neither the judge nor the prosecutor raised any questions about the client's dangerousness. Eight days after his release, Hawkins assaulted his mother and attempted suicide. The Hawkinses then brought suit naming the attorney as one of the defendants. They alleged two theories: First, that the attorney violated a duty imposed by rules of ethics and court rules to disclose to the court information about his client's dangerousness. Second, based on *Tarasoff*, the attorney should be held liable for failure to warn of his client's dangerousness. The court rejected the first theory. It found no specific provision in either the rules of ethics or court rules that required a lawyer to reveal adverse information about a client:

> We believe that the duty of counsel to be loyal to his client and to represent zealously his client's interest overrides the nebulous and unsupported theory that our rules and ethical code mandate disclosure of information which counsel considers detrimental to his client's stated interest. Because disclosure is not "required by law," appellants' theory of liability on the basis of ethical or court rule violations fails for lack of substance.[80]

As to the *Tarasoff* theory, the court appeared to hold that on appropriate facts a cause of action could be stated against an attorney for failure to warn, but that the case before it was distinguishable from *Tarasoff*:

> In the instant case Michael Hawkins' potential victims, his mother and sister, knew he might be dangerous and that he had

---

that attorneys should not have a common law or ethical duty to disclose that a client is HIV-positive).

79. 602 P.2d 361 (Wash. Ct. App. 1979).
80. Id. at 365.

been released from confinement, contrary to Tatiana Tarasoff's ignorance of any risk of harm. Thus, no duty befell Sanders to warn Frances Hawkins of a risk of which she was already fully cognizant. Further, it must not be overlooked that Sanders received no information that Hawkins planned to assault anyone, only that he was mentally ill and likely to be dangerous to himself and others. That Sanders received no information directly from Michael Hawkins is the final distinction between the two cases.

The common law duty to volunteer information about a client to a court considering pretrial release must be limited to situations where information gained convinces counsel that his client intends to commit a crime or inflict injury upon unknowing third persons. Such a duty cannot be extended to the facts before us.[81]

In addition to tort law, statutes may impose an obligation on lawyers to disclose confidential information to prevent or rectify harm. For example, in a few states statutes may require attorneys to reveal confidential information to prevent child abuse.[82]

If a statute *expressly* requires a lawyer to disclose information, the lawyer must comply with the statute, unless compliance would violate the client's constitutional rights, a point discussed below. The situations in which a statute expressly imposes a disclosure obligation on an attorney are rare. Far more common are statutes that apply broadly to "any person" and do not include a specific exemption for attorneys. A famous example is the *Lake Pleasant bodies* case, People v. Belge.[83] Two lawyers, Armani and Belge, were representing a defendant accused of murder when the defen-

---

81. Id. at 365-366. Cf. State v. Hansen, 862 P.2d 117 (Wash. 1993) (en banc) (attorney has duty to warn judge of client's intention to attack judge; *Hawkins* distinguished because mother and sister were aware of danger while judge was not).

82. See Ellen Marrus, Please Keep My Secret: Child Abuse Reporting Statutes, Confidentiality, and Juvenile Delinquency, 11 Geo. J. Legal Ethics 509, 515-520 (1998). See also Robin A. Rosencrantz, Note, Rejecting "Hear No Evil Speak No Evil": Expanding the Attorney's Role in Child Abuse Reporting, 8 Geo. J. Legal Ethics 327 (1995) (arguing that lawyers should be added to list of statutory mandatory reporters).

83. 372 N.Y.S.2d 798 (County Ct.), *aff'd*, 376 N.Y.S.2d 771 (App. Div. 1975), *aff'd*, 359 N.E.2d 377 (N.Y. 1976). For a personal view of the case coauthored by one of the lawyers, see Tom Alibrandi & Frank H. Armani, Privileged Information (1984). See also Richard Zitrin & Carol M. Langford, The Moral Compass of the American Lawyer ch. 1 (1999).

dant informed them that he had committed three unsolved murders. The defendant told his lawyers of the location of one victim's body. Belge went to the location and inspected the body to verify the client's story. The lawyers did not reveal the information, but their knowledge later became public during the defendant's trial as part of their insanity defense. Because of public outrage against the lawyers' conduct, the district attorney presented the matter to a grand jury, which returned an indictment against Belge, but not against Armani, for violation of two provisions of the New York Public Health Law, one requiring that the dead be given a decent burial, the other directing any person knowing of the death of a person without medical assistance to report the matter to the authorities. Neither statute expressly referred to attorneys. While the trial court dismissed the indictment and the appellate division affirmed, the victory for the duty of confidentiality was far from clear cut. The trial court did not decide that the attorneys' conduct was clearly proper. Instead, it concluded that it must balance the rights of the defendant against the interests of society. The court seemed particularly influenced by the fact that the grand jury had returned an indictment against Belge but not against Armani, characterizing the grand jury as "grasping at straws." The court went on to state that Belge's conduct amounted to obstruction of justice and that the decision of the court would have been much more difficult if he had been indicted on that ground.

The appellate court was equally lukewarm in its support of Belge. While finding that the attorney-client privilege protected Belge from responsibility under the public health law, the court stated:

> In view of the fact that the claim of absolute privilege was proffered, we note that the privilege is not all-encompassing and that in a given case there may be conflicting considerations. We believe that an attorney must protect his client's interests, but also must observe basic human standards of decency, having due regard to the need that the legal system accord justice to the interests of society and its individual members.

> We write to emphasize our serious concern regarding the consequences which emanate from a claim of an absolute attorney-client privilege. Because the only question presented, briefed and argued on this appeal was a legal one with respect to the sufficiency

of the indictments, we limit our determination to that issue and do not reach the ethical questions underlying this case.[84]

What should be the scope of the duty of confidentiality?

Advocates of a strict view of confidentiality have made two arguments in support of their position. One argument rests on the "rights" of clients, either legal rights or more broadly defined moral rights. The other argument rests on the social utility of client confidentiality.

Proponents of a strong view of confidentiality have argued that clients have constitutional rights to confidentiality based on the Fifth Amendment privilege against self-incrimination and the Sixth Amendment right to counsel. In Fisher v. United States[85] the Supreme Court held that the privilege against self-incrimination protected information that a client had given to a lawyer (1) if the attorney-client privilege applied to the conveyance of the information from the client to the lawyer, and (2) if the information could not have been obtained directly from the client because of the privilege against self-incrimination. (We will consider *Fisher* in more detail in connection with Problems 2-4 and 2-5.) Under *Fisher* a rule requiring or allowing a lawyer to reveal confidential information to prevent a criminal or wrongful act would almost never violate the privilege against self-incrimination. First, the attorney-client privilege may not apply to the information. If the client does not convey the information for the purpose of seeking legal advice, the privilege does not apply.[86] Thus, if the client simply "blurts out" his plans, the privilege may not apply. Even if the client is seeking legal advice about his plans, then the privilege may still not apply because one of the well-recognized exceptions to the attorney-client privilege is the "crime-fraud exception." Under this exception a client's communications are not privileged when the client is seeking legal advice to enable or assist

[handwritten margin note: must be in process of seeking legal advice]

---

84. 376 N.Y.S.2d at 772.
85. 425 U.S. 391 (1976).
86. Unif. R. Evid. 502, 13A U.L.A. 518 (1994); 1 McCormick on Evidence §88.

B. Confidentiality

Crime fraud exception - exception to Atty. Client priv.

- No priv. when client seeks legal advice to enable commission of crime

the client in committing a crime or fraud.[87] Recall, however, that *Purcell* rejected both of these arguments. Second, the privilege against self-incrimination applies only if the information is incriminating. To the extent that the attorney's disclosure prevents a crime (or the attempt to commit a crime), there is no incrimination. Further, disclosure of information to prevent noncriminal conduct would not implicate the privilege against self-incrimination. Finally, disclosure would not violate the privilege against self-incrimination if the client received "use immunity" against being prosecuted based on the disclosed information. The attorney could request such immunity from the authorities before revealing the client's intention to commit a crime.[88]

Similarly, the Sixth Amendment right to counsel does not prevent disclosure of information to prevent harm. First, the right to counsel does not attach in criminal cases until the initiation of adversary judicial proceedings.[89] A rule that required disclosure of information prior to that time would not implicate the Sixth Amendment. Even if the disclosure obligation attached after initiation of formal proceedings, the Sixth Amendment does not guarantee a right to a particular counsel, only a right to effective representation. Any Sixth Amendment problem with a rule requiring lawyers to disclose information to prevent serious harm could be resolved, therefore, by appointing another lawyer to represent the client.[90]

A broader statement of the clients' rights argument focuses on moral rather than legal rights.[91] Under this view the client's moral rights to privacy and autonomy justify an obligation of confidentiality.[92] But moral philosophy recognizes that rights such as privacy and autonomy may be limited in various situations, in par-

---

87. Unif. R. Evid. 502(d)(1), 13A U.L.A. 519 (1994); 1 McCormick on Evidence §95.

88. See Harry I. Subin, The Lawyer as Superego: Disclosure of Client Confidences to Prevent Harm, 70 Iowa L. Rev. 1091, 1120-1127 (1985).

89. See Moran v. Burbine, 475 U.S. 412, 428 (1986).

90. See Subin, The Lawyer as Superego, 70 Iowa L. Rev. at 1127-1132; see also Crystal, Confidentiality Under the Model Rules of Professional Conduct, 30 Kan. L. Rev. 215.

91. See generally Nancy J. Moore, Limits to Attorney-Client Confidentiality: A "Philosophically Informed" and Comparative Approach to Legal and Medical Ethics, 36 Case W. Res. L. Rev. 177 (1985).

92. Id. at 188-191.

ticular when a person intends to harm others.[93] Thus, neither constitutional nor moral rights justify a strict rule of confidentiality.

The social utility argument for confidentiality claims that if
clients are encouraged to reveal confidential information, including information about wrongdoing, lawyers will be in a position to
dissuade them from wrongful conduct. Thus, a rule of confidentiality is more likely to prevent harm than a rule of disclosure. The
social utility argument is based on assumptions that are both un-
proven and of doubtful validity.[94] First, the argument assumes that
clients will be deterred from seeking legal advice about wrongful
conduct if lawyers have an obligation to disclose the intention of
their clients to commit wrongs. In many cases, clients have no
choice about seeking representation. In addition, law-abiding clients have an incentive to seek legal advice regardless of the disclosure rule in order to conform their conduct to the law. Second,
the argument assumes that lawyers can be effective in dissuading
clients from engaging in wrongful conduct. In many cases, however, the wrongful nature of the conduct and the possible consequences are clear. Rather, the client intends to commit the act
regardless of the consequences.[95] Further, limited empirical studies of attorney-client confidentiality lend little support to the need
for strict confidentiality.[96]

Even if one accepts the conclusion that a rule of strict confidentiality is not justified by either clients' rights or social utility,

93. Id. at 194.
94. See Daniel R. Fischel, Lawyers and Confidentiality, 65 U. Chi. L. Rev.
1 (1998) (confidentiality rules benefit lawyers but are of dubious value to clients
and society as a whole).
95. See Crystal, Confidentiality Under the Model Rules of Professional
Conduct, 30 Kan. L. Rev. at 225-226 (using a hypothetical analysis of types of
clients that lawyers represent to conclude that a disclosure rule is more likely to
reduce harm than a rule of confidentiality); Subin, The Lawyer as Superego, 70
Iowa L. Rev. at 1166-1172 (instrumental defense less persuasive than rights-
based argument for confidentiality). See also Steven Shavell, Legal Advice About
Contemplated Acts: The Decision to Obtain Advice, Its Social Desirability, and
Protection of Confidentiality, 17 J. Legal Stud. 123 (1988) (developing model
dealing with effect of advice and confidentiality on rational decisionmaking).
96. See Fred C. Zacharias, Rethinking Confidentiality, 74 Iowa L. Rev.
351 (1989). But see Leslie C. Levin, Testing the Radical Experiment: A Study
of Lawyer Response to Clients Who Intend to Harm Others, 47 Rutgers L. Rev.
81 (1994) (survey of lawyer responses under New Jersey rule requiring lawyers
to reveal confidential information to prevent clients from committing criminal,
fraudulent, or illegal acts that would seriously harm others, casting doubt on
wisdom of mandatory disclosure rule).

a more difficult question remains: What should be the scope of
the duty of confidentiality? In particular, how far should the "harm
prevention" principle be taken? Professor Harry Subin argues that
lawyers should have a duty to reveal confidential information to
prevent clients from committing a felony.[97] Other scholars have
argued for even broader rules of disclosure.[98]

Confidentiality problems are, of course, not unique to the
area of criminal defense practice. We will also encounter confidentiality problems in the context of civil litigation and in connection with business practice.

─────────────── **Problem 2-4** ───────────────

Dealing with Physical Evidence, Fruits, and Instrumentalities of Crimes

You represent Robert Williams, a young man accused
of armed robbery of a local convenience store. Your client was identified by the store clerk as the robber, but
you think the identification is weak, and you may well
be able to obtain an acquittal or at least negotiate a favorable plea bargain.

Your client first denied that he was involved in the
robbery, but at your last meeting he admitted that he
committed the crime. He said he put the money from
the robbery in a bag in a closet at his girlfriend's apartment. She doesn't know that it is there, but he thinks
she may find it. He wants to know what to do. What
advice would you give and what steps would you take?

Suppose the girlfriend comes to your office with the
bag of money that she has found and asks you what to
do with it. What would you do?

Read Model Rules 1.2(d), 2.1, 4.3, 8.4, and comments.

97. Subin, The Lawyer as Superego, 70 Iowa L. Rev. at 1172-1176.
98. See Crystal, Confidentiality Under the Model Rules of Professional
Conduct, 30 Kan. L. Rev. 215; Moore, Limits to Attorney-Client Confidentiality, 36 Case W. Res. L. Rev. 177.

The obligations of lawyers regarding tangible criminal material in their possession

We saw in Problem 2-3 that under the Model Rules of Professional Conduct, lawyers have discretion to reveal confidential information to prevent clients from committing criminal acts that are likely to involve death or serious bodily harm, but lawyers have an ethical obligation to maintain confidentiality of information regarding past crimes. Suppose, however, a lawyer has more than information about a past crime. Suppose a lawyer obtains possession of tangible property related to a crime. Lawyers can come into possession of fruits of criminal conduct (stolen money, for example), instrumentalities of crimes (such as weapons), contraband (material the possession of which is illegal, such as narcotics), or tangible evidence of crimes (for example, incriminating documents or tape recordings). The discussion that follows uses the term "tangible criminal material" to refer to these items collectively. Lawyers can obtain possession of tangible criminal material in a variety of ways: from clients, from third parties, or as a result of their own investigation. What are a lawyer's legal and ethical obligations if the lawyer comes into possession of tangible criminal material?

Lawyers may not assist their clients by actively concealing tangible criminal material. The leading case establishing this proposition is In re Ryder.[99] Ryder represented an individual accused of bank robbery with a sawed-off shotgun. The FBI told Ryder that his client had bills taken in the bank robbery in his possession when he was arrested. Ryder's client told him that a man whom he would not identify had paid him $500 to put a package in a safety deposit box, a story Ryder did not believe. Ryder had his client sign a power of attorney so that he could obtain possession of the client's safety deposit box. When Ryder opened his client's box, he found a sawed-off shotgun and a bag of money, among other items. Ryder transferred the contents of his client's box to a new box that he had opened in his name. The FBI later discovered Ryder's box containing the money and gun. Ryder testified that he intended to return the money to the true owner. He claimed

---

99. 263 F. Supp. 360 (E.D. Va.), *aff'd*, 381 F.2d 713 (4th Cir. 1967).

that his purpose in transferring the money and gun to his own box was to support an argument that the money and gun were inadmissible in a prosecution against his client because of the attorney-client privilege. The court removed Ryder from the case, and later the United States attorney instituted disciplinary proceedings against him. The district court suspended Ryder from practice for 18 months. The court ruled that Ryder had gone far beyond the receipt of confidential information to become an active participant in concealment of a crime. On appeal the Fourth Circuit approved the district court's order:

> It is an abuse of a lawyer's professional responsibility knowingly to take possession of and secrete the fruits and instrumentalities of a crime. Ryder's acts bear no reasonable relation to the privilege and duty to refuse to divulge a client's confidential communication. Ryder made himself an active participant in a criminal act, ostensibly wearing the mantle of the loyal advocate, but in reality serving as accessory after the fact.[100]

A number of courts have gone beyond the decision in *Ryder* and have held that attorneys who come into possession of tangible criminal material have an obligation to turn the material over to the authorities. In State ex rel. Sowers v. Olwell,[101] Olwell, an attorney representing a suspect in a murder, came into possession of a knife. It was unclear from the case whether Olwell obtained the knife from his client or from another source. A few days before a coroner's inquest into the death, Olwell received a subpoena duces tecum, directing him to produce "all knives in your possession" that related to the death. Olwell refused to comply with the subpoena, claiming a confidential relationship of attorney and client. The court held Olwell in contempt for his refusal to comply with the subpoena. On appeal the Washington Supreme Court reversed. The court's decision balanced the attorney's obligations as an officer of the court and the attorney-client privilege:

---

100. 381 F.2d at 714. *Accord* State ex rel. Oklahoma Bar Assn. v. Harlton, 669 P.2d 774, 777 (Okla. 1983) (attorney received five-year suspension after pleading guilty to charge of hindering prosecution by concealing shotgun; attorney "embraced the role of an accessory to a crime as a personal accommodation to its perpetrator").

101. 394 P.2d 681 (Wash. 1964).

We are in agreement that the attorney-client privilege is applicable
to the knife held by appellant, but do not agree that the privilege
warrants the attorney, as an officer of the court, from withholding
it after being properly requested to produce the same. The attorney
should not be a depository for criminal evidence (such as a knife,
other weapons, stolen property, etc.), which in itself has little, if
any, material value for the purposes of aiding counsel in the preparation of the defense of his client's case. Such evidence given the
attorney during legal consultation for information purposes and
used by the attorney in preparing the defense of his client's case,
whether or not the case ever goes to trial, could clearly be withheld
for a reasonable period of time. It follows that the attorney, after a
reasonable period, should, as an officer of the court, on his own
motion turn the same over to the prosecution.

We think the attorney-client privilege should and can be preserved even though the attorney surrenders the evidence he has in
his possession. The prosecution, upon receipt of such evidence
from an attorney, where charge against the attorney's client is contemplated (presently or in the future), should be well aware of the
existence of the attorney-client privilege. Therefore, the state, when
attempting to introduce such evidence at the trial, should take extreme precautions to make certain that the source of the evidence
is not disclosed in the presence of the jury and prejudicial error is
not committed. By thus allowing the prosecution to recover such
evidence, the public interest is served, and by refusing the prosecution an opportunity to disclose the source of the evidence, the
client's privilege is preserved and a balance is reached between these
conflicting interests. The burden of introducing such evidence at a
trial would continue to be upon the prosecution.[102]

Although Olwell was under subpoena, the court stated that he had
an obligation "on his own motion" to turn the material over to
the authorities after a reasonable period of time for examination.
The court also held that the client's privilege against self-
incrimination did not prevent Olwell from having to turn the material over to the authorities because the privilege against
self-incrimination was personal to the client and could not be as-
serted by the lawyer.[103] (The United States Supreme Court later
rejected this view of the privilege against self-incrimination in

102. Id. at 684-685.
103. Id. at 686.

Fisher v. United States.[104] *Fisher* is discussed in more detail later in this problem.)

Several courts have applied the *Olwell* approach to other types of tangible criminal material and in a variety of other settings. In Morrell v. State[105] the defendant Morrell was charged with kidnapping and rape. A public defender was appointed to represent Morrell. About a month later, the lawyer received a telephone call from a friend of Morrell's who had been living in Morrell's home with his consent while Morrell was awaiting trial. The friend told the lawyer that he had found a legal pad that appeared to have a kidnapping plan written on it. The lawyer took possession of the pad and asked his client about it. Morrell denied that the plan implicated him; he said that he had written the plan in response to a television report about an earlier kidnapping. Unsure how to proceed, the lawyer sought the advice of the Ethics Advisory Committee of the Alaska Bar Association. The committee advised the lawyer to return the plan to the friend, to advise the friend about the law on concealment of evidence, and to withdraw from the case if it became obvious that a violation of rules of ethics would occur. The lawyer basically followed this advice. The friend decided to turn the pad over to the police, and it was introduced into evidence at Morrell's trial, at which he was convicted. Morrell argued on appeal that his former attorney's conduct had denied him effective assistance of counsel. The Alaska Supreme Court rejected this argument, relying on *Olwell*, *Ryder*, and other cases:

> From the foregoing cases emerges the rule that a criminal defense attorney must turn over to the prosecution real evidence that the attorney obtains from his client. Further, if the evidence is obtained from a non-client third party who is not acting for the client, then the privilege to refuse to testify concerning the manner in which the evidence was obtained is inapplicable.[106]

In dictum, the court stated that the attorney's obligation would have been the same even if he had received the evidence directly from his client rather than from a third party.[107] Similarly, in State

---

104. 425 U.S. 391 (1975).
105. 575 P.2d 1200 (Alaska 1978).
106. Id. at 1210.
107. Id. at 1211.

v. Carlin[108] the defendant was prosecuted for making terroristic threats. The defendant had made tape recordings of his conversations, which he had turned over to his attorney. The court ordered the attorney to produce the tapes for the prosecution, but the attorney objected, claiming that he had obtained the tapes in a privileged communication. The court of appeals affirmed: "Since the appellant's attorney had a duty to turn over the evidence under the line of cases mentioned above, there was no error in the court ordering him to do so."[109]

Section 179 of the Restatement of the Law Governing Lawyers incorporates the line of cases discussed above:

§179. Physical Evidence of Client Crime

With respect to physical evidence of a client crime, a lawyer:

(1) may, when reasonably necessary for purposes of the representation, take possession of the evidence and retain it for the time reasonably necessary to examine it and subject it to tests that do not alter or destroy material characteristics of the evidence; but

(2) following possession under Subsection (1), the lawyer must:

(a) return the evidence to the site from which it was taken, when that can be accomplished without destroying or altering material characteristics of the evidence; or

(b) notify prosecuting authorities of the lawyer's possession of the evidence or turn the evidence over to them.

While most of the cases have involved situations in which lawyers have been subject to subpoena or in which defendants have made claims of ineffective assistance of counsel, lawyers who keep possession of tangible criminal material run the risk of criminal prosecution for violation of statutes dealing with obstruction of justice, concealment of evidence, and similar crimes. In *Morrell* the court discussed the application of criminal statutes as follows:

While statutes which address the concealing of evidence are generally construed to require an affirmative act of concealment in ad-

108. 640 P.2d 324 (Kan. Ct. App. 1982).
109. Id. at 328. See also Henderson v. State, 962 S.W.2d 544 (Tex. Ct. Crim. App. 1997) (en banc), *cert. denied*, 119 S. Ct. 437 (1998) (trial court properly required production of maps in lawyers' possession showing where baby was buried because privilege must yield when possible to prevent death or serious injury).

dition to the failure to disclose information to the authorities, taking possession of evidence from a non-client third party and holding the evidence in a place not accessible to investigating authorities would seem to fall within the statute's ambit.[110]

In Commonwealth v. Stenhach[111] two public defenders were prosecuted for hindering prosecution and tampering with evidence because they kept possession of a rifle stock used in a homicide committed by their client. The lawyers had learned of the existence and location of the weapon in a confidential communication from their client. The jury found the defendants guilty. The appellate court first joined the "overwhelming majority of states which hold that physical evidence of crime in the possession of a criminal defense attorney is not subject to a privilege but must be delivered to the prosecution."[112] The court, however, then went on to reverse the defendants' convictions on the ground that the statutes as applied to them were vague and overbroad.

Attorneys facing the question of how to deal with tangible criminal material, however, can take little comfort from *Stenhach*. First, the attorneys were convicted at trial and only obtained a reversal on appeal. The emotional and financial costs to them were undoubtedly great. Second, given the body of law now on the books requiring lawyers to turn over tangible criminal material to the authorities, future courts are much less likely to be sympathetic to due process claims.

Despite the widespread acceptance of the attorney's duty to turn over physical evidence as articulated by the court in *Olwell*,[113] lawyers confronted with actual or potential possession of tangible criminal material may face a number of questions regarding the application of the doctrine.

110. 575 P.2d at 1212. See also State ex rel. Oklahoma Bar Assn. v. Harlton, 669 P.2d 774 (Okla. 1983) (disciplinary proceeding based on attorney's pleading guilty to charge of hindering prosecution by concealing shotgun).

111. 514 A.2d 114 (Pa. Super. Ct. 1986).

112. Id. at 119.

113. For a criticism of the duty to turn over tangible criminal material and a recommendation that attorneys be granted, by legislation if necessary, a limited privilege to possess such material, see Jane M. Graffeo, Note, Ethics, Law, and Loyalty: The Attorney's Duty to Turn Over Incriminating Physical Evidence, 32 Stan. L. Rev. 977 (1980). A similar approach is recommended by Stephanie J. Frye, Comment, Disclosure of Incriminating Physical Evidence Received from a Client: The Defense Attorney's Dilemma, 52 U. Colo. L. Rev. 419 (1981).

Application of the attorney-client privilege after tangible criminal material is turned over to the authorities

Olwell held that the confidentiality of communications between client and lawyer would be protected after the attorney turned over any tangible criminal material to the authorities. An important question remains, however, about the application of the privilege. Suppose the authorities cannot link the tangible criminal material to the defendant except through the testimony of the defendant's lawyer. May the state require the defense either to stipulate about the source of the tangible criminal material or require the lawyer to testify about the source? If the state cannot do this, then the attorney's obligation to turn over the material will often be a hollow one since the prosecution can make no use of the material unless it can independently establish the source of the material. Indeed, in some cases it may be strategically desirable for attorneys to take possession of tangible criminal material, to turn over evidence to the authorities, and then to claim the privilege to prevent the prosecution from being able to locate independently the material and tie it to the defendant. Yet if the defendant can be forced to choose between stipulating as to the source of the material or having defense counsel called as a witness, then attorney-client confidentiality has been seriously infringed.[114]

In People v. Meredith[115] one of two codefendants was accused of conspiracy to murder. A crucial fact in the case was the location of the victim's wallet. The defendant had told his lawyer that the wallet was in a trash can behind his residence. The lawyer's investigator retrieved the wallet and the attorney then turned it over to authorities. At trial the defense and prosecution agreed that the prosecution could introduce the wallet into evidence and that the conversations between the defendant and his lawyer were privileged. The issue in the case was whether the prosecution could call the investigator to testify regarding his observation of the location of the wallet. The court first held that the attorney-client privilege applied not just to communications between attorney and client but also to observations made as a consequence of protected communications. The court also held, however, that an

---

114. See Norman Lefstein, Incriminating Physical Evidence, The Defense Attorney's Dilemma, and the Need for Rules, 64 N.C. L. Rev. 897, 909-910 (1986).

115. 631 P.2d 46 (Cal. 1981).

observation by a lawyer or his agent would lose its privileged character if "the defense by altering or removing physical evidence has precluded the prosecution from making that same observation."[116]

It should also be noted that a defendant can waive the attorney-client privilege by disclosing information to a third party. If the privilege has been waived, attorneys may be called as witnesses regarding delivery of tangible criminal material.[117]

Application of the Fifth Amendment privilege against self-incrimination

The court in *Olwell* held that the privilege against self-incrimination was not infringed when a lawyer was required to produce tangible criminal material because the privilege against self-incrimination was personal to the client. The court decided *Olwell*, however, prior to the Supreme Court's opinion in Fisher v. United States.[118]

Fisher involved an investigation of possible civil and criminal violations of the federal income tax laws. The taxpayers obtained their accountants' work papers relating to the preparation of their tax returns and turned the documents over to their attorneys for assistance in the investigation. The Internal Revenue Service subsequently issued subpoenas to the attorneys seeking production of these documents. When the attorneys refused to comply, the government brought enforcement actions against them. The Supreme Court held that the Fifth Amendment privilege against self-incrimination protects a person from being *compelled* to give *incriminating testimony*. The Court ruled that the privilege, therefore, did not prevent enforcement of the subpoenas against the attorneys because it did not compel the taxpayers to do anything.[119]

The Court went on to consider the relationship between the attorney-client privilege and the privilege against self-incrimination. It ruled that the taxpayers did not lose the privilege against self-incrimination by turning over the documents to their

116. Id. at 48. See also Hitch v. Pima County Superior Court, 708 P.2d 72 (Ariz. 1985) (en banc) (defendant forced to choose between having lawyer testify or stipulation regarding original location of material).

117. Commonwealth v. Ferri, 599 A.2d 208 (Pa. Super. Ct. 1991), *cert. denied*, 510 U.S. 1164 (1994).

118. 425 U.S. 391 (1975).

119. Id. at 397.

lawyers. Accordingly, the lawyers could assert the attorney-client privilege as to any documents in their possession that would be subject to the privilege against self-incrimination if the documents had been retained by the taxpayers:

> Where the transfer is made for the purpose of obtaining legal advice, the purposes of the attorney-client privilege would be defeated unless the privilege is applicable. "It follows, then, that *when the client himself would be privileged* from production of the document, . . . [because of] self-incrimination, the attorney having possession of the document is not bound to produce."[120]

The Court then had to address the issue of the extent to which the privilege against self-incrimination applied to the documents. Returning to the foundations of the privilege against self-incrimination, the Court reiterated that the privilege only prohibits a person from being compelled to give testimony against himself; it does not bar the use of incriminating evidence against a person. The Court concluded that the accountants' work papers did not involve any testimony by the taxpayers and were not, therefore, subject to the privilege against self-incrimination.[121] In its discussion the Court confirmed that "[p]urely evidentiary (but 'nontestimonial') materials, as well as contraband and fruits and instrumentalities of crime, may now be searched for and seized under proper circumstances."[122]

The Court noted, however, that the *act of production* of the documents (as opposed to their substantive content) could have testimonial aspects, depending on the circumstances. In some cases, production of documents or other evidence could establish their *existence, possession or control* by the taxpayer, or *authentication*.[123] The Court then went on to conclude that on the facts of the case, none of these testimonial factors was present:

> The papers belong to the accountant, were prepared by him, and are the kind usually prepared by an accountant working on the tax returns of his client. Surely the Government is in no way relying on the "truthtelling" of the taxpayer to prove the existence of or his access to the documents. . . . The existence and location of the papers are a foregone conclusion and the taxpayer adds little or noth-

120. Id. at 404 (emphasis in original).
121. Id. at 409-410.
122. Id. at 407.
123. Id. at 410.

ing to the sum total of the Government's information by conceding that he in fact has the papers. . . .

As for the possibility that responding to the subpoena would authenticate the workpapers, [t]he taxpayer would be no more competent to authenticate the accountant's workpapers or reports by producing them than he would be to authenticate them if testifying orally.[124]

In a subsequent case, United States v. Doe,[125] the Court refined two aspects of its holding in *Fisher*. The case involved subpoenas directed to the owner of sole proprietorships seeking production of his business records in connection with a grand jury investigation of corruption in the awarding of county and municipal contracts. The Court in *Fisher* had left open the question of whether the Fifth Amendment protected against production of an individual's own records rather than those of a third party. In *Doe* the Court ruled that the privilege did not apply to the defendant's own records when they had been voluntarily prepared because there was no element of compulsion present.[126]

In *Fisher* the Court had also recognized that, depending on the facts, the act of production could amount to compelled testimony in violation of the Fifth Amendment. The Court in *Doe* ruled that the act of production in that case did indeed violate the Fifth Amendment because it forced the defendant to admit the existence of the records, the defendant's possession, and their authenticity.[127] The Court decided that the government could enforce the subpoena only if it granted the defendant "use immunity" from any incrimination resulting from the production of the material.[128]

It is unclear whether *Fisher* and *Doe* apply to lawyers' duty to deliver to the authorities tangible criminal material in their possession. On one hand, if attorneys have an obligation to turn tangible criminal material over to the authorities (as *Olwell* and *Morrell* indicate), then under *Fisher* and *Doe* the act of production would amount to a violation of the privilege against self-incrimination if the production established the existence of the material, the defendant's possession or control of the material, or authenticity of

124. Id. at 411-413.
125. 465 U.S. 605 (1984).
126. Id. at 611-612.
127. Id. at 613.
128. Id. at 616-617.

the material. The state could respond to this potential problem by granting use immunity against any information obtained as a result of the production of the material. This would require the state to establish the existence of the material and to authenticate the material from sources other than the compelled disclosure.

On the other hand, it could be argued that the attorneys' obligations under the cases discussed in this problem do not violate the privilege against self-incrimination. First, in some cases the attorney receives the material in a communication that is not subject to the attorney-client privilege. Under *Fisher* the privilege against self-incrimination does not apply unless the attorney received the material in a communication that was subject to the attorney-client privilege. Thus, if the attorney received the material from a third party, not the client, the privilege would generally not apply.[129] Second, arguably there is no violation of the privilege because neither the attorney nor the client is compelled (an essential element for a violation of the privilege against self-incrimination) to turn the material over to the authorities: The material can be returned to its source.

Professor Kevin Reitz has argued that the duty to turn over material recognized by *Olwell* is fundamentally inconsistent with the privilege as recognized by *Fisher* and *Doe*. As a result he argues for a modification of both the privilege against self-incrimination and the lawyer's duty to produce tangible criminal material.[130]

How should attorneys comply with an obligation to turn tangible criminal material over to the authorities?

Assuming lawyers have an obligation to turn tangible criminal material in their possession over to the authorities, rarely will it make sense for lawyers voluntarily to take possession of such ma-

---

129. See People v. Sanchez, 30 Cal. Rptr. 2d 111 (Ct. App., *review denied* (1994)) (no violation of privilege against self-incrimination when defense counsel turned over incriminating diaries that he received from defendant's sisters to court).

130. Kevin R. Reitz, Clients, Lawyers and the Fifth Amendment: The Need for a Protected Privilege, 41 Duke L.J. 572 (1991). See also Kenneth J. Melilli, Act-of-Production Immunity, 52 Ohio St. L.J. 223 (1991) (discussing whether act of production immunity extends to derivative use of material produced).

terial.[131] One reason for doing so would be if the material could be exculpatory. In some cases, however, the attorney may not have a choice about obtaining or keeping possession. The material may be delivered anonymously to the lawyer or the party making the delivery may refuse to keep it.

What should the lawyer do if the lawyer does have possession of tangible criminal material? One possibility would be to return the material to its original location rather than to the authorities. Such an approach finds support in the *Meredith* case, which held that the privilege is lost if the attorney prevents the authorities from being able to obtain the material through an independent investigation. The ABA Standards for the Defense Function and the Restatement of the Law Governing Lawyers also recognize return of the property to its original location as an option.[132] The court in Hitch v. Pima County Superior Court[133] adopted the approach recommended by the ABA Standards, but this approach may be questionable in other jurisdictions where decisions such as *Olwell* seem to impose a duty on lawyers to turn the material over to the authorities. Indeed, even in California returning the material to its original location may not be proper. A California appellate decision states that if a lawyer takes possession of physical evidence, the lawyer must immediately notify the court so that the prosecution can have access to the evidence.[134] In addition, if substantial risk exists that the material will be destroyed or will be used to harm someone if it is returned to its original location, it seems improper for the lawyer to take that step.[135]

Another option would be to turn the material over to the authorities anonymously to protect client confidentiality to the maximum extent possible. Defense counsel could hire another attorney for the purpose of delivering the materials to the authorities. Normally, the identity of a client is not subject to the attorney-

131. See Barry S. Martin, Incriminating Criminal Evidence, Practical Solutions, 15 Pacific L.J. 807 (1984).

132. ABA Standards for Criminal Justice, Defense Function Standard 4-4.6(b) (3d ed. 1993); Restatement (Third) of the Law Governing Lawyers §179(2)(a).

133. 708 P.2d 72 (Ariz. 1985) (en banc).

134. See People v. Superior Court (In re Fairbank), 237 Cal. Rptr. 158 (Ct. App., *review denied* (1987)).

135. ABA Standards for Criminal Justice, Defense Function Standard 4-4.6(c) (3d ed. 1993).

client privilege, but at least one court has held that the identity of
a client from whom an attorney received stolen property was privileged.[136] On the other hand, an anonymous return may effectively
deprive the prosecution of evidence of a crime: What is a prosecutor to do with a gun returned anonymously without any identification of the crime to which the gun is related?[137]

──────────── **Problem 2-5** ────────────

Perjury in Criminal Cases

Melinda Lee represents Neil Denny in a prosecution for
robbery of a convenience store. At the initial interview,
Denny told Lee that he was nowhere near the convenience store and that he did not commit the robbery.
When Lee asked Denny where he was, Denny was vague
and hesitant, but he finally said that he was "with some
friends." Lee interviewed the friends that Denny identified and learned that Denny was with them from about
8:00 P.M. until about 10:30 P.M., but that he had left
them before the robbery occurred at 11:00.

At a subsequent meeting Lee informs Denny of the
results of her investigation. Denny says that he now re-
members that he was with his friends early in the evening, but that he spent the rest of the evening with his
girlfriend, Robin Gayle, at her apartment. Lee then interviews Gayle, who says that she and Denny were together the entire evening from about 7:30 until 1:00
A.M. watching television. She doesn't remember, however, what they watched, and her recall of the evening
is sketchy. Lee concludes that Gayle is lying to protect
Denny.

a.   What would you do if you were in Lee's position and Denny insists on taking the stand to present his

136. Anderson v. State, 297 So. 2d 871 (Fla. Dist. Ct. App. 1974).
137. See Norman Lefstein, Incriminating Physical Evidence, The Defense
Attorney's Dilemma, and the Need for Rules, 64 N.C. L. Rev. 897, 936-937
(1986).

alibi defense and demands that Lee call Gayle as a witness on his behalf? Why?

    b.   Suppose Lee counsels Denny that he must tes-
tify truthfully and informs him of the possible consequences of presenting false testimony. Nonetheless,
Denny insists on taking the stand to present his alibi
defense and on offering Gayle as a witness in his behalf.
Suppose Lee then informs the court that Denny is planning to testify falsely and to offer the false testimony of
an alibi witness. If you were the judge, what would you
do?

    c.   Suppose Lee counsels Denny that he must tes-
tify truthfully, that false testimony has a number of adverse consequences, and that Lee will inform the court
if Denny insists on offering perjured testimony. As a result, Denny does not take the stand and does not present
Gayle as an alibi witness. The jury convicts Denny of
armed robbery. Denny then files a petition seeking postconviction relief on the ground that Lee's actions violated Denny's Sixth and Fourteenth Amendment right
to effective assistance of counsel. Analyze whether
Denny's right to effective assistance of counsel has been
violated.

    d.   Suppose Lee counsels Denny that he must tes-
tify truthfully and informs him of the possible consequences of presenting false testimony. Nonetheless,
Denny insists on taking the stand to present his alibi
defense and on offering Gayle as a witness in his behalf.
Suppose Lee then informs the court that Denny is planning to testify falsely and to offer the false testimony of
an alibi witness. The judge advises Denny of his obligation to testify truthfully and warns Denny that if he
commits perjury, Denny may be prosecuted; the judge
also advises Denny that the judge may take the perjury
into account in sentencing if Denny is convicted. The
judge further rules that Lee has the authority to decide
whether to offer Gayle as a witness. Denny testifies in
his own behalf and presents his alibi defense, but Lee

refuses to offer Gayle as a witness. The jury convicts Denny of armed robbery. Denny then files a petition seeking postconviction relief on the ground that Lee's actions violated his Fifth and Fourteenth Amendment privilege against self-incrimination. Analyze whether Denny's privilege against self-incrimination has been violated.

e.   Based on your analysis of the situations above, how would you as defense counsel handle an initial client interview? What, if anything, would you say about confidentiality when you first meet with the defendant? What would you say if the defendant said to you: "Everything I tell you is confidential, right?"

f.   You are a member of a bar committee appointed by your state supreme court to review the rules of ethics in your state. Which approach to the problem of perjury by a criminal defendant would you favor? Why?

Read Model Rules 1.2, 1.16, 2.1, 3.3, and comments.

Approaches to the problem of perjury by the criminal defendant

What should defense counsel do when the defendant insists on taking the stand and testifying perjuriously (contemplated perjury) or when defense counsel learns that the defendant has testified perjuriously (completed perjury)?[138] Put aside for the moment the question of when a lawyer "knows" that a client will testify perjuriously. We will consider that point later in the discussion. Assume that, by whatever standard of knowledge is applicable, the lawyer does know that the client will commit or has committed perjury. Five approaches have been suggested for how defense

---

138.   For an historical survey of some of the most important cases involving perjured testimony, see Richard H. Underwood, Perjury: An Anthology, 13 Ariz. J. Intl. & Comp. L. 307 (1996).

counsel should respond either to contemplated or completed perjury by a criminal defendant.

   1. *Full representation.* In a famous 1966 article Professor
Monroe Freedman argued that if a criminal defendant insists on
taking the stand and testifying perjuriously, defense counsel
should not move to withdraw from the case and should not inform
the court of the perjury. Instead, defense counsel should allow the
defendant to take the stand and to testify; defense counsel should
not do anything that would either explicitly or implicitly disclose
the attorney's knowledge to the judge or jury. More specifically,
Freedman's approach meant that the attorney would examine the
defendant in the normal fashion, even if the defendant's answers
were perjurious, and that the attorney would make normal closing
arguments to the finder of fact, including arguments based on perjured testimony.[139] In later works Professor Freedman explained
the basis for his position. At its deepest level, his view of the obligations of defense counsel is founded on the value of the "dignity
of the individual in a free society." Constitutional rights, such as
due process of law, right to counsel, and the privilege against self-
incrimination, express this basic value. Confidentiality of communications between lawyer and client is central to all of these
rights, since without client trust and complete information, lawyers cannot adequately defend their clients' rights.[140] In addition,
Professor Freedman has criticized the practicality and constitutionality of the alternatives that others have proposed for dealing
with the issue of perjury by criminal defendants.[141]

   2. *Disclosure to the court.* Professor Freedman's position
met with immediate criticism from then United States Circuit
Judge (later Chief Justice of the United States Supreme Court)

---

   139. Monroe H. Freedman, Professional Responsibility of the Criminal
Defense Lawyer: The Three Hardest Questions, 64 Mich. L. Rev. 1469, 1475-
1478 (1966).
   140. Freedman, Understanding Lawyers' Ethics 13-17. See also Jay S.
Silver, Truth, Justice, and the American Way: The Case *Against* the Client Perjury Rules, 47 Vand. L. Rev. 339 (1994) (criticizing the disclosure obligations of
the Model Rules because they impede the discovery of truth, subvert the rights
of the accused, and undermine the adversarial process).
   141. See Monroe H. Freedman, Lawyers' Ethics in an Adversary System
27-42 (1975) and Freedman, Understanding Lawyers' Ethics 109-141.

Warren Burger. Justice Burger claimed that a lawyer could never under any circumstances participate in a fraud on the court, and that for a lawyer to ask questions of a client that would elicit perjured testimony was clearly improper.[142] Logically, the opposite position to Freedman's position of full representation would be full disclosure by defense counsel to the court of the defendant's contemplated or completed perjury. Although Justice Burger did not go that far in his 1966 article, he later came to endorse that position in his opinion in Nix v. Whiteside,[143] discussed in detail below.

Professor Freedman's and Justice Burger's views on the issue of perjury by the criminal defendant represent the polar positions for dealing with the problem. Each has the advantage of being clear in its direction to counsel, but each can be criticized for ignoring an important competing value: the integrity of the adversarial system in Freedman's case and the importance of client confidentiality to individual liberty in Justice Burger's case. Not surprisingly, other courts and scholars have attempted to find a middle ground that balances or accommodates in some fashion these competing values. Three alternatives to the full representation position of Professor Freedman and the disclosure position of Justice Burger are the following: withdrawal without disclosure, narrative testimony, and avoidance of knowledge.

3. *Withdrawal without disclosure.* An attorney confronted with a client who plans to take the stand and commit perjury or who has already testified perjuriously could move to withdraw from the case and still protect the confidentiality of client communications. The lawyer could, for example, move to withdraw because of "ethical reasons" or because of a "conflict of interest" or because of "privileged reasons."[144] Professor Freedman has

---

142. Warren E. Burger, Standards of Conduct for Prosecution and Defense Personnel: A Judge's Viewpoint, 5 Am. Crim. L.Q. 11, 13 (1966). For a history of the Freedman-Burger dispute, see Lyle Denniston, When Your Client Lies, 6 Cal. Law. 55, 57 (July 1986).

143. 475 U.S. 157 (1986).

144. See Manfredi & Levine v. Superior Court (Barles), 78 Cal. Rptr. 2d 494 (Ct. App. 1998) (decision to grant motion to withdraw within discretion of trial court; court should ordinarily accept representations of counsel that confidentiality precludes disclosure of specific reasons for motion when court con-

criticized the withdrawal solution on a number of grounds, including the following: First, if the court grants the motion, the problem is simply passed on to successor counsel who will either face the same dilemma or who will not learn of the perjury because the client has now been educated about what can and cannot be told to a lawyer. If the latter occurs, the withdrawal solution is no solution at all since it allows perjury to take place, but adds cost to the operation of the judicial system. Second, if the matter occurs on the eve of or during the trial, the judge will almost certainly deny the motion. The "withdrawal approach" does not guide the attorney about how to act in that event. Third, if the attorney moves to withdraw, the court may order the lawyer to reveal the reason, so it may be impossible to maintain confidentiality.[145] In addition, if the lawyer does reveal the reason for moving to withdraw, and the client takes the stand, the judge may take the client's perjury into account in sentencing.[146]

4. *Narrative testimony.* In 1971 the American Bar Association adopted Defense Function Standard 7.7 to guide defense lawyers in dealing with perjury by the criminal defendant. In 1979 the ABA Committee on Standards for Criminal Justice proposed a revised version of 7.7, but then withdrew this proposal from consideration by the ABA on the understanding that the issue of perjury by the criminal defendant would be considered by the ABA committee working on the Model Rules of Professional Conduct. Revised Defense Function Standard 7.7, however, did provide a detailed statement of the narrative approach to perjury by the criminal defendant.

Revised Standard 7.7 granted lawyers discretion to move to

---

cludes counsel is acting in good faith). See also Lawyer Disciplinary Board v. Farber, 488 S.E.2d 460 (W. Va. 1997) (lawyer received four-month suspension for disclosure of confidential information in connection with motion to withdraw in criminal case because disclosure went beyond what was necessary and was accompanied by threats to client).

145. Freedman, Understanding Lawyers' Ethics 115-116.

146. See United States v. Dunnigan, 507 U.S. 87 (1993) (upholding trial judge's enhancement of defendant's sentence under federal sentencing guidelines because of perjury committed at trial); United States v. Grayson, 438 U.S. 41 (1978) (upholding sentencing increase because of defendant's perjury).

withdraw if the issue of client perjury arose before trial. If withdrawal was not feasible or was denied by the court, the standard provided as follows:

> (c) If withdrawal from the case is not feasible or is not permitted by the court, or if the situation arises immediately preceding trial or during the trial and the defendant insists upon testifying perjuriously in his or her own behalf, it is unprofessional conduct for the lawyer to lend aid to the perjury or use the perjured testimony. Before the defendant takes the stand in these circumstances, the lawyer should make a record of the fact that the defendant is taking the stand against the advice of counsel in some appropriate manner without revealing the fact to the court. The lawyer may identify the witness as the defendant and may ask appropriate questions of the defendant when it is believed that the defendant's answers will not be perjurious. As to matters for which it is believed the defendant will offer perjurious testimony, the lawyer should seek to avoid direct examination of the defendant in the conventional manner; instead, the lawyer should ask the defendant if he or she wishes to make any additional statement concerning the case to the trier or triers of the facts. A lawyer may not later argue the defendant's known false version of the facts to the jury as worthy of belief, and may not recite or rely upon the false testimony in his or her closing argument.

Standard 7.7 represents an effort to walk a tightrope between the full representation and the disclosure approaches to perjury by the criminal defendant. Under the narrative approach defense counsel should not reveal client perjury, but at the same time defense counsel must strictly avoid any involvement in client perjury.
The principal objection to the narrative testimony approach is that it sacrifices both of the principles it seeks to protect: The solution does not prevent perjury from taking place, and it infringes confidentiality because both the judge and jury are almost certain to know that defendant's lawyer does not trust his own client's testimony.[147] Moreover, the narrative solution does not address the question of what the lawyer should do when the lawyer learns that the client has already testified perjuriously. Nevertheless, several courts have adopted the narrative solution as an eth-

---

147. Freedman, Understanding Lawyers' Ethics 117-119.

ically proper way for defense counsel to deal with the problem[148] and it has been incorporated in the District of Columbia Rules of Professional Conduct.[149] Some commentators also support the narrative approach.[150]

5. *Avoidance of knowledge.*   Some commentators have suggested that the most practical way for a lawyer to deal with the problem of perjury by a criminal defendant is to make sure that the lawyer avoids knowing that the client intends to commit perjury. For example, if defense lawyers ask their clients to inform them about "what the prosecution is likely to say" and "tell me your memory of what happened," rather than "what happened," then defense counsel can obtain all the facts without committing their clients to a particular version of what occurred. Professor Freedman characterizes this as "sophistry" and a "disingenuous evasion" designed to achieve the same result that he advocates openly and defends on the basis of fundamental values.[151] Further, this solution does not address the issue of the lawyer's obligation if the lawyer learns of perjury despite efforts to avoid knowledge.

The approach of the Model Rules of Professional Conduct and the Restatement of the Law Governing Lawyers

The lawyer's obligations regarding perjury by the criminal defendant depend on whether the perjury is contemplated or completed. Under Model Rule 3.3, when the lawyer knows of contemplated perjury, the lawyer's course of action is to attempt to dissuade the

148. People v. Guzman, 755 P.2d 917 (Cal. 1988) (en banc), *cert. denied,* 488 U.S. 1050 (1989); Shockley v. State, 565 A.2d 1373 (Del. 1989); Commonwealth v. Jermyn, 620 A.2d 1128 (Pa. 1993), *cert. denied,* 510 U.S. 1049 (1994); In re Goodwin, 305 S.E.2d 578 (S.C. 1983). See also People v. Johnson, 72 Cal. Rptr. 2d 805 (Ct. App.), *cert. denied,* 119 S. Ct. 262 (1998) (court adopts narrative solution after comprehensive review of other options; court finds, however that even though defendant did not testify, error was harmless beyond a reasonable doubt because of other evidence).

149. D.C. R. Prof. Conduct 3.3(b).

150. The most extensive defense of the narrative approach can be found in Norman Lefstein, Client Perjury in Criminal Cases: Still in Search of an Answer, 1 Geo. J. Legal Ethics 521 (1988). See also Crystal, Confidentiality Under the Model Rules of Professional Conduct, 30 Kan. L. Rev. at 236-244.

151. Freedman, Understanding Lawyers' Ethics 119, 141.

client from testifying falsely, and, if this fails, to move to withdraw if that step is feasible.[152]

Criminal defendants have a constitutional right to testify in their own behalf, so neither defense counsel nor the court has the right to stop a defendant from testifying, even if the defendant intends to testify perjuriously.[153] If the client takes the stand and testifies perjuriously, ABA Model Rule 3.3(a)(4) requires the lawyer to take "reasonable remedial measures":

> A lawyer shall not knowingly . . . offer evidence that the lawyer knows to be false. If a lawyer has offered material evidence and comes to know of its falsity, the lawyer shall take reasonable remedial measures.

While the language of the rule is less than clear in its use of the term "reasonable remedial measures," the comments are clear that the rule is intended to adopt Justice Burger's position requiring full disclosure if necessary to correct the perjury.[154] See Comments 7-11.[155] In particular, note that Comment 11 states: "If withdrawal will not remedy the situation or is impossible, the advocate should make disclosure to the court." Comments 9 and 10 express reasons for the ABA's adoption of the disclosure approach.

The Restatement of the Law Governing Lawyers also adopts the view that lawyers have a duty to disclose client perjury if other remedial measures are insufficient to remove the false impression

152. Model Rule 3.3, cmt. 7. In Formal Opinion 87-353, the ABA Committee on Ethics and Professional Responsibility ruled that a lawyer normally need not move to withdraw after a defendant initially states an intention to testify falsely because the lawyer can ordinarily conclude that a warning about the consequences of perjury, including the lawyer's duty to reveal the perjury to the court, will be sufficient to dissuade the client from committing perjury. If the client continues to insist on testifying falsely despite the lawyer's warnings, however, the lawyer should move to withdraw.

153. Rock v. Arkansas, 483 U.S. 44 (1987).

154. Prior to the adoption of the Model Rules, the ABA's position on the problem of client perjury reflected an oscillation between protection of client confidentiality and avoidance of lawyer involvement in perjury. For a history of these developments, see Jeffrey L. Dunetz, Surprise Client Perjury: Some Questions and Proposed Solutions to an Old Problem, 29 N.Y.L. Sch. L. Rev. 407, 410-420 (1984).

155. In Formal Opinion 87-353 the ABA committee opined that Rule 3.3(a)(4) does require disclosure to the court if that is the only way to correct the perjury. Id. at 4.

caused by the client's testimony.[156] The Restatement explains that the preservation of the integrity of the tribunal is superior to any interest the client might have in the loyalty of and confidentiality of communications with counsel regarding false testimony.[157] Once false evidence has been introduced withdrawal is not a reasonable remedial measure.[158] However, the lawyer may be able to take remedial measures that do not involve disclosure of confidential information. The lawyer could attempt to persuade the client to take the stand and correct the client's false testimony. In some instances the lawyer may be able to move to strike or withdraw the evidence.[159]

If a lawyer informs the court that a defendant either intends to or has testified falsely, what should the court do about the matter? Comment 11 to Model Rule 3.3 provides only a small degree of guidance: "It is for the court then to determine what should be done — making a statement about the matter to the trier of fact, ordering a mistrial or perhaps nothing." In United States v. Scott,[160] defendant's public defender moved to withdraw for unspecified ethical reasons. The trial judge informed the defendant that he had the choice of either proceeding pro se or with the assistance of counsel who would make the decision about whether to allow the defendant to testify. The defendant chose to continue the case pro se. The Eleventh Circuit reversed the defendant's conviction, holding that the trial judge had put the defendant to an unconstitutional choice between the constitutional rights to testify and to effective assistance of counsel. The court stated that the trial judge should have simply decided the issue of whether to grant counsel's motion to withdraw. The court also held that without more information the trial court should have denied the motion to withdraw.[161] The court conceded, however, that "a much more difficult case would have resulted had it been established on the record that defendant intended to commit perjury."[162]

---

156. Restatement (Third) of The Law Governing Lawyers §180(2). On remedial measures available to an attorney prior to disclosing confidential information, see id. §180, cmt. *h.*
157. Id. cmt. *b.*
158. Id. cmt. *h.*
159. Id.
160. 909 F.2d 488 (11th Cir. 1990).
161. Id. at 493.
162. Id. at 493-494.

Client perjury and the constitutional rights to effective assistance of counsel, the privilege against self-incrimination, and due process of law

As discussed above, Professor Freedman based his full representation approach on various constitutional rights of criminal defendants, including the Sixth Amendment right to effective assistance of counsel and the Fifth Amendment privilege against self-incrimination.

In Nix v. Whiteside[163] the Supreme Court considered the relationship between client perjury and the Sixth Amendment right to effective assistance of counsel. The defendant Whiteside along with two companions came to the apartment of Calvin Love seeking marijuana. Love was in bed at the time, and the two men argued. Love got up from bed, asked his girlfriend to get his "piece," and then returned to bed. According to Whiteside's testimony, he saw Love reach under his pillow. Whiteside then stabbed Love fatally in the chest.[164]

Whiteside was charged with murder. He told his court-appointed lawyer, Gary Robinson, that he had not actually seen Love pulling a gun, but he was convinced that Love had a pistol. None of the witnesses had seen a pistol, and the police did not find one on the premises. Robinson advised Whiteside that to establish self defense Whiteside need not show that Love actually had a gun, only that Whiteside had a reasonable belief that Love had a weapon.[165]

About a week before trial Whiteside told Robinson that he had seen something "metallic" in Love's hand. When Robinson questioned Whiteside about the change in his story, Whiteside said: "If I don't say I saw a gun, I'm dead." Robinson told Whiteside that this testimony would amount to perjury, that it was unnecessary to establish self-defense, that as a lawyer he would be involved in suborning perjury, that he would inform the court if Whiteside testified in this fashion, and that Robinson would probably be allowed to testify to impeach Whiteside's testimony. Robinson also indicated that he would attempt to withdraw if Whiteside persisted in this testimony.[166]

---

163. 475 U.S. 157 (1986).
164. Id. at 160.
165. Id.
166. Id. at 161.

At trial Whiteside testified that he "knew" Love had a gun
and that he believed Love was reaching for a gun under his pillow,
but he admitted on cross-examination that he had not actually
seen a gun. Robinson presented evidence to substantiate Whiteside's belief that Love had a weapon. Nonetheless, Whiteside was
convicted of second-degree murder. Both on direct appeal and in
subsequent habeas corpus proceedings, he contended that Robinson's conduct had denied him effective assistance of counsel.[167]

The Supreme Court found that Robinson's conduct did not
amount to ineffective assistance of counsel. The Court's majority
opinion, written by Chief Justice Burger, judged Robinson's actions under the test for ineffective assistance of counsel set forth
in Strickland v. Washington.[168] (Recall our discussion of *Strickland*
in connection with Problem 2-2).

The majority first concluded that Robinson's actions
amounted to a reasonable professional response to Whiteside's in-
dication that he planned to give false testimony. The opinion noted
that the Court's role was not to constitutionalize particular standards of professional conduct.[169] After making this concession,
however, the opinion proceeded to consider various professional
norms and to cite with approval Model Rule 3.3, requiring disclosure to the court to rectify client perjury.[170] Based on this review,
the Court found that Robinson had acted reasonably:

> Whether Robinson's conduct is seen as a successful attempt to dis-
> suade his client from committing the crime of perjury, or whether
> seen as a "threat" to withdraw from representation and disclose the
> illegal scheme, Robinson's representation of Whiteside falls well
> within accepted standards of professional conduct and the range of
> reasonable professional conduct acceptable under *Strickland*.[171]

The Court also found that Whiteside had not suffered prejudice,
the second prong of the *Strickland* test, because of Robinson's conduct.[172] It is noteworthy that Whiteside did testify and presented
the substance of his self-defense argument to the jury.

In a concurring opinion written by Justice Blackmun and

167. Id. at 161-62.
168. 466 U.S. 668 (1984).
169. 475 U.S. at 165.
170. Id. at 168.
171. Id. at 171.
172. Id. at 175-176.

joined by Justices Brennan, Marshall, and Stevens, these justices
agreed that Whiteside had failed to show any prejudice but they
criticized the majority opinion for implicitly defining as a matter
of constitutional law the appropriate standard of conduct for lawyers in dealing with perjury by criminal defendants. Justice Blackmun argued that states should be free to adopt "differing
approaches" to a complex ethical problem: "The signal merit of
asking first whether a defendant has shown any adverse prejudicial
effect before inquiring into his attorney's performance is that it
avoids unnecessary federal interference in a State's regulation of
its bar."[173]

While *Nix* found no constitutional violation on the facts of
the case, it is possible to imagine cases in which a defendant could
establish a constitutional violation. Suppose Robinson had acted
based on his belief that his client was committing perjury rather
than his client's admission, and suppose the substance of the client's claim of self-defense had not been presented to the jury. In
such a case the defendant might be able to establish both prongs
of the *Strickland* test for ineffective assistance of counsel.[174]

Nix was a Sixth Amendment case. The Supreme Court has
yet to address the question of the relationship between the Fifth
Amendment privilege against self-incrimination and client perjury.[175] As we saw in connection with Problem 2-4, the leading
Supreme Court case on the privilege against self-incrimination is
Fisher v. United States.[176] In *Fisher* the Supreme Court held that
information conveyed to an attorney by a client is subject to the
privilege against self-incrimination if two requirements are met:
First, the conveyance of the information from the client to the

173. Id. at 190.
174. *Compare* State v. Jones, 923 P.2d 560 (Mont. 1996) (defendant's
Sixth Amendment right violated when lawyer moved to withdraw on unsubstan-
tiated belief that defendant intended to commit perjury) *with* State v. Berrysmith,
944 P.2d 397 (Wash. Ct. App. 1997), *review. denied*, 954 P.2d 277 (Wash. 1998)
(no violation of defendant's constitutional rights under *Nix* when lawyer moved
to withdraw because of reasonable belief that client intended to commit perjury
and could not be dissuaded from doing so; court also rules that defendant did
not have constitutional right to be present at hearing on motion because issue
was lawyer's reasonable belief, not whether defendant would actually commit
perjury).
175. See Monroe H. Freedman, Client Confidences and Client Perjury:
Some Unanswered Questions, 136 U. Pa. L. Rev. 1939 (1988).
176. 425 U.S. 391 (1976).

attorney must be protected by the attorney-client evidentiary privilege. Second, the information sought from the attorney must be subject to the privilege against self-incrimination if the government had attempted to obtain the information directly from the client. Information obtained directly from the client is subject to the privilege against self-incrimination if the production of the information compels the client to give incriminating testimony.[177]

Whether a lawyer's revelation of a criminal defendant's contemplated or completed perjury violates the defendant's privilege against self-incrimination turns on the answer to two questions. Did the attorney receive the information from the client in a privileged communication? If the attorney's knowledge of the perjury comes from a source other than the client, the communication is not subject to the attorney-client privilege, and the attorney's disclosure would not violate the client's privilege against self-incrimination. In addition, if the attorney is revealing contemplated rather than completed perjury, the disclosure may fall within the crime/fraud exception to the attorney-client privilege.[178] Would the revelation incriminate the client? If the revelation prevents or rectifies false testimony, it is difficult to see how the revelation is incriminating. But, if the revelation results in a prosecution for perjury or sentencing enhancement, then the defendant has been incriminated by the lawyer's revelation.

177. Id. at 397, 404-405.
178. In an ethics advisory opinion, the National Association of Criminal Defense Lawyers ruled that an attorney who knows that a criminal defendant intends to commit perjury should not reveal the client's intention to the court because the revelation would violate the client's privilege against self-incrimination, and the privilege took priority over any rule of ethics that required disclosure. Adv. Op. 92-2, The Champion 23 (March 1993). The opinion discussed the application of the crime/fraud exception as follows:

It is important to consider . . . whether a lawyer's knowledge of a client's intention to commit perjury is within the future crime exception to the lawyer-client privilege.
     In fact, perjury has been construed as falling outside of the future crime exception. One reason is that it is "intrinsically and inextricably" related to the crime for which the defendant is being tried. In this respect, it is like the future crime of concealing the proceeds of a theft — that is, to reveal the future crime (ongoing concealment) is to implicate the client in the past crime (theft). This is not true, of course, of the future crime of bribing a juror. To reveal the client's intent to commit the bribery does not require revealing any confidences regarding his guilt of the past crime that is being tried.

Id. at 26.

If the case is being tried before a judge rather than a jury, defense counsel's disclosure of false testimony by the defendant poses an additional constitutional problem. The defendant's right to due process of law may be infringed because the judge as trier of fact has been prejudiced. In such cases defense counsel must take special care to avoid informing the court of the defendant's perjury. Use of the narrative solution is one possibility available to defense counsel. If defense counsel decides to move to withdraw or to inform the court, defense counsel must adopt a procedure that avoids informing the judge trying the case. This could be done in either of two ways. The motion could be made to a judge not trying the case. The chief administrative judge for the court would be the natural choice. In the alternative the lawyer could make the motion to the judge who has been assigned the case, but ask the judge to certify the case to another judge for trial.[179]

When does a lawyer "know" that a defendant intends to or has committed perjury?

Model Rule 3.3 requires lawyers to take action to deal with client perjury only if the lawyer "knows" that the client intends to or has committed perjury. When does a lawyer have knowledge of perjury? The terminology section of the Model Rules states:

> "Knowingly," "Known," or "Knows," denotes actual knowledge of the fact in question. A person's knowledge may be inferred from circumstances.

What does "actual knowledge" mean in the context of the issue of perjury by a criminal defendant? It would be absurd to suggest that actual knowledge requires the lawyer to have been a witness to the underlying crime so as to have personal knowledge of the falsity of the client's statements. A personal knowledge standard would negate the obligations of Rule 3.3 since the rule would apply

---

179. For cases on the due process problems facing defense counsel when client perjury occurs in bench trials, see Lowery v. Cardwell, 575 F.2d 727 (9th Cir. 1978); State v. Jefferson, 615 P.2d 638 (Ariz. 1980) (en banc); Butler v. United States, 414 A.2d 844 (D.C. 1980) (en banc).

only when a attorney could not represent a defendant because the
lawyer would be a witness in the case. In Formal Opinion 87-353
the ABA stated that a lawyer should take action only when the
client had a "clearly stated intention" to testify falsely at trial.
Proposed ABA Defense Function Standard 7.7 went further,
adopting a two-part test to determine when lawyers were required
to take action in response to threatened perjury: "If the defendant
has admitted to defense counsel facts which establish guilt and
counsel's independent investigation established that the admissions are true but the defendant insists on the right to trial."

The courts have not been quite that stringent. Several courts
have said that the attorney must have a "firm factual basis" before
taking any action to prevent or rectify perjury by the defendant[180]
and this is the view adopted by the Restatement.[181] Other courts
have adopted a requirement that the lawyer have evidence establishing "beyond a reasonable doubt" that the defendant has or will
commit perjury.[182]

Disclosure of client perjury by defense counsel can result in
serious prejudice to the defendant. It seems reasonable that the
standard of disclosure should be at least as demanding as that
required to convict the defendant, that is, beyond a reasonable
doubt. Under this standard the mere fact that a client has given
the attorney inconsistent statements should not in and of itself be
sufficient to amount to knowledge of perjury.[183] If a lawyer concludes that he has sufficient knowledge of perjury to bring the
matter to the attention of the court, it may be necessary for the
court to hold a hearing to determine if there is adequate evidence
of perjury to require some action.[184]

180. United States v. Long, 857 F.2d 436, 445 (8th Cir. 1988); United
States ex rel. Wilcox v. Johnson, 555 F.2d 115, 122 (3d Cir. 1977).
181. Restatement (Third) of The Law Governing Lawyers §180, cmt. c.
182. E.g., Shockley v. State, 565 A.2d 1373, 1379 (Del. 1989). Advisory
Opinion 92-2 of the National Association of Criminal Defense Lawyers also
adopts the "beyond a reasonable doubt" standard. See Adv. Op. 92-2, The
Champion 29 (March 1993). See also Harry I. Subin, The Criminal Lawyer's
"Different Mission": Reflections on the "Right" to Present a False Case, 1 Geo.
J. Legal Ethics 125, 142 (1987).
183. See People v. Schultheis, 638 P.2d 8, 11 (Colo. 1981) (en banc).
184. The possibility of having such hearings is discussed in Carol T. Rie-
ger, Client Perjury: A Proposed Resolution of the Constitutional and Ethical
Issues, 70 Minn. L. Rev. 121 (1985).

Perjury by witnesses other than criminal defendants

Suppose the defendant wishes to call a witness that defense counsel reasonably believes will be testifying falsely. What should the lawyer do? While criminal defendants have the right to decide whether to testify in their own behalf, lawyers have the authority to determine which witnesses to call. See Model Rule 1.2(a). Similarly, ABA Defense Function Standard 4-5.2(b) provides as follows:

> Strategic and tactical decisions should be made by defense counsel after consultation with the client where feasible and appropriate. Such decisions include what witnesses to call, whether and how to conduct cross-examination, what jurors to accept or strike, what trial motions should be made, and what evidence should be introduced.

Further, Model Rule 3.3(c) states "[a] lawyer may refuse to offer evidence that the lawyer reasonably believes is false."[185] Thus, if a lawyer knows that a witness will testify falsely, the lawyer has the authority and duty simply to refuse to call the witness.[186] As stated in Model Rule 1.2(a) and Defense Function Standard 4-5.2(b), the lawyer should take this step only after consultation with the client. If a lawyer learns that a witness has already testified falsely, the lawyer would have a duty to take reasonable remedial measures, including disclosure of the false testimony to the tribunal if necessary. See Model Rule 3.3(a)(4).[187]

The lawyer's refusal to call a witness could prompt a confrontation between lawyer and client that could in turn lead to the client's demand that the lawyer withdraw. The matter would then be brought to the attention of the court, which could take such action as it thought appropriate, including granting counsel permission to withdraw, directing counsel to call the defense witness, or allowing counsel to proceed without calling the witness.

---

185. See also Restatement (Third) of the Law Governing Lawyers §180(3).

186. See People v. Flores, 538 N.E.2d 481 (Ill. 1989), *cert. denied,* 497 U.S. 1031 (1990) (lawyer has discretion not to call nonclient witness in criminal case).

187. See Restatement (Third) of the Law Governing Lawyers §180(2).

The ethics of the lawyer's "lecture"

In cases like Nix v. Whiteside, the lawyer responded to a client's decision to testify falsely. In other cases, however, lawyers face decisions about how active they can be in coaching clients about their testimony. In the novel and movie *Anatomy of a Murder*, attorney Paul Biegler has been asked to represent Lieutenant Frederic Manion, who is accused of murdering Barney Quill. Quill raped Manion's wife, Laura. After considering the facts published in the newspapers, Biegler concludes that the only defense available to Manion is insanity at the time of the homicide. Before asking Manion to tell him about the murder, Biegler lectures Manion on the various legal defenses to homicide, leading Manion to shape his testimony to establish the defense of insanity.

Professor Monroe Freedman has argued that the ethical propriety of using the lecture depends on the circumstances. In many cases, he contends, the lawyer should inform the client of the legal significance of facts because it is necessary for the lawyer to do so to overcome various psychological barriers to a person's accurate recollection of events. The lawyer in these cases is not trying to create false testimony, but rather is simply seeking to obtain from the client accurate information necessary to represent the client competently. He discusses three potential psychological barriers to clients (or witnesses) giving accurate facts:

First, memory is affected by various factors such as temperament, biases, expectations, and experience. As a result people reconstruct past events, often without being aware that they are doing so. Because of this "imaginative reconstruction" a person's memory may be *"subjectively* accurate but *objectively* false."[188] Second, people tend to remember in ways that are consistent with their own interests. Freedman notes that this often amounts to "wishful thinking" rather than deliberate dishonesty.[189] Third, people tend to respond confidently to questions about what they remember even when the actual circumstances should make them cautious about the accuracy of their recollections. Freedman concludes his discussion of the psychology of memory as follows:

---

188. Freedman, Understanding Lawyers' Ethics 153 (quoting Gardner, The Perception and Memory of Witnesses, 18 Cornell L. Rev. 391 (1933)).
189. Id. at 154.

To sum up, remembering is not analogous to playing back a videotape or retrieving information from a computer. Rather, it is a process of active, creative reconstruction, which begins at the moment of perception. Moreover, this reconstructive process is significantly affected by the form of the questions asked and by what we understand to be in our own interest — even though, on a conscious level, we are responding as honestly as we can.[190]

Freedman admits however, that there are cases in which giving information about the law cannot be justified on the ground of overcoming psychological barriers, and he treats the lecture in *Anatomy of a Murder* in that second category.[191]

C. Conflicts of Interest

Problem 2-6
Defendants with Mental Disabilities

You represent Henrietta Krindler, who is accused of murdering her husband. The state contends that Krindler killed her husband to collect substantial insurance proceeds on his life. Krindler has admitted to you that she killed her husband. She says that he was suffering from terminal liver cancer and that she killed him to save him from a painful death. In fact, Krindler's husband was not ill at all. Krindler, who has a history of mental illness, suffered from a delusion about her husband's condition.

You have considered raising the issue of whether Krindler is competent to stand trial. Under your state statute, which is similar to section 4.04 of the Model Penal Code, a defendant is incompetent to stand trial if the defendant "lacks capacity to understand the proceedings against him or to assist in his own defense." You have concluded, however, that it is probably not in

190. Id. at 155.
191. Freedman, Lawyers' Ethics in an Adversary System at 73.

Krindler's interest to claim that she is incompetent to stand trial. First, you think that it is extremely unlikely that the court will find Krindler incompetent under this statute. Second, if Krindler is found incompetent, she will be institutionalized indefinitely and will still be subject to trial. Third, you believe that you have a good chance of being able to convince the jury that Krindler should be found guilty of manslaughter rather than murder because she lacks the mens rea required for murder. Fourth, if you raise the incompetency issue, any statements Krindler makes to doctors who examine her to determine her competency will probably not be privileged.[192] An examination could reveal information that would be helpful to the prosecution if the case goes to trial.

You have also considered whether to raise the defense that Krindler was not criminally responsible at the time she killed her husband. Your state supreme court has ruled that a defendant is not criminally responsible if "the defendant lacks substantial capacity either to appreciate the criminality of his conduct or to conform his conduct to the requirements of the law." You doubt that Krindler meets the requirements of this statute because it appears that she knew right from wrong when she killed her husband and that she was able to conform her conduct to the law. She acted on a mistaken belief about her husband's condition, but even if she had not been mistaken about his health, her action would still not have been justified under the law. In addition, if you enter a plea of not guilty by reason of insanity, Krindler will have to undergo examination by the state's doctors.

You have concluded, therefore, that the best strategy to follow is not to raise either a claim that Krindler is incompetent to stand trial or a defense of insanity, but

---

192. *Compare* Buchanan v. Kentucky, 483 U.S. 402 (1987) (state's use of psychiatric report to rebut mental status defense did not violate privilege against self-incrimination) *with* Estelle v. Smith, 451 U.S. 454 (1981) (Fifth Amendment violation for prosecutor to use statements made by defendant to court-appointed psychiatrist at sentencing hearing to establish future dangerousness when defendant had not put incompetency at issue).

instead to enter a plea of not guilty to murder and then to contend at trial that Krindler should be found guilty of at most manslaughter because she lacked the mens rea necessary for murder.

You have tried to discuss these considerations with Krindler, and she seems to understand the issues, but she has insisted that you not put up any defense on her behalf. She wants to enter a plea of guilty to murder, and she does not want you to introduce any evidence in mitigation at her sentencing hearing. Krindler says that she committed the crime and should be punished, that she does not want to be locked away in an institution for the rest of her life, and that her husband has told her that he wants her to join him. How should you proceed?

Read Model Rules 1.2(a), 1.14, 1.16, and comments.

Determining the client's competency

The rules of professional conduct generally assume that lawyers represent clients who are able to communicate with their lawyers and to make fundamental decisions about their cases based on the advice of counsel. See Model Rule 1.2(a).[193] Suppose this assumption fails: A lawyer represents a client who the lawyer believes is not fully competent and who is making decisions that may be harmful to the client, such as refusing to raise certain defenses or refusing to accept a favorable plea bargain. A client's incompetency could be caused by mental illness or retardation, physical disability, or addiction to drugs. In addition, lawyers who represent children also face the issue of dealing with clients who may have less than full capacity.

Model Rule 1.14 provides some general guidance to lawyers facing such problems. (EC 7-11 and 7-12 of the Code of Professional Responsibility are similar in many respects to Rule 1.14.) The rule envisions two possibilities: (a) clients who suffer from

---

193. See also ABA Standards for Criminal Justice, Defense Function Standard 4-5.2 (3d ed. 1993) (distinguishing fundamental decisions that clients are entitled to make based on lawyers' advice from strategic and tactical decisions that lawyers are authorized to make after consultation with clients when feasible).

impaired capacity but are capable of participating in a client-lawyer relationship to some degree, and (b) clients who "cannot adequately act in [their] own interest." Thus an initial issue a lawyer must resolve is whether the client is impaired or incompetent. Model Rule 1.14 does not address this issue, but Comment 1 provides some guidance. It focuses on three factors that are significant in deciding whether a client is incompetent or simply impaired: the ability of the client to "understand, deliberate upon, and reach conclusions about matters affecting the client's own well-being." In Dusky v. United States,[194] the Supreme Court articulated the following standard for determining the defendant's competency to stand trial:

[Test for incompetent]

> whether he has sufficient present ability to consult with his lawyer with a reasonable degree of rational understanding — and whether he has a rational as well as factual understanding of the proceedings against him.[195]

[How much of proceeding must client understand]

The Model Penal Code provision quoted in the problem adopts this test focusing on the defendant's ability to *understand the proceeding* and to *assist in the defense*.[196]

Suppose a lawyer is unsure whether a client is competent to stand trial or to make other decisions. How should the lawyer proceed? As an initial step the lawyer may want to consult with a psychiatrist or psychologist to obtain medical advice about the defendant's condition. May the lawyer do so if the client refuses to consent to such a consultation? In Informal Opinion 89-1530 the ABA Committee on Ethics and Professional Responsibility advised that lawyers may do so and that any disclosures they made would not violate their duty of confidentiality:

> [D]isclosures necessary for the lawyer to seek expert advice when there is reason to suspect impairment threatening serious harm to

---

194. 362 U.S. 402 (1960).

195. Id. Scholars have criticized the current formulation of the standard of competency to stand trial. *Compare* Richard J. Bonnie, The Competence of Criminal Defendants: Beyond *Dusky* and *Drope*, 47 U. Miami L. Rev. 539 (1993) *with* Bruce J. Winick, Reforming Incompetency to Stand Trial and Plead Guilty: A Restated Proposal and a Response to Professor Bonnie, 85 J. Crim. L. & Criminology 571 (1995).

196. See also ABA, Criminal Justice Mental Health Standard 7-4.1 (2d ed. 1986).

Co'n see
a psychiatrist
to determine
competency
for representation
purposes
- still
protected

the client are impliedly authorized in order to carry out the representation within the meaning of Model Rule 1.6. Otherwise, Rule
1.14 could not work effectively and the Model Rules would be in-
ternally inconsistent. Disclosures necessary under Rule 1.14 would
be prohibited by the provisions of Model Rule 1.6.[197]

See also Model Rule 1.14, cmt. 5. Suppose that the lawyer, based
either on the lawyer's own observations or on the advice of a doctor, concludes that substantial doubt exists about the defendant's
competency to stand trial. What should the lawyer do? Due process requires that criminal defendants be competent to stand
trial.[198] If a lawyer in a criminal case believes that the client is incompetent, the lawyer can deal with the problem by informing the
court so that the court can hold a hearing on the defendant's competency to stand trial.[199] In some cases, however, defense counsel
may conclude that it is more advantageous for an incompetent defendant to proceed to trial than to raise an incompetency issue.
The ABA's Criminal Justice Mental Health Standards summarize
the reasons why defense counsel could reach this conclusion:

> An involuntary commitment for treatment to restore competence
> may extend well beyond the maximum sentence imposable for a
> relatively minor offense. A defendant could view the stigma flowing
> from a finding of mental illness as more opprobrious than that gen-
> erated by a criminal conviction. An evaluation may force a defen-
> dant to reveal to a court-appointed expert information the
> defendant would prefer to keep secret. . . . A defendant might even
> prefer to be punished through imprisonment than to experience
> commitment to a mental hospital for treatment, given the marginal
> conditions in many public mental institutions. If the prosecution

197. ABA Comm. on Ethics and Prof. Resp., Informal Op. 89-1530, at
3. In Formal Opinion 96-404, the ABA committee reaffirmed Informal Opinion
89-1530 and discussed other issues facing lawyers who represent clients with
disabilities. See also Restatement (Third) of the Law Governing Lawyers §35,
cmt. *d*.

198. Drope v. Missouri, 420 U.S. 162 (1975); Pate v. Robinson, 383 U.S.
375 (1966).

199. See James A. Cohen, The Attorney-Client Privilege, Ethical Rules,
and the Impaired Criminal Defendant, 52 U. Miami L. Rev. 529 (1998) (arguing
that lawyers should be able to reveal confidential information to court to assist it
in making competency determination).

case against a defendant is weak, or if a defendant's assistance is not actually required during trial, defense counsel may believe that an acquittal is likely even though defendant is incompetent.[200]

One federal study has shown that confinement for mental illness typically exceeds that for the underlying offense. The study found that in felony cases the median length of commitment for patients found not guilty by reason of insanity was 49.2 months, while jail sentences for convicted felons was 33.4 months.[201]

May defense counsel decide as a matter of strategy not to inform the court when counsel has substantial doubts about a criminal defendant's competence to stand trial? (Of course, even if defense counsel does not raise the issue, either the prosecutor or the court on its own motion may do so.[202]) Despite the considerations noted above, the ABA Criminal Justice Mental Health Standards require defense counsel to move the court for a competency determination when "defense counsel has a good faith doubt as to the defendant's competence."[203] While recognizing that in some cases it may not be to the advantage of a defendant to raise the issue of competency, the commentary to the standards justifies imposing a duty on defense counsel to inform the court of the defendant's incompetency because of counsel's duty to the system: "Because the trial of an incompetent defendant necessarily is invalid as a violation of due process, a defense lawyer's duty to maintain the integrity of judicial proceedings requires that a trial court be advised of the defendant's possible incompetence."[204]

Model Rule 1.14, in contrast to the Mental Health Standards, does not impose on the lawyer a duty of disclosure. Comment 5 to Rule 1.14 states simply that the "lawyer's position in such cases is an unavoidably difficult one." The Restatement states that lawyers do not have a duty to inform a tribunal of a defendant's possible incompetency when the lawyer concludes

---

200. ABA, Criminal Justice Mental Health Standard 7-4.2, cmt. (2d ed. 1986).

201. Paul A. Chernoff & William G. Schaffer, Defending the Mentally Ill: Ethical Quicksand, 10 Am. Crim. L. Rev. 505, 523-524, n.65 (1972).

202. See ABA, Criminal Justice Mental Health Standard 7-4.2 (2d ed. 1986).

203. Id. 7-4.2(c).

204. Id. cmt.

that such disclosure would not be in the client's interest, unless law imposes such an obligation.[205]

In United States v. Boigegrain,[206] the Tenth Circuit ruled that a criminal defendant was not denied effective assistance of counsel when defense counsel raised the issue of his competency to stand trial over the defendant's objection. Relying on the ABA Criminal Justice Mental Health Standards, the court stated that defense counsel had a duty to bring the issue of the defendant's competency to the attention of the court: "Of all the actors in a trial, defense counsel has the most intimate association with the defendant. Therefore, the defendant's lawyer is not only allowed to raise the competency issue, but, because of the importance of the prohibition on trying those who cannot understand proceedings against them, she has a professional duty to do so when appropriate."[207] Similarly, in State v. Johnson,[208] the Wisconsin Supreme Court held that a defendant had been denied effective assistance of counsel in a murder case when his lawyer did not inform the court that the defendant might not be competent to stand trial. The court rejected arguments that defense counsel had acted properly because he had concluded that the defendant was competent and because he had decided that it was not strategically wise to raise the incompetency issue. The court held that when defense counsel has "reason to doubt the competency of his client to stand trial, he must raise the issue with the trial court."[209]

Professor Rodney Uphoff has criticized *Johnson* because it undercuts the defendant's right to zealous representation. He would allow lawyers to make case-by-case determinations of what their role should be:

205. Restatement (Third), of the Law Governing Lawyers §35, cmt. *d*.
206. 155 F.3d 1181 (10th Cir. 1998), *cert. denied*, 119 S. Ct. 828 (1999).
207. 155 F.3d at 1188. Judge Holloway, concurring in part and dissenting in part, agreed that defense counsel did have a duty to raise the issue of the defendant's competency, but argued that this resulted in a conflict of interest when defense counsel proceeded to advocate the defendant's incompetency against the defendant's wishes. Judge Holloway argued that defense counsel should have been allowed to withdraw. The trial court should have appointed new counsel who would have advocated defendant's position that he was competent to stand trial. Id. at 1190-1193.
208. 395 N.W.2d 176 (Wis. 1986).
209. Id. at 182.

The decision as to whether to respect a client's questionable decision, assume a more paternalistic role, or raise competency depends on the lawyer's careful analysis of the degree of the client's mental impairment, the importance of the decision being considered, the type of case, and the costs and benefits to the client of the alternative courses of action.[210]

Representing competent but possibly impaired clients

Suppose counsel represents a defendant whom the court has found competent to stand trial but whose decisionmaking capacities the lawyer still question. What, if anything, should the lawyer do if the defendant insists on entering a plea or demands that the lawyer conduct the case in a fashion that the lawyer concludes is clearly not in the client's best interest? Competent clients generally have the authority to make ultimate decisions about their cases. See Model Rule 1.2(a). ABA Defense Function Standard 4-5.2 provides as follows:

(a) Certain decisions relating to the conduct of the case are ultimately for the accused and others are ultimately for defense counsel. The decisions which are to be made by the accused after full consultation with counsel include:
(i) what pleas to enter;
(ii) whether to accept a plea agreement;
(iii) whether to waive jury trial;
(iv) whether to testify in his or her own behalf; and
(v) whether to appeal.
(b) Strategic and tactical decisions should be made by defense counsel after consultation with the client where feasible and appropriate. Such decisions include what witnesses to call, whether and how to conduct cross-examination, what jurors to accept or strike, what trial motions should be made, and what evidence should be introduced.
(c) If a disagreement on significant matters of tactics or strategy arises between defense counsel and the client, defense counsel

---

210. Rodney J. Uphoff, The Role of the Criminal Defense Lawyer in Representing the Mentally Impaired Defendant: Zealous Advocate or Officer of the Court? 1988 Wis. L. Rev. 65, 99-108. For a contrary view see Norma Schrock, Note, Defense Counsel's Role in Determining Competency to Stand Trial, 9 Geo. J. Legal Ethics 639 (1996) (arguing that lawyers should have duty to bring to attention of court issue of defendant's competency to stand trial).

should make a record of the circumstances, counsel's advice and reasons, and the conclusion reached. The record should be made in a manner which protects the confidentiality of the lawyer-client relationship.

Federal and state courts have held that competent defendants cannot be compelled to raise insanity defenses against their wishes.[211] This view finds support in the Supreme Court's decision in Faretta v. California,[212] in which the Court held that the Sixth Amendment guarantees criminal defendants the right to proceed without counsel when they voluntarily and intelligently elect to do so.

If a competent defendant has the right to decide whether to plead guilty or to raise an insanity defense, defense counsel who strongly disagrees with the decision has a limited number of options: attempt to persuade the defendant otherwise, bring the matter to the attention of the court so that the court can determine the defendant's competency to make the decision, move to withdraw on the ground that the client "insists upon pursuing an objective that the lawyer considers repugnant or imprudent" under Model Rule 1.16(b)(3), or follow the client's directions.[213] Even though the defendant may have the right to make ultimate decisions about the case, lawyers still retain the authority to make tactical decisions that are binding on their clients, at least until they are discharged.[214]

211. United States v. Marble, 940 F.2d 1543 (D.C. Cir. 1991); People v. Bloom, 774 P.2d 698 (Cal. 1989) (en banc), *cert. denied*, 494 U.S. 1039 (1990) (defendant cannot be compelled to present a defense in a death penalty case).

212. 422 U.S. 806 (1975).

213. See Red Dog v. State, 625 A.2d 245 (Del. 1993) (defendant has right to forgo appeals and accept death penalty; defense counsel who finds client's decision repugnant should move to withdraw; defense counsel who has "reasonable and objective basis" to doubt client's competency must in a timely fashion inform trial court and request competency determination).

214. Faretta v. California, 422 U.S. at 820; Model Rule 1.2(a) and ABA Standards for Criminal Justice, Defense Function Standard 4-5.2 (3d ed. 1993). For discussions of the lawyer's role in representing criminal defendants who do not wish to assert possible defenses, see Josephine Ross, Autonomy Versus a Client's Best Interests: The Defense Lawyer's Dilemma When Mentally Ill Clients Seek to Control Their Defense, 35 Am. Crim. L. Rev. 1343 (1998); Anne C. Singer, The Imposition of the Insanity Defense on an Unwilling Defendant, 41 Ohio St. L.J. 637 (1980); and Richard C. Dieter, Note, Ethical Choices for Attorneys Whose Clients Elect Execution, 3 Geo. J. Legal Ethics 799 (1990).

Probably the most dramatic example of a defendant who decided, against the advice of his lawyers, to forgo his legal rights and to accept the death penalty was Gary Gilmore.[215] Gilmore was convicted and sentenced to death for two brutal murders. Gilmore's lawyers told him that he had an excellent chance of having his sentence reversed because the Utah statute under which he was sentenced was constitutionally defective in that it failed to provide for mandatory appellate review of death sentences. In addition, at the sentencing hearing the trial judge had erroneously admitted evidence of another murder that Gilmore had committed.

Gilmore looked at his situation quite differently from his lawyers. He found life in prison intolerable. Gilmore told his lawyers that he needed to atone for a crime he had committed in eighteenth-century England, a crime for which he believed he had already been executed.

Gilmore finally decided to accept execution rather than to appeal his conviction, and he ordered his lawyers not to file an appeal on his behalf. When they refused because they doubted his competency, he fired them and hired another lawyer, who had written to Gilmore and had volunteered to assist him in accepting his punishment.

The Utah Supreme Court accepted Gilmore's decision not to appeal his conviction and lifted a stay to allow his execution to proceed. His mother then filed a petition as "next friend" before the United States Supreme Court. The Court initially granted a stay, but lifted the order after reviewing the record and finding that Gilmore had made a knowing and intelligent waiver of his rights.[216] The State of Utah then executed Gilmore.

In the Unabomber case, the defendant, Theodore Kaczynski, was found competent to stand trial. He directed his lawyers not to raise an insanity defense to the murder charges against him. They strongly disagreed with this decision because they believed it was the only viable defense available to him. The lawyers finally reached an agreement with Kaczynski not to raise a formal defense of insanity but instead to claim that his mental illness negated his intent to murder. They would have supported this position by tes-

215.   Norman Mailer, The Executioner's Song (1979). For a review of the book highly critical of the conduct of the various lawyers who represented Gilmore, see Barbara A. Babcock, Book Review, 32 Stan. L. Rev. 865 (1980).
216.   Gilmore v. Utah, 429 U.S. 1012 (1976).

timony of lay rather than expert witness, but this became unnecessary when the defense reached a plea bargain with the
government.[217]

Issues involving representation of clients with diminished capacity can occur in civil litigation and in nonlitigation matters.
Problem 3-10 deals with the topic in the context of marital practice.

Problem 2-7

Multiple Representation of Codefendants

Two brothers, Andre and Ronald Martinez, have been
indicted on charges of securities fraud in connection
with a shopping mall that went bankrupt. They have
asked you to defend them in the case. How would you
decide whether you could legally and ethically represent
them?

Read Model Rule 1.7 and comments.

Multiple representation in criminal cases and the Sixth
Amendment right to counsel

Conflicts of interest present some of the most pervasive and difficult ethical problems that lawyers face in practice. In Chapter 3
we will examine a variety of conflicts of interest in civil litigation:
adverse representation against a current client, multiple representation of clients in a single matter, representation against a former
client, advocate-witness conflicts, and conflicts involving the lawyer's own personal or financial interest.

In criminal cases lawyers may also face conflicts of interest.
For example, codefendants in a criminal case may ask a lawyer to
represent them in the matter. Defendants may seek the representation of a single lawyer for a variety of reasons: for example, con-

---

217. Ross, Autonomy Versus a Client's Best Interests, 35 Am. Crim. L.
Rev. at 1344 n.2. See also Joel S. Newman, Doctors, Lawyers, and the Unabomber, 60 Mont. L. Rev. 67 (1999).

fidence in the lawyer, desire to present a united front, and the need to share expenses. Multiple representation in criminal cases involves not only issues of professional ethics but also issues of constitutional law — the defendants' Sixth Amendment right to effective assistance of counsel. Some scholars have argued that conflicts of interest are so pervasive in the representation of multiple criminal defendants that such representation should be prohibited either as a matter of constitutional law or under rules of ethics.[218]

Despite these arguments, neither the rules of ethics nor constitutional decisions create a per se prohibition on multiple representation, although multiple representation is discouraged. Model Rule 1.7(b) deals with multiple representation of clients in a single matter. While the text of Rule 1.7 makes no distinction between civil and criminal cases, Comment 7 states: "The potential for conflict of interest in representing multiple defendants in a criminal case is so grave that ordinarily a lawyer should decline to represent more than one codefendant." Similarly, ABA Defense Function Standard 4-3.5(c) provides as follows:

> The potential for conflict of interest in representing multiple defendants is so grave that ordinarily defense counsel should decline to act for more than one of several codefendants except in unusual situations when, after careful investigation, it is clear either that no conflict is likely to develop at trial, sentencing, or at any other time in the proceeding or that common representation will be advantageous to each of the codefendants represented and, in either case, that:
>
> (i) the several defendants give an informed consent to such multiple representation; and
> (ii) the consent of the defendants is made a matter of judicial record. In determining the presence of consent by the defendants, the trial judge should make appropriate inquiries respecting actual or potential conflicts of interest of counsel and whether the defendants fully comprehend the difficulties that defense counsel sometimes encounters in defending multiple clients.

218. See John S. Geer, Representation of Multiple Criminal Defendants: Conflicts of Interest and the Professional Responsibilities of the Defense Attorney, 62 Minn. L. Rev. 119 (1978); Gary T. Lowenthal, Joint Representation in Criminal Cases: A Critical Appraisal, 64 Va. L. Rev. 939 (1978).

The Restatement also warns about the dangers of multiple representation of criminal defendants.[219]

In a line of cases the Supreme Court has examined the impact of the Sixth Amendment right to counsel on the issue of multiple representation in criminal cases. The Court first dealt with situations in which the trial court had appointed counsel to represent codefendants over the objection of one of the defendants or defense counsel.[220] The Court held that trial courts had the obligation to inquire into whether a conflict of interest existed. In addition, when an actual conflict occurs, the defendant need not show prejudice resulting from the attorney's representation to establish a Sixth Amendment violation.[221]

In later cases the Court considered whether a Sixth Amendment violation occurred when the defendants had voluntarily hired counsel to represent them jointly rather than having counsel appointed over the objections of one of them.[222] The Court ruled that a different, more demanding standard applies in voluntary multiple representation cases. In these cases the defendant must show that "an actual conflict of interest adversely affected his lawyer's performance."[223]

In the most recent of its multiple representation cases, Wheat v. United States,[224] the Court held that trial courts have the authority at the pretrial stage to reject waivers of conflicts of interest

219. Restatement (Third) of the Law Governing Lawyers §210.

220. Glasser v. United States, 315 U.S. 60 (1942); Holloway v. Arkansas, 435 U.S. 475 (1978).

221. *Glasser*, 315 U.S. at 71, 76; *Holloway*, 435 U.S. at 488-489.

222. Cuyler v. Sullivan, 446 U.S. 335 (1980); Burger v. Kemp, 483 U.S. 776 (1987).

223. *Cuyler*, 446 U.S. at 350. See Burger v. Kemp, 483 U.S. 776 (1987) (counsel's failure to make "lesser culpability" argument on appeal insufficient to establish either actual conflict or prejudice). Although the Court in *Burger* failed to find a Sixth Amendment violation resulting from multiple representation, lower courts have done so in some cases. E.g., Griffin v. McVicar, 84 F.3d 880 (7th Cir. 1996), *cert. denied*, 520 U.S. 1139 (1997) (ineffective assistance of counsel shown when lawyer adopted common defense strategy for defendants with different degrees of culpability); Hoffman v. Leeke, 903 F.2d 280 (4th Cir. 1990) (ineffective assistance of counsel when lawyer represented codefendants in murder case and negotiated plea bargain in which one defendant implicated other).

224. 486 U.S. 153 (1988).

by codefendants and to require separate rather than multiple representation whenever multiple representation involves either an actual or a serious potential for a conflict of interest.[225]

As we will see in the civil litigation context, conflicts of interest can arise in forms other than multiple representation of defendants. The same is true in criminal litigation. For example, prior representation of a witness in a criminal case may disqualify the attorney from representing the defendant because the attorney may be placed in the position of either using confidential information to the detriment of the former client or sacrificing the current client's right to effective assistance of counsel.[226] Similarly, a lawyer in a criminal case may have a disqualifying "positional" or "issue" conflict of interest.[227]

Deciding whether to undertake multiple representation

In light of this body of law, how should a lawyer proceed in deciding whether to undertake multiple representation in a criminal case? Lawyers in private defense practice face an initial personal decision: Am I willing to undertake the risk of multiple representation, even if it is ethically and constitutionally permitted? On one hand, some lawyers believe that representing multiple defendants is so likely to involve an actual conflict of interest that such

225. Id. at 163-164. For a criticism of the Court's decision in *Wheat* arguing that it fails to give proper weight to the right to counsel, see Bruce A. Green, "Through a Glass, Darkly": How the Court Sees Motions to Disqualify Criminal Defense Lawyers, 89 Colum. L. Rev. 1201 (1989). See also Bruce A. Green, Her Brother's Keeper: The Prosecutor's Responsibility When Defense Counsel Has a Potential Conflict of Interest, 16 Am. J. Crim. L. 323 (1989).

226. E.g., United States v. Moscony, 927 F.2d 742 (3d Cir.), *cert. denied*, 501 U.S. 1211 (1991); People v. Holmes, 565 N.E.2d 950 (Ill. 1990); People v. Ortiz, 564 N.E.2d 630 (N.Y. 1990). See Gary T. Lowenthal, Successive Representation by Criminal Lawyers, 93 Yale L.J. 1 (1983).

227. E.g., McConico v. State, 919 F.2d 1543 (11th Cir. 1990) (conflict of interest for lawyer to represent defendant in murder prosecution raising claim of self-defense when lawyer represented beneficiary of insurance policy on life of victim in claim against insurer which might have been lost if victim had been aggressor; beneficiary was also witness for prosecution).

representation should always be avoided. In addition, if a lawyer undertakes multiple representation, a conviction will often produce a claim of ineffective assistance of counsel, requiring the lawyer to withdraw from further representation in the matter and involving the lawyer in time-consuming postconviction relief proceedings. On the other hand, the potential clients may be financially unable to afford separate counsel, and joint representation may be strategically desirable because it facilitates a common defense.

If a lawyer is willing to undertake multiple representation, or if the lawyer is appointed to represent multiple clients, the lawyer must then decide whether such representation is ethically and constitutionally permitted. Under *Wheat* a Sixth Amendment violation occurs if the lawyer represents multiple defendants who have an actual conflict of interest or a serious potential conflict of interest. How does a lawyer determine whether either of these situations exists? Professors Fortune, Underwood, and Imwinkelried offer the following checklist of questions to consider in deciding whether multiple representation of criminal defendants is permissible:

1. Does one defendant have evidence to offer that inculpates the codefendant?
2. Is one defendant more culpable than the other? If so, conflict is almost inevitable, either because the prosecution will offer a deal to the one less culpable or because distinctions will need to be drawn during the case.
3. Are the defenses inconsistent in any way?
4. Will one testify and the other not? A defendant who testifies inevitably calls attention to the failure of the other defendant to take the stand. This problem is exacerbated by joint representation.
5. Will the prosecution's evidence strike the defendants unequally? If a prosecution witness implicates *A*, but not *B*, the attorney is put in the position of attacking the witness on behalf of *A*, but implying that he is telling the truth about *B*.
6. Should distinctions be drawn in closing argument? The attorney representing codefendants cannot do so.
7. Should distinctions be drawn at sentencing because of

either the defendants' relative culpability or their different backgrounds?[228]

Lawyers who conclude that they may not undertake multiple representation because of an actual or serious potential conflict must decline representation and should move to have separate counsel appointed to represent the defendants. The failure of the trial court to appoint separate counsel on motion by defense counsel because of a conflict of interest would be a Sixth Amendment violation under *Holloway*.

Suppose the lawyer, after considering the facts and potential conflicts, concludes that multiple representation would be proper. The lawyer may do so, provided the clients consent after consultation with the lawyer. The Model Rules state that "consultation shall include explanation of the implications of the common representation and the advantages and risks involved." Model Rule 1.7(b). Advantages of multiple representation typically include pooling resources, obtaining the benefit of counsel with particular expertise or with knowledge of the case, and presenting a united defense front. The lawyer should be careful to point out the disadvantages of multiple representation. In broad terms multiple representation precludes defense counsel from advocating a position on behalf of one defendant that casts the blame on another represented defendant, whether in plea bargaining, witness selection, witness examination, argument, sentencing, or appeal. The defendants must understand that the lawyer will zealously represent their interests but will not favor one defendant at the expense of another. If the defendants foresee the possibility of an actual conflict of interest, they should not consent to multiple representation. The defendants should also be informed that communications with the lawyer by either defendant will not be privileged as to the other. If the defendants conclude that the advantages of multiple representation outweigh any disadvantages, and if they are willing to consent to multiple representation, the lawyer may proceed. Although the Model Rules do not require written consent, prudent lawyers will obtain consent in writing. The consent should acknowledge a full consultation with the lawyer about the advantages and disadvantages of multiple representation, and

228. William H. Fortune et al., Modern Litigation and Professional Responsibility Handbook §14.3.1, at 461-462 (1996).

should provide that the defendants have been advised of their right to retain independent counsel.

In federal court the rules of criminal procedure require trial judges to inquire into the propriety of multiple representation. Federal Rule of Criminal Procedure 44(c) provides as follows:

> Whenever two or more defendants have been jointly charged pursuant to Rule 8(b) or have been joined for trial pursuant to Rule 13, and are represented by the same retained or assigned counsel or by retained or assigned counsel who are associated in the practice of law, the court shall promptly inquire with respect to such joint representation and shall personally advise each defendant of the right to the effective assistance of counsel, including separate representation. Unless it appears that there is good cause to believe no conflict of interest is likely to arise, the court shall take such measures as may be appropriate to protect each defendant's right to counsel.

The inquiry by the court under Rule 44 should be designed to prevent disclosure of confidential information to the prosecution. The Advisory Committee's notes state:

> Whenever it is necessary to make a more particularized inquiry into the nature of the contemplated defense, the court should "pursue the inquiry with defendants and their counsel on the record but in chambers" so as "to avoid the possibility of prejudicial disclosures to the prosecution."

In state court, lawyers must, of course, follow state rules of criminal procedure.[229] In the absence of a court rule, a lawyer who has accepted multiple representation should make the clients' consent a matter of judicial record as recommended by ABA Defense Function Standard 4-3.5(c).[230]

---

229. See, e.g., People v. Mroczko, 672 P.2d 835 (Cal. 1983) (en banc) (trial court must initially appoint separate counsel with an instruction to inform the court if counsel, after investigation and consultation with their clients, conclude that the interests of justice and of their clients will best be served by multiple representation; court will then make such on-the-record disposition as is appropriate).

230. See Shongutsie v. State, 827 P.2d 361 (Wyo. 1992) (consent should preferably be in writing and should be included in the record).

D.   Limitations on Litigation Tactics by the Prosecution and by the Defense

—————————— **Problem 2-8** ——————————

Trial Publicity

a.   You represent Nicholas Donetti, who has been under investigation in connection with the death of his wife, Myra. Myra drowned in what Donetti says was a boating accident. The police have been suspicious of Donetti's story from the beginning. This morning the prosecutor held a press conference to announce Donetti's indictment for murder. The prosecutor informed reporters that the couple's eight-year-old child, Michael, who was with them in the boat, had told the police that his father had killed his mother. The prosecutor also said that the police had uncovered a motive for the murder: only a month before Myra's death, Donetti had taken out a large insurance policy on her life.

You and your client are outraged at the prosecutor's conduct because the information given to the press was, in your opinion, grossly misleading. Donetti tells you that Michael did not see his mother fall into the water. What he saw was Donetti extending an oar for his wife to grab. Michael was confused as to what was happening and said, "Don't hurt mommy." Donetti also tells you that he did not take out a new insurance policy on his wife's life; he converted an existing term policy into a whole life policy.

You have just received a telephone call from a reporter for one of the local television stations. The reporter says that her station will be running the prosecutor's news conference on the 6:00 news. She wants to know if you have any comments. What would you say?

b.   Suppose defense counsel holds a press conference responding to the prosecutor's press conference.

Prosecutions statements serve no legitimate other purpose than to cause prejudice

The trial judge, angered by the publicity, calls both lawyers to court and issues an order prohibiting both the prosecutor and defense counsel from "commenting publicly about the witnesses or evidence in the case." Be prepared to present an oral argument in support of and in opposition to the judge's order.

Read Model Rules 3.6, 3.8, and comments.

Interests involved in trial publicity

The issue of the extent to which trial publicity should be regulated involves a tension both among and within several competing interests. First, the public has a legitimate interest in obtaining information about legal proceedings. Several aspects of the "public's right to know," as it is often put, should be distinguished. The public has a legitimate interest in the just functioning of the legal system. Only to the extent that the public has information about the system can it evaluate the justice of legal proceedings. The public also has legitimate health and safety concerns that relate to matters being considered by the legal system. In addition, although some may question the legitimacy of this interest, matters occurring in court may be interesting to the public because they provide glimpses into the lives of others. The public interest regarding trial publicity does not, however, always support unrestricted publicity. As noted above, the public has an interest in the fairness of legal proceedings. To the extent that trial publicity prejudices proceedings and prevents justice from being done, the public has an interest in reasonable restrictions on publicity.

Second, the litigants themselves, particularly defendants in criminal cases, also have interests in trial publicity. As is true with the public interest, the interests of litigants do not point clearly in one direction. Criminal defendants certainly have an interest in not having their trials prejudiced by publicity. Indeed, as discussed below, this is not simply an interest of the criminal defendant, but a constitutional right. Yet in some cases criminal defendants may have an interest in promoting publicity about their cases, particularly when they feel that existing public information or perceptions are inaccurate or when they feel that vindication in the public forum is essential to their defense.

Finally, the various official participants in legal proceedings have an interest in trial publicity, although their interests may be entitled to somewhat lesser consideration than those of the public or the defendant. Judges, jurors, witnesses, and lawyers retain First Amendment rights even though they are involved in legal proceedings. They may feel strongly about issues in which they participate and may have unique perspectives or insights that they wish to share with the public.[231]

A brief history of the restrictions on lawyer participation in trial publicity

The current restrictions on lawyer participation in trial publicity can be traced to the Supreme Court's decision in Sheppard v. Maxwell.[232] Dr. Sam Sheppard was accused of bludgeoning his pregnant wife, Marilyn, to death. He claimed that he was innocent and that his wife had been killed by an unidentified intruder. The case appealed to the public's interest because of the wealth of the defendant, the mystery surrounding the case, and the fact that the defendant was having an affair. (The case later became the basis of the highly popular television show "The Fugitive" and the 1993 movie of the same name.) In describing the extent of publicity in the case, the Supreme Court referred to five volumes of clippings from the Cleveland newspapers, almost all of which were prejudicial to Sheppard; the Court also noted that this material did not include the radio and television coverage, which it assumed to be at least as extensive. The Court reversed Sheppard's conviction. Referring to the "carnival atmosphere" at trial, the Court held the trial judge had failed to protect the defendant's right to due process of law. The Court outlined various measures that the trial judge should have taken, including stricter rules governing the use of the courtroom by the media; insulation of witnesses from press contacts; and some control over the "release of leads, information, and gossip to the press by police officers, witnesses, and the counsel for both sides."[233]

As a result of the *Sheppard* case the ABA undertook a study

231. For a discussion of the various interests involved in the issue of trial publicity, see Joel H. Swift, Restraints on Defense Publicity in Criminal Jury Cases, 1984 Utah L. Rev. 45, 67-84.

232. 384 U.S. 333 (1966).

233. Id. at 359.

of the fair trial–free press issue. This study led to the adoption of ABA Standards in 1968 and of DR 7-107 of the Code of Professional Responsibility in 1969.[234] Disciplinary Rule 7-107 applied to all types of legal proceedings, but the bulk of the rule applied to criminal cases. Two major decisions from the Fourth and Seventh Circuits dealt with the constitutionality of DR 7-107: Hirschkop v. Snead[235] and Chicago Council of Lawyers v. Bauer.[236] Both courts held that it was constitutionally permissible for the state to adopt rules regulating extrajudicial statements by counsel in connection with criminal jury trials. Both courts also held, however, that it would be unconstitutional to apply these rules in a per se fashion. The *Bauer* court held that a lawyer could be disciplined for an extrajudicial statement only if the statement posed a "serious and imminent" threat to the trial process.[237] *Hirschkop* adopted a lesser standard: Discipline was proper if the statement posed a "reasonable likelihood" of prejudice to the administration of justice.[238]

The drafters of the Model Rules attempted to construct a trial publicity rule that balanced fair trial and free expression rights. See Model Rule 3.6, cmt. 1. They were, of course, aware of the *Bauer* and *Hirschkop* decisions, but they felt relatively free to adopt the rule that they thought best because these decisions differed in many respects. Rule 3.6(a), as originally adopted in 1983 (the 1994 amendment is discussed below), stated that a lawyer may not make an extrajudicial statement if the statement has a "substantial likelihood of materially prejudicing an adjudicative proceeding." This test lies somewhere between the *Bauer* test of "serious and imminent threat" and the *Hirschkop* test of "reasonable likelihood" of prejudice to a fair trial. Section 3.6(b) listed a number of statements that "ordinarily" have a substantial likelihood of materially prejudicing a proceeding. This flexible approach responded to the holdings in *Bauer* and *Hirschkop* that the rules could not be applied in a per se fashion. Rule 3.6(c) provided a "safe haven" list of statements that lawyers could make.

234. Wolfram, Modern Legal Ethics §12.2.2, at 633.
235. 594 F.2d 356 (4th Cir. 1979) (per curiam).
236. 522 F.2d 242 (7th Cir. 1975), *cert. denied sub nom.* Cunningham v. Chicago Council of Lawyers, 427 U.S. 912 (1976).
237. 522 F.2d at 249.
238. 594 F.2d at 370.

The constitutionality of Model Rule 3.6: Gentile v. State Bar of Nevada

In Gentile v. State Bar of Nevada[239] the Supreme Court considered the constitutionality of Model Rule 3.6. On January 31, 1987, the Las Vegas Police Department reported the theft of large amounts of cocaine and travelers' checks from a safety deposit vault at Western Vault Company. The drugs and checks had been used in an undercover operation. Attorney Dominic Gentile's client, Grady Sanders, owned Western Vault. The sheriff originally named Sanders and police officers involved in the undercover operation as suspects, but the investigation quickly began to focus on Sanders rather than the police officers.

While two police officers had ready access to the safety deposit box, the sheriff stated that he had complete confidence in his officers. Media reports after the theft indicated that other customers of Western Vault had reported money missing. The police opened other boxes to search for the stolen items. The media reported that they seized $264,000 from a box that was listed as unrented. Subsequent reports identified the owner of this box and provided details of her drug-related background.

The sheriff soon informed the media that the two police officers had been "cleared" after taking polygraph tests. Press reports stated that Sanders could not be reached for comment and that he had refused to take a lie detector test.

Hours after his client was indicted, Gentile, a well-known criminal defense lawyer in the Las Vegas area and the former associate dean of the National College for Criminal Defense Lawyers and Public Defenders, called a press conference and delivered the following statement:

> *Mr. Gentile*: I want to start this off by saying in clear terms that I think that this indictment is a significant event in the history of the evolution of sophistication of the City of Las Vegas, because things of this nature, of exactly this nature have happened in New York with the French connection case and in Miami with cases — at least two cases there — have happened in Chicago as well, but all three of those cities have been honest enough to indict the people who did it; the police department, crooked cops.
>
> When this case goes to trial, and as it develops, you're going

239. 501 U.S. 1030 (1991).

to see that the evidence will prove not only that Grady Sanders is an innocent person and had nothing to do with any of the charges that are being leveled against him, but that the person that was in the most direct position to have stolen the drugs and money, the American Express Travelers' checks, is Detective Steve Scholl.

There is far more evidence that will establish that Detective Scholl took these drugs and took these American Express Travelers' checks than any other living human being.

And I have to say that I feel that Grady Sanders is being used as a scapegoat to try to cover up for what has to be obvious to people at the Las Vegas Metropolitan Police Department and at the District Attorney's office.

Now, with respect to these other charges that are contained in this indictment, the so-called other victims, as I sit here today I can tell you that one, two — four of them are known drug dealers and convicted money launderers and drug dealers; three of whom didn't say a word about anything until after they were approached by Metro and after they were already in trouble and are trying to work themselves out of something.

Now, up until the moment, of course, that they started going along with what detectives from Metro wanted them to say, these people were being held out as being incredible and liars by the very same people who are going to say now that you can believe them.

Another problem that you are going to see develop here is the fact that of these other counts, at least four of them said nothing about any of this, about anything being missing until after the Las Vegas Metropolitan Police Department announced publicly last year their claim that drugs and American Express Travelers' checks were missing.

Many of the contracts that these people had show on the face of the contract that there is $100,000 in insurance for the contents of the box.

If you look at the indictment very closely, you're going to see that these claims fall under $100,000.

Finally, there were only two claims on the face of the indictment that came to our attention prior to the events of January 31 of '87, that being the date that Metro said that there was something missing from their box.

And both of these claims were dealt with by Mr. Sanders and we're dealing here essentially with people that we're not sure if they ever had anything in the box.

That's about all that I have to say.

[Questions from the floor followed.][240]

240. Id. at 1059-1060.

This was the first time in Gentile's professional career that he had called a formal press conference. He testified at his subsequent disciplinary hearing that he decided to call the conference because of "concern that, unless some of the weaknesses in the State's case were made public, a potential jury venire would be poisoned by repetition in the press of information being released by the police and prosecutors, in particular the repeated press reports about polygraph tests and the fact that the two police officers were no longer suspects." Gentile gave as a second reason for calling the press conference the serious toll that the investigation had taken on his client.[241]

Before calling the press conference, Gentile researched the issue of whether the press conference would be likely to prejudice the trial. Considering the length of time before the trial was scheduled to begin (six months), the size of the community and prior First Amendment cases, he concluded that his statements would not be prejudicial.[242] The case went to trial on schedule six months later. All of the evidence referred to in Gentile's press conference was admitted into evidence, and his client was acquitted.[243]

The state bar subsequently instituted disciplinary proceedings against Gentile for violation of Nevada Supreme Court Rule 177, which was practically identical to the 1983 version of ABA Model Rule 3.6. The Nevada Disciplinary Board found that Gentile had violated the rule and the Nevada Supreme Court affirmed. The United States Supreme Court reversed in a 5-4 decision.

The opinions of Justice Anthony Kennedy and Chief Justice William Rehnquist largely agreed that the standard set forth in Rule 3.6 of a "substantial likelihood of materially prejudicing an adjudicative proceeding" was constitutional.[244] The opinions differed on the constitutionality of the application of this standard, and on the significance of due process (fair notice), to the facts of the case. Four members of the Court (opinion of Justice Kennedy joined by Justices Blackmun, Marshall, and Stevens) would allow a state to impose discipline for pretrial statements by a lawyer only if there was a clear showing of the likelihood of material prejudice. They found Rule 3.6 as applied to the facts of this case to be

241. Id. at 1042-1043.
242. Id. at 1044.
243. Id. at 1047.
244. Id. at 1036-1037 (opinion of Justice Kennedy) and 1075 (opinion of Justice Rehnquist).

unconstitutional because the likelihood of prejudice was small.[245] These four justices also found an independent due process basis for setting aside the decision of the Nevada Supreme Court. They found that Rule 3.6(c) "misled petitioner into thinking that he could give his press conference without fear of discipline. . . . [because the rule] provides that a lawyer 'may state without elaboration . . . the general nature of the . . . defense.' "[246]

Four other members of the Court (opinion of Justice Rehnquist joined by Justices Scalia, Souter, and White) would give the states practically blanket authority to regulate pretrial speech by attorneys. Rather than requiring a clear showing of material prejudice, these justices focused on the special role of attorneys and the substantial state interest in protecting the integrity of criminal trials.[247] In light of the greater leeway that these justices would give to the states, they found no due process violation in the wording of the Nevada rule.[248]

Justice O'Connor cast the deciding vote in the case. While agreeing with the Rehnquist opinion, which gave states substantial leeway in regulating pretrial speech by lawyers, she also agreed with the Kennedy opinion that the wording of Rule 3.6 did not give Gentile fair notice that he would be subject to discipline.[249]

What conclusions can one draw from the *Gentile* case? First, it is clear that the standard of "substantial likelihood of materially prejudicing an adjudicative proceeding" is constitutional, having been accepted by all nine justices. Second, it also seems reasonably clear that a lawyer who gave a press conference like the one in *Gentile* could be subject to discipline if the applicable disciplinary rule did not have the due process infirmity that troubled Justice O'Connor.[250]

245. Id. at 1037-1048.
246. Id. at 1048.
247. Id. at 1065-1076.
248. Id. at 1078-1079.
249. Id. at 1081-1082.
250. See In re Morrissey 168 F.3d 134 (4th Cir.), *cert. denied*, 119 S. Ct. 2394 (1999) (lawyer held in criminal contempt for violation of local rule prohibiting release of information by lawyer involved in criminal case if reasonable likelihood that such dissemination would interfere with a fair trial or otherwise prejudice the due administration of justice); United States v. Cutler, 58 F.3d 825 (2d Cir. 1995) (attorney found guilty of criminal contempt for violation of local rule prohibiting extrajudicial statements that have reasonable likelihood of interfering with fair trial).

ABA amendments to Rule 3.6 in 1994

In response to the Supreme Court's decision in *Gentile*, the ABA adopted a revised version of Model Rule 3.6.[251] The new rule continues to use the "substantial likelihood of material prejudice standard" that was approved by the Supreme Court in *Gentile*. See Model Rule 3.6(a). Revised Rule 3.6(b) creates a "safe harbor" of statements that lawyers may make; these are substantially the same as under the former rule. Among the statements that are allowed are the following:

- 3.6(b)(1): "the claim, offense or defense involved and, except when prohibited by law, the identity of the persons involved"
- 3.6(b)(2): "the information contained in a public record"

The most significant change made in the new rule is the addition of Rule 3.6(c), which provides lawyers with a "right of reply":

> Notwithstanding paragraph (a), a lawyer may make a statement that a reasonable lawyer would believe is required to protect a client from the substantial undue prejudicial effect of recent publicity not initiated by the lawyer or the lawyer's client. A statement made pursuant to this paragraph shall be limited to such information as is necessary to mitigate the recent adverse publicity.

While the provision is not limited to criminal cases, it will be particularly important to criminal defense counsel. It appears that *Gentile*'s statements would have been protected under this rule.

Former Rule 3.6(b) contained a list of statements that were ordinarily likely to result in material prejudice of an adjudicative proceeding. This list has been deleted from the text of the rule, but the list reappears in Comment 5; prudent lawyers should continue to consult this list for statements to avoid.

In connection with its amendments of Rule 3.6, the ABA also amended Rule 3.8, which deals with the ethical obligations of prosecutors, to include a new provision, Rule 3.8(g):

---

251. The Restatement generally follows Model Rule 3.6. See Restatement (Third) of the Law Governing Lawyers §169.

The prosecutor in a criminal case shall: . . .

> (g) except for statements that are necessary to inform the public of the nature and extent of the prosecutor's action and that serve a legitimate law enforcement purpose, refrain from making extrajudicial comments that have a substantial likelihood of heightening public condemnation of the accused.

Comment 5 to the rule, however, makes it clear that prosecutors may ethically make statements allowed by revised Rule 3.6(b) or (c).

Not all states have adopted right of reply

It is unclear whether most states will adopt the ABA's revised Model Rule 3.6 with its right of reply.[252] In states that have not adopted the ABA's amendment to Model Rule 3.6, a lawyer who makes an extrajudicial statement like the one that Gentile made is at disciplinary risk.

Several commentators have criticized Rule 3.6. Professor Joel Swift argues that the rule is too restrictive of First Amendment rights of lawyers. He argues that the only justification for restrictions on trial publicity is jury impartiality, but Rule 3.6 is not narrowly drawn to achieve that purpose.[253] Professor Monroe Freedman, while agreeing with this point, also argues that Rule 3.6 is not evenhanded. The rule grants prosecutors a great deal of leeway because they can determine what is in the public record through a "speaking indictment," while defense counsel do not have this flexibility. Freedman argues that it is more important in our system to limit trial publicity by prosecutors than by defense counsel.[254]

Some jurisdictions have rejected the "substantial likelihood of material prejudice" test of Model Rule 3.6 in favor of a "clear

---

252. For many years California did not have a trial publicity rule. In response to the extensive publicity surrounding the *O. J. Simpson* case, the California Supreme Court adopted a trial publicity rule based on ABA Model Rule 3.6 including its right of reply. Cal. R. Prof. Conduct 5-120. For a discussion of the ethics of the public statements made by counsel in the *O. J. Simpson* case, see Kevin Cole & Fred C. Zacharias, The Agony of Victory and the Ethics of Lawyer Speech, 69 S. Cal. L. Rev. 1627 (1996).

253. Joel H. Swift, Model Rule 3.6: An Unconstitutional Regulation of Defense Attorney Trial Publicity, 64 B.U. L. Rev. 1003 (1984). See generally Jonathan M. Moses, Note, Legal Spin Control: Ethics and Advocacy in the Court of Public Opinion, 95 Colum. L. Rev. 1811 (1995) (tracing history of restrictions on extrajudicial statements by lawyers and arguing for change in rules in light of new role of lawyers as advocates for clients in arena of public opinion).

254. Freedman, Understanding Lawyers' Ethics 228-236.

and present danger" test.[255] This test gives lawyers more freedom to engage in extrajudicial statements. For example, given the timing of Gentile's statement and the size of the Las Vegas community, it is extremely doubtful that Gentile's press conference posed a clear and present danger to the integrity of his client's trial.

Gag orders

Gentile dealt with the constitutionality of disciplinary action against an attorney for engaging in trial publicity. To prevent prejudicial pretrial publicity from occurring, many judges will consider imposing "gag" orders on all counsel involved in the proceeding. Because a gag order amounts to a prior restraint on free speech, the standard for imposition of a gag order is quite high. In United States v. Salameh,[256] the judge in the trial of defendants accused of the bombing of the World Trade Center in New York issued an order prohibiting defense counsel from making statements in the press or media that "may have something to do with the case." The Second Circuit ruled that prior restraints on speech carry a "heavy presumption" against their constitutionality. The court stated that limitations on speech must be "no broader than necessary to protect the integrity of the judicial system and the defendant's right to a fair trial." In addition, the court must explore other available remedies.[257] The Second Circuit vacated the trial judge's order because it failed to meet these standards.[258]

In United States v. Cutler,[259] however, the Second Circuit upheld a contempt conviction of an attorney who repeatedly violated district court orders to comply with New York District Court

255. See Twohig v. Blackmer, 918 P.2d 332 (N.M. 1996) (relying on N.M.R. Prof. Conduct 16-306). See also Committee on Prof. Resp., Assn. of Bar of City of New York, The Need for Fair Trials Does Not Justify a Disciplinary Rule That Broadly Restricts an Attorney's Speech, 20 Fordham Urb. L.J. 881 (1993) (proposing amendment to New York Code of Professional Responsibility that would adopt "clear and present danger" test).
256. 992 F.2d 445 (2d Cir. 1993).
257. Id. at 447.
258. See also Monroe H. Freedman & Janet Starwood, Prior Restraints on Freedom of Expression by Defendants and Defense Attorneys: *Ratio Decidendi v. Obiter Dictum*, 29 Stan. L. Rev. 607 (1977).
259. 58 F.3d 825 (2d Cir. 1995).

Local Criminal Rule 7, which prohibits extrajudicial statements that have a reasonable likelihood of interfering with a fair trial. The trial judge in that case had characterized the rule as "a kind of gag order."[260]

Problem 2-9
Limitations on Trial Tactics

The college town of Anderson was shocked when Thomas McSwaine, the son of one of Anderson's prominent business leaders, was arrested for rape of a young woman, Brenda Cain, at a fraternity party. Cain was badly bruised about the face and neck after the incident. You are a member of the defense team. McSwaine admits having intercourse with Cain. He also admits that they had "rough sex," but he denies the charge of rape. He claims that Cain consented to having intercourse with him and begged him to "do it like in *Rising Sun*."[261]

With regard to the consent theory, you have hired investigators to inquire into Cain's sexual history. In particular, you were looking for information showing Cain had engaged in "rough sex" in the past or that she had had sex based on movies she had seen. Your investigation revealed two fraternity brothers of McSwaine, both of whom are prepared to testify that they had had sex with Cain and that "she liked it hard and rough." Your investigation also located a former boyfriend who will testify that the couple had watched pornographic movies and that she had asked to have sex the way it was done in the movies. Your defense strategy is to use this information in an aggressive cross-examination of Cain and to introduce the testimony of these three witnesses as part of your case in chief.

In preparing this strategy, you are concerned about the possible application of your state's rape shield law.

260. Id. at 830.
261. The novel by Michael Crichton and the movie based on the novel. A prominent scene in the book and movie involves sexual intercourse while the girl is being strangled, supposedly to heighten the experience.

That law, which is based on Rule 412 of the Federal Rules of Evidence, provides as follows:

Rule 412. Sex Offense Cases; Relevance of Alleged Victim's Past Sexual Behavior or Alleged Sexual Predisposition

(a) Evidence generally inadmissible. The following evidence is not admissible in any civil or criminal proceeding involving alleged sexual misconduct except as provided in subdivisions (b) and (c):

(1) Evidence offered to prove that any alleged victim engaged in other sexual behavior.

(2) Evidence offered to prove any alleged victim's sexual predisposition.

(b) Exceptions. —

(1) In a criminal case, the following evidence is admissible, if otherwise admissible under these rules:

(A) evidence of specific instances of sexual behavior by the alleged victim offered to prove that a person other than the accused was the source of semen, injury or other physical evidence;

(B) evidence of specific instances of sexual behavior by the alleged victim with respect to the person accused of the sexual misconduct offered by the accused to prove consent or by the prosecution; and

(C) evidence the exclusion of which would violate the constitutional rights of the defendant.

(2) In a civil case, evidence offered to prove the sexual behavior or sexual predisposition of any alleged victim is admissible if it is otherwise admissible under these rules and its probative value substantially outweighs the danger of harm to any victim and of unfair prejudice to any party. Evidence of an alleged victim's reputation is admissible only if it has been placed in controversy by the alleged victim.

(c) Procedure to determine admissibility. —

(1) A party intending to offer evidence under subdivision (b) must —

(A) file a written motion at least 14 days before trial specifically describing the evidence and stating the purpose for which it is offered unless the court, for good cause requires a different time for filing or permits filing during trial; and

(B) serve the motion on all parties and notify the alleged victim or, when appropriate, the alleged victim's guardian or representative.

(2) Before admitting evidence under this rule the court must conduct a hearing in camera and afford the victim and parties a right to attend and be heard. The motion, related papers, and the record of the hearing must be sealed and remain under seal unless the court orders otherwise.

As the defense team prepares its case for trial, the following dialogue occurs between two members of the team:

L1:   Let's discuss how we might handle the testimony of the boyfriend and the fraternity brothers. It seems to me that we have to file a motion under the rape shield law to offer this evidence, but our prospects don't look too good. As I read the statute, the only possible ground for admitting the evidence is under (b)(1)(C), where we have to establish a violation of Tom's constitutional rights.

L2:   I think that's right. My research indicates that our confrontation clause argument is 50-50 at best. If we lose, we're in trouble, but I've come up with a backup strategy. At trial we can cross-examine Cain about whether she said anything to McSwaine about liking rough sex. We can also cross-examine her about the statement that Tom said she made: "do it like in *Rising Sun*." If she admits either or both of these matters, then I think we've got a good shot at an acquittal. If she denies either or both, we can then ask her if she ever engaged in rough sex in the past, or if she ever asked a partner to engage in sex like in a movie. If they object to this, we can argue that the questions are being asked not to obtain evidence in violation of section (a) of the statute, but rather as part of an inquiry into her credibility. De-

pending on her answers, we can then offer
the testimony of her boyfriend and of the two
fraternity brothers, also arguing that this testimony is being offered not as evidence of
sexual behavior but to show prior inconsistent statements by Cain.

L1: Well, the court might not let us go into prior
sexual history for the purpose of testing her
credibility. It also might be a problem getting
in the testimony of the boyfriend and the two
fraternity brothers, because as I understand
the rules, you can't generally introduce any
collateral evidence to impeach a witness's
credibility. [See Fed. R. Evid. 608(b).]

L2: That's true, but we can do several things.
First of all I don't think the rule about collateral attacks on credibility prevents testimony about the witness's reputation for
truth and veracity. We could put the boyfriend on the stand and have him testify that
she has a reputation for lying; that's probably
better than if he just testified that she liked
to do it based on movies. Also, even if none
of this gets in, just asking the questions or
having the boyfriend and the fraternity
brothers there at trial could affect the jury.

L1: One other idea. When we put the boyfriend
and the fraternity brothers on our witness
list, the prosecutor will have to ask Cain
about them. If Cain tells the prosecutor what
these guys told us, then the prosecutor will
have to make sure she admits this stuff on
cross, which is just what we want. The prosecutor may even decide to bring it out on
direct because it might be less damaging.
Also, when they know about these witnesses,
Cain or the prosecutor might get scared and
be more willing to negotiate a plea.

L2: I like it.

After developing this strategy, the defense team
files a motion to allow the testimony of the boyfriend

and the two fraternity brothers under the rape shield law. You have argued in the motion that exclusion of the evidence would violate your client's rights under the confrontation clause of the Sixth Amendment as applied to the states through the Fourteenth Amendment. After you filed your memorandum, you learned of a recent decision from the United States Court of Appeals for the Seventh Circuit holding that application of the Illinois rape shield law did not violate the defendant's right to confrontation. Ironically, the prosecution has found a case that the defense team has not uncovered, Olden v. Kentucky.[262] In *Olden* the Supreme Court held that the trial court's refusal to permit the defendant to cross-examine the alleged rape victim about her cohabitation with her boyfriend violated the defendant's Sixth Amendment right to confront witnesses when the defendant claimed that the alleged victim had concocted the charge of rape because of fear of her boyfriend's reaction if he knew that she had voluntarily engaged in sexual relations with the defendant.

Not wishing to rely solely on the consent theory, McSwaine's defense team has come up with a second theory of defense, one that McSwaine did not suggest but that defense counsel believe is plausible based on the facts. The defense plans to contend that the alleged rape was a "setup" by Cain to extort money from McSwaine's wealthy family. With regard to the "setup" theory, you plan to cross-examine Cain to inquire into whether Cain has hired a lawyer to represent her in a possible civil action against McSwaine. You plan to ask questions about her finances and about whether she has brought any other lawsuits or made any other charges of rape or assault. You also plan to inquire about how she came to know members of McSwaine's fraternity as well as McSwaine. The purpose of these questions is to try to portray Cain as an extortionist looking for a chance to get money from the family of an innocent, nice young man.

262. 488 U.S. 227 (1988).

Under local rules you have received a list of potential jurors several weeks before trial. The list gives the names and addresses of the jurors, but no other information. To prepare for jury selection the defense has hired an investigator who will do the following: purchase credit reports that contain personal and financial information about each juror; drive by each juror's home and make observations that might be indicative of the juror's attitudes; and in some cases interview neighbors of the juror to determine the juror's attitudes and any possible grounds of bias or prejudice.

During the course of your investigation, you learn that one juror, Donald Spade, is employed by Anderson Supply Company. Anderson Supply is a subsidiary of McSwaine Enterprises, the company owned by Thomas McSwaine's father. During voir dire the jurors are asked: "Are you or any member of your immediate family employed by Quinton McSwaine or by McSwaine Enterprises? If so, please identify yourself." Spade does not respond.

Read Model Rules 3.3, 3.4, 3.5, 4.4, and comments.

Improper contacts with jurors and improper methods of jury selection

Neutral decisionmakers who resolve disputes based on the law and facts presented at trial rather than on extrajudicial influences are central to the concept of an adversarial system of justice.[263] The Model Rules recognize the importance of the integrity of decisionmakers in Model Rule 3.5, which provides as follows:

Rule 3.5. Impartiality and Decorum of the Tribunal

A lawyer shall not:

(a) seek to influence a judge, juror, prospective juror or other official by means prohibited by law;

---

263. 1 Hazard & Hodes, The Law of Lawyering §3.5:301, at 658.1.

(b) communicate ex parte with such a person except as permitted by law; or

(c) engage in conduct intended to disrupt a tribunal.[264]

Model Rules 3.5(a) and (b) refer lawyers to "law" to determine whether attempts to influence or to communicate with judges, jurors, prospective jurors, and other officials are improper. Such law includes statutes, court decisions, or court rules regarding contact with jurors. By making lawyers' obligations dependent on "law," however, the Model Rules may leave lawyers in doubt about the scope of their obligations when other law is silent or uncertain.

In the absence of specific law on improper contacts, several principles can guide lawyers in dealings with jurors. First, any form of communication with jurors or prospective jurors, except in the course of official proceedings, or unless specifically authorized by law, is improper. This restriction obviously includes communications that relate to the merits of the case, but it also includes pleasantries that have nothing to do with substance. The rule operates as a prophylactic to prevent the possibility of improper influence. This prohibition on all communications except in the course of official proceedings carries forward the rules found in DR 7-108(A), (B), and (C) of the Code of Professional Responsibility.[265] Trial judges should instruct jurors of this prohibition so that a juror will not take a lawyer's failure to respond to pleasant conversation as rudeness.

Second, the prohibition on communication or improper influences does not prohibit lawyers from investigating the backgrounds of jurors for the purpose of jury selection so long as there is no communication with the juror and so long as the investigation does not violate other law. Under DR 7-108(E) of the Code of Professional Responsibility, lawyers were permitted to investigate jurors so long as the inquiry was not "vexatious or harassing." In the absence of clear guidance by statute, court rule, or case law, this standard may be helpful to lawyers under Rule 3.5.[266]

264. See also Restatement (Third) of the Law Governing Lawyers §§173(1) (prohibition on ex parte communication with judge or official before whom case is pending), 175(1), (2) (prohibition on communication with prospective and sitting jurors).

265. See 1 Hazard & Hodes, The Law of Lawyering §3.5:201, at 655.

266. See also id. at 655 n.1. See generally Fortune et al., Modern Litigation and Professional Responsibility Handbook §9.3, at 331.

In some jurisdictions, it is common practice for lawyers to interview jurors after the conclusion of the case for the purpose of improving their trial skills or perhaps for the purpose of determining whether the jury may have acted improperly in reaching its decision. Are such contacts improper? DR 7-108(D) of the Code of Professional Responsibility provided:

> After discharge of the jury from further consideration of a case with which the lawyer was connected, the lawyer shall not ask questions of or make comments to a member of that jury that are calculated merely to harass or embarrass the juror or to influence his actions in future jury service.

Model Rule 3.5 does not speak clearly on the issue. In State v. Furutani,[267] however, the defendant was prosecuted for a variety of crimes including theft and tax fraud. After the defendant's conviction, a member of the jury panel informed the court and defense counsel that she had been pressured into voting to convict in part because the defendant had failed to take the stand in his own defense. The prosecution hired a private investigator to interview the foreman of the jury regarding these allegations. The Hawaii Supreme Court had this to say about the prosecutor's ex parte contact with the foreman:

> [Although the Code of Professional Responsibility] did not prohibit the kind of post-trial ex parte communication with a juror involved in the present matter, it is clear that HRPC 3.5(b) and 8.4(a) do. Subsequent to January 1, 1994, all post-trial communications between attorneys and jurors, relating to the subject matter of the trial, must be in the presence of all parties to the proceeding or their legal representatives.

> This does not mean, however, that HRPC 3.5(b) and 8.4(a) would necessarily preclude the discovery of the kind of juror misconduct involved in this appeal. Rather than being subjected to an ex parte interview in the first instance, a juror could be simultaneously contacted by all parties on an informal basis, or, as in the present case, the juror could be questioned on the record in open court.

> As an aside, we acknowledge our awareness of the legitimate collateral benefits — to attorneys, judges, and jurors alike — that

---

267. 873 P.2d 51 (Haw. 1994).

accrue from post-trial jury "debriefings." Assuming that they do not occur ex parte or otherwise violate the HRPC, such "debriefings" are not prohibited.[268]

The Massachusetts version of Rule 3.5 prohibits lawyers from contacting jurors after they have been discharged from the case without leave of court, but the Restatement adopts an approach similar to the position of the Code, prohibiting contacts that are intended to harass jurors or influence their conduct in future cases.[269]

Jury selection is a growth industry. Especially in high profile cases, parties commonly hire jury consultants to assist in jury selection. Are there any ethical restrictions on such practices? The Model Rules do not have a specific provision on ethical obligations of lawyers in connection with jury selection. Model Rule 3.4(c) states that a lawyer should not "knowingly disobey an obligation under the rules of a tribunal except for an open refusal based on an assertion that no valid obligation exists." Thus, it appears that ethical obligations in jury selection follow the procedural rules applicable to jury selection.

In a series of cases beginning with Batson v. Kentucky,[270] the Supreme Court has attempted to address the problem of discriminatory exercise of peremptory challenges. The *Batson* Court held that the prosecution violates the defendant's right to equal protection when it exercises peremptory challenges to remove jurors solely on the ground of race. In subsequent cases, the Court has dramatically expanded its scrutiny of the use of peremptory challenges, although the rationale for the decisions has shifted. The Court held that exercise of peremptory challenges based on race by private litigants in civil cases is unconstitutional because this use of peremptory challenges violates *the equal protection rights of jurors.*[271] Similarly, the Court held that the defendant's exercise of peremptory challenges based on race in a criminal case was unconstitutional because it also infringed the jurors' right to equal protection. The Court rejected the argument that restriction of the

---

268. Id. at 56 n.8. In Rapp v. Disciplinary Bd., 916 F. Supp. 1525 (D. Haw. 1996), however, the Hawaii federal district court declared Rule 3.5, which prohibits communications with jurors "except as permitted by law," unconstitutionally vague.

269. Restatement (Third) of the Law Governing Lawyers §175(3).

270. 476 U.S. 79 (1986).

271. Edmonson v. Leesville Concrete Co., 500 U.S. 614 (1991).

defendant's right to use peremptory challenges amounted to a violation of the defendant's constitutional right to due process, reasoning that the defendant does not have a constitutional right to any particular system of peremptory challenges.[272] The Court has expanded the prohibition on the discriminatory use of peremptory challenges to include strikes based on gender as well as race,[273] but the Court has refused to extend the right to cover the use of peremptory challenges based on religion.[274]

[handwritten margin note: cannot use preemptory challenge based on race, or gender but can use it on religion.]

Model Rule 3.5 prohibits ex parte contacts not only with jurors but also with judges and officials. We will examine ex parte communications with judges in more detail in Problem 6-1, which deals with conduct of judges in their official capacities.

Duty to disclose adverse facts and law

Under the Model Rules, lawyers do not have an obligation to disclose voluntarily either to the court or to the opposing side adverse factual information, even if the information is material and even if the information is not known by the court or the other side.[275] The absence of a duty of disclosure of adverse facts can be justified on several grounds. First, a duty to disclose would be inconsistent with the concept of an adversarial system of justice in which each side has the obligation to investigate and to present its case. Second, clients often communicate adverse information in confidence to their lawyers. A duty to disclose would undermine the attorney-client privilege. Further, in criminal cases, imposing a duty to disclose on defense counsel would be inconsistent with the defendant's privilege against self-incrimination and other constitutional rights.

---

272. Georgia v. McCollum, 505 U.S. 42 (1992). For a criticism of the application of the *Batson* rule to defense counsel and an argument that it should not be unethical for defense counsel to use race and gender in jury selection, see Abbe Smith, "Nice Work If You Can Get It": "Ethical" Jury Selection in Criminal Defense, 67 Fordham L. Rev. 523 (1998). But see Andrew G. Gordon, Note, Beyond Batson v. Kentucky: A Proposed Ethical Rule Prohibiting Racial Discrimination in Jury Selection, 62 Fordham L. Rev. 685 (1993).

273. J. E. B. v. Alabama ex rel T.B., 511 U.S. 127 (1994).

274. Davis v. Minnesota, 511 U.S. 1115 (1994) (denial of certiorari in case involving exercise of peremptory challenge based on religion).

275. See Wolfram, Modern Legal Ethics §12.3.2, at 639.

The proposition that lawyers do not have a duty to disclose adverse facts is qualified, however, by several obligations. First, lawyers and their clients have an obligation to comply with various discovery rules requiring production of information in response to inquiries from the opposing side. See Model Rule 3.4(d), which states that a lawyer shall not "fail to make reasonably diligent effort to comply with a legally proper discovery request by an opposing party." Problem 4-4 examines lawyers' legal and ethical obligations in connection with discovery in civil cases. Second, lawyers have a duty not to engage personally in fraud or criminal conduct. See Model Rules 8.4(b), (c).[276] Nor can the absence of a duty to disclose be used to justify assisting the client in conduct that is criminal or fraudulent. See Model Rule 3.3(a)(2) (lawyer must disclose material fact to a tribunal when necessary to avoid assisting the client in a criminal or fraudulent act).[277] Third, lawyers are obligated to disclose to a tribunal the commission of perjury by their clients when disclosure is the only "reasonable remedial measure." See Model Rule 3.3(a)(4). Recall Problem 2-5.[278] Fourth, in ex parte proceedings (for example, if a lawyer is seeking a temporary restraining order), lawyers must disclose all material facts. See Model Rule 3.3(d).[279] Because ex parte proceedings do not involve an adversarial process, the rationale for nondisclosure does not apply. Cf. Model Rule 3.9 (duty to disclose representative capacity when lawyer appears in nonadjudicative proceeding). Finally, prosecutors have a duty to disclose to defense counsel exculpatory material. See Model Rule 3.8(d) and Problem 2-10.

Under the Code of Professional Responsibility lawyers had

276. See United States v. Thoreen, 653 F.2d 1332 (9th Cir. 1981), *cert. denied*, 455 U.S. 938 (1982) (improper for defense counsel to substitute individual for defendant at counsel table to test ability of witnesses to identify defendant).

277. See ABA Comm. on Ethics and Prof. Resp., Formal Op. 98-412 (lawyer who learns that client has violated court order in civil case prohibiting transfer of assets must disclose violation to court if necessary to correct prior representation by lawyer or to prevent assisting criminal or fraudulent conduct by client).

278. See also ABA Comm. on Ethics and Prof. Resp., Formal Op. 93-376 (duty to disclose client perjury applies to deposition as well as trial testimony).

279. See Jill M. Dennis, Note, The Model Rules and the Search for Truth: The Origins and Applications of Model Rule 3.3(d), 8 Geo. J. Legal Ethics 157 (1994).

an obligation to disclose juror misconduct to tribunals. The Code's DR 7-108(G) stated: "A lawyer shall reveal promptly to the court improper conduct by a venireman or a juror, or by another toward a venireman or a juror or a member of his family, of which the lawyer has knowledge." For example, in In re R.[280] the accused lawyer represented the plaintiff in a personal injury case. During the trial, the plaintiff happened to give a ride to one of the jurors, who was hitchhiking to court. The plaintiff and juror did not immediately recognize each other; when they did, they were both embarrassed. From the opinion it appears that the plaintiff did not inform his lawyers of the contact until after a verdict was returned and then set aside on unrelated grounds. The plaintiff's lawyer, after consultation with his partners, decided not to inform the court because the verdict had been set aside and because no impropriety was involved in that the plaintiff and the juror had not discussed the case. The Oregon Supreme Court disagreed: "[I]f an attorney learns of improper conduct at any time that any court can rectify the effect of that conduct, the attorney has an obligation to inform such court. . . . If there is the slightest bit of doubt in an attorney's mind whether he is obligated to inform the court of juror misconduct, that doubt should be resolved in favor of disclosure."[281] The court did, however, dismiss the complaint because it found no improper conduct by the plaintiff and the juror.

It is unclear whether the duty to disclose juror misconduct found in the Code survives the adoption of the Model Rules. The Model Rules do not have a provision equivalent to DR 7-108(G). In State v. Cady,[282] however, the Kansas Supreme Court held that the prosecutor had a duty to disclose to the trial court information that the prosecutor had received regarding juror misconduct during the trial.

While the Model Rules do not generally require lawyers to disclose adverse factual information, the rules do impose a limited obligation to disclosed adverse law. Model Rule 3.3(a)(3) states that a lawyer must disclose legal authority in the controlling jurisdiction that is directly adverse to the position of the client and not disclosed by the opposing lawyer. DR 7-106(B)(1) of the Code is

280. 554 P.2d 522 (Or. 1976) (en banc).
281. Id. at 524.
282. 811 P.2d 1130 (Kan. 1991).

identical. The duty to disclose adverse law under Rule 3.3 continues until the conclusion of the proceeding. See Model Rule 3.3(b).[283]

The duty to disclose adverse law can be distinguished from the obligation not to disclose adverse facts in at least two respects. First, because the duty applies to law, issues of attorney-client confidentiality are not implicated. Second, if a court decides a case based on an error of law, the decision affects third parties who must rely on and use the law. By contrast, an erroneous decision on the facts affects only the parties involved in the case.

Note that the duty to disclose is limited to authority in the "controlling jurisdiction" and to authority that is "directly adverse." Hazard and Hodes state:

> The "controlling" jurisdiction normally means the same state as the pending case for state law issues, and the same District or Circuit for federal law issues. In either event, of course, applicable decisions of the United States Supreme Court would be considered controlling.[284]

The meaning of the term "directly adverse" in Rule 3.3(a)(3) is unclear. Some might argue that any case that can be distinguished is not directly adverse. If so, however, the disclosure obligation of Rule 3.3(a)(3) is meaningless because a competent lawyer can always develop a plausible distinction. Hazard and Hodes argue that lawyers should use the standard articulated in ABA Formal Opinion 280:

> An attorney should advise the court of decisions adverse to his case which opposing counsel has not raised if the decision is one which the court should clearly consider in deciding the case, if the judge might consider himself misled by the attorney's silence, or if a reasonable judge would consider an attorney who advanced a proposition contrary to the undisclosed opinion lacking in candor and fairness to him.[285]

---

283. See also ABA Comm. on Ethics and Prof. Resp., Informal Op. 84-1505 (lawyer must disclose appellate decision directly adverse to lawyer's position in motion to dismiss even though motion had earlier been denied by trial court if the issue raised in the motion to dismiss can be revived because not final and appealable).

284. 1 Hazard & Hodes, The Law of Lawyering §3.3:206, at 592.

285. ABA, Opinions on Prof. Ethics, Formal Op. 280, at 618 (1967).

Query whether this standard is consistent with the history of Model Rule 3.3(a)(3). This definition comes very close to the proposed Model Rule that was withdrawn due to criticism of its breadth. That proposed rule stated:

> If a lawyer discovers that the tribunal has not been apprised of legal authority known to the lawyer that would probably have a substantial effect on the determination of a material issue, the lawyer shall advise the tribunal of that authority.[286]

Professor Daisy Floyd has argued that courts are using their power to award sanctions for litigation misconduct under Rule 11 of the Federal Rules of Civil Procedure and similar rules to enforce a duty to disclose adverse authority that is broader than Model Rule 3.3. She warns lawyers that they are acting at their peril if they rely on the narrow standard of disclosure reflected in that rule.[287]

While Model Rule 3.3(a)(3) requires lawyers to disclose adverse law in some situations, lawyers also have a duty not to engage in misleading argument. For example, partial quotations that are misleading or citations of cases that have been overruled or questioned would be improper because they amount to misleading argument. See Model Rule 3.3, cmt. 3.

One special application of the duty to disclose adverse law in criminal cases involves the "*Anders* brief." In Anders v. California,[288] the Supreme Court held that appointed counsel who moves to withdraw from handling an appeal because counsel has concluded that the appeal is frivolous cannot simply file a "no-merit letter," but must instead accompany the motion with "a brief referring to anything in the record that might arguably support the appeal."[289] The Court made clear that the purpose of the *Anders* brief was not to require counsel to act as advocate against the client, but rather to provide information so that the appellate court could more easily assess whether to appoint counsel to handle the

---

286. ABA Commn. on Evaluation of Prof. Standards, Rule 3.1(c) (Discussion Draft January 30, 1980). See Geoffrey C. Hazard, Jr., Arguing the Law: The Advocate's Duty and Opportunity, 16 Ga. L. Rev. 821 (1982).

287. Daisy H. Floyd, Candor Versus Advocacy: Courts' Use of Sanctions to Enforce the Duty of Candor Toward the Tribunal, 29 Ga. L. Rev. 1035 (1995).

288. 386 U.S. 738 (1967).

289. Id. at 744.

appeal. Further, the brief requirement served as a mechanism to assure that appointed counsel had thoroughly reviewed the record.[290] In McCoy v. Court of Appeals[291] the Supreme Court upheld the constitutionality of a Wisconsin rule requiring appointed counsel to include in the *Anders* brief a discussion of why issues that might arguably support the appeal lacked merit. Three justices dissented on the ground that the decision in *McCoy* effectively turned appointed counsel into an advocate against the client. Several state supreme courts have rejected the *Anders* approach of filing a no-merit letter along with a brief on the ground that the filing of the letter makes the lawyer an advocate against the client. These courts require counsel to make the best arguments that can be made from the record without conceding that they are frivolous.[292]

Dealing with documents and witness examination

Under an adversarial system of justice, attorneys are granted wide latitude in the presentation of cases on behalf of their clients, subject to general rules of law, court rules, and court orders.[293] Nonetheless, some specific restrictions apply to attorney conduct in dealing with documents and other real evidence, examination of witnesses, and advocacy.

Destruction or falsification of evidence directly undermines the truthfulness of legal proceedings and is both unethical[294] and illegal.[295] Many companies have document destruction programs, and lawyers can face the difficult question whether a client's compliance with such a program is improper. If the documents are subject to subpoena or court order, they clearly cannot be de-

---

290. Id. at 745.

291. 486 U.S. 429 (1988).

292. State v. McKenney, 568 P.2d 1213 (Idaho 1977); Ramos v. State, 944 P.2d 856 (Nev. 1997); State v. Cigic, 639 A.2d 251 (N.H. 1994).

293. See Model Rule 3.4(c); Restatement (Third) of the Law Governing Lawyers §165.

294. See Model Rule 3.4(a); In re Barrow, 294 S.E.2d 785 (S.C. 1982) (discipline for failure to inform court that client had removed warning label in products liability case).

295. American Law Inst., Model Penal Code §241.7 (1962) (offense of tampering with or fabricating evidence). See also Restatement (Third) of the Law Governing Lawyers §178.

stroyed, but prudent lawyers would counsel clients against destruction of documents when the lawyer knows that legal proceedings in which the documents would have substantial evidentiary value are likely to occur within a reasonable period of time.[296] As discussed in Problem 2-4 lawyers who obtain possession of stolen property or of physical evidence of a crime have a duty to turn this material over to the authorities within a reasonable period of time.[297]

A number of ethical and legal restrictions apply when lawyers deal with or examine witnesses. See Problem 3-7 dealing with the ethical propriety of a lawyer appearing as both a witness and an advocate at trial. Lawyers may not unlawfully interfere with the other side's access to a witness.[298] Further, lawyers may not request a witness to refrain from voluntarily giving information to the other side unless the witness is a client or the relative, employee, or agent of a client and the lawyer reasonably believes that the person will not be materially and adversely affected by a refusal to give information.[299]

In preparing witnesses for trial, lawyers must draw a fine line between legitimate preparation and improper encouragement of false testimony. We encountered this issue in connection with the lawyer's lecture (Problem 2-5). See also the material on improper witness coaching in Problem 4-4.

In examining witnesses, lawyers are bound to follow the rules of civil procedure and evidence in the applicable jurisdiction. Model Rule 3.4(c) provides that a lawyer shall not "knowingly disobey an obligation under the rules of a tribunal except for an open refusal based on an assertion that no valid obligation exists."[300] In addition, Rule 3.4(e) provides that a lawyer shall not

in trial, allude to any matter that the lawyer does not reasonably believe is relevant or that will not be supported by admissible evidence, assert personal knowledge of facts in issue except when testifying as a witness, or state a personal opinion as to the justness of

296. Restatement (Third) of the Law Governing Lawyers. §178, cmt. *c*.
297. Id. §§57, cmt. *f* (stolen property), 179 (physical evidence of crime).
298. Id. §176(2).
299. Model Rule 3.4(f); Restatement (Third) of the Law Governing Lawyers §176(4).
300. See generally Fortune et al., Modern Litigation and Professional Responsibility Handbook chs. 9-13.

a cause, the credibility of a witness, the culpability of a civil litigant or the guilt or innocence of an accused.

The Restatement expresses similar obligations.[301] If a lawyer anticipates that opposing counsel may attempt to engage in examination or offer evidence that is inadmissible, counsel should file a motion in limine seeking judicial determination of the issue in advance of trial.[302]

May a lawyer cross-examine a witness that the lawyer knows is telling the truth for the purpose of undermining the credibility of the witness? The basis for a lawyer's conclusion that a witness is telling the truth will often flow from confidential communications with the client. If lawyers are precluded from examining witnesses because of information gained from their clients, clients will become reluctant to share damaging information and the attorney-client relationship will be undermined.[303] The Model Rules support the view that lawyers may properly attempt to undermine the credibility of a witness that the lawyer knows is telling the truth. Model Rule 4.4 states:

> In representing a client, a lawyer shall not use means that have no substantial purpose other than to embarrass, delay, or burden a third person, or use methods of obtaining evidence that violate the legal rights of such a person.

Cross-examination of the truthful witness, however, has a substantial purpose other than harming the witness: calling into question the witness's credibility.[304] Similarly, the Restatement provides that lawyers may attempt to discredit a witness the lawyer knows is telling the truth, although the Restatement indicates that lawyers retain professional discretion whether to exercise this power.[305] The ABA Standards for the Prosecution and the Defense

301. Restatement (Third) of the Law Governing Lawyers §§165 (compliance with law, rules, and tribunal rulings), 167 (prohibition on reference to inadmissible evidence and expression of personal opinion).
302. See Fortune et al., Modern Litigation and Professional Responsibility Handbook §11.6, at 370-371.
303. For a philosophical and moral justification for lawyers' cross-examination of truthful witnesses, see Freedman, Understanding Lawyers' Ethics 161-168.
304. See 2 Hazard & Hodes, The Law of Lawyering §4.4:102, at 756.
305. Restatement (Third) of the Law Governing Lawyers §166, cmt. *c*.

Functions express different positions on the issue of cross-examination of the truthful witness. ABA Prosecution Function Standard 3-5.7(b) states:

> The prosecutor's belief that the witness is telling the truth does not preclude cross-examination, but may affect the method and scope of cross-examination. A prosecutor should not use the power of cross-examination to discredit or undermine a witness if the prosecutor knows the witness is testifying truthfully.

ABA Defense Function Standard 4-7.6(b), however, states: "Defense counsel's belief or knowledge that the witness is telling the truth does not preclude cross-examination."

Improper argument

While scores of books have been written on argumentative technique, the rules of ethics regarding argument are relatively sparse. Lawyers must, of course, comply with rules of procedure in connection with their arguments.[306] For example, this prohibition makes improper any argument based on inadmissible evidence or that appeals to bias or prejudice.[307] The rules prohibit lawyers from expressing personal belief or personal opinion regarding the merits of the case, although lawyers who are unable to convey (as opposed to voicing) genuine belief in their clients' cases are unlikely to be successful advocates.[308]

May a lawyer argue for inferences that the lawyer knows are false but that are reasonably supportable by the evidence? This question is similar to the question of whether it is proper for a lawyer to cross-examine a witness the lawyer knows is telling the truth. Case law seems to support the proposition that defense counsel may do so, but that it is improper for a prosecutor to adopt

---

306. See Model Rule 3.4(c); Restatement (Third) of the Law Governing Lawyers §165. See generally Fortune et al., Modern Litigation and Professional Responsibility Handbook ch. 13.

307. Fortune et al., Modern Litigation and Professional Responsibility §§13.3.6., 13.6.4.

308. Model Rule 3.4(e) and Restatement (Third) of the Law Governing Lawyers §167(1).

this tactic. An interesting example is United States v. Latimer,[309] a prosecution for bank robbery. At trial, two tellers testified that they had activated the bank's camera system during the robbery. The government failed to introduce any pictures because the camera malfunctioned, but it also failed to offer evidence of the malfunction. In closing argument, defense counsel contended that the jury should draw the inference from the government's failure to offer the film that the film did not identify the defendant, even though defense counsel knew that the camera was not working. In rebuttal, the U.S. attorney explained to the jury that the camera was inoperative.[310] The Tenth Circuit held that defense counsel properly argued for a favorable inference from the evidence. The court went on to find that the prosecutor had acted improperly. The court noted that even if defense counsel had made an improper argument, that does not open the door for an improper response by the prosecutor.[311] The court then discussed two ways in which the prosecutor's argument was improper:

> First, the argument went outside the record and made statements as to facts not proven. . . . Second, the statement put the personal knowledge and belief of the prosecuting attorney on the scales, which is also clearly improper.[312]

As a result the court remanded for a new trial.

Problem 2-10

Special Duties of Prosecutors

a.   You are an assistant state attorney general handling the prosecution for armed robbery of a filling station. The defendant in the case is Alan Swaine. At a police lineup the store clerk, Mable Jones, identified Swaine as the robber. A customer who was in the store

---

309. 511 F.2d 498 (10th Cir. 1975).
310. Id. at 502 nn.5-6.
311. Id. at 503. See also United States v. Young, 470 U.S. 1 (1985).
312. 511 F.2d at 503.

at the time, Alicia Chin, also independently identified Swaine as the robber.

In preparing your case for trial you have met with Jones, Chin, and the arresting officers. During the course of these meetings, one of the officers told you that when the police interviewed Jones immediately after the robbery, she told them that she thought that she had seen the robber in the store before and that she thought some of his friends had called him "Shooter." The police investigated this, but it turned out that "Shooter" was another youth and had nothing to do with the robbery. Despite this mixup about "Shooter," Jones is positive of her identification of Swaine, as is Chin.

You have received a request from the defense for "all *Brady* material." How do you plan to handle the information regarding Jones's mistake about "Shooter"?

b. You are an assistant state attorney general in charge of prosecution of white-collar crimes. Your office has been handling the investigation of a major securities fraud case. You have recently begun plea negotiations with lawyers for one of the defendants. You have informed the lawyers that your office will be willing to accept a plea of guilty to securities fraud, but that if the defendant is unwilling to do so, the indictment will include both securities fraud and criminal racketeering charges. A defendant convicted under your state's criminal racketeering law faces the possibility of substantially more severe penalties than one convicted of securities fraud. Defense counsel has complained bitterly about your threat to use the criminal racketeering law if the defendant does not plead guilty.

Read Model Rule, 3.8, 4.2, and comments.

The prosecutor's ethical obligation to do justice

It is a well-accepted proposition that prosecutors have broader ethical obligations than defense counsel. While defense counsel are obligated to represented their clients zealously within the bounds of law, prosecutors have an obligation to seek justice.[313] One of the most frequently cited statements of this principle is from Berger v. United States:[314]

> The United States Attorney is the representative not of an ordinary party to a controversy, but of a sovereignty whose obligation to govern impartially is as compelling as its obligation to govern at all; and whose interest, therefore, in a criminal prosecution is not that it shall win a case, but that justice shall be done. As such, he is in a peculiar and very definite sense the servant of the law, the twofold aim of which is that guilt shall not escape or innocence suffer. He may prosecute with earnestness and vigor — indeed, he should do so. But, while he may strike hard blows, he is not at liberty to strike foul ones. It is as much his duty to refrain from improper methods calculated to produce a wrongful conviction as it is to use every legitimate means to bring about a just one.[315]

The ABA Standards for the Prosecution Function and the Model Rules both incorporate the prosecutor's obligation to justice. Standard 3-1.2(c) states: "The duty of the prosecutor is to seek justice, not merely to convict." Comment 1 to Model Rule 3.8 provides: "A prosecutor has the responsibility of a minister of justice and not simply that of an advocate."

The general obligation of prosecutors to "do justice" is relatively uncontroversial. Problems arise, however, in making this general principle specific and in devising an appropriate remedial system to deal with violations of prosecutorial duties. Model Rule 3.8 provides a limited number of special obligations that apply to prosecutors. More detail and specificity can be found in the ABA Standards for the Prosecution Function and in the National Prosecution Standards of the National District Attorneys Association.[316] Like private counsel, prosecutors can also encounter many

313. See Bruce A. Green, Why Should Prosecutors "Seek Justice"? 26 Fordham Urb. L.J. 607 (1999).

314. 295 U.S. 78 (1935).

315. Id. at 88.

316. Analysis of the ethical obligations of prosecutors can be found in Bennett L. Gershman, Prosecutorial Misconduct (1985); John S. Edwards, Professional Responsibilities of the Federal Prosecutor, 17 U. Rich. L. Rev. 511 (1983); Monroe H. Freedman, The Professional Responsibility of the Prosecuting Attorney, 55 Geo. L.J. 1030 (1967); H. Richard Uviller, The Vir-

and varied conflict-of-interest situations.[317] In these materials we will focus on four issues: disclosure of exculpatory evidence, exercise of prosecutorial discretion, ex parte contacts with defendants, and prosecutorial trial conduct.

Disclosure of exculpatory evidence

We saw earlier in these materials that defense counsel in a criminal case does not have the obligation (or even the right) to disclose incriminating information that defense counsel receives in confidence. Recall Problem 2-3. Remember, however, that a distinction must be drawn between incriminating information and tangible criminal material (such as the instrumentality or fruits of a crime). A defense lawyer who obtains possession of tangible criminal material generally must turn this material over to the prosecution. Recall Problem 2-4. Note also that a distinction must be drawn between an attorney's knowledge of adverse facts and the attorney's knowledge of adverse law. Both prosecutors and defense counsel have an obligation, although a fairly limited one, to disclose adverse legal authority. See Model Rule 3.3(a)(3).

The duty of prosecutors regarding adverse facts contrasts sharply with that of defense counsel. Prosecutors have both a constitutional and a professional obligation to disclose "exculpatory" material. The leading case dealing with the due process effect of a prosecutor's failure to disclose exculpatory material is Brady v. Maryland,[318] a prosecution for murder in which defense counsel asked the prosecution to be allowed to examine extrajudicial statements made by defendant's companion. The prosecution showed defense counsel several statements, but did not disclose one statement in which the companion admitted committing the homicide. The Supreme Court held that "suppression by the prosecution of evidence favorable to an accused upon request violates due process

---

tuous Prosecutor in Quest of an Ethical Standard: Guidance from the ABA, 71 Mich. L. Rev. 1145 (1973).

317. See generally Susan W. Brenner & James G. Durham, Towards Resolving Prosecutor Conflicts of Interest, 6 Geo. J. Legal Ethics 415 (1993); Richard H. Underwood, Part-Time Prosecutors and Conflicts of Interest: A Survey and Some Proposals, 81 Ky. L.J. 1 (1992-1993).

318. 373 U.S. 83 (1963).

where the evidence is material either to guilt or to punishment, irrespective of the good faith or bad faith of the prosecution."[319]

In subsequent cases the Court has refined the scope of the *Brady* rule. The duty to turn over exculpatory evidence applies even if the prosecution has not suppressed the evidence and even if the defense does not file a *Brady* motion.[320] The duty applies to evidence that can be used to impeach government witnesses as well as to exculpatory evidence.[321] While the scope of the duty of disclosure is broad, a conviction will be set aside only if the evidence is "material." Evidence is material when there is a "reasonable probability" that the outcome would have been different had the evidence been disclosed.[322] Given the uncertainty about whether the materiality test has been met, the Court has warned that the "prudent prosecutor will resolve doubtful questions in favor of disclosure."[323]

Note that the constitutional duty of disclosure does not turn on the bad faith of the prosecutor. The prosecutor has "a duty to learn of any favorable evidence known to the others acting on the government's behalf in the case, including the police."[324] The *Brady* rule only applies, however, if the evidence is in the possession of the government. If the government has failed to preserve the evidence, the defendant's constitutional rights have not been violated unless the defendant establishes that the prosecution acted in bad faith.[325]

319. Id. at 87.
320. United States v. Agurs, 427 U.S. 97, 106-107 (1976).
321. United States v. Bagley, 473 U.S. 667, 676 (1985).
322. Id. at 682. See also Strickler v. Greene, 119 S. Ct. 1936 (1999); Kyles v. Whitley, 514 U.S. 419 (1995). For criticism of this standard, see *Bagley*, 473 U.S. at 696, 707 (Brennan and Marshall, J J., dissenting) (if prosecution fails to comply with duty to reveal all information that might reasonably be considered favorable to defense, conviction should be set aside unless prosecution establishes beyond reasonable doubt that new evidence, if developed by reasonably competent counsel, would not have affected outcome of trial).
323. 514 U.S. at 439 (quoting United States v. Agurs, 427 U.S. at 108).
324. Kyles v. Whitley, 514 U.S. 419, 437 (1995). See also Giglio v. United States, 405 U.S. 150 (1972) (assistant U.S. Attorney who presented case to grand jury had promised witness that he would not be prosecuted if he testified before grand jury and at trial; conviction of defendant reversed because of failure to disclose this promise even though assistant who made promise did not have authority to do so and even though promise was not known by U.S. Attorney or trial counsel).
325. Arizona v. Youngblood, 488 U.S. 51 (1988) (failure of prosecution to preserve semen samples and clothing of victim in child molestation case held

Some prosecutors have decided to comply with the *Brady* rule by implementing an "open file policy." Even under an open file policy, a *Brady* violation can occur if exculpatory or impeachment evidence is not in the prosecution's files but is in the hands of the police.[326] The prosecutor's duty to disclose exculpatory evidence does not, however, apply to grand jury proceedings because the grand jury is a separate constitutional body not subject to direct judicial supervision.[327]

The Model Rules of Professional Conduct and the ABA Standards for the Prosecution Function both include rules setting forth a prosecutorial obligation to disclose exculpatory material. Model Rule 3.8(d) provides that a prosecutor in a criminal case shall

> make timely disclosure to the defense of all evidence or information known to the prosecutor that tends to negate the guilt of the accused or mitigates the offense, and, in connection with sentencing, disclose to the defense and to the tribunal all unprivileged mitigating information known to the prosecutor, except when the prosecutor is relieved of this responsibility by a protective order of the tribunal.

ABA Prosecution Function Standard 3-3.11(a) is substantially the same. Rule 3.8(d) differs from the constitutional standard in at least two respects. First, the ethical duty applies only to evidence or information "known to the prosecutor," while the constitutional standard applies to any evidence in the hands of the government, even if not known by the prosecutor. Second, the "tends to" standard of the rule appears to require greater disclosure than the constitutional standard. A study of disciplinary sanctions against prosecutors for *Brady* violations, however, finds that cases are rarely brought and sanctions are light.[328]

---

not to violate defendant's right to due process absent showing of prosecutorial bad faith even though expert testimony indicated that timely performance of tests could have exonerated defendant). On the application of the *Brady* rule to plea bargains, see Note, The Prosecutor's Duty to Disclose to Defendants Pleading Guilty, 99 Harv. L. Rev. 1004 (1986).

326. Strickler v. Greene, 119 S.Ct. 1936 (1999).

327. United States v. Williams, 504 U.S. 36 (1992).

328. Richard A. Rosen, Disciplinary Sanctions Against Prosecutors for *Brady* Violations: A Paper Tiger, 65 N.C. L. Rev. 693 (1987) (recommending independent review of reported criminal cases by bar counsel for *Brady* violations and automatic reversal when prosecutors act in bad faith). For a recent case in which a prosecutor had his license suspended for making false statements to a

For years knowledgeable observers of the criminal justice system have contended that police perjury ("testilying") is widespread.[329] Several highly publicized cases, including the O. J. Simpson trial and the case of Randall Adams (documented in the movie *The Thin Blue Line*), have given the issue greater publicity, but prosecutors have done little to address the issue.

Prosecutorial discretion

Prosecutors have broad discretionary power at almost every stage of criminal proceedings, including investigation, charging, and plea bargaining. How should this power be exercised? The Model Rules provide that prosecutors should not institute criminal proceedings without "probable cause." Model Rule 3.8(a). Is this standard for the charging function sufficiently stringent?[330] One former assistant U.S. Attorney claims that the first concern of most prosecutors is whether the defendant is guilty of the crime with which he or she may be charged.[331] The ABA Standards for the Prosecution Function adopt the probable cause standard but impose some additional obligations on prosecutors in connection with the charging function.[332]

The Supreme Court has imposed some limits on prosecutorial discretion when prosecutorial "vindictiveness" is present. In Blackledge v. Perry[333] the Court ruled that it was unconstitutional for a prosecutor to bring felony charges against a prisoner for as-

---

court and for failing to disclose material exculpatory evidence, see Committee on Prof. Ethics & Conduct v. Ramey, 512 N.W.2d 569 (Iowa 1994). See also Stanley Z. Fisher, "Just the Facts, Ma'am": Lying and the Omission of Exculpatory Evidence in Police Reports, 28 New Eng. L. Rev. 1 (1993).

329. Alan Dershowitz, Is Legal Ethics Asking The Right Questions? 1 J. Inst. for Study Legal Ethics 15 (1996); Richard H. Underwood, The Professional and the Liar, 87 Ky. L.J. 919, 966-999 (1998-1999).

330. Consider Kenneth J. Melilli, Prosecutorial Discretion in an Adversary System, 1992 B.Y.U. L. Rev. 669 (prosecutors should charge only in cases in which they are convinced of defendant's guilt beyond a reasonable doubt).

331. John Kaplan, The Prosecutorial Discretion — A Comment, 60 Nw. U. L. Rev. 174, 178 (1965).

332. See ABA Standards for Criminal Justice, Prosecution Function Standard 3-3.9 (3d ed. 1993). See also Natl. Dist. Atty. Assn., National Prosecution Standards (2d ed. 1991).

333. 417 U.S. 21 (1974).

sault with a deadly weapon after the defendant exercised his statutory right to a trial de novo on appeal from a misdemeanor conviction for the same conduct. While the Court held that there was no evidence that the prosecutor acted in bad faith, it ruled that such a "potential for vindictiveness" must not enter into the defendant's decision.[334]

Subsequently, however, the Court ruled that the doctrine did not apply when the prosecutor informed the defendant during plea bargaining that he would face higher charges if he did not agree to the bargain offered by the prosecutor.[335] The Court found the prosecutor's actions to be part of the "give-and-take" negotiation common in plea bargaining rather than evidence of vindictiveness.[336]

In United States v. Goodwin[337] the Court discussed when a presumption of vindictiveness would arise such that actual proof of vindictiveness was unnecessary. *Goodwin* involved a decision by a U.S. Attorney to file felony charges against the defendant after the defendant had rejected a plea bargain. While the decision was not part of the give-and-take of plea bargaining, the Court found nothing in the case to warrant a presumption of vindictiveness. The Court drew a distinction between allegations of vindictiveness pretrial (as in *Goodwin*) and those made posttrial (as in *Blackledge*). The Court found the possibility of vindictiveness to be greater in the posttrial rather than in the pretrial stage.[338]

Should a prosecutor confess error when the prosecutor is convinced of the defendant's innocence? Suppose, for example, DNA evidence developed after the defendant's conviction shows that the defendant could not have committed the crime. Neither the Rules of Professional Conduct nor the ABA Standards refer to the issue.[339]

---

334. Id. at 28.
335. Bordenkircher v. Hayes, 434 U.S. 357 (1978).
336. Id. at 363.
337. 457 U.S. 368 (1982).
338. Id. at 381. On prosecutorial vindictiveness, see Ellen S. Podgor & Jeffrey S. Weiner, Prosecutorial Misconduct: Alive and Well, and Living in Indiana? 3 Geo. J. Legal Ethics 657, 661-664 (1990).
339. See Mark Hansen, A Prosecutor's Duty, 78-Jun A.B.A. J. 28 (1992) (assistant attorney general resigned rather than defend conviction she felt was wrong).

Ex parte communications with defendants

Model Rule 4.2 provides the following prohibition on ex parte communications between lawyers and other represented persons:

> In representing a client, a lawyer shall not communicate about the subject of the representation with a person the lawyer knows to be represented by another lawyer in the matter, unless the lawyer has the consent of the other lawyer or is authorized by law to do so.

At its August 1995 meeting, the ABA amended Model Rule 4.2 to substitute the word *person* for *party*. The amendment was intended to make it clear that the rule is not limited to formal parties to litigation but applies to persons represented by counsel prior to the institution of formal legal proceedings and also to persons represented by counsel in transactional rather than litigation matters.[340] In jurisdictions that have not adopted this amendment, Model Rule 4.2 may be limited to parties to litigation.[341]

The anticontact rule serves several purposes. First, it prevents a lawyer from intruding into the client-lawyer relationship and perhaps obtaining privileged information. Second, it prohibits a lawyer from obtaining admissions or otherwise taking advantage of the opposing party while that party does not have the benefit of counsel.[342] The rule has stirred considerable controversy in the context of civil litigation, particularly on the issue of whether the rule prohibits a lawyer from interviewing current or former employees of corporate parties. We will consider this issue in Problem 4-2.

Model Rule 4.2 also has evoked controversy in the criminal context, particularly between the defense bar and federal prosecutors. The controversy began with the Second Circuit's decision

---

340. Even prior to this amendment, the ABA Committee on Ethics and Professional Responsibility had issued a formal opinion interpreting the word *party* to mean *person*. ABA Comm. on Ethics and Prof. Resp., Formal Op. 95-396.

341. See Grievance Comm. for the S. Dist. of N.Y. v. Simels, 48 F.3d 640 (2d Cir. 1995) (no violation of DR 7-104(A)(1), the Code equivalent of Model Rule 4.2, to interview represented witness and potential codefendant in drug case because rule uses term "party" and should be narrowly construed).

342. 2 Hazard & Hodes, The Law of Lawyering §4.2:101, at 730.

in United States v. Hammad,[343] which held that an informant's contact with the suspect of a criminal investigation who was represented by counsel at the prosecutor's direction violated the no-communication rule. The Justice Department considered this to be a significant impediment to its law enforcement activities because major criminals were often represented by counsel while they were under investigation. In response, then Attorney General Richard Thornburgh issued an internal memorandum purporting to exempt all Justice Department lawyers from the ethics rule on the ground that by virtue of federal law their law enforcement activities were "authorized by law" within the meaning of the rule. The defense bar objected to this position, and the ABA adopted a resolution opposing the Thornburgh memorandum on the ground that it attempted to exempt Justice Department lawyers from ethical obligations generally applicable to attorneys.[344]

The controversy continues to rage. The Second Circuit withdrew its earlier decision in *Hammad*. Its revised opinion provided that "legitimate investigative techniques" fell within the "authorized by law" exception, although cases could arise in which prosecutors overstepped their authority, leading to the suppression of evidence.[345] Other courts have rejected the position that the rule applies at all until formal adversary proceedings have commenced against the defendant.[346] The Justice Department, under the Clinton administration, continued to assert the government's right to exempt U.S. Attorneys from the operation of state ethics rules under the Supremacy Clause; the department issued a new regulation defining the scope of permissible contacts by government attorneys with individuals and organizations who are represented by counsel.[347] Several court decisions, however, rejected the Justice Department's position that it had the authority to exempt U.S.

---

343. 846 F.2d 854 (2d Cir. 1988) (later withdrawn, see note 345, below).

344. For different perspectives on the issue, see Symposium on Ethical Obligations of Prosecutors, 53 U. Pitts. L. Rev. 271 (1992).

345. United States v. Hammad, 858 F.2d 834, 839 (2d Cir. 1988), *cert. denied*, 498 U.S. 871 (1990).

346. See United States v. Balter, 91 F.3d 427 (3d Cir.), *cert. denied*, 519 U.S. 1011 (1996); United States v. Heinz, 983 F.2d 609 (5th Cir. 1993); United States v. Ryans, 903 F.2d 731 (10th Cir.), *cert. denied*, 498 U.S. 855 (1990).

347. 59 Fed. Reg. 39,910 (August 4, 1994) (to be codified at 28 C.F.R. pt. 77).

Attorneys from regulation by state courts.[348] In 1999 Congress entered the fray, passing legislation (the McDade Act) that overturned the Justice Department's regulations and subjected U.S. Attorneys to the full authority of state courts.[349] Model Rule 4.2 is being revised by the ABA Ethics 2000 commission, however, and the rule likely will be rewritten to authorize legitimate law enforcement investigative activities for both federal and state prosecutors, although the exact scope of that authorization is still unclear.

Courtroom misconduct by prosecutors

Berger v. United States, discussed above, provides a good example of prosecutorial overzealousness in the courtroom:

> That the United States prosecuting attorney overstepped the bounds of that propriety and fairness which should characterize the conduct of such an officer in the prosecution of a criminal offense is clearly shown by the record. He was guilty of misstating the facts in his cross-examination of witnesses; of putting into the mouths of such witnesses things which they had not said; of suggesting by his questions that statements had been made to him personally out of court, in respect of which no proof was offered; of pretending to understand that a witness had said something which he had not said and persistently cross-examining the witness upon that basis; of assuming prejudicial facts not in evidence; of bullying and arguing with witnesses; and, in general, of conducting himself in a thoroughly indecorous and improper manner. . . .
>
> The prosecuting attorney's argument to the jury was undignified and intemperate, containing improper insinuations and assertions calculated to mislead the jury. . . . The following is an illustration: A witness by the name of Goldie Goldstein had been

---

348. United States ex rel. O'Keefe v. McDonnell Douglas Corp., 132 F.3d 1252 (8th Cir. 1998) (Justice Department does not have power by regulation to exempt U.S. Attorneys from state ethics rules absent specific statutory authorization); In re Howes, 940 P.2d 159 (N.M. 1997) (discipline of federal prosecutor on basis of conduct in District of Columbia in accepting telephone calls from represented defendant, rejecting respondent's defense that contacts were authorized by law).

349. 28 U.S.C. §530B and interim final regulations, 64 Fed. Reg. 19,273 (April 20, 1999) (requiring federal prosecutors to comply with state ethics laws and rules as well as federal rules).

called by the prosecution to identify the petitioner. She apparently had difficulty in doing so. The prosecuting attorney, in the course of his argument, said (italics added).

> Mrs. Goldie Goldstein takes the stand. She says she knows Jones, *and you can bet your bottom dollar she knew Berger.* She stood right where I am now and looked at him and was afraid to go over there, and when I waved my arm everybody started to holler, "Don't point at him. You know the rules of law." Well, it is the most complicated game in the world. I was examining *a woman that I knew knew Berger and could identify him,* she was standing right here looking at him, and I couldn't say, "Isn't that the man?" Now, imagine that! But that is the rules of the game, and I have to play within those rules.

The jury was thus invited to conclude that the witness Goldstein knew Berger well but pretended otherwise; and that this was within the personal knowledge of the prosecuting attorney.

Again, at another point in his argument, after suggesting that defendants' counsel had the advantage of being able to charge the district attorney with being unfair "of trying to twist a witness," he said:

> But, oh, they can twist the questions, . . . *they can sit up in their offices and devise ways to pass counterfeit money;* "but don't let the Government touch me, that is unfair; please leave my client alone."[350]

The ABA Standards for the Prosecution Function provide fairly detailed guidance to prosecutors on impermissible trial conduct.[351] Professor Fred Zacharias argues that the general prosecutorial obligation to "do justice" is too vague. He reasons that a more precise concept would require prosecutors to assure defendants that the basic elements of the adversary system exist at trial. Zacharias contends that this perspective would assist rule drafters in preparing more precise rules.[352]

The fundamental problem with prosecutorial misconduct in

---

350. 295 U.S. 78, 84-88 (1935).

351. ABA Standards for Criminal Justice, Prosecution Function Standards 3-5.1 to 3-5.10 (3d ed. 1993).

352. Fred C. Zacharias, Structuring the Ethics of Prosecutorial Trial Practice: Can Prosecutors Do Justice? 44 Vand. L. Rev. 45 (1991). Zacharias expands the argument of this article to develop a general framework for code drafting in Specificity in Professional Responsibility Codes: Theory, Practice, and the Paradigm of Prosecutorial Ethics, 69 Notre Dame L. Rev. 223 (1993).

the courtroom may be not in defining it but in devising remedies to deal with it. One study considered a number of possible remedies for dealing with the problem, including greater use of the contempt power by courts and structural reform of the prosecutor's office to reduce the pressures that can lead to overzealous tactics.[353]

Should prosecutors be subject to greater regulation?

The investigation of President Bill Clinton by independent special prosecutor Kenneth Starr brought to the public attention the question of whether prosecutorial power is subject to abuse.[354] Even before "Starr Wars," a number of commentators had begun questioning the wisdom of prosecutors having the broad, relatively unchecked power that they have traditionally exercised.[355] For example, Bruce Fein has argued that some prosecutors are deflected from seeking justice by a variety of motives: "a desire for fame and remembrance; the potential for book and movie royalties created by attacking publicly prominent personalities; vaulting political ambitions; ideological hostility towards the accused; or, vindictiveness."[356] After giving a number of recent examples of this overzealousness, Fein offers a number of possible remedies:

> Opportunities or incentives for abuses can be curbed without impairing energetic discharge of prosecutorial duties. Prosecutors should enjoy a qualified good-faith immunity from damage suits

353. Albert W. Alschuler, Courtroom Misconduct by Prosecutors and Trial Judges, 50 Tex. L. Rev. 629 (1972). See also Podgor & Weiner, Prosecutorial Misconduct, 3 Geo. J. Legal Ethics at 686-688.

354. See Ellen Yaroshefsky, Starr Wars: Aberrational or Routine Exercise of Prosecutorial Discretion (Presentation to ABA 25th Nat. Conf. on Prof. Resp., June 4, 1999).

355. See, e.g., Bennett L. Gershman, The New Prosecutors, 53 U. Pitt. L. Rev. 393 (1992); Walter W. Steele, Jr., Unethical Prosecutors and Inadequate Discipline, 38 Sw. L.J. 965 (1984); James Vorenberg, Decent Restraint of Prosecutorial Power, 94 Harv. L. Rev. 1521 (1981). But see Frank O. Bowman, III, A Bludgeon by Any Other Name: The Misuses of "Ethical Rules" Against Prosecutors to Control the Law of the State, 9 Geo. J. Legal Ethics 665 (1996).

356. Bruce Fein, Time to Rein in the Prosecution, 80-July A.B.A. J. 96 (1994).

based on violations of constitutional rights in the exercise of prosecutorial functions, not the current absolute immunity.

Prosecutors should be barred from nonprosecutorial electoral
office for five years following a resignation. They should be prohibited from commercial exploitation of particular criminal investigations or prosecutions.

Professional disciplinary rules should forbid prosecutors from
broadcast appearances to discuss ongoing investigations or pending
indictments, even if statements are confined to matters of public
record. They also should visit automatic disbarment for prosecutorial assertions of guilt against any person not convicted in accordance with due process. Finally, judges should be entrusted with
discretion to award attorneys' fees to targets of criminal investigations or to defendants who are not proven guilty.[357]

Prosecutors do enjoy absolute immunity "in initiating a prosecution and in presenting the State's case" at trial.[358] Outside of trial,
however, the Supreme Court has limited prosecutorial immunity.
In Buckley v. Fitzsimmons[359] the Court held that prosecutors were
entitled only to qualified rather than to absolute immunity for investigative conduct and for statements made at press conferences.
In Kalina v. Fletcher[360] the Court held that prosecutors were protected by absolute immunity in connection with preparation and
filing of charging documents, but they were not entitled to such
immunity with respect to executing certifications for determination of probable cause because such certificates were not part of
the traditional functions of advocates.

Prosecutors have qualified immunity not absolute

Problem 2-11

Fee Forfeiture and Lawyer Subpoenas

    a.   Norman Schwartz has asked your firm to de-
fend him in a prosecution for violation of federal drug
felony statutes. You have told Schwartz that your firm
charges $25,000 to take the case, plus $5,000 advanced
expenses, plus fees determined on an hourly basis.

357. Id.
358. Imbler v. Pachtman, 424 U.S. 409, 431 (1976).
359. 509 U.S. 259 (1993).
360. 522 U.S. 118 (1997).

Schwartz agrees to these financial arrangements. The next day he delivers to your office three checks: a personal check in the amount of $10,000 and two cashiers' checks in the amount of $10,000 each. All of the checks are drawn on different banks. Do you have any ethical or legal problems taking the three checks from Schwartz?

b. During the course of investigation of the Schwartz case, an informant tells the prosecutors that Schwartz has invested the proceeds of his drug transactions in various real estate developments. The informant also says that he believes that the Fleming Law Firm has represented Schwartz in connection with these investments. The prosecutors then issue a subpoena duces tecum to the Fleming firm directing it to produce before the grand jury the following:

> all files relating to representation by any current or former lawyer in the Fleming Law Firm of Norman Schwartz or of any entity with which Schwartz is affiliated. As used in this subpoena, the term "affiliated" includes without limitation any form of affiliation including, by way of example, serving as an officer, director, employee, shareholder, general or limited partner, managing agent, or joint venturer.

What should the Fleming firm do in response to this subpoena? As defense counsel, what advice would you give Schwartz about the subpoena? Be prepared to argue on Schwartz's behalf in support of a motion to quash the subpoena and on behalf of the prosecution against the motion.

Read Model Rules 1.6, 3.8(f), 8.4, and comments.

Money laundering and fee forfeiture

One of a lawyer's fundamental professional obligations is the duty not to engage in criminal misconduct. Model Rule 8.4(b). See also

Model Rule 1.2(d) (lawyer may not counsel or assist client in criminal or fraudulent conduct). For two reasons, the area of criminal defense practice raises the issue of lawyer participation in criminal conduct perhaps more directly than other areas of practice. First, by definition criminal defense practice involves representation of individuals who are under investigation for criminal violations or who have been charged with criminal conduct. The closer one is to criminality, the more likely one is to become involved. Recall Problem 2-4 in which we considered the ethical and legal problems facing lawyers when they obtain possession of fruits, instrumentalities, or evidence of crimes. Second, in many cases defendants are charged with crimes that involve money. The fact that the accused may have tainted funds raises the possibility that the attorney fees may be derived from criminal activity.

What criminal statutes apply to the payment of fees to lawyers? One type of statute that could apply to payments of legal fees is one prohibiting "money laundering." At the federal level, 18 U.S.C. §1957 makes it a crime if any person "knowingly engages or attempts to engage in a monetary transaction in criminally derived property that is of a value greater than $10,000 and is derived from specified unlawful activity."[361] The statute is extremely broad in two respects. First, the term "monetary transaction" refers to any deposit, withdrawal, transfer, or exchange of funds in a financial institution.[362] A deposit or withdrawal of a fee from a federally insured institution will do. Second, the government need not prove that the recipient knew the specific crime from which the funds were derived, only that the funds came from specified unlawful activity.[363] Section 1957 provides an exception for "any transaction necessary to preserve a person's right to representation as guaranteed by the sixth amendment to the Constitution."[364] This exception would probably be of little use to attorneys prosecuted under the statute, however, because the Supreme Court has held that the Sixth Amendment is not infringed when a statute prevents defendants from using money that does not belong to them to hire attorneys. See the cases dealing with the forfeiture statutes discussed below. Thus, if an attorney were charged with

---

361. A related money laundering statute is 18 U.S.C. §1956.
362. 18 U.S.C. §1957(f)(1).
363. Id. §1957(c).
364. Id. §1957(f)(1).

committing a federal crime by receiving as a fee funds derived from criminal activity, the only defense available to the lawyer would be that the lawyer did not "knowingly" receive property derived from illegal activity.

The Justice Department in its manual for U.S. Attorneys takes the position that there is no statutory prohibition on the application of the statute even to bona fide legal fees paid to defense counsel if defense counsel receives the fees knowing that they have been derived from illegal activity.[365] The department also takes the view that there is no constitutional barrier to prosecuting attorneys for receiving criminally derived funds.[366] The Justice Department recognizes, however, that attorneys must investigate matters that they handle and that the failure to do so would be a breach of their ethical obligations and a violation of defendants' constitutional right to effective assistance of counsel.[367] As part of an investigation, attorneys may acquire information that could be used to establish that they know that their fees have been paid from property derived from illegal activity. In order to avoid hampering lawyers in their ability to represent criminal defendants, the department as a matter of policy will not prosecute attorneys under section 1957 for receipt of bona fide attorney fees except under the following circumstances:

> (1) there is proof beyond a reasonable doubt that the attorney had actual knowledge of the illegal origin of the specific property received (prosecution is not permitted if the only proof of knowledge is evidence of willful blindness); and (2) such evidence does not consist of (a) confidential communications made by the client preliminary to and with regard to undertaking representation in the criminal matter; or (b) confidential communications made during the course of representation in the criminal matter; or (c) other information obtained by the attorney during the course of the representation and in furtherance of the obligation to effectively represent the client.[368]

---

365. Department of Justice, United States Attorneys' Manual, tit. 9-105.600 (1997).
366. Id.
367. Id.
368. Id.

Under general criminal standards a person is treated as having knowledge if the person exhibits "willful blindness," an intentional effort to avoid gaining knowledge.[369] As the policy states, however, the Justice Department will not prosecute attorneys under section 1957 unless attorneys have actual knowledge that the property was derived from criminal activity. In other words, the Government does not take the position that attorneys have a duty to investigate the source of the funds used to pay their fees, at least under this statute. The 1977 edition of the Justice Department manual stated that extensive prerepresentation publicity about the defendant and his affairs is "never sufficient by itself to establish actual knowledge."[370] The 1997 edition does not contain this statement, but it is difficult to see how statements in the media could ever amount to actual knowledge. As an additional protection for attorneys, U.S. Attorneys cannot prosecute attorneys for receiving fees in violation of section 1957 unless the Criminal Division in Washington approves the prosecution in accordance with the policies discussed above.[371] While the Justice Department's interpretation of the money laundering statute provides defense counsel with a number of protections, the department's policy is not binding, nor does it have the force of law.[372]

Although state statutes dealing with money or property derived from illegal activity vary considerably, many states make it a crime for a person knowingly to receive or to possess stolen property.[373] State prosecutors typically do not operate under policy restrictions like those governing U.S. Attorneys, so a lawyer could be subject to state prosecution for receiving stolen property by taking a fee, with the only defense available that the lawyer did not know that the property was stolen. Prosecutors are attorneys too, however, and since many prosecutors become defense attorneys after they leave government service, they may tend to be sympathetic to the argument that defense attorneys should not be

---

369. See generally John P. Freeman & Nathan M. Crystal, Scienter in Professional Liability Cases, 42 S.C. L. Rev. 783, 833-838 (1991).

370. Department of Justice, United States Attorneys' Manual, tit. 9-105.430 (1977).

371. Id. tit. 9-105.300 (1997).

372. Id. tit. 1-1.100.

373. E.g., Cal. Penal Code §496; N.Y. Penal Law §§165.40 et seq.; Model Penal Code §223.6, 10 U.L.A. 278 (Supp. 1999).

charged with committing crimes simply because they are paid to represent defendants in criminal cases. This may explain why there has been no reported prosecution of an attorney for obtaining a fee in violation of a statute prohibiting receipt of stolen property.[374]

Even though a lawyer may not be prosecuted by federal or state authorities, the true owner of any stolen money or property could bring an action against the attorney to recover any money or property conveyed to the attorney. In the case of money, the true owner would have to trace the funds into the lawyer's possession, which might be difficult to do.

A second class of statutes affecting fee payments to lawyers in criminal defense practice provide for forfeiture of property derived from certain illegal activity. Two federal statutes have been particularly important in connection with fee payments to attorneys: 18 U.S.C. §1963(c), which provides for forfeiture of property used in or derived from criminal activity in violation of RICO (Racketeer Influenced and Corrupt Organizations), and 21 U.S.C. §853(c), which provides for forfeiture of property used in or derived from violation of drug felony statutes. Section 853(c) provides as follows:

Third Party Transfers

All right, title, and interest in property [subject to criminal forfeiture] vests in the United States upon the commission of the act giving rise to forfeiture under this section. Any such property that is subsequently transferred to a person other than the defendant may be the subject of a special verdict of forfeiture and thereafter shall be ordered forfeited to the United States, unless the transferee establishes in a hearing . . . that he is a bona fide purchaser for value of such property who at the time of purchase was reasonably without cause to believe that the property was subject to forfeiture under this section.

Note that the statute states that title to the property vests in the United States when the crime is committed, not when the defendant is found guilty. Because of this "relation back" of the statute, fee payments to attorneys are subject to forfeiture.

The Justice Department has been much more aggressive in

---

374. Cf. Cardin v. State, 533 A.2d 928 (Md. Ct. Spec. App. 1987), *cert. denied*, 488 U.S. 827 (1988) (attorney convicted of theft when he received fees from savings and loan institution without performing services).

its use of the forfeiture statutes than it has been in using section 1957, the money laundering statute, against attorneys. In response, defense attorneys have vigorously contested efforts by the government seeking forfeiture of their fees, arguing that such efforts were inconsistent with the intent of these statutes and violated defendants' Sixth Amendment right to counsel.

In United States v. Monsanto[375] the Supreme Court rejected arguments that section 853 (the drug forfeiture statute) was not intended to reach attorney fees. Finding the statutory language to be "plain and unambiguous" in its coverage of "all property," the Court noted:

> In enacting §853, Congress decided to give force to the old adage that "crime does not pay." We find no evidence that Congress intended to modify that nostrum to read, "crime does not pay, except for attorney's fees."[376]

In a companion case to *Monsanto*, Caplin & Drysdale, Chartered v. United States,[377] the Court considered and rejected both Fifth and Sixth Amendment arguments against application of the forfeiture statutes to attorney fees. As to the Sixth Amendment argument, the Court ruled that nothing in the statute prevented defendants from hiring the counsel of their choice out of nonforfeitable assets.[378] The fact that the statute prevented defendants from using forfeitable assets to hire attorneys did not infringe the Sixth Amendment: "A defendant has no Sixth Amendment right to spend another person's money for services rendered by an attorney, even if those funds are the only way that that defendant will be able to retain the attorney of his choice."[379] The Court also rejected the argument that the application of the statute to attorney fees violated the Due Process Clause of the Fifth Amendment because it upset the balance of forces between the prosecution and the defense.[380] The Court noted that any weapon in the war on crime was subject to prosecutorial abuse, but abuse should be

---

375. 491 U.S. 600 (1989).
376. Id. at 614.
377. 491 U.S. 617 (1989).
378. Id. at 626.
379. Id.
380. Id. at 633.

judged on a case-by-case basis, not by invalidation of the statute as a whole.[381]

The Court dealt with one final constitutional question in *Monsanto*: the validity of the statutory provision allowing court orders freezing defendants' assets before the assets are finally adjudged to be forfeitable.[382] The Court found no constitutional prohibition against the issuance of a restraining order based on a finding of probable cause.[383] In *Monsanto* the Court did not address the need for or extent of a hearing required to restrain disposition of assets.[384] On remand the Second Circuit ruled that assets could be subject to an ex parte restraining order on a showing of probable cause by the prosecution, but that the Fifth and Sixth Amendments required a prompt adversary, postrestraint, pretrial hearing on the issues whether there was probable cause that the defendant committed the crime of which she was accused and whether the assets were probably subject to forfeiture.[385]

The Justice Department has also articulated policies regarding when it will bring actions against attorneys seeking forfeiture of fees. Any action seeking forfeiture of payments made to attorneys as legal fees requires approval from Washington by the assistant attorney general of the Criminal Division.[386] The department has articulated the following general policy on actions to forfeit attorney fees:

> While there are no constitutional or statutory prohibitions to application of the third party forfeiture provisions to attorney fees, the Department recognizes that attorneys, who among all third parties uniquely may be aware of the possibility of forfeiture, may not be able to meet the statutory requirements for relief for third party transferees without hampering their ability to represent their clients. In particular, requiring an attorney to bear the burden of proving lack of reasonable cause to believe that an asset was subject to for-

381. Id. at 634-635.
382. 21 U.S.C. §853(e).
383. 491 U.S. at 616.
384. Id. at 615 n.10.
385. United States v. Monsanto, 924 F.2d 1186 (2d Cir.) (en banc), *cert. denied*, 502 U.S. 943 (1991). See also United States v. James Daniel Good Real Property, 510 U.S. 43 (1993) (government may not seize assets without preseizure hearing unless extraordinary circumstances are present).
386. Department of Justice, United States Attorneys' Manual, tit. 9-119.104 (1997).

feiture may prevent the free and open exchange of information between an attorney and a client. The Department recognizes that the
proper exercise of prosecutorial discretion dictates that this be taken
into consideration in applying the third party forfeiture provisions
to attorney fees. See the Criminal Resource Manual at 2301
through 2303. Accordingly, it is the policy of the Department that
application of the forfeiture provisions to attorney fees be carefully
reviewed and that they be uniformly and fairly applied.[387]

In addition, subject to approval in Washington, U.S. Attorneys
may enter into agreements to exempt legitimate fee payments from
forfeiture actions.[388]

In United States v. Moffitt, Zwerling & Kemler, P.C.,[389] the
Moffitt law firm was retained to represent a defendant charged
with drug trafficking and money laundering. The firm required the
defendant to pay an up-front fee of $100,000. The defendant paid
the fee in two installments of $17,000 and $86,800. Much of the
$103,800 payment was in the form of $100 bills. The Fourth Circuit rejected the firm's argument that it was an innocent transferee
entitled to take the payment free of the government's claim of
forfeiture:

> The firm contends that its partners believed, based on their exten-
> sive interviews with him, that Covington had "squirreled" away
> substantial assets from legitimate business activity. And the firm
> asserts that Covington was informed that he could not pay in
> "funny money." The district court found, however, that Covington
> advised the firm's partners that he was broke, and for that reason
> continued to engage in illegal activity. . . . In addition, during the
> supposedly extensive interviews with Covington, the firm's partners
> tiptoed around the most pertinent questions. They did not even ask
> Covington what legitimate sources of income he had. And, con-
> spicuously, they avoided asking Covington exactly where he had
> obtained the $103,800 in cash to pay his legal fee. . . . In their meet-
> ings with Covington the lawyers did not seek to obviate doubts that
> any person would have had about the source of Covington's sub-
> stantial cash payment. The meetings, in fact, create the impression
> that the participants were engaging in some sort of wink and nod
> ritual whereby they agreed not to ask — or tell — too much. . . .

387. Id. tit. 9-119.200. The Department's Criminal Resource Manual establishes detailed guidelines to implement this policy. Id. tit. 9-119.202.
388. Id. tit. 9-119.203.
389. 83 F.3d 660 (4th Cir. 1996), cert. denied, 519 U.S. 1101 (1997).

> Both what the law firm knew in August, 1991, and what it declined
> to inquire about, convinces us that it reasonably had cause to know
> that the $103,800 was subject to forfeiture. . . .[390]

The Court also held that the Government could pursue common
law claims for conversion and detinue against the firm even though
the forfeiture statute did not apply because the law firm no longer
had possession of the specific cash received from the defendant.

Note that the Fourth Circuit did not mention the Justice Department's guidelines for seeking forfeiture of attorney fees. Arguably the proceeding was proper under the guidelines because
the government had reasonable grounds to believe that the law
firm had actual knowledge that the fee payment was subject to
forfeiture. The district court had cited the guidelines, stating that
they are for internal guidance of the Justice Department and are
not intended to create a legal standard.[391]

Even if fees are not subject to forfeiture under federal law,
they may be subject to forfeiture under state law. A number of
states have enacted forfeiture statutes that could also apply to attorney fees.[392]

Another federal statute, 26 U.S.C. §6050I, applies to fees
paid to lawyers (principally in connection with criminal matters,
although the statute could also apply to fees paid in civil cases as
well). The statute requires reporting of "cash payments" in excess
of $10,000.

> Any person —
>
>> (1) who is engaged in a trade or business, and
>> (2) who, in the course of such trade or business, receives
>> more than $10,000 in cash in 1 transaction (or in 2 or more
>> related transactions),
>
> shall make the return . . . with respect to such transaction (or related transactions) at such time as the Secretary may by regulations
> prescribe.

While the statute uses the word "cash," the statute defines
the term more broadly than is commonly understood. "Cash" in-

---

390. 83 F.3d at 666.
391. In re Moffitt, Zwerling & Kemler, P.C., 846 F. Supp. 463, 475 (E.D.
Va. 1994).
392. E.g., Cal. Penal Code §186; N.Y. Civ. Prac. Law §§1310 et seq.

cludes foreign currency and "any monetary instrument (whether or not in bearer form) with a face amount of not more than $10,000." Thus, cashiers' checks, travelers' checks, or money orders in the amount of $10,000, but not more, are included within the term "cash."[393] (The statutory limitation of instruments to not more than $10,000 may appear to be odd, but the reason for this limitation is that cash payments of more than $10,000 to a financial institution must be reported by the institution so it is unnecessary to impose reporting requirements on recipients of instruments issued by the institution.) Payment by an ordinary check drawn on the writer's account in a financial institution is not, however, subject to reporting.[394] The reporting requirement applies even if the attorney does not receive any single payment of $10,000 or more if the payments are part of a series of connected transactions. Thus the reporting requirement would apply if the client paid two monthly installments, one for $7,500 in cash, the other with a $7,500 bank check.[395] The statute also prohibits structuring transactions to evade the reporting requirement.[396] In addition, the IRS form for reporting cash payments, Form 8300, provides: "This form may be filed voluntarily for any suspicious transaction . . . even if it does not exceed $10,000."

Form 8300 requires the person reporting the transaction to disclose the identity of the individual from whom cash was received, the identity of the person on whose behalf the transaction was conducted, the nature of the transaction and the method of payment, and the business reporting the transaction. Some criminal defense counsel have argued that these requirements violate the attorney-client privilege and their clients' constitutional rights; they refused to complete the portions of the form requiring disclosure of the identity of their clients and the method of payment of their fees. Several appellate courts have ruled in favor of the IRS on the issue.[397] These courts applied traditional doctrine that the client's identity and the fees paid by the client are usually

393. Treas. Reg. §1.6050I-1(c).
394. 26 U.S.C. §6050I(d).
395. Treas. Reg. §1.6050I-1(b).
396. 26 U.S.C. §6050I(f)(1). See Office of Disciplinary Counsel v. Massey, 687 N.E.2d 734 (Ohio 1998) (lawyer disciplined for attempting to structure fee payments to avoid IRS disclosure requirements).
397. Gerald B. Lefcourt, P. C. v. United States, 125 F.3d 79 (2d Cir. 1997), *cert. denied*, 118 S. Ct. 2341 (1998); United States v. Sindel, 53 F.3d 874

not subject to the attorney-client privilege because such information is generally not given in confidence or for the purpose of obtaining legal advice. The next section discusses the application of the attorney-client privilege to client identity and fee payments.

In a comprehensive analysis of the impact of the federal money laundering, forfeiture, and reporting statutes on lawyers, Professors Eugene Gaetke and Sarah Welling conclude that the laws require lawyers to act cautiously but they do not force lawyers to act unethically.[398] They point out, however, that these laws may produce a number of practical problems, including less informed defense counsel, reluctance of lawyers to take on certain cases, and increased use of disqualification motions by prosecutors. They find these practical problems to be disturbing because they may reduce the quality of representation received by defendants and may tip the balance between the prosecution and the defense unfairly in the prosecution's favor. Professor Ellen Podgor takes an even more critical view of the IRS reporting requirement, arguing that it undermines the adversarial system and places lawyers in the position of being government agents.[399]

The attorney-client privilege and subpoenas directed at lawyers

As discussed above, the Internal Revenue Code requires lawyers to report cash payments received from clients that exceed $10,000. In addition, as part of criminal investigations both federal and state prosecutors have on occasion subpoenaed information from lawyers about the identities of their clients or about payments of their

(8th Cir. 1995); United States v. Ritchie, 15 F.3d 592 (6th Cir.), *cert. denied,* 513 U.S. 868 (1994); United States v. Leventhal, 961 F.2d 936 (11th Cir. 1992).

398. Eugene R. Gaetke & Sarah N. Welling, Money Laundering and Lawyers, 43 Syracuse L. Rev. 1165, 1242 (1992).

399. Ellen S. Podgor, Form 8300: The Demise of Law as a Profession, 5 Geo. J. Legal Ethics 485 (1992). See also Matthew P. Harrington & Eric A. Lustig, IRS Form 8300: The Attorney-Client Privilege and Tax Policy Become Casualties in the War Against Money Laundering, 24 Hofstra L. Rev. 623 (1996) (criticizing section 6050I as applied to attorneys and offering proposals for reform by courts or Congress).

fees. Such subpoenas raise issues of the application of the attorney-client privilege. Recall our discussion in connection with Problem 2-3 dealing with the distinction between the evidentiary attorney-client privilege and the ethical duty of confidentiality. On the distinction between the ethical duty and the evidentiary privilege, see Model Rule 1.6, cmt. 5.

If the government seeks information about a client from a lawyer in connection with a contemplated or pending legal proceeding, both the ethical duty and the evidentiary privilege are involved, but in different ways. Comment 19 to Rule 1.6 indicates how a lawyer should proceed in such a case. Initially, the ethical duty is involved. The ethical duty to protect confidential information requires the lawyer to invoke the evidentiary privilege and to refuse to provide information until the lawyer has an opportunity to consult with the client about the matter.[400] The client after consultation with the lawyer could, of course, decide to waive the evidentiary privilege and provide the information to the government. If the client wishes to invoke the privilege, the attorney could seek to quash any subpoena that had been issued. Arguments to quash the subpoena would be based on the scope of the evidentiary privilege. What should the lawyer do if the trial court denies the motion to quash? Discovery orders are normally not immediately appealable, and a party who is subject to such an order can usually only obtain immediate appellate review by refusing to comply with the order, becoming subject to a contempt sanction, and then appealing the finding of contempt.[401] Most courts, however, have created an exception allowing immediate appeal by the client when a subpoena compels a lawyer to reveal documents or information that is subject to an arguable claim of privilege. As the First Circuit said:

[A]llowing an appeal only if the attorney accepts a contempt citation pits lawyers against their clients in a manner that we do not believe is in the interests of justice. . . . A lawyer should not be required to choose between the interests of his or her client and his

---

400. ABA Comm. on Ethics and Prof. Resp., Formal Op. 94-385.
401. See United States v. Ryan, 402 U.S. 530 (1971); In re Grand Jury Subpoena (Horn), 976 F.2d 1314 (9th Cir. 1992).

or her own interests. A rule that promotes conflicts of interest hinders the fair representation of the client and makes it less likely that clients will be well served by their attorneys.[402]

If the appellate court then rejects the claim of privilege, the attorney ethically is required to comply with the court order. See Rule 1.6, cmt. 19.

Does the attorney-client evidentiary privilege prevent disclosure of information regarding the identity of the client or payment of legal fees from the client to the lawyer? Courts have generally held that information about fee payments and client identity are not subject to the attorney-client privilege because such communications ordinarily do not reveal any confidential information.[403] Courts have recognized, however, some limited situations in which information about client identity or fee payments is protected by the privilege because revelation of such information would convey confidential information. In Baird v. Koerner,[404] the Ninth Circuit recognized a "legal advice" exception, although the term is not particularly descriptive of the scope of the exception. The case involved delinquent taxpayers who, based on the advice of their attorney, tendered past-due taxes. The government attempted to learn from the attorney the names of the taxpayers. The court upheld the claim of privilege because revealing the identities would clearly be revealing confidential information. Other courts have articulated "last link" or "communication" exceptions to the attorney-client privilege.[405]

402. In re Grand Jury Subpoenas, 123 F.3d 695, 699 (1st Cir. 1997). Not all courts agree. See United States v. Amlani, 169 F.3d 1189 (9th Cir. 1999) (client can only appeal subpoena directed to former not current counsel).

403. See Clarke v. American Commerce Natl. Bank, 974 F.2d 127 (9th Cir. 1992); In re Grand Jury Matter (Doe), 926 F.2d 348 (4th Cir. 1991); In re Criminal Investigation No. 1/242Q, 602 A.2d 1220 (Md. 1992).

404. 279 F.2d 623 (9th Cir. 1960).

405. For a general discussion of these exceptions, see In re Grand Jury Subpoenas (Anderson), 906 F.2d 1485 (10th Cir. 1990) (recognizing legal advice, last link, and confidential communication exceptions to general rule that attorney-client privilege does not apply to client identity or fee payments) and In re Criminal Investigation No. 1/242Q, 602 A.2d 1220 (Md. 1992). Compare In re Subpoena to Testify Before Grand Jury (Alexiou v. United States), 39 F.3d 973 (9th Cir. 1994), cert. denied, 514 U.S. 1097 (1995) (lawyer may be compelled to disclose to grand jury identity of client who gave him counterfeit bill because that would not establish "last link" necessary to convict client; prosecution must

Despite different formulations, these exceptions all have a common core of operative facts. When a court has upheld a claim of privilege regarding client identity or fee information, it is because disclosure of the identity of the client or of the fees paid would reveal confidential information in addition to the client's identity or fee payments, often the client's motive for seeking legal advice.[406] Of course, even if the attorney-client privilege applies to either the identity of the client or the fees that were paid, it is possible that some exception to the privilege applies, such as waiver of the privilege or if the client sought legal advice for the purpose of committing a crime or fraud (the "crime/fraud" exception). We have already encountered the crime-fraud exception to the attorney-client privilege in connection with the *Purcell* case, discussed in Problem 2-3. We will consider the scope and exceptions to the attorney-client privilege in civil cases in Problem 3-3.

Professor Steven Goode argues that the case law on when client identity and fee payments are privileged is in disarray. He advocates a new approach in which the client's identity and fee payments are privileged "whenever it is the client's status as a client that is the relevant information sought."[407] Under his status-as-client approach, Goode would hold that the attorney-client privilege applies to a situation in which the plaintiffs in a civil suit seek the identity of a hit-and-run driver from his lawyer, but not to completion by attorneys of IRS Form 8300 requiring reporting of cash payments from clients.[408]

At its February 1990 meeting, the American Bar Association adopted Model Rule 3.8(f) to regulate the issuance of subpoenas by prosecutors seeking information about client representation. As approved in 1990, the rule required prior judicial approval for subpoenas directed at lawyers about past or present clients. Several

---

still prove knowledge and intent) *with* Dietz v. Doe, 935 P.2d 611 (Wash. 1997) (identity of client in hit-and-run accident can be subject to privilege under legal advice exception if revelation would implicate client in crime for which advice was sought).

406. See In re Grand Jury Subpoena for Attorney Representing Criminal Defendant Reyes-Requena (DeGeurin), 926 F.2d 1423 (5th Cir. 1991); In re Grand Jury Proceeding (Cherney), 898 F.2d 565 (7th Cir. 1990). See generally 1 Hazard & Hodes, The Law of Lawyering §1.6:105.

407. Steven Goode, Identity, Fees, and the Attorney-Client Privilege, 59 Geo. Wash. L. Rev. 307, 311 (1991).

408. Id. at 311-312.

states embraced this rule,[409] and some federal district courts issued similar rules. Federal prosecutors have attacked these rules as inconsistent with federal law. Professors Hazard and Hodes argue that Rule 3.8(f) is clearly invalid to the extent it interferes with federal grand jury investigations.[410] Other commentators argue that current law imposes no substantial restriction on the use of subpoenas directed at attorneys, so to restore a proper balance between governmental and individual interests, limitations on the use of subpoenas, including judicial screening, should be adopted.[411] At its August 1995 meeting the ABA amended Model Rule 3.8(f) to delete the requirement that a prosecutor seeking to subpoena a lawyer about a past or present client obtain prior judicial approval for the subpoena. Federal courts were divided on the validity of state or federal district court rules that attempted to limit the power of prosecutors to issue subpoenas directed at attorneys. The McDade Act, which subjects U.S. attorneys to state ethics rules, has probably resolved the issue.[412]

The Justice Department has established a policy for issuance of subpoenas by U.S. Attorneys to lawyers for information regarding representation of clients.[413] Under the policy, no subpoena can be issued except with the approval of the assistant attorney general

---

409. See Laws. Man. on Prof. Conduct (ABA/BNA) 55:1303. See In re Grand Jury Investigation, 556 N.E.2d 363 (Mass. 1990). But see State ex rel. Doe v. Troisi, 459 S.E.2d 139 (W. Va. 1995) (rejecting need for preliminary showing by prosecutors to subpoena attorneys to testify before grand juries, holding that attorney-client privilege provides sufficient protection to clients).

410. 1 Hazard & Hodes, The Law of Lawyering §3.8:701, at 702.

411. See Max D. Stern & David A. Hoffman, Privileged Informers: The Attorney Subpoena Problem and a Proposal for Reform, 136 U. Pa. L. Rev. 1783 (1988). See also Ellen Y. Suni, Subpoenas to Criminal Defense Lawyers: A Proposal for Limits, 65 Or. L. Rev. 215 (1986).

412. Compare Whitehouse v. United States Dist. Ct. for the Dist. of R.I., 53 F.3d 1349 (1st Cir. 1995) (district court has authority to adopt ethics rule requiring federal prosecutors to seek judicial approval before obtaining subpoenas against lawyers) with Baylson v. Disciplinary Bd., 975 F.2d 102 (3d Cir. 1992) (holding that state rule was invalid as applied to federal prosecutors under the Supremacy Clause), cert. denied, 507 U.S. 984 (1993). In United States v. Colorado Supreme Court, 189 F.3d 1281 (10th Cir. 1999), the Tenth Circuit held that federal prosecutors were subject to Colorado Rule of Professional Conduct 3.8(f) by virtue of the McDade Act, 28 U.S.C. §530B.

413. Department of Justice, United States Attorneys' Manual, tit. 9-13.410 (1997).

for the Criminal Division in Washington.[414] The policy requires the assistant attorney general to apply a number of principles before approving issuance of a subpoena:

- The information sought must not be protected by a valid claim of privilege.
- All reasonable efforts must have been used to obtain the information from other sources or voluntarily from the attorney.
- In a criminal investigation, the information sought must be reasonably necessary for the successful completion of an investigation or prosecution. Peripheral or speculative information should not be sought.
- In a civil investigation, the information must be reasonably necessary to the successful completion of the litigation.
- The need for the subpoena must outweigh the potential impact on the client-lawyer relationship, including the possible disqualification of defense counsel.
- The subpoena must be narrowly drawn as to subject matter and time.[415]

E.   Delivery of Legal Services to Indigents in Criminal Cases

—————— **Problem 2-12** ——————

Evaluation of Delivery of Defense Services in Criminal Cases

You are a member of a task force of your state bar appointed to evaluate the delivery of criminal defense services in your state. The chairperson of your committee will assign you a topic for evaluation. Be prepared to report to the committee your evaluation of how well

414. Id. tit. 9-13.410(A).
415. Id. tit. 9-13.410(C).

your state complies with ABA standards on the topic
that has been assigned to you.

Methods of delivering defense services

In Gideon v. Wainwright[416] the Supreme Court held that the
Sixth and Fourteenth Amendments guaranteed indigent defendants a right to appointed counsel in criminal prosecutions in state
courts. *Gideon* was a felony prosecution. The Court subsequently
held in Argersinger v. Hamlin[417] that the right to counsel applied
to misdemeanor as well as to felony cases if the defendant was
incarcerated as a result of the proceeding. Later decisions, however, have watered down the right to counsel in misdemeanor
cases.[418] Other cases have defined the types of proceedings to
which the right to counsel is applicable.[419] The right to counsel
attaches at any "critical stage" of the proceeding.[420]

States use three basic systems to implement the constitutional
right to counsel in criminal cases. Each of these systems has suffered from problems. *Public defender programs* are used principally
in large cities. Public defenders must often deal with excessive
caseloads. In addition, the method of selection of the chief public
defender may undermine the independence of the program. In
contract defense programs, counsel receive fixed fees for agreeing to

---

416.   372 U.S. 335 (1963).

417.   407 U.S. 25 (1972).

418.   In Scott v. Illinois, 440 U.S. 367 (1979), the Court held that the
conviction of a defendant in a misdemeanor case was not unconstitutional when
the defendant was not afforded the right to counsel if no prison sentence was
actually imposed even if the defendant was subject to incarceration for the crime.
Further, in Nichols v. United States, 511 U.S. 738 (1994), the Court held that
a conviction under *Scott* in which the defendant was not provided with counsel
could nonetheless be used in a subsequent criminal proceeding to enhance the
defendant's sentence.

419.   See, e.g., In re Gault, 387 U.S. 1 (1967) (right to counsel applicable
to juvenile delinquency proceedings). An ABA study 30 years after *Gault* concluded that a crisis of poor access and quality of legal services exists in juvenile
delinquency proceedings. See Patricia Puritz et al., A Call for Justice: An Assessment of Access to Counsel and Quality of Representation in Delinquency Proceedings (1995).

420.   See Wolfram, Modern Legal Ethics §14.3.2, at 795-796 (catalogue
of critical stages).

handle certain matters. Contract defense programs can be used in combination with defender programs to deal with excessive caseloads or conflict of interest situations. Contract defense is also used in smaller communities that are unable to afford a defender program. Critics of contract defense fear that contracts are awarded to the lowest bidder without regard to qualifications. Most small jurisdictions make use of *assigned counsel programs*. In some jurisdictions, assigned counsel receive no compensation; representation is treated as part of the lawyer's pro bono obligation. Even in jurisdictions where assigned counsel receive compensation, fees are typically capped or limited to very low hourly rates. Funds for expert witnesses and other litigation costs may be available but are severely limited.[421]

ABA Standards for Providing Defense Services

In 1992 the ABA released revised Standards for Providing Defense Services. The ABA concluded that full-time defender organizations were the most desirable method of providing defense services to indigents, but that participation by the organized bar through either assignment or contract system was also desirable.[422] Standard 5-1.2 provides as follows:

> (a) The legal representation plan for each jurisdiction should provide for the services of a full-time defender organization when population and caseload are sufficient to support such an organization. Multi-jurisdictional organizations may be appropriate in rural areas.
>
> (b) Every system should include the active and substantial participation of the private bar. That participation should be

---

421. See Stephen J. Schulhofer & David D. Friedman, Rethinking Indigent Defense: Promoting Effective Representation Through Consumer Sovereignty and Freedom of Choice for All Criminal Defendants, 31 Am. Crim. L. Rev. 73, 83-96 (1993).

422. A 1992 study of indigent defense systems in nine state courts of general jurisdiction found that indigent defenders handled their cases more expeditiously and at least as competently as private counsel. Roger Hansen et al., Indigent Defenders Get the Job Done and Done Well 103-104 (1992). For a study of constitutional and ethical problems under contract delivery systems, see Kelly A. Hardy, Comment, Contracting for Indigent Defense: Providing Another Forum for Skeptics to Question Attorneys' Ethics, 80 Marq. L. Rev. 1053 (1997).

through a coordinated assigned-counsel system and may also include contracts for services. No program should be precluded from representing clients in any particular type or category of case.

The comments explain the justification for a mixed system as follows:

When adequately funded and staffed, defender organizations employing full-time personnel are capable of providing excellent defense services. By devoting all of their efforts to legal representation, defender programs ordinarily are able to develop unusual expertise in handling various kinds of criminal cases. Moreover, defender offices frequently are in the best position to supply counsel soon after an accused is arrested. By virtue of their experience, full-time defenders are also able to work for changes in laws and procedures aimed at benefitting defendants and the criminal justice system.

There are also definite purposes served by retaining the presence of substantial private bar participation in the system for criminal defense. Just as private attorneys often can learn from the full-time lawyers of defender organizations, there are many private attorneys, qualified by training and experience, who can contribute substantially to the knowledge of defenders. In addition, a "mixed" system of representation consisting of both private attorneys and full-time defenders offers a "safety valve," so that the caseload pressures on each group are less likely to be burdensome.

In some cities, where a mixed system has been absent and public defenders have been required to handle all of the cases, the results have been unsatisfactory. Caseloads have increased faster than the size of staffs and necessary revenues, making quality legal representation exceedingly difficult. Furthermore, the involvement of private attorneys in defense services assures the continued interest of the bar in the welfare of the criminal justice system. Without the knowledgeable and active support of the bar as a whole, continued improvements in the nation's justice system are rendered less likely.

Finally, private attorney representation in criminal cases is essential because of new and stricter policies within defense services programs regarding conflicts of interest, primarily in representation of codefendants. In some cases, these policies can result in the declaration of conflicts of interest in more than 25 percent of all cases assigned to a public defender program.[423]

423. ABA Standards for Criminal Justice, Providing Defense Services Standard 5-1.2, cmt. (1992).

The Standards then set forth guidelines for various aspects of defense services systems. Some of the more important guidelines include the following:

    1. Funding and eligibility. The Standards call for funding of the full cost of defense services sufficient to provide quality representation to all eligible persons. Standard 5-1.6.[424] The Standards go on to define eligible persons as those "who are financially unable to obtain adequate representation without substantial hardship." Standard 5-7.1. The commentary stresses the need for adoption of detailed written guidelines to implement the eligibility standard.

    2. Professional independence. Standard 5-1.3 provides that lawyers should be "free from political influence and should be subject to judicial supervision only in the same manner and to the same extent as are lawyers in private practice." Selection of lawyers for specific cases should be made by administrators of the state's plan for providing defense services rather than by the judiciary or elected officials. To support the independence of public defender organizations, the Standard recommends that they be governed by independent boards of trustees that have the power to set general policy but not to interfere in particular cases.

    3. Assigned counsel. The Standards call for a plan for assignment of counsel implemented by administrators rather than ad hoc assignments by judges. Standard 5-2.1. Eligibility for assignments should be as widely distributed as possible among qualified members of the bar, but the Standards reject the notion that cases should be assigned to all members of the bar regardless of qualifications. Standard 5-2.2. The Standards state that cases should be assigned to lawyers "experienced and active in trial practice, and familiar with the practice and procedure of the criminal courts." Standard 5-2.2. The assignment plan should set forth specific qualification standards for particular types of cases. The Standards state that a lawyer "should not seek to avoid appointment by a tribunal to represent a person except for good cause."

424. The ABA has conducted a number of studies showing persistent underfunding of the justice system. See ABA, Special Comm. on Funding the Justice System, Striving for Solutions: An Overview of Crisis Points in America's System of Justice (1995).

Model Rule 6.2 is similar. Assigned counsel should receive prompt compensation at reasonable hourly rates and should be reimbursed for out-of-pocket expenses. Compensation should be paid for all hours necessary to provide quality representation. Standard 5-2.4.

4.   *Defender systems.*   The Standards call for the selection of the chief defender and staff on the basis of merit, and prohibit their selection by judges. Compensation for the chief defender and staff should be comparable to that for prosecutors. Standard 5-4.1.

5.   *Workload.*   The Standards provide that regardless of the type of system, whether defender, assigned counsel, or contract, lawyers should not accept excessive workloads that interfere with rendering quality representation. Standard 5-5.3. The comments refer to various methods for measuring caseloads and workloads. One standard mentioned as a rough measure of caseload for full-time attorneys was that of the National Advisory Commission on Criminal Justice:

- 150 felonies per attorney per year
- 400 misdemeanors per attorney per year
- 200 juvenile cases per attorney per year
- 200 mental commitment cases per attorney per year
- 25 appeals per attorney per year

Attorneys employed less than full time or who handled a mix of cases would handle a proportionate caseload. The commentary refers to a Florida study indicating that in capital cases an appropriate caseload was five cases per attorney per year when the defendant was not under a warrant of death and three cases per attorney per year when a warrant for execution had been issued.[425]

425. For a criticism of inadequate funding of indigent defense and a call for systemic litigation to alleviate the problem, see Richard Klein, The Eleventh Commandment: Thou Shalt Not Be Compelled to Render the Ineffective Assistance of Counsel, 68 Ind. L.J. 363 (1993). See also Charles J. Ogletree, Jr., An Essay on the New Public Defender for the 21st Century, 58 Law & Contemp. Probs. 81, 93 (Winter, 1995)(discussing problems facing public defenders and proposing creation of Defender Services Center that "would focus on providing pervasive ongoing defense attorney training and on developing and sustaining a positive office culture").

Chapter 3

Ethical Issues in Civil Litigation: The Client-Lawyer Relationship, Confidentiality, and Conflicts of Interest

This chapter turns from criminal to civil litigation. Section A examines various aspects of the fiduciary relationship between lawyers and clients, including attorney fees, scope of representation, authority of attorneys, and withdrawal from representation. Confidentiality is the topic of section B, which includes problems on the use of the Internet, the scope of the attorney-client privilege, and the work product doctrine. Section C addresses the various types of conflicts of interest: representation against current clients, representation against former clients, and conflicts when the lawyer may be required to be a witness in a case. Further, some areas of practice, such as tort litigation, insurance defense, and marital practice, pose special conflict of interest problems.

A. The Client-Lawyer Relationship

─────────────── **Problem 3-1** ───────────────

Contingent Fees, Expenses, and Fee Splitting

Harriet Carnes, an employee of Johnson Manufacturing Company, injured her leg while working on the job. Evidence indicates that the doctor who treated her injury, Ronald Dawson, was negligent, resulting in the amputation of her leg.

Carnes retained Isabel Lopez to represent her in obtaining workers' compensation benefits for her injury. Because Lopez does not handle medical malpractice cases, she suggested that Carnes retain a medical malpractice expert. Lopez recommended Herbert Atlee and offered to contact him on Carnes's behalf. Carnes agreed, and Lopez discussed the case with Atlee. Atlee said that his standard fee for medical malpractice cases was a 45 percent contingent fee, which included a 10 percent fee to the referring lawyer, with the client being responsible for all expenses. Lopez informed Carnes of Atlee's fee arrangements, and told Carnes that she would continue to be involved in the case on a consulting basis. Carnes then met with Atlee and signed a written contingent fee agreement providing for a 45 percent contingent fee and stating that Carnes was responsible for all expenses.

Atlee was able to negotiate a settlement of the medical malpractice action for $100,000, which Carnes agreed to accept. Carnes signed a general release and received a check for $40,000. When Carnes received the check, she was uncertain how Atlee had computed her $40,000 payment, but she was hesitant to ask. A few days later she was still troubled by the amount of the check, so she called Atlee's office and spoke to his secretary, who told Carnes that the amount of her check was determined as follows:

Settlement proceeds	$100,000
Less 45% fee	(45,000)
Less expert witness fee of 10%	(10,000)
Less other expenses	(5,000)
Proceeds to client	$40,000

Carnes asked about the "other expenses" and was told that these included copying, travel, and overhead. Carnes has come to you for advice about her settlement. She says that she doesn't feel that she was fairly treated and she wants to know what, if anything, she can do about it.

Read Model Rules 1.5, 1.8(e), 1.15, 3.4, and comments.

The ethical obligation to charge reasonable fees

Disciplinary Rule 2-106(A) of the Code of Professional Responsibility provided that a lawyer "shall not enter into an agreement for, charge, or collect an illegal or clearly excessive fee." The Model Rules include a somewhat more stringent standard for legal fees. Model Rule 1.5(a) states that a "lawyer's fee shall be reasonable" (as contrasted with the "clearly excessive" standard of the Code).

Courts regulate the reasonableness of lawyers' fees in three important ways.[1] First, courts can discipline lawyers for charging excessive fees.[2] Unfortunately, some studies have provided distressing documentation of lawyers' improper billing practices, such as double billing (for example, billing two clients for the time spent in preparing a research memo involving an issue applicable

---

1. See generally Wolfram, Modern Legal Ethics §9.1 (discussing supervisory power that courts exercise over fee agreements).
2. E.g., Bushman v. State Bar, 522 P.2d 312 (Cal. 1974) (en banc) (exorbitant fee in divorce case); In re Teichner, 470 N.E.2d 972 (Ill. 1984) (improper to charge 25 percent contingent fee for collection of life insurance proceeds when no dispute with company), *cert. denied,* 470 U.S. 1053 (1985); see Dale R. Agthe, Annotation, Attorney's Charging Excessive Fee as Ground for Disciplinary Action, 11 A.L.R.4th 133 (1982).

to both clients) and undisclosed markups on costs.[3] In response to these abuses, the ABA Committee on Ethics and Professional Responsibility issued Formal Opinion 93-379 in which it addressed a number of issues regarding fees and expenses. The ABA committee advised lawyers who bill strictly on an hourly basis that it is improper for lawyers to charge more than the actual time expended. Thus lawyers who have agreed to charge their clients on an hourly basis could not ethically double bill for court appearances, travel time, or for work product used in more than one case. The ABA's opinion indicated, however, that lawyers could agree to alternative methods of billing that were not strictly time based, provided the method was fully disclosed to the client. Similarly, the committee reasoned that lawyers could not charge more than the actual cost of expenses, absent full disclosure to the client. Other professional organizations have also taken steps to control improper billing practices.[4]

Second, courts have the power to reduce the amount of fees charged by attorneys if the court finds the fee to be unreasonable. The issue could arise in a variety of ways: in an action by the client to recover from the attorney an excessive fee retained by the attorney, in an action by the attorney to collect a fee, or in a collateral proceeding or motion incident to a matter already in court.[5] In

3. The seminal work has been done by Lisa Lerman. See Lisa G. Lerman, Lying to Clients, 138 U. Pa. L. Rev. 659 (1990) and Scenes from a Law Firm, 50 Rutgers L. Rev. 2153 (1998). See also William G. Ross, The Honest Hour: The Ethics of Time-Based Billing by Attorneys (1996); Sonia S. Chan, ABA Formal Opinion 93-379: Double Billing, Padding and Other Forms of Overbilling, 9 Geo. J. Legal Ethics 611 (1996); Conference on Gross Profits, 22 Hofstra L. Rev. 625 (1994). See In re Disciplinary Proceeding Against Haskell, 962 P.2d 813 (Wash. 1998) (en banc) (only attorney in firm authorized to do work for insurance company suspended for two years for having associates use his initials on their bills, for charging personal expenses to client, and for billing for unauthorized travel expenses).

4. See ABA, Task Force on Lawyer Business Ethics, Statements of Principles, 51 Bus. Law. 745 (1996) (statements on billing for legal services, billing disbursements and other charges, and marketing legal services).

5. E.g., In re A. H. Robins Co. (Bergstrom v. Dalkon Shield Claimants Trust), 86 F.3d 364 (4th Cir.), *cert. denied*, 519 U.S. 993 (1996) (courts have inherent power to determine reasonableness of contingent fees; 10 percent limit for supplementary distribution in Dalkon Shield case); McKenzie Constr., Inc. v. Maynard, 758 F.2d 97, 101 (3d Cir. 1985) (in action by client to recover portion of contingent fee retained by lawyer, court should determine reasonableness of fee based on circumstances surrounding negotiation and performance,

addition, fee disputes between lawyer and client can be resolved through arbitration before a fee dispute resolution board established pursuant to court rule.[6] Third, in some cases the court must determine a reasonable fee because the fee will be paid by the defendant pursuant to statute, court rule, or contract.[7] Problem 6-4 deals with determination of legal fees under statutes providing for "fee shifting."

The ethical duty to inform the client of the basis or rate of the fee

Model Rule 1.5(b) imposes obligations on lawyers to reach clear agreements with their clients about the manner in which lawyers charge for their services: "When the lawyer has not regularly represented the client, the basis or rate of the fee shall be communicated to the client, preferably in writing, before or within a reasonable time after commencing the representation." Lawyers charge fees for their services in a wide variety of ways. The fee can be determined strictly on an *hourly basis*; under this method, the fee is computed by multiplying the number of hours worked on the matter by each lawyer (or paralegal) times the hourly rate for that provider. Hourly rates for lawyers and paralegals are set based on their experience and type of practice in comparison with the fees commonly charged by other lawyers and paralegals providing similar services. Hourly fees are quite common in business and tax matters; lawyers engaged in civil defense litigation also typically bill on a hourly basis.

Contingent fees are normally used by plaintiffs' lawyers in personal injury matters. The essence of the contingent fee is that the lawyer's right to receive compensation is contingent on the client's receiving an award, either by settlement or judgment. Typically, contingent fees are based on a percentage of the amount recov-

---

but "courts should be reluctant to disturb contingent fee arrangements freely entered into by knowledgeable and competent parties"); Kirby v. Liska, 351 N.W.2d 421 (Neb. 1984) (in action by attorney to collect fee in quiet title action, court reduced fee from $65,340 to $6,500 based on time and difficulty of matter).

6. See ABA Model Rules for Fee Arbitration, Laws. Man. on Prof. Conduct (ABA/BNA) 01:4001 et seq.

7. See, e.g., Evans v. Jeff D., 475 U.S. 717 (1986) (dealing with recovery of attorney fees under federal fee-shifting statutes).

ered, and normally the fee varies depending on the stage at which the matter is concluded. Thus, a common contingent fee in a personal injury action is 25 percent if the matter is settled before trial, 33 percent if the matter is settled after a jury is selected, and 50 percent if the matter is concluded after appeal.

The major justification for contingent fees is that they allow people who could not afford an attorney to obtain access to the legal system for vindication of their rights. It is interesting to note that contingent fees are considered improper in many other countries. The difference in attitude toward contingency fees between the United States and other nations reflects deeper cultural factors and institutional arrangements. In many other countries, litigation is viewed as an evil, while in the United States litigation is often a mechanism for vindication of important rights. In addition, many other countries provide access to the legal system by regulating legal fees and by providing for shifting of fees to the losing party.[8] Although the United States is experiencing trends in those directions, legal fees in this country continue to be largely a matter of contract between the client and the lawyer.

While the use of contingent fees in the United States is well established, contingent fees have been criticized on the ground that in some cases they are unreasonable when compared to the risk of nonrecovery.[9] To take an extreme example, suppose a widow retained an attorney to represent her regarding administration of her husband's estate. If the attorney charged the client a contingency fee for collecting life insurance proceeds on the husband's estate when no bona fide dispute with the insurance company existed, the attorney fee would clearly be excessive.[10] As a result, some scholars have proposed limitations on contingent fees.[11]

8. Restatement (Third) of the Law Governing Lawyers §47, cmt. *b*.

9. See Frederick B. MacKinnon, Contingent Fees for Legal Services 157-211 (1964). See also Restatement (Third) of the Law Governing Lawyers §47, cmt. *b*.

10. See White v. McBride, 937 S.W.2d 796 (Tenn. 1996) (one-third contingent-fee for estate administration was clearly excessive; quantum meruit recovery also denied).

11. Lester Brickman, Contingent Fees Without Contingencies: *Hamlet Without the Prince of Denmark?* 37 UCLA L. Rev. 29 (1989) (contingent fees proper only when case involves risk and fee must be proportional to risk); Kevin M. Clermont & John D. Currivan, Improving on the Contingent Fee, 63 Cornell

The Restatement of the Law Governing Lawyers indicates that contingent fees can be unreasonable in two situations: "those in which there was a high likelihood of substantial recovery by trial or settlement, so that the lawyer bore little risk of nonpayment; and those in which the client's recovery was likely to be so large that the lawyer's fee would clearly exceed the sum appropriate to pay for services performed and risks assumed."[12]

One recent proposal has attempted to resolve the problem of determining the risk-free amount of damages involved in personal injury litigation by imposing a duty on plaintiff's counsel to seek early settlement offers from the defendant.[13] The amount of the early settlement offer would then become the riskless amount against which plaintiff's counsel could not ethically charge a contingency fee. The principal features of the proposal are as follows:

(1)   Contingency fees cannot be charged against settlement offers made prior to the retention of counsel by personal injury claimants.

(2)   Defendants in personal injury cases receive the opportunity to make early settlement offers in personal injury cases, but only if made within 60 days from receipt from plaintiffs' counsel of a demand for compensation. If the offer is accepted, plaintiffs' counsel fees are limited to hourly rate charges and are capped at 10 percent of the first $100,000 of the offer and 5 percent of any greater amounts.

L. Rev. 529 (1978) (proposing contingent fee consisting of two components: hourly charge plus small percentage of amount by which recovery exceeds time charge); Stewart Jay, The Dilemmas of Attorney Contingent Fees, 2 Geo. J. Legal Ethics 813 (1989) (contingent fees should be eliminated in wide range of cases); Murray L. Schwartz & Daniel J. B. Mitchell, An Economic Analysis of the Contingent Fee in Personal-Injury Litigation, 22 Stan. L. Rev. 1125 (1970) (using economic analysis to analyze justifications for contingency fees and arguing for experimentation with alternative methods because risk of nonrecovery has diminished). See also Thomas J. Miceli, Do Contingent Fees Promote Excessive Litigation? 23 J. Legal Stud. 211 (1994) (economic analysis does not support the conclusion that contingent fees lead to excessive litigation).

12.   Restatement (Third) of the Law Governing Lawyers §47, cmt. *c*.

13.   For a description of one insurance company's effort to eliminate lawyers by making early settlement offers to accident victims, see Richard C. Reuben, Insurer Out to Eliminate Middleman, 82-Sept. A.B.A. J. 20 (1996) (Allstate's early settlement offer program). See also Annette Wencl & David Strickland, Allstate's "Customer Service" Charade, Trial 42 (September 1999).

(3)   Demands for settlement by plaintiffs' counsel must include basic, routinely discoverable information in order to assist defendants in evaluating plaintiffs' claims. To assist plaintiffs in evaluating defendants' offers, discoverable material "in the . . . [defendant's] possession concerning the alleged injury upon which [the defendant] relied in making his offer of settlement" must be made available to plaintiffs for a settlement offer to be effective.

(4)   If early offers are rejected, contingency fees may only be charged against net recoveries in excess of those offers.

(5)   If no offer is made within the 60-day period, contingency fee contracts are unaffected by the proposal.[14]

In Formal Opinion 94-389, the ABA Committee on Ethics and Professional Responsibility rejected the proposal. The committee decided that contingent fees were generally proper even in cases in which liability was clear and some recovery certain, provided the client was fully informed of and consented to the contingency fee:

[T]he Committee is of the view that the argument may rest on a faulty notion as to the number of cases regarding which at the onset of the engagement the lawyer can say with certainty that the client will recover. Defendants often vigorously defend and even win cases where liability seems certain. Additionally, a previously undiscovered fact or an unexpected change in the law can suddenly transform a case that seemed a sure winner at the outset of representation into a certain loser. . . .

Moreover, even in cases where there is no risk of nonrecovery, and the lawyer and client are certain that liability is clear and will be conceded, a fee arrangement contingent on the amount recovered may nonetheless be reasonable. As the increasing popularity of reverse contingent fees demonstrates, for almost all cases there is a range of possible recoveries. Since the amount of the recovery will be largely determined by the lawyer's knowledge, skill,

14. See Michael Horowitz, Making Ethics Real, Making Ethics Work: A Proposal for Contingency Fee Reform, 44 Emory L. J. 173, 175-176 (1995). (proposal made by Mr. Horowitz, Professor Jeffrey O'Connell of the University of Virginia Law School, and Professor Lester Brickman of Cardozo Law School). For a more detailed presentation of the proposal in the form of a proposed court rule or statute, see id. at 194-211.

experience and time expended, both the defendant and the plaintiff may best be served by a contingency fee arrangement that ties the lawyer's fee to the amount recovered.

Also, an early settlement offer is often prompted by the defendant's recognition of the ability of the plaintiff's lawyer fairly and accurately to value the case and to proceed effectively through trial and appeals if necessary. There is no ethical reason why the lawyer is not entitled to an appropriate consideration for this value that his engagement has brought to the case, even though it results in an early resolution.[15]

The committee also found no support in the Model Rules or the Model Code for imposing an obligation on plaintiff's counsel to solicit early settlement offers.[16] The committee did note in its opinion that rules of ethics impose some limitations on contingency fees, including the requirement of reasonableness. See Model Rule 1.5(a). Professor Lester Brickman, one of the authors of the proposal submitted to the ABA committee, has criticized the ABA opinion for ignoring the fundamental issue: whether it is proper for lawyers to charge a *standard* contingency fee in cases in which liability is certain. Brickman contends that the ABA committee acts in the financial and political interests of lawyers rather than the public.[17]

Fixed fees are often employed in routine estate planning and real estate matters. Thus, a lawyer might charge a fee of $500 to examine title and prepare documents to close a residential real estate transaction. A fixed fee could also be based on a percentage of the value of the transaction. Thus, in some jurisdictions lawyers charge a fixed percentage of the value of the assets in an estate to handle the legal work involved in administration of a decedent's estate. We will consider in Problem 5-4 the propriety of such a percentage fee. One point to note here is that although this fee is expressed as a percentage, it is not a contingent fee.

Some lawyers use a *value-billing* approach. Under this method the lawyer does not set the fee in advance but rather determines the fee at the conclusion of the matter, taking into account a variety

15. ABA Comm. on Ethics and Prof. Resp., Formal Op. 94-389, at 8-9.
16. Id. at 8.
17. Lester Brickman, ABA Regulation of Contingency Fees: Money Talks, Ethics Walks, 65 Fordham L. Rev. 247 (1996).

of factors. A common method of setting a fee under a value-billing approach involves two steps. First, the lawyer computes the "lodestar" fee (i.e., a fee determined by multiplying the hours worked on the matter by the hourly rates of the attorneys and paralegals who performed services in the matter). Second, the lawyer adjusts the lodestar fee either upward or downward depending on various factors, such as results obtained and the time pressure for handling the matter.

Various combinations of fees are also possible. For example, in a personal injury matter, a lawyer might charge a client a fixed fee of a certain amount coupled with a percentage of the recovery. Presumably, the percentage in this case would be less than in a pure contingency matter since the lawyer would face less risk because of the fixed fee. Some lawyers have begun charging fees based on a *blended rate*, a single rate that applies to both lawyers and paralegals. This method of billing may be attractive to clients because the hourly rate for services rendered is less than that charged for lawyers, while also being desirable for lawyers because it allows lawyers to increase their profit margins by having the work done by employees who cost the least. Some firms have also experimented with fees computed on an hourly basis, coupled with a bonus for a successful outcome.[18]

For a number of years in many jurisdictions, bar associations established minimum *fee schedules* that lawyers were required to use in setting their fees. In 1975 the Supreme Court declared fee schedules to be invalid in violation of the antitrust laws.[19]

In some cases a prevailing party may be entitled to court-awarded fees. In Evans v. Jeff D.[20] the Supreme Court held that court-awarded fees belong to the plaintiff. The plaintiff in turn is required to compensate her attorney pursuant to the engagement agreement between them. Thus, court-awarded fees are a credit against the amount the plaintiff owes her attorney; if the

[handwritten margin note: Minimum Fee Structures are invalid]

---

18. For a discussion of innovative billing techniques, see Bradford W. Hildebrandt ed., Alternative Pricing Practices (PLI 1995); Richard C. Reed ed., Billing Innovations (ABA 1996). For a discussion of the ethical implications of alternative billing methods for business lawyers, see Committee on Lawyer Business Ethics, Business and Ethics Implications of Alternative Billing Practices: Report on Alternative Billing Arrangements, 54-Nov. Bus. Law. 175 (1998).

19. Goldfarb v. Virginia State Bar, 421 U.S. 773 (1975).

20. 475 U.S. 717 (1986).

court-awarded fees exceed the contractual amount, the plaintiff keeps the excess. Hazard & Hodes point out, however, that the parties should be free to contract for a different arrangement. For example, the plaintiff and her lawyer could agree that court-awarded fees go "into the pot" with other damages, all subject to a percentage fee. Or, the parties could agree that the court-awarded fee would be the only amount that the attorney would receive.[21]

Recall that in connection with Problem 2-2 we discussed the use of retainers and lawyers' trust account obligations.

Special ethical duties regarding contingent fees

Model Rule 1.5(c) imposes special requirements with regard to contingent fees. Agreements for contingent fees must

- be in writing
- state the method by which the fee is computed, including the percentages if the matter is concluded by settlement, trial, or appeal
- identify litigation or other expenses that the client is responsible to pay
- state whether expenses are deducted before or after the contingent fee percentage is computed

The rule also requires lawyers to provide clients with a written settlement statement at the conclusion of the matter stating the outcome and showing how the client's remittance is computed. Violation of these requirements will not necessarily result in forfeiture of the lawyer's fee. For example, if the lawyer fails to obtain a written contingency fee agreement, but the client does not contest the amount of the fee, the lawyer will probably be able to recover at least for the reasonable value of the lawyer's services.[22]

---

21. 1 Hazard & Hodes, The Law of Lawyering §1.5:104.

22. Restatement (Third) of the Law Governing Lawyers §46, cmt. *g*. But see Estate of Pinter v. McGee, 679 A.2d 728 (N.J. Super. Ct. App. Div. 1996) (failure to put contingency fee agreement in writing bars claim for quantum meruit).

Some states, either by statute or court rule, have imposed limitations on contingent fee percentages.[23]

When a client receives a lump-sum settlement, the lawyer's contingent fee, like other expenses, is paid at the time of the settlement. But suppose the client agrees to a structured settlement. In the typical structured settlement, the client receives a lump-sum payment coupled with periodic payments either directly from the defendant or perhaps through an annuity issued by an insurance company. When is the attorney's contingent fee paid under a structured settlement? Courts have generally upheld fee agreements in which the client agrees to pay the lawyer's contingent fee out of any lump-sum payment, even if the lawyer would be receiving the bulk of the lump sum. If the fee agreement provides for payment of the lawyer's contingent fee out of the lump-sum settlement, the amount of fee would be based on the present value of the settlement or the cost of the annuity if the settlement was being funded through an annuity.[24] In the absence of an agreement allowing the lawyer to be paid out of the lump-sum payment, the lawyer's contingent fee would be paid pro rata out of each payment received by the client.[25]

In certain cases contingent fee agreements are professionally improper. We have already encountered the rule that prohibits a lawyer from receiving a contingent fee in a criminal case. Model Rule 1.5(d)(2). See Problem 2-2. Rule 1.5(d)(1) states that contingent fees are improper in domestic relations matters when the amount of the fee is "contingent upon the securing of a divorce or upon the amount of alimony or support, or property settlement in lieu thereof." Two rationales support the rule. First, public policy favors reconciliation in domestic cases. If contingent fees were

23. See Fla. R. Prof. Conduct 4-1.5(f)(4); N.J. Sup. Ct. R. 1:21-7. See also Cal. Bus. & Prof. Code §6146 (limitations on contingent fees in claims against health care providers).

24. See Nguyen v. Los Angeles County Harbor/UCLA Medical Center, 48 Cal. Rptr. 2d 301 (Ct. App. 1996); Restatement (Third) of the Law Governing Lawyers §47, cmt. *e*. See also In re Fox, 490 S.E.2d 265 (S.C. 1997) (lawyer disciplined for taking fee up-front on basis of full amount of structured settlement; court holds that cost method is proper approach for valuation of structured settlements).

25. In re Myers, 663 N.E.2d 771 (Ind. 1996) (in absence of agreement lawyer cannot take total fee in structured settlement out of initial payment to client). See Restatement (Third) of the Law Governing Lawyers §47, cmt. *e*.

permitted in divorce cases, the lawyer's financial interest would be inconsistent with that public policy. Second, contingent fees are unnecessary to secure counsel in divorce cases. A spouse with assets can afford counsel, and in most jurisdictions courts will require the spouse with assets to pay a reasonable attorney fee if the other spouse is unable to afford counsel.[26] Since the rule applies only when the fee is contingent on divorce or settlement in lieu of divorce, it should not prohibit contingent fees to collect past-due alimony and child support because the policy in favor of reconciliation is not involved in these cases.

Divorce statutes usually allow the court to award either of the parties attorney fees or "suit money." Under such statutes, courts must determine the amount of a reasonable attorney fee. Some courts have held that a judicial enhancement of the lodestar amount to take into account the results obtained in the case constitutes an improper contingent fee in a domestic case.[27]

Contingent fees are typically charged by plaintiff's counsel. May a defense attorney charge a contingent fee? In Wunschel Law Firm, P. C. v. Clabaugh,[28] the Iowa Supreme Court held that a defense contingent fee based on a percentage of the difference between the amount demanded by the plaintiff in the complaint and the amount the defendant was required to pay was void as against public policy. The court reasoned that a defense percentage contingent fee in unliquidated tort cases was likely to produce unreasonable fees because the amount demanded in the complaint does not bear a logical relationship to the amount of any recovery. The Model Rules do not address the issue, but in Formal Opinion 93-373 the ABA Committee on Ethics and Professional Responsibility ruled that defense contingent-fee contracts were not unethical per se under the Model Rules. The committee stated that "the *Wunschel* court quite properly condemned the use of the prayer for relief as the sole basis for calculating a reverse contingent fee," but the committee went on to assert that in other cases defense contingent fees could be reasonable and in the best interest of the client.

---

26. Restatement (Third) of the Law Governing Lawyers §47, cmt. *g.*
27. State ex rel. Oklahoma Bar Assn. v. Fagin, 848 P.2d 11 (Okla. 1992); Glasscock v. Glasscock, 403 S.E.2d 313 (S.C. 1991). *Contra* Eckell v. Wilson, 597 A.2d 696 (Pa. Super. Ct. 1991), *appeal denied,* 607 A.2d 253 (Pa. 1992).
28. 291 N.W.2d 331 (Iowa 1980).

Comment 3 to Rule 1.5 states: "When there is doubt whether a contingent fee is consistent with the client's best interest, the lawyer should offer the client alternative bases for the fee and explain their implications." In Informal Opinion 86-1521, the ABA Committee on Ethics and Professional Responsibility ruled that an attorney should not unilaterally set a contingent fee but should give a client who is in a position to pay a fixed fee the option of either a reasonable fixed fee or a contingent fee.

Ethical obligations regarding expenses

Deposition costs, expert witness fees, copying charges, and travel expenses all make litigation costly. Who is responsible for these expenses? Lawyers act as agents for their clients; since the client is the principal, the client is legally responsible for the expenses of litigation. If the lawyer has advanced the expense on behalf of the client, the client is legally obligated to indemnify the lawyer.[29] Although the client is ultimately responsible for these expenses, the lawyer may also be liable to the provider of the service. For example, in Cahn v. Fisher[30] the Arizona Court of Appeals held that while a client is responsible for litigation costs, based on "custom and usage," an attorney was also legally responsible for paying a court reporter's charges when the attorney orders a transcript.[31]

While the client is legally responsible for expenses of litigation, many clients may not be able to afford these costs. May lawyers lend or advance litigation expenses on behalf of their clients? At common law the crime of *maintenance* prohibited advances of money to pay expenses or otherwise support litigation. A related offense, *champerty,* involved the purchase of a portion of the lawsuit. The evil to be prevented in both cases was "stirring up" litigation.[32] A more modern rationale for the prohibition against

29. Restatement (Third) of the Law Governing Lawyers §29(2).

30. 805 P.2d 1040 (Ariz. Ct. App. 1991, *review denied*).

31. See Boesch v. Marilyn M. Jones & Assocs., 712 N.E.2d 1061 (Ind. Ct. App. 1999) (lawyer liable for court reporter's fee when lawyer retained reporter without expressly disclaiming responsibility for payment); Restatement (Third) of the Law Governing Lawyers §42(2)(b) (lawyer liable to third person who provides goods or services used by lawyer and who relies on lawyer's credit unless liability is disclaimed).

32. Wolfram, Modern Legal Ethics §8.13, at 489-490.

lawyers' advancing expenses (other than expenses of litigation) to their clients is that lawyers become creditors, with interests adverse to those of their clients. An adverse financial interest may cause the lawyer to conduct the litigation to protect the lawyer's rather than the client's interest. This justification is weak, however, because advances of litigation expenses are often quite substantial. In addition, contingent fee agreements also give lawyers an interest in litigation that may cause them to conduct the litigation to protect their interests over those of their clients. Yet contingent fee agreements are ethically permissible. The traditional prohibitions have been gradually relaxed so that lawyers can now advance "court costs and expenses of litigation," with repayment contingent on the outcome of the case. See Model Rule 1.8(e)(1).[33] The Model Rules go even further in the case of indigent clients, allowing lawyers to agree to pay litigation expenses with no responsibility for repayment. Model Rule 1.8(e)(2). While the rules of professional conduct allow lawyers to advance litigation expenses, lawyers are not required to do so. Lawyers may demand that clients make expense deposits and may bill them periodically for expenses incurred in their cases.

Although the rules of ethics permit lawyers to advance litigation expenses on behalf of clients, the rules still prohibit attorneys from making general advances or loans. Thus, in Formal Opinion 288, the ABA Committee on Ethics and Professional Responsibility stated:

> For a lawyer to make advances to an injured client to cover subsistence for him and for the members of his family while the case is pending, does not constitute the advancement of expenses, the latter term referring to court costs, witness fees and expenses resulting from the conduct of the litigation itself, and not expenses unconnected with the litigation, although resulting from the accident.

The prohibition against advancing living expenses to clients appears to extend to loan guarantees as well. Disciplinary Rule 5-103(B) states that a lawyer must not "advance or guarantee financial assistance." Model Rule 1.8(e) states that a lawyer may not "provide financial assistance," without mentioning guarantees,

---

33. See also Restatement (Third) of the Law Governing Lawyers §48(2)(a).

but Professor Wolfram argues that the change in wording is not significant and that the Model Rules as well as the Code were intended to prohibit a lawyer from helping the client to obtain a loan on the lawyer's credit.[34] Presumably a lawyer could, however, assist a client in obtaining a loan for living expenses so long as the lawyer did not make a guarantee to the lender.

Early drafts of the Model Rules would have allowed lawyers to advance living expenses to clients, but this proposal was rejected in Model Rule 1.8(e).[35] The drafters of the Restatement of the Law Governing Lawyers proposed to change the rule. Proposed section 48(2) would have allowed a lawyer to

> [m]ake or guarantee a loan on fair terms, the repayment of which to the lawyer may be contingent on the outcome of the matter, if: (i) the loan is needed to enable the client to withstand delay in litigation that otherwise might unjustly induce the client to settle or dismiss a case because of financial hardship rather than on the merits; and (ii) if the lawyer does not promise or offer the loan before being retained.

The American Law Institute, however, ultimately decided to reject this proposal in favor of the traditional prohibition against advancement of living expenses. Some courts have allowed lawyers to advance living expenses to their clients for humanitarian reasons, while others continue to apply the traditional prohibition.[36] What litigation expenses may lawyers properly charge to their clients? Expenses involved in litigation commonly include the following: filing fees, costs of transcribing depositions, fees of expert witnesses, travel expenses, photocopying, long-distance telephone or fax charges, and computer research charges. In Formal Opinion 93-379, the ABA Committee on Ethics and Professional Responsibility considered various billing practices by lawyers. The com-

---

34. Wolfram, Modern Legal Ethics §9.2.3, at 509 n.87.

35. ABA Comm. on Evaluation of Prof. Standards, Model Rules of Prof. Conduct Rule 1.8(e)(1) (Prop. Final Draft, May 30, 1981).

36. See Florida Bar v. Taylor, 648 So. 2d 1190 (Fla. 1994) (lawyer not subject to discipline for providing needy client with used clothing and $200 loan when lawyer acted for humanitarian reasons). But see In re Minor Child K.A.H., 967 P.2d 91 (Alaska 1998), cert. denied, 120 S. Ct. 57 (1999) (reimbursement denied to lawyer who advanced living expenses to client); Mississippi Bar v. Attorney HH, 671 So. 2d 1293 (Miss. 1995) (advancement of living expenses even for humanitarian purposes is improper).

mittee ruled that general office overhead (library, insurance, rent, utilities, and similar items) was not properly chargeable as an expense to clients absent disclosure to the client in advance of the engagement.[37] The committee also decided that lawyers could not ethically charge clients for expenses in excess of actual disbursements, absent disclosure to the contrary.[38] In other words, markups or surcharges on expenses are improper unless the client consents after clear disclosure from the lawyer. The committee also considered in-house provision of services, such as photocopying, in-house meals, and similar items. As to these expenses, absent agreement to the contrary, lawyers may not ethically charge more than "the direct cost associated with the service (i.e., the actual cost of making a copy on the photocopy machine) plus a reasonable allocation of overhead expenses directly associated with the provision of the service (e.g., the salary of a photocopy machine operator)," as determined by standard accounting methods.[39] In its opinion, the committee emphasized the lawyer's duty to disclose to clients at the beginning of the representation the basis of the fee and other charges to the client.[40]

An issue that comes up quite frequently in personal injury matters deals with a lawyer's obligation to make payments to third parties out of the proceeds of personal injury settlements. Clients often make assignments of a portion of the proceeds of their personal injury claims to providers of medical services or to businesses (for example, the client might assign proceeds to purchase a vehicle or to pay a debt). When the case is settled, however, the client may object to the lawyer honoring the assignment. Model Rule 1.15(b) provides that "a lawyer shall promptly deliver to the client or third person any funds or other property that the client or third person is entitled to receive." The rule recognizes that parties other than the client may have an interest in money that comes into the lawyer's possession. Comment 3 to Rule 1.15 provides that "under applicable law" a lawyer may have a duty to a third party that precludes the lawyer from surrendering funds to the client. When does applicable law provide such a duty? In some

---

37. ABA Comm. on Ethics and Prof. Resp., Formal Op. 93-379, at 8. See also Restatement (Third) of the Law Governing Lawyers §50(3)(a).

38. Formal Op. 93-379, at 9.

39. Id.

40. Id. at 3.

cases, statutes may provide for subrogation or lien rights of third-party providers. Courts have held that lawyers have a legal and ethical duty to honor any valid contractual assignment or statutory lien of which the lawyer has received notice.[41] In the event of a dispute between the client and a third party, a lawyer should hold the funds in trust until the dispute is resolved. See Model Rule 1.15(c).

Witness fees are a common litigation expense. Witnesses fall into two broad categories: fact witnesses and expert witnesses. The Model Rules provide that lawyers may not pay witnesses fees that are prohibited by law. Model Rule 3.4(b). As comment 3 indicates, the rule in most jurisdictions is that fact witnesses cannot be paid a fee for testifying, but they may be paid their expenses and any lost wages because of time spent in testifying.[42] In Formal Opinion 96-402, the ABA committee decided that lawyers could ethically pay fact witnesses a reasonable amount for their time in preparing for and in attending depositions. Expert witnesses may be paid reasonable fees for testifying, but the general rule is that expert witnesses may not be paid a fee contingent on their testimony or on the outcome of the case. Comment 3 to Rule 3.4(b).[43] The Restatement of the Law Governing Lawyers follows the Model Rules.[44]

41. E.g., Kaiser Found. Health Plan, Inc. v. Aguiluz, 54 Cal. Rptr. 2d 665 (Ct. App. 1996, *review denied*) (lawyer who disbursed entire settlement to client was liable to health care provider when lawyer had received notice of client's assignment to provider); Herzog v. Irace, 594 A.2d 1106 (Me. 1991) (lawyers liable to doctor for failure to honor assignment); Leon v. Martinez, 638 N.E.2d 511 (N.Y. 1994) (lawyer required to honor assignment of portion of personal injury proceeds made by client).

42. See Golden Door Jewelry Creations, Inc. v. Lloyds Underwriters Non-Marine Assn., 865 F. Supp. 1516 (S.D. Fla. 1994) *aff'd in part, rev'd in part*, 117 F.3d 1328 (11th Cir. 1997) (defendant violated Rule 3.4(b) by paying fact witnesses for their testimony; court ordered all testimony tainted by improper payments to be stricken).

43. See Swafford v. Harris, 967 S.W.2d 319 (Tenn. 1998) (contingency fee contract for services of physician acting as medico-legal expert in personal injury case is void as against public policy; physician also denied quantum meruit recovery). The District of Columbia Rules of Professional Conduct provide that an expert witness's fee may be contingent on the outcome of the case provided that the fee is not a percentage of the recovery. See D.C.R. Prof. Conduct 3.4, cmt. 8.

44. Restatement (Third) of the Law Governing Lawyers §177.

Fee splitting

The term *fee splitting* can refer to transactions with both nonlawyers and lawyers. Fee splitting with nonlawyers has traditionally been improper because the practice can undermine the independence of lawyers and promote the unauthorized practice of law. See Model Rule 5.4(a). We will examine the wisdom of the rules prohibiting fee splitting with nonlawyers in Chapter 7.

Fee splitting between lawyers occurs when lawyers who are not members of a firm divide a fee in a matter. Fee splitting can arise in a variety of ways, for example, referral of a matter from one lawyer to another, association of attorneys in a case to handle different aspects of the matter, completion of a case by a second lawyer after the first lawyer withdrew from representation or after the client discharged the lawyer, and continuation of compensation to a retired member by the lawyer's former firm.

The most controversial aspect of fee splitting arises when a lawyer receives a pure referral or forwarding fee without performing any services. For example, suppose a lawyer who practices business and commercial law has a client with a personal injury claim. The lawyer might refer the case to a litigation specialist and seek a referral fee, typically one-third of the personal injury lawyer's one-third contingent fee.

The argument against allowing lawyers to pay and to receive referral fees rests on two concerns: First, referral fees result in clients paying excessive legal fees. If the lawyer performing services can afford to pay the referring lawyer a fee when the referring lawyer has performed no service, then the client is being overcharged. Second, allowing referral fees could result in such unethical practices as solicitation of business.

Critics of the prohibition on referral fees respond, however, that these concerns do not justify the prohibition. First, if rules permitted referral fees, clients would not be overcharged because referral fees would give lawyers a financial incentive to turn matters over to specialists, who presumably can handle matters more efficiently and with a higher degree of competence than generalists. Second, any concern about unethical practices should be dealt with by regulating those practices directly. Critics of the prohibition on pure referral fees also point out that it creates an arbitrary discrimination against sole practitioners and small firms because it applies only to lawyers who are not members of a firm. Lawyers in large firms are free to divide fees based on their partnership or shareholder agreements.

Under the Code of Professional Responsibility a pure referral fee — one in which the referring lawyer did nothing more than make the referral and did not perform any substantial services in the matter — was unethical. The Code provided that lawyers not in the same firm could divide fees only if the "division is made in proportion to the services performed and responsibility assumed by each." DR 2-107(A)(2). (The Code also required that the client consent to the division and that the total fee be reasonable.) Despite this prohibition, the practice of referral fees appeared to be fairly widespread in the profession.[45]

The Model Rules have loosened the restriction on referral fees from that found in the Code of Professional Responsibility. Under Rule 1.5(e) a referral fee is permitted if:

(1) The division is in proportion to the services performed by each lawyer *or*, by written agreement with the client, each lawyer assumes joint responsibility for the representation;

(2) The client is advised of and does not object to the participation of all the lawyers involved; and

(3) The total fee is reasonable. [Emphasis added.]

The key change from the Code is that the Model Rules allow a referral fee even in the absence of services performed by the referring lawyer if by written agreement with the client, each lawyer assumes joint responsibility for the matter. When does a referring lawyer assume joint responsibility for the matter? Comment 4 provides: "Joint responsibility for the representation entails the obligations stated in Rule 5.1 for purposes of the matter involved." Rule 5.1, which deals with the obligations of partners and supervisory lawyers, states that a partner must take reasonable steps to ensure compliance by members of the firm with the Rules of Professional Conduct. Thus, a referring lawyer would assume joint responsibility if the lawyer undertook reasonable steps to make sure the lawyer handling the matter complied with the Rules of Professional Conduct. Periodic consultations on the strategy and progress of the matter should meet this requirement. When attor-

---

45. Wolfram, Modern Legal Ethics §9.2.4, at 510 (practice "both rife and virtually respectable in many communities").

neys not in the same firm enter into fee-splitting agreements, the referring attorney is likely to be liable for the malpractice of the attorney handling the matter.[46]

Professors Hazard and Hodes argue that the prohibition on pure referral fees should be repealed and lawyers allowed to act as "talent scouts."[47] Professor Wolfram argues that the Model Rule does not adequately address the issue of client consent because it only requires clients to be advised of the referral arrangement and "not object." He argues in favor of rules, like those adopted in California and Illinois, that require client consent after the client is fully informed about the terms and reasons for the fee-sharing arrangement.[48] It should be noted that many states in addition to California and Illinois have modified the ABA's version of Rule 1.5(e).[49]

Suppose lawyers enter into a fee-splitting agreement that violates Rule 1.5(e) (for example, suppose the lawyers fail to obtain a written agreement with the client regarding their joint responsibilities). Is the agreement between the lawyers unenforceable? The courts are divided on the issue of the contractual effect of a fee-splitting agreement that violates the Rules of Professional Conduct. Some courts refuse to enforce such an agreement because it violates public policy, while others will enforce the agreement under principles of estoppel to prevent unjust enrichment.[50]

46. See Noris v. Silver, 701 So. 2d 1238 (Fla. Dist. Ct. App. 1997).
47. 1 Hazard & Hodes, The Law of Lawyering §1.5:601.
48. Wolfram, Modern Legal Ethics §9.2.4, at 512.
49. See Laws. Man. on Prof. Conduct (ABA/BNA) 41:702-704.
50. *Compare* Christensen v. Eggen, 577 N.W.2d 221 (Minn. 1998) (fee-splitting agreement that violated Rule 1.5(e) was unenforceable) *with* King v. Housel, 556 N.E.2d 501 (Ohio 1990) (attorney estopped from claiming that fee-splitting agreement was invalid). See also Alan F. Post, Chartered v. Bregman, 707 A.2d 806 (Md. 1998) (depending on facts and circumstances, violation of ethics rule on division of fees may render fee-splitting agreement between lawyers not in same firm unenforceable).

———————— **Problem 3-2** ————————

Engagement and Nonengagement Agreements

MEMORANDUM

To: Associate
From: Partner
Date: —
Re: Engagement and nonengagement agreements

  a.   Approximately 90 percent of our firm's practice is personal injury. For a variety of reasons, our firm declines many more cases than it accepts. At our last partnership meeting, we discussed the firm's ethical obligations and possible malpractice liability when it rejects cases. Some firms use "nonengagement" letters when they reject cases. Please advise whether the firm has any malpractice exposure when it turns down cases, and please draft a nonengagement letter for consideration by the firm. In connection with this assignment, see the *Togstad* case, a summary of which is attached.

  b.   Attached also is a copy of the fee agreement that our firm is currently using in contingent fee matters. I would appreciate your reviewing the agreement and giving me your suggestions for revisions or additions.

———————————————————————————————

Read Model Rules 1.2(a), 1.4, 1.5, 1.8, 1.15, 1.16, 2.1, and comments.

TOGSTAD V. VESELY, OTTO, MILLER & KEEFE, 291 N.W.2d 686 (Minn. 1980): Ms. Togstad consulted with attorney Miller about a possible medical malpractice action involving her husband. She testified that after an interview lasting about 45 minutes, Miller told her "he did not think we had a legal case, however, he was going to discuss this with his partner." When she did not hear anything further from the attorney, Togstad assumed

that the attorney and his partner had concluded that they did not
have a cause of action. Ms. Togstad did not consult with another
attorney until a year later, when the statute of limitations had run.

Miller testified that he told Togstad at the conclusion of the
interview that "there was nothing related in her factual circumstances that told me that she had a case that our firm would be
interested in undertaking." He also testified that because of the
serious injuries her husband had suffered, he advised her to obtain
an opinion from another attorney and to do so promptly. Miller
further testified that he told Ms. Togstad that his firm did not have
expertise in medical malpractice actions and that it associated
counsel in cases of that nature. Finally, Miller said that he would
talk with associate counsel about Togstad's case and would inform
her if the opinion of that counsel differed from Miller's. Miller's
"impression" was that he did discuss the matter with associate
counsel and that associate counsel thought that there was no liability for medical malpractice. Accordingly, Miller did not communicate further with Togstad.

The jury returned a verdict of $610,500 for Mr. Togstad and
$39,000 for his wife. The Minnesota Supreme Court affirmed. It
found that there was sufficient evidence on which the jury could
conclude that Miller was negligent: first, in giving advice that the
Togstads did not have a cause of action without adequate factual
investigation; second, in failing to inform Togstad of the upcoming
expiration of the statute of limitations.

CONTINGENT FEE AGREEMENT

_____ (Date)

Re: [Matter Description]
      C.A. No. _____

Dear _____

This letter is to acknowledge and thank you for your request
that _____ represent you in the above-referenced
matter. We are pleased to have this opportunity to assist you and
want to acquaint you with our manner of handling your case. This
letter of engagement is being sent to you pursuant to the
_____ Rules of Professional Conduct.

Scope of Representation

Our representation of you is in connection with the above-captioned matter only, unless we otherwise agree in writing.

Firm Representation

While [NAME OF OTHER ATTORNEY(S) IN OFFICE WHO WILL BE ASSISTING] _____ and I will be primarily responsible for your case, other attorneys in the firm may, from time to time, be involved in the event we are out of town or otherwise unavailable. Should we be unavailable when you call, please feel free to refer any questions to our secretaries. If they are unavailable to answer any immediate concern, [NAME OF OTHER ATTORNEY(S) IN OFFICE WHO WILL BE ASSISTING] _____ or I will be in touch with you as quickly as possible.

Efforts on Your Behalf

We will strive to complete your work as expeditiously as possible and at a fair and reasonable cost to you. We do represent other clients, and there will be times when we will be giving your work priority over others. But the converse is also true, and we trust that you will understand if reasonable delays occur in completion of your work.

(a) **Investigation.** We will investigate to the extent we deem appropriate the liability and damages aspects of this matter.

(b) **Evaluation.** Once the available and appropriate information is assimilated, we will discuss with you our evaluation of your case. This will include an evaluation of the liability aspects of this matter, as well as that of damages. Evaluations are nothing more than our prediction, based on our experience, of what we believe a final award might be. Our evaluation of your case may change from time to time as new information becomes available, or new developments occur in the law.

(c) **Negotiation.** Once we have discussed our evaluation of this matter with you, we will, with your permission, attempt to negotiate a settlement. We will keep you advised of all offers of settlement.

(d) **Filing of Suit.** If we are unable to settle this matter amicably on your behalf, it will be necessary for us to file suit. At present, it is anticipated that suit will be filed in _____ court. From our experience, it is likely to take approximately ____ months before this matter will be ready for trial.

(e)   **Status.** We will keep you advised of the status of this matter and significant developments as they occur. We ask that you keep us advised of any changes or developments of which you become aware that affect this matter or our representation of you. This would include, but not be limited to, any changes in your condition, any information affecting either liability or damages, changes of address, etc. If, at any time, you have any questions, we invite you to call [NAME OF OTHER ATTORNEY(S) IN OFFICE WHO WILL BE ASSISTING] _____ or me.

(f)   **Discovery.** Our Rules of Civil Procedure provide for a procedure called "discovery." This is a process by which each side can discover the facts and claims relied upon by the other in order to expedite the settlement process or to narrow the issues to be tried. Discovery takes many forms, and may include interrogatories, requests for production, and depositions. The other side may request that your deposition be taken. In a deposition, the other side's attorney will ask you questions under oath before a court reporter. This is typically done in one of the attorney's offices. Should the other side ask to take your deposition, we will of course let you know and discuss this with you.

Billing Basis

Attorney time for handling this matter will be charged on a contingent fee basis. Our fee will be _____ percent of any recovery obtained before trial, and _____ percent of any recovery obtained after trial of the case begins. In addition to the firm's percentage of any recovery, you will be responsible for all costs such as filing fees, depositions, travel expenses, retention of experts, court costs, witness fees, etc. For example, if your case were settled for $10,000 prior to trial, our fee would be $2,500 plus any costs incurred. On the other hand, if the case were tried and we recovered $10,000, our fee would be $3,333 plus any costs and expenses incurred. If the case is tried and we receive nothing, you will not have to pay attorney fees, but you will still be responsible for paying costs.

Billing

Since we are handling this case on a contingent fee basis, we will bill you for any fees only at the end of the case. The firm, in its discretion, may advance costs associated with this matter. Though typically we will not bill you for these advances until the end of the case, we retain the right to submit an interim bill for costs should we determine it is necessary. Once the case is ended, we will prepare a bill outlining your recovery, our attorney's fees, any costs you are required to reimburse the firm, and any other expenses deducted from your recovery. You will be provided a copy of this bill.

Appeal

Should the case be tried and lost, or should any recovery not meet our and your expectations, an appeal may be available if the court committed some error during the course of the trial. Should an adverse verdict occur, we will evaluate the merits of an appeal and advise you of our evaluation. Under the terms of this agreement, we are not required to pursue an appeal on your behalf, but will do so upon mutual agreement.

Termination

You shall at all times have the right to terminate our services upon written notice to that effect. Should you terminate our representation of you, the fee and cost arrangements discussed above will continue in effect. We shall, subject to the Rules of Professional Conduct and to applicable court requirements with respect to withdrawal, have the right to terminate our services upon reasonable written notice to you. Should we terminate our services, you will still be responsible for costs incurred in your behalf, but not for any fees.

Very truly yours,

For the firm

I AGREE TO THE TERMS OF REPRESENTATION
AND ENGAGEMENT AS OUTLINED ABOVE.

[IF CLIENT A CORPORATION,
CORPORATE NAME HERE]

_____

[Name of Individual Signing]

Scope of representation

Client-lawyer agreements are contracts, subject to the rules of contract law, but are also governed by a number of special rules that
apply because of the fiduciary relationship between attorney and
client.[51] The agreement between the client and the lawyer determines the matters in which the lawyer represents the client. Courts
are likely, however, to resolve any ambiguities·and uncertainties in
the agreement against the lawyer;[52] thus, lawyers must define
clearly the matters for which they are agreeing to represent their
clients. For example, if a lawyer agrees to represent a client in
"your suit," a court is likely to conclude that the lawyer has agreed
to represent the client in any appeal arising from the action.[53] Even
if the agreement between the client and the lawyer provided that
the lawyer agreed to represent the client only at trial, the lawyer
would still be required to move to withdraw from the case after
trial and to take reasonable steps to protect the client's right to
appeal if the lawyer did not plan to handle the appeal.[54]

When a client comes to a lawyer with a legal problem, the
problem may involve several distinct legal matters. Consider a case
in which a worker is seriously injured on the job from a defective
machine and then dies in the hospital as a result of medical malpractice. This one incident involves at least four different legal

---

51. Restatement (Third) of the Law Governing Lawyers §29A, cmt. *c.* See
Joseph M. Perillo, The Law of Lawyers' Contracts Is Different, 67 Fordham L.
Rev. 443 (1998).

52. Restatement (Third) of the Law Governing Lawyers §29A(2) (agreement should be construed from the standpoint of a reasonable person in the
client's circumstances).

53. Id. §29A, cmt. *h* and illus. 4.

54. See id. §45.

matters: a products liability case against the manufacturer of the defective machine, a worker's compensation claim, a medical malpractice claim against the doctors and hospital, and administration of the decedent's estate. The lawyer should reach a clear understanding with the client regarding the matters that the firm is handling, and any matters for which the client will not be retaining the firm's services. Lawyers who fail to do so face a risk of malpractice liability.[55]

While it is clearly permissible for the client and lawyer to define the matters in which the attorney is undertaking representation, may they agree to limit the extent of the lawyer's duties in handling a matter? A lawyer may not enter into an agreement with the client prospectively limiting the lawyer's liability for malpractice.[56] Such an agreement undermines the lawyer's duty to represent the client competently and diligently; moreover, clients may not have sufficient information to evaluate the reasonableness of such a disclaimer.[57] Thus, it would be unethical and contractually unenforceable for an engagement agreement to disclaim liability for malpractice. An agreement to submit fees disputes or malpractice claims to arbitration may, however, be enforceable, depending on the jurisdiction.[58]

---

55. See Meighan v. Shore, 40 Cal. Rptr. 2d 744 (Ct. App. 1995, *review denied*) (lawyer who represents husband in medical malpractice action has duty to inform wife of possible loss of consortium claim); Nichols v. Keller, 19 Cal. Rptr. 2d 601 (Ct. App. 1993, *review denied*) (lawyer retained to handle workers' compensation matter had duty either to investigate claims against third parties arising from occurrence or to advise client to seek other counsel for such claims).

56. Model Rule 1.8(h). The Model Rule qualifies the prohibition by stating "unless permitted by law and the client is independently represented in making the agreement." The Restatement (Third) of the Law Governing Lawyers, however, contains an absolute prohibition in Section 76(1) because no such law exists. Section 76, Reporter's Notes to cmt. *b*.

57. Id. cmt. *b*.

58. *Compare* Powers v. Dickson, Carlson & Campillo, 63 Cal. Rptr. 2d 261 (Ct. App. 1997) (under California law agreements to submit malpractice claims to arbitration are enforceable) *with* Alternative Sys., Inc. v. Carey, 79 Cal. Rptr. 2d 567 (Ct. App. 1998) (engagement agreement requiring arbitration of fee disputes was unenforceable because inconsistent with statutory system for mandatory fee arbitration, which provided clients with greater protections than under agreement). See also N.Y. County Lawyers' Assn. Comm. on Prof. Ethics, Op. 723 (1997) (outside domestic relations area, where special rules apply, lawyers may ethically include arbitration provisions in engagement agreements, provided lawyer fully discloses consequences of provision and gives client

Suppose, however, that the agreement does not go this far. For example, may the lawyer and client agree that the lawyer will "spend no more than five hours on this matter"? On one hand, agreements that limit the scope of a lawyer's duties can be beneficial to clients because they allow clients to obtain the degree of representation that they desire. Clients, like buyers of other goods and services, should be entitled to purchase different degrees of quality. On the other hand, some clients, particularly unsophisticated ones, may not understand the level of service that they are purchasing. The Model Rules are unclear on whether agreements that limit the scope of a lawyer's duties are valid. Model Rule 1.2(c) states that a "lawyer may limit the objectives of the representation if the client consents after consultation." The comments, however, state that an agreement that limits the scope of representation so as to violate the duty of competency is unenforceable under Model Rule 1.1. See Comments 4 and 5.

The Restatement of the Law Governing Lawyers is more tolerant of agreements limiting the scope of representation. Section 30 of the Restatement allows such agreements if (1) the client is adequately informed and consents and (2) the terms of the limitation are reasonable in the circumstances. The comments elaborate on the reasonableness requirement:

> When the client is sophisticated in such waivers, informed consent ordinarily permits the inference that the waiver is reasonable. For other clients, the requirement is met if, in addition to informed consent, the benefits supposedly obtained by the waiver — typically, a reduced legal fee or the ability to retain a particularly able lawyer — could reasonably be considered to outweigh the potential risk posed by the limitation.[59]

Allocation of authority between lawyer and client

Issues of authority between attorney and client can arise in two ways. First, as between lawyer and client, has the attorney acted with authority? Second, is the client bound to a third party by

---

opportunity to obtain independent advice; if New York law does not allow arbitrators to award punitive damages, arbitration clause may be unenforceable limitation on attorney liability).

59. Restatement (Third) of the Law Governing Lawyers §30, cmt. *c*.

virtue of an agreement or action taken by the lawyer, even if the lawyer acted without authority?[60]

As to the allocation of authority between client and lawyer, traditionally many attorneys viewed themselves as experts entrusted to handle their clients' matters as they thought to be in the best interest of the client.[61] The Model Rules and the Restatement of the Law Governing Lawyers reject this paternalistic view of the client-lawyer relationship because it suffers from fundamental defects. The expert model subordinates the actual client to the lawyer's view of the client's interests. In addition, this approach ignores the fact that the full participation of clients can improve the quality of the lawyer's representation because clients have information and perspectives that lawyers lack.[62]

Under the Model Rules and principles of agency law, a distinction is drawn between objectives of representation and means to achieve those objectives. Thus Model Rule 1.2(a) provides: "A lawyer shall abide by a client's decisions concerning the objectives of representation [subject to certain limitations] and shall consult with the client as to the means by which they are to be pursued."[63] Model Rule 1.2(a) identifies the following matters as decisions for the client to make: whether to accept an offer of settlement in a civil case, and in criminal cases, the plea to be entered, whether to waive jury trial, and whether the client will testify.[64] While the Model Rules do not mention the determination whether to appeal as a decision for the client to make, most other authorities do so.[65] Some scholars have argued that the Model Rules do not sufficiently recognize the autonomy of clients and that the principle of "informed consent," which has been applied to the relationship

60. Compare Restatement (Third) of the Law Governing Lawyers ch. 2, topic 3 (Authority to Make Decisions) and topic 4 (Lawyer's Authority to Act for Client).

61. See Douglas E. Rosenthal, Lawyer and Client: Who's in Charge? 7 (1974).

62. See Restatement (Third) of the Law Governing Lawyers ch. 2, topic 3, Introductory note.

63. See ABA Standards for Criminal Justice, Defense Function Standard 4-5.2 (3d ed. 1993) (distinguishing fundamental decisions that clients are entitled to make based on advice of lawyers from strategic and tactical decisions that lawyers are authorized to make after consultation with clients where feasible).

64. See also Restatement (Third) of the Law Governing Lawyers §33.

65. See id. §33(1); ABA Defense Function Standard 4-5.2.

between doctor and patient, should be applied to the relationship between lawyer and client.[66]

Although clients are entitled to make decisions regarding the objectives of representation, lawyers have a duty to counsel their clients regarding these matters. See Model Rule 2.1.[67] The role of counselor gives lawyers broad authority to advise their clients on both legal and nonlegal considerations involved in a proposed course of action. Model Rule 2.1 states that in providing advice, "a lawyer may refer not only to law but to other considerations such as moral, economic, social and political factors, that may be relevant to the client's situation."[68] The client's right to make decisions regarding the objectives of representation does not mean, however, that lawyers must follow every decision that clients make. In representing clients lawyers may not counsel or assist them to engage in conduct that the lawyer knows to be criminal, fraudulent, or in violation of a court order; lawyers who do so face the possibility of professional discipline[69] and civil liability either to the client or to third persons.[70]

A vast number of decisions in a case are strategic or tactical rather than relating to the objectives of representation. What causes of action should be included in the complaint? How many expert witnesses should the client retain? What discovery should be done? What witnesses will be called to testify at trial? Should counsel object to a question at trial? Lawyers have broad authority to make strategic and tactical decisions in connection with the representation to advance their clients' interests.[71] The lawyer's authority to make these decisions can be limited in several ways. Clients and lawyers are generally free to allocate the authority to

---

66. Susan R. Martyn, Informed Consent in the Practice of Law, 48 Geo. Wash. L. Rev. 307 (1980); Marcy Strauss, Toward a Revised Model of Attorney-Client Relationship: The Argument for Autonomy, 65 N.C. L. Rev. 315 (1987). But see Judith L. Maute, Allocation of Decisionmaking Authority Under the Model Rules of Professional Conduct, 17 U.C. Davis L. Rev. 1049 (1984) (arguing that joint venture framework adopted by Model Rules is flexible enough to accommodate attorney, client, and social interests).

67. See Restatement (Third) of the Law Governing Lawyers §31(3).

68. See also id. §151(3).

69. See Model Rule 1.2(d); Restatement (Third) of the Law Governing Lawyers §151(2).

70. See Restatement (Third) of the Law Governing Lawyers §151(1).

71. See Model Rule 1.2(a); Restatement (Third) of the Law Governing Lawyers §32(3) and cmt. e.

make strategic and tactical decisions by contract.[72] The lawyer's engagement agreement could, for example, specify that the lawyer may not employ an expert witness without the client's approval, or it could authorize the lawyer to engage in such discovery as the lawyer believes necessary, subject to a budget. Further, lawyers are required to keep their clients reasonably informed about the client's matter.[73] Clients may give lawyers instructions during the course of representation regarding strategic and tactical decisions, and lawyers are generally bound to follow these instructions, unless the client directs the lawyer to act unethically or illegally.[74] Thus, a client could instruct the lawyer that the client does not want to go to the expense of taking the deposition of an expert witness. Some tactical matters require immediate action — for example, the decision whether to object to a question at trial — so that consultation with the client is impractical. In these situations, lawyers have the authority to make the decision without client consultation.[75]

Suppose a lawyer believes that the client's instructions are "tying my hands" so that the lawyer cannot effectively carry out the representation? The lawyer may counsel the client about the wisdom of the client's decision. See Model Rule 2.1. If the issue involves a litigation expense that the client is unwilling to incur, with client consent the lawyer could advance the expense. See Model Rule 1.8(e). Finally, the lawyer could move to withdraw from the matter if the client's instructions make it unreasonably difficult for the lawyer to carry out the representation.[76]

The principles discussed above govern allocation of authority between lawyer and client. Under what circumstances is a client legally bound to a third person as a result of the lawyer's actions on behalf of the client? When a lawyer proceeds with express authority, the lawyer's action binds the client.[77] In addition, agency

---

72. Restatement (Third) of the Law Governing Lawyers §32(1) and cmt. *c*.

73. See Model Rule 1.4; Restatement (Third) of the Law Governing Lawyers §31(1).

74. Restatement (Third) of the Law Governing Lawyers §32(2), cmt. *d* and §34.

75. See id. §32, cmt. *e* and §34, cmt. *d*.

76. See Model Rule 1.16(b), which allows a lawyer to withdraw if the client decides on a course of action that the lawyer believes is "imprudent" or if "good cause" exists for withdrawal. See also Restatement (Third) of the Law Governing Lawyers §44(3).

77. Restatement (Third) of the Law Governing Lawyers §38 and cmt. *d*.

law provides that the actions of an agent bind the principal when the agent acts with implied or apparent authority, when the principal ratifies the agent's conduct, or when the principal is estopped from denying the agent's authority. For example, normally an attorney would have apparent authority to agree to a trial date.[78]

Settlement of a lawsuit involves both authority between lawyer and client and effect on third parties. The Model Rules provide that a client has the prerogative to decide whether to accept an offer of settlement in a civil case. Model Rule 1.2(a). The client's right to decide whether to accept a settlement imposes a duty on a lawyer to convey information to the client about a settlement offer. See Model Rule 1.4, cmt. 1. Recall that the rights of defendants in criminal cases are somewhat broader. See Model Rule 1.2(a) and Problem 2-6.

Suppose the plaintiff authorizes a lawyer to settle a case for any amount in excess of $200,000. The client is bound if the lawyer agrees to such a settlement. If the client then refuses to proceed with the settlement, the opposing party could take legal steps to enforce the settlement (for example, a motion to the tribunal before which the case is pending to compel settlement). Suppose a lawyer agrees to a settlement that the client has *not* authorized. Normally, an attorney does not have apparent authority to settle a case on behalf of a client.[79] Thus the client is not bound by the settlement. A lawyer who acts without authority is subject to disciplinary action, legal liability to the client, and legal liability to third persons harmed by the lawyer's unauthorized action.[80]

In contingent fee cases lawyers often have a substantial financial interest in the matter, resulting from time expended and expenses advanced in the case. Some lawyers have attempted to protect themselves against what they consider to be unreasonable rejections of settlement offers by their clients, but these efforts have met with little success. In Cincinnati Bar Assn. v. Shultz,[81] a disciplinary proceeding, the lawyer included in her contingent fee agreement a provision for payment of hourly fees if the client discharged her firm. The court held that this provision was improper

---

78. See id. §§38, 39, and illus. 1.
79. Id. §39, cmt. *d*. But see Koval v. Simon Telelect, Inc., 693 N.E.2d 1299 (Ind. 1998) (lawyers generally do not have inherent authority to settle, but exception for "in court" actions, including settlements pursuant to rules for alternative dispute resolution).
80. See Restatement (Third) of the Law Governing Lawyers §42(3).
81. 643 N.E.2d 1139 (Ohio 1994).

because it was inconsistent with the shared risk concept, which is the essence of a contingent fee agreement.

Termination of the client-lawyer relationship: discharge and withdrawal

Almost all jurisdictions follow the rule that a client has the absolute right to discharge an attorney, regardless of cause. Courts reason that the relationship of client and attorney is highly personal and that clients should not be limited in their right to select counsel of their choice.[82] Recognition that the client has the right to discharge an attorney at any time for any reason, however, creates a potential problem of unfairness to the attorney. How should an attorney be compensated when the client has exercised the right to discharge the attorney?

Courts typically allow discharged attorneys to recover the reasonable value of their services, i.e., on a quantum meruit basis.[83] This method of compensation protects the client's right to discharge an attorney and protects the attorney's right to compen-

82. See Wolfram, Modern Legal Ethics §9.5.2, at 545; Restatement (Third) of the Law Governing Lawyers §44(1) and cmt. b. See also Cohen v. Radio-Elecs. Officers Union, Dist. 3, NMEBA, 679 A.2d 1188 (N.J. 1996) (retainer agreement may not limit client's right to discharge lawyer but agreement may provide for compensation to attorney when client exercises right; six months' notice of termination held to be unreasonable, but court finds one month's notice reasonable).

83. See generally George L. Blum, Annotation, Limitation to Quantum Meruit Recovery, Where Attorney Employed Under Contingent-Fee Contract Is Discharged Without Cause, 56 A.L.R.5th 1 (1998). Some of the recent cases on the rights of discharged lawyers include the following: Greer, Klosik & Daugherty v. Yetman, 496 S.E.2d 693 (Ga. 1998) (firm entitled to quantum meruit not amount of contingent fee when client discharged firm after favorable jury verdict while case on appeal); Reynolds v. Polen, 564 N.W.2d 467 (Mich. Ct. App. 1997) (discharged contingent-fee firm entitled to be compensated on quantum meruit basis when firm acted unreasonably, but not unethically or against public policy, by being dilatory in providing notice of conflict of trial date); Cohen v. Grainger, Tesoriero & Bell, 622 N.E.2d 288 (N.Y. 1993) (discharged lawyer has statutory lien for unpaid fee; as against client, lawyer may recover on quantum meruit basis; as against successor attorney, lawyer may elect to receive either quantum meruit immediately or percentage based on proportionate share of work performed on entire case when case finally concluded). See generally Lester Brickman, Setting the Fee When the Client Discharges a Contingent Fee Attorney, 41 Emory L. J. 367 (1992).

sation for services rendered. Extreme cases could justify deviation from the quantum meruit rule. For example, if the client discharged the attorney because of the attorney's serious misconduct, a court might find that fee forfeiture was appropriate.[84] At the other extreme, if the client discharged an attorney shortly before concluding a settlement, to deprive the attorney of a contingent fee that was all but earned, a court might allow the attorney to receive the full contractual amount.[85] In this situation, the client typically has acted in bad faith to deprive the lawyer of her fee. Moreover, allowing recovery at the full contractual rate does not burden the client's right to select counsel because the matter has been completed.[86]

In deciding the amount of quantum meruit recovery, courts will not necessarily determine the amount of recovery mechanically, based simply on the number of hours that the attorney worked on the case. Instead, courts will probably examine a variety of factors, including the number of hours worked, the lawyer's hourly rate, the difficulty of the case, the stage of the case at which the lawyer was discharged, and the benefits received by the client.[87] A number of courts limit the amount of quantum meruit

84. See White v. McBride, 937 S.W.2d 796 (Tenn. 1996) (charging of excessive contingent fee in probate case was improper and justifies forfeiture of all compensation, including quantum meruit) and Restatement (Third) of the Law Governing Lawyers §49.

85. See Wegner v. Arnold, 713 N.E.2d 247 (Ill. App. Ct. 1999, *appeal denied*) (where attorney is fired immediately before settlement, factors involved in determining reasonable fee would justify awarding entire contract fee as reasonable value of services rendered); Taylor v. Shigaki, 930 P.2d 340 (Wash. Ct. App.), *review denied,* 940 P.2d 654 (Wash. 1997) (under doctrine of substantial performance lawyer entitled to full contingent fee when client discharged lawyer nine days before trial date, after substantial offer of settlement had been made, and six hours before client met with claims adjuster to negotiate final settlement); Restatement (Third) of the Law Governing Lawyers §52(2). The client is liable to the discharged attorney, but the liability of successor counsel is uncertain. *Compare* Pryor v. Merten, 490 S.E.2d 590 (N.C. Ct. App. 1997), *review denied,* 502 S.E.2d 597 (N.C. 1998) (discharged contingent-fee attorney may recover in quantum meruit from successor counsel and need not bring suit directly against client) *with* Fowkes v. Shoemaker, 661 A.2d 877 (Pa. Super. Ct. 1995), *appeal denied,* 674 A.2d 1072 (Pa. 1996) (successor counsel not liable in quantum meruit to discharged attorney).

86. See Restatement (Third) of the Law Governing Lawyers §52(2) and cmt. *c.*

87. See Searcy, Denney, Scarola, Barnhart & Shipley, P. A. v. Poletz, 652 So. 2d 366 (Fla. 1995) (quantum meruit compensation to discharged contingent-

recovery to the ratable portion of the contract that has been performed (not always an easy task) on the theory that a discharged attorney should not receive a benefit in excess of the contract amount. In addition, allowing recovery in excess of the contract amount would burden the client's right to select new counsel. The Restatement of the Law Governing Lawyers adopts the view that a discharged attorney is entitled to recover quantum meruit, limited by the ratable portion of the contract that has been performed.[88] When awarding quantum meruit compensation under a contingent fee contract, it seems appropriate to defer the lawyer's right to recover in quantum meruit until the client receives an award, otherwise the client's right to discharge the attorney would be burdened by the obligation to pay the attorney immediate quantum meruit compensation.[89]

Withdraw   The rules on withdrawal by attorneys are divided into two categories: mandatory and permissive withdrawal. Under Model Rule 1.16(a), a lawyer must withdraw from representation if the representation will result in a violation of the Rules of Conduct (for example, if the lawyer faces a conflict of interest or if the client demands that the lawyer engage in illegal conduct). In addition, a lawyer must withdraw if the client discharges the lawyer or if the lawyer's physical or mental condition impairs the lawyer's ability to represent the client.[90] When a matter is pending before a tribunal, a lawyer who is ethically required to withdraw must still file a motion with the tribunal to obtain permission to withdraw.

Model Rule 1.16(b) deals with permissive withdrawal. The rule gives lawyers broad power to withdraw if "withdrawal can be accomplished without material adverse effect on the interests of the client." In addition to withdrawal without material adverse effect, Rule 1.16(b) specifies six situations in which withdrawal is permissive.[91] These include the client's insistence on following a course of conduct that the lawyer considers to be "repugnant or imprudent"; the client's failure to pay fees or expenses, provided the client has been given reasonable warning that the lawyer will

---

fee attorney measured by variety of factors rather than simply "lodestar," i.e. hourly rate, amount).

88. Restatement (Third) of the Law Governing Lawyers §52(1).
89. See Rosenberg v. Levin, 409 So. 2d 1016 (Fla. 1982).
90. See also Restatement (Third) of the Law Governing Lawyers §44(2).
91. Restatement (Third) of the Law Governing Lawyers §44(3) is substantially similar to Model Rule 1.16(b).

withdraw unless the client makes payment; the client has made representation "unreasonably difficult"; and in case of "other good cause."

The proper scope of the withdrawal rules has engendered a good deal of discussion and debate. When the client is abusing the professional relationship, by demanding that the lawyer engage in illegal or unethical conduct, the lawyer's duty or right to withdraw is clear. May a lawyer withdraw if the client's conduct does not rise to this level? As we saw in Chapter 2, a lawyer may withdraw if the client insists on conduct that the lawyer considers to be "repugnant or imprudent."[92] Is this ground for withdrawal determined subjectively by the lawyer or is it subject to an objective standard? The Restatement takes the view that right to withdraw on this ground is limited to cases in which the client is demanding that the lawyer engage in conduct that no reasonable lawyer should be required to do.[93]

If the lawyer simply disagrees with the client's decision, even if the disagreement is strongly held, ground for withdrawal does not exist. For example, suppose a lawyer who represents a client in a personal injury action receives an offer to settle the case that the lawyer believes is reasonable but that the client is unwilling to accept. Since the client retains the right to accept or reject settlement offers, a lawyer would not be justified in withdrawing if the client refused to accept the lawyer's recommendation regarding the settlement offer. Some courts have held that lawyers who withdraw under such circumstances forfeit their right to receive any fee.[94]

By agreeing to accept representation, attorneys make commitments to their clients to provide personal services. In addition, as discussed previously, in many cases attorneys agree to advance expenses on behalf of their clients. Sometimes cases turn out to be less valuable or more expensive than the attorney anticipated when the litigation began. May an attorney withdraw due to ex-

---

92. See Model Rule 1.16(b)(3); Restatement (Third) of the Law Governing Lawyers §44(3)(f).

93. See Restatement (Third) of the Law Governing Lawyers §44, cmt. *j*.

94. See Augustson v. Linea Aerea Nacional-Chile, S.A., 76 F.3d 658 (5th Cir. 1996) (when law firm withdraws from case in dispute with client over settlement, firm is not entitled to any fee). But see Kannewurf v. Johns, 632 N.E.2d 711 (Ill. App. Ct. 1994) (lawyer who withdrew over fundamental disagreement about settlement of case entitled to quantum meruit compensation).

treme financial hardship? The Model Rules allow an attorney to withdraw in such a situation provided court approval is obtained, Rule 1.16(b)(5); but the Restatement of the Law Governing Lawyers takes the position that financial hardship alone is not sufficient to justify withdrawal, although financial hardship is a factor that along with other factors can establish good cause for withdrawal.[95] Some courts have allowed lawyers to withdraw if continued representation would constitute an extreme financial hardship to the lawyer.[96] If the attorney voluntarily withdraws without cause, however, the lawyer may forfeit all right to compensation.[97]

Both the Model Rules and the Restatement of the Law Governing Lawyers allow a lawyer to withdraw if withdrawal can be accomplished without material adverse effect on the client.[98] For example, suppose a law firm represents corporate client *A* in a minor litigation matter that is in its early stages. Corporation *B* approaches the law firm to seek representation against client *A* in a major matter that is unrelated to the matter the firm is handling for client *A*. The firm seeks client *A*'s consent to undertake the representation, but client *A* refuses to consent. May the firm withdraw from representation of client *A* in order to take on the more lucrative representation of Corporation *B*, provided substitute counsel can be retained to represent *A* without material adverse effect on *A*? Professors Hazard and Hodes argue that the rules allow a lawyer to drop a client like a "hot potato" if withdrawal can be accomplished without material harm to the client, even if the lawyer is motivated solely by economic considerations.[99] The Model Rules and the Restatement of the Law Governing Lawyers seem to support this view by allowing a lawyer to withdraw for any reason, provided withdrawal can be accomplished without

95. Restatement (Third) of the Law Governing Lawyers §44, cmt. *m*.

96. *Compare* Haines v. Liggett Group, Inc., 814 F. Supp. 414 (D.N.J. 1993) (withdrawal denied; court notes absence of provision in contingent-fee agreement allowing for withdrawal in event of financial hardship) *with* Smith v. R. J. Reynolds Tobacco Co., 630 A.2d 820 (N.J. Super. Ct. App. Div. 1993) (withdrawal for financial hardship permissible but case remanded for determination of probable recovery and anticipated litigation costs).

97. See Faro v. Romani, 641 So. 2d 69 (Fla. 1994).

98. See Model Rule 1.16(b); Restatement (Third) of the Law Governing Lawyers §44(3)(a).

99. See 1 Hazard & Hodes, The Law of Lawyering §1.16:302 (authors recognize, however, that many courts and commentators disagree with this view).

material adverse effect on the interests of the client.[100] The Restatement recognizes that withdrawal in this case constitutes a breach of contract, but refers to the breach as "nominal." Query whether this approach is correct. First, the rule almost certainly violates reasonable client expectations. Most clients surely believe that when a lawyer has agreed to represent them, the lawyer cannot withdraw from representation for the lawyer's own financial interest, even if the client would not be harmed. Second, it is unlikely that many cases would arise in which a lawyer could withdraw because of lack of material adverse effect. In almost any case that has gone beyond its earliest stages, withdrawal would result in material harm to the client. Finally, the rule does not serve any substantial lawyer interest. Lawyers can avoid the problem of undertaking representation during early stages by using *investigation agreements,* in which the lawyer agrees to investigate the matter before undertaking representation.

In terminating representation an attorney must take reasonable steps to protect the client's interest from prejudice.[101] Thus, if the time for filing an appeal is about to run out, an attorney whose representation has terminated should nonetheless file notice of the appeal to protect the client's interest.[102] The lawyer could then file a motion with the appellate court to withdraw from representation.

Liens

Model Rule 1.8(j) prohibits lawyers from acquiring a proprietary interest in the cause of action or subject of litigation except for reasonable contingent fees in civil cases and "a lien granted by law to secure the lawyer's fee or expenses."[103] Courts have generally

---

100. See Model Rule 1.16(b); Restatement (Third) of the Law Governing Lawyers §44(3)(a) and cmt. *h(ii).*
101. Restatement (Third) of the Law Governing Lawyers §45.
102. Id. §45, cmt. *b.*
103. See Restatement (Third) of the Law Governing Lawyers §48(1). Lawyers may acquire an interest in a client's venture that is not subject to litigation. Thus, a lawyer may obtain an ownership interest in a client's business while representing the client provided the lawyer complies with the stringent requirements for business transactions between lawyer and client. See Model Rule 1.8(a) and Problem 5-1.

recognized two types of lawyers' liens. The *retaining lien* is the attorney's right to retain client papers or other valuable client property in the lawyer's possession as security for any unpaid amount the client owes the lawyer.[104] The lien arises as a matter of law rather than pursuant to contract and is based on equitable principles: The attorney has rendered substantial services or advanced expenses on the client's behalf and should be entitled to compensation. The lien is purely possessory; the lawyer may not sell the client's property to satisfy the client's debt to the lawyer. Because of the coercive aspects of the lien, some jurisdictions no longer recognize it, and others have cautioned lawyers against exercising the lien when the client would be prejudiced. For example, In re White was a disciplinary proceeding in which the South Carolina Supreme Court held that the exercise of a retaining lien was not per se unethical. The court, however, warned lawyers to be careful in asserting such liens and outlined factors for lawyers to weigh in making that decision.[105]

When a lawyer has been discharged, the lawyer may consider asserting a retaining lien until the lawyer has been paid. As discussed above, lawyers must be cautious in asserting such a lien to avoid prejudice to the clients. As a condition for releasing the file, some lawyers have demanded that clients sign a release of liability. Such releases are generally unethical and unenforceable, unless the client is independently represented by counsel.[106]

The Restatement of the Law Governing Lawyers rejects the general concept of a retaining lien unless established by statute because of its coercive aspects, although the drafters recognize that their position represents a minority view.[107] Under the Restatement, however, a lawyer may retain a document prepared by the lawyer for which the client has not paid the lawyer, but even

---

104. On the retaining lien, see generally Wolfram, Modern Legal Ethics §9.6.3, at 559-560.

105. 492 S.E.2d 82 (S.C. 1997).

106. See Committee on Legal Ethics v. Hazlett, 367 S.E.2d 772 (W. Va. 1988) (attorney's demand for release from liability before surrendering file was improper); Model Rule 1.8(h); Restatement (Third) of the Law Governing Lawyers §76. The Restatement draws distinctions between the enforceability of such releases and standards for professional discipline. *Compare* §§76(2) *and* 76(3)(b).

107. Restatement (Third) of the Law Governing Lawyers §55(1) and cmts. *a, b.*

in this situation the lawyer cannot do so if retention of the document will unreasonably harm the client.[108] Thus, a lawyer may not refuse to record a deed because the client has not paid the lawyer's fee.[109]

The second form of lien is the *charging lien,* which is applied against the proceeds of any settlement or judgment for the amount of any unpaid fees or expenses due the attorney. Where recognized, the charging lien is generally based on statute.[110] When created by statute, lawyers must obviously comply with statutory requirements for perfection and enforcement of a charging lien.[111]

May a lawyer ethically enter into a fee agreement that provides for a contractual charging lien? Professor Wolfram argues that contractual charging liens are of doubtful validity because Model Rule 1.8(j) prohibits a lawyer from acquiring an interest in the client's cause of action, except for liens recognized by law.[112] In a few jurisdictions, however, courts recognize contractually created liens,[113] and the Restatement of the Law Governing Lawyers would allow lawyers to contract with clients for charging liens, unless prohibited by statute or court rule.[114] For a lien to be effective against a third party (for example, an insurance company or a successor counsel), a lawyer must give notice of a charging lien to such party.[115]

Lawyers may also enter into contracts with their clients in which they obtain a security interest or mortgage in the clients' property to secure payment of their fees. Because security agreements between clients and lawyers are somewhat unusual, courts are likely to scrutinize such a security arrangement under fiduciary

---

108. Id. §55, cmt. *c.*

109. Id.

110. Wolfram, Modern Legal Ethics §9.6.3, at 561-562.

111. See In re Marriage of Etcheverry, 921 P.2d 82 (Colo. Ct. App. 1996) (against public policy to allow statutorily created charging lien to attach to child support payments).

112. Wolfram, Modern Legal Ethics §9.6.3, at 562.

113. See Eleazer v. Hardaway Concrete Co., 315 S.E.2d 174 (S.C. Ct. App. 1984) (recognizing common law charging lien on settlement or judgment for expenses, but not for legal fees; attorney and client may agree that attorney has lien on settlement or judgment).

114. Restatement (Third) of the Law Governing Lawyers §55(2) and cmts. *d, e.*

115. Id. §55, cmt. *e.*

principles of fairness and full disclosure.[116] Some states may prohibit or limit lawyers from obtaining security interests or mortgages to secure payment of their fees. For example, in domestic cases in New York, lawyers may obtain a mortgage or security interest to secure their fees only when the retainer agreement provides for such an interest, notice of an application for a security interest has been given to the other spouse, and the court grants approval for the application of a security interest after submission of an application for counsel fees. In addition, a lawyer in New York may not foreclose a mortgage on a primary residence while the consenting spouse remains in the residence.[117]

The client's file

The Model Rules do not speak directly to lawyers' obligations regarding the client's file, but section 58 of the Restatement of the Law Governing Lawyers does provide some specific standards. Lawyers have a duty to take reasonable steps to safeguard documents in the lawyer's possession relating to representation of a client.[118] Clients ordinarily have the right to inspect and copy documents in their files, but a lawyer may refuse to allow the client to do so when a substantial reason exists, for example if the file contains documents subject to a protective order.[119] Clients do not have a right, however, to inspect or copy internal firm memoranda (as distinguished from research memoranda) that may be in the file.[120] On termination of representation, the client is entitled to receive all documents in the file, except internal firm memoranda.[121] The firm may not charge the client for making copies of documents that the client is entitled to receive; if the firm wishes to retain copies, it may do so at its own expense.[122] As noted above,

116. See id. §55(4) and cmt. *i.*
117. Procedure for Attorneys in Domestic Relations Matters, N.Y. Sup. Ct. R. §1400.5.
118. Restatement (Third) of the Law Governing Lawyers §58(1).
119. Id. §58(2) and cmt. *c.*
120. Id.
121. Id. §58(3).
122. Id. cmt. *e.* See In re Admonition Issued to X. Y., 529 N.W.2d 688 (Minn. 1995) (absent specific provision in engagement agreement lawyer may not charge client for copying file on withdrawal because file belongs to client).

some jurisdictions recognize a retaining lien that allows lawyers to retain possession of the file until outstanding fees and expenses are paid. The Restatement rejects the general concept of a retaining lien, but the Restatement allows lawyers to retain specific documents that they have prepared when the client has not paid the fee or expenses associated with preparation of the document, provided that nondelivery would not substantially harm the client.[123]

B. Confidentiality

Problem 3-3

The Ethical Duty of Confidentiality, the Attorney-Client Privilege, and the Work Product Doctrine

a. You are an associate in a large law firm working in products liability defense. One of the shareholders in your firm has expressed concern that the firm's use of e-mail, cellular telephones, and perhaps even fax machines to communicate with clients may be inconsistent with the firm's ethical duty of confidentiality to its clients. You have been asked to draft a policy for the firm's consideration on the use of such technology. Prepare an outline of the central points that you believe such a policy should cover and an explanation of these principles.

b. The firm represents International Motors, Inc. (IM), a multinational manufacturer of automobiles. In a series of cases plaintiffs have alleged that IM produced vehicles with defective fuel tanks. Plaintiffs have sought to obtain various documents involved in the design of the fuel tank. IM has resisted these efforts, claiming that the documents are covered by the attorney-client privilege and the work product doctrine. All design decisions made by IM are the responsibility of its Design Review

---

123. Restatement (Third) of the Law Governing Lawyers §55(1).

Committee (DRC), the chairman of which has always been an attorney. All documents presented to the DRC are marked "CONFIDENTIAL MATERIAL PROTECTED BY THE ATTORNEY-CLIENT PRIVILEGE AND THE WORK PRODUCT DOCTRINE." IM has refused to produce any DRC documents (except for ones that it voluntarily produced in connection with filings with regulatory bodies), claiming that such documents are privileged. What arguments would you expect plaintiffs to make in an effort to overcome claims of privilege? What responses would you make?

Read Model Rule 1.6 and comments.

Confidentiality and the use of e-mail, faxes, and cellular telephones

Model Rule 1.6(a) provides that a "lawyer shall not reveal information relating to representation of a client unless the client consents after consultation, except for disclosures that are impliedly authorized in order to carry out the representation [subject to certain exceptions in section b]." The rule could be read literally to impose strict liability on attorneys for any revelation of client information unless the disclosure was expressly or impliedly authorized by the client or unless one of the exceptions set forth in section (b) applies. The rule is being interpreted, however, as having a negligence standard. Lawyers must take reasonable steps to preserve client confidentiality. If a lawyer uses a means of communication that has a reasonable expectation of privacy, the lawyer complies with the obligation of confidentiality even though client information might be revealed either inadvertently or through intentional interception by another person. Thus, the Restatement of the Law Governing Lawyers provides that confidential client information must be "acquired, stored, retrieved, and transmitted under systems and controls that are reasonably designed and managed to maintain confidentiality."[124]

Use of land-line telephones and fax machines is well estab-

---

124. See Restatement (Third) of the Law Governing Lawyers §112, cmt. d. *Accord* ABA Comm. on Ethics and Prof. Resp., Formal Op. 99-413.

lished in the practice of law, and both enjoy a reasonable expectation of privacy, even though such communications may be intercepted or misdirected.[125] The federal wiretapping act, the Electronic Communications Privacy Act (the ECPA), supports this expectation of privacy in two ways.[126] First, the act makes interception of wire communications a crime and imposes civil liability unless one of the parties to the communication consents to the interception.[127] Second, information gained from an unlawful interception is inadmissible in evidence.[128]

The expectation of privacy associated with cordless or cellular telephones is less certain.[129] While both cordless and cellular telephones enjoy the protection of the ECPA,[130] devices for the interception of the radio waves that transmit cordless or cellular calls are available commercially, and unauthorized interception of such communications is not uncommon. Some court decisions have held that cordless telephone calls are entitled to an expectation of privacy.[131] Ethics advisory opinions have cautioned lawyers about the use of cellular or cordless telephones. Some opinions have decided that lawyers should not use such devices for confidential communications.[132] Other opinions, while concluding that lawyers may ethically use these devices, have warned lawyers about the risk of interception and have advised that at a minimum a lawyer should inform the other party to the communication that the communication may not be considered to be confidential.[133]

125. See Katz v. United States, 389 U.S. 347 (1967) (telephone call from booth where listening device had been attached entitled to Fourth Amendment protection); State v. Canady, 460 S.E.2d 677 (W. Va. 1995) (facsimile transmission held subject to attorney-client privilege).

126. 18 U.S.C. §§2510 et seq.

127. Id. §2511.

128. Id. §2515.

129. See Laws. Man. on Prof. Conduct (ABA/BNA) 55:404-408.

130. Cordless telephone calls were originally not protected by the ECPA, but amendments to the act in 1994 expanded its coverage to include cordless telephone calls. See McKamey v. Roach, 55 F.3d 1236, 1238 n.1 (6th Cir. 1995).

131. See State v. McVeigh, 620 A.2d 133, 147 (Conn. 1993); State v. Faford, 910 P.2d 447, 451-452 (Wash. 1996) (en banc).

132. E.g., Massachusetts Ethics Opinion 94-5 (1994) (lawyer should not use if risk that third party will overhear confidential communication is "nontrivial").

133. N.C. Ethics Adv. Op. 215 (1995). See also Minn. Lawyers Prof. Resp. Board Op. 19 (1999) (lawyers may ethically use analog cordless or cellular telephones only with client consent after consultation).

In a comprehensive opinion, the ABA Committee on Ethics and Professional Responsibility has examined the ethical propriety of lawyers' use of e-mail.[134] The committee first discussed the characteristics of four types of e-mail transmissions: "direct" e-mail; "private system" e-mail; on-line service provider (OSP) e-mail; and Internet service provider (ISP) e-mail. All forms of e-mail have the risk of unauthorized interception. E-mail sent through on-line service providers or over the Internet is also subject to monitoring by the service provider. The committee decided that neither of these risks was sufficient to destroy the reasonable expectation of privacy. Telephone conversations can be intercepted illegally, but that risk does not mean that lawyers act unethically when using the telephone to discuss client matters. Monitoring of e-mail by OSPs and ISPs is restricted by law and does not lessen the reasonable expectation of privacy. The committee concluded that lawyers may ethically use e-mail to convey confidential information without use of encryption or other technology:

> Lawyers have a reasonable expectation of privacy in communications made by all forms of e-mail, including unencrypted e-mail sent on the Internet, despite some risk of interception and disclosure. It therefore follows that its use is consistent with the duty under Rule 1.6 to use reasonable means to maintain the confidentiality of information relating to a client's representation.[135]

Even if a method of communication is ethically permissible because a reasonable expectation of privacy exists, as a matter of prudence lawyers may need to refrain from using a method of communication or adopt additional precautions (such as the use of scrambling devices or encryption technology[136]) for particularly

134. ABA Comm. on Ethics and Prof. Resp., Formal Op. 99-413.

135. Id. at 11. A number of state bar ethics opinions have adopted an approach similar to the ABA committee's: use of any form of e-mail is consistent with a lawyer's obligations under Rule 1.6 without the need for encryption or client consent. Opinions in Pennsylvania and Arizona recommended that lawyers obtain client consent or use encryption. Opinions in Iowa and North Carolina took the position that lawyers should not transmit sensitive client information by e-mail. Id. at 11-12 n.40.

136. On encryption technology, see David Hricik, Lawyers Worry Too Much About Transmitting Client Confidences by Internet E-mail, 11 Geo. J. Legal Ethics 459, 493-496 (1998).

sensitive information.[137] While ABA Formal Opinion 99-413 and most state opinions do not require client consent, it would be prudent for lawyers to include in their engagement agreements a provision in which clients authorize use of various forms of communication with appropriate warnings to the client. To reinforce claims of confidentiality, communications by fax or e-mail should contain confidentiality notices.[138]

Scope and exceptions to the attorney-client privilege

The attorney-client privilege is one of the pillars on which the legal profession rests.[139] As the Supreme Court recently stated in Swidler & Berlin v. United States:[140]

> The attorney-client privilege is one of the oldest recognized privileges for confidential communications. . . . The privilege is intended to encourage "full and frank communication between attorneys and their clients and thereby promote broader public interests in the observance of law and the administration of justice."[141]

Courts and commentators have defined the attorney-client privilege in various ways. Problem 2-3 quoted Professor Wigmore's widely cited version. The Restatement of the Law Governing Lawyers contains the following formulation:

> [The] attorney-client privilege may be invoked . . . with respect to:
>
> (1) a communication
> (2) made between privileged persons
> (3) in confidence

---

137. ABA Formal Opinion 99-413 at. 2.

138. Amy M. Fulmer Stevenson, Comment, Making a Wrong Turn on the Information Superhighway: Electronic Mail, the Attorney-Client Privilege and Inadvertent Disclosure, 26 Cap. U.L. Rev. 347, 375 n.159 (1997).

139. See generally Edna S. Epstein, The Attorney-Client Privilege and the Work Product Doctrine (ABA 3d ed. 1997).

140. 524 U.S. 399 (1998) (holding that the privilege survives death of client, in this case former Deputy White House counsel Vincent Foster).

141. Id. at 403 (quoting from Upjohn v. United States, 449 U.S. 383, 389 (1981)).

(4) for the purpose of obtaining or providing legal assistance for the client.[142]

The attorney-client privilege does not apply if any of these elements is absent. Thus if the communication is with a third person rather than with the client, or if the communication is not for the purpose of giving legal advice, the communication is not privileged.[143] For example, in United States v. Ackert[144] the Second Circuit held that corporate counsel's discussions with an investment banker were not protected by the attorney-client privilege even though the lawyer's goal was to obtain information to help him advise his client. The court stated "the privilege protects communications between a client and an attorney, not communications that prove important to an attorney's legal advice to a client."[145]

In addition, courts have recognized several exceptions to the privilege, the two most important of which are waiver and the crime-fraud exception. The Restatement provides that the attorney-client privilege can be waived in several ways: by agreement, disclaimer, or failure to object;[146] by voluntary disclosure by the client, the client's lawyer, or another authorized agent of the client;[147] or by raising the lawyer's communication or assistance as an issue in the proceeding.[148]

The Restatement provides that the attorney-client privilege does not apply to a communication occurring when a client:

---

142. Restatement (Third) of the Law Governing Lawyers §118.
143. Section 120 of the Restatement defines "privileged persons" as follows:

> Privileged persons within the meaning of §118 are the client (including a prospective client), the client's lawyer, agents of either who facilitate communications between them, and agents of the lawyer who facilitate the representation.

144. 169 F.3d 136 (2d Cir. 1999).
145. Id. at 139.
146. Restatement (Third) of the Law Governing Lawyers §128.
147. Id. §129.
148. Id. §130. See Frontier Ref., Inc. v. Gorman-Rupp Co., 136 F.3d 695 (10th Cir. 1998) (discussing various approaches to issue of waiver of privilege by filing lawsuit to which privileged material is relevant).

(a) consults a lawyer for the purpose, later accomplished, of obtaining assistance to engage in a crime or fraud or aiding a third person to do so, or

(b) regardless of the client's purpose at the time of consultation, uses the lawyer's advice or other services to engage in or assist a crime or fraud.[149]

We have already encountered the application of the crime-fraud exception in Problem 2-3 in connection with *Purcell*. Another highly publicized application of the exception occurred in connection with tobacco litigation. In American Tobacco Co. v. State[150] the State of Florida brought suit against various tobacco manufacturers, seeking to recover health care expenses it incurred in treating diseases of Medicaid smokers. The state subpoenaed various documents to which the tobacco companies raised claims of privilege. The state contended that the crime-fraud exception applied because the documents would show that the tobacco companies defrauded the American public about the risks of smoking. The court of appeals agreed. The opinion focused on the procedure and standard of proof necessary to establish the exception. The court held that the procedure for determining the application of the exception was an adversarial hearing in which each party could present evidence and argument, and the standard for application of the exception was the "prima facie" evidence standard:

> [T]he party opposing the privilege on the crime-fraud exception has the initial burden of producing evidence which, if unexplained, would be prima facie proof of the existence of the exception. The burden of persuasion then shifts to the party asserting the privilege to give a reasonable explanation of the conduct or communication. If the court accepts the explanation as sufficient to rebut the evidence presented by the party opposing the privilege, then the privilege remains. However, if after considering and weighing the explanation the court does not accept it, then a prima facie case exists as to the exception, and the privilege is lost. Thus, the trial court must consider the evidence and argument rebutting the ex-

149. Restatement (Third) of the Law Governing Lawyers §132.
150. 697 So. 2d 1249 (Fla. Dist. Ct. App. 1997).

istence of the crime-fraud exception and must weigh its sufficiency against the case made by the proponent of the exception.[151]

Scope and exceptions to the work product doctrine

The attorney work product doctrine has its genesis in the Supreme Court's decision in Hickman v. Taylor.[152] *Hickman* was an action for wrongful death of a seaman against the owners of a tug that sank. Plaintiffs sought to obtain by discovery copies of all written statements from members of the crew taken by defendants. The Court first held that the statements were not protected by the attorney-client privilege since they did not involve confidential communications from the client.[153] The Court went on to hold, however, that the material sought by the plaintiff was still not subject to discovery:

> Historically, a lawyer is an officer of the court and is bound to work for the advancement of justice while faithfully protecting the rightful interests of his clients. In performing his various duties, however, it is essential that a lawyer work with a certain degree of privacy, free from unnecessary intrusion by opposing parties and their counsel. Proper preparation of a client's case demands that he assemble information, sift what he considers to be the relevant from the irrelevant facts, prepare his legal theories and plan his strategy without undue and needless interference. That is the historical and the necessary way in which lawyers act within the framework of our system of jurisprudence to promote justice and to protect their clients' interests. This work is reflected, of course, in interviews, statements, memoranda, correspondence, briefs, mental impressions, personal beliefs, and countless other tangible and intangible ways — aptly though roughly termed by the Circuit Court of Appeals in this case . . . as the "Work product of the lawyer." Were such materials open to opposing counsel on mere demand, much of what is now put down in writing would remain unwritten. An attorney's thoughts, heretofore inviolate, would not be his own. Inefficiency, unfairness and sharp practices would inevitably develop in the giving of legal advice and in the preparation of cases for trial. The

---

151. Id. at 1256. See also Haines v. Liggett Group, Inc., 975 F.2d 81 (3d Cir. 1992) (adopting "prima facie" evidence standard).
152. 329 U.S. 495 (1947).
153. Id. at 508.

effect on the legal profession would be demoralizing. And the interests of the clients and the cause of justice would be poorly served.[154]

The Court concluded that work product material was not absolutely immune from discovery: "Where relevant and non-privileged facts remain hidden in an attorney's file and where production of those facts is essential to the preparation of one's case, discovery may properly be had."[155]

The work product doctrine is embodied in Rule 26(b)(3) of the Federal Rules of Civil Procedure:

> Trial Preparation: Materials. Subject to the provisions of subdivision (b)(4) of this rule, a party may obtain discovery of documents and tangible things otherwise discoverable under subdivision (b)(1) of this rule and prepared in anticipation of litigation or for trial by or for another party or by or for that other party's representative (including the other party's attorney, consultant, surety, indemnitor, insurer, or agent) only upon a showing that the party seeking discovery has substantial need of the materials in the preparation of the party's case and that the party is unable without undue hardship to obtain the substantial equivalent of the materials by other means. In ordering discovery of such materials when the required showing has been made, the court shall protect against disclosure of the mental impressions, conclusions, opinions, or legal theories of an attorney or other representative of a party concerning the litigation.

[margin note: If discoverable + unable to be acquired elsewhere it is subject]

Two aspects of the work product doctrine should be noted. First, for the doctrine to apply, the material must be prepared "in anticipation of litigation." Second, a party may obtain discovery of work product material by showing "substantial need" coupled with "undue hardship."[156]

[margin note: sub need + undue hardship]

In applying the work product doctrine courts have developed a distinction between ordinary and opinion work product. The Restatement provides the following definition: "Opinion work product consists of the opinions or mental impressions of a lawyer;

154. Id. at 510-511.
155. Id. at 511.
156. The Restatement of the Law Governing Lawyers contains an extensive discussion of the elements of the work product doctrine. See Restatement (Third) of the Law Governing Lawyers §§136-142.

all other work product is ordinary work product."[157] Opinion work product receives greater protection than ordinary work product. While a party may obtain ordinary work product if the party can establish substantial need for the material and inability to obtain equivalent material without undue hardship, a party may obtain opinion work product only if "extraordinary circumstances justify disclosure," unless an exception exists.[158] The work product doctrine is subject to many of the same exceptions as the attorney-client privilege. The protections of the work product doctrine can be waived,[159] and most courts recognize that the crime-fraud exception applies.[160]

Internal investigations: scope of the attorney-client privilege

When allegations of serious wrongdoing are made against corporate employees, corporations will usually investigate the charges. Are the results of such internal investigations discoverable by the opposing party, or are they protected by the attorney-client privilege or the work product doctrine? In Upjohn v. United States,[161] the Supreme Court dealt with the issue of whether under the Federal Rules of Evidence the Internal Revenue Service could subpoena written questionnaires sent by the corporation's general counsel to various middle managers as part of the corporation's internal investigation into questionable foreign payments made by one of its subsidiaries. The questionnaire sought detailed factual information about the payments. The court of appeals held that the questionnaire was not privileged because the privilege applies only to members of the "control group," not to lower-level employees. The Supreme Court reversed. It held that the control group test "overlooks the fact that the privilege exists to protect not only the giving of professional advice to those who can act on it but also the giving of information to the lawyer to enable him to give sound and informed advice."[162] The Court did not specify a

157. Id. §136(2).
158. Id. §138.
159. Id. §§140 (waiver by voluntary act), 141 (waiver by use in litigation).
160. Id. §142.
161. 449 U.S. 383 (1981).
162. Id. at 390.

clear rule for the scope of the privilege, indicating that the privilege must be decided on a case-by-case basis, but the Court did hold that the privilege could apply to communications made by both middle- and lower-level employees.

Corp privileg cdn exist at every level of corp

While *Upjohn* appears to provide broad protection for communications by all corporate employees to corporate counsel in federal court, *Upjohn* has not been widely followed in the state courts.[163] Some courts have accepted the control group test.[164] Others follow a "subject matter test":

> [A]n employee of a corporation, though not a member of its control group, is sufficiently identified with the corporation so that his communication to the corporation's attorney is privileged where the employee makes the communication at the direction of his superiors in the corporation and where the subject matter upon which the attorney's advice is sought by the corporation and dealt with in the communication is the performance by the employee of the duties of his employment.[165]

C. Conflicts of Interest

─────────────── **Problem 3-4** ───────────────

Representation Against Current Clients

You are a member of the professional responsibility committee of the law firm of Knight & McLaughlin.[166]

---

163. See Alexander C. Black, Annotation, What Corporate Communications Are Entitled to Attorney-Client Privilege — Modern Cases, 27 A.L.R.5th 76 (1995).

164. See, e.g., Consolidation Coal Co. v. Bucyrus-Erie Co., 432 N.E.2d 250 (Ill. 1982).

165. Southern Bell Tel. & Tel. Co. v. Deason, 632 So. 2d 1377, 1383 (Fla. 1994) (quoting Harper & Row Publishers, Inc. v. Decker, 423 F.2d 487 (7th Cir. 1970), *aff'd per curiam by an equally divided court*, 400 U.S. 348 (1971)). Compare Samaritan Found. v. Goodfarb, 862 P.2d 870 (Ariz. 1993) (en banc) (adopting narrow version of subject-matter test in which communication must relate to employee's own activities).

166. Mallen and Smith, the authors of the leading treatise on legal malpractice, recommend that a law firm create a committee, which they refer to as the "quality control committee," to engage in malpractice prevention. They iden-

The committee's functions include making decisions on conflicts of interest and other issues of professional ethics that the firm faces. How would you decide the following issues that have been presented to the committee?

a. During the previous two years the firm has done a small amount of legal work for the Velasquez Steel Company. The work involved some tax issues and questions under the Fair Labor Standards Act. The firm has not done any work for Velasquez Steel this year. Fees paid by Velasquez during the last two years total about $25,000. Recently, General Contractors, Inc. has asked Knight & McLaughlin to represent it in a major breach of warranty action against Velasquez. The partner in the firm who would be in charge of the matter estimates that the case would generate more than $1 million in fees for the firm.

b. The firm is handling the formation of NYM Associates, a limited partnership with ten doctors as limited partners. The partnership owns and operates sophisticated equipment used in medical testing and diagnosis. Oldtown Hospital has asked the firm to defend it in a malpractice action filed against the hospital and several doctors, one of whom is a 10 percent owner in NYM Associates. The hospital will need to argue in the litigation that if any malpractice occurred, it was the fault of the doctor and that the hospital bears no responsibility.

c. The firm represents the American Plumbing Contractors Association, a national association with more than 1,000 members, in connection with federal, state, and local legislative and regulatory matters. Harriet Clawson, a discharged former executive of one of the companies in the association, has asked the firm to

tify 21 functions for such a committee, including analysis of potential ethical problems. 1 Mallen & Smith, Legal Malpractice §2.4.

represent her in a wrongful discharge action against her former company.

d. The firm represents Johnson Control Company, a manufacturer of electronic parts, in a products liability action. Johnson Control is a wholly owned subsidiary of National Electric, Inc. American Computer Components has asked the firm to defend it in a products liability action brought by Wilson Disk Company. Wilson Disk Company is also a wholly owned subsidiary of National Electric. Thus, Johnson Control and Wilson Disk are both subsidiaries of National Electric.

e. One of the firm's rapidly growing clients is computerservices.com, a company that provides a variety of hardware, software, and Internet services to businesses. Computerservices has asked the firm to represent it in an appeal to the United States Court of Appeals for the Sixth Circuit involving the application of the Fair Labor Standards Act. When the matter was listed in the firm's new business report, another partner raised a question about the matter, because he represents a number of business clients in Fair Labor Standards Act cases; he was concerned that the firm might be representing clients with inconsistent legal positions.

f. The committee is considering recommending to the litigation section that the firm include the following prospective waiver of conflicts of interest in its retainer agreements. The provision would be used only with sophisticated entities that have in-house counsel:

> It is understood and agreed that the firm represents [name of entity, hereinafter referred to as "Client"] and not any of its officers, directors, shareholders, employees, subsidiaries, affiliates, or members, unless the firm specifically agrees in writing to undertake representation of any such person.
> It is further understood and agreed that the firm reserves the right to represent existing or new clients in matters against Client, so long as such representation is

not substantially related to any matter that the firm is handling for Client, and Client hereby expressly waives any claim that such representation involves a conflict of interest or disqualifies the firm from such representation. **PLEASE CONSULT WITH YOUR IN-HOUSE COUNSEL REGARDING THIS WAIVER OF CONFLICTS OF INTEREST.**

  g.   The committee has been struggling with articulating a principle for deciding doubtful conflict-of-interest questions. Some more traditional members of the firm believe that the firm should turn down any matter that involves even a remote possibility of a conflict of interest, absent the consent of all affected clients, in order to avoid any appearance of impropriety. Other members of the firm point to the competitive environment in which law firms function and argue that the firm should not turn down substantial matters when the risk of disqualification or other charge of unethical conduct is small. What approach would you favor?

Read Model Rules 1.7, 1.9, 1.13, and comments.

Representation of one client against another client in a single matter and in unrelated matters

Conflicts of interest come in a variety of forms: adverse representation against a current client, multiple representation of clients in a single matter, representation against a former client, advocate-witness conflicts, and conflicts involving the lawyer's own personal or financial interest.[167] Problem 3-4 posed several situations involving adverse representation against a "current" client.

Model Rule 1.7(a) deals with adverse representation against current clients. That rule provides that a lawyer may not undertake representation that is "directly adverse" to another client unless

---

167. See generally Samuel R. Miller et al., Conflicts of Interest in Corporate Litigation, 48 Bus. Law. 141 (1992). See also ABA, Task Force on Conflicts of Interest, Conflict of Interest Issues, 50 Bus. Law. 1381 (1995) (discussion of principles and suggested agreements for medium and large firms in dealing with common conflict-of-interest problems).

certain conditions are met. In applying Rule 1.7(a) a distinction should be drawn between conflicts involving representation against a current client in a *single contested litigation matter* and in *unrelated matters*.

Cases in which lawyers are asked to undertake representation on behalf of one client against another client in a single contested litigation matter are rare but do occur occasionally. For example, a lawyer may be asked to represent a driver and a passenger in an automobile accident involving another driver, when the passenger has a claim against the driver of her vehicle.[168] See Problem 3-8. Lawyers have sometimes been asked to represent both spouses in divorce cases.[169] See Problem 3-10.

Both the Restatement of the Law Governing Lawyers and the Model Rules adopt the position that representation of interests that are directly adverse in a contested litigation matter is improper, even with the consent of all affected clients. The Restatement states:

> Notwithstanding the informed consent of each affected client or former client, a lawyer may not represent a client if: . . .
>
> (b)   one client will assert a claim against the other in the same litigation;[170]

Two justifications can be given for prohibiting representation of adverse clients in a single matter, even with their consent. First, the rules dealing with conflicts of interest are based on the lawyer's duty of loyalty. See Model Rule 1.7, cmt. 1. In single-matter conflicts the lawyer cannot carry out the duty of loyalty owed to both clients. Whatever the lawyer does for one client will of necessity harm the other client in the matter. In addition, for systemic

---

168. E.g., In re Shaw, 443 A.2d 670 (N.J. 1982); Fugnitto v. Fugnitto, 452 N.Y.S.2d 976 (App. Div. 1982). See also Chateau de Ville Prods., Inc. v. Tams-Witmark Music Library, Inc., 474 F. Supp. 223 (S.D.N.Y. 1979) (law firm could not represent plaintiff and alleged coconspirator of defendant).

169. Klemm v. Superior Court, 142 Cal. Rptr. 509 (Ct. App. 1977) (lawyer may not represent both husband and wife in contested divorce).

170. Restatement (Third) of the Law Governing Lawyers §202(2)(b) & cmt. *g(iii)*. For a review of the Restatement's provisions on conflicts of interest, see Nancy J. Moore, Restating the Law of Lawyer Conflicts, 10 Geo. J. Legal Ethics 541 (1997).

reasons representation of adverse parties in a single matter is improper. Our legal system produces decisions that serve as guidance for future conduct by third parties and as means for vindication of public interests. The adversarial nature of the system is based on the assumption of zealous representation by lawyers of the interests of their clients. If a lawyer's representation of a client is infected by a conflict of interest, the adversarial nature of the representation is undermined, and the public benefits flowing from the adversarial system may be reduced.[171] As the Restatement of the Law Governing Lawyers puts it, "the institutional interest in vigorous development of each client's position renders the conflict nonconsentable."[172]

The Model Rules express the same prohibition against representation of adverse parties in a single contested litigation more obliquely than the Restatement. Rule 1.7(a) states that a lawyer may not represent a client whose interest is "directly adverse" to another client unless (1) "the lawyer reasonably believes the representation will not adversely affect the relationship with the other client" and (2) "each client consents after consultation." While the text of the rule seems to allow such representation with client consent, Comment 7 states that "[p]aragraph (a) prohibits representation of opposing parties in litigation." In addition, Comment 5 states that "when a disinterested lawyer would conclude that the client should not agree to the representation under the circumstances, the lawyer involved cannot properly ask for such agreement or provide representation on the basis of the client's consent." Given the nature of the adversarial system, a disinterested lawyer would not approve of representation of clients with directly adverse interests in a single contested litigation matter.

Note also that, in general, if the rules of ethics prohibit a lawyer's conduct, that prohibition extends to all members of the lawyer's firm. See Model Rule 1.10. We will discuss the rationale, scope, and limitations of this rule of "vicarious" or "imputed" disqualification in later problems in these materials.

---

171. Professor Nancy Moore, however, has criticized the "public interest" justification for limiting client consent to multiple representation. She argues that the focus should be on the client's capacity for informed and voluntary consent. Nancy J. Moore, Conflicts of Interest in the Simultaneous Representation of Multiple Clients: A Proposed Solution to the Current Confusion and Controversy, 61 Tex. L. Rev. 211, 229-230 (1982).

172. Restatement (Third) of the Law Governing Lawyers §202, cmt. *g(iii)*.

The rule prohibiting lawyers and members of their firms from undertaking representation adverse to current clients applies not only to adverse representation in a single matter but also to adverse representation in unrelated matters. For example, if a member of a firm represents client *A* in one matter, a member of that firm may not generally represent client *B* against *A* in an unrelated matter even though the firm does not represent *A* in that second matter. See Model Rule 1.7, cmt. 8. Grievance Committee v. Rottner illustrates this type of conflict.[173] In *Rottner,* Twible retained a law firm to represent him in a minor collection matter. While this case was pending, O'Brien asked the same firm to represent him in an action for assault and battery against Twible. Although the firm informed O'Brien that it had represented Twible in prior matters and was currently representing him in the collection case, the firm did not discuss O'Brien's case with Twible, nor did the firm obtain Twible's consent to representation. The firm then filed suit on O'Brien's behalf against Twible. The complaint sought both actual and punitive damages, claiming that Twible's conduct was "wilful, wanton, malicious, premeditated and vindictive."[174] Despite protests from Twible, the firm continued representing O'Brien and even proceeded to attach Twible's home in connection with the case.

In finding that the lawyers involved in the matter were guilty of misconduct, the Connecticut Supreme Court discussed how a lawyer's representation against a client in an unrelated matter violates the principle of loyalty:

> When a client engages the services of a lawyer in a given piece of business he is entitled to feel that, until that business is finally disposed of in some manner, he has the undivided loyalty of the one upon whom he looks as his advocate and his champion. If, as in this case, he is sued and his home attached by his own attorney, who is representing him in another matter, all feeling of loyalty is necessarily destroyed, and the profession is exposed to the charge that it is interested only in money.[175]

173. 203 A.2d 82 (Conn. 1964).
174. Id. at 83.
175. Id. at 84. See also Committee on Legal Ethics v. Frame, 433 S.E.2d 579 (W. Va. 1993) (improper for lawyer to represent controlling shareholder of corporation in her divorce action while another lawyer in firm represented plaintiff in personal injury action against her corporation).

As *Rottner* shows, a lawyer's duty of loyalty precludes the lawyer from undertaking representation of one client against another client even if the matters are unrelated to one another. Conflicts involving unrelated matters differ in two respects, however, from cases of adverse representation against a client in a single matter. First, because the matters are unrelated, the impact on the duty of loyalty is decreased. Second, the adverse representation in unrelated matters does not undermine the integrity of an adversarial presentation. Because of these differences, with informed client consent a lawyer may undertake representation of clients in unrelated matters, although it may be difficult to obtain consent from both clients.[176]

Determining who is a current client

Rule 1.7(a) applies only if the clients are both current clients. If the adverse client is a former client rather than a current one, a less restrictive rule applies: A lawyer may ethically undertake representation against a former client, even without that former client's consent, if the current and former matters are not "substantially related" to each other. Model Rule 1.9. We will consider the substantial relationship test in Problem 3-5.

Determining whether a client is a current or former client is not always straightforward. If a firm is currently doing work for a client, then the client is quite clearly a current client. Even if the firm is not currently doing work for a client, however, courts will treat a client as a current client when an ongoing professional relationship exists between the client and the firm such that the client reasonably expects that the firm is its lawyer. This continuous relationship is clearly present when the client hires the firm pursuant to a general retainer, a fee paid to the firm to ensure its availability to handle work for the client, but it can also occur even when the

---

176. Model Rule 1.7(a) and cmt. 8; Restatement (Third) of the Law Governing Lawyers §209(2). Professor Tom Morgan argues that representation of one client against another client in unrelated matters should be improper, even if the consent of both clients cannot be obtained, only if the lawyer's representation would be materially limited. Thomas D. Morgan, Suing a Current Client, 9 Geo. J. Legal Ethics 1157 (1996).

client has not paid the firm a general retainer. (Recall the discussion of general and special retainers in Problem 2-2.)

A leading case on the issue of whether a client-lawyer relationship remains current is International Business Machines Corp. v. Levin,[177] an action brought under the federal antitrust laws by the plaintiffs, Levin and Levin Computer Corporation (LCC). The plaintiffs were represented by a law firm that had represented Levin since 1965. Beginning in 1971, the firm represented Levin and LCC in negotiations with IBM to purchase certain computer equipment on credit. IBM refused to grant purchasers of equipment financing terms as favorable as those offered to lessees. As a result Levin and LCC filed suit in June 1972, claiming that IBM had committed antitrust violations. Beginning in April 1970, other lawyers in the same firm had been representing IBM in unrelated labor matters. On the date when the firm filed the antitrust action, the firm was not handling a specific matter for IBM, but it did undertake labor work for IBM after commencing the litigation.

IBM representatives were originally unaware of the firm's dual representation. When they learned of the conflict, almost five years after the antitrust action was filed, IBM moved to disqualify the firm in the antitrust action. The firm argued that the dual representation would not have an adverse effect on its independent professional judgment on behalf of IBM. The Court of Appeals for the Third Circuit disagreed: "[A] possible effect on the quality of the attorney's services on behalf of the client being sued may be a diminution in the vigor of his representation of the client in the other matter."[178]

The court also held that there was a client-lawyer relationship between the law firm and IBM even though the firm was not currently handling a matter for IBM at the time the firm filed suit on behalf of Levin and Levin Computer Corporation against IBM. The court stated:

> Although [the law firm] had no specific assignment from IBM on hand on the day the antitrust complaint was filed and even though [it] performed services for IBM on a fee for service basis rather than

177. 579 F.2d 271 (3d Cir. 1978).
178. Id. at 280.

pursuant to a retainer arrangement, the pattern of repeated retainers, both before and after the filing of the complaint, supports the finding of a continuous relationship.[179]

Determining who is a current client in "entity" representation cases

Determining whether a person is a current client can also be complex when the client is an entity such as a partnership, corporation, or association. Merely because a law firm represents an entity does not mean that the firm has a client-lawyer relationship with every member of the entity. For example, in Formal Opinion 91-361 the ABA Committee on Ethics and Professional Responsibility addressed the question whether an attorney who represents a partnership has a client-lawyer relationship with its partners. The committee first noted that the Rules of Professional Conduct adopt in Rule 1.13(a) the concept of "entity" representation, which means that a lawyer employed by an entity represents it rather than any of its members or constituents.

The committee went on to hold, however, that an attorney who represents a partnership could also have a client-lawyer relationship with a partner, depending on the facts and circumstances:

> Whether such a relationship has been created almost always will depend on an analysis of the specific facts involved. The analysis may include such factors as whether the lawyer affirmatively assumed a duty of representation to the individual partner, whether the partner was separately represented by other counsel when the partnership was created or in connection with its affairs, whether the lawyer had represented an individual partner before undertaking to represent the partnership, and whether there was evidence of reliance by the individual partner on the lawyer as his or her separate counsel, or of the partner's expectation of personal representation.[180]

Numerous cases follow the general approach reflected in Formal Opinion 91-361.[181]

179. Id. at 281.
180. ABA Comm. on Ethics and Prof. Resp., Formal Op. 91-361, at 4.
181. See Hopper v. Frank, 16 F.3d 92 (5th Cir. 1994) (summary judgment for law firm affirmed in legal malpractice action claiming that law firm that

A similar facts-and-circumstances analysis applies to closely held corporations and to associations. For example, in Meyer v. Mulligan[182] the Wyoming Supreme Court reversed a trial court's decision granting summary judgment for a lawyer in a claim for legal malpractice brought by a shareholder in a closely held corporation. Relying on ABA Formal Opinion 91-361, the court held that summary judgment was inappropriate because it was unclear whom the lawyer represented.[183] Similarly, in Formal Opinion 92-365, the ABA Committee on Ethics and Professional Responsibility ruled that an attorney does not automatically have a client-lawyer relationship with a member of an association simply because the attorney represents the association, but such a relationship can arise from the facts and circumstances. The committee quoted with approval the factors that it had referred to in the partnership setting. It also indicated that another factor was the size of the association.

A leading case dealing with the existence of a client-lawyer relationship in the context of representation of associations is Westinghouse Electric Corp. v. Kerr-McGee Corp.[184] In *Westinghouse* an association of petroleum producers retained the Washington office of Kirkland & Ellis as independent special counsel to prepare a report on competition in the industry. To collect information for the report, the firm sent a questionnaire to oil companies that were members of the association; the firm also interviewed representatives of some of these companies. The firm told the companies that all information divulged to the law firm

---

represented limited partnership in securities offering had client-lawyer relationship with general partners of partnership); Responsible Citizens v. Superior Court, 20 Cal. Rptr. 2d 756 (Ct. App. 1993, *review denied*) (attorney that represents partnership does not per se have client-lawyer relationship with partners; such relationship can be formed based on express or implied agreement); Security Bank v. Klicker, 418 N.W.2d 27 (Wis. Ct. App. 1987, *review denied*) (lawyer does not have client-lawyer relationship with partners merely by virtue of representation of partnership; whether firm has client-lawyer relationship with partners depends on facts and circumstances of dealings between attorney and individual partners).

182. 889 P.2d 509 (Wyo. 1995).

183. But see Brennan v. Ruffner, 640 So. 2d 143 (Fla. Dist. Ct. App. 1994) (summary judgment granted for lawyer in legal malpractice action brought by shareholder in closely held corporation on ground that lawyer represented corporation, not individual shareholders).

184. 580 F.2d 1311 (7th Cir.), *cert. denied*, 439 U.S. 955 (1978).

would be confidential. The final report released by the firm presented facts and arguments to show that legislation to break up the oil companies was unnecessary in light of overall competitive conditions in the energy industry. Subsequently, the firm's Chicago office filed a complaint on behalf of Westinghouse against a number of defendants, several of whom were members of the petroleum association, charging violations of the federal antitrust laws. The complaint presented theories diametrically opposed to those set forth in the report that the firm had prepared for the association. The Court of Appeals for the Seventh Circuit ruled that a client-lawyer relationship existed between the law firm and the members of the association and that the firm should therefore be disqualified from handling the antitrust case. If Kirkland & Ellis had done nothing more than represent the association, it would not have had a client-lawyer relationship with the members of the association. The firm, however, held itself out as independent counsel, communicated directly with members of the association, and assured them of confidentiality, one of the hallmarks of a client-lawyer relationship.[185]

In contrast to the facts-and-circumstances approach for partnerships and associations, a number of courts have held that when a lawyer represents a member of a corporate group, the lawyer will be treated as having a client-lawyer relationship with subsidiaries, affiliates, or other members of the corporate group. In McCourt Co. v. FPC Properties, Inc.,[186] the Massachusetts Supreme Court stated the principle as follows:

> A law firm that represents client *A* in the defense of an action may not, at the same time, be counsel for a plaintiff in an action brought against client *A*, at least without the consent of both parties. . . . Nor does it matter that client *A* is a corporation or that client *A* consists, collectively, of a parent corporation and various wholly owned subsidiaries.[187]

185. For a somewhat different approach to the issue of whether a client-lawyer relationship exists between a firm representing an association and members of the association, see Glueck v. Jonathan Logan, Inc., 653 F.2d 746 (2d Cir. 1981) ("substantial relationship" test used to determine whether law firm that represented association should be disqualified from representation of plaintiff in action against defendant member of association).

186. 434 N.E.2d 1234 (Mass. 1982).

187. Id. at 1235.

Similarly, in Stratagem Development Corp. v. Heron International N.V.[188] the court held that a law firm was per se ineligible to represent the plaintiff when the firm also represented a wholly owned subsidiary of the defendant. This was true although the litigation concerned matters unrelated to the representation of the subsidiary. A law firm's obligation to an existing client must be measured "not so much against the similarities in litigation, as against the duty of undivided loyalty," a duty that "applies with equal force where the client is a subsidiary of the entity to be sued."[189]

The corporate group cases seem inconsistent with the general principles governing formation of client-lawyer relationships. Indeed, the corporate group cases are probably weaker ones for creation of client-lawyer relationships because the connection between the attorney and the purported corporate client is likely to be more remote than in partnerships or in closely held corporations. Recent decisions have indicated a willingness to apply a facts-and-circumstances test to determine whether a law firm that represents a member of a corporate group has a client-lawyer relationship with other members of the group.[190] Further, in Formal Opinion 95-390 the ABA Committee on Ethics and Professional Responsibility supported use of a facts-and-circumstances test rather than a per se rule to determine formation of client-lawyer relationships in corporate groups.

188.   756 F. Supp. 789 (S.D.N.Y. 1991).
189.   Id. at 792. See also Hartford Accident & Indemnity Co. v. RJR Nabisco, Inc., 721 F. Supp. 534 (S.D.N.Y. 1989) (parent corporation was client of law firm by virtue of firm's representation of its wholly owned subsidiary; had law firm not earlier terminated its representation of subsidiary, it would have been disqualified from representing plaintiff in suit against parent).
190.   See Reuben H. Donnelley Corp. v. Sprint Publishing & Advertising, Inc. 1996 WL 99902 (N.D. Ill. 1996) (law firm that represented one of Sprint's more than 250 subsidiaries not disqualified from representing client in litigation against another subsidiary when subsidiaries were separate entities and not alter egos); Brooklyn Navy Yard Cogeneration Partners, L.P. v. Superior Court, 70 Cal. Rptr. 2d 419 (Ct. App. 1997) (law firm not disqualified from representing client against parent corporation when firm represented parent's subsidiary in unrelated matters; court adopts "alter ego" test to determine whether affiliated entities should be treated as one client under conflict of interest rules). Cf. ABA Comm. on Ethics and Prof. Resp., Formal Op. 97-405 (lawyer may represent one government agency while representing a client against another agency, unless engagement agreement with government provides for broader definition of client).

The Restatement of the Law Governing Lawyers adopts a facts-and-circumstances test for determining whether a client-lawyer relationship exists, focusing on the reasonable expectations of the client:

§26   Formation of Client-Lawyer Relationship

A relationship of client and lawyer arises when:

> (1) a person manifests to a lawyer the person's intent that the lawyer provide legal services for the person; and either
>> (a) the lawyer manifests to the person consent to do so; or
>> (b) the lawyer fails to manifest lack of consent to do so, and the lawyer knows or reasonably should know that the person reasonably relies on the lawyer to provide the services; or
> (2) a tribunal with power to do so appoints the lawyer to provide the services.

Positional conflicts

Sometimes a conflict of interest can arise when a lawyer takes a legal position on behalf of one client that is adverse to the interests of another client. The term *positional conflict of interest* has been coined to refer to such conflicts. Positional conflicts can arise in a variety of ways: The purest form involves a firm taking opposing legal positions on behalf of different clients in different courts. A subtler form of positional conflict occurs when a firm represents one client in a matter that can harm the economic interests of another client.[191]

The Model Rules do not have a specific provision dealing with positional conflicts, but comment 9 to Model Rule 1.7 states:

> A lawyer may represent parties having antagonistic positions on a legal question that has arisen in different cases, unless representation of either client would be adversely affected. Thus, it is ordinarily not improper to assert such positions in cases pending in different trial courts, but it may be improper to do so in cases pending at the same time in an appellate court.

191. See John S. Dzienkowski, Positional Conflicts of Interest, 71 Tex. L. Rev. 457 (1993).

The Restatement elaborates on when representation of adverse legal positions would be improper:

> [A] conflict is presented when there is a substantial risk that a lawyer's action in Case A will materially and adversely affect another of the lawyer's clients in Case B. Factors relevant in determining the risk of such an effect include whether the issue is before a trial court or an appellate court; whether the issue is substantive or procedural; the temporal relationship between the matters; the practical significance of the issue to the immediate and long-run interests of the clients involved; and the clients' reasonable expectations in retaining the lawyer.[192]

If advocacy of one client's legal position would materially and adversely affect another client, the lawyer may proceed only with the informed consent of both clients.[193]

Sometimes a positional conflict of interest arises not because of adverse legal positions but because the lawyer represents competing economic interests. Comment 3 to Model Rule 1.7 states that representation of competing economic interests is generally proper without the need for client consent: "On the other hand, simultaneous representation in unrelated matters of clients whose interests are only generally adverse, such as competing economic enterprises, does not require consent of the respective clients."

In Maritrans GP, Inc. v. Pepper, Hamilton & Scheetz[194] the Pennsylvania Supreme Court stirred a good deal of concern in the profession when it held that under some circumstances it was a conflict of interest and breach of fiduciary duty for a law firm to represent competitors. In Maritrans the defendant law firm had been Maritrans's labor counsel for a number of years, and then began representing some of Maritrans's competitors. The firm and Maritrans initially reached an understanding in which Pepper, Hamilton agreed not to represent Maritrans's chief competitor, while Maritrans consented to the firm's representation of lesser competitors, provided the firm put in place screening mechanisms to prevent confidential information from passing between the lawyers representing Maritrans and those representing the competi-

---

192. Restatement (Third) of the Law Governing Lawyers §209, cmt. *f.*

193. See id.; ABA Comm. on Legal Ethics and Prof. Resp., Formal Op. 93-377.

194. 602 A.2d 1277 (Pa. 1992).

tors. Pepper, Hamilton, however, reneged on the agreement by "parking" the chief competitor with a labor lawyer in another firm who soon joined the firm. Maritrans sought an injunction to prevent Pepper, Hamilton from representing its competitors. The firm argued that the case involved a "business conflict" between competitors rather than an ethical violation. The Pennsylvania Supreme Court, however, enjoined Pepper, Hamilton from representing Maritrans's competitors because the firm was using confidential information gained during its prior representation against a former client. The court stated that it was not adopting a per se rule prohibiting a lawyer from undertaking representation of competitors, but it noted that each case must be judged on its facts. While *Maritrans* has generated a good deal of discussion, the case should not be read as prohibiting representation of clients with competing economic interests. The facts of *Maritrans* were extreme, involving abuse of a fiduciary relationship, misrepresentation to a client, and misuse of confidential information. Such conduct is far more egregious than simply representing clients with competing economic interests.

Consentable conflicts

Rule 1.7(a) allows a lawyer to represent one client against a current client provided (1) the lawyer reasonably believes that the representation of one client will not adversely affect the representation of the other and (2) each client consents after consultation. The possibility of consentable conflicts raises several questions: Why should a lawyer ever be able to undertake representation against a client even with that client's consent? Why shouldn't a lawyer always be able to undertake representation against a client provided the client is willing to consent? What steps must the lawyer take to have effective consent?[195]

Why should a lawyer ever be able to undertake representation against a client? The rationale for allowing representation against a client with the consent of that client follows from the interests of both clients. The client seeking the lawyer's services has an interest in being able to retain the lawyer of its choice. The client

195. See generally Fred C. Zacharias, Waiving Conflicts of Interest, 108 Yale L. J. 407 (1998).

against whom the lawyer would be undertaking representation has an interest in the loyalty of its counsel. In some cases, however, the impact of the representation on the lawyer's duty of loyalty to that client is farfetched. If the potentially adversely affected client is willing to "waive" any objection to the representation because it does not believe that the representation will have an impact on the lawyer's duty of loyalty to it, then the interests of both clients are being advanced. Consider the following example given by the ABA Committee on Ethics and Professional Responsibility in Formal Opinion 93-372:

> [T]he idea that . . . a corporation in Miami retaining the Florida office of a national law firm to negotiate a lease should preclude that firm's New York office from taking an adverse position in a totally unrelated commercial dispute against another division of the same corporation strikes some as placing unreasonable limitations on the opportunities of both clients and lawyers.[196]

Why shouldn't all conflicts be subject to waiver or consent? We have already seen that in cases in which a lawyer is asked to represent clients who have adverse interests in a single contested litigation matter, representation is improper even with client consent. In these situations it is impossible for the lawyer to comply with the duty of loyalty to both clients; in addition, the systemic interest in the proper functioning of the adversarial situation justifies a per se prohibition. In most conflict situations, however, including those involving unrelated-matter conflicts, representation of both clients is permissible with their consent.

Assuming then that some, but not all, conflicts are subject to waiver or consent, what must a lawyer do to obtain effective client consent? A good example of informed consent by a client to representation against it in unrelated matters is Unified Sewerage Agency v. Jelco, Inc.[197] In *Unified Sewerage* a law firm was representing Teeples & Thatcher, a client that the firm had represented for more than 10 years, in an embryonic dispute with its general contractor, Jelco, when Jelco asked the same firm to represent it in a dispute with an electrical subcontractor. The firm advised Jelco of its representation of Teeples & Thatcher and informed

196. ABA Comm. on Ethics and Prof. Resp., Formal Op. 93-372, at 2.
197. 646 F.2d 1339 (9th Cir. 1981).

Jelco that it could not undertake representation unless Jelco consented to the firm's continued representation of Teeples & Thatcher. Jelco's management, with full knowledge of the firm's representation of Teeples & Thatcher and with the advice of its general counsel, consented to the law firm's representation of Teeples & Thatcher. Subsequently, the firm filed suit in the name of Unified Sewerage for the benefit of Teeples & Thatcher against Jelco. The firm again asked Jelco whether it consented to the firm's continued representation of Teeples & Thatcher and Jelco once again gave its consent. A few months later, however, Jelco discharged the firm from handling the matter with the electrical subcontractor and also moved to disqualify the firm in the pending action brought by Unified.

The Court of Appeals for the Ninth Circuit affirmed the trial court's decision denying the motion for disqualification. While recognizing the general rule precluding representation against a present client, the court held that such representation was proper because Jelco had given informed consent. The court noted that the attorney must do more than simply inform the client of the conflict and obtain approval of the representation. The lawyer must explain the implications of the conflict to the client. On the facts of the case the court found that this requirement was satisfied. The court placed particular emphasis on the fact that Jelco's consent had been obtained after Jelco had consulted with its general counsel about the matter.

By contrast to *Unified Sewerage*, the court in International Business Machines Corp. v. Levin, discussed above, held that the firm had not effectively obtained IBM's consent. Two partners in the law firm testified that they had independently obtained IBM's consent to the firm's representation of Levin, but representatives of IBM denied that they had given their consent. The Court of Appeals for the Third Circuit rejected the consent argument because it concluded that the law firm had not carried its burden of proving a "full disclosure" to IBM as required by DR 5-105(C) (the predecessor to Model Rule 1.7). The court noted that the alleged consent occurred during a telephone call that took at most three minutes.

Consent: validity of prospective waivers

In cases like *Unified Sewerage,* the consent occurred after the conflict situation arose. May a law firm effectively obtain a prospective waiver of future conflicts? In Formal Opinion 93-372, the ABA Committee on Ethics and Professional Responsibility noted that the impetus for prospective waivers has arisen from the dramatic change in the practice of law that has occurred in the last few decades:

> In an era when law firms operated in just one location, when there were few mega-conglomerate clients and when clients typically hired only a single firm to undertake all of their legal business, the thought of seeking prospective waivers rarely arose.[198]

Recognizing these changes, the committee gave limited endorsement to prospective waivers. The committee ruled that it was "not ordinarily impermissible to seek such prospective waivers" but "the mere existence of a prospective waiver will not necessarily be dispositive of the question whether the waiver is effective." The waiver will not be effective as to matters not reasonably contemplated at the time the waiver was executed. In addition, the waiver will not be effective to allow use of confidential information.

Consider the following analysis of the enforceability of prospective waivers:

> A blanket waiver . . . should not be enforced. Central to the effectiveness of client consent is communication of information sufficient to enable the client to make an informed decision. It is difficult to believe that a client can receive sufficient information to make an informed decision when the client, at the time of the consent, knows neither the nature of the conflict nor the person or entity with whom the conflict exists.
>
> Moreover, the argument in support of judicial recognition of a blanket waiver is weak. The argument is based on the policy in favor of selection of counsel; it posits that if such waivers are not valid, a law firm may be unwilling to undertake representation of a new client in a matter because it fears that the new representation may require the firm's disqualification in a matter on behalf of a more substantial client who has or may have an interest adverse to

198. ABA Comm. on Ethics and Prof. Resp., Formal Op. 93-372, at 2.

that of the new client. Thus, clients may be deprived of the opportunity of obtaining the services of law firms with particular expertise.

This argument in favor of the validity of a blanket waiver ignores the economic forces that drive law firms. . . . To say that the firm would refuse to undertake representation in that matter because of some unknown, future conflict is to say that firms will refuse to take on new business because a new client might some day have a conflict with an existing client. While such a conflict might develop, the client also represents new business to the firm. Therefore, the economic drive of firms will give them a powerful incentive to take on such new business. . . .

While courts should refuse to enforce blanket prospective waivers, it would be appropriate for courts to accept more limited prospective consents. A good example of such a situation is City of Cleveland v. Cleveland Elec. Illuminating Co. [440 F. Supp. 193 (N.D. Ohio 1976), aff'd, 573 F.2d 1310 (6th Cir. 1977), cert. denied, 435 U.S. 996 (1978)]. In that case the law firm of Squire, Sanders & Dempsey had represented Cleveland Electric Company for over 65 years when the City asked the firm to handle a bond matter involving the City's competing utility company. The City was well aware of the law firm's long-time representation of Cleveland Electric because of numerous prior dealings with the Electric Company; it wished to retain the firm's services, however, because it was one of the few firms in Ohio that handled sophisticated bond work. Squire, Sanders was willing to take on the bond work only if the City waived any objection to future conflicts. The City had independent advice from its law department and waived its objections to any conflict of interest. Subsequently, the City moved to disqualify the firm in an antitrust action brought by the City against Cleveland Electric. The United States District Court for the Northern District of Ohio denied the motion for disqualification. In a lengthy opinion the court held that the City had waived any conflict of interest. The court also ruled that the City failed to show that the firm was using confidential information against its interests.

In cases like City of Cleveland a prospective consent should be enforced. The client was a sophisticated corporate entity with independent legal advice about the waiver. The waiver itself was limited to the firm's representation of an identified long-term client rather than a blanket prospective consent. When such factors are present, it seems reasonable to conclude that the client has sufficient information to consent to the dual representation. Moreover, unless the City had agreed to the waiver it would have been unable to obtain representation in specialized bond work. Thus, the policy argument in favor of recognizing a waiver in such a case, which rests on the ability of a client to retain counsel of its choice, seems strong. Finally, the case did not involve the use of confidential information against the client.[199]

The Restatement of the Law Governing Lawyering generally adopts this approach. The Restatement provides that a consent to future conflicts is ineffective unless the client "possesses sophistication in the matter in question and has had the opportunity to receive independent legal advice about the consent." The Restatement also recognizes the possibility that in a continuing client-lawyer relationship, the client might consent in advance to types of conflicts with which it is familiar.[200]

─────────────── **Problem 3-5** ───────────────

Representation Against Former Clients

For eight years the law firm of Carson, Fender & Sink was local counsel for National Securities, Inc., one of the country's largest brokerage firms. The firm defended National in a variety of securities matters, principally arbitrations of claims by customers. Three years ago National had a change of management and decided to replace many of its local counsel, including the Carson firm.

   Recently, Marian Enderson, the chief executive officer of one of Carson's corporate clients, has encountered problems with one of National's brokers, Ronald Benson, an employee of National for a number of years. Enderson claims that Benson gave her misleading information about a company that has since gone bankrupt. Enderson asked the Carson firm to represent her in arbitration against National. The firm advised Enderson

199. Nathan M. Crystal, Disqualification of Counsel for Unrelated Matter Conflicts of Interest, 4 Geo. J. Legal Ethics 273, 307-309 (1990). See Worldspan, L.P. v. Sabre Group Holdings, Inc., 5 F. Supp. 2d 1356 (N.D. Ga. 1998) (general conflicts waiver in engagement agreement ineffective when applied to conflict that arises five years later).
200. Restatement (Third) of the Law Governing Lawyers §202, cmt. *d.*

of its prior representation of National, but Enderson
stated that she wanted the firm to represent her even if
there was a risk that the firm might face a disqualification motion. Carson has filed the claim in arbitration
against National. The claim alleges that National is responsible for Benson's fraud, based on agency and securities   theories.   National   denies   that   Benson
committed any fraud. It also argues that even if Benson
did engage in fraud, it maintains proper procedures for
preventing fraud and therefore is not responsible for
Benson's actions. When the Carson firm filed the complaint in arbitration, counsel for National objected to the
firm's representation of Enderson. After the Carson firm
refused to withdraw, National filed a motion to disqualify the firm. Be prepared to argue in support of the
motion to disqualify on behalf of National and in opposition to the motion on behalf of the Carson firm.

Read Model Rule 1.9 and comments.

Origin and justification for the substantial relationship test

Neither the Code of Professional Responsibility nor the 1908 Canons of Ethics had a specific rule dealing with representation against
a former client. In T.C. Theatre Corp. v. Warner Bros. Pictures,
Inc.,[201] however, Judge Weinfeld articulated a principle for deciding when a lawyer could properly undertake representation against
a former client:

> I hold that the former client need show no more than that the mat-
> ters embraced within the pending suit wherein his former attorney
> appears on behalf of his adversary are substantially related to the
> matters or cause of action wherein the attorney previously repre-
> sented him, the former client. The court will assume that during
> the course of the former representation confidences were disclosed
> to the attorney bearing on the subject matter of the representation.
> It will not inquire into their nature and extent. Only in this manner

201. 113 F. Supp. 265 (S.D.N.Y. 1953).

can the lawyer's duty of absolute fidelity be enforced and the spirit of the rule relating to privileged communications be maintained.

. . . In cases of this sort the court must ask whether it can reasonably be said that in the course of the former representation the attorney might have acquired information related to the subject of his subsequent representation. If so, then the relationship between the two matters is sufficiently close to bring the later representation within the prohibition of Canon 6 [which prohibited lawyers from representing clients with conflicting interest and from revealing confidential information].[202]

Judge Weinfeld developed what is now widely referred to as the "substantial relationship" test for deciding when representation against a former client is permissible. Several aspects of the substantial relationship test developed by Judge Weinfeld are worth noting. Implicit in this test is recognition of the principle that if the matters are not substantially related, representation against a former client is permissible, even without the consent of that former client. Why should this be the case? Shouldn't a lawyer be absolutely precluded from undertaking representation against a former client? Even putting aside the possible misuse of confidential information, isn't representation against a former client disloyal, and doesn't it create an appearance of wrongdoing that should be avoided? While these points have merit, there are competing considerations. First, a duty of absolute loyalty to a former client would mean that a lawyer could never undertake representation against a former client without that client's consent. This rule would substantially limit the ability of other clients to select counsel of their choice. Second, a per se prohibition on representation against former clients might deter lawyers from taking on representation in relatively small matters because of concern that the representation would disqualify the lawyer from handling all unknown future matters against that client. Third, unless some limitation were established, lawyers would owe former clients a lifetime duty of loyalty. The existence of such a duty would almost certainly increase legal fees because lawyers would be forced to take into account the preclusive effect of representation of a client in deciding how much to charge the client for the lawyer's services. Finally, lawyers serve as agents for their clients. Under agency law,

202. Id. at 268-269.

an agent after termination of employment may not use confidential information against the principal, but the agent is not prevented from competing with the principal.[203]

Judge Weinfeld also stated that if the current and former matters were substantially related, a court should make no further inquiry to determine whether confidential information is actually being used. To engage in such an inquiry would defeat the very confidentiality that the rule is designed to protect. Thus, the substantial relationship test in its original form amounted to an "irrebuttable presumption" that confidential information was likely to be used if the matters were substantially related. As noted below, however, some courts have moved away from this view and will allow the attorney to offer evidence to rebut the presumption that confidential information will be used in the subsequent representation. Finally, the remedy most frequently used for violation of the substantial relationship test has been disqualification of the lawyer and the lawyer's firm from continuing the representation of the current client in the substantially related matter against the former client.[204]

Application of the substantial relationship test

Model Rule 1.9(a) codifies the substantial relationship test first developed by Judge Weinfeld. While the test itself is widely accepted, courts have adopted differing interpretations of its meaning.[205] Some courts focus on the *facts* involved in the two matters to determine if they are substantially related. For example, in Kaminski Brothers, Inc. v. Detroit Diesel Allison[206] the law firm representing the plaintiff in a products liability case involving design and installation of a fuel line in heavy equipment had previously represented the defendant in 15 cases that involved passenger ve-

203. Restatement (Second) of Agency §396 (1958).
204. A lawyer who violates the substantial relationship test may also be subject to malpractice liability to the former client. Damron v. Herzog, 67 F.3d 211 (9th Cir. 1995), *cert. denied*, 516 U.S. 1117 (1996).
205. See generally Chrispens v. Coastal Ref. & Mktg., Inc., 897 P.2d 104 (Kan. 1995) (discussing various approaches to meaning of the substantial relationship test and adopting facts-and-circumstances test); Charles W. Wolfram, Former-Client Conflicts, 10 Geo. J. Legal Ethics 677 (1997).
206. 638 F. Supp. 414 (M.D. Pa. 1985).

hicles or lightweight trucks. In denying the motion for disqualification, the court focused on the factual difference between
passenger vehicles and heavy equipment. The court also rejected
the defendant's argument that the firm should be disqualified because it may have been privy to negotiation techniques or defense
theories.[207] In Trone v. Smith[208] the Ninth Circuit stated the following fact-based application of the substantial relationship test:

> The substantial relationship test does not require that the issues in
> the two representations be identical.
>   The relationship is measured by the allegations in the com-
> plaint and by the nature of the evidence that would be helpful in
> establishing those allegations.[209]

> By contrast, other courts focus on the *legal issues* involved in
> the two matters. For example, the Second Circuit has ruled that
> disqualification is justified only when the relationship between the
> issues involved in the two matters is "patently clear."[210]
>   The Seventh Circuit has developed a three-pronged test that
> combines both factual and legal analysis:

> Initially, the trial judge must make a factual reconstruction of the
> scope of the prior legal representation. Second, it must be deter-
> mined whether it is reasonable to infer that the confidential infor-
> mation allegedly given would have been given to a lawyer
> representing a client in those matters. Finally, it must be deter-
> mined whether that information is relevant to the issues raised in
> the litigation pending against the former client.[211]

The courts are divided on whether the attorney's representation of a former client over an extended period of time in matters

---

207. Id. at 417. See also Ciba-Geigy Corp. v. Alza Corp., 795 F. Supp.
711 (D.N.J. 1992).
208. 621 F.2d 994 (9th Cir. 1980).
209. Id. at 1000.
210. Government of India v. Cook Indus., Inc., 569 F.2d 737, 740 (2d
Cir. 1978).
211. Novo Terapeutisk Laboratorium A/S v. Baxter Travenol Labs., Inc.,
607 F.2d 186, 190 (7th Cir. 1979). See also State ex rel. Wal-Mart Stores, Inc.
v. Kortum, 559 N.W.2d 496 (Neb. 1997) (matters are substantially related if
combination of factual and legal issues creates genuine threat that confidential
information may be used against former client).

that are similar to the current representation is sufficient to amount to a substantial relationship. In Duncan v. Merrill Lynch, Pierce, Fenner & Smith, Inc.[212] the Fifth Circuit held that a law firm was not disqualified from representing the plaintiff in a securities fraud action arising from the sale of municipal bonds even though the firm had previously represented Merrill Lynch in 10 different securities matters over a 10-year period. The court stated that the firm's representation of "Merrill Lynch, even on a variety of matters and over a relatively long period of time, is alone insufficient to establish the required nexus with the present case." The court decided that Merrill Lynch had done nothing more than offer a "catalogue of such generalities," when disqualification required a "painstaking analysis of the facts."[213] Other courts, however, have held that representation over an extended period of time in similar matters is sufficient to warrant disqualification because the prior representation gives insight and understanding of the client's business practices and legal strategy and such information can be used to the disadvantage of a former client.[214]

The Restatement of the Law Governing Lawyers adopts a functional definition of a substantial relationship. Under the Restatement approach, a substantial relationship between the current and former representation exists if "there is a substantial risk that representation of the present client will involve the use of information acquired in the course of representing the former client, unless that information has become generally known."[215] The Restatement also rejects the view that general insight or understanding of the client gained during the prior representation are sufficient to amount to a substantial relationship:

212. 646 F.2d 1020 (5th Cir.), *cert. denied,* 454 U.S. 895 (1981).
213. 646 F.2d at 1029.
214. Kaselaan & D'Angelo Assocs., Inc. v. D'Angelo, 144 F.R.D. 235, 240-241 (D.N.J. 1992). *Accord* Cardona v. General Motors Corp., 942 F. Supp. 968 (D.N.J. 1996) (plaintiff's law firm disqualified in lemon law suit against GM when lawyer hired by firm had previously represented GM in similar litigation even though the lawyer was screened from participation; counsel was aware of defendant's claims and litigation philosophy, as well as its methods and procedures for defending claims).
215. Restatement (Third) of the Law Governing Lawyers §213(2) and cmt. *d(iii).* See also Jamaica Pub. Serv. Co. v. AIU Ins. Co., 707 N.E.2d 414 (NY 1998) (plaintiff's law firm not disqualified for disclosure of generally known information when member of firm was former in-house counsel of defendant).

A lawyer might also have learned a former client's preferred approach to bargaining in settlement discussions or negotiating business points in a transaction, willingness or unwillingness to be deposed by an adversary, and financial ability to withstand extended litigation or contract negotiations. Only when such information will be directly in issue or of unusual value in the subsequent matter will it be independently relevant in assessing a substantial relationship.[216]

Does the existence of a substantial relationship operate as a per se bar or can a lawyer rebut the application of the test by showing that confidential information was not in fact received? Most courts, following Judge Weinfeld's original formulation, appear to hold that the presumption is conclusive. For example, in Allegaert v. Perot[217] the Court of Appeals for the Second Circuit stated:

> Our rule . . . is that an attorney may be disqualified . . . if he has accepted employment adverse to the interests of a former client on a matter substantially related to the prior litigation. Once the substantial relationship is established, the court need not inquire whether the attorney in fact received confidential information, because the receipt of such information will be presumed.[218]

Other courts allow former counsel to rebut the presumption of receipt of confidential information.[219]

Whether the presumption of receipt of confidential information should be rebuttable turns on the foundation of the substantial relationship test. If the test is based solely on the duty of confidentiality, then it makes sense for the presumption to be rebuttable. Several courts have indicated, however, that the test is based both on the duty of confidentiality and on the duty of loyalty

---

216. Restatement (Third) of the Law Governing Lawyers §213, cmt. *d(iii)*.

217. 565 F.2d 246 (2d Cir. 1977).

218. Id. at 250. See also In re American Airlines, Inc., 972 F.2d 605, 614 (5th Cir. 1992), *cert. denied,* 507 U.S. 912 (1993); Sullivan Country Regional Refuse Disposal Dist. v. Acworth, 686 A.2d 755 (N.H. 1996) (when substantial relationship exists, presumption of use of confidential information is irrebuttable).

219. See LaSalle Natl. Bank v. County of Lake, 703 F.2d 252, 256 (7th Cir. 1983).

owed to the former client. As the court said in *Casco Northern Bank v. JBI Associates, Ltd.*:[220]

> The rule addresses the reasonable expectations of the average client that his attorney, who is both counsellor and confidante, will remain loyal. The rule protects the integrity of the judicial system and the public's view of the legal profession; it is necessary to counteract the perception of attorneys as simply "hired guns," who can and do change sides at will, subject only to the highest bidder.[221]

The Restatement warns that extensive inquiry into the confidences of the former client would undermine the very interest the substantial relationship test is designed to protect.[222] Thus, "[w]hen the prior matter involved litigation, it will be conclusively presumed that the lawyer obtained confidential information about the issues involved in the litigation."[223] In other cases, the inquiry should be on "the work that the lawyer undertook and the array of information that a lawyer ordinarily would have obtained to carry out that work."[224] To the extent that inquiry into specific confidential information is necessary, the Restatement suggests the use of in-camera proceedings to protect the former client's right to confidentiality.[225]

Normally, the application of the substantial relationship test requires the party seeking disqualification to show that a client-lawyer relationship formerly existed. In some cases, however, disqualification may be appropriate even when a client-lawyer relationship was not formed. If the attorney acquired information from a nonclient pursuant to a joint defense agreement, courts will apply the substantial relationship to prevent breach of the agreement.[226]

Another situation in which the substantial relationship test may be applied even though a client-lawyer relationship was not formed involves prospective clients. Suppose a lawyer is not en-

220. 667 A.2d 856 (Me. 1995).
221. Id. at 860. *Accord* In re American Airlines, Inc., 972 F.2d 605, 616-621 (5th Cir. 1992), *cert. denied*, 507 U.S. 912 (1993).
222. Restatement (Third) of the Law Governing Lawyers §213, cmt. *d(iii)*.
223. Id.
224. Id.
225. Id.
226. See National Medical Enters., Inc. v. Godbey, 924 S.W.2d 123 (Tex. 1996).

gaged after preliminary discussions with a prospective client. The lawyer may be unable to undertake the representation because of a conflict of interest between the prospective client and another client of the lawyer's firm. Sometimes the client may decide to retain other counsel; in an increasingly competitive market for legal services, many corporate clients shop around through a series of "beauty contests" before retaining counsel.[227] The Model Rules do not address the issue of duties owed to a former prospective client. The courts are divided on the issue of whether a preliminary consultation with a client is sufficient to invoke the former client disqualification rule.[228] Under the Restatement a lawyer is disqualified from undertaking representation against a former prospective client in a substantially related matter only if the lawyer acquired information that would be "significantly harmful" to the former prospective client. Even then the lawyer's firm is not disqualified if it screens the lawyer from participation in the matter.[229]

Appearance of impropriety as a basis for disqualification

Canon 9 of the Code of Professional Responsibility provided that a lawyer should avoid "even the appearance of professional impropriety." Some courts relied on this concept to disqualify law-

227. See Kenneth D. Agran, Note, The Treacherous Path to the Diamond-Studded Tiara: Ethical Dilemmas in Legal Beauty Contests, 9 Geo. J. Legal Ethics 1307 (1996).

228. *Compare* Derrickson v. Derrickson, 541 A.2d 149 (D.C. 1988) (attorney was not disqualified from representing wife in motion seeking increase in alimony when husband had consulted with attorney about seeking divorce from his wife eight years previously, when consultation lasted for approximately one hour, and when husband decided not to retain attorney) and State ex rel. DeFrances v. Bedell, 446 S.E.2d 906 (W. Va. 1994) (preliminary consultation does not result in disqualification) *with* Bays v. Theran, 639 N.E.2d 720 (Mass. 1994) (lawyer's receipt of letter and two or three telephone calls from party regarding possible hiring and basic legal considerations established client-lawyer relationship and precluded firm from undertaking representation against client). See also ABA Comm. on Ethics and Prof. Resp., Formal Op. 90-358 (information imparted by would-be client seeking legal representation is confidential, but will not result in disqualification from representation of other parties in matter unless information is critical to representation; opinion outlines steps to take to avoid disqualification) and Debra B. Perschbacher & Rex R. Perschbacher, Enter at Your Own Risk: The Initial Consultation & Conflicts of Interest, 3 Geo. J. Legal Ethics 689 (1990).

229. Restatement (Third) of the Law Governing Lawyers §27 and cmt. *c*.

yers from undertaking representation against former clients, even without an inquiry into whether the current and former representations were substantially related.[230]

Many commentators and courts criticized the use of the appearance of impropriety as a basis for disqualification principally because of its vagueness: From whose perspective — the public, the bar, reasonable people, the former client — is the appearance to be judged?[231] The Model Rules do not include the concept of the appearance of impropriety, and Comment 5 to Rule 1.9 specifically rejects this principle as a basis for analysis.[232] Similarly, the Restatement also rejects the appearance of impropriety as a basis for prohibiting representation against former clients.[233]

Despite this widespread rejection, occasional decisions still rely on the appearance of impropriety as a basis of disqualification. For example, in Crawford W. Long Memorial Hospital of Emory University v. Yerby[234] the hospital moved to disqualify plaintiff's attorney, who had previously represented the hospital in 18 medical malpractice actions. In 1984, when the attorney was representing the hospital on other medical malpractice claims, Yerby entered the hospital for back surgery and died the same day. The court found that it was unnecessary to decide if the matters were substantially related:

> In this case, we need not determine whether the medical-malpractice claim that Bennett has brought *against* the hospital is "substantially related" to any of the eighteen medical-malpractice claims that he had defended *on behalf* of the hospital. The circumstance of representing a client against a former client in an action that is of the same general subject matter, and grows out of an event that occurred *during the time* of such representation, creates an impermissible appearance of impropriety.[235]

230. E.g., Renshaw v. Ravert, 460 F. Supp. 1089 (E.D. Pa. 1978) (in civil rights case substantial relationship test does not require disqualification of plaintiff's attorney, but disqualification is warranted under Canon 9 because attorney represented one of defendant police officers 10 years previously).

231. Wolfram, Modern Legal Ethics §7.1.4, at 319-323.

232. See Schwartz v. Cortelloni, 685 N.E.2d 871 (Ill. 1997) (rejecting appearance of impropriety standard).

233. Restatement (Third) of the Law Governing Lawyers §201, cmt. *c(iv)*.

234. 373 S.E.2d 749 (Ga. 1988).

235. Id. at 751.

Problem 3-6

Imputation of Disqualification

For six years Anne Reynor has been an associate with
Chen & Rivera, where she has worked in the insurance
defense section, principally defending medical malpractice actions. Reynor has decided to leave the firm and
join a plaintiff's litigation firm. Her new firm, Coles,
Howe & Sanchez, handles a variety of plaintiff's matters
including medical malpractice. The firm is now handling several cases in which Chen & Rivera represents
the defendant doctor and the insurance carrier. Coles,
Howe & Sanchez wants to avoid any problem of disqualification because of Reynor's joining the firm. What
advice would you give to the firm?

Read Model Rules 1.9, 1.10, and comments.

The imputation principle

Both the Code of Professional Responsibility in DR 5-105(D) and
the Model Rules of Professional Conduct in Rule 1.10(a) recognize a principle of "imputed" or "vicarious" disqualification. Under this principle, when lawyers are currently associated in a firm,
and one of the lawyers is disqualified from handling a matter, that
disqualification is imputed to disqualify all members of the firm.
The rationale for the rule of imputed disqualification is based on
the fact that lawyers practicing in a firm have access to firm files
and have mutual financial interests. As a result, it is assumed that
any confidential information that one member of the firm has is
accessible to other members of the firm and that any conflict of
interest that affects a member of the firm will also affect other
members. One can question the validity of these assumptions, especially in large firms, but the principle of imputed disqualification
seems to be firmly established in the law of professional ethics. It
should be noted that the concept of a "firm" is broader than private legal firms, and can include cocounsel relationships. See
Model Rule 1.10, cmt. 1. In People ex rel. Department of Cor-

porations v. Speedee Oil Change Systems, Inc.[236] the California Supreme Court held that the rule of imputed disqualification extends to lawyers who are "of counsel" to firms, a relationship that is "close, personal, continuous, and regular." There are, however, qualifications and limitations to the principle of imputed disqualification.

Imputed disqualification and movement between firms

One of the most important limitations on the rule of imputed disqualification deals with movement of a lawyer from one firm to another. Strictly applied, the rule of imputed disqualification could lead to extreme instances of disqualification, even when no realistic risk of use of confidential information exists. Consider this example: Lawyer works for Old Firm. Lawyer leaves Old Firm to join New Firm. Arguably, all lawyers in New Firm are precluded from undertaking representation against any client of Old Firm on a matter that is substantially related to any matter that Old Firm was handling while Lawyer was a member of the firm, *even if Lawyer was not involved in the matter.* This result could flow from a "double imputation" of disqualification: Lawyer would be disqualified vicariously because of her membership in Old Firm. Lawyer's vicarious disqualification would then be imputed to all members of New Firm when Lawyer joins the firm.

This "double imputation" (from Old Firm members to Lawyer and from Lawyer to New Firm members) was questionable as a matter of policy. First, the risk of misuse of confidential information in this situation is small because Lawyer was not directly privy to any confidential information. Second, the use of imputed disqualification could unfairly restrict the mobility of lawyers between firms and unnecessarily limit the ability of clients to select counsel.

The leading case dealing with application of the rule of imputed disqualification when lawyers move between firms is Silver Chrysler Plymouth, Inc. v. Chrysler Motors Corp.[237] Silver Chrysler Plymouth sued Chrysler Motors for breach of contract. The Kelley Drye law firm represented its long-time client, Chrysler

236. 980 P.2d 371 (Cal. 1999).
237. 518 F.2d 751 (2d Cir. 1975).

Motors, in the action. The firm of Hammond & Schreiber, P.C. represented the plaintiff. Dale Schreiber, a member of that firm, had worked as an associate at Kelley Drye. The defendant moved to disqualify the plaintiff's firm because of Schreiber's prior employment with Kelley Drye. The Court of Appeals for the Second Circuit rejected the notion that Schreiber should be conclusively presumed to have received confidential information:

> It is . . . well known that the larger firms in the metropolitan areas have hundreds (collectively thousands) of clients. It is unquestionably true that in the course of their work at large law firms, associates are entrusted with the confidences of some of their clients. But it would be absurd to conclude that immediately upon their entry on duty they become the recipients of knowledge as to the names of all the firm's clients, the contents of all files relating to such clients, and all confidential disclosures by client officers or employees to any lawyer in the firm. Obviously such legal osmosis does not occur. The mere recital of such a proposition should be self-refuting. And a rational interpretation of the Code of Professional Responsibility does not call for disqualification on the basis of such an unrealistic perception of the practice of law in large firms.[238]

The court ruled that Schreiber should be disqualified only if he had actually acquired confidential information. While Schreiber had worked on some Chrysler matters, his involvement was relatively minor, consisting principally of limited research.[239] Accordingly, the court found that Schreiber had rebutted any inference that he had received confidential information and would not be disqualified.

The *Silver Chrysler Plymouth* decision has been codified in Model Rule 1.9(b). If a lawyer who has had no involvement or only minor involvement in a client's matters changes firms, the lawyer is disqualified from handling a matter against the client of the lawyer's old firm only if the new matter is substantially related to a matter involving the client of the former firm and if the lawyer received confidential information related to the matter. The lawyer is not disqualified simply based on her membership in the old firm.

238. Id. at 753-754.
239. Id. at 756.

If the lawyer is not disqualified under Rule 1.9(b), then her new firm is also not disqualified under Rule 1.10(a).[240]

Imputed disqualification and "screening" of disqualified lawyers

Silver Chrysler Plymouth dealt with a situation in which the lawyer moving to the new firm was not personally disqualified. Suppose, however, that the lawyer is personally disqualified, either because he acquired confidential information or because the matter that he is being asked to handle is substantially related to a matter that he handled while a member of his old firm. While the lawyer cannot personally handle the matter, can another member of his new firm do so, or is the lawyer's disqualification imputed to the new firm? Strict application of the rule of imputed disqualification would disqualify all members of the new firm. It has been suggested, however, that this is an overly broad application of the rule of imputed disqualification and that the new firm should not be disqualified from handling a matter if the personally disqualified lawyer is "screened" from any involvement in the matter (the term *Chinese Wall* is also used).

The drafters of the Model Rules debated whether screening should be allowed when a disqualified lawyer moves from one firm to another. Strong arguments were made in favor of this approach. First, the argument for absolute disqualification of the new firm was based on the assumption that the lawyer joining the new firm would violate his ethical obligation to maintain confidences of the former client. Advocates of screening argued that it was not reasonable to base rules of ethics on the assumption that lawyers would generally violate such a fundamental duty. Second, a rule of absolute disqualification unfairly penalizes clients of the new firm, who are deprived of the counsel of their choice. Third, the rule is unfair to lawyers seeking a change in employment since firms may be unwilling to hire them because of the risk of disqualification

---

240. But see State ex rel. FirsTier Bank, N. A. v. Buckley, 503 N.W.2d 838 (Neb. 1993) (adopting "bright line" test disqualifying new firm in matter substantially related to matter handled by lawyer's former firm regardless of whether lawyer received confidential information).

of the entire firm. Such lawyers would be viewed as "typhoid Marys."[241] In addition, it was pointed out that the Model Rules did allow screening in another context, when a lawyer moved from government service to private practice, although the interests involved in that situation are somewhat different. See Model Rule 1.11(a) and Problem 6-3. Despite these arguments, the drafters of the Model Rules chose to reject the possibility of screening when a disqualified lawyer joined a firm. Apparently, the drafters concluded that clients were entitled to assurances of confidentiality, and that this was possible only by a rule that disqualified the entire firm that hired a personally disqualified lawyer.[242]

Although the Model Rules reject screening as a way of dealing with conflicts of interest when a lawyer moves from one firm to another, the issue continues to be debated and litigated. Some courts follow the Model Rules approach and reject screening.[243] Other courts hold that despite the Model Rules, screening should be permitted.[244] In Cromley v. Board of Education of Lockport Township High School District 205,[245] the Seventh Circuit elaborated on what would be required to screen the attorney effectively and thereby avoid disqualification:

The types of institutional mechanisms that have been determined to protect successfully the confidentiality of the attorney-client relationship include: (1) instructions, given to all members of the new firm, of the attorney's recusal and of the ban on exchange of information; (2) prohibited access to the files and other information on the case; (3) locked case files with keys distributed to a select few; (4) secret codes necessary to access pertinent information on electronic hardware; and (5) prohibited sharing in the fees derived from such litigation. . . . Moreover, the screening devices must be employed "as soon as the 'disqualifying event occurred.' " . . . Other

241. 1 Hazard & Hodes, The Law of Lawyering §1.10:207, at 336.
242. Id.
243. E.g., Roberts v. Hutchins, 572 So. 2d 1231, 1234 n.3 (Ala. 1990).
244. E.g., Manning v. Waring, Cox, James, Sklar & Allen, 849 F.2d 222 (6th Cir. 1988); Kala v. Aluminum Smelting & Ref. Co., 688 N.E.2d 258 (Ohio 1998) (screening generally available to prevent disqualification of firm that hires personally disqualified lawyer; on facts of case, however, firm disqualified despite screening because of appearance of impropriety caused by lawyer abandoning client two weeks after seeking continuance to file appeal).
245. 17 F.3d 1059 (7th Cir.), cert. denied, 513 U.S. 816 (1994).

factors have been considered helpful in determining whether adequate protection of the former client's confidences has been achieved: the size of the law firm, its structural divisions, the "screened" attorney's position in the firm, the likelihood of contact between the "screened" attorney and one representing another party, and the fact that a law firm's and lawyer's most valuable asset is "their reputations for honesty and integrity, along with competence." . . . In addition, the attorneys in question must have affirmed these screening devices under oath.[246]

The Restatement of the Law Governing Lawyers has also approved of the use of screening to avoid disqualification of a firm when a disqualified lawyer joins the firm.[247] Under the Restatement approach, however, screening may be used only when the confidential information held by the personally disqualified lawyer is "unlikely to be significant in the subsequent matter."[248] The New York Court of Appeals has adopted the Restatement approach.[249]

The Restatement authorizes an even broader use of screening when a lawyer obtained confidential information from a former *prospective client*. In that case, the lawyer's firm may undertake representation against the former prospective client even if the lawyer obtained confidential information that could be significantly harmful to the former prospective client, provided the lawyer who received the information is screened from any participation in the matter.[250] If the information would not be significantly harmful, the lawyer could personally undertake representation against the former prospective client.[251]

Disqualification of a law firm can result from hiring paralegals or other nonlawyer employees who previously worked for an adverse party in substantially related matters. Here also the courts are divided on whether screening should be permitted.[252] If the

246. 17 F.3d at 1065.
247. Restatement (Third) of the Law Governing Lawyers §204(2).
248. Id. §204(2)(a). Comment *d* outlines certain factors that can be used to determine whether the information is significant.
249. Kassis v. Teacher's Ins. & Annuity Assn., 717 N.E.2d 674 (N.Y. 1999).
250. Restatement (Third) of the Law Governing Lawyers §27(1)(b)(i).
251. Id. §27(1)(b).
252. *Compare* Phoenix Founders, Inc. v. Marshall, 887 S.W.2d 831 (Tex. 1994) and ABA Comm. on Ethics and Prof. Resp., Informal Op. 88-1526

firm does not adopt adequate screening procedures, disqualification is likely to result.[253]

Imputation when a disqualified lawyer leaves a firm

Imputation of disqualification issues can also arise as to the former firm when a lawyer leaves the firm and takes cases with her. Is the former firm precluded from handling a new matter against the former client if the new matter is substantially related to work done by the former lawyer for the client during the course of the firm's representation? Considering the approach of the Model Rules to imputation when a lawyer joins a firm, the answer should not be surprising. The old firm is not disqualified from handling a matter against a former client when the matter was handled by a departed lawyer unless the current matter is substantially related to the prior representation *and* some lawyer still remaining with the firm actually received confidential information regarding the former client. Model Rule 1.10(b).[254]

(1988) (allowing screening) *with* Koulisis v. Rivers, 730 So. 2d 289 (Fla. Dist. Ct. App. 1999) and Ciaffone v. Eighth Judicial Dist. Court (Skyline Restaurant & Casino), 945 P.2d 950 (Nev. 1997) (screening not permitted).

253. See In re Complex Asbestos Litig. (Widger v. Owens-Corning Fiberglas Corp.), 283 Cal. Rptr. 732 (Ct. App. 1991, *review denied*) (law firm disqualified when it hired paralegal employed by opposing counsel without obtaining consent or establishing appropriate screening); Grant v. Thirteenth Court of Appeals, 888 S.W.2d 466 (Tex. 1994) (disqualification of firm that hired legal secretary who had done extensive work for opposing side).

254. See Novo Terapeutisk Laboratorium A/S v. Baxter Travenol Labs., Inc., 607 F.2d 186 (7th Cir. 1979) (law firm not disqualified from representing plaintiff when former partner of firm, while member of firm, had conference with defendant but had not shared confidential information with other members of the firm); Solow v. W.R. Grace & Co., 632 N.E.2d 437 (N.Y. 1994) (law firm not disqualified from representing plaintiff in asbestos case against manufacturer when member of firm who previously represented manufacturer has departed firm and no evidence exists that confidential information was shared with other members of firm).

─────────────── **Problem 3-7** ───────────────

Advocate-Witness Conflicts of Interest

MEMORANDUM

To: Associate
From: Partner
Date: —
Re: Staley Manufacturing v. Bowers Chemical
         Corp.

Bowers Chemical Corporation is one of our firm's long-time clients. We have represented the company for almost 20 years in a wide variety of business and litigation matters. Five years ago Bowers entered into a long-term supply contract with Staley under which Bowers agreed to supply all of Staley's requirements of a certain chemical.

Until about a year ago both parties performed their obligations under the contract without problem, but at that time a dispute developed because Staley had increased its requirements to a level that Bowers claims is unreasonable. We tried unsuccessfully to negotiate the matter, and now Staley has filed suit against Bowers, claiming that Bowers has breached the contract by failing to meet its requirements.

We just received answers to our first set of interrogatories. In response to our request for a list of witnesses that Staley plans to call, the company included me as a potential witness to testify about the negotiations leading up to the execution of the contract. I'm concerned that this will necessitate our firm's withdrawal from the case. Please be prepared to meet with me tomorrow to advise whether we will need to withdraw from the case.

Read Model Rule 3.7 and comments.

The advocate-witness rule under the Code of Professional Responsibility

The Code of Professional Responsibility provided that it was unethical for a lawyer to accept or to continue representation of a client if the lawyer or a member of the lawyer's firm "ought to be called as a witness" on behalf of the client. DR 5-101(B), 5-102(A). If the testimony was at the request of the opposing party rather than on behalf of the client, the Code provided that the lawyer could continue representation unless the testimony was prejudicial to the client. DR 5-102(B). It is important to note that under the Code, if the lawyer would be a witness, the lawyer's entire firm would be disqualified from appearing as counsel. In addition, unlike other conflict-of-interest rules, the client could not consent to an advocate-witness conflict.

Disciplinary Rule 5-101(B) listed four exceptions to the prohibition against a lawyer serving as both advocate and witness: (1) testimony about uncontested matters, (2) testimony regarding matters of formality when the lawyer had no reason to believe that substantial evidence would be offered in opposition, (3) testimony about the nature and value of legal services, and (4) substantial hardship to the client because of distinctive value of the lawyer or the lawyer's firm as counsel.

Ethical Consideration 5-9 offered several rationales for the advocate-witness rule:

> Occasionally a lawyer is called upon to decide in a particular case whether he will be a witness or an advocate. If a lawyer is both counsel and witness, he becomes more easily impeachable for interest and thus may be a less effective witness. Conversely, the opposing counsel may be handicapped in challenging the credibility of the lawyer when the lawyer also appears as an advocate in the case. An advocate who becomes a witness is in the unseemly and ineffective position of arguing his own credibility. The roles of an advocate and of a witness are inconsistent; the function of an advocate is to advance or argue the cause of another, while that of a witness is to state facts objectively.

A leading example of the application of the Code's advocate-witness rule is Comden v. Superior Court.[255] In *Comden* the actress

---

255. 576 P.2d 971 (Cal.) (en banc), *cert. denied*, 439 U.S. 981 (1978).

Doris Day entered into a contract with Doris Day Distributing Company, authorizing the company to distribute pet products bearing her name and likeness. A dispute developed over performance of the contract, and Ms. Day brought suit seeking to enjoin the company from using her name. In support of a motion for preliminary injunction, two of Ms. Day's attorneys filed declarations. One attorney stated that he had heard one of the defendant's investors state that he had acquired a 50 percent interest in the company; this transaction violated the contract between Ms. Day and the defendant. Another attorney stated that the defendant had refused to allow the inspection of its records as provided by the contract with Ms. Day. The defendant moved to disqualify the law firm in which these two lawyers were members on the ground that they were likely to be called as witnesses. The trial court granted the motion. Ms. Day sought review by way of petition for writ of mandamus. The California Supreme Court affirmed the trial court's disqualification order under Rule 2-111(A)(4) of the California Rules of Professional Conduct, which was substantially the same as the provisions of the Code of Professional Responsibility.

In its opinion the California Supreme Court rejected several arguments against disqualification. Petitioners first argued that it was premature to order disqualification because subsequent discovery might eliminate the need for testimony by the attorneys. The court ruled that the trial court was within its discretion in ordering immediate disqualification when it was uncertain whether the lawyers would testify because "delaying the decision creates the issue of hardship."[256]

The court then rejected petitioners' argument that disqualification should be denied because of substantial hardship to Ms. Day resulting from the "distinctive value" of the services of the firm. While finding some inconvenience present, the court ruled that "impressions and rapport with the people involved" was insufficient to establish substantial hardship. The court noted that "[i]f we were to hold that interview, research, and preliminary discussion on trial strategy are sufficient to cloak a firm with such 'distinctive value' that a loss of its service results in substantial hardship within the meaning of the rule, the latter will be consumed by exception."[257]

256. 576 P.2d at 974.
257. Id. at 975.

Finally, the court considered the petitioners' argument that the disqualification motion was a tactical device and deprived Ms. Day of the counsel of her choice. Although recognizing that disqualification motions can be employed for tactical reasons, the court pointed out that the fundamental issue was a conflict between the client's right to counsel of its choice and the preservation of ethical standards of the profession. The court ruled that the client's right to select counsel must yield under these circumstances.[258] In *Comden* the disqualification applied to the entire firm and was enforced even over the objections and despite the consent of Ms. Day.

The California Rules of Professional Conduct have been amended since *Comden* was decided. Current Rule 5-210 allows a lawyer to serve as an advocate when the lawyer is a witness in the case if the client gives informed, written consent. In addition, any disqualification under the rule applies only to the lawyer personally, not to the lawyer's firm.

Rationales for the advocate-witness rule

The rationales for the advocate-witness rule have been subject to extensive scrutiny by scholars. In a leading article, Professor Arnold Enker offered the following criticism:

> Ethical Consideration 5-9 . . . asserts that the lawyer who testifies and appears as advocate in the same case "may be a less effective witness" because he is "more easily impeachable for interest." . . . But this is hardly a persuasive argument on which to ground an ethical duty for the lawyer to withdraw from the case. It is at best a tactical consideration that counsel and client should weigh together to determine how serious the risks are in the given situation and whether they are outweighed by the advantages to the client of being represented in court by this particular lawyer. The argument fails to explain why the rule is not subject to exception with the client's consent as are [other conflicts of interest].
>
> Nor is withdrawal from the trial of the case, which constitutes the specific ethical duty, likely to cure the problem in most in-

258. Id.

stances. The lawyer's personal familiarity with the facts of the case will usually stem from his representation of the client in earlier stages of the same matter. Withdrawal from the trial of the case will not significantly alter his vulnerability because of interest. It is more likely to injure the client's representation than strengthen his witness.[259]

Professor Enker then considered the rationale set forth in EC 5-9 that the opposing counsel might be "handicapped in challenging the credibility of the lawyer when the lawyer also appears as an advocate in the case." He rejected this justification because it was based on an erroneous premise: that "opposing counsel's sense of professional fraternity will overcome his partisan duty to his client and prevent him from arguing his adversary's interest."[260] Further, even if accurate, this concern was a problem for opposing counsel, not a basis for disqualification of the advocate-witness.[261]

Ethical Consideration 5-9 also stated that "[a]n advocate who becomes a witness is in the unseemly and ineffective position of arguing his own credibility." He found this "too insubstantial a basis on which to ground such a firmly held rule."[262] Enker also rejected the justification originally set forth by Professor Wigmore that the rule was designed to protect the image of the profession from public fear that lawyers might lie to advance their clients' interests. After noting that this justification was conspicuously absent from EC 5-9, Enker found it to be "at best a makeweight."

In the last sentence of EC 5-9, however, Enker found what he considered to be the best justification for the advocate-witness rule: the distinction between testimony and advocacy. A witness testifies as to his personal knowledge and belief. A lawyer, by contrast, argues based on fact and reason, not based on her personal belief. Indeed, it is ethically improper for a lawyer to state her personal belief in the merits of the client's case. See DR 7-106(C)(3) of the Code and Model Rule 3.4(e).

---

259. Arnold N. Enker, The Rationale of the Rule That Forbids a Lawyer to Be Advocate and Witness in the Same Case, 1977 Am. Bar Found. Res. J. 455, 457.
    260. Id. at 457-458.
    261. Id. at 458.
    262. Id.

>   This distinction between the two roles of advocate and witness
> is essential to enable the lawyer to maintain independence from his
> client while advocating his cause. Were the lawyer to combine the
> two roles, the assessment of his integrity and credibility in evalu-
> ating his testimony would likely affect the evaluation of his argu-
> ment.[263]

Enker drew two implications from this analysis. First, since the basis of the rule was preservation of the role of the attorney, the advocate-witness rule should not be subject to client consent or waiver. Second, since the basis of the rule was the prohibition on mixing roles, the rule should not prevent a lawyer in a firm from serving as advocate when another lawyer was a witness.[264]

By contrast to Professor Enker, the author of a lengthy student note argued that the basis of the rule was protection of the client from either diminished effectiveness of counsel or weakened credibility of the advocate-witness. Since client protection was the basis of the rule, the author argued that the rule should be subject to the client's informed consent.[265] Other commentators have argued that the rationales for the rule are so weak that it should be repealed.[266]

The advocate-witness rule under the Model Rules: scope and exceptions

Despite arguments that the rule should be repealed, the drafters of the Model Rules decided to retain it.[267] The Restatement of the Law Governing Lawyers also continues to adhere to the rule.[268] The drafters of the Model Rules focused on two justifications for

263. Id. at 463.

264. Id. at 465.

265. Note, The Advocate-Witness Rule: If Z, Then X. But Why? 52 N.Y.U. L. Rev. 1365, 1394-1400 (1977).

266. Harold A. Brown & Louis M. Brown, Disqualification of the Testifying Advocate — A Firm Rule? 57 N.C. L. Rev. 596 (1979); Jeffrey A. Stonerock, The Advocate-Witness Rule: Anachronism or Necessary Restraint? 94 Dickinson L. Rev. 821 (1990).

267. For a comparison of the Code and the Model Rules, see Richard C. Wydick, Trial Counsel as Witness: The Code and the Model Rules, 15 U.C. Davis L. Rev. 651 (1982).

268. Restatement (Third) of the Law Governing Lawyers §168.

the advocate-witness rule. Model Rule 3.7, cmt. 1. First, the opposing party may be prejudiced when an advocate serves as a witness because it becomes unclear whether the statement of the advocate-witness "should be taken as proof or as an analysis of the proof." Model Rule 3.7, cmt. 2. Second, serving as both advocate and witness may create a conflict of interest between lawyer and client when the lawyer's testimony would be adverse to the client. Model Rule 3.7, cmt. 5. Sections (a) and (b) of Rule 3.7 reflect these justifications. Since section (a) is based on the policy of preventing prejudice to the opposing party rather than protecting the client from harm, it is not subject to client consent. Section (b), however, is based on the principle of avoiding harm to the client and is thus subject to consent by the client after consultation.[269]

Rule 3.7 applies only if the lawyer is "likely to be a necessary witness." The Restatement agrees with this test.[270] This represents a change in language from the Code of Professional Responsibility, which provided that the lawyer must withdraw if "it is obvious that he or a lawyer in his firm ought to be called as a witness." DR 5-101(B). Under the Code some courts had ruled that the lawyer was disqualified if the lawyer's testimony could conceivably be used at trial. See Comden v. Superior Court, discussed above. The drafters of the Model Rules intended to narrow the scope of the advocate-witness rule.[271] One important application of the "necessary witness" requirement is that the lawyer is not disqualified from serving as an advocate if the lawyer's testimony would be cumulative with that of other witnesses. An example is Cannon Airways, Inc. v. Franklin Holdings Corp.,[272] which was a suit for breach of an aircraft lease agreement. The agreement provided for recovery of "reasonable attorneys' fees." Defendant moved to disqualify plaintiff's counsel because a dispute existed regarding the scope of the clause; defendant contended that plaintiff's counsel would be required to testify about the negotiations that resulted in the clause. The court denied this motion because the attorney was not the only witness available to testify about the negotiations

---

269. See generally 1 Hazard & Hodes, The Law of Lawyering §3.7:103.
270. Restatement (Third) of the Law Governing Lawyers §168(1)(b) and cmt. e.
271. 1 Hazard & Hodes, The Law of Lawyering §3.7:201.
272. 669 F. Supp. 96 (D. Del. 1987).

on behalf of the plaintiff, and the defendant had failed to show that the attorney's testimony was "necessary to supplement or to corroborate" testimony of plaintiff's other witness about the negotiations.[273]

Both the Code and the Model Rules contain similar exceptions to the advocate-witness rule. Compare Code of Professional Responsibility DR 5-101(B)(1)-(4) and Model Rule 3.7(a)(1)-(3). The exceptions dealing with uncontested matters and with testimony regarding legal fees have generated little litigation and should provide few problems in application. Thus, if a lawyer must testify to identify a document so that it can be offered into evidence and there is no dispute about the authenticity of the document, the lawyer is not disqualified from continuing as an advocate in the matter because of this testimony. Similarly, in a suit for breach of contract or for collection of a note in which the contract or note provides for recovery of legal fees, testimony by the trial attorney to establish these fees is permissible and does not require disqualification of the attorney as advocate in the case.

The broadest exception to the prohibition against serving as both advocate and witness occurs when disqualification involves "substantial hardship" to the client. Here there is a modest change from the Code to the Model Rules. Under the Code the substantial hardship had to result from the "distinctive value of the lawyer or his firm as counsel in the particular case." DR 5-101(B)(4). This exception was narrowly construed by the courts and the ABA to apply only in unusual circumstances. See *Comden*, discussed above. In Formal Opinion 339 the ABA Committee on Ethics and Professional Responsibility stated:

> [E]xceptional situations may arise when . . . disadvantages to the client would clearly be outweighed by the real hardship to the client of being compelled to retain other counsel in the particular case. For example, where a complex suit has been in preparation over a long period of time and a development which could not be anticipated makes the lawyer's testimony essential, it would be manifestly unfair to the client to be compelled to seek new trial counsel at substantial additional expense and perhaps to have to seek a delay

---

273. Id. at 102. See also Chappell v. Cosgrove, 916 P.2d 836 (N.M. 1996) (lawyer who accompanied client to meeting not disqualified; because four other witnesses could testify about what took place at meeting, lawyer's testimony was cumulative).

of the trial. Similarly, a long or extensive professional relationship with a client may have afforded a lawyer, or a firm, such an extraordinary familiarity with the client's affairs that the value to the client of representation by that lawyer or firm in a trial involving those matters would clearly outweigh the disadvantages of having the lawyer, or a lawyer in the firm, testify to some disputed and significant issue.[274]

Both the Model Rules and the Restatement broaden somewhat the substantial hardship exception by deleting the requirement of "distinctive value" and focusing instead on balancing of various factors.[275]

Suppose a lawyer is disqualified from being an advocate at a trial because the lawyer is likely to be a necessary witness and none of the exceptions in Rule 3.7 applies. Is the lawyer's entire firm disqualified, or may another lawyer in the firm handle the trial? Disciplinary Rule 5-102(A) of the Code of Professional Responsibility provided that the disqualification of a lawyer from handling a case because of the advocate-witness rule was imputed to the entire firm, preventing any lawyer in the firm from continuing the representation. The rule stated:

> If, after undertaking employment in contemplated or pending litigation, a lawyer learns or it is obvious that he *or a lawyer in his firm* ought to be called as a witness on behalf of his client, he shall withdraw from the conduct of the trial *and his firm, if any, shall not continue representation in the trial.* [Emphasis added.]

Even under the Code, however, some courts had refused to disqualify a firm simply because a member of the firm would be a witness.[276]

Both the Model Rules and the Restatement reject the principle of imputation of disqualification when one lawyer will be appearing as a witness while another attorney in the lawyer's firm

---

274. ABA Comm. on Ethics and Prof. Resp., Formal Op. 339, at 3 (1975).

275. See Model Rule 3.7, cmt. 4; Restatement (Third) of the Law Governing Lawyers §168, cmt. *h.* See also McElroy v. Gaffney, 529 A.2d 889 (N.H. 1987) (disqualification of plaintiff's lawyer in shareholders' derivative action denied; attorney's knowledge of transactions, complexity of litigation, and expense to plaintiff to hire new counsel are factors supporting denial of motion).

276. E.g., S & S Hotel Ventures Ltd. Partnership v. 777 S.H. Corp., 508 N.E.2d 647 (N.Y. 1987).

will serve as the client's advocate, unless a conflict of interest exists. Rule 3.7(b) provides that "[a] lawyer may act as advocate in a trial in which another lawyer in the lawyer's firm is likely to be called as a witness unless precluded from doing so by Rule 1.7 or Rule 1.9." As Comment 4 to Rule 3.7 states: "The principle of imputed disqualification stated in Rule 1.10 has no application to this aspect of the problem." The Restatement agrees.[277]

A conflict of interest is most obvious when the lawyer's testimony would be adverse to the client's interests. Even in this case, the firm would not necessarily be disqualified if the lawyer's testimony, although adverse, plays a relatively minor role in the case and the client consents after being counseled about the conflict.[278] If the lawyer's testimony would have a substantial effect on the case, however, the lawyer's firm should be disqualified even if the client were willing to consent. Under Rule 1.7(b) a client may consent to a conflict of interest, but only if the "lawyer reasonably believes the representation will not be adversely affected." It is hard to imagine that this condition could ever be met if the lawyer would be testifying adversely to the interests of the client on a significant issue in the case.[279]

If an attorney is disqualified from serving as an advocate in the case because the attorney is likely to be a necessary witness, may the attorney continue to provide legal services during discovery and after trial on appeal? In Culebras Enterprises Corp. v. Rivera-Rios[280] the First Circuit ruled that disqualification applied only at trial, not to pretrial matters, because representation at pretrial did not involve any of the purposes generally served by the rule, and the Restatement adopts this view.[281] Other courts, how-

277. Restatement (Third) of the Law Governing Lawyers §168(3) and cmts. *f, i.*

278. See Model Rule 3.7, cmt. 5 (representation is improper when there is likely to be a substantial conflict between the testimony of the client and the lawyer); 1 Hazard & Hodes, The Law of Lawyering §3.7:301, at 686.1 (consent permissible if the client is adequately counseled).

279. See Klupt v. Krongard, 728 A.2d 727 (Md. Ct. Spec. App.), *cert. denied,* 735 A.2d 1107 (Md. 1999) (lawyer disqualified from representation of patent licensor when contingent licensee planned to call lawyer as witness to testify about statements made by lawyer that would conflict with testimony of licensor; conflict was not waivable by licensor).

280. 846 F.2d 94 (1st Cir. 1988).

281. Restatement (Third) of the Law Governing Lawyers §168, cmt. *c.* See also ABA Comm. on Ethics and Prof. Resp., Informal Op. 83-1503 (lawyer

ever, disagree and have disqualified counsel from participation in pretrial matters.[282]

Avoiding advocate-witness conflicts during investigation

While rejection of the rule of imputed disqualification in the Model Rules and the Restatement has substantially reduced the impact of the advocate-witness rule, the rule still applies to a lawyer who personally will be a witness. As a result, attorneys who engage in trial practice need to be aware of the possible disqualifying effect of the rule and to guard against this eventuality when participating in matters that may lead to litigation or when interviewing witnesses in matters that are in litigation. Consider the following advice from Professors Fortune, Underwood, and Imwinkelried for dealing with this problem:

> In interviewing witnesses, however, it is prudent to assume that the witness will give a different version of the facts at a later time, and that the attorney may become a necessary witness to challenge the turncoat. . . .
> What precautions can be taken to guard against being considered a necessary impeachment witness? First, consider having someone else conduct witness interviews, either an employee or an independent investigator. Second, have someone else present when interviewing a witness who may deny or vary a statement. Third, reduce the interview to a signed statement.[283]

---

who has withdrawn as trial counsel because of advocate-witness rule may prepare brief and argue case on appeal so long as lawyer's testimony is not in issue and no conflict of interest is present); Informal Op. 89-1529 (lawyer who anticipates testifying at trial may represent party in discovery and other pretrial matters if client consents after consultation).

282. World Youth Day, Inc. v. Famous Artists Merchandising Exch., Inc., 866 F. Supp. 1297 (D. Colo. 1994) (lawyer disqualified from handling depositions because of likelihood that depositions would be used at trial, revealing lawyer's dual role); Freeman v. Vicchiarelli, 827 F. Supp. 300 (D.N.J. 1993) (early application of rule is necessary for smooth operation of adversarial system).

283. William H. Fortune et al., Modern Litigation and Professional Responsibility Handbook §4.5, at 169-170 (1996). See also Restatement (Third) of the Law Governing Lawyers §168, cmt. *j* (advocate-witness rule does not apply to testimony by nonlawyer employee who does not sit at counsel table or act in advocacy support role).

--------------------------- **Problem 3-8** ---------------------------

Simultaneous Representation of Plaintiffs in Tort Cases

Scene: Office of Sandra Lawson, Esq.

Lawson: Come in, Ms. Downing and Mr. Partee. Please sit down. I understand that you were involved in an automobile accident. Why don't you tell me what happened.

Downing: We were going to a friend's house on Friday afternoon. I had stopped at a red light at the corner of Barian Way and North Druid Street. The light turned green, and I started to enter the intersection when a truck came barreling through the intersection. He obviously ran the red light because my light was already green. He slammed into the side of the car where Ed was riding.

Lawson: *(to Mr. Partee)* Did you see what happened?

Partee: No. I was trying to change the radio station, and the next thing I knew, we had been hit.

Lawson: Did the police charge anyone in the accident?

Downing: The driver of the truck got a ticket for running a red light.

Lawson: Were you charged?

Downing: No.

Lawson: Tell me about your injuries.

Downing: I was shaken up pretty bad and went to the emergency room. They X-rayed me but didn't find any broken bones or other problems. I missed a few days of work.

Lawson: And you, Mr. Partee?

Partee: I had a broken arm and a concussion.

> I have been out of work for four weeks.
> I feel pretty good now and plan to go
> back to work next week.

Lawson: You want me to represent you in this
matter, is that right?

Partee: Yes.

Downing: That's right.

Lawson: I will need to get your medical records
and the accident report. Would you
please sign these medical and police au-
thorizations so that I can obtain the records?

Be prepared to evaluate how Lawson handled the interview. What would you have done?

Read Model Rule 1.7(b) and comments.

Simultaneous representation of clients in a single matter

In earlier problems we discussed conflicts of interest involving representation against current and former clients. Problem 3-8 deals
with another type of client conflict: simultaneous representation
of clients in a single matter. This type of conflict differs from the
two that we have already considered because in those situations
the lawyer was clearly undertaking representation *against* a client.
In the simultaneous representation situation, the adversity between the clients is not readily apparent. In the case of representation of the driver and passenger in an automobile accident with
another driver, both the driver and passenger appear to have a
harmony of interests in establishing that the other driver was at
fault. Despite this apparent unity of interests, representation of
coplaintiffs, such as driver and passenger, poses a number of potential conflicts of interest, ones that may well ripen into actual
conflicts.

Model Rule 1.7(b) governs the situation of simultaneous representation of potentially conflicting interests. (Note that Rule
1.7(b) also deals with situations in which the lawyer's personal
interest or that of a third person may have an impact on the lawyer's representation of a client. We will consider these situations

in later problems.) Interestingly, the structure of the rule is remarkably similar to Rule 1.7(a), which deals with direct adverse representation. Both rules allow representation despite the conflict if the lawyer "reasonably believes" that she can undertake the representation without adverse impact on the clients and if the clients consent after consultation. Nonetheless, important differences exist between Rules 1.7(a) and 1.7(b). First, when the interests of the clients are not directly adverse, Rule 1.7(b) prohibits representation only if the lawyer's representation of one client would be "materially limited" by the representation of the other. Second, Rule 1.7(b) specifies the disclosures that the attorney should make to obtain informed consent from the clients.

Simultaneous representation of coparties in tort litigation

A number of courts and ethics opinions have addressed the possible conflict between driver and passenger arising from an automobile accident. These authorities have held that a lawyer may not undertake simultaneous representation of both a driver and passenger when the passenger has a claim against the driver for negligence.[284] If such a claim is unlikely, simultaneous representation is permitted provided both the driver and passenger consent to the representation after the lawyer fully discloses the advantages and risks involved.[285]

Figueroa-Olmo v. Westinghouse Electric Corp.[286] illustrates the application of the conflict-of-interest rules in tort litigation involving multiple plaintiffs with potential claims against each other. In *Figueroa-Olmo* four individuals were killed when the truck in which they were riding collided with one of Westinghouse's trailers at an intersection near San Juan. Consolidated actions were brought by 40 relatives of the decedents; all the plaintiffs were represented by one law firm. Westinghouse filed counterclaims claiming that the driver and passengers of the truck were contrib-

---

284. E.g., In re Thornton, 421 A.2d 1 (D.C. 1980); In re Shaw, 443 A.2d 670 (N.J. 1982); Fugnitto v. Fugnitto, 452 N.Y.S.2d 976 (App. Div. 1982); Jedwabny v. Philadelphia Transp. Co., 135 A.2d 252 (Pa. 1957), *cert. denied*, 355 U.S. 966 (1958).

285. See In re Aguiluz, 3 Cal. St. Bar Ct. Rep. 41 (Bar Ct. 1994).

286. 616 F. Supp. 1445 (D.P.R. 1985).

utorily negligent. Some of the plaintiffs were heirs of the decedents, while others were not. Under Puerto Rico law an heir who accepted an interest in an estate (filing of a lawsuit on behalf of the estate amounted to acceptance of an interest in the estate) also became legally responsible for any claims against the estate. Westinghouse filed a motion to disqualify the law firm from representing all of the plaintiffs because of a conflict of interest, claiming that the plaintiffs who were not heirs had potential cross-claims against the plaintiffs who were heirs and had accepted an interest in the estate.

The law firm filed written statements with the court in which each plaintiff consented to representation by the firm. Westinghouse objected to the statements on the ground that they did not show that the firm had made the full disclosure required by the rules of professional conduct. The district court ruled that the potential for a conflict of interest between the plaintiffs did not automatically prevent multiple representation and result in disqualification. The court discussed the circumstances under which multiple representation of potentially conflicting interests would be permitted:

> According to Model Rule 1.7(b), disqualification of counsel on grounds of potential conflicting interests in multiple client representation in the same lawsuit is not automatic but may depend on whether the clients agree to being so represented after having been informed of all the risks and disadvantages involved. . . . The premise behind this pragmatic approach is to safeguard a person's right to hire a particular attorney of certain expertise who may not be affordable except by the joint resources of various litigants who team up as plaintiffs or as defendants. . . . Parties also have a right to control their litigation in light of whatever interests they consider more important and worthy of litigating. . . . However, the right to be represented by a particular attorney is not an unfettered one. Even informed consent may be insufficient to prevent disqualification, if it is not obvious to the court that the attorney will be able to represent all clients adequately, . . . or if the court believes no waiver may cure the damage to the integrity of the judicial process that such joint representation will cause. . . . The court may also examine the circumstances surrounding the consent to determine if it was truly voluntary and informed. . . . It has also been held that if the conflicts of interest involve abuse of confidential information from the client rather than the mere possibility of disloyalty in advocacy during a litigation, the client's consent might be insufficient. . . . If the simultaneously represented clients' interests are or be-

come actually opposed or directly adverse, then disqualification should be ordered. . . . Our circuit has cautioned that it is "more important that unethical conduct be prevented than that defendant have an unfettered right to counsel of its choice."[287]

The court ruled, however, that the plaintiffs' lawyers had failed to comply with the obligation of consultation required by Rule 1.7(b); it ordered plaintiffs' counsel to conduct meetings with the plaintiffs to explain their legal rights, and to file with the court written consents in a format specified by the court.[288]

Informed consent to simultaneous representation

Assuming that a lawyer reasonably believes that the lawyer may permissibly represent both the driver and passenger because no actual conflict is present, the lawyer must obtain the consent of the clients after consultation.

Rule 1.7(b)(2) states that "the consultation shall include explanation of the implications of the common representation and the advantages and risks involved." What are the implications, advantages, and risks that should be disclosed?[289] One advantage that is often mentioned in connection with simultaneous representation is the reduction of legal fees by having one lawyer involved instead of two. While this may well be an advantage in a matter in which the client pays for the lawyer's services on an hourly basis, it is questionable whether it is an advantage in tort matters, which are usually handled on a contingency basis. For example, if one lawyer represents both the driver and passenger, recovers $5,000 for the driver and $10,000 for the passenger, and charges a one-third fee, the legal fees will be the same as when two lawyers independently represent the driver and the passenger, obtain the same recoveries, and charge their clients the same one-third fee.

Expense sharing is another possible advantage of simultane-

287. Id. at 1451-1452.
288. See Gustafson v. City of Seattle, 941 P.2d 701 (Wash. Ct. App. 1997) (attorney must obtain informed consent before representing driver and passenger unless it reasonably appears that other parties are solely liable).
289. See Zador Corp. v. Kwan, 37 Cal. Rptr. 2d 754 (Ct. App. 1995) (quoting well-drafted consent form with detailed explanations of advantages and disadvantages of multiple representation of codefendants in real estate litigation).

ous representation. Lawyers normally charge their clients for expenses incurred in a matter, such as filing fees, deposition costs, and costs of expert witnesses. If one lawyer rather than several handles the case, the clients could share the expenses, rather than each being required to pay her own expenses.

In addition to expense sharing, there are other possible advantages to the clients of simultaneous representation. Dealings between opposing sides in the case and particularly with the insurance carrier for the defendant may be simplified and thereby expedited if one lawyer is involved for the plaintiffs rather than two. Further, both the driver and passenger may have trust and confidence in the particular lawyer. Permitting simultaneous representation allows both to have the lawyer of their choice.

Disadvantages to multiple representation exist as well. While the matter may not seem initially to involve an actual conflict between the clients, during the progress of the case a conflict may arise. For example, discovery may produce evidence showing that the driver of the vehicle in which the passenger was riding may have been at fault and that the passenger therefore has a claim against the driver. Comment 7 to Model Rule 1.7 identifies other possible conflicts when a lawyer represents multiple parties in litigation:

> An impermissible conflict may exist by reason of substantial discrepancy in the parties' testimony, incompatibility in positions in relation to an opposing party or the fact that there are substantially different possibilities of settlement of the claims or liabilities in question.

Representation of multiple parties can produce "aggregate settlement" conflicts. Suppose the defendant offers a lump sum to settle the entire case. A lawyer representing multiple plaintiffs cannot ethically agree to an aggregate settlement unless each client consents after consultation. Model Rule 1.8(g). The settlement desires of one client may therefore lead to rejection of a settlement that the other client considers advantageous.

If an actual conflict develops between the driver and passenger, the lawyer will be required to withdraw from representation. On withdrawal the lawyer could not represent either party unless both consented to the representation. After withdrawal both the clients would then be former clients. As discussed previously, a lawyer may not undertake representation against a former client in the same or substantially related matter without the consent of that client. Model Rule 1.9(a).[290] Both would be forced to hire new lawyers. At a minimum this would cause delay in their case and might well result in additional expenses. The lawyer must disclose to potential coclients the possible conflicts that may arise and inform them that she would be required to withdraw from representation of both of them if an actual conflict arose.

The lawyer should also advise the driver and passenger of another aspect of joint representation — the impact on the attorney-client privilege. It is well established as a matter of evidence law that no attorney-client privilege exists between joint clients as to communications made by either client to the lawyer should a dispute develop between the joint clients.[291] For example, if a driver provides a lawyer with information showing that the driver was negligent, this information would not be privileged should the passenger later file a cross-claim against the driver. The parties should be advised about this limitation on the attorney-client privilege before they agree to simultaneous representation. A lawyer who fails to obtain informed consent is exposed to the risk of malpractice liability.[292]

What form should consent to simultaneous representation take? Rule 1.7(b) does not require the consent of the clients to be in writing. (Compare Rule 1.5(c), which requires contingent fee agreements to be in writing.) Thus, oral consent by the clients after consultation with the lawyer about the advantages, risks, and implications of multiple representation is sufficient. Prudent lawyers, however, do not rely on oral consent. Should a client later charge the lawyer with misconduct or sue for malpractice, the lawyer

290. See 1 Hazard & Hodes, The Law of Lawyering §1.7:307. But see Zador Corp. v. Kwan, 37 Cal. Rptr. 2d 754 (Ct. App. 1995) (law firm represented multiple defendants in real estate litigation; firm was allowed to represent one defendant after withdrawing from representation of other defendant due to conflict of interest because written consent to multiple representation specified which defendant law firm could continue to represent if conflict developed).

291. 1 McCormick on Evidence §91 (5th ed. 1999); cf. Model Rule 2.2, cmt. 6.

292. See Woodruff v. Tomlin, 616 F.2d 924 (6th Cir.), *cert. denied,* 449 U.S. 888 (1980) (cause of action for legal malpractice stated against attorney who represented two sisters — one the driver and the other a passenger — in collision case without disclosure of possible claim that passenger had against driver).

would not have any documentation of the client's consent. Instead, lawyers should obtain their clients' consent in writing. Ideally the lawyer should write a letter to the clients outlining the advantages and disadvantages of multiple representation and ask the clients to sign the letter if they consent to multiple representation.

Conflicts of interest in class actions

The contemporary legal scene has witnessed an explosive growth of mass tort litigation involving products such as asbestos, tobacco, and contraceptive devices. Procedurally, many of these cases have been brought as class actions under Rule 23 of the Federal Rules of Civil Procedure and corresponding state rules, but others involve mass consolidations of thousands of individual claims. Regardless of the procedural device used, mass torts present a host of unique ethical problems, including conflicts of interest.[293] Federal district judge Jack B. Weinstein, who has presided over a number of significant mass tort cases, has identified three major types of conflicts of interest in mass torts: between lawyer and client, among present clients, and between present and future claimants.[294]

Because of the vast sums of money involved in class-action mass torts, class counsel may have a financial interest to settle the case and thereby obtain an early payment of substantial fees, even if the settlement does not fairly compensate the members of the class for their injuries. Conflicts of interest among current clients and between current and future claimants are also significant problems in mass torts. Most mass torts involve claimants with different degrees of injury. In addition, because of the long latency period involved in discovery of injuries caused by some products,

293. The leading article is Jack B. Weinstein, Ethical Dilemmas in Mass Tort Litigation, 88 Nw. U. L. Rev. 469 (1994). The literature on class actions in mass torts is voluminous. See Symposium, Mass Tortes: Serving Up Just Desserts, 80 Cornell L. Rev. 811 (1995); Symposium, The Institute of Judicial Administration Research Conference on Class Actions, 71 N.Y.U. L. Rev. 1 (1996). See also Vincent R. Johnson, Ethical Limitations on Creative Financing of Mass Tort Class Actions, 54 Brooklyn L. Rev. 539 (1988).

294. Weinstein, Ethical Dilemmas in Mass Tort Litigation, 88 Nw. U. L. Rev. at 502-510.

many such cases include future claimants as well as those with current injuries. Even among future claimants, conflicts can develop. Some future claimants may be identifiable as having been exposed to the product causing the illness but may not exhibit disease, while other claimants may be unidentified or even unidentifiable (the unborn, for example).

Parties to mass tort litigation have argued that these conflicts can be overcome by judicial oversight of class action settlements.[295] The Supreme Court, however, has rejected this solution. The Court has refused to approve settlements of class-action mass torts unless all the requirements of Rule 23 have been met, including representation by class counsel that does not suffer from conflicts of interest.[296] The Court has ruled that when such conflicts exist, as is often the case, subclasses with independent representation must be created.[297]

―――――――― **Problem 3-9** ――――――――

Insurance Defense Practice

*Scene: Office of Roberto Sanchez, defense counsel
Others present: Joseph Taylor, truck driver for Freight
Lines, Inc. and Elaine Voss, Vice President of Operations
for Freight Lines*

Sanchez: Come in, Mr. Taylor and Ms. Voss. I appreciate your coming down here. Freight Lines's insurance carrier, Interstate Insurance, has sent this suit to our firm to defend you, Mr. Taylor, and Freight Lines. Please understand that even though the insurance company is paying my fee, I am your lawyer. Anything you tell me will be kept in confidence. Mr. Taylor, why don't you tell me what happened?

295. Id. at 507.
296. See Ortiz v. Fibreboard Corp., 119 S. Ct. 2295 (1999); Amchem Prods., Inc. v. Windsor, 521 U.S. 591 (1997).
297. See *Ortiz*, 119 S. Ct. at 2319; *Amchem Prods.*, 521 U.S. at 627-628.

Taylor: Well, I had just delivered a load to Charleston and was on the way back to the warehouse when this guy in a little car pulled out in front of me. I hit the brakes but nothing happened. . . . *(To Voss)* I told you those brakes were going bad. . . . *(To Sanchez)* Anyway, I hit him broadside and can't remember anything else. I was in the hospital for two months. Just got out last week and I still have a lot of pain.

Sanchez: I'm sorry you've had so much trouble. Hopefully, this case will settle soon and you can put all of this behind you.

Taylor: What about my case against that other driver? My doctor said that some of my injuries may be permanent.

Sanchez: I've looked at the accident report and unfortunately it appears that the driver did not have any insurance. Freight Lines does have uninsured motorist coverage under its policy.

Voss: How would that affect our rates?

Sanchez: Well, any claim under a policy will increase your rates, but I'm not sure how much.

Voss: I don't believe the company could authorize a claim under the uninsured motorist provision if it would substantially affect our rates. . . . There is one other thing I want to mention to you. The truck that was involved in this accident had been retired from our fleet about a month ago and removed from the list of trucks covered under the policy. We just used it that day because one of our other trucks was broken down. Fortunately, the company doesn't know about this, but I wanted to let you know about it so that you wouldn't raise it as an issue if it comes up.

> *Sanchez:* Um. I'll have to give both of these mat-
> ters some thought. . . .

Mr. Sanchez asks your advice about how he should proceed. What advice would you give?

Read Model Rule 1.7(b) and comments.

Relationship between insured, insurance company, and defense counsel

The standard liability policy is a contract between the insurance company and the insured. For a specified premium, the insurance company agrees (a) to defend any suit against the insured within the coverage of the policy regardless of the merit of the suit (commonly called the "duty to defend") and (b) to pay any judgment against the insured up to the applicable policy limit. Under the typical policy, the insurance company reserves the right to control the defense, including the right to accept or reject any offer of settlement, and to select counsel to defend the insured. In addition to paying the premium, the insured promises to give the insurer prompt notice of any claim or occurrence within the coverage of the policy, to cooperate fully in the defense, and to subrogate the insurance company for any amount paid on behalf of the insured.[298]

Traditionally courts and commentators have viewed defense counsel as representing *both* the insured and the insurance company (sometimes referred to as the "two-client" model or "tripartite relationship").[299] Dual representation has been justified on the

---

298. See generally ABA Comm. on Prof. Ethics and Griev., Formal Op. 282 (1950).

299. See, e.g., State Farm Mut. Auto. Ins. Co. v. Federal Ins. Co., 86 Cal. Rptr. 2d 20 (Ct. App. 1999, *review denied*) (lawyer retained by insurance company to defend insured represents both and is accordingly disqualified from suing insurer in unrelated matter). ABA Formal Opinion 96-403 states that by express agreement insurer, insured, and defense counsel could agree that counsel represents (1) only the insured, (2) both insured and the insurer for all purposes, (3) both insured and insurer for all purposes except settlement, in which case counsel represents the insurer. As discussed subsequently, the one-client model

ground that the insurance company and insured generally have a "community of interest" with respect to any claim brought by a third party within the policy coverage: Both the insurance company and the insured have an interest in defeating the claim or in minimizing the amount of the recovery.[300]

While normally a harmony of interests exists between insurer and insured, a number of situations can develop in which the harmony of interests disintegrates.[301] The most common such situations are the following:

- *Coverage disputes.* The insurer's contractual obligation is limited to amounts that the insured is legally liable to pay and that fall within the scope of the policy's coverage. Intentional torts and punitive damages typically are excluded from coverage under liability policies. Sometimes the existence of a coverage issue is apparent to the insurer at the outset of the case (for example, if the policy excludes coverage for intentional torts and punitive damages and the complaint alleges a cause of action for both). In other cases, however, facts that could establish lack of coverage may come to the attorney in confidence and may not be known by the insurer.
- *Excess claims.* In an "excess" situation, the plaintiff is seeking damages that exceed the policy limits, but has made a settlement offer that is within the policy limits. The insured has an interest in having the insurer accept this settlement since the insured will not suffer any financial loss. The insurer may have an interest in rejecting the offer, however, if the insurer believes the offer is excessive, even though within the policy limits.
- *Uninsured or underinsured motorist claims.* Many automobile policies have uninsured or underinsured coverage. Under

---

in which defense counsel represents only the insured offers a number of advantages over the current two-client model.

300. See ABA Comm. on Prof. Ethics and Griev., Formal Op. 282 (1950); Fortune et al., Modern Litigation and Professional Responsibility Handbook §15.3.1, at 502-505; 3 Mallen & Smith, Legal Malpractice §28.14, at 553-554.

301. See generally Douglas R. Richmond, Lost in the Eternal Triangle of Insurance Defense Ethics, 9 Geo. J. Legal Ethics 475 (1996); Symposium: Liability Insurance Conflicts and Professional Responsibility, 4 Conn. Ins. L.J. 101 (1997-1998).

such a provision, if the other driver does not have insurance (or is underinsured), the insured's own company
provides coverage subject to the limits in the policy. As a
result the same insurance company may be defending the
insured and the opposing party.

- *Counterclaims.* As noted above, the typical liability policy
provides that the insurance company has a "duty to defend" the insured. Suppose the insured has a counterclaim
against the opposing party. The insured has an interest in
pursuing this claim, but the insurance company has no
financial interest in paying for an attorney to obtain recovery on behalf of the insured.

- *Fraud or collusion by the insured.* In some cases (if the plaintiff is a friend or relative, for example), the insured may
have an interest in conceding liability or in colluding with
the plaintiff.

- *Multiple insureds.* In some cases, the insurance company
may have multiple insureds in a single matter. For example, an insurance company may issue medical malpractice
policies that cover several doctors involved in a malpractice case. The insureds may have conflicting interests if
their degrees of fault or amount of coverage differ.

- *Subrogation.* Insurance policies typically provide that the
insurance company is "subrogated" to the rights of the
insured. This means that if the insurance company makes
a payment to the insured (for example, for property damage), the insurance company takes over any rights that the
insured may have against a third party. A conflict of interest may develop between the insured and the insurer if
the insured also has claims against the third party that are
not covered by the policy.

Each of these situations represents a potential conflict of interest between insurance company and insured. Under standard
conflict-of-interest principles, a lawyer may represent multiple
clients with potential conflicts of interest in a single matter provided the lawyer fully explains to the clients the advantages, disadvantages, and risks of multiple representation, and provided
both clients consent to the representation. See Model Rule 1.7(b).
Surprisingly, insurance defense counsel have largely ignored these
obligations of full disclosure and consent. Instead, when suit is

filed against the insured, the insurance company typically forwards the case to defense counsel selected by it. Defense counsel then contacts the insured and proceeds to defend the case with little if any explanation of the relationship between defense counsel, insured, and insurance company. Failure by defense counsel to make full disclosure of their role and to obtain consent by the insured to multiple representation has been justified on the ground that the insured has given "consent" to the representation by forwarding court papers to the insurance company,[302] but this consent is implied rather than expressed and in any event does not include a full disclosure of defense counsel's role.[303]

Dealing with conflicts of interest between insured and insurer

Assuming defense counsel has undertaken representation, what action should counsel take if one of the potential conflicts of interest outlined above ripens into an actual conflict? Under standard principles of lawyer's obligations, when a lawyer faces an actual conflict of interest between two clients, the lawyer must withdraw from representation of both. Applied to insurance defense counsel, however, this approach is unsatisfactory. If defense counsel is required to withdraw, new defense counsel must be appointed at additional expense to the company and ultimately to its insureds. Thus, insurance defense practice has developed a different approach.

In almost all of the conflict situations outlined above, the conflict between insured and insurance company does not involve confidential information that defense counsel has received from the insured. For example, excess claims, uninsured or underinsured motorist claims, counterclaims, multiple insureds, and subrogation situations rarely involve any confidential information. In addition, many coverage disputes do not involve confidential in-

302. See ABA Comm. on Prof. Ethics and Griev., Formal Op. 282, at 3 (1950).
303. See ABA Comm. on Ethics and Prof. Resp., Formal Op. 96-403, at 3-5 (defense counsel should communicate to insured nature and limits on representation at earliest possible opportunity; insured consents by accepting defense).

formation. In these nonconfidential information situations, the standard practice for dealing with the conflict is for the insurance company to notify the insured in writing and to inform the insured that it should consider retaining independent counsel at its own expense to protect its interests.[304] For example, when the plaintiff makes a settlement demand within the policy limits, the insurer will send the insured an *excess letter* informing the insured of its potential liability if the case is not settled and the plaintiff obtains a recovery in excess of the policy limits.[305] Similarly, when coverage is in doubt, the insurance company will send the insured a *reservation of rights letter*, informing the insured that the company is defending the claim but is reserving its right to contest coverage, typically in an independent declaratory judgment action.[306] Defense counsel will continue to handle the case on behalf of both the insurer and the insured. The insured, with its own counsel, can participate in the proceedings to the extent appropriate to protect the insured's interest that is in conflict with the insurer's. Independent counsel can, for example, advocate on behalf of the insured that the insurer accept a settlement offer within the policy limits; similarly, independent counsel may represent the insured in any declaratory judgment action to determine coverage.

Liability insurance policies typically do not provide coverage for counterclaims by the insured. If the insured defendant has a

---

304. Guidance for defense counsel in dealing with standard conflict-of-interest situations can be found in the Guiding Principles of the National Conference of Lawyers and Liability Insurers, reprinted in 20 Fedn. Ins. Couns. Q. 93 (#4, 1970). The ABA approved the principles in 1972. The ABA rescinded its approval of the principles in 1980 under pressure from the Justice Department because of concern about the anticompetitive effect of intraprofessional agreements, not because of substantive problems with the principles. Wolfram, Modern Legal Ethics §8.4.2, at 429 n.97. Nonetheless, the Guiding Principles provide a set of standards for the most common problems that defense counsel face. The Guiding Principles begin by recognizing the traditional principle that both the insurer and the insured are clients of defense counsel. Guiding Principle I.

305. Guiding Principles II and III deal with excess situations. If the insured retains separate counsel after receiving an excess letter, the insured's attorney has the right to be informed of settlement negotiations, but the insurer retains the right to decide whether to accept settlement offers and to otherwise control the defense, pursuant to the terms of the insurance policy. (Note that some insurance policies, particularly those involving professionals, provide that the insurer may not agree to settle the case without the consent of the insured.)

306. See Guiding Principles IV and V.

counterclaim against the plaintiff, defense counsel should notify the insured that the policy does not cover this matter and that the insured should seek independent representation for this claim.[307] On occasion, the same insurance company may insure multiple parties in the case. The company should inform the insureds of this fact, each insured should be separately represented, and the company should share with the insureds its factual investigation in the matter (except that statements by any insured or employees of an insured should not be given to parties with adverse interests to the insured).[308] The company should provide separate counsel to defend the company in claims by the insured for uninsured motorist coverage.[309]

What should defense counsel do when counsel learns of a conflict between insured and insurance company in confidence? Suppose, for example, the insured tells defense counsel of facts unknown to the insurer that would constitute a defense of lack of coverage. If the facts show that the insured is engaged in fraud or collusion, defense counsel should at a minimum withdraw from representation. Further, depending on the confidentiality rule that applies in the jurisdiction where the lawyer practices, the lawyer may be authorized to reveal the insured's confidences to prevent a crime or fraud. See Problem 2-3 on the scope of the duty of confidentiality. If the facts revealed to defense counsel simply establish a possible coverage defense but do not involve fraud by the insured, defense counsel faces a fundamental conflict between two clients. The traditional answer to such a conflict is for the lawyer to withdraw, but in insurance defense practice this solution would do nothing but increase the cost of handling the case. In this difficult situation, the best solution is probably for defense counsel to continue the representation without revealing the insured's confidences to the insurer.[310]

Should the insurer be required to pay for the insured's independent counsel when the insured is notified of a conflict of

307. See Guiding Principle VII.
308. See Guiding Principle VIII.
309. See Guiding Principle X.
310. The Guiding Principles recognize that cases can arise in which defense counsel learns of coverage issues through confidential communications with the insured. In this situation, the Principles state that defense counsel should not reveal the information to the company nor should counsel advise the insured regarding coverage matters. Guiding Principle VI.

interest? A growing number of courts have so held.[311] The argument for imposing the cost of hiring conflict counsel on the insurer is that the insurer has a contractual duty to defend. If the insured must pay for conflict counsel, the insured is not receiving its contractual right to a defense. At the same time, good arguments can be made against imposing the cost of conflict counsel on the insurer. First, the relationship between insurer and insured is a matter of contract. If the contract clearly provides that the insured must bear the expense of hiring its own counsel when a conflict arises, it is inconsistent with the contract for courts to impose this expense on insurers. Second, if insurance companies must pay for independent defense counsel every time one of the standard insurance defense conflicts arises, insureds have no incentive not to retain counsel. As a result, total defense fees and insurance premiums are likely to increase. A better approach might be to place the cost of hiring independent counsel on insureds, who can then determine whether hiring counsel to deal with the particular conflict is truly cost effective. In addition, if a sufficient market for insurance for conflicts counsel exists, insurance companies will respond to the demand by offering riders providing for such coverage on payment of an additional premium.

The most common failing of defense counsel: protecting the interests of the insurer over the insured

Defense counsel typically has an ongoing financial relationship with the insurance company. The company will be referring matters to defense counsel on a regular basis and paying its fees. In contrast, defense counsel's relationship with the insured is usually transitory, lasting only for the one case, and the insured does not pay any fees. As a result, it is not surprising that some defense counsel have fallen into the ethical trap of protecting the interests of the insurance company over those of the insured.

For example, in Parsons v. Continental National American Group[312] the insured was a 14-year-old charged with assault and

---

311. San Diego Navy Fed. Credit Union v. Cumis Ins. Socy., 208 Cal. Rptr. 494 (Ct. App. 1984). *Accord* CHI of Alaska, Inc. v. Employers Reins. Corp., 844 P.2d 1113 (Alaska 1993).

312. 550 P.2d 94 (Ariz. 1976) (en banc).

battery of his neighbors. The liability policy issued by CNA had a $25,000 limit and excluded intentional torts. The attorney retained by the insurance company obtained the child's confidential file from a boys' school were he was being kept. The attorney wrote the insurer advising it that the file showed that the boy was "fully aware of his acts" and that "the assault he committed on claimants can only be a deliberate act on his part." In preparing for trial, the attorney interviewed the child and received a narrative statement from him. In a letter to CNA, he wrote as follows: "His own story makes it obvious that his acts were willful and criminal."[313] At trial the attorney offered no evidence on the child's behalf, and a judgment was entered against the child in the amount of $50,000. The plaintiffs then brought a garnishment action against CNA seeking the amount of the policy.[314] CNA defended on the ground that the policy excluded intentional torts. The Arizona Supreme Court ruled that the company was estopped from denying liability because the attorney retained by the insurance company to defend the insured had violated his duty of confidentiality by revealing information obtained from the insured to the insurer in an effort to help the insurer establish a defense of lack of coverage:

> The attorney in the present case continued to act as Michael's attorney while he was actively working against Michael's interests. When an attorney who is an insurance company's agent uses the confidential relationship between an attorney and a client to gather information so as to deny the insured coverage under the policy in the garnishment proceeding we hold that such conduct constitutes a waiver of any policy defense, and is so contrary to public policy that the insurance company is estopped as a matter of law from disclaiming liability under an exclusionary clause in the policy.[315]

The court warned that an attorney confronted with such a conflict — confidential information received from the insured showing

313. Id. at 96.
314. In many jurisdictions, issues of coverage are resolved by declaratory judgment action. E.g., Employers Cas. Co. v. Tilley, 496 S.W.2d 552 (Tex. 1973) (declaratory judgment action brought by insurer against insured seeking determination whether insured's failure to give timely notice as required by policy relieved insurer of obligations under policy).
315. 550 P.2d at 99.

lack of coverage — should withdraw from representation of the insurer.[316] The insurance company was held liable for the full $50,000, an amount in excess of the policy limit, because the company had rejected an opportunity to settle the case for $25,000.

In *Parsons* the insurance company was estopped from denying coverage because of defense counsel's misconduct.[317] Most jurisdictions recognize that an insurance company can be held liable to its insured for bad faith refusal to settle claims under insurance policies.[318] In many cases such bad faith claims exceed the limits of the insurer's policy. When defense counsel purports to represent both the insured and insurer in settlement and favors the interests of the insurer, defense counsel may be liable for malpractice.[319]

The possibility of a one-client model

One way of eliminating the conflicts of interest facing defense counsel in representation of both the insured and the insurer is to change from a two-client to a one-client model of representation.[320] Indeed, some decisions indicate movement in this direc-

316. Id. at 98.

317. *Accord* Employers Cas. Co. v. Tilley, 496 S.W.2d 552 (Tex. 1973) (insurer estopped from denying coverage when attorney hired by insurer to defend insured worked on behalf of company to obtain statements from insured's employees establishing lack of coverage because of failure to file timely notice of claim).

318. See Douglas R. Richmond, An Overview of Insurance Bad Faith Law and Litigation, 25 Seton Hall L. Rev. 74, 80 n.33 (third-party claims) and 104 n.170 (first-party claims) (1994). See also Roger C. Henderson, The Tort of Bad Faith in First-Party Insurance Transactions After Two Decades, 37 Ariz. L. Rev. 1153, 1153-1154 (1995).

319. See Lysick v. Walcom, 65 Cal. Rptr. 406 (Ct. App. 1968) (defense counsel liable for malpractice when counsel protected interests of insurer rather than insured in excess situation).

320. Robert E. O'Malley, Ethics Principles for the Insurer, the Insured, and Defense Counsel: The Eternal Triangle Reformed, 66 Tul. L. Rev. 511 (1991) (proposing set of Guiding Principles II based on one-client model); see also Douglas R. Richmond, Lost in the Eternal Triangle of Insurance Defense Ethics, 9 Geo. J. Legal Ethics 475 (1996) (surveying problem areas, but arguing that primary duty must be to insured). *Compare* Charles Silver & Kent Syverud,

tion.[321] Under a one-client model, defense counsel would represent only the insured and would be required to take into account only the insured's interests, not those of the insurer. The insurance company would pay the fees of defense counsel pursuant to its duty to defend under the policy. The one-client model would be fully consistent with the rules of ethics. Model Rule 1.8(f) provides that a lawyer may represent a client while receiving payment from a third party so long as the client consents after consultation, the payor does not interfere with the lawyer's independent professional judgment on behalf of the client, and the lawyer adheres to the duty of confidentiality.

Insurance companies are likely to object to proposals for a one-client model on several grounds. First, companies might contend that under the one-client model they would lose the ability to select competent counsel. If the choice were left to the insured, companies would have no guarantee that the insured would select capable counsel. The result might well be less capable representation, harming both the insured and the insurer.[322] Selection of counsel and identification of the client, however, are different issues. Insurers could protect their legitimate interest in competent counsel by reserving in their policies the right either to select counsel or to approve counsel selected by the insured.

Second, companies might argue that the one-client model would deprive them of their contractual right to control the defense because counsel of record would owe its allegiance only to the insured. The one-client model does not, however, limit the insurer's contractual right to control the defense. For example, under the policy the insurer could reserve the right to establish a reasonable budget for the defense of the case. Further, as is the

---

The Professional Responsibilities of Insurance Defense Lawyers, 45 Duke L.J. 255 (1995) (insurance contract should control responsibilities of defense counsel).

321. See Atlanta Intl. Ins. Co. v. Bell, 475 N.W.2d 294 (Mich. 1991) (insurer may not bring malpractice action against defense counsel because counsel represents only insured not insurer). See also San Diego Navy Fed. Credit Union v. Cumis Ins. Socy., 208 Cal. Rptr. 494 (Ct. App. 1984) (when insurer defends under reservation of rights because of a coverage issue, insured is entitled to retain counsel at insurer's expense).

322. See Ronald E. Mallen, A New Definition of Insurance Defense Counsel, 53 Ins. Couns. J. 108 (1986).

case now, insurance policies could provide that any settlement offer is subject to the insurer's acceptance.

Third, insurers might argue that a change to the one-client model would mean that they would lose the ability to receive objective advice from defense counsel on whether to accept a settlement offer. This argument is correct, but the benefits of the change may well outweigh the costs. Under the current two-client model, defense counsel has a difficult task when the insurer asks for advice about acceptance of a settlement offer. Defense counsel represents both the insured and the insurer. As attorney for the insured, defense counsel should advocate acceptance of any settlement that the insured finds favorable. As attorney for the insurer, however, defense counsel should give objective advice about the advantages and disadvantages of the settlement. Under the one-client model defense counsel would become an advocate for the insured rather than an objective advisor to the insurer. How significant would be the loss of advice from defense counsel? Insurers could still rely on advice from adjusters and in-house counsel, but their analysis of the case is unlikely to be as deep as that of defense counsel, who is more familiar with the facts and context of the case. The one-client model, however, might reduce the amount of bad faith litigation growing out of insurance defense.

Emerging conflicts of interest

Like other fields of law, insurance defense practice changes, producing new types of conflicts of interest.[323] In the past few years insurers have attempted to control escalating defense costs by adopting various management techniques, including audits of defense counsel's fees by outside consultants and establishment of litigation management guidelines. The following are some typical provisions:

- We will not pay for file reviews by attorneys after the initial assignment and file review has been made.

---

323. See Douglas R. Richmond, Emerging Conflicts of Interest in Insurance Defense Practice, 32 Tort & Ins. L.J. 69 (1996).

- Paralegals should answer interrogatories and respond to requests to produce.
- We will not pay for proofreading or redrafts of legal documents.
- We will not pay for trial preparation unless trial is imminent.
- We will not pay for legal research in excess of two hours without advance approval. When seeking advance approval, identify the issue or issues to be researched, the relationship between that issue and the case you are handling, the impact that issue will have on the outcome of the case, the likelihood of a favorable result of such research, and the time you anticipate spending on such research, and indicate whether or not such an issue has been previously researched and is not available to you. A copy of any research memoranda is to be provided to us.
- We will not pay for time spent traveling unless actual work on our behalf is being performed.[324]

Many defense counsel have complained that such guidelines are inconsistent with their duties of competence (Model Rule 1.1), confidentiality (Model Rule 1.6), and loyalty (Model Rule 1.7) to their insured clients. The conflict between the duties of defense counsel to the insured and the interest of insurers in controlling litigation costs is unresolved.

─────────── **Problem 3-10** ───────────

Family Practice

   a.   Ellen Andrews and her husband, Samuel, have asked you to represent them in obtaining a no-fault divorce, which is recognized in your jurisdiction. You represented the parties previously in the purchase of their home and the preparation of their wills, but you have done no other legal work for them. They tell you that they have been married for five years, that they do not

---

324. Robert C. Heist, The Tripartite Relationship and the Insurer's Duty to Defend Contrasted with Its Desire to Manage and Control Litigation Through the Introduction of the Legal Audit, 602 PLI/Lit 221, 230-233 (1999) (on Westlaw).

have any animosity toward each other, but that the marriage has just not worked out for them. There are no children. They also tell you that financial problems have been a factor in the divorce. Samuel was in the real estate development business, but his company failed, and he has been out of work now for more than a year. Ellen works full time as a bookkeeper in a doctor's office.

Ellen and Samuel have agreed on a division of their assets. They give you the following sheet of paper:

DIVISION OF ASSETS

1. House, 711 Camellia Drive. Approximate value $250,000. Subject to mortgage to Second Union Bank in amount of $210,000. Property to be sold. Equity used to pay off credit card debt and remaining equity divided. Ellen to live in house until sold.

2. Furnishings in house to go to Ellen except that Samuel will take the following:

Lounge chair in living room
Double bed in guest room
Samuel's chest of drawers in bedroom
GE TV and VCR
Computer and printer

3. We will each keep our cars and take over payments.

4. Credit card debt to be paid when house is sold:

VISA: $2,200
MasterCard: $3,500
Various merchants: about $5,000

What would you say to them? *Need 2nd lawyer?*

b. You are an attorney practicing domestic relations law. You have an interview with a new client, Melissa Carter, who wishes to obtain a divorce from her husband, Carl. Melissa's father, Alan Frank, accompanies her to the interview. Melissa tells you that Carl has been mentally and physically abusing her. Frank expresses hostility toward Carl. He says that he wants to make sure that Carl pays financially for what he has done to his daughter. When you raise the issue of fees, Frank states that he will be responsible for the fees. Be prepared to continue the interview from this point.

    c.   You are an attorney appointed by the family court to represent Susan Van Ness, age 14, in an abuse and neglect case filed by the Department of Family and Children Services against Susan's father, Harold, and also in connection with a divorce action filed by Susan's mother, Emily. Harold denies the allegations of abuse and has sought custody of Susan in the divorce case. In his answer Harold claims that his wife is a "pathological liar" who dominates and controls Susan. You have met with Susan, the parents, a social worker, and two psychiatrists; one doctor is treating Susan, while the other psychiatrist is an expert hired by Harold. The allegations of sexual abuse originally came from the mother. Susan initially denied that the abuse occurred, but she later told her psychiatrist that the allegations were true. The treating psychiatrist is prepared to testify that in his opinion the abuse occurred. The psychiatrist for the defense disagrees and will testify that the abuse has been fabricated by the mother and indoctrinated in Susan. Susan has told you very strongly that she wants to live with her mother, not her father. You are not sure whether the allegations of abuse are true, but you believe that they probably are. You are also not sure who should have custody of Susan, but you tend to believe that she would be better off not living with either parent. Two possible choices are the wife's mother or the husband's sister, both of whom you find acceptable. How would you proceed in light of your uncertainties in the case?

Read Model Rules 1.7, 1.8(f), 1.14. 2.2, 4.3, and comments.

Is multiple representation of spouses per se improper?

According to some authorities, it is ethically improper for an attorney to represent both the husband and wife in a divorce or separation, regardless of the circumstances.[325] The Bounds of Advocacy, standards of conduct adopted by the American Academy of Matrimonial Lawyers in 1991, also condemns multiple representation. Standard 2.20 provides: "An attorney should not represent both husband and wife even if they do not wish to obtain independent representation." The comment offers the following rationale: "[I]t is impossible for the attorney to provide impartial advice to both parties, and even a seemingly amicable separation or divorce may result in bitter litigation over financial matters or custody."

Despite these authorities, a number of leading courts have held that it is not per se improper for a lawyer to represent both spouses in a separation or divorce matter. In Klemm v. Superior Court[326] the attorney represented both the husband and wife in a divorce action. The parties had agreed to joint custody without child support. The trial judge granted an interlocutory decree and awarded custody in accordance with the agreement, but because the wife was receiving welfare payments from the county, the judge referred the case to the county's family support division. The division recommended that the court order the husband to pay $50 per month in child support to the county as reimbursement for past and present payments made by the county to the wife. The attorney filed an objection to this recommendation. At the hearing on the issue, counsel filed written consents by both spouses to joint representation and indicated to the court that she was prepared to proceed to contest the support division's recommendation on behalf of both parties. The trial court refused to allow the attorney to proceed on behalf of both parties because of a conflict between the husband and wife. The court ruled that at some point the wife might no longer qualify for welfare payments, in which event a support order would accrue to her benefit.[327]

The California Court of Appeals reversed. The court drew a distinction between marital cases in which an actual rather than a potential conflict of interest exists. If an actual conflict exists, multiple representation, even with client consent, is improper:

---

325. See Holmes v. Holmes, 248 N.E.2d 564 (Ind. Ct. App. 1969); Hale v. Hale, 539 A.2d 247 (Md. Ct. Spec. App.), *cert. denied*, 542 A.2d 857 (Md. 1988).

326. 142 Cal. Rptr. 509 (Ct. App. 1977).

327. Id. at 511 n.1.

Consent to dual adverse representation is neither intelligent nor informed

As a matter of law a purported consent to dual representation of litigants with adverse interests at a contested hearing would be neither intelligent nor informed. Such representation would be per se inconsistent with the adversary position of an attorney in litigation, and common sense dictates that it would be unthinkable to permit an attorney to assume a position at a trial or hearing where he could not advocate the interests of one client without adversely injuring those of the other.[328]

When a potential rather than an actual conflict exists, however, multiple representation with informed client consent is permissible. On the facts of the case the court found that the conflict was potential rather than actual: "While on the face of the matter it may appear foolhardy for the wife to waive child support, other values could very well have been more important to her than such support — such as maintaining a good relationship between the husband and the children and between the husband and herself despite the marital problems — thus avoiding . . . backbiting, acrimony and ill will. . . ."[329] Several commentators have also argued that simultaneous representation of spouses should be permissible in appropriate cases.[330]

When is simultaneous representation ethically proper?

Assuming that simultaneous representation in a divorce or separation matter is not per se improper, when may an attorney undertake such representation? As noted above, if an actual conflict

---

328. Id. at 512.

329. Id. at 513. The court also noted that the parties' agreement to waive child support would not prevent the court from ordering support at a later date if necessary. Other cases finding multiple representation in marital matters to be proper include Levine v. Levine, 436 N.E.2d 476 (N.Y. 1982) (fact that same attorney represented both parties in preparation of separation agreement does not, without more, establish overreaching on part of husband) and Halvorsen v. Halvorsen, 479 P.2d 161 (Wash. Ct. App. 1970, *review denied*) (fact that both parties to divorce were represented by same attorney did not show inadequacy of representation or justify setting aside separation agreement).

330. Nathan M. Crystal, Ethical Problems in Marital Practice, 30 S.C. L. Rev. 321, 325-328 (1979); Nancy J. Moore, Conflicts of Interest in the Simultaneous Representation of Multiple Clients: A Proposed Solution to the Current Controversy, 61 Tex. L. Rev. 211, 245-258 (1982).

of interest exists between husband and wife, simultaneous representation is unethical. Even in the absence of an actual conflict, the attorney may not undertake simultaneous representation unless the attorney is able to comply with the requirements of Rule 1.7(b) or Rule 2.2. Professors Hazard and Hodes point out that the standards for intermediation under Rule 2.2 and for simultaneous representation of potentially conflicting interests under Rule 1.7(b) are essentially the same. They offer the same analysis under both sections of multiple representation of spouses in divorce cases.[331] As they point out, the reason the Model Rules include both Rules 1.7 and 2.2 is to emphasize the different roles performed by lawyers. Rule 1.7 appears in the section of the rules dealing with the client-lawyer relationship, while Rule 2.2 appears in the section dealing with the lawyer as counselor.[332] The analysis here follows Rule 2.2 because the standards in that rule are more specific.

Under Rule 2.2(a)(2) a lawyer may not act as an intermediary unless the lawyer "reasonably believes that the matter can be resolved on terms compatible with the clients' best interests, that each client will be able to make adequately informed decisions in the matter and that there is little risk of material prejudice to the interest of any of the clients if the contemplated resolution is unsuccessful." Cases will arise in which a lawyer could not have the reasonable belief required by the rule:

> [An] attorney should decline dual representation because of her inability to represent adequately the interests of both spouses if it is likely that (1) advocacy will be needed, (2) independent counseling will be necessary, or (3) the lawyer will not be able to function as a neutral intermediary.

1. The Need for Advocacy. If a contested issue develops in a divorce case, advocacy will be required. In deciding whether it is likely that a contested issue will develop, the attorney should consider the following:

> (a) The degree to which the parties have discussed significant issues and reached agreement on them, at least in principle. . . .
>
> (b) The presence of minor children, substantial debts, or

---

331. See 1 Hazard & Hodes, the Law of Lawyering §2.2:204.
332. Id. §2.2:101.

substantial assets. As the divorce becomes more complex, the potential for a contest increases. While mere complexity of the case should not preclude dual representation, if complexity is coupled with lack of agreement or consideration of basic issues, dual representation should be declined because a contested issue is likely.

2. *The Need for Independent Counsel.* If either spouse is in a dependent condition, the spouse needs the services of an independent advisor. Whether a spouse is in this condition depends on the following:

(a)   The emotional condition of the parties. If either person is severely emotionally disturbed because of the crisis of the divorce or otherwise, the lawyer should not undertake dual representation.

(b)   The relationship between the spouses. It is not uncommon for one spouse to dominate the other. If the lawyer perceives that one spouse dominates the decision making of the other, dual representation should not be accepted.

3. *The Lawyer's Ability to Act Neutrally.* As the representative of the spouses, the lawyer has obligations of loyalty and care to both. The lawyer should not undertake dual representation if his personal relationship with either spouse is such that he cannot fulfill this role. A dangerous situation exists if the lawyer has had a close relationship with one of the parties, for example, as business counselor to the husband, and is asked to handle the divorce on behalf of both. The prior relationship, coupled with the prospects for future legal work from the husband, may undermine the lawyer's neutrality.[333]

Assuming the lawyer reasonably believes that she can act as an intermediary between divorce clients under Rule 2.2, the lawyer must obtain the clients' consent to intermediation after consultation. Consultation should include a full explanation of "the implications of the common representation, including the advantages

---

333. Nathan M. Crystal, Ethical Problems in Marital Practice, 30 S.C. L. Rev. 321, 329-330 (1979).

and risks involved, and the effect on the attorney-client privileges." Consider the following analysis of this requirement:

   1. *Advantages of Dual Representation.* — Clients usually give two reasons for wanting dual representation: a desire to save legal fees, and trust and confidence in the attorney. If one lawyer handles a complex divorce, legal fees are saved in one sense: the total dollar amount paid for legal services is less than if two attorneys are employed. In another sense, however, fees are not saved. [W]hen a lawyer represents both spouses he owes duties to both. The lawyer functions like a mediator rather than an advocate or independent counselor. While clients may rationally prefer to pay X dollars for these services rather than X plus Y dollars for the services of two independent attorneys, they should be aware that it is misleading to state that fees are being saved; different services are being purchased.

   Clients should be advised that their goal of obtaining a divorce for one legal fee could be achieved even if the lawyer does not represent both. The lawyer could represent one spouse, leaving the other unrepresented. This approach offers the advantage that the lawyer would not be forced to withdraw if a contested issue developed. It has disadvantages, however. While the attorney may communicate with the unrepresented party, he is ethically prohibited from giving legal advice to that party. Although this is not a major consideration in simple divorces, in complex cases the unrepresented party is probably seriously disadvantaged by lack of counsel. Moreover, regardless of the complexity of the divorce, the unrepresented party may be troubled by his lack of representation. This may cause the divorce to proceed less smoothly than if the attorney represented both parties.

   Trust and confidence of both spouses in a specific lawyer is the second reason usually given by clients who want dual representation. For some clients this reason actually represents an underlying fear that if two lawyers are participating the divorce will become formalized and adversarial. The parties should be informed that the question whether the participation of two lawyers makes a divorce more or less adversarial is problematic. Evidence indicates that some lawyers fail to consider that divorces can be resolved in a cooperative rather than adversarial spirit. On the other hand, lawyers often help promote agreements that clients could not have reached on their own.

   2. *Disadvantages of Dual Representation.* — The clients should be informed of three possible detrimental effects of dual represen-

tation. First, although the parties intend a friendly divorce, a dispute may arise. If this should occur, the lawyer would be required to withdraw from the case. Each of the parties would then be forced to hire new counsel. As a result, total legal fees would probably exceed the fees that would have been paid if separate counsel had been hired initially. Second, several court decisions have overturned separation agreements when one lawyer handled the divorce on the ground that the lawyer did not adequately protect the interests of both parties. While having one lawyer handle the case does not automatically make the agreement invalid, the parties should be aware that dual representation makes it more likely that a court will not enforce the agreement if one of the parties subsequently becomes dissatisfied with it. Third, by asking the lawyer to represent both, the parties waive their attorney-client privilege for communications made to the attorney by either of them. The attorney might be forced to testify to damaging information if the divorce becomes contested.

3. *Consent.* — If the clients decide that they want the lawyer to represent both of them after the lawyer has fully discussed the advantages and disadvantages of dual representation, the lawyer should obtain their written consent at the time representation is undertaken. The consent should state that the lawyer has explained the advantages and risks of dual representation. A clause evincing consent to the representation should also be included in the separation agreement, and the lawyer should disclose the dual representation to the court at the time of the final decree.[334]

The Restatement of the Law Governing Lawyers partially approves of a lawyer's acting as an intermediary in an uncontested divorce. Section 211 offers the following illustration:

Husband and Wife have agreed to obtain an uncontested dissolution of their marriage. They have consulted Lawyer to help them reach an agreement on disposition of their property. A conflict of interest clearly exists between the prospective clients. . . . If reasonable prospects of an agreement exist, Lawyer may accept the joint representation with the effective consent of both. . . . However, in the later dissolution proceeding, Lawyer may represent only one of the parties . . . and Lawyer must withdraw from representing both clients if their efforts to reach an agreement fail.[335]

334. Id. at 330-332.
335. Restatement (Third) of the Law Governing Lawyers §211, illus. 6.

The Restatement approach is a creative compromise between absolute prohibition and blanket endorsement of representation of spouses in domestic cases. Under the Restatement view, a lawyer could act as an intermediary between a husband and wife who seek an uncontested divorce in negotiating an agreement to resolve differences between them, but the lawyer avoids representing opposite sides in litigation.

An alternative to simultaneous representation: representation of one party with the other party being unrepresented

Even if simultaneous representation is ethically permissible, many lawyers may not be willing to run the risks that such representation entails. Indeed, even courts that have permitted simultaneous representation have warned lawyers of the potential risks of this course of action, including malpractice liability, disciplinary proceedings, and invalidation of any agreement entered into between the jointly represented parties.[336]

In light of these risks, one approach that many attorneys have used is to refuse to represent both spouses, advising the unrepresented spouse to obtain independent counsel. If the unrepresented spouse refuses to obtain counsel, the attorney proceeds with the matter on behalf of the client, dealing with the other spouse as an unrepresented party. Ethically, an attorney may represent one client and deal with an unrepresented party, provided the attorney complies with Model Rule 4.3 (dealing with unrepresented persons).

May a lawyer prepare a separation agreement and present it to the unrepresented party for that party's signature? In Formal Opinion 84-350, the ABA Committee on Ethics and Professional Responsibility withdrew two earlier opinions prohibiting lawyers who represented one spouse in a divorce case from presenting

---

336. See Klemm v. Superior Court, 142 Cal. Rptr. 509, 514 (Ct. App. 1977). See also Ishmael v. Millington, 50 Cal. Rptr. 592 (Dist. Ct. App. 1966) (summary judgment for attorney reversed in malpractice action brought by wife claiming that attorney favored interests of husband in preparation of agreement); Columbus Bar Assn. v. Grelle, 237 N.E.2d 298 (1968) (attorney reprimanded because of misunderstandings resulting from multiple representation).

waivers or responsive pleadings to the other spouse for signature. Thus, under the Model Rules, it is apparently permissible for a lawyer to present to an unrepresented party a document for execution.[337] Suppose, however, the unrepresented spouse asks questions about the documents that are presented. Here the lawyer faces a difficulty. The comment to Rule 4.3 provides as follows: "During the course of a lawyer's representation of a client, the lawyer should not give advice to an unrepresented person other than the advice to obtain counsel." Answering questions beyond the most routine or straightforward would seem to be giving advice.

As discussed above, the Bounds of Advocacy of the American Academy of Matrimonial Lawyers state that a lawyer should not represent both spouses in a domestic matter. These standards also deal with the situation in which the lawyer represents one spouse, while the other is unrepresented:

2.21 An Attorney Should Not Advise an Unrepresented Party

COMMENT

Once it becomes apparent that an opposing party intends to proceed without a lawyer, the attorney should, at the earliest opportunity, inform the opposing party in writing as follows:

1. I am your spouse's lawyer.
2. I do not and will not represent you.
3. I will at all times look out for your spouse's interests, not yours.
4. Any statements I make to you about this case should be taken by you as negotiation or argument on behalf of your spouse and not as advice to you as to your best interest.
5. I urge you to obtain your own lawyer.

While the "one client only" approach is an option for attorneys who do not want to run the risks of dual representation, some

---

337. See also Dolan v. Hickey, 431 N.E.2d 229, 231 (Mass. 1982) ("acts of drafting documents and presenting them for execution, without more, do not amount to 'advice,' and are proper as long as the attorney does not engage in misrepresentation or overreaching"). But see Lawyer Disciplinary Board v. Frame, 479 S.E.2d 676 (W. Va. 1996) (lawyer publicly reprimanded for preparing answer for defendant wife in divorce case).

commentators have questioned whether the unrepresented client will fully understand the situation.[338]

Third-party control

Normally, the client who retains a lawyer will also pay the lawyer's fee. Situations arise, however, in which attorney fees are paid by a third party rather than by the client. For example, in Chapter 4 we will consider group legal services plans, in which a sponsor organizes a plan that provides for designated legal services to be rendered by lawyers to members of the plan.

The presence of third-party payors can raise ethical problems if the third party attempts to control the client-lawyer relationship or seek confidential information. Recall the litigation management guidelines adopted by insurers discussed in Problem 3-9. Model Rule 1.8(f) provides some guidance to lawyers for dealing with these issues. Under that rule a lawyer may ethically receive payment of legal fees from someone other than the client so long as the client consents after consultation with the lawyer about the arrangement, the third party does not interfere with the lawyer's independent professional judgment on behalf of the client, and the third person recognizes that the lawyer is bound by rules of confidentiality. When a third-party payor is involved, it would be prudent for the lawyer to obtain in writing the client's consent to payment of fees by the third party. In addition, the lawyer should notify the payor in writing of the lawyer's ethical obligations under Rule 1.8(f).

Representation of clients with diminished capacity

We saw in connection with Problem 2-6 that lawyers in criminal defense practice may face problems of representing clients with diminished capacity. The issue also arises in civil litigation. In civil cases, unlike criminal cases, the Constitution does not require deferral of the trial until a party is competent to stand trial. Instead,

338. James C. Hagy, Note, Simultaneous Representation: Transaction Resolution in the Adversary System, 28 Case W. Res. L. Rev. 86, 97 (1977).

if a party to a civil matter is incompetent, the court may appoint a guardian ad litem to protect the interests of that party.

In civil cases it is helpful to distinguish four roles that lawyers perform. First, in some cases a court may appoint a lawyer to serve as guardian ad litem for an incompetent client. When appointed as a guardian, the lawyer is no longer acting in a legal capacity. The guardian's role is to determine what is in the best interest of the ward and to report those findings to the court.[339] Second, in some cases a court may appoint both a guardian ad litem and an attorney to represent the guardian in court. The appointment of a separate guardian and lawyer clarifies the lawyer's responsibilities. In this situation the lawyer is acting in a legal capacity as attorney for the guardian. Generally, the lawyer should look to the guardian to make recommendations to the court that affect the ward. After all, the court has appointed the guardian to make recommendations. See Model Rule 1.14, cmt. 3.[340] Occasions will arise, however, when lawyers may need to take action to protect the interests of the ward against misconduct by the guardian. The clearest case occurs when the guardian is improperly using the ward's money or property. See Model Rule 1.14, cmt. 4.

Third, sometimes a court may appoint three representatives: a guardian for the ward, an attorney for the guardian, and an attorney for the ward. The court may find it necessary to appoint an attorney for the ward when the ward strongly disagrees with the guardian's recommendations. In this situation the attorney for the ward has the duty to advocate the ward's position, even if the lawyer disagrees with that position, so that the court can decide between the recommendation of the guardian and the ward's desires.

Finally, the most difficult role for an attorney occurs when the court appoints an attorney to represent the client but does not appoint a guardian ad litem for the client. Such cases are troublesome because the lawyer has not been appointed as guardian for

339. See Paige K. B. v. Molepske, 580 N.W.2d 289 (Wis. 1998) (lawyer who serves as guardian ad litem for children in divorce case enjoys absolute immunity because lawyer serves as arm of court to advocate best interests of children). See also Roy T. Stuckey, Guardians ad Litem as Surrogate Parents: Implications for Role Definition and Confidentiality, 64 Fordham L. Rev. 1785 (1996).

340. See also 1 Hazard & Hodes, The Law of Lawyering §1.14:302; Restatement (Third) of the Law Governing Lawyers §35(3).

the client and is therefore not authorized to make recommendations on the client's behalf, yet at the same time the client is not fully competent to make decisions. Typical situations in which lawyers can face this problem are domestic cases involving custody of minor children,[341] cases involving developmentally disabled clients, and civil commitment proceedings.

As a general proposition lawyers should maintain a normal client-lawyer relationship with an impaired client to the maximum extent possible. Model Rule 1.14(a).[342] Thus, the lawyer is required to communicate information to the client and to assist the client in making decisions regarding the representation. This view is based on two propositions, one empirical, the other normative. Empirically, clients suffer from different degrees of impairment, from the relatively mild to the incapacitating. Many clients with some degree of impairment can participate in decisions affecting their lives. Normatively, even when a client suffers from an impairment, the client is still entitled to exercise personal liberty to the maximum extent possible.[343] In In re M.R.,[344] the New Jersey Supreme Court described the role of an attorney appointed to represent the interests of a developmentally disabled client:

> [A] declaration of incompetency does not deprive a developmentally-disabled person of the right to make all decisions. The primary duty of the attorney for such a person is to protect that person's rights, including the right to make decisions on specific matters. Generally, the attorney should advocate any decision made by the developmentally-disabled person. On perceiving a conflict between that person's preferences and best interests, the attorney may in-

---

341. See generally Special Issue, Ethical Issues in the Legal Representation of Children, 64 Fordham L. Rev. 1281 (1996). Both the ABA and the American Academy of Matrimonial Lawyers have adopted standards to guide lawyers who represent children in nondelinquency proceedings. See ABA, Standards of Practice for Lawyers Who Represent Children in Abuse and Neglect Cases, 29 Fam. L.Q. 375 (1995); Representing Children: Standards for Attorneys and Guardians ad Litem in Custody or Visitation Proceedings (with Commentary), 13 J. Am. Acad. Matrimonial Law. 1 (1995). For a comparison of these standards, see Ann M. Haralambie, In Whose Best Interest? 34-June Trial 42 (1998).

342. See also Restatement (Third) of the Law Governing Lawyers §35(1).

343. See Model Rule 1.14, cmt. 2; Restatement (Third) of the Law Governing Lawyers §35, cmt. c.

344. 638 A.2d 1274 (N.J. 1994).

form the court of the possible need for a guardian ad litem. . . . Our endeavor is to respect everyone's right of self-determination, including the right of the developmentally disabled.[345]

If a lawyer concludes that the client is incompetent and is unable to make decisions regarding the representation, the lawyer has several choices on how to proceed. The lawyer could seek the appointment of a general guardian for the client's property (referred to as a conservator in many jurisdictions) or a guardian ad litem to determine the client's interest in litigation. See Model Rule 1.14(b).[346] When a guardian has been appointed, the guardian is then legally authorized to make decisions on behalf of the client. The lawyer should generally follow the decisions of the guardian unless the guardian is engaged in conduct that amounts to a breach of fiduciary duty.[347]

Appointment of a guardian is a serious step that deprives the client of a substantial degree of personal liberty. Comment 3 to Model Rule 1.14 notes that appointment of a guardian may be "expensive or traumatic for the client." Thus, lawyers must exercise professional discretion in deciding whether to seek the appointment of a guardian, considering the costs and benefits to the client, along with the other possible options for dealing with the client's incompetency.[348]

What options other than appointment of a guardian ad litem should a lawyer consider? Some clients may be willing to execute general or limited powers of attorney giving another person the power to make decisions on their behalf.[349] The attorney may enlist the participation of family members to assist the client in making decisions. Finally, the attorney may assume greater decisionmaking authority, deciding what a reasonable person in

---

345. Id. at 1285. See also Stanley S. Herr, Representation of Clients with Disabilities: Issues of Ethics and Control, 17 N.Y.U. Rev. L. & Soc. Change 609 (1990). For a discussion of the lawyer's role in civil commitment proceedings, see Natalie Wolf, Note, The Ethical Dilemmas Faced by Attorneys Representing the Mentally Ill in Civil Commitment Proceedings, 6 Geo. J. Legal Ethics 163 (1992) (arguing that lawyers in civil commitment proceedings should act as advocates for their clients rather than assume the role of guardians).

346. See also Restatement (Third) of the Law Governing Lawyers §35(4).

347. See id. §35(3) and cmt. *f*.

348. See Model Rule 1.14(b) and cmt. 3.

349. Restatement (Third) of the Law Governing Lawyers §35, cmt. *e*.

the client's position would do, even if that decision conflicts with the view expressed by the client.[350] Acting as a "de facto" guardian is obviously an extreme step that lawyers should take only under unusual circumstances. In Formal Opinion 96-404, the ABA Committee on Ethics and Professional Responsibility advised lawyers that the "action taken should be the least restrictive of the client's autonomy that will yet adequately protect the client in connection with the representation."[351]

Other ethical problems in family practice

In addition to the topics discussed above, family practitioners face many other ethical problems.[352] Issues covered in other problems in these materials include the following: May a lawyer reveal confidential information received from a client to prevent child abuse? Problem 2-3. Are nonrefundable retainers and contingent fees proper in domestic relations cases? Problems 2-2 and 3-1. What are the limitations on negotiation tactics in divorce cases? Problem 4-5. When are sexual relations between a lawyer and client improper? Problem 7-1.

350. See Model Rule 1.14, cmt. 2 (lawyer must sometimes act as de facto guardian). See also Restatement (Third) of the Law Governing Lawyers §35(2) and cmt. *d*.

351. ABA Comm. on Ethics and Prof. Resp., Formal Op. 96-404, at 9. See also Paul R. Tremblay, On Persuasion and Paternalism: Lawyer Decision-making and the Questionably Competent Client, 1987 Utah L. Rev. 515. Working from a premise of informed consent by clients, Tremblay argues that all the choices available to lawyers who represent questionably competent clients are troublesome, but that some of the choices are ethically more defensible than others. He would prohibit lawyers from acting as de facto guardians except in emergencies and would allow lawyers to seek the appointment of guardians only in extreme cases. He favors enlisting the support of family members and persuasion for dealing with clients who have diminished capacity.

352. See generally Symposium, The Pursuit of Professionalism, 9 J. Am. Acad. Matrimonial Law. (Fall 1992). New York has adopted special rules that closely regulate professional and personal relationships between matrimonial lawyers and their clients. See Sup. Ct. App. Div. R., pt. 1400.

Chapter 4

Ethical Issues in Civil Litigation: Limitations on Zealous Representation, Alternative Dispute Resolution, and Delivery of Legal Services

In Chapter 3 we focused on the client-lawyer relationship, confidentiality, and conflicts of interest in civil litigation. In this chapter we turn to issues involving limitations on zealous representation and delivery of legal services in civil cases. While client obligations are an important element of these issues, these topics also implicate duties to third parties and the system of justice. Section A examines limitations on lawyers' conduct in connection with commencement, investigation, and discovery in civil matters. Section B considers ethical problems in dispute settlement, including negotiation, mediation, and arbitration. Section C focuses on issues of delivery of legal services, including advertising and solicitation, group legal services, and pro bono obligations.

An important point to keep in mind is that while lawyers must represent their clients with loyalty and zealousness, limitations nonetheless exist on what lawyers can do on behalf of their clients. Lawyers function in an adversarial system, but they must "play by the rules." Professors Hazard and Hodes offer the following justifications for rules that limit zealous representation:

> The justification for imposing additional limitations on advocacy — which concededly can work to the disadvantage even of clients who have engaged in no wrongdoing — is twofold. First, society at large has an interest in maintaining the efficiency of its tribunals. Second, society has an interest in assuring that its most coercive processes are, and are perceived to be, fair. The notion that lawyers have an enforceable duty to be "fair" to non-clients contradicts the simplistic conception of the lawyer as hired gladiator, but it has always been a fundamental theme of the law of lawyering, as opposed to professional mythology.[1]

As we examine the rules that limit lawyers' conduct, ask yourself whether the rules limiting zealous representation draw the line at the appropriate place. If not, are the rules insufficiently sensitive to the interests of society and third parties or, on the contrary, do they excessively limit zealous representation?[2]

A.   Commencement of Actions, Investigation, and Discovery

———————— Problem 4-1 ————————

Frivolous Claims

    a.   Erin Mueller has asked you to represent her in a medical malpractice action arising from back surgery.

---

1. 1 Hazard & Hodes, The Law of Lawyering §3:102, at 537.
2. See Eugene R. Gaetke, Lawyers as Officers of the Court, 42 Vand. L. Rev. 39 (1989) (arguing that rules of professional conduct give insufficient substantive content to principle that lawyers are officers of courts).

Potential defendants in the case are Dr. Nancy Seiquera, the surgeon; Dr. Robert Smith, the anesthesiologist; and Metropolitan Hospital.

> (1) What investigation should you conduct before taking the case and before filing suit?
> (2) Would it be proper for you to try to arrange an interview with the doctors about the surgery before filing suit?

b. You represent Ronald LeBanc, the defendant in a divorce action brought by his wife, Helen. After Helen told Ronald she wanted a divorce, Ronald learned that Helen had been having an affair with another man. Ronald is outraged by the affair, and he has told you that he wants to do everything he can to get back at his wife. He wants to bring an action against his wife's lover, Charles Wenrow, for "alienation of affections." How would you handle Ronald's desire that you bring suit against Wenrow?

Read Model Rules 2.1, 3.1, 3.2, 4.3, and comments.

Frivolous actions and delay: ethical duties and discovery sanctions

The duty of lawyers not to engage in frivolous legal proceedings represents one of the most important limitations on adversarial representation. Rule 3.1 of the Model Rules expresses the ethical obligation of lawyers not to engage in frivolous legal proceedings. Rule 3.2 sets forth a related obligation: lawyers shall exercise reasonable efforts to expedite litigation.

Several points about Model Rule 3.1 are worth noting. First, the concept of frivolousness applies not only to complaints but also to answers, motions, and other steps in a legal proceeding. Thus, both counsel for plaintiffs and defendants are subject to the obligation not to engage in frivolous representation. Second, the rule contains an exception for defense of criminal proceedings. Presumably this exception reflects the criminal defendant's constitutional right to a presumption of innocence. Third, the rule does not define a frivolous action, although the comments to the rule provide some guidance. Comment 2 states that an action is not frivolous simply because the facts have not been fully developed or because the lawyer expects to develop evidence in support of the contention during discovery. Further, an action is not frivolous "even though the lawyer believes that the client's position ultimately will not prevail." Fourth, a claim is not frivolous even if the claim is not warranted under existing law if the lawyer can make a "good faith argument for extension, modification or reversal of existing law." While the rule alludes to the concept of good faith, the Model Code comparison that accompanies the rule states: "[T]he test in Rule 3.1 is an objective test. . . ." Finally, a claim may be frivolous if it is brought for an improper purpose, even if the claim has legal and factual merit. Comment 2 to Model Rule 3.1 states: "The action is frivolous, however, if the client desires to have the action taken primarily for the purpose of harassing or maliciously injuring a person. . . ."

The bulk of litigation dealing with frivolous actions by lawyers has developed under Rule 11 of the Federal Rules of Civil Procedure, not under Model Rules 3.1 and 3.2. Rule 11 applies only to actions in federal court, but many states have rules of civil procedure modeled on federal Rule 11, and state courts have usually relied on federal court decisions in interpreting their rules.[3] The reason that Rule 11 has been the vehicle for development of the law dealing with frivolous actions is that unlike Rules 3.1 and 3.2, which are enforced through the disciplinary process, Rule 11 provides for monetary sanctions. Thus, lawyers and their clients who have felt that they have been the victims of frivolous proceedings have had a financial incentive to seek relief under Rule 11. The incentive for lawyers and their clients to seek sanctions may diminish as a result of amendments to the rule in 1993, discussed below.

The amount of case law applying Rule 11 is staggering, and an introductory course on professional ethics cannot possibly

---

3. E.g., Bryson v. Sullivan, 412 S.E.2d 327 (N.C. 1992); Jandrt v. Jerome Foods, Inc., 597 N.W.2d 744 (Wis. 1999). See also Van Christo Advertising, Inc. v. M/A-COM/LCS, 688 N.E.2d 985 (Mass. 1998) (under Massachusetts version of Rule 11, which is based on pre-1983 federal rule, subjective rather than objective standard applies).

cover the entire range of issues raised by the rule.[4] Unlike Model Rule 3.1, which fails to provide a clear definition of frivolousness, Rule 11 contains four specific obligations that lawyers have when they present a matter to a court, by filing documents or otherwise:

- First, "after an inquiry reasonable under the circumstances," the lawyer believes that the document "is not being presented for any improper purpose, such as to harass or to cause unnecessary delay or needless increase in the cost of litigation."
- Second, "after an inquiry reasonable under the circumstances," the lawyer believes that the legal contentions "are warranted by existing law or by a nonfrivolous argument for the extension, modification, or reversal of existing law or the establishment of new law."
- Third, "after an inquiry reasonable under the circumstances," the lawyer believes "the allegations and other factual contentions have evidentiary support or, if specifically so identified, are likely to have evidentiary support after a reasonable opportunity for further investigation or discovery."
- Fourth, "after an inquiry reasonable under the circumstances," the lawyer believes "the denials of factual contentions are warranted on the evidence or, if specifically so identified, are reasonably based on a lack of information or belief."

A lawyer's obligations under Rule 11 are governed by an objective rather than a subjective standard, but in determining compliance courts generally look to determine whether the pleading or paper is frivolous as a whole rather than whether any particular claim or argument is frivolous.[5] The Advisory Committee notes to

4. For comprehensive treatments of the rule, see Jerold S. Solovy et al., Sanctions Under Rule 11, 601 PLI/Lit 105 (1999) (on Westlaw); Georgene M. Vairo, Rule 11 Sanctions: Case Law Perspectives & Preventive Measures (2d ed. 1992) (with bibliography). See also Gregory P. Joseph, Sanctions: The Federal Law of Litigation Abuse (2d ed. 1994).

5. See, e.g., Golden Eagle Distrib. Corp. v. Burroughs Corp., 801 F.2d 1531 (9th Cir. 1986). See also 1 Hazard & Hodes, The Law of Lawyering §3.1: 102, at 546.

the 1993 amendments to Rule 11 state that the purpose of the amendment was to eliminate the "empty-head pure-heart" justification for a frivolous argument.

The Restatement of the Law Governing Lawyers also provides some guidance on the meaning of frivolousness. Comment *d* to section 170 states: "A frivolous position is one that a lawyer of ordinary competence would recognize as so lacking in merit that there is no substantial possibility that the tribunal would accept it."

A good example of the application of Rule 11 is White v. General Motors Corp.[6] *White* involved a suit by two former employees of General Motors Corp. (GM). The employees had terminated their employment with GM under its Special Incentive Separation Program. They received $60,000 in cash and signed general releases in which they gave up all claims, both known and unknown, based on their cessation of employment, whether arising under common law, statute, or administrative rule or regulation. Both employees subsequently filed suit claiming that they were discharged because they had complained to management about defective brake work in their plant. White also alleged that GM had slandered him by referring to him as a "troublemaker" when he gave GM as a reference for a job application at another company, Westlake Hardware.

The court of appeals affirmed the district court's decision finding that plaintiffs' attorney had violated Rule 11 in several ways. First, the attorney had failed to conduct a reasonable investigation into the facts forming the basis for the slander claim against GM. Under Kansas law, which governed the case, a slander claim must state the words spoken, the name of the person to whom they were spoken, and the time and place of publication. White's attorney failed to contact anyone at Westlake Hardware to determine whether a GM employee had made the statement that White was a troublemaker.[7] The attorney also continued to assert the slander claim even after GM's lawyers presented an affidavit from a Westlake Hardware employee that she had made no inquiry at GM and even though the attorney had no evidence to support her allegations.[8]

6. 908 F.2d 675 (10th Cir. 1990), *cert. denied,* 498 U.S. 1069 (1991).
7. 908 F.2d at 681.
8. Id.

Second, the attorney had filed claims for wrongful discharge that were unwarranted under existing law because such claims were barred by the general releases signed by the plaintiffs. The court addressed the issue of the attorney's duty regarding affirmative defenses as follows:

Part of a reasonable attorney's prefiling investigation must include determining whether any obvious affirmative defenses bar the case. . . . An attorney need not forbear to file her action if she has a colorable argument as to why an otherwise applicable affirmative defense is inapplicable in a given situation. For instance, an otherwise time-barred claim may be filed, with no mention of the statute of limitations if the attorney has a nonfrivolous argument that the limitation was tolled for part of the period. The attorney's argument must be nonfrivolous, however; she runs the risk of sanctions if her only response to an affirmative defense is unreasonable. . . .

The court rejected plaintiffs' arguments that they had executed the releases under duress and found their arguments regarding Kansas law on duress so poorly framed and so negligently made as to be sanctionable. We agree. Among the arguments made to the district court was that the Kansas Supreme Court case of Hastain v. Greenbaum, 205 Kan. 475, 470 P.2d 741 (1970), which is binding on this court, was distinguishable because the West Publishing Company classified it as a "Bills and Notes" case in formulating its Headnotes. . . .

The district court also sanctioned plaintiffs for alleging that the releases were void due to ambiguity. Plaintiffs point out that the exact duties of GM are not set out in the releases. But the releases clearly state that all present and future claims, known and unknown, were released by White and Staponski. Further, plaintiffs failed to allege any real confusion caused by any ambiguities in the releases. There is no substantial disagreement between the parties on the terms of the contract.

[T]here were arguments to set aside the releases that could have been made that would not have warranted sanctions. A reasonably competent attorney could have filed a colorable, nonfrivolous ADEA [Age Discrimination in Employment Act] case against GM. Although it would be more difficult, a nonfrivolous common law whistleblowing claim also might have been brought. Thus, we have the tragedy of inept lawyers who failed to investigate their claims, and who compounded the court's and the defendant's problems in dealing with the case by adopting an extremely aggressive approach. Rule 11 should not be used to discourage advocacy, including that which challenges existing law. Nevertheless, the court is entitled to expect a reasonable level of competence and care on the part of the attorneys who appear before it, and to expect that claims submitted for adjudication by those attorneys will have a rational basis. We cannot find the district court's decision to award sanctions an abuse of discretion.[9]

Third, the attorney filed the action for an improper purpose. The court found evidence to support the district court's finding of improper purpose in the fact that the attorney threatened to utilize the media to create adverse publicity against GM and in the fact of unwarranted discovery requests filed by the attorney. The lack of prefiling investigation and the unwarranted nature of the claims also supported the finding of improper purpose.[10] The attorney in *White* was later ordered to pay $50,000 for violation of Rule 11,[11] and she was subsequently disbarred for misconduct in several cases, including *White*.[12]

While Rule 11 is the best-known provision regulating improper litigation tactics, it is only one of an arsenal of weapons that federal courts (or state courts whose procedural systems are based on the Federal Rules) can use to punish litigation abuse, either through the award of attorney fees or other sanctions: Rule 16(f) (failure to abide by pretrial order), 26(g) (improper discovery requests or objections), 30(g) (failure to attend a deposition or serve a subpoena on a witness to be deposed), 37 (improper failure to respond to discovery), 41(b) (dismissal of action or claim when a party fails to comply with the Federal Rules or court order), 45(e) (contempt for failure to obey subpoena), and 56(g) (presentation of affidavit in summary judgment motion in bad faith or for the purpose of delay); see also Federal Rule of Appellate Procedure 38 (power to award damages and costs for a frivolous appeal). In addition, a federal statute, 28 U.S.C. §1927, provides as follows:

Any attorney or other person admitted to conduct cases in any court of the United States or any Territory thereof who so multiplies the

9. Id. at 682-683.
10. Id. at 683. But see Sussman v. Bank of Israel, 56 F.3d 450 (2d Cir.), *cert. denied*, 516 U.S. 916 (1995) (district court erred in awarding sanctions for improper purpose in filing complaint — threatening negative publicity to force settlement of related litigation — when complaint was not substantively frivolous).
11. White v. General Motors Corp., 977 F.2d 499 (10th Cir. 1992).
12. In re Caranchini, 956 S.W.2d 910 (Mo. 1997) (en banc), *cert. denied*, 118 S. Ct. 2347 (1998).

proceedings in any case unreasonably and vexatiously may be required by the court to satisfy personally the excess costs, expenses, and attorneys' fees reasonably incurred because of such conduct.[13]

Finally, in Chambers v. Nasco, Inc.[14] the Supreme Court in a 5-4 decision ruled that federal courts have inherent power to impose sanctions for bad faith conduct even when the conduct is not specifically covered by rules of procedure or statutory provisions, including fraud that occurs outside court.[15]

Criticism of Rule 11, the 1993 amendment, and the Private Securities Litigation Reform Act of 1995

Rule 11 has been extensively studied and frequently criticized. Some opponents of the rule argue that it grants judges too much discretion, with the result that the application of the rule varies widely.[16] Other critics challenge the efficiency of the rule. Since the rule spawns ancillary proceedings at the trial court level and appeals to determine both violations and sanctions, these commentators question whether the benefits of the rule in deterring frivolous conduct outweigh the costs of administration.[17] Finally, other scholars charge that the rule has a deterrent effect on innovative advocacy, and that this impact may be especially significant in new and evolving areas of law.[18]

---

13. For a comparison of Rule 11 and 28 U.S.C. §1927, see Ridder v. City of Springfield, 109 F.3d 288 (6th Cir. 1997), *cert. denied*, 118 S. Ct. 687 (1998).

14. 501 U.S. 32 (1991).

15. A circuit-by-circuit comparison of sanctions under Rule 11 and under these other sources of law can be found in American Bar Association Section of Litigation, Sanctions: Rule 11 & Other Powers (Melissa L. Nelken ed., 3d ed. 1992).

16. For a study supporting this conclusion, see Saul M. Kassin, An Empirical Study of Rule 11 Sanctions (1985).

17. For an analysis of whether the costs of the rule exceed its benefits, with a conclusion that they do not, at least in the Third Circuit, see Third Circuit Task Force on Federal Rule of Civil Procedure 11, Rule 11 in Transition (Stephen B. Burbank Rep. 1989).

18. Melissa L. Nelken, Sanctions Under Amended Federal Rule 11 — Some "Chilling" Problems in the Struggle Between Compensation and Punishment, 74 Geo. L.J. 1313 (1986). See also Jeffrey A. Parness, More Stringent Sanctions Under Federal Civil Rule 11: A Reply to Professor Nelken, 75 Geo. L.J. 1937 (1987). See generally Byron C. Keeling, Toward a Balanced Approach

In 1993 the Supreme Court approved a revised Rule 11 based on recommendations of the Judicial Conference of the United States. While the substantive standards of the new rule are quite similar to those under previous Rule 11, the new rule makes a number of important changes in application. The rule provides that a motion seeking sanctions under the rule cannot be filed in court until the other party has been served with the motion and given 21 days to correct any violation.[19] Second, sanctions under the rule may be imposed not only on individual attorneys but also on their law firms.[20] This change overrules the Supreme Court decision in Pavelic & LeFlore v. Marvel Entertainment Group.[21] Third, the new rule makes explicit that the purpose of sanctions is deterrence rather than compensation. The rule allows monetary sanctions, but ordinarily payments are made to the court as a penalty.[22] Fourth, under the new rule sanctions are discretionary with the court. Fifth, the rule requires specificity in court orders imposing sanctions.[23] These changes have substantially reduced the amount of Rule 11 litigation.[24]

In 1995 Congress moved to toughen the application of Rule 11 to securities cases by enacting the Private Securities Litigation Reform Act of 1995.[25] The act responded to what Congress determined to be abuses in securities litigation, including routine filing of securities fraud cases whenever a company's stock price changed, targeting of deep-pocket defendants, use of the discovery system to impose costs on defendants and thereby induce settlement, and improper control of class actions by class counsel. The act changed the procedure for imposing Rule 11 sanctions and made sanctions mandatory rather than discretionary. Further, the

---

to "Frivolous" Litigation: A Critical Review of Federal Rule 11 and State Sanctions Provisions, 21 Pepp. L. Rev. 1067 (1994).

19. Fed. R. Civ. P. 11(c)(1)(A). See Hadges v. Yonkers Racing Corp. (In re Kuntsler), 48 F.3d 1320 (2d Cir. 1995) (district court improperly imposed sanctions when moving party failed to comply with 21-day safe harbor provision of Rule 11).

20. Fed. R. Civ. P. 11(c).

21. 493 U.S. 120 (1989).

22. Fed. R. Civ. P. 11(c)(2).

23. Id. 11(c)(3).

24. See Georgene Vairo, Rule 11 and the Profession, 67 Fordham L. Rev. 589 (1998).

25. Pub. L. No. 104-67, 109 Stat. 737 (1995).

act presumed that the opposing party's attorney fees will be the sanction.[26]

Tort liability of attorneys for frivolous actions

Not only are attorneys subject to disciplinary action under Model Rule 3.1 and to sanctions under federal Rule 11 for asserting frivolous positions, the possibility of tort liability also exists. Section 674 of the Restatement (Second) of Torts defines malicious prosecution as follows:

> **§674. General Principle**
>
> One who takes an active part in the initiation, continuation or procurement of civil proceedings against another is subject to liability to the other for wrongful civil proceedings if
>
> (a) he acts without probable cause, and primarily for a purpose other than that of securing the proper adjudication of the claim in which the proceedings are based, and
>
> (b) except when they are ex parte, the proceedings have terminated in favor of the person against whom they are brought.

Comment *d* to that section amplifies its application to attorneys, making clear that attorneys are not liable for malicious prosecution simply because they act in their professional capacity:

> d. *Attorneys.* An attorney who initiates a civil proceeding on behalf of his client or one who takes any steps in the proceeding is not liable if he has probable cause for his action (see §675); and even if he has no probable cause and is convinced that his client's claim is unfounded, he is still not liable if he acts primarily for the purpose of aiding his client in obtaining a proper adjudication of his claim. (See §676.) An attorney is not required or expected to prejudge his client's claim, and although he is fully aware that its chances of success are comparatively slight, it is his responsibility to present it to the court for adjudication if his client so insists after he has explained to the client the nature of the chances.
>
> If, however, the attorney acts without probable cause for belief in the possibility that the claim will succeed, and for an improper

---

26. See Solovy et al., Sanctions Under Rule 11, 601 PLI/Lit at 116-125 (on Westlaw).

purpose, as, for example, to put pressure upon the person proceeded against in order to compel payment of another claim of his own or solely to harass the person proceeded against by bringing a claim known to be invalid, he is subject to the same liability as any other person. . . . [27]

Related to malicious prosecution is the tort of abuse of process. The Restatement defines abuse of process as follows:

§682.   General Principle

One who uses a legal process, whether criminal or civil, against another primarily to accomplish a purpose for which it is not designed, is subject to liability to the other for harm caused by the abuse of process.

Comparison of the elements of the two torts indicates that it should be easier to establish a claim for abuse of process than a claim for malicious prosecution. Both malicious prosecution and abuse of process call for an improper purpose. Malicious prosecution, however, requires termination of the proceeding in favor of the plaintiff, while abuse of process does not. In addition, malicious prosecution requires that the proceeding be brought without probable cause. Abuse of process does not have this requirement; the tort occurs when process is used for a purpose other than that for which it was intended.

With increasing frequency, disgruntled defendants have brought claims for malicious prosecution and abuse of process against attorneys for opposing parties.[28] Such claims involve a tension between two important public policies. On one hand, the public has an interest in open access to courts. If courts hold attorneys liable for actions that they bring on behalf of clients, a "chilling effect" on the use of the judicial process may result. On the other hand, the judicial process should be used to resolve bona

---

27. The Restatement of Torts focuses on malicious prosecution of claims, but one court has recognized a cause of action for malicious defense. See Aranson v. Schroeder, 671 A.2d 1023 (N.H. 1995).

28. On attorney liability for malicious prosecution and abuse of process, see Debra E. Wax, Annotation, Liability of Attorney, Acting for Client, for Malicious Prosecution, 46 A.L.R.4th 249 (1986); Debra T. Landis, Annotation, Civil Liability of Attorney for Abuse of Process, 97 A.L.R.3d 688 (1980). See also 1 Mallen & Smith, Legal Malpractice §6.6-6.22.

fide disputes rather than as a weapon to coerce defendants into paying money or for other improper purposes. Not surprisingly, the courts have struck a balance between these two policies, recognizing the possibility of attorney liability for malicious prosecution or abuse of process but indicating that liability will be imposed only in extreme cases. While such claims have rarely been successful, on occasion courts have found liability. For example, in Crowley v. Katleman[29] the California Supreme Court held that the plaintiff, an attorney, stated a cause of action for malicious prosecution against the defendant and her attorneys for challenging a will that left the defendant's husband's estate to the plaintiff attorney. The plaintiff attorney and the decedent had been good friends; the plaintiff had not drafted the will; the decedent executed the will before he married the defendant; and the decedent did not revoke or revise the will during their marriage. The defendant wife had challenged the will on multiple grounds, including fraud, undue influence, and lack of mental capacity. The California Supreme Court found that a malicious prosecution claim could still be brought even though not all of the grounds were without probable cause. In addition, the court rejected the defendant's arguments that the appropriate remedy for frivolous claims was through court-imposed sanctions rather than by a tort action.

By contrast, in Detenbeck v. Koester[30] the Texas Court of Appeals held that the plaintiff doctor failed to state a cause of action for abuse of process against the defendant and his attorneys for bringing a medical malpractice action against the plaintiff. The court ruled that bringing suit was not using process other than the purpose for which it was intended. The court also stated that if the suit were groundless the defendant could seek appropriate sanctions.[31]

---

29. 881 P.2d 1083 (Cal. 1994) (en banc).

30. 886 S.W.2d 477 (Tex. Ct. App. 1994, no writ).

31. Id. at 482. See also Dutt v. Kremp, 894 P.2d 354 (Nev. 1995) (reversing jury verdict in malicious prosecution and abuse-of-process action arising from attorney's representation of plaintiff in medical malpractice action; objective facts showed probable cause and lack of ulterior motive for bringing malpractice action; probable cause does not require attorney to consult with medical expert before bringing malpractice action).

Investigative contacts with potential witnesses or potential defendants prior to filing suit

We will see in the next problem that the rules of professional conduct prohibit a lawyer from communicating with a person the lawyer knows is represented by counsel in the matter without the consent of the person's attorney, unless the communication is authorized by law. Model Rule 4.2. Further, when an entity is involved in the matter, the no-communication rule applies to some current employees of the entity, even if the employee is not personally involved in the matter or personally represented by counsel.

Does the no-communication rule apply prior to the filing of a lawsuit? If not, plaintiffs' counsel could avoid the rule by conducting extensive interviews before bringing suit. Yet as we have seen, plaintiffs' counsel have an ethical and legal obligation to investigate the facts of the case before filing suit to determine if the action is meritorious. Courts have accommodated these conflicting considerations by allowing plaintiffs' counsel to engage in investigation prior to filing suit so long as they do not have actual knowledge that the person contacted is represented by counsel. For example, in Jorgensen v. Taco Bell Corp.,[32] a sexual harassment case, plaintiff's counsel hired a private investigator who interviewed the alleged harasser and two of Taco Bell's employees before plaintiff filed suit. Taco Bell subsequently moved to disqualify plaintiff's counsel. The court of appeals recognized that the anticontract rule might apply before suit was filed if the attorney had actual knowledge that the person contacted was represented by counsel.[33] The court concluded, however, that plaintiff's counsel did not have actual knowledge that the employees were represented by counsel; it rejected on policy grounds Taco Bell's argument that counsel "should have known" that the employees would be represented by counsel for Taco Bell:

> Frivolous litigation is frequently avoided by a careful lawyer's investigation of a client's claims before filing suit. Rule 2-100 [the California version of the no-communication rule] should not be applied to require that investigation of such claims not be undertaken before suit is filed because the party or employee investigated

32. 58 Cal. Rptr. 2d 178 (Ct. App. 1996).
33. Id. at 180.

may be expected to obtain counsel at a future time. This file-first investigate-later result which appellant would generate through its application of rule 2-100 is practically capable of compulsorily producing the type of frivolous litigation for which the Legislature has authorized the imposition of sanctions.[34]

The court in *Jorgensen* also mentioned ways that employers could protect themselves against communications with their employees before suit was filed. The rules of ethics allow an employer to request that its employees not discuss the matter with plaintiff's counsel. See Model Rule 3.4(f)(1). An employer could also have its attorney send the other party a warning letter stating that its employees were represented by counsel in the matter and that any communications should be made through employer's counsel.[35] On receipt of such a letter, counsel would have actual knowledge that the employees were represented by counsel.

When a lawyer has actual knowledge that an employee is represented by counsel, communications prior to filing suit are improper. In Shoney's, Inc. v. Lewis[36] the Kentucky Supreme Court ordered disqualification of the lawyer for the plaintiff in a sexual harassment case for taking precomplaint statements from two of defendant's managers. The plaintiff's lawyer knew that the employer would be represented by counsel in the matter and had even had discussions with the employer's lawyer about the case before taking the statements.[37] The court also ordered sup-

34. Id. at 181. Other courts have agreed that the anticontact rule requires the lawyer to have actual knowledge that the person contacted is represented by counsel. See Johnson v. Cadillac Plastic Group, Inc., 930 F. Supp. 1437 (D. Colo. 1996); Weider Sports Equip. Co. v. Fitness First, Inc., 912 F. Supp. 502 (D. Utah 1996); Gaylard v. Homemakers of Montgomery, Inc., 675 So. 2d 363 (Ala. 1996). Like the court in *Jorgensen* these courts have emphasized the attorney's obligation to investigate the facts before filing suit.

35. 58 Cal. Rptr. 2d at 181.

36. 875 S.W.2d 514 (Ky. 1994).

37. In K-Mart Corp. v. Helton, 894 S.W.2d 630 (Ky. 1995), plaintiff's attorney took a statement from a managerial employee of K-Mart in connection with a false imprisonment case prior to filing suit. The Kentucky Supreme Court distinguished *Shoney's* and refused to disqualify plaintiff's counsel. The court stated that in *Shoney's* the attorney knew that the employees were represented by corporate counsel. By contrast, in *K-Mart* the company had done nothing to indicate to plaintiff's counsel that its employees were represented by counsel; in fact, K-Mart had asked the employee to contact the plaintiff to try to "smooth over" the situation. Id. at 631.

pression of the statements because of counsel's unethical conduct.[38]

Even if the anticontact rule does not apply, a lawyer contacting a witness or a potential defendant must keep in mind the obligations with regard to unrepresented parties set forth in Rule 4.3. In addition, the comment to Rule 4.3 provides: "During the course of a lawyer's representation of a client, the lawyer should not give advice to an unrepresented person other than the advice to obtain counsel." Thus, under the rule it is proper for the attorney to communicate with a witness or even with a potential defendant, but the attorney must use care in doing so. The attorney may not mislead the person about the attorney's role nor may the attorney give the other party legal advice.[39] Indeed, some attorneys may feel that some form of "*Miranda* warning" is called for whenever meeting with a witness or potential defendant.

Problem 4-2

Investigation: Contacts with Employees

A massive fire at the International Hotel killed 15 guests and injured many more. The estate of one of the deceased guests has retained you to represent its interests. You have sent your investigator to the scene of the fire, and he learned the names of a number of the hotel's employees. Some of them worked in the kitchen where the fire began, while others worked in other parts of the hotel.

When your investigator tried to arrange an interview with one of the employees, he was told by the employee that "the hotel's lawyers told us not to talk to anyone about the case." You have learned that International has retained Steve Fairey of Wilson & Farr to represent it in the fire litigation. You called Fairey to

38. 875 S.W.2d at 516.
39. See W. T. Grant Co. v. Haines, 531 F.2d 671, 675-676 (2d Cir. 1976) (outside counsel did not violate rule prohibiting advice and misrepresentation to unrepresented person, but methods used were "at least inappropriate and certainly not to be encouraged").

complain about his attempts to silence International's employees.

During the course of your investigation of the fire, you learned that three months ago the hotel fired its manager, Anita Allen. You contacted Allen, who told you that the hotel fired her after she complained about the hotel's unwillingness to spend money on maintenance. Allen said that the hotel had experienced some electrical problems in the kitchen, and she suspected that this may have caused the accident. She gave you a copy of a memorandum that she sent to the home office of International complaining about the lack of maintenance and raising safety concerns. Wilson & Farr has learned that you have interviewed Allen and has filed a motion to disqualify you from handling this case because of your ex parte contact with Allen.

Read Model Rules 3.4(f), 4.2, and comments.

Prohibition of communication with a party represented by counsel in general

An established rule of professional conduct is that a lawyer may not communicate with a person who is represented by counsel in a matter without the consent of that person's lawyer. Model Rule 4.2 provides as follows:

> In representing a client, a lawyer shall not communicate about the subject of the representation with a person the lawyer knows to be represented by another lawyer in the matter, unless the lawyer has the consent of the other lawyer or is authorized by law to do so.[40]

The rule is substantially similar to DR 7-104(A)(1) of the Code of Professional Responsibility, except that DR 7-104(A)(1) used the term *party*, while Model Rule 4.2, as amended at the August 1995 meeting of the ABA, uses the word *person*. The amendment was intended to make it clear that the rule is not limited to formal parties to litigation; it also applies to persons represented by coun-

---

40. See also Restatement (Third) of the Law Governing Lawyers §158.

sel prior to the institution of formal legal proceedings and also to persons represented by counsel in transactional rather than litigation matters. In jurisdictions that have not adopted this amendment, however, Model Rule 4.2 may be limited to parties to litigation.[41] The Restatement of the Law Governing Lawyers is in accord with the ABA's 1995 amendment to Model Rule 4.2.[42]

The rationale of the no-communication rule is that it protects people who are represented by counsel from the harm they can suffer if they deal with a lawyer who represents an opposing person without receiving the advice of counsel. A client might reveal privileged information or might agree to an unwise settlement without the advice of counsel.[43]

The no-communication rule applies in a wide variety of settings. For example, in a divorce case, it is unethical for a lawyer representing one spouse to meet with the other spouse in an effort to negotiate a settlement without the consent of the other spouse's attorney.[44] Similarly, in a personal injury case, a lawyer representing the plaintiff may not meet with an adjuster from an insurance company without consent of the insurer's counsel.[45] Controversy has raged between the criminal defense bar and prosecutors over the issue of whether federal prosecutors and their agents may contact individuals who are represented by counsel during the course of criminal investigations without the consent of their attorneys. See Problem 2-10. The application of the no-communication rule

---

41. See Grievance Comm. for the S. Dist. of N.Y. v. Simels, 48 F.3d 640 (2d Cir. 1995) (no violation of DR 7-104(A)(1), the Code equivalent of Model Rule 4.2, to interview represented witness and potential codefendant in drug case because rule uses term *party* and should be narrowly construed); Gaylard v. Homemakers of Montgomery, Inc., 675 So. 2d 363 (Ala. 1996) (not improper under Rule 4.2 to contact employee of defendant prior to filing suit because defendant not a "party" and lawyer did not know that employer was represented by counsel in matter).

42. Restatement (Third) of the Law Governing Lawyers §158, cmt. *c*.

43. See John Leubsdorf, Communicating with Another Lawyer's Client: The Lawyer's Veto and the Client's Interests, 127 U. Pa. L. Rev. 683, 686 (1979); Stephen M. Sinaiko, Note, Ex Parte Communication and the Corporate Adversary: A New Approach, 66 N.Y.U. L. Rev. 1456, 1463-1476 (1991).

44. E.g., In re Wehringer, 525 N.Y.S.2d 604 (App. Div.), *cert. denied*, 488 U.S. 988 (1988).

45. In re Illuzzi, 616 A.2d 233 (Vt. 1992) (lawyer violated DR 7-104(A)(1) by meeting with insurance adjuster after company had retained counsel, even though such contacts were an "accepted practice" in state).

normally occurs in litigation settings, but the rule also applies to any situation in which an adverse person is represented by counsel, even if it does not involve pending litigation.[46]

The no-communication rule is subject to some exceptions. Communication is permitted when authorized by law, for example, a communication pursuant to court rule or court order.[47] In our society, open access to government is a fundamental value, so the rule allows lawyers to communicate directly with governmental officials even when those officials are represented by counsel.[48] The rule applies only to lawyers, not to their clients.[49] Thus, in a divorce case one spouse is free to negotiate directly with the other spouse. Lawyers may advise clients of their right to communicate directly with the opposing party but should not assist them in such a communication.[50] Communication in an emergency is also permissible.[51]

Application of the prohibition on communications with an opposing party to current employees of corporate parties

The application of Rule 4.2 to represented individuals is relatively uncontroversial, but substantial dispute exists about the wisdom of applying the rule to employees of represented corporate parties (or other entities). It is important to distinguish situations in which individual employees of a corporation are named as parties along with the corporation from cases in which only the corporation is named. If an individual employee is a named party and is represented by counsel, Rule 4.2 clearly applies and prohibits a lawyer for the opposing party from communicating with the employee-party without the consent of the employee-party's counsel. Sup-

---

46. Cf. United States v. Galanis, 685 F. Supp. 901, 902 (S.D.N.Y. 1988) (DR 7-104(A)(1) "applies to persons retained to handle real estate transactions, administer estates for an executor, seek legislative relief, or any other of the myriad tasks for which lawyers are employed").

47. Restatement (Third) of the Law Governing Lawyers §158, cmts. *g, m*.

48. Model Rule 4.2, cmt. 1; Restatement (Third) of the Law Governing Lawyers §161.

49. Restatement (Third) of the Law Governing Lawyers §158, cmt. *k*.

50. Id.

51. Id. cmt. *i*.

pose, however, that only the corporation is a named party. Does Rule 4.2 prohibit an attorney for the opposing party from communicating with any of the employees of the corporation on the ground that they are "alter egos" of the corporation?

The issue of the scope of permissible informal contacts that an investigating lawyer may make with employees of corporate parties involves a tension between competing policies. On one hand, lawyers representing clients against corporations need to be able to investigate the facts fully to properly represent their clients. Indeed, Rule 11 of the Federal Rules of Civil Procedure and ABA Model Rule 3.1 require adequate investigation. A rule that prohibits communication with employees of a corporate party who may have been witnesses to an accident or who may otherwise have relevant information interferes with the opposing counsel's ability to investigate the facts. While an attorney could always take the deposition of an employee after a suit has been filed, depositions are more expensive than interviews and may be impractical when large numbers of employees are involved. Also, in most jurisdictions an attorney cannot take a deposition or use other discovery devices prior to filing suit. On the other hand, corporations, like individuals, have a right to be represented by counsel. Ex parte contacts between lawyers for opposing parties and corporate employees can interfere with the corporation's right to have legal assistance.[52]

Since artificial entities like corporations can act only through agents, all courts agree that some corporate employees are subject to the no-communication rule. Courts and commentators differ, however, on how broadly to define the class of covered employees. The most favorable approach from the perspective of opposing counsel wishing to obtain information from corporate employees is the "control group" test.[53] Under this test, only upper-level management in position to make decisions on behalf of the corporation is subject to the no-communication rule. All lower-level employees are subject to informal interviews. Some commentators

52. For a discussion of these competing policies, see Jerome N. Krulewitch, Comment, Ex Parte Communications With Corporate Parties: The Scope of the Limitations on Attorney Communications with One of Adverse Interest, 82 Nw. U. L. Rev. 1274, 1277-1285 (1988); Sinaiko, Note, Ex Parte Communication and the Corporate Adversary, 66 N.Y.U. L. Rev. at 1463-1481.

53. Fair Automotive Repair, Inc. v. Car-X Serv. Sys., Inc., 471 N.E.2d 554 (Ill. App. Ct. 1984).

have criticized the "control group" test because it fails to provide sufficient protection to corporations.[54] At the opposite extreme, some authorities argue that the no-communication rule should apply to all corporate employees.[55]

Not surprisingly, neither of the extreme approaches has found much acceptance, and other authorities have searched for a middle ground. For example, in Wright v. Group Health Hospital[56] the Washington Supreme Court adopted a "managing-speaking agent" test. Under this test, if the employee has managing authority sufficient to speak for and bind the corporation in the matter in question, then the no-communication rule applies. This approach extends the no-communication rule beyond the control group to some management employees, but it would not cover lower-level employees who might have been involved in the matter or who were mere witnesses to the matter. Other authorities have argued for a "scope of employment" test or for a "balancing" test.[57]

Model Rule 4.2, Comment 4 adopts a broad no-communication rule, one that applies to most, but not necessarily all, employees of a corporation. The comment refers to three classes of employees, all of whom are covered by the no-communication rule:

> In the case of an organization, this Rule prohibits communications by a lawyer for another person or entity concerning the matter in representation with persons having managerial responsibility

54. See Krulewitch, Comment, Ex Parte Communications With Corporate Parties, 82 Nw. U. L. Rev. at 1286-1290; Sinaiko, Note, Ex Parte Communication and the Corporate Adversary, 66 N.Y.U. L. Rev. at 1481-1484.

55. See Sinaiko, Note, Ex Parte Communication and the Corporate Adversary, 66 N.Y.U. L. Rev. at 1490-1493; see also David A. Green, Balancing Ethical Concerns Against Liberal Discovery: The Case of Rule 4.2 and the Problem of Loophole Lawyering, 8 Geo. J. Legal Ethics 283 (1995) (arguing for a total ban on ex parte contacts in commercial litigation).

56. 691 P.2d 564 (Wash. 1984) (en banc).

57. See Krulewitch, Comment, Ex Parte Communications with Corporate Parties, 82 Nw. U. L. Rev. at 1285-1297; Ernest F. Lidge III, The Ethics of Communicating with an Organization's Employees: An Analysis of the Unworkable "Hybrid" or "Multifactor" Managing-Speaking Agent, ABA, and *Niesig* Tests and a Proposal for a "Supervisor" Standard, 45 Ark. L. Rev. 801 (1993); Sinaiko, Note, Ex Parte Communication and the Corporate Adversary, 66 N.Y.U. L. Rev. at 1482-1495.

on behalf of the organization, and with any other person whose act or omission in connection with that matter may be imputed to the organization for purposes of civil or criminal liability or whose statement may constitute an admission on the part of the organization.

Thus, under Comment 4, management-level employees and employees who were involved in the matter (that is, ones whose act or omission may be imputed to the organization) are subject to the no-communication rule. Further, even employees who were not involved in the matter but who are mere witnesses are also covered by the rule if any statement by such an employee would "constitute an admission on the part of the organization."

When does a statement by an employee constitute an admission against the organization? The rule followed in many states is that a statement by an employee does not constitute an admission unless the employee was authorized to make the statement.[58] Under this rule, a statement by an ordinary employee would not be an admission against the organization. The Federal Rules of Evidence have broadened the category of employee statements that can constitute admissions against the organization. Federal Rule of Evidence 801(d) provides as follows (with emphasis added):

(d) Statements which are not hearsay. — A statement is not hearsay if — . . .

(2) Admission by party-opponent. — The statement is offered against a party and is
(A) the party's own statement, in either an individual or a representative capacity, or
(B) a statement of which the party has manifested an adoption or belief in its truth, or
(C) *a statement by a person authorized by the party to make a statement concerning the subject,* or
(D) *a statement by the party's agent or servant concerning a matter within the scope of the agency or employment, made during the existence of the relationship,* or
(E) a statement by a coconspirator of a party during the course and in furtherance of the conspiracy.

58. Sinaiko, Note, Ex Parte Communication and the Corporate Adversary, 66 N.Y.U. L. Rev. at 1459 n.16.

Under Federal Rule 801, therefore, statements made by employees concerning matters within the scope of their employment made while the employment relationship continues constitute admissions against the organization. Even under this broader admission rule, however, not all employee statements constitute admissions. For example, in Wilkinson v. Carnival Cruise Lines, Inc.[59] a passenger was injured when an electronically activated sliding glass door leading to a swimming pool closed on her foot. At trial the plaintiff offered the statement of a cabin steward made to plaintiff's traveling companion that the defendant had been having problems with the door. The Eleventh Circuit held that the statement was inadmissible under Rule 801(d) because the door was in an area in which the steward was not authorized to work; thus, the statement did not concern a matter that was within the scope of the steward's employment.

Depending on the scope of the rules of evidence dealing with admissions by employees of corporations, Rule 4.2 provides a broad prohibition against ex parte communication with employees of a corporate party. Moreover, Comment 4 to Rule 4.2 refers to Rule 3.4(f). That rule states that it is improper for a lawyer to request that a person "refrain from voluntarily giving relevant information to another party," but it goes on to provide an exception if the person is "a relative or an employee or other agent of a client." Therefore, an attorney for a corporation could ask all of its employees, whether covered by Rule 4.2 or not, to voluntarily refrain from giving information to opposing counsel except through formal discovery.

The Restatement of the Law Governing Lawyers narrows the scope of the anticontact rule from that found in Model Rule 4.2. Section 159 provides as follows:

[A] represented non-client includes . . .

(2) a representative of an organization represented by a lawyer:
(a) who supervises, directs or regularly consults with the lawyer concerning the matter or who has power to compromise or settle the matter;
(b) whose acts or omissions may be imputed to the organization for purposes of civil or criminal liability in the matter; or

59. 920 F.2d 1560 (11th Cir. 1991).

> (c) whose statements, under applicable rules of evidence,
> would have the effect of binding the organization with respect
> to proof of the matter.

The Restatement rejects a broad anticontact rule because there is "no justification for permitting one party thus to control entirely the flow of information to opposing parties."[60] In two respects the Restatement narrows the categories of employees subject to the noncontact rule from Model Rule 4.2. First, under section (a) not all managers are subject to the rule.[61] Second, employees who make statements are covered by the Restatement rule only if the statement would be binding on the organization (in the sense that the organization could not introduce evidence to refute the statement) rather than simply being admissible against the entity. The Restatement explains that a "contrary rule would essentially mean that most employees with relevant information would be within the anticontact rule, contrary to the policies described in Comment b."[62]

Courts are, of course, free to craft the scope of their anticontact rule. In Niesig v. Team I[63] the New York Court of Appeals adopted the following test:

> The test that best balances the competing interests, and incorporates the most desirable elements of the other approaches, is one that defines "party" to include corporate employees whose acts or omissions in the matter under inquiry are binding on the corporation (in effect, the corporation's "alter egos") or imputed to the corporation for purposes of its liability, or employees implementing the advice of counsel. All other employees may be interviewed informally.[64]

The Niesig test is closer to the Restatement approach than to Rule 4.2.[65] Unlike the comment to that rule, this test allows interviews with employees whose statements would be admissible against the

---

60. Restatement (Third) of the Law Governing Lawyers §159, cmt. b.
61. Id. cmt. c and illus. 1, 2.
62. Id. cmt. e.
63. 558 N.E.2d 1030 (N.Y. 1990).
64. Id. at 1035.
65. Restatement (Third) of the Law Governing Lawyers §159, Reporter's Note.

organization, unless the employee is in one of the three categories listed by the court.[66]

During the course of an otherwise permissible communication with a current employee, a lawyer may not seek to obtain privileged information.[67] Further, even if an attorney may properly communicate with an employee, it may be improper for the attorney to seek documents from the employee because such a request circumvents the discovery process and prevents opposing counsel from raising objections to the discoverability of documents.[68]

Application of the prohibition on communications with an opposing party to former employees of corporate parties

Does Rule 4.2 apply to former rather than current employees? The argument against applying the rule to former employees is that they are no longer in a position to make a decision or admission on behalf of the corporation. Yet if the former employee was involved in the matter in controversy, his conduct is still attributed to the corporation even though he has left employment. Further, an attorney communicating with a former employee could learn confidential information or could obtain privileged documents. A number of cases have considered the issue, and the vast majority have ruled that an attorney may communicate with a former employee so long as the attorney does not try to obtain confidential or privileged information.[69]

66. See also Dent v. Kaufman, 406 S.E.2d 68 (W. Va. 1991) (following *Niesig* test, indicating that under this test employees who are mere witnesses can be interviewed).

67. Restatement (Third) of the Law Governing Lawyers §162.

68. See In re Shell Oil Refinery (Adams v. Shell Oil Co.), 143 F.R.D. 105 (E.D. La. 1992) (protective order entered requiring disclosure of documents obtained through ex parte contact with employee and prohibiting their use in case).

69. Recent cases include Brown v. Oregon Dep. of Corrections, 173 F.R.D. 265 (D. Or. 1997); H.B.A. Management, Inc. v. Estate of Schwartz, 693 So. 2d 541 (Fla. 1997) (no prohibition on communication with former employees because employee cannot bind entity). See generally Benjamin J. Vernia, Annotation, Right of Attorney to Conduct Ex Parte Interviews with Former Corporate Employees, 57 A.L.R.5th 633 (1998). For an argument that contact with former employees should be regulated by amendment to the rules of civil procedure, see John E. Iole & John D. Goetz, Ethics or Procedure? A Discovery-Based Approach

In Formal Opinion 91-359, the ABA Committee on Ethics and Professional Responsibility adopted this majority view and ruled that lawyers were not prohibited from communicating with former employees under Model Rule 4.2, but the committee cautioned attorneys about the possible application of other rules:

> With respect to *any* unrepresented former employee, of course, the potentially communicating adversary attorney must be careful not to seek to induce the former employee to violate the privilege attaching to attorney-client communications. . . . Such an attempt could violate Rule 4.4 (requiring respect for the rights of third persons).
>
> The lawyer should also punctiliously comply with the requirements of Rule 4.3, which addresses a lawyer's dealings with unrepresented persons. That rule, insofar as pertinent here, requires that the lawyer contacting a former employee of an opposing corporate party make clear the nature of the lawyer's role in the matter giving occasion for the contact, including the identity of the lawyer's client and the fact that the witness's former employer is an adverse party.[70]

A few cases have gone somewhat further than the majority of cases and ABA Formal Opinion 91-359 in prohibiting communications with former employees. A leading example is Camden v. Maryland,[71] an employment discrimination case. The former employee contacted by plaintiff's counsel had been the affirmative action coordinator for the defendant and was responsible for handling the Camden case while employed by defendant. He prepared reports on the case for defendant's top management and met regularly with defendant's counsel, engaging in strategy sessions about the strengths and weaknesses of Camden's claims. He also signed defendant's response to the complaint filed by Camden with the EEOC. The court in *Camden* accepted the proposition that communications with former employees were generally permissible without consent of the attorney for the former employer, but the court held that such contacts were improper when the employee had been "extensively exposed" to confidential infor-

---

to Ex Parte Contacts with Former Employees of a Corporate Adversary, 68 Notre Dame L. Rev. 81 (1992).

70. ABA Comm. on Ethics and Prof. Resp., Formal Op. 91-359, at 6.
71. 910 F. Supp. 1115 (D. Md. 1996).

mation.[72] Further, in *Camden* plaintiff's counsel intentionally sought and obtained confidential information, including documents that were marked as confidential.[73]

The Restatement of the Law Governing Lawyers provides that communication with former employees is generally proper except under limited circumstances, for example, if the former employee continues to consult with counsel for the entity.[74] The Restatement also seems to adopt the view of the court in Camden v. Maryland that a lawyer may not communicate with a former employee who has been "extensively exposed" to privileged information.[75]

Other applications of Rule 4.2: settlement offers, expert witnesses, and treating physicians

As we saw previously, attorneys have an ethical obligation to convey settlement offers to their clients. Model Rule 1.4 and cmt. 1. Suppose a lawyer believes that opposing counsel has not conveyed a settlement offer to his client. May the attorney communicate the offer directly to the opposing party? In Formal Opinion 92-362 the ABA Committee on Ethics and Professional Responsibility dealt with the application of Rule 4.2 in the context of settlement offers. The committee first concluded that Rule 4.2 does not allow an attorney to make a direct communication of a settlement offer to the opposing party. The committee also reaffirmed Informal Opinion 1348 (1975), which held that it was improper for an attorney to send to the opposing party copies of settlement offers made to opposing counsel. The committee did note several options available to an attorney who believes that opposing counsel is not conveying settlement offers to his client. First, the attorney could serve an "offer of judgment" on the opposing party, with copy to opposing counsel, if authorized by rules of civil procedure.[76] An offer of judgment sent to the opposing party does not violate Rule 4.2 because it is a communication "authorized by

---

72. Id. at 1116.
73. Id. at 1118 n.5, 1123.
74. Restatement (Third) of the Law Governing Lawyers §159, cmt. *g*.
75. Id. §162, cmt. *d*.
76. See Fed. R. Civ. P. 68.

law.["77] Second, the attorney may file a copy of the settlement offer with the court.[78] Finally, the attorney could advise his client that the client has the right to convey a settlement offer directly to the opposing party. In reaching this conclusion the committee pointed out that while Rule 4.2 prohibits a lawyer from communicating with the opposing party, the rule does not apply to clients. Comment 1 states that "parties to a matter may communicate directly with each other." The committee also referred to various rules of ethics that require lawyers to counsel clients about their rights. As a result, the committee concluded as follows:

> In the Committee's view, fulfillment of the duties imposed by these Rules requires that the lawyer for the offeror-party advise that party with respect to the lawyer's belief as to whether the offers are in fact being communicated to the offeree-party. Likewise, the offeror-party's lawyer has a duty to that party to discuss not only the limits on the lawyer's ability to communicate with the offeree-party, but also the freedom of the offeror-party to communicate with the opposing offeree-party.[79]

Although the committee recognized that Rule 8.4(a) prohibits a lawyer from violating the rules of professional conduct "through the acts of another," it decided that Rule 8.4 did not apply in the context of advising a client about the client's right to convey a settlement offer to the opposing party when the lawyer has good reason to believe that the opposing counsel has not done so.

Discovery of opinions of expert witnesses is subject to specific limitations under discovery rules,[80] so a lawyer may not informally interview an expert for the opposing party without consent of opposing counsel.[81]

In cases involving personal injuries, a common issue is whether defense counsel may informally interview the injured party's treating physician. The jurisdictions are fairly evenly di-

---

77. ABA Comm. on Prof. Ethics, Informal Op. 985 (1967).
78. ABA Comm. on Ethics and Prof. Resp., Informal Op. 1348 (1975).
79. ABA Comm. on Ethics and Prof. Resp., Formal Op. 92-362, at 5.
80. See Fed. R. Civ. P. 26(b)(4).
81. See Erickson v. Newmar Corp., 87 F.3d 298 (9th Cir. 1996); In re Firestorm 1991, 916 P.2d 411 (Wash. 1996) (en banc); ABA Comm. on Ethics and Prof. Resp., Formal Op. 93-378; see generally William H. Fortune et al., Modern Litigation and Professional Responsibility Handbook §5.6, at 211-214 (1996).

vided on whether such interviews are proper.[82] When courts have found such contacts to be improper, they have generally emphasized the physician-patient privilege and the physician's ethical duty of confidentiality. Courts that have permitted such interviews have usually found that the patient waived confidentiality by bringing the lawsuit and thereby putting his physical condition in issue.

━━━━━━ Problem 4-3 ━━━━━━

Investigation: Secret Tape Recording and Inadvertent Disclosures

   a.   Sally Pender works in the underwriting division of DAC Insurance Company. For over a year Pender's supervisor, Herbert Foster, has been making sexual advances toward her that she has rebuffed. With each of Pender's refusals, Foster has become increasingly belligerent. Pender fears for her job and even her safety. Uncertain what to do, Pender has consulted with Roberta Slinger, a local attorney who handles discrimination cases.

   Slinger and Pender discuss the possibility of reporting Foster's conduct to higher officials in the company, but Pender says that she is reluctant to do that because "it's her word against his," and Foster is very well respected in the company. As they mull over how they might get concrete evidence of Foster's conduct, it occurs to Slinger that one possibility would be for Pender secretly to tape record an encounter in which Foster makes sexual advances. If you were Slinger, how would you handle this situation? Why?

   b.   Suppose Slinger has filed suit on Pender's behalf against Foster and DAC Insurance. DAC and Foster are represented by Daniel R. Chin, of the firm Chin

   82. J. Christopher Smith, Comment, Recognizing the Split: The Jurisdictional Treatment of Defense Counsel's Ex Parte Contact with Plaintiff's Treating Physician, 23 J. Legal Prof. 247 (1999). See Daniel P. Jones, Annotation, Discovery: Right to Ex Parte Interview with Injured Party's Treating Physician, 50 A.L.R.4th 714 (1986).

& Rivera. One morning, Slinger's secretary, Ronald Best, comes into her office.

Best: Roberta, I reviewed your morning e-mail. I printed out one from Dan Chin addressed to Milton Rodriguez, president of DAC Insurance. It indicates a copy to you. I think Chin must have listed you to receive a copy by mistake.

Slinger: Let's see . . .

Re: Pender v. Foster and DAC Insurance

Dear Milton:

I met with Melinda Dasher's attorney today. I think we can settle her claim against DAC and Foster on the terms we discussed, and they are agreeable to a confidentiality agreement. I'll keep you advised.

If you were Slinger, how would you proceed? Why?

_____

Read Model Rules 1.1, 1.2(d), 8.4, and comments.

Legality of secret tape recording

Model Rule 8.4(b) provides that it is professional misconduct for a lawyer to "commit a criminal act that reflects adversely on the lawyer's honesty, truthworthiness or fitness as a lawyer in other respects." Model Rule 1.2(d) provides that a lawyer "shall not counsel a client to engage, or assist a client, in conduct that the lawyer knows is criminal or fraudulent." Does secret tape recording amount to criminal conduct?

The federal wiretapping statute, 18 U.S.C. §2511, prohibits interception and disclosure of wire, oral, or electronic communications. Among the statutory exceptions, however, is a section allowing recording by a party to the conversation:

It shall not be unlawful under this chapter for a person not acting under color of law to intercept a wire, oral, or electronic communication where such person is a party to the communication or where one of the parties to the communication has given prior consent to such interception unless such communication is intercepted for the purpose of committing any criminal or tortious act in violation of the Constitution or laws of the United States or of any State.[83]

Thus, recording of a conversation with "one-party consent" is not a violation of the federal statute. A lawyer who personally records a conversation with a client or other person, or who assists a client in doing so, would not, therefore, be committing a federal crime.

Some states, however, have more restrictive statutes prohibiting recording without "two-party consent." For example, the Illinois law on electronic eavesdropping provides as follows:

A person commits eavesdropping when he: (a) Uses an eavesdropping device to hear or record all or any part of any conversation unless he does so (1) with the consent of all of the parties to such conversation or (2) [in accordance with certain statutory procedures for use of eavesdropping devices by law enforcement officials].[84]

In states with two-party consent laws, a lawyer could not record a conversation without the consent of all parties to the conversation, and could not assist a client in doing so.

The ethical propriety of participation by lawyers in secret tape recording that is not illegal

Model Rule 8.4(c) provides that it is professional misconduct for a lawyer to "engage in conduct involving dishonesty, fraud, deceit or misrepresentation." Does secret tape recording amount to dishonesty or deceit even if the recording would not be illegal under federal or state law? In Formal Opinion 337 (1974), the ABA Committee on Ethics and Professional Responsibility ruled that it

---

83. 18 U.S.C. §2511(2)(d).
84. Ill. Ann. Stat. ch. 720, para. 5/14-2. Oregon law permits recording of telephone conversations with one-party consent but prohibits recording of in-person private conversations without two-party consent. Or. Rev. Stat. §165.540.

was unethical for a lawyer to record a conversation with a client or third person without that person's consent even though the recording was not a crime. The committee reasoned that "conduct which involves dishonesty, fraud, deceit or misrepresentation . . . clearly encompasses the making of recordings without the consent of all parties."[85] The committee noted a possible exception for lawyers involved in law enforcement activities:

> There may be extraordinary circumstances in which the Attorney General of the United States or the principal prosecuting attorney of a state or local government or law enforcement attorneys or officers acting under the direction of the Attorney General or such principal prosecuting attorneys might ethically make and use secret recordings if acting within strict statutory limitations conforming to constitutional requirements.

Some courts and ethics committees have followed ABA Formal Opinion 337.[86] For example, in In re Anonymous Member of the South Carolina Bar, the South Carolina Supreme Court stated:

> [W]e reaffirm our prior rulings that an attorney shall not record a conversation or any portion of a conversation of any person whether by tape or other electronic device, without the prior knowledge and consent of all parties to the conversation. . . . Henceforth, this rule shall be applied irrespective of the purpose(s) for which such recordings were made, the intent of the parties to the conversation, whether anything of a confidential nature was discussed, and whether any party gained an unfair advantage from the recordings.[87]

Other courts and ethics committees, however, have rejected ABA Formal Opinion 337. In Attorney M v. Mississippi Bar[88] an

---

85. ABA Comm. on Ethics and Prof. Resp., Formal Op. 337, at 3 (1974).
86. People v. Selby, 606 P.2d 45 (Colo. 1979) (en banc); Iowa Supreme Court Bd. of Professional Ethics & Conduct v. Plumb, 546 N.W.2d 215 (Iowa 1996); In re Anonymous Member of the S.C. Bar, 404 S.E.2d 513 (S.C. 1991); Ariz. State Bar Comm. on Rules of Prof. Conduct, Op. 95-3; Minn. Lawyers Prof. Resp. Bd., Secret Recordings of Conversations, Op. No. 18 (1996) (generally improper in accordance with Formal Opinion 337, but certain limited exceptions exist).
87. 404 S.E.2d 513, 514 (S.C. 1991).
88. 621 So. 2d 220 (Miss. 1992).

attorney was charged with misconduct because he secretly tape recorded a telephone conversation with a doctor who was a potential defendant in a malpractice case. In finding that the attorney had not engaged in misconduct, the Mississippi Supreme Court rejected the per se prohibition on secret recording by lawyers expressed in Formal Opinion 337. Instead, the court adopted a facts-and-circumstances test to determine whether the lawyer's conduct amounted to dishonesty, fraud, deceit, or misrepresentation. The court concluded:

> [W]e find that Attorney M's conduct did not rise to the level of "dishonesty, fraud, deceit, or misrepresentation." First, the express purpose of each telephone call was to obtain a statement from Dr. C concerning the physical condition of Attorney M's client upon leaving Dr. C's care. Such information is indisputably "of such a nature as reasonably to import to the person called the probability, if not certainty, that it would be taken down in some manner for future use." Further, the circumstances surrounding the incident do not suggest dishonesty, fraud, deceit, or misrepresentation. In fact, the circumstances were such that Dr. C admittedly assumed that he was being taped. During one of the telephone conversations, Attorney M expressly stated that he wished to record Dr. C's statement. In addition, there is no indication that Attorney M planned to use the recordings for any improper purpose. Contrary to the finding of the Complaint Tribunal, Attorney M did not violate MRPC Rule 8.4.[89]

In a companion case, however, the Mississippi Supreme Court ruled that an attorney was guilty of misconduct when he lied to a police chief about secretly recording their discussion of his client's prosecution. The court rejected the lawyer's argument

___

89. Id. at 224-225. Ethics committees rejecting the per se approach of ABA Formal Opinion 337 include the following: State Bar of Mich. Standing Comm. on Prof. and Jud. Ethics, Op. No. RI-309 (1998) (rejecting Formal Opinion 337 as overbroad; whether secret recording is improper must be determined on case-by-case basis); Supreme Court of Ohio Bd. of Commissioners on Grievances and Discipline, Op. No. 97-3 (1997) (generally secret recording is improper but certain recognized exceptions to prohibition exist: the prosecuting and law enforcement attorney exception, the criminal defense attorney exception, and the extraordinary circumstances exception); Utah State Bar Ethics Adv. Op. Comm., Op. No. 96-04 (rejecting Formal Opinion 337 as overbroad; secret tape recording generally permissible if actual deceit or misrepresentation not involved).

that it was necessary for him to misrepresent the taping because that was the only way in which he could gain evidence to protect his client.[90]

Counseling or assisting a client in secret tape recording

As discussed above, in some cases secret recording by a lawyer or client would be illegal under either federal or state law. In these situations a lawyer must not counsel or assist a client in such illegal conduct. By contrast, a few jurisdictions permit lawyers to engage in secret recording. In those jurisdictions, then, it follows that it would be ethically permissible for the lawyer to counsel or assist a client to engage in such recording.

Suppose, however, that a client suggests the possibility of making a secret recording that would be legal for the client to do, but unethical for the lawyer to do. On one hand, a lawyer cannot engage indirectly through the actions of another in conduct that it would be unethical for the lawyer to do directly. For example, in Gunter v. Virginia State Bar[91] the Virginia Supreme Court suspended a lawyer for 30 days for hiring an investigator to install a recording device on the telephone of the home of his client, the husband in a divorce case. The court stated:

> The surreptitious recordation of conversations authorized by Mr. Gunter in this case was an "underhand practice" designed to "ensnare" an opponent. It was more than a departure from the standards of fairness and candor which characterize the traditions of professionalism. We hold that it was deceitful conduct proscribed by DR 1-102(A)(4) [the provision of the Code of Professional Responsibility corresponding to Model Rule 8.4(c)].[92]

On the other hand, a lawyer has the right and obligation to counsel a client about the client's legal rights. For example, in Miano v. AC & R Advertising, Inc.,[93] an age discrimination suit, plaintiffs had secretly recorded some conversations they had with certain of defendant's key employees. The court held that the tapes

90. Mississippi Bar v. Attorney ST, 621 So. 2d 229 (Miss. 1993).
91. 385 S.E.2d 597 (Va. 1989).
92. 385 S.E.2d at 600.
93. 148 F.R.D. 68 (S.D.N.Y. 1993).

were admissible in evidence and that the plaintiffs' lawyer had not engaged in unethical conduct in connection with the taping. In its opinion the court discussed the lawyer's obligations when a client suggests secret recording of a conversation with the defendant:

> [I]t is not improper for an attorney to advise his client of the legality of taping activity by the client. . . . The lawyer need not discourage or deter such activity, but he also may not assist, direct or otherwise participate in it so that, in effect, he is using the client as a vehicle to do what he cannot do.[94]

In its opinion the court relied on New York State Bar Opinion No. 515 (1979), which held that an attorney may counsel a client fully about the client's right to engage in secret tape recording. Similarly, ABA Model Rule 1.2(d) states that a lawyer "may discuss the legal consequences of any proposed course of conduct with a client and may counsel or assist a client to make a good faith effort to determine the validity, scope, meaning or application of the law."

Inadvertent disclosures of confidential information

A number of recent cases have dealt with the issue of whether an inadvertent disclosure of confidential information waives the attorney-client privilege. Courts apply three approaches to waiver of the privilege.[95] The traditional approach was that any disclosure results in a loss of the privilege because the purpose of the privilege was to protect confidential communications; by definition, a communication that has been disclosed is no longer confidential.[96] Other courts have held that the purpose of the privilege is to protect the client's reasonable expectations. Under this limited waiver approach, the privilege is lost only if the client intends to waive the privilege.[97] Finally, the modern ap-

---

94. Id. at 83.

95. For a discussion of the case law on these three approaches, see Harry M. Gruber, Note, E-Mail: The Attorney-Client Privilege Applied, 66 Geo. Wash. L. Rev. 624, 646-656 (1998).

96. 8 Wigmore on Evidence §2325, at 633, (McNaughton ed. 1961).

97. See Berg Elecs., Inc. v. Molex, Inc., 875 F. Supp. 261 (D. Del. 1995) (after discussing rationales for three approaches, court adopts limited waiver principle).

proach looks at the precautions taken to determine whether the privilege should apply.[98]

What are a lawyer's ethical obligations if an attorney receives documents that appear on their face to be subject to a legitimate claim of privilege? In Formal Opinion 92-368, the ABA Committee on Ethics and Professional Responsibility gave this advice:

> A lawyer who receives materials that on their face appear to be subject to the attorney-client privilege or otherwise confidential, under circumstances where it is clear they were not intended for the receiving lawyer, should refrain from examining the materials, notify the sending lawyer and abide [by] the instructions of the lawyer who sent them.[99]

While recognizing that the issue could not be answered by a "literalistic reading of the black letter of the Model Rules," the committee based its decision on a variety of factors: the importance the Model Rules give to confidentiality, the law governing waiver of the attorney-client privilege, the law governing missent property, the similarity between the behavior in this situation and "other conduct the profession universally condemns," and the receiving lawyer's obligations to the client.[100] Several courts have followed the approach recommended in ABA Formal Opinion 92-368.[101] If the documents are clearly not privileged, however, at least one court has held that the attorney may properly use the information contained in the documents without notifying the sender,[102] although an attorney who follows this course of action runs the risk that a court may later find that the documents were privileged.

---

98. See Abamar Housing & Dev., Inc. v. Lisa Daly Lady Decor, Inc., 698 So. 2d 276 (Fla. Dist. Ct. App.), *review denied*, 704 So. 2d 520 (Fla. 1997) (adopting "relevant circumstances test" and finding no waiver of privilege because reasonable precautions were exercised).

99. ABA Comm. on Ethics and Prof. Resp., Formal Op. 92-368, at 1.

100. Id. at 2.

101. American Express v. Accu-Weather, Inc., 1996 WL 346388 (S.D.N.Y. 1996); State Compensation Ins. Fund v. WPS, Inc., 82 Cal. Rptr. 2d 799 (Ct. App. 1999); In re Meador, 968 S.W.2d 346 (Tex. 1998).

102. Aerojet-General Corp. v. Transport Indemnity Ins., 22 Cal. Rptr. 2d 862 (Ct. App. 1993) (lawyer did not act improperly in failing to disclose receipt of memorandum revealing identity of witness because such information was not privileged).

─────────────── **Problem 4-4** ───────────────

Discovery: Interrogatories, Document Production, and Depositions

a. Your firm represents a manufacturer of children's toys, All the Best, Inc., in a products liability action brought in federal court by parents of a child who suffered serious injury from using one of your client's products. You are local counsel in the case. Strawberry & DeWitt represents All the Best nationally and supervises its product liability litigation throughout the country. You have received the plaintiff's first set of interrogatories. Among the 25 is the following:

> 3. Please IDENTIFY all tests or inspections used by the defendant for the manufacture of the product. As used in this interrogatory, the term IDENTIFY means to state the manner in which each such test or inspection was performed and the stage of the product process at which the test or inspection was performed, the purpose of the tests or inspections, the names and last known addresses of the persons in charge of the tests or inspections at the time the product was manufactured or assembled by the defendant, whether any records of any tests or inspections performed by the defendant exist, attaching a copy to the answers to these interrogatories of all such records or stating where and when such records may be examined by counsel, and a description of each change made in the product or any part thereof as a result of any test or inspection performed on the product.

You forwarded the interrogatories to Strawberry & DeWitt. Strawberry & DeWitt has directed that you file the following objection to the interrogatory:

> Defendant objects to interrogatory number 3 on the ground that it is vague, overbroad, and burdensome. In addition, the interrogatory is objected to on the ground that the definition of "identify" creates discrete subparts of the interrogatory which, taken with the other interrogatories served on defendant, exceed the maximum of 25 allowed by Federal Rule 33.

How would you proceed? Consider ABA Model Rule 3.4 and Rule 33 of the Federal Rules of Civil Procedure, which provides as follows:

Rule 33.   Interrogatories to Parties

(a) Availability. Without leave of court or written stipulation, any party may serve upon any other party written interrogatories, not exceeding 25 in number including all discrete subparts, to be answered by the party served or, if the party served is a public or private corporation or a partnership or association or governmental agency, by any officer or agent, who shall furnish such information as is available to the party. . . .

(b) Answers and Objections.

(1) Each interrogatory shall be answered separately and fully in writing under oath, unless it is objected to, in which event the objecting party shall state the reasons for objection and shall answer to the extent the interrogatory is not objectionable.

(2) The answers are to be signed by the person making them, and the objections signed by the attorney making them.

(3) The party upon whom the interrogatories have been served shall serve a copy of the answers, and objections if any, within 30 days after the service of the interrogatories. A shorter or longer time may be directed by the court or, in the absence of such an order, agreed to in writing by the parties subject to Rule 29.

(4) All grounds for an objection to an interrogatory shall be stated with specificity. Any ground not stated in a timely objection is waived unless the party's failure to object is excused by the court for good cause shown.

(5) The party submitting the interrogatories may move for an order under Rule 37(a) with respect to any objection to or other failure to answer an interrogatory.

(c) Scope; Use at Trial. Interrogatories may relate to any matters which can be inquired into under Rule 26(b)(1), and the answers may be used to the extent permitted by the rules of evidence. . . .

(d) Option to Produce Business Records. . . .

Suppose you were counsel for the plaintiff and received the answer to the interrogatory given above. How
would you proceed?

b.   You represent the estate of an individual killed
in an explosion at a plant. You have noticed the deposition of the defendant's supervisor, who was on duty at
the time the explosion occurred. The firm that represents the defendant has a reputation for "hard ball" litigation tactics. You want to be prepared to deal with
such tactics if they arise during the deposition. What
types of problems can you anticipate? How would you
plan to respond to these problems?

Read Model Rules 3.4, 4.4, and comments.

The problem of discovery abuse

The philosophy of litigation underwent a radical transformation
with the adoption of the Federal Rules of Civil Procedure in 1938.
Prior to the approval of the Federal Rules, the pleadings served
the function of defining and narrowing the issues in a case; pretrial
discovery was extremely limited. The Federal Rules changed the
role of pleadings to that of providing notice to the opposing side
of claims and defenses, and the Rules broadly expanded the scope
of pretrial discovery.[103]
   Liberal discovery and the adversary system, however, are in
tension with each other. On one hand, the discovery rules require
lawyers to reveal information that is often damaging to their clients' cases. On the other hand, an adversarial mentality may lead
some lawyers to engage in "discovery abuse." While discovery
abuse is difficult to define, the term refers to "behavior motivated
by goals other than the exchange of information fairly related to
the issues in dispute."[104] Discovery abuse generally falls into two

---

103. See William A. Glaser, Pretrial Discovery and the Adversary System
15-25 (1968).
   104. Earl C. Dudley, Jr., Discovery Abuse Revisited: Some Specific Proposals to Amend the Federal Rules of Civil Procedure, 26 U.S.F. L. Rev. 189,
193 (1992).

categories: "(1) propounding unnecessarily broad discovery requests; and (2) withholding information from the propounding
party to which that party is entitled."[105]

Civil discovery has been studied extensively.[106] The conclusions of these studies are remarkably uniform. In routine cases,
discovery produces few problems, probably because little discovery takes place in such cases.[107] Discovery problems do exist, however, in high-stakes, high-conflict cases.[108]

The most frequently used discovery tools are written interrogatories under Rule 33 of the Federal Rules of Civil Procedure,
requests for production of documents under Rule 34, and oral
depositions under Rule 30. What types of problems can lawyers
anticipate in using these discovery tools? What steps can lawyers
take when they encounter what they believe to be discovery abuse?

Discovery abuse in connection with interrogatories and requests for production of documents

The problem of discovery abuse in response to interrogatories and
requests for production of documents is illustrated in Washington

105. Id. at 194.
106. Recent studies were conducted by the RAND Institute and by the
Federal Judicial Center. See James S. Kakalik et al., Rand Inst. for Civil Justice,
Discovery Management: Further Analysis of the Civil Justice Reform Act Evaluation Data, 39 B.C. L. Rev. 613 (1998); Thomas E. Willging et al., Federal
Judicial Center, An Empirical Study of Discovery and Disclosure Practice Under
the 1993 Federal Rule Amendments, 39 B.C. L. Rev. 525 (1998). Earlier studies
include the following: Paul R. Connolly et al., Federal Judicial Center, Judicial
Controls and the Civil Litigative Process: Discovery (1978); Wayne D. Brazil,
Views from the Front Lines: Observations by Chicago Lawyers About the System
of Civil Discovery, 1980 Am. Bar Found. Res. J. 217; Wayne D. Brazil, Civil
Discovery: Lawyers' Views of Its Effectiveness, Its Principal Problems and
Abuses, 1980 Am. Bar Found. Res. J. 787; Wayne D. Brazil, Improving Judicial
Controls over the Pretrial Development of Civil Actions: Model Rules for Case
Management and Sanctions, 1981 Am. Bar Found. Res. J. 875. See also Louis
Harris & Assocs., Judges' Opinions on Procedural Issues: A Survey of State and
Federal Trial Judges Who Spend at Least Half Their Time on General Civil
Cases, 69 B.U. L. Rev. 731 (1989).
107. See Linda S. Mullenix, The Pervasive Myth of Pervasive Discovery
Abuse: The Sequel, 39 B.C. L. Rev. 683 (1998).
108. See Bryant G. Garth, Two Worlds of Civil Discovery: From Studies
of Cost and Delay to the Markets in Legal Services and Legal Reform, 39 B.C.
L. Rev. 597 (1998).

State Physicians Insurance Exchange & Assn. v. Fisons Corp.[109]
In 1986 two-year-old Jennifer Pollock suffered seizures and permanent brain damage caused by excessive amounts of the drug
theophylline in her system. Jennifer's parents brought suit against
her pediatrician, Dr. Klicpera, who had prescribed Somophyllin,
a theophylline-based medication, for her, and against the drug's
manufacturer, Fisons Corporation. Dr. Klicpera cross-claimed for
contribution and damages from Fisons. In January 1989, the Pollocks settled with Dr. Klicpera. More than a year later, an attorney
for the Pollocks supplied Dr. Klicpera with a copy of a letter received from an anonymous source. The letter dated June 30, 1981,
indicated that Fisons knew in 1981 of "life-threatening theophylline toxicity" in children who received the drug while suffering
from viral infections. Fisons had sent the letter to a small number
of what the company considered to be "influential physicians."[110]
The Pollocks and Dr. Klicpera claimed that their discovery requests should have resulted in production of the letter, and they
moved for sanctions against Fisons and its attorneys. The trial
court denied the motion, but the Washington Supreme Court reversed. In its opinion the court cited numerous examples of discovery abuse by Fisons and its attorneys:

> In November 1986 the doctor served his first requests for pro-
> duction on the drug company. Four requests were made. Three
> asked for documents concerning Somophyllin. Request 3 stated:
>
> > 3. Produce genuine copies of any letters sent by your company to
> > physicians concerning theophylline toxicity in children.
>
> The drug company's response was:
>
> > Such letters, *if any*, regarding Somophyllin Oral Liquid will be
> > produced at a reasonable time and place convenient to Fisons and
> > its counsel of record. . . .
>
> Had the request, as written, been complied with, the first
> smoking gun letter . . . would have been disclosed early in the liti-
> gation. That June 30, 1981 letter concerned theophylline toxicity
> in children; it was sent by the drug company to physicians.
>
> The child's first requests for production, and the responses
> thereto, included the following: . . .

---

109. 858 P.2d 1054 (Wash. 1993) (en banc).
110. Id. at 1058.

REQUEST FOR PRODUCTION NO. 13: All documents of any clinical investigators who at any time stated or recommended to the defendant that the use of the drug Somophyllin Oral Liquid might prove dangerous.

RESPONSE: Fisons objects to this request as overbroad in time and scope for the reasons identified in response to request number 2 hereby incorporated by reference. Fisons further objects to this request as calling for materials not within Fisons' possession, custody or control. Fisons further objects to this request to the extent it calls for expert disclosures beyond the scope of [Rule] 26(b)(4) or which may be protected by the work-product and/or attorney-client privilege. *Without waiver of these objections and subject to these limitations, Fisons will produce documents responsive to this interrogatory* at plaintiffs' expense at a mutually agreeable time at Fisons' headquarters. (Italics ours.) . . .

It appears clear that no conceivable discovery request could have been made by the doctor that would have uncovered the relevant documents, given the above and other responses of the drug company. The objections did not specify that certain documents were not being produced. Instead the general objections were followed by a promise to produce requested documents. These responses did not comply with either the spirit or letter of the discovery rules and thus were signed in violation of the certification requirement.

The drug company does not claim that its inquiry into the records did not uncover the smoking gun documents. Instead, the drug company attempts to justify its responses by arguing as follows: (1) The plaintiffs themselves limited the scope of discovery to documents contained in Somophyllin Oral Liquid *files*. (2) The smoking gun documents were not intended to relate to Somophyllin Oral Liquid, but rather were intended to promote another product of the drug company. (3) The drug company produced all of the documents it agreed to produce or was ordered to produce. (4) The drug company's failure to produce the smoking gun documents resulted from the plaintiffs' failure to specifically ask for those documents or from their failure to move to compel production of those documents. (5) Discovery is an adversarial process and good lawyering required the responses made in this case.[111]

Court sanctions for discovery abuse can include fines against the offending lawyers, permission for the opposing party to engage in liberal cross-examination of witnesses on issues related to the

111. Id. at 1081-1083.

abuse, and in extreme cases dismissal of the action.[112] Some cases have gone further than imposing sanctions and have found that lawyers may be held liable in tort[113] or subject to professional discipline for improper discovery conduct.[114]

Discovery abuse in deposition practice

Deposition practice is another area where problems of discovery abuse exist.[115] A leading case exemplifying problems that can develop in depositions is Eggleston v. Chicago Journeymen Plumbers' Local Union No. 130,[116] a civil rights class action brought by five named plaintiffs seeking to represent African Americans and Latinos alleging employment discrimination in their attempts to gain entry to the plumbing trade. Discovery in the case became confrontational and ultimately collapsed. One type of abuse involved the manner in which defense counsel conducted depositions of the named plaintiffs:

> *Q*   Is any ancestor of yours Caucasian?
> *A*   I rather not answer.

---

112. See United States v. Shaffer Equip. Co., 158 F.R.D. 80 (S.D. W. Va. 1994), *on remand from* 11 F.3d 450 (4th Cir. 1993) (two U.S. attorneys were required to pay sanctions of $2,000 and $2,500 each, without reimbursement from government, for failing to comply with their ethical duty of candor under Model Rule 3.3 by continuing litigation even though they knew that their expert witness had lied about his credentials); Berkey Photo, Inc. v. Eastman Kodak Co., 603 F.2d 263 (2d Cir. 1979), *cert. denied*, 444 U.S. 1093 (1980) (trial judge did not abuse his discretion in allowing plaintiff's lawyer to cross-examine defendant's expert regarding concealment and destruction of documents that defendant failed to reveal in response to discovery requests); Lipin v. Bender, 644 N.E.2d 1300 (N.Y. 1994) (dismissal of action because plaintiff took copies of privileged documents from defendant during deposition).

113. See Cresswell v. Sullivan & Cromwell, 668 F. Supp. 166 (S.D.N.Y. 1987).

114. Crowe v. Smith, 151 F.3d 217 (5th Cir 1998), *cert. denied*, 119 S. Ct. 2047 (1999); Mississippi Bar v. Land, 653 So. 2d 899 (Miss. 1994); Cincinnati Bar Assn. v. Wallace, 700 N.E.2d 1238 (Ohio 1998).

115. See generally A. Darby Dickerson, The Law and Ethics of Civil Depositions, 57 Md. L. Rev. 273 (1998). For a discussion of the problem, existing remedies, and proposed solutions, see Jean M. Cary, Rambo Depositions: Controlling an Ethical Cancer in Civil Litigation, 25 Hofstra L. Rev. 561 (1996).

116. 657 F.2d 890 (7th Cir. 1981), *cert. denied*, 455 U.S. 1017 (1982).

          Q I think it is a proper question. I believe you should answer the question, Mr. Eggleston.

Mr. Miner: If you know. If you have first-hand knowledge.

By the Witness: A I can only go by what my grandmother tells me, you know. I don't know if it is true or not.

By Mr. Barron: Q What did your grandmother tell you, sir?

          A Well, she said our — she said yes.

          Q That some of your ancestors were Caucasian?

          A Yes.

          Q And is this your mother's mother or your father's mother who told you that?

          A My father's mother.

          Q Is she still living?

          A Yes.

          Q What is her name?

          A Berta Eggleston. Berta or Bertie.

          Q Would you tell us what she said to you about your ancestors?

Mr. Miner: Listen. I am going to cut this off right now, and I will just instruct him not to answer any further questions. If you want to raise some doubt as to whether or not Mr. Eggleston is a black man, Howard, you are free to do so; but you have established that both his mother and father are members of the Negro race, and whether some hundred years ago he had some white blood introduced into his system is, I think, irrelevant, and I will instruct him not to answer any more questions.

By Mr. Barron: Q Would you answer the question, please, Mr. Eggleston?

Mr. Miner: I have instructed him not to answer. You can tell him that you are not going to answer the questions when I instruct you not to.

By the Witness: A I rather not answer.

By Mr. Barron: Q What is your grandfather's name, Mr. Eggleston?

          A Josef Eggleston.

> Q Do you know your great grandfather, Mr.
> Eggleston, on your father's side?
> Mr. Miner: Listen, Howard. This is getting bizarre. I
> am going to instruct him not to answer
> any more questions about anything be-
> yond his grandparents just so that we
> might finish this in less than the time it
> took us to get through Mr. Plummer's
> deposition.
> Mr. Barron: We are not through with Mr. Plummer's
> deposition, Mr. Miner.

Apart from the racial probing, other avenues of defendants' inquiry deserve examination. Although the deposition was not scheduled as a bar examination, Eggleston and Rose were asked questions some members of the bar might have difficulty answering correctly.

Religion also got some attention. Eggleston was asked if he purported to represent Jews as well as Buddhists. We find no issue of religion in the case.[117]

The court concluded, however, that the collapse of discovery could not be attributed solely to the defendants. Plaintiffs refused to answer a large number of deposition questions, engaged in private off-the-record conferences, and aborted many depositions unilaterally.[118]

Other cases have shown even more outrageous forms of misconduct during depositions. In Paramount Communications Inc. v. QVC Network Inc.[119] the Delaware Supreme Court strongly condemned the deposition conduct of well-known Texas attorney Joseph Jamail. Jamail referred to opposing counsel as an "asshole" and told him that he could "gag a maggot off a meat wagon."[120] While the court was unable to impose sanctions on Jamail because

117. Id. at 897-898 n.12.
118. Id. at 901-902.
119. 637 A.2d 34 (Del. 1994).
120. Id. at 54. See also Mullaney v. Aude, 730 A.2d 759 (Md. Ct. Spec. App.), cert. denied, 736 A.2d 1065 (1999) (male lawyer sanctioned for referring to female lawyer as "babe" at deposition); In re Golden, 496 S.E.2d 619 (S.C. 1998) (gratuitously insulting, threatening, and demeaning comments in the course of two depositions held to constitute misconduct warranting public reprimand for violating South Carolina Rules of Professional Conduct 4.4 and 8.4).

he was not admitted to practice in Delaware either by regular or pro hac vice admission, the court expressed its strong opposition to such tactics and warned Delaware lawyers against participating in such misconduct.[121]

As *Eggleston* points out, one form of improper deposition conduct involves inappropriate coaching of a witness during breaks in a deposition after a question has been posed. Improper witness coaching can also take place before the deposition (or before trial) when lawyers prepare witnesses for their appearances. But what is improper witness-coaching? Lawyers generally have substantial leeway in helping prepare witnesses to testify so long as they do not attempt to have a witness testify falsely. The Restatement of the Law Governing Lawyers provides the following helpful comment:

> In preparing a witness to testify, a lawyer may invite the witness to provide truthful testimony favorable to the lawyer's client. Preparation consistent with the rule of this Section may include the following: discussing the role of the witness and effective courtroom demeanor; discussing the witness's recollection and probable testimony; revealing to the witness other testimony or evidence that will be presented and asking the witness to reconsider the witness's recollection or recounting of events in that light; discussing the applicability of law to the events in issue; reviewing the factual context into which the witness's observations or opinions will fit; reviewing documents or other physical evidence that may be introduced; and discussing probable lines of hostile cross-examination that the witness should be prepared to meet. Witness preparation may include rehearsal of testimony. A lawyer may suggest choice of words that might be employed to make the witness's meaning clear. However, a lawyer may not assist the witness to testify falsely as to a material fact.[122]

If a lawyer directs a client to lie, the lawyer's misconduct is clear, but lawyers can suggest false testimony in more subtle ways. Although such conduct is difficult to detect or to police, it is none-

---

121. 637 A. 2d at 53-56.
122. Restatement (Third) of the Law Governing Lawyers §176, cmt. *b*. See Richard C. Wydick, The Ethics of Witness Coaching, 17 Cardozo L. Rev. 1 (1995).

theless improper.[123] In 1998 the Texas law firm of Baron & Budd became involved in controversy over a memorandum entitled, "Preparing for Your Deposition," which it used to prepare clients to testify in asbestos cases. The memorandum advised clients that it was important for them to testify that they never saw any warning labels on asbestos products and cautioned them against saying that they saw more than one brand name.[124]

In Problem 2-5 we examined the issue of lawyers' ethical obligations when a defendant in a criminal case threatens to or does in fact testify perjuriously. Perjury can, of course, occur in civil cases. In Formal Opinion 93-376, the ABA Committee on Ethics and Professional Responsibility discussed a lawyer's obligations when a client commits perjury during a deposition. The committee concluded that under Model Rule 3.3, the lawyer has an obligation to advise the client to correct the perjury and to disclose the perjury if the client refuses to do so.

Techniques for dealing with discovery abuse

How can lawyers deal with discovery abuse? Possible responses fall into two broad categories: formal and informal. The most obvious formal response is a motion for sanctions, typically under Federal Rule 37. A motion for sanctions is always a possibility, but attorneys should be aware of problems with this approach. First, given the demands on the judiciary, it may be difficult to obtain judicial time to consider a motion for sanctions. Second, even when the matter comes before a court, many judges are likely to be impatient with "discovery spats" because they consume judicial time, are collateral to the merits of the case, and force judges to deal with issues that they think lawyers should handle on their own. Third, except in extreme cases courts are usually unwilling to impose harsh sanctions on lawyers.[125] A court is far more likely

123. See Liisa Renee Salmi, Note, Don't Walk the Line: Ethical Considerations in Preparing Witnesses for Deposition and Trial, 18 Rev. Litig. 135 (1999).

124. The full text of the memo is available on the Internet at ⟨http://www.dallasobserver.com/1998/081398/feature1-1.html⟩. See also Michael Higgins, Fine Line, 84-May A.B.A. J. 52 (1998).

125. See Charles Yablon, Stupid Lawyer Tricks: An Essay on Discovery

simply to order the offending party to comply with the discovery request.

Aside from sanctions, attorneys can resort to various other formal devices to avoid or deal with discovery abuse. For example, in some cases courts may be willing to issue orders defining the scope of discovery or to appoint special masters to oversee discovery and resolve discovery disputes. The administrative judge of a court may be available by telephone to resolve immediately disputes that arise during depositions.

Often, however, lawyers must use informal methods for dealing with discovery problems. The most effective informal method for dealing with discovery issues is mutual agreement of counsel. An early meeting with opposing counsel to discuss discovery before formal discovery requests are filed may eliminate many problems. Indeed, the 1993 amendments to the Federal Rules of Civil Procedure require counsel to have a discovery conference.[126] If discovery disputes develop, a frank meeting with opposing counsel to discuss the scope and objections to discovery may produce a compromise that both parties can accept. Prudent lawyers should reduce all agreements to writing either immediately or by confirming letter to avoid misunderstandings, to encourage compliance, and to provide a foundation for a motion for sanctions if the other attorney fails to live up to the agreement.

In some jurisdictions bar associations have established committees to deal with discovery disputes. Resort to such a committee may be an option for dealing with some discovery problems.

Responding in kind is rarely an effective device for dealing with discovery abuse by the opposing party. Attorneys who engage in retaliation commit ethical misconduct themselves. In addition, they help poison the atmosphere of the case, often to the disadvantage of their clients. Moreover, they weaken their legal position should they wish to seek sanctions against the offending lawyer.

One possible response to discovery abuse is to look for opportunities to use the discovery abuse against the opposing party. Answers to interrogatories, responses to requests for production of documents, and oral depositions are all admissible in evidence against the party providing the answers. Unreasonable responses

---

Abuse, 96 Colum. L. Rev. 1618 (1996) (arguing that judges should consider less extreme sanctions to control discovery abuse).
    126. Fed. R. Civ. P. 26(f).

or answers that are obvious attempts to avoid supplying information may be used in cross-examination to undermine the credibility of the party making those answers before the trier of fact.

As the material above illustrates, deposition practice can be a troubling and unpleasant experience, particularly for young lawyers, because of the face-to-face encounter with opposing counsel in a forum without a neutral decisionmaker. Knowledge of proper objections and improper deposition conduct is essential to dealing with these problems.[127] A number of federal district courts have adopted guidelines for conducting depositions to deal with some of the problems that have arisen.[128] In Hall v. Clifton Precision[129] the court adopted the following guidelines:

1. At the beginning of the deposition, deposing counsel shall instruct the witness to ask deposing counsel, rather than the witness's own counsel, for clarifications, definitions, or explanations of any words, questions, or documents presented during the course of the deposition. The witness shall abide by these instructions.

2. All objections, except those which would be waived if not made at the deposition under Federal Rules of Civil Procedure 32(d)(3)(B), and those necessary to assert a privilege, to enforce a limitation on evidence directed by the court, or to present a motion pursuant to Federal Rules of Civil Procedure 30(d), shall be preserved. Therefore, those objections need not and shall not be made during the course of depositions.

3. Counsel shall not direct or request that a witness not answer a question, unless that counsel has objected to the question on the ground that the answer is protected by a privilege or a limitation on evidence directed by the court.

4. Counsel shall not make objections or statements which might suggest an answer to a witness. Counsels' statements when making objections should be succinct and verbally economical, stating the basis of the objection and nothing more.

5. Counsel and their witness-clients shall not engage in private, off-the-record conferences during depositions or during breaks or recesses, except for the purpose of deciding whether to assert a privilege.

127. See William J. Snipes et al., Successful Techniques for Dealing with the Difficult Adversary, 585 PLI/Lit 167 (1998) (on Westlaw).
128. See Standing Orders of the Court on Effective Discovery in Civil Cases, 102 F.R.D. 339 (E.D.N.Y. 1984).
129. 150 F.R.D. 525 (E.D. Pa. 1993).

6. Any conferences which occur pursuant to, or in violation of, guideline (5) are a proper subject for inquiry by deposing counsel to ascertain whether there has been any witness-coaching and, if so, what.

7. Any conferences which occur pursuant to, or in violation of, guideline (5) shall be noted on the record by the counsel who participated in the conference. The purpose and outcome of the conference shall also be noted on the record.

8. Deposing counsel shall provide to the witness's counsel a copy of all documents shown to the witness during the deposition. The copies shall be provided either before the deposition begins or contemporaneously with the showing of each document to the witness. The witness and the witness's counsel do not have the right to discuss documents privately before the witness answers questions about them.[130]

Not all courts agree with the strict requirements set down by the court in *Hall*. For example, in In re Stratosphere Corp. Securities Litigation[131] the court disagreed with the prohibition on all private off-the-record conferences during breaks in depositions. The court ruled that neither a lawyer nor a client could demand a break in a deposition while a question was pending except to discuss a possible claim of privilege, but concluded that otherwise the right to counsel allowed lawyers to discuss testimony with their clients.[132]

---

130. Id. at 531-532.

131. 182 F.R.D. 614 (D. Nev. 1998).

132. Id. at 619-621. *Compare* State ex rel. Means v. King, 520 S.E. 2d 875 (W. Va. 1999) (attorney may confer with client during recess or break in discovery deposition so long as attorney does not request break in questions or request a conference between question and answer for improper purpose; such a right does not apply, however, to evidence deposition or to testimony at trial) *with* In re PSE & G Shareholder Litig., 726 A.2d 994 (N.J. Super. Ct. Ch. Div. 1998) (counsel and client may not discuss testimony during deposition breaks but may confer at end of each day to prepare for witness's testimony the following day).

B. Alternative Dispute Resolution

―――――――― **Problem 4-5** ――――――――

Negotiation

Analyze and be prepared to discuss the ethical issues raised by the following negotiation situations:

a.   In a personal injury case, the insurance company has authorized defense counsel, Dorn, to settle the case for a maximum of $100,000. At a negotiation session with plaintiff's counsel, Phillips, Dorn states, "I am authorized to settle this case for $50,000." Later in the session, Phillips states, "My client won't accept less than $75,000." In fact, Phillips has discussed settlement with the client, and the client is willing to accept $60,000 to settle the case.

b.   In a wrongful discharge case, may Phillips, counsel for the plaintiff, make a claim in negotiation for plaintiff's reinstatement to his job even though the plaintiff does not want his job back, using this demand as a bargaining chip for increased damages? May Phillips claim that the discharge has caused the plaintiff "emotional distress" when in fact the plaintiff has taken the loss of his job in stride?

c.   An automobile accident occurred between two vehicles driven by Adams and Waring. Benson was a passenger in Adams's vehicle. Benson's attorney, Phillips, is negotiating with Dorn, counsel for defendant Waring. During the course of negotiation, Dorn states that Waring's insurer is willing to tender its policy limits of $300,000 to settle the case in exchange for a covenant not to sue. Dorn tells Phillips that "you should also be able to get Adams's policy limits of $100,000 to settle your claim against him." Dorn is mistaken about the limits of Adams's policy. In fact, Phillips knows that Adams has a $1,000,000 umbrella policy in addition to a basic $100,000 policy.

d.   Emerson is president and chief executive officer of More for Less, Inc., a national retail chain. The audit committee of the company's board of directors learned recently that Emerson has been embezzling substantial sums of money for several years. Matthews, an attorney retained by More for Less, has been meeting with Emerson's lawyers. Matthews says that the company would be willing not to file criminal charges against Emerson if Emerson resigns as president and transfers to the company all stock that Emerson owns in the company.

e.   Dorn, counsel retained by the defendant's insurance company in an automobile accident case, has a meeting with plaintiff's counsel, Phillips. When Phillips enters the room, Dorn smells alcohol on Philips's breath and observes that Phillips is extremely disheveled. Before Dorn can say much, Phillips expresses a willingness to settle the case for $10,000 if Dorn gets Phillips a check "right away." While outwardly calm, Dorn is shocked by this offer. Dorn and the insurance company had evaluated the case as having a settlement value of $25,000 to $50,000. Dorn suspects that Phillips is looking for a quick fee.

f.   Dorn represents defendant Harrison in a divorce proceeding brought by Harrison's wife. Dorn is about to meet with opposing counsel to see if they can work out a settlement. Harrison is extremely angry with his wife, and he has evidence of an affair. He tells Dorn, "I want her to get as little as possible out of this divorce. Use all the dirt we've got and anything else you can come up with to make them settle on our terms. Don't pull any punches."

Read Model Rules 1.2(a), 3.3, 4.1, 4.3, 4.4, 8.4, and comments.

Regardless of the type of practice — civil litigation, criminal defense or prosecution, business, or labor — negotiation is an extremely important part of the work of lawyers.[133] Ethical issues in negotiation fall into two broad categories: honesty and fairness.

Honesty in negotiation: the duty not to engage in misrepresentation

To what extent must lawyers be honest in negotiations? The question can be refined into two questions: To what extent are lawyers prohibited from making false representations in negotiations? When must a lawyer disclose material information to the opposing party in negotiation?

A plausible answer to the question of when lawyers are allowed to make false representations (or, more bluntly, to lie in negotiations) is "never." In an influential article on negotiation, however, Professor James White argues that while lawyers do have a general obligation not to engage in fraud or deceit in negotiation, it is erroneous to claim that lawyers should never engage in misrepresentation in negotiation. According to White, misrepresentation of one's position is essential to negotiation, just as it is to a game like poker:

> Like the poker player, a negotiator hopes that his opponent will overestimate the value of his hand. Like the poker player, in a variety of ways he must facilitate his opponent's inaccurate assessment. The critical difference between those who are successful negotiators and those who are not lies in this capacity both to mislead and not to be misled.
>
> Some experienced negotiators will deny the accuracy of this assertion, but they will be wrong. I submit that a careful examination of the behavior of even the most forthright, honest, and trustworthy negotiators will show them actively engaged in misleading

---

133. For an empirical study of lawyer practices in negotiation, see Scott S. Dahl, Ethics on the Table: Stretching the Truth in Negotiations, 8 Rev. Litig. 173 (1989).

their opponents about their true positions. That is true of both the plaintiff and the defendant in a lawsuit. It is true of both labor and management in a collective bargaining agreement. It is true as well of both the buyer and the seller in a wide variety of sales transactions. To conceal one's true position, to mislead an opponent about one's true settling point, is the essence of negotiation.[134]

Some scholars have criticized White's view that negotiation inherently involves a degree of misrepresentation. These scholars have argued that White has an adversarial conception of negotiation; they contend that negotiation can and should be cooperative rather than adversarial. In cooperative negotiations, the effectiveness of misrepresentation is substantially diminished.[135] Other scholars have argued that it is simply wrong for lawyers to lie in negotiation, and to the extent that current practice or rules allow misrepresentation and deceit, these rules should be changed. The leading article expressing this view is Alvin B. Rubin, A Causerie on Lawyers' Ethics in Negotiation.[136]

The Model Rules seem to adopt White's view that lawyers have a general obligation of honesty in negotiation but that deceit and misrepresentation are to some degree part of the rules of the game. Model Rule 4.1(a) states that in representing a client a lawyer shall not knowingly "make a false statement of material fact or

---

134. James J. White, Machiavelli and the Bar: Ethical Limitations on Lying in Negotiation, 1980 Am. Bar Found. Res. J. 926, 927-928. See also Eleanor Holmes Norton, Bargaining and the Ethic of Process, 64 N.Y.U. L. Rev. 493 (1989) (necessities of bargaining process produce ethical functionalism with minimal truthfulness and fairness).

135. See generally Carrie Menkel-Meadow, Toward Another View of Legal Negotiation: The Structure of Problem Solving, 31 UCLA L. Rev. 754 (1984). For an interesting discussion of this issue, see the exchange between Professor White and Professor Roger Fisher, coauthor with William Ury of Getting to Yes (1981), a leading work on cooperative negotiation, in James J. White, Essay Review, The Pros and Cons of "Getting to Yes," 34 J. Legal Educ. 115 (1984).

136. 35 La. L. Rev. 577 (1975). See also Reed E. Loder, Moral Truthseeking and the Virtuous Negotiator, 8 Geo. J. Legal Ethics 45 (1994); Gary T. Lowenthal, The Bar's Failure to Require Truthful Bargaining by Lawyers, 2 Geo. J. Legal Ethics 411 (1988); Walter W. Steele, Jr., Deceptive Negotiating and High-Toned Morality, 39 Vand. L. Rev. 1387 (1986); Gerald B. Wetlaufer, The Ethics of Lying in Negotiations, 75 Iowa L. Rev. 1219 (1990). For an analysis of the legal obligations imposed on lawyers in negotiation, see Rex R. Perschbacher, Regulating Lawyers' Negotiations, 27 Ariz. L. Rev. 75 (1985).

law to a third person."[137] The comment to Rule 4.1, however, makes clear that some false statements are permissible because they do not amount to statements of material fact. Comment 2 states that "[u]nder generally accepted conventions in negotiation, certain types of statements ordinarily are not taken as statements of material fact."

How does a lawyer decide what misrepresentations under "accepted conventions" do not amount to statements of fact? Comment 2 to Rule 4.1 gives a few examples but does not provide a definition or any criteria for distinguishing permissible from prohibited misrepresentations. Case law, however, does offer some guidance. Improper misrepresentation clearly occurs when a lawyer makes a false statement about the material facts of the case — the testimony of a witness or the existence or contents of a document, for example. Improper misrepresentation also occurs when a lawyer makes false statements about the effect of provisions of an agreement, about procedural aspects of the case, or about insurance coverage. Such a misrepresentation can result in rescission of the agreement,[138] subject the lawyer to disciplinary action,[139] or produce civil liability.[140] Note also that a lawyer's duty not to engage in misrepresentation in negotiations parallels a lawyer's duty not to engage in misrepresentation in court proceedings.[141]

Lawyers do not act improperly, however, when they misrepresent their true *opinions* about the relative strengths of each side

137. See Restatement (Third) of the Law Governing Lawyers §157(1). See also ABA Comm. on Ethics and Prof. Resp., Formal Op. 94-387 (lawyer may negotiate regarding claim that is barred by statute of limitations and may file suit of time-barred claim so long as lawyer does not make any false representations; same rules apply to government lawyers).

138. See Carlson v. Carlson, 832 P.2d 380 (Nev. 1992) (wife entitled to relief from property settlement agreement based on representations by husband and his attorney that division was essentially equal).

139. See In re Broome, 615 So. 2d 1333 (La. 1993) (lawyer disciplined for obtaining personal injury settlement based on false representation that suit had been timely filed).

140. See Fire Ins. Exch. v. Bell, 643 N.E.2d 310 (Ind. 1994) (lawyer subject to liability for misrepresenting limits of insurance policy; as matter of law lawyers have right to rely on representations made by opposing counsel about amount of insurance).

141. See Model Rule 3.3(a)(1); In re Neitlich, 597 N.E.2d 425 (Mass. 1992) (one-year suspension administered to lawyer who misrepresented terms of client's pending real estate transaction to court in postdivorce proceeding).

of a case. Lawyers may permissibly say to their opponents that they believe they have very strong cases even though they actually believe that there are serious problems with their positions. Further, in negotiations lawyers may argue for interpretations of relevant law that are most favorable to their clients, even when lawyers believe that their opponents' positions are correct.[142]

Representations regarding settlement authority could arise in two ways. First, a lawyer could make a representation regarding settlement authority for the purpose of inducing agreement by the opposing side. Second, the opposing party may ask a question about the lawyer's settlement authority. In either situation, is it improper for a lawyer to make misrepresentations about settlement authority? Comment 2 to Rule 4.1 states that a lawyer may make misrepresentations about a "party's intentions as to an acceptable settlement of a claim." Yet while misrepresentations of opinions about the merits of the case are essential to the negotiation process, misrepresentations of settlement authority are not. Further, settlement authority is a matter of fact, not opinion.

Responses to requests by the other side for information about settlement authority pose a more subtle problem. A lawyer's settlement authority will come from discussions with the client. These discussions will often involve confidential information — information received from the client that is subject to either the attorney-client privilege or the work product doctrine, or both. Thus, a question about settlement authority inquires into privileged matters and seeks information that the other party is not entitled to know.[143] In addition, if lawyers and clients know that lawyers must respond truthfully to questions about authority, they can easily devise ways to avoid having to answer the question. Thus, good reasons exist why lawyers should not be required to answer truthfully questions about their settlement authority. At the same time, it is probably unnecessary for the rules to permit lawyers to lie in response to inquiries about settlement authority because such questions can easily be deflected.

Another misrepresentation that is problematic involves a

142. See White, Machiavelli and the Bar, 1980 Am. Bar Found. Res. J. at 931-932. See also Restatement (Second) of Contracts §§168, 169 (1979); Restatement (Second) of Torts §542 (1977) (reliance on statements of opinion not justified except in limited situations).

143. Cf. ABA Comm. on Ethics and Prof. Resp., Formal Op. 93-370 (judge does not have right to require lawyer to reveal settlement authority absent client's consent).

"false demand," a contention injected into the negotiation process, not because it expresses a serious position by the side making the demand but because a false demand can be used as a bargaining chip to improve the overall settlement. Professor White argues that the false demand is a misrepresentation in the broadest sense because a person making a demand "implicitly or explicitly states his interest in the demand and his estimation of it," but he goes on to conclude that such demands are "not thought to be inappropriate," at least in labor negotiations.[144]

Honesty in negotiation: the duty of disclosure

So far we have discussed the question of when misrepresentation by lawyers in negotiation is improper. The issue of honesty in negotiation also raises a question of disclosure. When are lawyers required to disclose information to the opposing party in connection with negotiation? Model Rule 4.1(b) states that a lawyer may not knowingly "fail to disclose a material fact to a third person when disclosure is necessary to avoid assisting a criminal or fraudulent act by a client, unless disclosure is prohibited by Rule 1.6." The "unless" clause was added to the rule during the floor debate before the House of Delegates on adoption of the Model Rules in 1983; the result is both confusing and contradictory. Professor Wolfram offers the following comment on the rule:

> Because MR 1.6 prohibits most if not all imaginable disclosures in the circumstances stated by the first part of MR 4.1(b), the "unless" clause entirely stops the lawyer's mouth from uttering the disclosures that the rule otherwise requires.[145]

Both the Wolfram and the Hazard & Hodes treatises argue that the only way for Rule 4.1(b) to make sense is to construe the rule to mean that a lawyer must disclose information when required by "other law," which includes the law of civil procedure and tort law dealing with actionable nondisclosure.[146]

While the Wolfram and the Hazard & Hodes treatises focus

144. White, Machiavelli and the Bar, 1980 Am. Bar Found. Res. J. at 932.

145. Wolfram, Modern Legal Ethics §13.5.8, at 724. See also 2 Hazard & Hodes, The Law of Lawyering §4.1:302, at 720.

146. Wolfram, Modern Legal Ethics §13.5.8, at 724. See also 2 Hazard & Hodes, The Law of Lawyering §4.1:303, at 721-723.

on the lawyer's implied obligation to obey other law as the basis
of a duty of disclosure, the author of this casebook has argued that
the lawyer's duty not to engage in misrepresentation under Model
Rule 4.1(a) will sometimes require disclosure of material information. Such a duty of disclosure arises when nondisclosure is
equivalent to misrepresentation.[147] Comment 1 to Model Rule 4.1
states: "Misrepresentations can also occur by failure to act." Similarly, Comment 2 to Model Rule 3.3 states: "There are circumstances where failure to make a disclosure is the equivalent of an
affirmative misrepresentation."[148] Note that when the duty of disclosure is based on the obligation not to engage in misrepresentation under Rule 4.1(a), the duty is not qualified by the obligation
of confidentiality.

Case law supports the analysis of the commentators rather
than the literal language of Model Rule 4.1(b). As a general proposition, lawyers do not have an obligation to disclose material information to the opposing side.[149] Numerous cases have held,
however, that under some circumstances lawyers have an ethical
duty to disclose information in connection with contract or settlement negotiations.[150] When does a lawyer have a duty of disclosure? The author of this casebook argues that the duty to disclose
arises in four situations:[151]

A duty of *corrective disclosure* arises when a lawyer made a
representation that the lawyer now learns was either false when
made or has become false because of changed circumstances.[152]

147. Nathan M. Crystal, The Lawyer's Duty to Disclose Material Facts
in Contract or Settlement Negotiations, 87 Ky. L.J. 1055, 1058 (1998–1999).

148. This comment to Rule 3.3 should also apply to Rule 4.1. The comment explains the meaning of Rule 3.3(a)(1), which prohibits lawyers from making a false statement of material fact or law to a tribunal. See ABA Comm. on
Ethics and Prof. Resp., Formal Op. 98-412 (disclosure obligations of a lawyer
who discovers that her client has violated court order during litigation). Model
Rule 4.1(a) imposes an identical obligation on lawyers not to make false statements of material fact or law to third parties.

149. See Restatement (Second) of Torts §551(1) (1977) and Restatement
(Second) of Contracts §161 (1979).

150. For a review of the case law, see Crystal, The Lawyer's Duty to Disclose Material Facts in Contract or Settlement Negotiations, 87 Ky. L.J. at 1059-
1074.

151. Id. at 1076-1082.

152. See In re Williams, 840 P.2d 1280 (Or. 1992) (lawyer represented
to landlord that he would hold tenant's rent payments in escrow pending reso-

If a lawyer knows that the other party is operating under a fundamental *mistake about the contents of a writing*, the lawyer has a duty to disclose the mistake to the other party. The mistake will typically arise as a result of a "scrivener's error."[153] The duty to disclose known mistakes in a writing also extends to situations in which a lawyer changes provisions in an agreement but fails to notify the other side of such modifications.[154]

Situations in which lawyers will have a *fiduciary duty to the opposing party to disclose material information* in negotiation will rarely occur. When the opposing party is represented by counsel, a lawyer does not have a fiduciary duty to the opposing party. If the lawyer is dealing with an unrepresented opposing party, the lawyer has an obligation to correct any misunderstanding that the other party may have about the lawyer's role in the negotiations.[155] See Model Rule 4.3. A lawyer may not give any advice to an unrepresented person, other than the advice to seek counsel.[156] In some limited circumstances, a lawyer may properly act as an intermediary between parties engaged in contract negotiations. See Model Rule 2.2 and Problem 5-1. Because lawyers who act as

---

lution of dispute; lawyer disciplined for failing to inform landlord that statement was no longer correct). See also Restatement (Third) of the Law Governing Lawyers §157, cmt. *d* (recognizing duty of corrective disclosure). Cf. Fed. R. Civ. P. 26(e) (duty to supplement responses in discovery).

153. See ABA Comm. on Ethics and Prof. Resp., Informal Op. 86-1518 (lawyer who receives contract containing scrivener's error should immediately notify other lawyer and need not consult with client because client does not have reasonable expectation of receiving erroneous provision); Stare v. Tate, 98 Cal. Rptr. 264 (Ct. App. 1971) (property settlement agreement set aside because of lawyer's failure to disclose mathematical mistake made by opposing party in its settlement offer).

154. Wright v. Pennamped, 657 N.E.2d 1223, *as modified on reh'g*, 664 N.E.2d 394 (Ind. Ct. App. 1996); In re Rothwell, 296 S.E.2d 870 (S.C. 1982).

155. See Hotz v. Minyard, 403 S.E.2d 634 (S.C. 1991) (summary judgment for lawyer reversed because material issues of fact exist on whether lawyer had fiduciary duty to daughter not to misrepresent terms of her father's will, which the lawyer had drafted, when the daughter consulted the lawyer about the terms of the will, the lawyer had an ongoing professional relationship with the daughter, and the lawyer failed to disclose that he was representing the father and not the daughter with regard to the will).

156. See Russell Engler, Out of Sight and Out of Line: The Need for Regulation of Lawyers' Negotiations with Unrepresented Poor Persons, 85 Cal. L. Rev. 79 (1997) (arguing that prohibition on giving advice is widely ignored and calling for a number of possible responses to deal with the problem).

intermediaries represent both parties, they have a fiduciary duty to disclose material information to both of them. Model Rule 2.2(b) and cmt. 6.

The broadest and vaguest category of cases in which lawyers have a duty of disclosure occurs when disclosure is necessary to correct a mistake by the other party about basic aspects of the transaction and the *failure to disclose violates standards of good faith and fair dealing.*[157] Probably the most blatant case of nondisclosure that violates the duty of good faith occurs when the lawyer's client dies, but the lawyer fails to reveal this information to the other side while negotiating a settlement agreement.[158] The duty of good faith disclosure extends further, however, to encompass failure to disclose major procedural developments,[159] mistakes about the amount of insurance coverage,[160] and recantation of testimony by a significant witness.[161]

In all the cases discussed in this section, the lawyers who failed to disclose information knew that the other party was operating under a mistake, and the mistake related to fundamental information. When these factors are absent, a duty to disclose does not arise. For example, in Brown v. County of Genesee[162] the Sixth Circuit held that a settlement agreement in an employment discrimination case should not be set aside because defense counsel and his client failed to reveal to the plaintiff and her attorney that

---

157. See Restatement (Second) of Torts §551(2)(e) (1977) and Restatement (Second) of Contracts §161(b) (1979).

158. See Virzi v. Grand Trunk Warehouse & Cold Storage Co., 571 F. Supp. 507 (E.D. Mich. 1983); Kentucky Bar Assn. v. Geisler, 938 S.W.2d 578 (Ky. 1997).

159. See Hamilton v. Harper, 404 S.E.2d 540 (W. Va. 1991) (lawyer failed to reveal that summary judgment had just been granted to insurer in federal court declaratory judgment action on issue of insurance coverage when lawyer accepted outstanding offer from insurance company).

160. See State ex rel. Neb. State Bar Assn. v. Addison, 412 N.W.2d 855 (Neb. 1987) (lawyer suspended for six months after failing to reveal to hospital administrator the existence of insurance policy in connection with negotiation of release of hospital's lien).

161. See Kath v. Western Media, Inc., 684 P.2d 98 (Wyo. 1984) (settlement invalidated because plaintiff's attorney failed to disclose existence of letter in which witness who was previously a lawyer for all parties to action contradicted testimony he had given in deposition).

162. 872 F.2d 169 (6th Cir. 1989).

they were mistaken about the highest pay level that plaintiff would have been entitled to had she been hired immediately. Defense counsel believed that it was "probable" that the plaintiff was mistaken about pay levels, but there was no way for counsel to know that a mistake had occurred. In addition, it was unclear to the court that the highest level of pay was fundamental to the agreement because there was no such condition in the settlement.[163]

One of the most extreme reported cases of nondisclosure is Spaulding v. Zimmerman.[164] In *Spaulding* the Minnesota Supreme Court held that a minor settlement in an accident case should be set aside because the lawyer for the defendant failed to disclose to the plaintiff a doctor's report showing that, unknown to the plaintiff, he was suffering from a life-threatening aneurysm that was probably caused by the accident. While the court set aside the settlement,[165] it held that defense counsel did not have an ethical duty to disclose plaintiff's condition.[166] The author of this casebook contends that the court in *Spaulding* incorrectly decided the ethical issue and that the result would be different under current rules. Under this analysis, the defense lawyers in *Spaulding* had a duty to disclose under Model Rule 4.1(a) because their failure to disclose amounted to misrepresentation:

> [T]he court was wrong in its characterization of the lawyers' conduct. Under the facts of the case, defense counsel's failure to disclose was the equivalent of a misrepresentation. Defense counsel had a duty to disclose because plaintiff's physical condition was a basic fact about which plaintiff was mistaken, and the failure to disclose violated principles of good faith and fair dealing. Indeed, *Spaulding* is probably the clearest case for disclosure that can be imagined because of the threat to the plaintiff's life.[167]

163. Id. at 174-175.
164. 116 N.W.2d 704 (Minn. 1962).
165. Id. at 709-710.
166. Id. at 710. In a comprehensive examination of the case, Professor Roger Cramton and Lori Knowles contend the court was correct that rules of ethics and discovery rules did not then and do not now require disclosure. They argue this result shows that the confidentiality rules are unsound and should be changed. Roger C. Cramton & Lori P. Knowles, Professional Secrecy and Its Exceptions: Spaulding v. Zimmerman Revisited, 83 Minn. L. Rev. 63 (1998).
167. See Crystal, The Lawyer's Duty to Disclose Material Facts in Contract or Settlement Negotiations, 87 Ky. L.J. at 1097.

Fairness of the settlement

The original draft of the Model Rules stated: "In conducting negotiations a lawyer shall be fair in dealing with other participants."[168] Whether the drafters truly intended to include a general obligation of fairness is doubtful since the comment stated that fairness in negotiations implies that representations shall be truthful. In any event, the idea of an obligation of fairness was quickly abandoned in favor of narrower rules focusing on misrepresentation and nondisclosure.[169]

Why shouldn't rules of ethics impose an obligation on lawyers to refuse to participate in agreements that are unfair? Three reasons could be given. First, there are no objective criteria of fairness that a lawyer or a disciplinary board could use to determine whether an agreement was fair. Thus, an ethical duty not to participate in an unfair outcome would be unworkable. Second, to the extent that rules of ethics prohibit lawyers from participating in settlement agreements that the lawyers know are invalid because of fraud, mistake, or other such cause, the rules already impose a substantial obligation of fairness. Third, a duty of fairness would be inconsistent with the adversarial system, under which the fairness of the outcome is judged by the fairness of the adjudication process. Rules of ethics do not prohibit lawyers from participating in adjudication that produces an outcome that some might consider substantively unfair so long as the process is a fair one. Similarly, the rules should not prohibit lawyers from engaging in negotiations that result in an agreement that some observers might consider unfair.

Some scholars, while agreeing that lawyers should not have an ethical duty to ensure the overall fairness of negotiations, have argued for a narrower proposition: Lawyers should have an obligation not to participate in an agreement that is unconscionable. Professor Lee Pizzimenti has proposed the adoption of the following rule of ethics:

---

168. ABA, Model Rules of Professional Conduct, Rule 4.2(a) (Discussion Draft 1980).

169. See Geoffrey C. Hazard, Jr., The Lawyer's Obligation to Be Trustworthy When Dealing with Opposing Parties, 33 S.C. L. Rev. 181 (1981) (legal regulation of trustworthiness cannot go further than to proscribe fraud because of substantial difference in technical sophistication among lawyers).

A lawyer shall not assist in the preparation of a written instrument containing terms which are unconscionable. A lawyer may assist in such preparation where there is a basis for concluding the terms are not unconscionable that is not frivolous, including a good faith argument for an extension, modification or reversal of existing law.[170]

Improper threats

Even though the Model Rules do not impose a general obligation of fairness in connection with negotiation, there are some limitations on negotiation tactics. One limitation deals with improper threats during negotiation. Disciplinary Rule 7-105(A) of the Code of Professional Responsibility prohibited lawyers from threatening to use the criminal process solely to obtain an advantage in a civil matter. Ethical Consideration 7-21 offered the following rationale for the prohibition:

> The civil adjudicative process is primarily designed for the settlement of disputes between parties, while the criminal process is designed for the protection of society as a whole. Threatening to use, or using, the criminal process to coerce adjustment of private civil claims or controversies is a subversion of that process; further, the person against whom the criminal process is so misused may be deterred from asserting his legal rights and thus the usefulness of the civil process in settling private disputes is impaired. As in all cases of abuse of judicial process, the improper use of criminal process tends to diminish public confidence in our legal system.

The drafters of the Model Rules intentionally omitted the ban on threats of criminal prosecution.[171] They believed that the prohibition found in the Code was unwise in two respects. First, the restriction was redundant because it was already covered by other rules, particularly by Model Rule 8.4(b), prohibiting lawyers from engaging in criminal conduct that reflects on their honesty, trustworthiness, or fitness to practice law, and by Model Rule 4.4, deal-

---

170. See Lee A. Pizzimenti, Prohibiting Lawyers from Assisting in Unconscionable Transactions: Using an Overt Tool, 72 Marq. L. Rev. 151, 174 (1989).

171. 2 Hazard & Hodes, The Law of Lawyering §4.4:103, at 759.

[handwritten margin note: threats of criminal action is sometimes proper]

ing with respect for the rights of third persons.[172] Second, the drafters concluded that the limitation was overbroad because some threats of criminal prosecution were proper tactics that lawyers should be allowed to use to protect clients' legitimate interests.[173]

In Formal Opinion 92-363, the ABA Committee on Ethics and Professional Responsibility discussed when a threat of criminal prosecution would be permissible under the Model Rules:

> Model Rule 8.4(b) provides that it is professional misconduct for a lawyer to "commit a criminal act that reflects adversely on the lawyer's honesty, trustworthiness or fitness as a lawyer in other respects." If a lawyer's conduct is extortionate or compounds a crime under the criminal law of a given jurisdiction, that conduct also violates Rule 8.4(b). It is beyond the scope of the Committee's jurisdiction to define extortionate conduct, but we note that the Model Penal Code does not criminalize threats of prosecution where the "property obtained by threat of accusation, exposure, lawsuit or other invocation of official action was *honestly claimed as restitution for harm done in the circumstances to which such accusation, exposure, lawsuit or other official action relates, or as compensation for property or lawful services.*" Model Penal Code, §223.4 (emphasis added). . . . [The committee then went on to discuss other provisions of the Model Rules that a threat of criminal prosecution might violate, depending on the circumstances.]
>
> Rule 4.4 (Respect for Rights of Third Persons) prohibits a lawyer from using means that "have no substantial purpose other than to embarrass, delay, or burden a third person. . . ." A lawyer who uses even a well-founded threat of criminal charges merely to harass a third person violates Rule 4.4. See also [2] Hazard & Hodes, [The Law of Lawyering] §4.4:104.
>
> Rule 4.1 (Truthfulness in Statements to Others) imposes a duty on lawyers to be truthful when dealing with others on a client's behalf. A lawyer who threatens criminal prosecution, without any actual intent to so proceed, violates Rule 4.1.
>
> Finally, Rule 3.1 (Meritorious Claims and Contentions) prohibits an advocate from asserting frivolous claims. A lawyer who

[handwritten margin note: MPC says it is not extortion if the payment is restitution]

---

172. See Wolfram, Modern Legal Ethics §13.5.5, at 718. See also ABA Comm. on Ethics and Prof. Resp., Formal Op. 94-383 (use of threat to file disciplinary charge against opposing lawyer to obtain advantage in civil matter is constrained by various provisions of Model Rules although not directly prohibited).

173. 2 Hazard & Hodes, The Law of Lawyering §4.4:103, at 760.

threatens criminal prosecution that is not well founded in fact and in law, or threatens such prosecution in furtherance of a civil claim that is not well founded, violates Rule 3.1.[174]

The committee concluded that if a lawyer did not violate any of these rules, a threat of criminal prosecution to settle a civil matter was proper if the crime was *related* to the civil matter. The committee also decided that a lawyer could agree not to report a criminal offense provided such an agreement did not amount to compounding a crime. The opinion refers to rules of ethics and criminal statutes in force in the jurisdiction in which the lawyer practices. The West Virginia Supreme Court largely adopted the approach of ABA Formal Opinion 92-363 in Committee on Legal Ethics v. Printz,[175] which held that an attorney may ethically threaten criminal prosecution to obtain restitution of embezzled funds.[176]

It should be noted that under the Model Rules a threat may sometimes be improper even if it does not involve a threat of criminal prosecution: for example, a threat that constitutes a tort or that is made for an improper purpose. Thus, courts have held that threats to give undue publicity to the other party's private matters in order to induce settlement are improper. In State v. Harrington[177] the Vermont Supreme Court held that a threat made by the wife's divorce lawyer to publicize her husband's adultery, a crime, in order to coerce settlement amounted to criminal extortion. Similarly, in In re Dienes[178] a lawyer received a public reprimand for making a veiled threat to inform the newspapers about his former employer's business unless the employer withdrew a motion seeking attorney fees from the lawyer.

174. ABA Comm. on Ethics and Prof. Resp., Formal Op. 92-363, at 4-5.
175. 416 S.E.2d 720 (W. Va. 1992).
176. See also Ruberton v. Gabage, 654 A.2d 1002 (N.J. Super. Ct. App. Div.), *cert. denied,* 663 A.2d 1358 (N.J. 1995) (in wrongful discharge case, threat by defense counsel to institute criminal charges unless plaintiff accepted settlement not actionable as abuse of process because process not used and because statements made in course of judicial proceeding are absolutely privileged).
177. 260 A.2d 692 (Vt. 1969). See generally Joseph M. Livermore, Lawyer Extortion, 20 Ariz. L. Rev. 403 (1978).
178. 571 A.2d 1303 (N.J. 1990).

Approaches to negotiation

Scholars who have studied lawyer negotiations have developed a typology of approaches to negotiation.[179] Fundamental to lawyer negotiation is a distinction between *style* and *strategy*. Negotiating style refers to the personality traits that the lawyer presents in negotiation.[180] Professor Gerald Williams has identified two basic negotiating styles: competitive (or adversarial) and cooperative (or problem solving). Williams listed the following as personality traits of effective competitive negotiators:

> dominating, forceful, attacking, aggressive, ambitious, clever, honest, perceptive, analytical, convincing, and self-controlled.[181]

He identified the following as personality traits of successful cooperative negotiators:

> trustworthy, fair, honest, courteous, personable, tactful, sincere, perceptive, reasonable, convincing, and self-controlled.[182]

Negotiation strategy refers to the goals of the negotiation. Building on Professor Williams's work, Professor Carrie Menkel-Meadow identified two negotiating strategies: adversarial and problem solving.[183] While the strategies appear to be identical to the styles of negotiating, a fundamental difference exists between technique of negotiation (style) and goals of negotiation (strategy). Professor Menkel-Meadow went on to discuss four possible approaches to negotiation that lawyers could adopt; these four approaches represent the logical combinations of the two styles and two strategies:

	Style	*Strategy*
(1)	Competitive	adversarial;
(2)	Cooperative	adversarial;

---

179. See Robert M. Bastress & Joseph D. Harbaugh, Interviewing, Counseling, and Negotiating 390-397 (1990).
180. Id. at 390.
181. Id. at 391.
182. Id.
183. Id. at 393.

(3) Competitive problem solvers;
(4) Cooperative problem solvers.[184]

For example, lawyers who approach negotiations with friendly, courteous, caring attitudes but use these techniques to achieve the highest possible settlements for their clients are employing cooperative adversarial negotiation methods.

How does a lawyer make a choice of negotiating style and strategy? Professors Bastress and Harbaugh argue that the choice of approach to a negotiation should be made carefully by the lawyer and client after considering the relevant factors, including the following:

1. The goals of the client and the needs of the opposing party. For example, if the client's only goal is to obtain as much of the only fungible commodity at issue as is possible, then an adversarial strategy is likely to produce the greater gain. On the other hand, if a continuing relationship between the parties is their primary aim, problem-solving may be more appropriate.

2. The configuration of shared, independent, and conflicting needs of the parties. For example, if the needs of the parties do not conflict but are shared or independent, it suggests that a cooperative problem-solving strategy could be very successful.

3. The resources, including money, personnel, time, and the like, available to your client and to the opposing party.

4. The ability of the parties to creatively generate additional issues and resources to expand the subject matter of the negotiation. The greater the number of issues and the amount of resources involved in the negotiation, the easier it is to move from adversarial to problem-solving.

5. The comfort or discomfort you (and your client) experience when you behave as a competitive versus cooperative bargainer. While we encourage you to experiment with the four unions of style and strategy, we acknowledge it is difficult to successfully use a negotiation model with which you are uncomfortable. Your client's needs must also be considered. The angry client in a wrongful death case, for instance, may not be satisfied with a cooperative problem-solving approach.

6. The style and strategy combination selected by your opponent. Professor Williams, for example, found that effective com-

184. Id. at 395.

petitive negotiators were quite successful when matched with co-operative bargainers.[185]

Bastress and Harbaugh go on to argue that the choice of approach to negotiation can change during the course of negotiation: Lawyers must plan for negotiation but should also remain flexible.

Model Rule 1.2(a) states that a lawyer must abide by the "client's decisions concerning the objectives of representation . . . and shall consult with the client as to the means by which they are to be pursued." The Bounds of Advocacy adopted by the American Academy of Matrimonial Lawyers contains the following provision on tactics in matrimonial cases:

> **2.27   An Attorney Should Refuse to Assist in Vindictive Conduct Toward a Spouse or Third Person and Should Not Do Anything to Increase the Emotional Level of the Dispute.**

> COMMENT
>
> Although the client has the right to determine the "objectives of representation," after consulting with the client the attorney may limit the objectives and the means by which the objectives are to be pursued. [See Model Rule 1.2(c).] The matrimonial lawyer should make every effort to lower the emotional level of the interaction between the parties and their counsel. Some dissension and bad feelings can be avoided by a frank discussion with the client at the outset of how the attorney handles cases, including what the attorney will and will not do regarding vindictive conduct or actions likely to adversely affect the children's interests. Although not essential, a letter to the client confirming the understanding, before specific issues or requests arise, is advisable. To the extent that the client is unwilling to accept any limitations on objectives or means, the attorney should decline the representation.
>
> If such a discussion did not occur, or the client despite a prior understanding asks the attorney to engage in conduct the attorney believes to be imprudent or repugnant, the attorney should attempt to convince the client to work toward family harmony or the interests of the children. Conduct in the interests of the children or family will almost always be in the client's long term best interests.

185. Id. at 402.

Similarly, Rule 2.25 of the Bounds of Advocacy provides as follows: "An attorney should not contest child custody or visitation for either financial leverage or vindictiveness."

In a study of lawyer negotiations, Professors Ronald Gilson and Robert Mnookin have developed a model for analyzing whether lawyers contribute to cooperation or conflict in resolving disputes. They conclude that lawyers can promote cooperation and thereby reduce the transaction costs involved in disputes. They also identify a number of institutional factors that are more conducive to cooperation.[186]

Problem 4-6

Mediation and Arbitration

    a. You represent Martinez Data Systems, Inc. (MDS), a closely held corporation that provides computer consulting services to a wide variety of clients. Raymond Martinez, the president of the company, has asked you to prepare a basic consulting contract that MDS can use when it enters into agreements with customers. In addition to reviewing MDS's current contract, you have researched various form books and checklists for ideas regarding the agreement. One issue raised in the form books is whether the agreement should include some form of alternative dispute resolution provision. Would you suggest that MDS consider including such a provision? If so, what advice would you give if Martinez asked for your recommendation regarding alternative dispute resolution?

    b. A partner in your firm has been appointed as a mediator in a divorce case pursuant to court rules that

---

186. Ronald J. Gilson & Robert H. Mnookin, Disputing Through Agents: Cooperation and Conflict Between Lawyers in Litigation, 94 Colum. L. Rev. 509 (1994). See also Russell Korobkin & Chris Guthrie, Psychology, Economics, and Settlement: A New Look at the Role of the Lawyer, 76 Tex. L. Rev. 77 (1997) (experimental evidence showing that lawyers share analytical approach that tends to promote higher rate of settlement than clients would achieve on their own).

call for court-annexed mediation in domestic cases. Court rules require the mediator to hold an orientation session in which the mediator explains the nature of the process to the parties and their lawyers. The partner has asked you to prepare a draft statement that he will use as the basis of his opening remarks.

Read Model Rules 1.1, 1.2, 1.4, 2.2, and comments.

Alternative dispute resolution in general

While *alternative dispute resolution* (ADR) is a rapidly growing field, most students still have little exposure to the area. We begin, then, with some basic ideas about ADR as an introduction to and background for discussion of several ethical issues. As you study this material, keep in mind that negotiation is one of the most important forms of ADR. We have already studied some of the major ethical problems in negotiation in Problem 4-5.

Alternative dispute resolution refers to various procedures other than litigation for resolving disputes.[187] The interest in and use of ADR has grown rapidly in recent years as public and professional dissatisfaction with delay, expense, and inflexibility of the judicial system has increased. ADR comes in a wide variety of forms and procedures.

The most common forms of ADR are *arbitration* and *mediation*. In arbitration a dispute is presented to a neutral decision-maker (or to a panel of decisionmakers) who has the authority to render a decision that is binding on the parties. Many controversies are submitted to arbitration pursuant to agreement of the parties. Agreements to arbitrate fall into two categories: predispute and postdispute. In predispute agreements, the parties contractually agree to submit to arbitration any disputes (or perhaps a defined category of disputes) that may arise in their relationship in the future. For example, the parties to a long-term supply con-

---

187. See Stephen B. Goldberg et al., Dispute Resolution: Negotiation, Mediation, and Other Processes 489-497 (2d ed. 1992) (with bibliography); PLI, What the Business Lawyer Needs to Know About ADR (William L. D. Barrett chair 1998); Nancy H. Rogers & Craig A. McEwen, Mediation: Law, Policy & Practice (2d ed. 1994).

tract could agree that if a dispute arises regarding performance of the agreement, the dispute will be submitted to arbitration. In postdispute arbitration agreements, the parties agree to submit to arbitration a controversy that has already arisen. For example, parties involved in a minor automobile accident could agree to submit their dispute to arbitration.

Controversies can also be submitted to arbitration by court rule rather than by agreement of the parties. A growing number of state and federal courts have adopted rules for court-annexed arbitration under which disputes that meet certain requirements are sent to arbitration.

Arbitration procedures and methods of selection of the arbitrators vary depending on how the arbitration arises. In court-annexed arbitration, court rules determine the procedure to be employed and the method of selection of the arbitrators. In predispute and postdispute agreements to arbitrate, the parties must specify the procedures to be used and the method of selection of the arbitrators. The disputants can, however, adopt rules of procedure prepared by private providers of arbitration services, such as the American Arbitration Association.

The fundamental difference between mediation and arbitration is that mediators do not have the power to render decisions that are binding on the parties. Instead, mediators attempt to assist the parties in reaching an agreement. This one difference, however, affects the entire process. Mediation tends to be more informal, with the mediator meeting both individually and collectively with the parties to gather information, gain understanding of the positions of the parties, and explore ideas for settlement. Arbitration, although less formal than adjudication, still usually involves adversarial presentations by the parties, often in the format of a traditional trial or hearing.

While arbitration and mediation are the most common forms of ADR, many other hybrid forms have been developed. For example, in *med-arb* the parties agree to mediation, but also agree that if mediation is unsuccessful for a certain period of time, the matter is then submitted to binding arbitration. Parties have used *summary jury trials* and *minitrials* to gain information about the likely result if their dispute were submitted to trial, but without the delay and expense involved in a full-fledged trial. The information gained from these mock trials often leads to a negotiated settlement. Indeed, parties have virtually unlimited flexibility to create dispute resolution mechanisms tailored to their particular needs.[188]

Ethical obligations of lawyers to advise clients regarding ADR

Do lawyers have an ethical obligation to advise clients of the availability of ADR? Rule 1.2(a) of the Model Rules provides that a lawyer "shall consult with the client as to the means by which [the objectives of representation] are to be pursued." Rule 1.4(b) states that a "lawyer shall explain a matter to the extent reasonably necessary to permit the client to make informed decisions regarding the representation." Some commentators reason that these current rules of ethics already require lawyers to inform clients of ADR.[189] Other writers have argued that the rules should be amended to make it clear that such an obligation exists.[190] In fact, some jurisdictions have done so.[191] For example, EC 7-5 of the Georgia Code of Professional Responsibility states: "A lawyer as adviser has a duty to advise the client as to various forms of dispute resolution. When a matter is likely to involve litigation, a lawyer has a duty to inform the client of forms of dispute resolution which might constitute reasonable alternatives to litigation." Moreover, it has been suggested that lawyers who fail to provide advice about ADR to their clients may be subject to malpractice liability.[192]

Model Rule 1.1 requires lawyers to provide competent representation to their clients. In advising clients regarding ADR,

188. Stephen P. Doyle & Roger S. Haydock, Without the Punches: Resolving Disputes Without Litigation 1-11 (Equilaw 1991).

189. See Robert F. Cochran, Jr., Must Lawyers Tell Clients About ADR? 48 Arb. J. 8 (June 1993).

190. Frank E. A. Sander & Michael L. Prigoff, Exchange, Professional Responsibility: Should There Be a Duty to Advise of ADR Options? 76-Nov. A.B.A. J. 50 (1990).

191. Monica L. Warmbrod, Comment, Could an Attorney Face Disciplinary Actions or Even Legal Malpractice Liability for Failure to Inform Clients of Alternative Dispute Resolution? 27 Cumb. L. Rev. 791, 813-814 (1996–1997).

192. Robert F. Cochran, Jr., Legal Representation and the Next Steps Toward Client Control: Attorney Malpractice for the Failure to Allow the Client to Control Negotiation and Pursue Alternatives to Litigation, 47 Wash. & Lee L. Rev. 819 (1990).

competent lawyers must be aware of and must be able to explain to their clients the advantages and disadvantages of ADR. Consider the following exchange on the advantages and disadvantages of arbitration:

> The scene is the law offices of Howland and Smith, a firm with 200 lawyers, including a large litigation section. Jane Garrity, a litigator, and Jim Smith, the firm's alternative dispute resolution specialist, are discussing how to handle a pending case involving one of Howland and Smith's clients, Bramson Ball Bearing Company. Bramson had sold 50,000 ball bearings to Jones Machine Company, a long-time customer, which Jones refused to pay for, claiming they were defective. Bramson denies any defects in the ball bearings and has asked Howland and Smith to bring suit against Jones for $75,000, the amount Jones had agreed to pay.

Smith: Jane, it seems to me this case would be ideal for arbitration. As you know we've got a three- or four-year delay before trial, and Bramson really wants to get its money. If we go to arbitration, we could wind this case up in six or seven months instead of waiting three or four years and then getting a settlement on the courthouse steps or going through litigation and a lengthy appeal. Moreover, there are likely to be difficult technical issues in connection with Jones's claim that the ball bearings were defective. If we go to court, we might have trouble explaining those issues to a judge or jury, but if we go to arbitration, we can choose an arbitrator with technical expertise.

Garrity: You ADR people are always singing the same tune: anything is better than the courts. My experience is that arbitration leaves a lot to be desired. First, it's not that easy to find a competent arbitrator. A lot of them really don't know what they're doing, and in the end they just split the difference.

Smith: I think you're too cynical about our ability to find a good arbitrator. For example, if you contact the American Arbitration Association or the Center for Public Resources they will send both parties a list of proposed arbitrators, with background material on each. Each party can strike one name from the list and rank the others in order of preference. The

AAA or CPR will appoint the highest mutual choice. Other dispute resolution organizations follow similar procedures to assist disputing parties in selecting a high-quality arbitrator.

Garrity: That's fine *if* the list of arbitrators they send you has high-quality people on it, but I've heard that's not always so. Then there's no appeal; if you get a bum award, one that's based on a misapplication of the law or is contrary to the weight of the evidence, you're just stuck with it.

Smith: But how important, as a practical matter, is a right of appeal in a case like this? Not only would an appeal add to our costs, but this is a straight breach of contract case with no novel legal issues. The likelihood that an appellate court would reverse the trial court in a case like this is surely not very substantial. From that perspective, it really doesn't matter much whether we're in court or before an arbitrator.

Garrity: Maybe you're right about that, but I think that the knowledge that an appellate court may be reviewing what he does motivates the trial judge to perform to the best of his ability. That's largely missing in arbitration, where there is no meaningful judicial review.

Smith: But if we're careful in selecting the arbitrator, that's much less of a concern. Besides, what we give up in terms of a right to appeal, we gain in finality. You've told me that we have a strong case here, and if we win we won't have to worry about Jones dragging things out by taking an appeal. They could, but the likelihood of success would be so low that it's not probable that they would.

Garrity: Well, I do think that we have a winner, but you never know what an arbitrator or judge, much less a jury, will do to you. That brings me to my next concern about going to arbitration. If I lose a case in court, I can blame the judge. But if we go to arbitration, and I've participated in selecting the arbitrator, I'm likely to get the blame if we lose. So while you praise arbitration because you can pick the arbitrator, that doesn't have much appeal to me.

Smith: Well, if you don't want to select the arbitrator, turn the entire selection procedure over to AAA or CPR.

	That way you can't be held responsible for who the arbitrator is.
Garrity:	That's a possible approach, but I'm not comfortable with turning the selection process completely over to someone else.
Smith:	But that's exactly what you do when you go to court! Still, I do have another approach for you. You could pick one arbitrator, the other side could pick one, and those two could agree on a third arbitrator. That would increase costs somewhat, but it would give you some input in selecting the crucial member of the panel. It would also ensure that at least one of the arbitrators is sympathetic to your arguments.
Garrity:	No, that's even worse than a single arbitrator. In addition to tripling the costs, a three-person panel more than triples the delays associated with arbitration. It's hard enough to find mutually agreeable hearing dates when you have to work with the schedules of two busy lawyers and one arbitrator: it's almost impossible if you add two more arbitrators. And, speaking of delay, I've heard of cases in which the defendant has tied up an arbitration almost indefinitely by running to court whenever there is some procedural dispute.
Smith:	I'm aware of cases like that, too, but they tend to be limited to situations in which arbitration takes place under a preexisting contractual commitment to arbitrate. Those commitments are usually honored, but sometimes when a dispute actually arises, one party sees an advantage in litigation rather than arbitration. In that situation, the reluctant party may resist arbitration in every way it can, including going to court to complain of alleged procedural irregularities in the arbitration. If, however, both parties voluntarily agree to arbitration at the time the dispute arises, neither of them is likely to go to court to block arbitration. In that situation, which is what we will have here if Bramson and Jones agree to arbitrate, a skilled arbitrator can dispose of the case quickly and effectively.
Garrity:	That's another problem. Those buzz words "quickly" and "effectively" mean something different to me — namely, that there's no attention paid

to the rules of evidence. In arbitration they use the "kitchen sink" approach: everything goes in.

Smith: Well, that's probably an overstatement. There are some arbitrators, particularly those who are lawyers, who are quite strict about what evidence they will admit. If you want an arbitrator like that, you can select one. Alternatively, you can provide that the arbitrator must abide by whatever evidentiary rules you adopt. I just can't emphasize strongly enough that the arbitration format is entirely within the control of the parties. You can make the arbitration as formal or informal, as much or as little like a federal court procedure as you wish. Just because you contact some arbitration agency to select the arbitrator and administer the proceedings doesn't mean you must adopt their rules. That's one of the virtues of arbitration, and I wish that more people would take advantage of it.

Still, I would not advise altering standard arbitration practice in this case. You are right in assuming that the general tendency of arbitrators is not to apply the rules of evidence strictly. As I see it, though, that's a plus for arbitration, not a minus. I've long found the rules of evidence to be a major cause of unnecessarily lengthy trials. Some trial lawyers even say that the rules don't always keep evidence out: they just ensure that it takes longer to get it in, particularly in a jury trial. Surely there are simpler ways of establishing the facts, and that's just what arbitration or a properly run bench trial does: it makes it possible to get to the heart of the matter quickly and without a lot of procedural folderol.

There's one other argument in favor of arbitration that we haven't talked about yet, and that is its privacy. This case involves Jones's complaints about the quality of Bramson's ball bearings, and I doubt that Bramson is very happy at the prospect of Jones spreading those complaints all over the court records, so any newspaper reporter who is interested can write about them. If we go to arbitration, the proceedings will be entirely private, and so will the arbitrator's decision.

Garrity: That's a nice point, but I have still another concern. There's a lot we don't know about this case yet. If we go to arbitration, won't we lose the discovery opportunities we'd have in court?

Smith: Once again, that depends on you and the other party. If you want some discovery, it's important to provide for it in your agreement to arbitrate. If you don't, you may not get any more than the other side will agree to, since many arbitrators will not compel discovery to which either party objects.

My advice on this point would be to provide for only as much discovery as you absolutely need to prepare for trial. One of the things that makes arbitration attractive is that discovery has gotten completely out of hand in court. If we were to go through normal court discovery in this case, say four or five depositions, plus the five or so days you've told me it should take to try it, that could cost Jones as much as $50,000. That just doesn't make sense in a case with a maximum recovery of $75,000. I'm sure that in arbitration, if we could agree on limited discovery — say, two depositions each — and then a skilled arbitrator who didn't waste time by strictly applying the rules of evidence and following formal court room procedures, we could try this case in a maximum of two days at a cost of approximately $20,000. Even adding the arbitrator's fee and an administrative fee for the organization supplying the arbitrator, which together would probably be less than $2,500, we'd still come out way ahead, and we wouldn't have to worry about the costs of an appeal. That's why I think it makes sense to arbitrate this case, not to litigate it. Indeed, I almost think that an attorney who doesn't at least advise his client about the alternatives to litigation for resolving disputes might be guilty of malpractice. So I think you should raise this possibility with Bramson, and if they are interested, discuss it with Jones's lawyer. You might even be surprised to find him receptive to this idea.[193]

---

193. Stephen B. Goldberg et al., Dispute Resolution: Negotiation, Mediation, and Other Processes 203-206 (2nd ed. 1992), adapted from 75-June A.B.A. J. 70 (1989).

The advantages and disadvantages of ADR depend, of course, on the type of ADR under consideration.[194] Some scholars have criticized the growing use of ADR.[195] In particular, the fairness of mediation, especially in divorce cases involving an imbalance of power between husband and wife, has been questioned.[196]

Ethical obligations of lawyers serving as mediators and arbitrators

With the growth of ADR it appears likely that lawyers will increasingly be called on to serve as mediators or arbitrators of disputes. What are the ethical obligations governing lawyers serving as "neutrals"? Model Rule 2.2 refers to lawyers acting as intermediaries. We will discuss this concept in more detail in connection with Problem 5-1. Despite the linguistic similarity, representation as an intermediary differs dramatically from service as a mediator. Comment 2 to Rule 2.2 provides as follows:

> The Rule does not apply to a lawyer acting as arbitrator or mediator between or among parties who are not clients of the lawyer, even where the lawyer has been appointed with the concurrence of the parties. In performing such a role the lawyer may be subject to applicable codes of ethics [prepared by organizations that provide ADR services].

When a lawyer acts as an intermediary under Rule 2.2, the lawyer serves as counsel for both parties. The lawyer provides legal advice

194. On the advantages and disadvantages of mediation, see Rogers & McEwen, Mediation: Law, Policy & Practice ch. 3. See also Special Issue, The Mediation Alternative, 49 Disp. Resol. J. 1 (March 1994).

195. See, e.g., Lisa Bernstein, Understanding the Limits of Court-Annexed ADR: A Critique of Federal Court-Annexed Arbitration Programs, 141 U. Pa. L. Rev. 2169 (1993).

196. See Penelope E. Bryan, Reclaiming Professionalism: The Lawyer's Role in Divorce Mediation, 28 Fam. L.Q. 177 (1994); Trina Grillo, The Mediation Alternative: Process Dangers for Women, 100 Yale L.J. 1545 (1991); Scott H. Hughes, Elizabeth's Story: Exploring Power Imbalances in Divorce Mediation, 8 Geo. J. Legal Ethics 553 (1995). But see Craig A. McEwen et al., Bring in the Lawyers: Challenging the Dominant Approaches to Ensuring Fairness in Divorce Mediation, 79 Minn. L. Rev. 1317 (1995) (arguing that lawyer-participant mandatory mediation in divorce cases properly balances fairness and efficiency considerations).

to both parties and may draft a document that expresses an agreement reached between the parties. By contrast, when a lawyer serves as a mediator, the lawyer is not representing either party. Instead, the lawyer serves as a neutral, assisting the parties in resolving a dispute.

The conclusion that a lawyer serving as a mediator is performing a different role from a lawyer functioning as an intermediary does little to determine what ethical obligations apply to lawyer-neutrals.[197] (A separate question is what ethical obligations should apply to nonlawyers functioning as neutrals.) One approach to defining the ethical obligations of lawyer-neutrals is to adopt a special rule of ethics that sets forth the duties of lawyers serving in this capacity. Such a rule has been proposed to the Ethics 2000 Commission.[198] A second approach is to reject a special rule governing lawyers serving as neutrals. This was the approach adopted by the Restatement[199] and appears to be the likely course that the Ethics 2000 Commission will follow. Under this approach the Model Rules would apply to lawyers serving as neutrals only to the extent that the rules apply to lawyers serving in a nonlegal capacity[200] or to the extent that a court extends the Model Rules by analogy to cover service as a neutral. Some courts have in fact done so. For example, in Poly Software International, Inc. v. Su[201] a lawyer who had served as a mediator in an intellectual

197. For a discussion of the range of ethical problems facing lawyer-neutrals, see Carrie Menkel-Meadow, Ethics in Alternative Dispute Resolution: New Issues, No Answers from the Adversary Conception of Lawyers' Responsibilities, 38 S. Tex. L. Rev. 407 (1997). Menkel-Meadow's article is part of a Symposium, The Lawyer's Duties and Responsibilities in Dispute Resolution, 38 S. Tex. L. Rev. 375 (1997).

198. See CPR-Georgetown Commission on Ethics and Standards in ADR, Proposed Model Rule of Professional Conduct for the Lawyer as Third Party Neutral (1999). See also Judith L. Maute, Public Values and Private Justice: A Case for Mediator Accountability, 4 Geo. J. Legal Ethics 503 (1991) (proposing rule for lawyers serving as mediators).

199. See Carrie Menkel-Meadow, The Silences of the Restatement of the Law Governing Lawyers: Lawyering as Only Adversary Practice, 10 Geo. J. Legal Ethics 631 (1997).

200. Some commentators have argued that Model Rule 5.7 dealing with ancillary services applies to mediation. See Fiona Furlan et al., Ethical Guidelines for Attorney-Mediators: Are Attorneys Bound by Ethical Codes for Lawyers When Acting as Mediators? 14 J. Am. Acad. Matrimonial Law. 267, 290-294 (1997). Very few states have adopted Rule 5.7. We will examine Model Rule 5.7 in Chapter 7.

201. 880 F. Supp. 1487 (D. Utah 1995).

property matter was disqualified from representing one party to the mediation against the coparticipant in a subsequent substantially related matter. The court relied by analogy on Model Rule 1.9(a). Finally, ethical standards applicable to lawyer-neutrals could be established either by court rule for court-annexed proceedings[202] or by private organizations that sponsor or promote alternative dispute resolution. Comment 2 to Rule 2.2 refers to specialized codes of ethics that apply to mediators and arbitrators. Some of the more important specialized codes of ethics include the following:

> ABA, Standards of Practice for Lawyer Mediators in Family Disputes (1984)
>
> American Arbitration Association, American Bar Association, and Society of Professionals in Dispute Resolution, Standards of Conduct for Mediators (1995)
>
> American Arbitration Association, Code of Ethics for Arbitrators in Commercial Disputes (1977)
>
> Society of Professionals in Dispute Resolution (SPIDR), Ethical Standards of Professional Responsibility (1986)

The ABA Standards of Practice for Lawyer Mediators in Family Disputes provide as follows (Specific Considerations are included for Standard I but are omitted for other standards.):

> I.   The mediator has a duty to define and describe the process of mediation and its cost before the parties reach an agreement to mediate.

Before the actual mediation sessions begin, the mediator shall conduct an orientation session to give an overview of the process and to assess the appropriateness of mediation for the participants. Among the topics covered, the mediator shall discuss the following:

A. The mediator shall define the process in context so that the participants understand the differences between mediation

---

202. See Robert B. Moberly, Ethical Standards for Court-Appointed Mediators and Florida's Mandatory Mediation Experiment, 21 Fla. St. U. L. Rev. 701 (1994). On the legal liability of court-appointed mediators, see Wagshal v. Foster, 28 F.3d 1249 (D.C. Cir. 1994) cert. denied, 514 U.S. 1004 (1995) (quasi-judicial absolute immunity for court-appointed mediators and neutral case evaluators).

and other means of conflict resolution available to them. In defining the process, the mediator shall also distinguish it from therapy or marriage counseling.

B. The mediator shall obtain sufficient information from the participants so they can mutually define the issues to be resolved in mediation.

C. It should be emphasized that the mediator may make suggestions for the participants to consider, such as alternative ways of resolving problems, and may draft proposals for the participants' consideration, but that all decisions are to be made voluntarily by the participants themselves, and the mediator's views are to be given no independent weight or credence.

D. The duties and responsibilities that the mediator and the participants accept in the mediation process shall be agreed upon. The mediator shall instruct the participants that either of them or the mediator has the right to suspend or terminate the process at any time.

E. The mediator shall assess the ability and willingness of the participants to mediate. The mediator has a continuing duty to assess his or her own ability and willingness to undertake mediation with the particular participants and the issues to be mediated. The mediator shall not continue and shall terminate the process, if in his or her judgment, one of the parties is not able or willing to participate in good faith.

F. The mediator shall explain the fees for mediation. It is inappropriate for a mediator to charge a contingency fee or to base the fee on the outcome of the mediation process.

G. The mediator shall inform the participants of the need to employ independent legal counsel for advice throughout the mediation process. The mediator shall inform the participants that the mediator cannot represent either or both of them in a marital dissolution or in any legal action.

H. The mediator shall discuss the issue of separate sessions. The mediator shall reach an understanding with the participants as to whether and under what circumstances the mediator may meet alone with either of them or with any third party. [ABA Commentary to Paragraph H: The mediator cannot act as lawyer for either party or for them jointly and should make that clear to both parties.]

I. It should be brought to the participants' attention that emotions play a part in the decision-making process. The mediator shall attempt to elicit from each of the participants a confirmation that each understands the connection between one's own emotions and the bargaining process.

II.   The mediator shall not voluntarily disclose information obtained through the mediation process without the prior consent of both participants.

III.   The mediator has a duty to be impartial.

IV.   The mediator has a duty to assure that the mediation participants make decisions based upon sufficient information and knowledge.

V.   The mediator has a duty to suspend or terminate mediation whenever continuation of the process would harm one or more of the participants.

VI.   The mediator has a continuing duty to advise each of the mediation participants to obtain legal review prior to reaching any agreement.

Because arbitrators, unlike mediators, have the power to render binding decisions, concerns about impartiality or conflicts of interest may be more worrisome in arbitration proceedings than in mediations. Canon II of the Code of Ethics of the American Arbitration Association for Arbitrators in Commercial Disputes (1977) provides as follows: "An arbitrator should disclose any interest or relationship likely to affect impartiality or which might create an appearance of partiality or bias." Disclosure is required for "(1) any direct or indirect financial or personal interest in the outcome of the arbitration; (2) any existing or past financial, business, professional, family or social relationships which are likely to affect impartiality or which might reasonably create an appearance of partiality or bias."[203]

An arbitrator's failure to disclose facts that could affect the arbitrator's impartiality will not necessarily invalidate any award. In Commonwealth Coatings Corp. v. Continental Casualty Co.[204] the Supreme Court invalidated an arbitration award under section 10 of the United States Arbitration Act, 9 U.S.C. §10, which provides that a court may vacate an award "[w]here there was evident

---

203. See Code of Ethics of the American Arbitration Association for Arbitrators in Commercial Disputes, Canon II(A) (1977). See also Ethical Standards of Professional Responsibility of the Society of Professionals in Dispute Resolution (SPIDR) (1986) (conflict of interest).

204. 393 U.S. 145 (1968).

partiality or corruption in the arbitrators, or either of them.''[205] In that case the neutral arbitrator (the one selected by the arbitrators chosen by each of the parties) was an engineering consultant who had substantial business ties with one of the parties. The arbitrator failed to disclose the relationship. The Court vacated the award, but the basis for its decision is obscure. Four Justices held that the award should be set aside because arbitrators, like judges, should disclose even the "slightest pecuniary interest."[206] Two concurring Justices disagreed with the plurality opinion that arbitrators should be treated like judges, but they agreed that the award should be set aside when the arbitrator failed to disclose a substantial interest.[207] Three dissenting Justices would have upheld the award because there was no evidence of "evident partiality" as required by the act. The award was unanimous and the nondisclosure was innocent.

By contrast, in Merit Insurance Co. v. Leatherby Insurance Co.[208] the Seventh Circuit refused to set aside an arbitration award in which the arbitrator failed to disclose that he had worked under the president and principal stockholder of one of the parties. The employment ended more than 10 years before the arbitration; both the president and the arbitrator testified that they had had little professional contact and no social contact.[209] The arbitrator had failed, however, to list the employment on forms required by the American Arbitration Association and he did not mention the relationship when the arbitration began even though he recognized the president.[210] Writing for the court, Judge Posner rejected Leatherby's argument that an arbitrator should be disqualified if his relationship with one of the parties was more than "trivial." Judge Posner noted that there were substantial differences be-

---

205. In addition to the federal arbitration act, most states have enacted arbitration statutes. Some state statutes and case law are more restrictive of arbitration than the federal act. The Supreme Court has broadly construed the federal act to preempt state law and to apply to the full extent of the Commerce Clause whenever a transaction affects interstate commerce, regardless of whether the parties contemplated an interstate transaction. See Allied-Bruce Terminix Cos. v. Dodson, 513 U.S. 265 (1995).

206. 393 U.S. at 148.

207. Id. at 150-152.

208. 714 F.2d 673 (7th Cir.), *cert. denied*, 464 U.S. 1009 (1983).

209. 714 F.2d at 677.

210. Id. at 678.

tween arbitration and litigation involving a trade-off between expertise and neutrality. In arbitration proceedings, parties select arbitrators because of their expertise; this necessitates a lessened expectation of impartiality. Accordingly, Posner adopted the following test for disqualification of arbitrators:

> [T]he test in this case is not whether the relationship was trivial; it is whether, having due regard for the different expectations regarding impartiality that parties bring to arbitration than to litigation, the relationship . . . was so intimate — personally, socially, professionally, or financially — as to cast serious doubt on [the arbitrator's] impartiality.[211]

Considering all the facts involved, particularly the passage of time, the court found no basis for disqualification of the arbitrator.

Moreover, the court went on to hold that even if the arbitrator had violated applicable ethical standards, that would not necessarily result in judicial nullification of the award. Citing section 10 of the United States Arbitration Act, the court ruled that the standard of "evident partiality or corruption" was more demanding than the ethical standard and required either proof of actual bias or at least that the "circumstances must be powerfully suggestive of bias."[212]

C.   Delivery of Legal Services in Civil Cases

1.   Advertising and Solicitation

─────────────── **Problem 4-7** ───────────────

Law Firm Marketing Practices

    a.   You are a member of a small, aggressive plaintiff's firm, Minelli & O'Hara, that wants to expand its personal injury and products liability practice. The firm

211. Id. at 680.
212. Id. at 681.

plans to run a series of television advertisements. Each ad will begin with a lawyer sitting on the side of his desk (in shirt-sleeves to convey the image of being hard-working), saying the following:

> If you have been injured in an accident or while at work, we at Minelli & O'Hara are available to meet with you to discuss your legal rights. There is no charge for an initial visit and no fees are due unless we secure a recovery on your behalf.

Each ad in the series will conclude as follows:

> Call Minelli & O'Hara at 1-800-MONEY NOW.

Between the opening and the conclusion, the ad will have a "How we're different" segment. The following are two of the segments that the firm plans to run:

> (1)   "How we're different: We offer discount fees. Most firms charge one-third or more to handle your case. At Minelli & O'Hara we will represent you for a 25 percent fee."
>
> (2)   "How we're different: With most other firms, you must wait until settlement or judgment to get any money. At Minelli & O'Hara, if your case is one of clear liability, we can help you get money within 60 days."

In addition to the television advertising, the firm will acquire names and addresses of victims from police department accident reports, which are a matter of public record. It will then send letters to individuals involved in accidents informing them that the firm is available for consultation about their legal rights arising out of the accident.

The firm would like your opinion about the ethical propriety of these plans.

b.   Because of the increased competitive environment for the practice of law, many law firms have begun aggressive marketing programs. The following is a list of some of the ways in which law firms are now marketing their services. Be prepared to discuss the ethical propriety or risks involved in these activities.

1. News releases highlighting activities of members of the firm, including recent litigation successes.
2. Client surveys to determine client needs and degree of satisfaction with the firm.
3. Cross-marketing, which involves contacting existing clients to advise them of services offered by the firm that the client is not currently using.
4. Client audits, in which the firm volunteers to audit the client's legal affairs searching for potential problems, at no cost or reduced cost to the client.
5. Offering to conduct a "mock trial" of a client's troublesome case to assist the client and current outside counsel to appraise the case.
6. Preparation of law firm brochures showing the backgrounds and areas of practice of the members of the firm along with a list of clients regularly represented.
7. Newsletters to current and potential clients advising them of recent developments of interest.
8. Sponsorship of seminars, to which potential clients are personally invited, on various legal topics presented by members of the firm.
9. Hiring public relations firms and marketing directors to develop the firm's marketing program.
10. Aggressive entertainment policies in which members of the firm invite officials of existing clients to accompany them on expense-paid trips.
11. Development of strategic alliances with other firms to refer and accept referrals in areas of expertise.
12. Creation of sophisticated Web pages that provide information about members of the firm and material about areas of law in which the firm practices (both directly and through links to other sites). Many Web pages are in-

teractive, allowing potential clients to make inquiries, to send information by completing forms on the Web page, and to arrange for electronic appointments. In addition, lawyers are participating in chat rooms and other real-time methods of communication with potential clients.

Advice?

    c. In 1991, the Florida Supreme Court amended its ethics rules to impose restrictions on electronic advertising.[213] The court revised the rules again in December 1999. Under the rules, information in the electronic media "shall be articulated by a single human voice, or on-screen text, with no background sound other than instrumental music." The rules prohibit use of a "person's voice or image, other than that of a lawyer who is a member of the firm whose services are advertised."[214] The comments justify these special restrictions as follows:

> [T]he unique characteristics of electronic media, including the pervasiveness of television and radio, the ease with which these media are abused, and the passiveness of the viewer or listener, make the electronic media especially subject to regulation in the public interest. Therefore, greater restrictions on the manner of television and radio advertising are justified than might be appropriate for advertisements in the other media. To prevent abuses, including potential interferences with the fair and proper administration of justice and the creation of incorrect public perceptions or assumptions about the manner in which our legal system works, and to promote the public's confidence in the legal profession and this country's system of justice while not inter-

---

    213. Florida Bar: Petition to Amend the Rules Regulating the Florida Bar — Advertising Issues, 571 So. 2d 451 (Fla. 1991). On the wisdom of the Florida rules as a matter of policy, see William E. Hornsby, Jr. & Kurt Schimmel, Regulating Lawyer Advertising: Public Images and the Irresistible Aristotelian Impulse, 9 Geo. J. Legal Ethics 325 (1996) (empirical study of lawyer advertising shows that public image of lawyers who use stylish advertisements is greater than those lawyers who use purely informational advertising).

    214. Fla. R. Prof. Conduct 4-7.5 (amended 1999).

fering with the free flow of useful information to prospective users of legal services, it is necessary also to restrict the techniques used in television and radio advertising.

Reginald Nason is the owner of the Nason Law Firm, which principally handles plaintiffs' cases arising out of mass disasters, such as hotel fires and plant explosions. The firm practices in a jurisdiction that has adopted the Florida amendments to the advertising rules. The firm has created several television advertisements that it has available to run whenever a mass disaster occurs. Each of the ads begins with a dramatization and is followed by a client testimonial, like the following:

should the comm be from the lawyers voice

> I'm Helen Andrews, and in 1999 I was almost killed in an explosion at the plant where I worked. I was in the hospital for more than three months. You wouldn't believe what the insurance company offered me. It was ridiculous. I went to Reginald Nason. He and the lawyers in his firm took my case to trial and I got twice as much as the insurance company offered me. The lawyers at the Nason Law Firm were there when I needed them.

In addition to television advertising, Nason takes other steps to obtain business whenever a mass disaster occurs. Shortly after a disaster takes place, Nason rents space at a hotel and conducts a seminar entitled, for example, "The Henderson Plant Explosion — Your Legal Rights." Nason advertises the seminar extensively on radio and television. At the seminar Nason and other members of his firm make presentations and provide materials to attendees. Nason and other members of his firm do not approach attendees personally, but Nason states publicly that he invites attendees to call his office for an appointment. The firm's business cards are readily available at the seminar.

A disciplinary proceeding has been filed against Nason for violation of the jurisdiction's rules regulating advertising and solicitation. Nason denies that he has violated the rules, but he also contends that, even if he did, his television advertising and seminars are constitutionally protected. Be prepared to discuss these constitutional issues.

Read Model Rules 7.1, 7.2, 7.3, 7.4, 7.5, and comments.

Basic constitutional principles governing regulation of lawyer advertising

Lawyers have long recognized that the practice of law is both a business and a profession and that success in the practice requires lawyers to be able to attract clients. The traditional view expressed by the profession, however, has been that commercial advertising or solicitation is unprofessional. Under this view, lawyers should attract clients through reputation rather than through marketing. Canon 27 of the original Canon of Ethics, adopted by the American Bar Association in 1908, provided as follows: "[S]olicitation of business by circulars or advertisements, or by personal communications, or interviews, not warranted by personal relations, is unprofessional."

During the last 25 years, however, the Supreme Court has established and expanded the constitutional right of lawyers to market their legal services. The genesis of this protection was the Court's decision in Virginia State Board of Pharmacy v. Virginia Citizens Consumer Council, Inc.[215] In *Virginia Pharmacy* the Court rejected the commercial speech exception to the First Amendment and held that commercial speech was entitled to some measure of First Amendment protection. The Court in *Virginia Pharmacy* reserved judgment, however, on whether its decision applied to other professions.

One year later, in Bates v. State Bar of Arizona,[216] the Court applied its holding in *Virginia Pharmacy* to lawyer advertising. In March 1974 two Arizona lawyers left their positions with the legal services program in Phoenix and opened a "legal clinic" through which they offered legal services at modest fees to people of moderate income. After two years, they decided that their practice could not survive unless they attracted a larger clientele. To do so,

---

215. 425 U.S. 748 (1976).
216. 433 U.S. 350 (1977).

they began advertising in one of the Phoenix newspapers, offering to provide various services for specified fees, including uncontested divorce, adoption, nonbusiness bankruptcy, and change of name. The Arizona Supreme Court censured the lawyers for conduct in violation of its code of professional responsibility. The United States Supreme Court reversed.

The question in *Bates* was whether the Arizona Supreme Court could constitutionally discipline lawyers for violating its Code of Professional Responsibility by making *truthful* newspaper advertisements about the *price* and *availability* of certain routine legal services. The Court noted that the consumer's interest in commercial speech is substantial and "often may be far keener than his concern for urgent political dialogue."[217] Further, commercial speech serves important societal interests by informing the public of the availability, nature, and prices of products and services.[218] The Court held that such advertising was constitutionally protected under the First Amendment and could not be prohibited by the state.[219] In its opinion, the Court considered and rejected six justifications offered by the state of Arizona to support its ban on advertising of legal services: the adverse effect on professionalism, the inherently misleading nature of attorney advertising, the adverse effect on the administration of justice, the undesirable economic effects of advertising, the adverse effect of advertising on the quality of service, and the difficulties of enforcement.[220]

The Court in *Bates* was careful, however, to indicate the limitations of its opinion. First, the decision did not prevent state

217. Id. at 364.
218. Id.
219. Id. at 383.
220. Id. at 368-379. For articles discussing the policy issues involved in lawyer advertising, see Geoffrey C. Hazard, Jr. et al., Why Lawyers Should Be Allowed to Advertise: A Market Analysis of Legal Services, 58 N.Y.U. L. Rev. 1084 (1983); Fred S. McChesney & Timothy J. Muris, The Effect of Advertising on the Quality of Legal Services, 65-Oct A.B.A. J. 1503 (1979). See also Richard J. Cebula, Does Lawyer Advertising Adversely Influence the Image of Lawyers in the United States? An Alternative Perspective and New Empirical Evidence, 27 J. Legal Stud. 503 (1998) (multiple regression study used to show that lawyer advertising enhances public image of profession). In 1995 the ABA issued a comprehensive report on lawyer advertising, ABA Commission on Advertising, Lawyer Advertising at the Crossroads (1995). The report outlines 18 considerations and 40 strategies to guide policymakers in dealing with the complex array of issues involved in lawyer advertising and solicitation.

regulation of false, deceptive, or misleading advertising.[221] The Court reserved judgment on claims about the quality of legal services: "[A]dvertising claims as to the quality of services — a matter we do not address today — are not susceptible of measurement or verification; accordingly, such claims may be so likely to be misleading as to warrant restriction."[222] Second, in-person solicitation posed unique problems that might warrant restriction. Third, the Court left open the possibility that warning or supplementation might be required, even as to advertising like that involved in *Bates*, to prevent consumers from being misled. Fourth, like other forms of speech, a state may impose reasonable "time, place, and manner" restrictions. Fifth, advertising concerning illegal transactions could be prohibited. Finally, "the special problems of advertising on the electronic broadcast media will warrant special consideration."[223]

In In re R. M. J.,[224] the Court broadened its holding in *Bates*, setting forth general principles for determining the constitutionality of restrictions on lawyer advertising. After the Supreme Court's decision in *Bates*, the Missouri Supreme Court amended its Code of Professional Responsibility to allow some lawyer advertising, but the rules continued to limit advertising to a significant degree. The rules allowed lawyers to publish in the print media 10 categories of information: name, address, and telephone number; areas of practice; date and place of birth; schools attended; foreign language ability; office hours; fee for an initial consultation; availability of a schedule of fees; credit arrangements; and the fixed fee to be charged for certain specified "routine" legal services. The state supreme court and the advisory committee charged with enforcing the rules interpreted them to mean that these 10 categories were exclusive; lawyers could not advertise in-

---

221. 433 U.S. at 383. See, e.g., In re Zang, 741 P.2d 267 (Ariz. 1987) (en banc), *cert. denied*, 484 U.S. 1067 (1988) (lawyers disciplined for misrepresentation in advertisements regarding ability and willingness to take cases to trial); Musselwhite v. State Bar of Tex., 786 S.W.2d 437 (Tex. Ct. App. 1990, writ denied), *cert. denied*, 501 U.S. 1251 (1991) (letters and advertisement soliciting claims of foreign tort victims were false and misleading in various respects, including suggestion that lawyer already had clients arising out of incident in question and prediction of high recoveries in American courts).

222. 433 U.S. at 383-384.

223. Id.

224. 455 U.S. 191 (1982).

formation beyond these categories. The Missouri rules also placed specific restrictions on the ways in which lawyers could advertise the areas in which they practiced.

Relying on its decision in Central Hudson Gas & Electric Corp. v. Public Service Commission,[225] the Court articulated three principles to be used in determining the constitutionality of restrictions on legal advertising:

- A state may constitutionally prohibit lawyers from engaging in false or inherently misleading advertising or "when experience has proven that in fact such advertising is subject to abuse."
- A state may not prohibit advertising that is potentially misleading, but may regulate such advertising by a method "no broader than reasonably necessary to prevent the deception," such as by explanation or disclaimer.
- States retain the right to regulate truthful advertising in some limited circumstances if the state establishes "a substantial interest and the interference with speech must be in proportion to the interest served."[226]

The Court then considered three charges against R. M. J. in light of these principles: listing the areas of his practice in language or in terms other than those provided by the rule; listing the courts and states in which he had been admitted to practice; and mailing announcement cards to persons other than "lawyers, clients, former clients, personal friends, and relatives." (R. M. J. conceded the constitutionality of the disclaimer requirement.) The Court found that none of the charges could be upheld constitutionally. None of the advertisements were false or inherently misleading, and the state failed to present any substantial state interest to justify the restrictions.[227]

Basic constitutional principles governing regulation of in-person solicitation by lawyers

Bates and *R. M. J.* dealt with the constitutionality of restrictions on lawyer advertising. In companion cases — Ohralik v. Ohio

225. 447 U.S. 557 (1980).
226. 455 U.S. at 203.
227. Id. at 205-207.

State Bar Assn.[228] and In re Primus[229] — the Court established constitutional principles governing in-person solicitation. *Ohralik* involved a classic case of "ambulance chasing." In casual conversation at a post office, attorney Ohralik heard about an automobile accident involving two young women. He telephoned the parents of the driver, learned that she was in the hospital, visited with the parents, and then met with their daughter in the hospital, where he offered to represent her on a contingency fee basis. Ohralik also contacted the passenger and volunteered to represent her as well. During these meetings, Ohralik secretly tape recorded the conversations. After both girls had signed contingency fee agreements, they decided that they did not want Ohralik to represent them, but he insisted that they were bound by their agreements with him.

The Supreme Court of Ohio indefinitely suspended Ohralik for solicitation of professional employment in violation of the Ohio Code of Professional Responsibility. The Supreme Court affirmed. The Court rejected Ohralik's argument that under the First Amendment, in-person solicitation was entitled to the same degree of protection as advertising. Instead, the Court found that in-person solicitation was distinguishable from advertising because it involved conduct as well as speech:

> In-person solicitation by a lawyer of remunerative employment is a business transaction in which speech is an essential but subordinate component. While this does not remove the speech from the protection of the First Amendment, as was held in *Bates* and *Virginia Pharmacy*, it lowers the level of appropriate judicial scrutiny.[230]

As a result, the state could constitutionally prevent solicitation in furtherance of important state interests. The Court found — indeed Ohralik conceded — that the state had an important interest in preventing those aspects of solicitation that involve fraud, undue influence, intimidation, overreaching, and other forms of "vexatious conduct."[231]

228. 436 U.S. 447 (1978).
229. 436 U.S. 412 (1978).
230. 436 U.S. at 457.
231. Id. at 462. A recent example of improper solicitation is In re Ravich, Koster, Tobin, Oleckna, Reitman & Greenstein, 715 A.2d 216 (N.J. 1998) (lawyers and law firm disciplined for solicitation after gas line explosion by setting up RV with signs across from emergency shelter, for conducting seminar in shelter, and for personal offers to provide legal services).

In re Primus[232] involved a radically different situation from *Ohralik*. Primus practiced with a public interest law firm that was affiliated with the American Civil Liberties Union; she also served as a lawyer for the South Carolina Council on Human Relations, a nonprofit organization. During the summer of 1973, local and national newspapers had reported that pregnant women in Aiken, South Carolina, were being sterilized as a condition for receiving continued medical benefits under the Medicaid program. Primus spoke at a meeting arranged by the Council on Human Relations to women who had been sterilized, including Mary Etta Williams. Ms. Primus informed the attendees of their legal rights, including the right to sue any doctor who had engaged in sterilization. Subsequently, the ACLU advised Ms. Primus that it was willing to provide representation to mothers in Aiken who had been sterilized. A representative of the Council on Human Relations told Ms. Primus that Ms. Williams wanted to bring suit. After Primus received this information, she wrote Williams a letter informing her of the ACLU's willingness to represent her in a suit against the doctor who had performed the sterilization.

The South Carolina Supreme Court publicly reprimanded Primus for solicitation in violation of the Code of Professional Responsibility. The Supreme Court reversed. The Court distinguished *Ohralik*. While *Ohralik* had involved solicitation for pecuniary gain, *Primus* involved solicitation for political purposes. In NAACP v. Button[233] and subsequent cases, the Court had held that under the associational freedom guaranteed by the First Amendment, organizations such as the NAACP could solicit clients as part of "collective activity undertaken to obtain meaningful access to the courts." The Court found that there was not a "meaningful distinction" between the ACLU and the NAACP.[234] In particular, the Court rejected the argument that the ACLU should be treated differently from the NAACP under the First Amendment because the ACLU has as one of its primary purposes the rendering of legal services and because the ACLU has a policy of seeking the award of attorney fees.[235] Since Primus's solicitation came within the core of First Amendment protection, the Court

232. 436 U.S. 412 (1978).
233. 371 U.S. 415 (1963).
234. 436 U.S. at 426-427.
235. Id. at 427-429.

ruled that she could be disciplined only if South Carolina established a compelling state interest and only if the means used were
"closely drawn to avoid unnecessary abridgment of associational
freedoms."[236] While the state could apply a prophylactic rule in
commercial solicitation cases like *Ohralik,* in political solicitation
cases like *Primus* the state must show actual injury.[237] The Court
found that the state had failed to establish that any such injury
occurred.[238]

The Court has not addressed the constitutionality of restrictions on in-person solicitation since the *Ohralik* and *Primus* cases,
but several questions remain unanswered. In *Ohralik* the Court
held that a state could adopt a per se rule prohibiting in-person
commercial solicitation. By contrast, in *Primus* the Court held that
solicitation by letter by a lawyer affiliated with a bona fide organization devoted to civil liberties (the ACLU) for the purpose of
providing access to legal services rather than for commercial gain
could not be prohibited unless the state showed actual harm resulting from the solicitation. It is unclear whether solicitation lacking some of the elements of *Primus* would be subject to the actual
harm standard or to a per se rule. Suppose Primus had engaged
in solicitation in person rather than by letter? Or suppose Primus
had been a member of a public interest law firm that was not
affiliated with an organization like the ACLU?

Another issue dealing with the scope of the constitutional
protection afforded in-person solicitation deals with what Justice
Marshall in *Ohralik* called "benign" solicitation:

> By "benign" commercial solicitation, I mean solicitation by advice
> and information that is truthful and that is presented in a noncoer-
> cive, nondeceitful, and dignified manner to a potential client who
> is emotionally and physically capable of making a rational decision
> either to accept or reject the representation with respect to a legal
> claim or matter that is not frivolous.[239]

The Court in *Ohralik* was not required to address the constitutionality of benign solicitation because the case dealt with in-

236. Id. at 432.
237. Id. at 434-435.
238. Id.
239. 436 U.S. at 472 n.3.

person solicitation under circumstances where actual overreaching was likely to occur and did in fact take place.

In Edenfield v. Fane[240] the Court considered the constitutionality of a Florida Board of Accountancy rule prohibiting in-person solicitation by accountants. In holding the rule unconstitutional, the Court pointed out that *Ohralik* did not hold that a state may constitutionally prohibit all in-person solicitation, but only in-person solicitation in situations "inherently conducive to overreaching and other forms of misconduct."[241] The Court struck down the Accountancy rule, but it distinguished accountants from lawyers on two grounds. First, "[u]nlike a lawyer, a CPA is not 'a professional trained in the art of persuasion.' " Second, the "typical client of a CPA is far less susceptible to manipulation than the young accident victim in *Ohralik*."[242] The Court, however, might apply the *Edenfield* approach if a lawyer solicited a sophisticated client rather than someone like the accident victim in *Ohralik*.[243]

Application and development: targeted advertising, direct mail advertising, and false or misleading communications

In subsequent cases, the Court has refined the application of the principles established in *Bates*, *R. M. J.*, *Ohralik*, and *Primus*. The type of advertising that came before the Court in *Bates* and in *R .M. J.* was relatively bland. In a series of cases, however, a sharply divided Supreme Court has considered the issue of the constitutionality of restrictions on targeted advertising, that is, advertising that deals with particular types of litigation, and direct mail advertising.

240. 507 U.S. 761 (1993).

241. Id. at 774.

242. Id. at 775. For a criticism of the Court's distinction between lawyers and accountants, see Jeffrey M. Brandt, Note, Attorney In-Person Solicitation: Hope for a New Direction and Supreme Court Protection after Edenfield v. Fane, 25 U. Tol. L. Rev. 783 (1994).

243. Rule 7.1(b) of the District of Columbia Rules of Professional Conduct allows lawyers to engage in benign solicitation. For an argument in support of this approach, see Kristina N. Bailey, Note, "Rainmaking" and D.C. Rule of Professional Conduct 7.1: The In-Person Solicitation of Clients, 9 Geo. J. Legal Ethics 1335 (1996).

Zauderer v. Office of Disciplinary Counsel[244] involved the constitutionality of restrictions on targeted advertising. Zauderer ran advertisements in Ohio newspapers publicizing his availability to represent, on a contingent fee basis, women who had been injured from using the Dalkon Shield contraceptive device. The advertisement included a drawing of the device with the question "DID YOU USE THIS IUD?"[245]

Before the Supreme Court, the State of Ohio conceded that Zauderer's Dalkon Shield advertisement was not false or misleading. Instead, it tried to justify discipline on three grounds. First, the state argued that Zauderer's advertisement should be treated the same as the in-person solicitation in *Ohralik*, subject to a prophylactic rule. The Court rejected this argument. The Court found that the concerns that supported the Court's decision in *Ohralik* — the possibility of overreaching coupled with the difficulty of enforcement — were not present when the lawyer used targeted advertising.[246] Second, the state argued that it could constitutionally prohibit the advertisement because it had a substantial interest in preventing lawyers from "stirring up litigation." In words that are sure to resonate with plaintiffs' lawyers, the Court stated: "[W]e cannot endorse the proposition that a lawsuit, as such, is an evil."[247] Finally, the Court found the state's claim of regulatory difficulties to be unpersuasive as a justification for prohibiting Zauderer's advertisement.[248]

The Court also held that illustrations were entitled to the same constitutional protection afforded textual communications, rejecting the argument that the state had a substantial interest in prohibiting the use of illustrations in order to uphold the dignity of the profession. After noting that there was no suggestion that Zauderer's illustration was undignified, the Court's opinion swept more broadly:

> [A]lthough the State undoubtedly has a substantial interest in ensuring that its attorneys behave with dignity and decorum in the courtroom, we are unsure that the State's desire that attorneys maintain their dignity in their communications with the public is

244. 471 U.S. 626 (1985).
245. Id. at 630.
246. Id. at 641-642.
247. Id. at 643.
248. Id. at 645-646.

an interest substantial enough to justify the abridgment of their First Amendment rights. Even if that were the case, we are unpersuaded that undignified behavior would tend to recur so often as to warrant a prophylactic rule.[249]

The Court also rejected Ohio's argument that the prohibition on illustrations was justified in that illustrations were misleading because they operate on an emotional or subconscious level:

> We are not convinced. The State's arguments amount to little more than unsupported assertions: nowhere does the State cite any evidence or authority of any kind for its contention that the potential abuses associated with the use of illustrations in attorneys' advertising cannot be combated by any means short of a blanket ban.[250]

In one respect, however, the Court found that Zauderer was subject to discipline. The Ohio Supreme Court had found that Zauderer violated its Code of Professional Responsibility by failing to disclose to potential clients that they would be liable for the expenses of litigation, even though they would not be liable for legal fees unless they obtained a recovery. The Court noted that "unjustified or unduly burdensome disclosure requirements might offend the First Amendment by chilling protected commercial speech." The Court ruled, however, that disclosure requirements, unlike prohibitions, were subject to less scrutiny and would be upheld "as long as [the] requirements are reasonably related to the State's interest in preventing deception of consumers."[251] The Court found that "the requirement that an attorney advertising his availability on a contingent-fee basis disclose that clients will have to pay costs even if their lawsuits are unsuccessful (assuming that to be the case) easily passes muster under this standard."[252]

In Shapero v. Kentucky Bar Assn.[253] the Court considered the constitutionality of restrictions on "direct mail advertising" by lawyers. Shapero applied to the Kentucky Attorneys Advertising Commission for permission to send the following letter to individuals against whom foreclosure proceedings had been instituted:

249. Id. at 647-648.
250. Id. at 648.
251. Id. at 651.
252. Id. at 652.
253. 486 U.S. 466 (1988).

It has come to my attention that your home is being foreclosed on. If this is true, you may be about to lose your home. Federal law may allow you to keep your home by ORDERING your creditor [*sic*] to STOP and give you more time to pay them.

You may call my office anytime from 8:30 A.M. to 5:00 P.M. for FREE information on how you can keep your home.

Call NOW, don't wait. It may surprise you what I may be able to do for you. Just call and tell me that you got this letter. Remember it is FREE, there is NO charge for calling.[254]

The matter ultimately went to the Kentucky Supreme Court. The Court found that Shapero's letter violated its Rule 7.3, which prohibited lawyers from engaging in solicitation and defined solicitation to include a "letter . . . directed to a specific recipient."[255]

The Supreme Court granted certiorari and reversed. Characterizing the case as nothing more than "*Ohralik* in writing," the State of Kentucky contended that Shapero's letter could be prohibited without a showing of actual harm because of the serious potential for abuse involved in solicitation. Finding that this suggestion "misses the mark," the Court pointed out that the ban on solicitation approved in *Ohralik* rested on two fundamental differences between advertising and solicitation. First, the in-person character of solicitation creates a situation "rife with possibilities for overreaching, invasion of privacy, the exercise of undue influence, and outright fraud." Second, solicitation poses unique enforcement difficulties because it is "not visible or otherwise open to public scrutiny." The Court found that targeted direct mail advertising was different from in-person solicitation in both respects.

The Court recognized that direct mail advertising could be subject to abuse: Recipients might overestimate the lawyer's familiarity with their problem or mistakenly assume that they have a legal problem (or a more serious legal problem) when this is not the case. The Court concluded, however, that these possibilities justified regulation, not prohibition; it suggested that states consider requiring lawyers to file their direct mail advertisements with a state agency to provide time and opportunity to review such mailings and consider forcing lawyers to identify direct mailings

254. Id. at 469.
255. Id. at 471.

as "advertising material."[256] The Court also pointed out that states could discipline lawyers for false or deceptive statements in direct mail advertising just as in media or print advertising, but it found nothing in the record to support the conclusion that Shapero's advertisement was overreaching or deceptive.

In a dissenting opinion in *Shapero*, Justice O'Connor criticized the line of decisions beginning with *Bates* because they failed to take into account fundamental differences between professional services and standardized consumer products. She also argued that the Court's decisions had failed to give sufficient weight to the substantial state interest in maintaining professional standards. She concluded: "In one way or another, time will uncover the folly of this approach. I can only hope that the Court will recognize the danger before it is too late to effect a worthwhile cure."[257]

Justice O'Connor's call in *Shapero* for a change in direction by the Supreme Court may have become a reality in the Court's decision in Florida Bar v. Went For It, Inc.[258] In 1989 the Florida Bar completed a two-year study of the effects of lawyer advertising on public opinion. Based on the study, the bar petitioned the Florida Supreme Court to adopt new restrictions on lawyer advertising.[259] As a result, the Florida Supreme Court issued new advertising rules, one of which prohibited for 30 days direct mail communications in wrongful death or personal injury cases.[260]

The lower courts found the restriction unconstitutional, but the Supreme Court reversed in a 5-4 decision. Writing for the majority, Justice O'Connor stated that the Court's commercial speech cases had held that commercial speech was entitled to some constitutional protection, but that such protection was more limited than that afforded speech at the "core" of the First Amendment. Accordingly, the Court engaged in "intermediate" rather than "strict" scrutiny of the Florida rule, using the framework established in *Central Hudson*:

> Under *Central Hudson*, the government may freely regulate commercial speech that concerns unlawful activity or is misleading. . . .

256. Id. at 476-477.
257. Id. at 491.
258. 515 U.S. 618 (1995).
259. Florida Bar: Petition to Amend the Rules Regulating the Florida Bar — Advertising Issues, 571 So. 2d 451 (Fla. 1991).
260. Fla. Sup. Ct. R. 4-7.4(b)(1).

Commercial speech that falls into neither of those categories, like
the advertising at issue here, may be regulated if the government
satisfies a test consisting of three related prongs: First, the government must assert a substantial interest in support of its regulation;
second, the government must demonstrate that the restriction on
commercial speech directly and materially advances that interest;
and third, the regulation must be "narrowly drawn."[261]

The majority found that the Florida Bar had satisfied the first
prong of the test because the rule was based on two substantial
state interests. First, the rule protected the "privacy and tranquility
of personal injury victims and their loved ones." Second, the rule
represented an "effort to protect the flagging reputations of Florida lawyers by preventing them from engaging in conduct that, the
Bar maintains, 'is universally regarded as deplorable and beneath
common decency because of its intrusion upon the special vulnerability and private grief of victims or their families.' "[262]
While stating that the second prong of the *Central Hudson* test
could not be satisfied by "mere speculation or conjecture," the
Court found that the Florida Bar's two-year study of the impact
of lawyer advertising on public opinion supported the conclusion
that the rule advanced the state interests in question "in a direct
and material way."[263] The Court distinguished Edenfield v.
Fane,[264] where the Court had invalidated a Florida rule prohibiting
in-person solicitation by accountants on the ground that the State
Board of Accountancy had presented no studies (or even any an-
ecdotal evidence) to support its regulation.[265] The Court in *Went
For It* also noted that the plaintiffs had failed to offer any evidence
to refute the studies presented by the Florida Bar.[266]
Turning to the third prong of the *Central Hudson* test, the
Court pointed out that the state was not required to meet a "least
restrictive means" test to regulate commercial speech. Instead, the
state was required to show only a reasonable "fit" between means
and ends:[267] "The Bar's rule is reasonably well tailored to its stated

261. 515 U.S. at 623-624.
262. Id. at 624-625.
263. Id. at 625-626.
264. 507 U.S. 761 (1993).
265. 515 U.S. at 626.
266. Id. at 628.
267. Id. at 632.

objective of eliminating targeted mailings whose type and timing are a source of distress to Floridians, distress that has caused many of them to lose respect for the legal profession."[268] The plaintiffs also argued that the rule "may prevent citizens from learning about their legal options, particularly at a time when other actors — opposing counsel and insurance adjusters — may be clamoring for victims' attentions."[269] The Court rejected this argument as well because it found that there were numerous other ways in which lawyers could inform individuals of their rights during the 30-day period, including by general advertising, billboards, untargeted letters directed to the general population, and telephone directories.[270]

The majority opinion distinguished Shapero v. Kentucky Bar Assn.,[271] which had invalidated restrictions on direct mail advertising. In *Shapero* the state did not seek to justify its regulation as a measure designed to prevent invasions of privacy. In addition, the restriction in *Shapero* was unlimited, while the Florida rule applied for only 30 days.[272]

Justice Kennedy's dissenting opinion agreed with the majority that the *Central Hudson* test should be used to evaluate the constitutionality of the Florida rule, but it disagreed with the majority on the application of every prong of the test. He found that protection of the privacy of recipients was not a substantial state interest because the state may not restrict speech that might offend the listener.[273] He pointed out that direct mail advertising provides important information to recipients.[274] He criticized the "studies" on which the bar based its rule.[275] Finally, Justice Kennedy argued that prohibition of direct mail advertising for 30 days was wildly disproportionate to any harm that might flow from such advertising.[276] In conclusion, the dissenting Justices saw the Court's decision as a major retreat from First Amendment protection for

268. Id. at 633.
269. Id.
270. Id. at 633-634.
271. 486 U.S. 466 (1988), discussed above.
272. 515 U.S. at 629.
273. Id. at 638.
274. Id. at 639-640.
275. Id. at 641.
276. Id. at 642.

commercial speech in general and lawyer advertising in particular.[277] After the Court upheld Florida's 30-day waiting period on direct mail advertising, Congress enacted legislation prohibiting communications with victims or their families for 30 days after an airplane crash involving an interstate or foreign carrier.[278]

In *Bates* and *R.M.J.*, the Court had indicated that states remained free to prohibit lawyers from engaging in false or misleading advertising, but the Court did not address what types of advertisements fell within those categories. In Peel v. Attorney Registration & Disciplinary Commission [279] the Court considered whether a lawyer's identification as a "certified civil trial specialist" was false and misleading when the state did not recognize certification of civil trial specialists, but the certification was issued by a bona fide organization with demanding standards, the National Board of Trial Advocacy. The State of Illinois contended that the use of the term "certified specialist" was inherently misleading and could therefore be prohibited, but the Supreme Court in a 5-4 decision disagreed. The Court agreed that if certifications were issued for a fee by organizations that did not enforce standards, a state could prohibit their use because they would be misleading, but the Court found that the NBTA certification was not misleading.[280] The Court considered the state's argument that the statement was, if not actually misleading, at least potentially misleading. The Court then referred to its earlier decisions holding that when statements are potentially misleading, the remedy is not outright ban but required disclaimer or disclosure.

---

277. Id. at 644-645.

278. 49 U.S.C.A. §1136(g)(2) provides as follows:

> In the event of an accident involving an air carrier providing interstate or foreign air transportation, no unsolicited communication concerning a potential action for personal injury or wrongful death may be made by an attorney or any potential party to the litigation to an individual injured in the accident, or to a relative of an individual involved in the accident, before the 30th day following the date of the accident.

The federal statute applies to any "potential party," so it would appear to prohibit efforts by defendants and their insurance carriers to settle cases during the 30-day period after an accident.

279. 496 U.S. 91 (1990).

280. Id. at 101-102.

Marketing on the Internet

Lawyers are using the Internet in a wide variety of ways to market their services, including passive Web pages, interactive Web pages, responses to e-mail inquiries, participation in chat rooms, and distribution of information to potential clients on commercially obtained lists. It is possible that the advertising and solicitation rules may be redesigned to deal with the special problems of marketing on the Internet.[281] In the meantime, regulatory authorities and lawyers must apply the existing rules to Internet advertising and solicitation.

Opinions from a number of state ethics advisory committees have stated that lawyers may use the Internet to market their services provided they comply with the rules on advertising and solicitation.[282] Like print or television advertising, Internet advertising can be false or misleading or can violate other advertising rules. For example, a lawyer who advertises that she is a specialist on her Web page in violation of a state's rules on certification of specialization is guilty of misconduct. See Model Rule 7.4.

The Internet has special characteristics, however, that cause problems in applying the traditional advertising and solicitation rules. The traditional rules assume a relatively limited amount of information supplied by the lawyer, while information on the Internet is vast and is typically available through links over which the lawyer has little control, other than providing the link. Unlike traditional advertising, Internet advertising contains hidden codes or tags. The traditional rules assume a communication that is relatively fixed in time, such as a newspaper or television advertisement, while advertising on the Internet changes frequently. Finally, traditional advertising is largely limited to the jurisdiction in which the lawyer practices (although advertisements by lawyers who practice at borders of states can be seen by residents of other

281. ABA Comm. on Advertising, A Re-examination of the ABA Model Rules of Professional Conduct Pertaining to Client Development in Light of Emerging Technologies (Discussion Draft July 1998). Available on the Web at ⟨http://www.abanet.org/legalservices/whitepaper.html.⟩

282. State Bar of Mich., Comm. on Prof. & Jud. Ethics, Op. No. RI-276 (July 11, 1996), 1996 WL 909975; N.Y. State Bar Assn., Comm. on Prof. Ethics, Op. No. 709 (Sept. 16, 1998), 1998 WL 957924; Pa. Bar Assn., Comm. on Legal Ethics & Prof. Resp., Op. No. 96-17 (May 3, 1996), 1996 WL 928126.

states). Advertising on the Internet is accessible in all states and throughout the world.

One problem in applying the false and misleading standard to lawyer Web advertisements deals with links. Are lawyers responsible for the accuracy of all sites to which they link their Web pages? If not, lawyers can use links to avoid the application of many of the advertising rules. If so, lawyers may be unduly cautious about including links on their Web pages. One way to deal with this issue is to provide that lawyers must exercise reasonable care in providing links on their Web pages and are required to act either to seek correction or to remove a link when they know the linked site contains false or misleading information.

Positioning Web pages for priority by search engines is crucial to the effectiveness of Internet advertising. Preparers of Web pages use various techniques to increase the prominence of the Web page for search engines, including repetitive words, meta tags, and invisible ink. If the use of such devices creates a false or misleading impression of the lawyer's practice, it should be treated as a violation of Rule 7.1. Similarly, a domain name can create a false or misleading impression of the nature of the firm's work or could create unjustified expectations about the results the lawyer could achieve.

Model Rule 7.2(b) provides: "A copy or recording of an advertisement or communication shall be kept for two years after its last dissemination along with a record of when and where it was used." Rules in some states such as Texas require filing of lawyer advertisements. The Texas Advertising Review Committee has ruled that the home page of a Web advertisement is subject to the Texas rules and must be filed for approval with a $50 fee, unless the home page is limited to certain information set forth in the Texas rules, in which case it is exempt from the filing requirement. Other pages are not subject to the filing requirement because they are treated as requested by the client, but these pages are subject to the advertising rules. Florida had a similar filing requirement until its rules were amended in 1999 to exempt Web pages.[283] Query whether these rules mean that a law firm must file its home page every time that page is modified? If so, is this a reasonable regulation of advertising?

---

283. The Florida and Texas rules are available on the Web pages of these bar associations, accessible through <http://www.legalethics.com>.

The accessibility of a lawyer's Web page or other advertising outside the jurisdiction in which the lawyer practices creates a number of intertwined problems. First, such an advertisement could be viewed as false or misleading to the extent that it implies that the lawyer can render services in jurisdictions where the lawyer is not admitted to practice. Lawyers should indicate the geographical limitations on their practice to avoid misleading potential viewers.[284] Second, lawyers who obtain clients in jurisdictions in which they are not admitted to practice may run afoul of the state's prohibitions on the unauthorized practice of law.[285] Third, it appears that some states will attempt to exercise jurisdiction over out-of-state lawyers who "target" their Web pages or other Internet advertising to potential clients in the state. For example, recently amended South Carolina rules provide that lawyers who are admitted in another jurisdiction must comply with the South Carolina rules if they use various specific forms of advertising directed to South Carolinians or "[a]ny other form of advertising or solicitation which is specifically targeted at potential clients in South Carolina."[286]

When is a communication targeted to residents of a state? The Web site may itself indicate the states to which it is directed. If not, disciplinary authorities may be able to infer the targeting of the site from review of the residence of clients obtained by the firm through the site. Prudent lawyers will take steps to limit the states to which they wish their sites to apply. For example, the home page could state: "This Web site is for residents of the following states only." Firms that wish to have their Web pages effective in states with more restrictive advertising rules than their home states may need to prepare separate Web pages for those states. For example: "Florida residents should click here."

Lawyers can also violate the solicitation rules when they use the Internet. An offer to provide legal services in a chat room or other real-time method of communication is similar to "live tele-

284. N.Y. State Bar Assn., Comm. on Prof. Ethics, Op. No. 709 (Sept. 16, 1998), 1998 WL 957924.
285. See Birbrower, Montalbano, Condon & Frank, P.C. v. Superior Court (ESQ Business Services, Inc.), 949 P.2d 1 (Cal. 1998). Problem 4-8 discusses the *Birbrower* case in more detail.
286. S. C. App. Ct. R. 418(b)(5) (amended May 12, 1999). On the jurisdictional issues, see Pa. Bar Assn., Comm. on Legal Ethics & Prof. Resp., Op. No. 98-85 (July 24, 1998), 1998 WL 988187.

phone contact" and should be subject to the solicitation rules.[287] See Model Rule 7.3(a). If a lawyer simply participates in a chat room without offering to provide services, however, the lawyer probably has not crossed the line of improper solicitation.

One of the leading cases involving professional discipline of a lawyer for Internet marketing is In re Canter.[288] In *Canter* the Tennessee Supreme Court imposed a one-year suspension on a lawyer who posted an advertisement about the green card lottery program on thousands of Internet newsgroups, including ones that were unrelated to the subject matter of the message. The court found that the respondent's advertisement was an improper intrusion into the privacy of the recipients because it was unsolicited and imposed a cost on recipients without their consent (cost of time of on-line use in reading or downloading the message). In addition, respondent had failed to identify the message as an advertisement (as required by Tennessee rules) and had failed to provide the Tennessee Board of Professional Responsibility with a copy of the advertisement within three days.

2.   *Group Legal Services*

The term *group legal services* refers to plans under which the sponsor of the plan contracts with a lawyer or law firm to provide designated legal services to members of the plan. Group legal services plans come in a wide variety of forms. Under most plans, the sponsor and the members have a preexisting relationship, such as employer and employee, labor union and member, or credit union and member. Methods of financing of plans vary considerably. In some plans, members may pay a premium for benefits (often referred to as "prepaid legal services" plans), while other plans offer their benefits to members without direct charge. Some plans may be insured to spread risk, while others are uninsured. Plans also differ in the range of choice offered to members to select counsel. "Closed panel" plans provide a list of attorneys from whom members must select. "Open panel" plans allow members to select

---

287. State Bar of Mich., Comm. on Prof. & Jud. Ethics, Op. No. RI-276 (July 11, 1996), 1996 WL 909975.

288. No. 95-831-O-H, Tenn. 6/5/97, Laws. Man. on Prof. Conduct (ABA/BNA), 13 Current Rep. 13 (July 23, 1997).

counsel of their choice so long as counsel is willing to agree to the terms and reimbursement limitations of the plan. Many plans will have a "gatekeeper" law firm that provides basic services under the plan. The gatekeeper firm will refer the member to a specialist when necessary.[289]

The essence of a group legal services plan is the tripartite relationship between sponsor, member, and lawyer. The injection of the sponsor into the attorney-client relationship, however, has made group legal services plans controversial within the profession. On one hand, a sponsor can provide valuable services to its members, such as negotiating lower attorney fees and overseeing the quality of legal services. On the other hand, because the sponsor pays the lawyers for the services that the lawyers render to their clients, this financial relationship may have an impact on the lawyers' independent professional judgment. Further, the presence of the third-party sponsor poses possible confidentiality and conflict-of-interest problems.[290]

The traditional attitude of the profession toward group legal services was one of hostility. Canon 35 of the ABA's Canons of Professional Ethics, entitled "Intermediaries," provided as follows:

> The professional services of a lawyer should not be controlled or exploited by any lay agency, personal or corporate, which intervenes between client and lawyer. A lawyer's responsibilities and qualifications are individual. He should avoid all relations which direct the performance of his duties by or in the interest of such intermediary.

In a series of decisions beginning in 1963, the Supreme Court considered the impact of the First Amendment on the bar's prohibition on cooperation with intermediaries. In NAACP v. Button[291] the NAACP provided attorneys to assist parents in challenging racial segregation in public schools. Typically, parents learned of the availability of legal assistance through meetings sponsored by the NAACP at which staff attorneys appeared and

---

289. For a description of the various types of group legal services plans, see Wolfram, Modern Legal Ethics §16.5.3, at 901-904.

290. For a discussion of the strengths and weaknesses of group legal services plans, see id. §16.5.4, at 904-910.

291. 371 U.S. 415 (1963).

spoke. Virginia argued that such activities amounted to improper solicitation, but the Supreme Court disagreed, holding that the NAACP's litigation activities were entitled to First Amendment protection:

> In the context of NAACP objectives, litigation is not a technique of resolving private differences; it is a means for achieving the lawful objectives of equality of treatment by all government, federal, state and local, for the members of the Negro community in this country. It is thus a form of political expression.[292]

In later cases the Court expanded the holding in *Button* to apply to labor unions, providing counsel either by referral or on salary, to assist their members in ordinary (rather than civil rights) litigation.[293] The Court summarized its holdings in these cases as follows: "The common thread running through our decisions . . . is that collective activity undertaken to obtain meaningful access to the courts is a fundamental right within the protection of the First Amendment."[294]

In light of these decisions, the ABA was forced to change its rules of professional conduct, but the change represented only a grudging acceptance of group legal services plans. The Model Code of Professional Responsibility adopted by the ABA in 1969 allowed lawyers to participate with group legal services plans provided that the plans met certain requirements, one of which was that cooperation was permissible "only in those instances and to the extent that controlling constitutional interpretation at the time of the rendition of the services requires the allowance of such legal service activities." DR 2-103(D)(5).[295]

During the next few years, the ABA faced continued pressure both from some ranks of the profession and from the Antitrust Division of the Justice Department to change its restrictive stance on group legal services plans. In response to these pressures, the

292. Id. at 429.
293. See United Transp. Union v. State Bar of Mich., 401 U.S. 576 (1971); United Mine Workers of America, Dist. 12 v. Illinois State Bar Assn., 389 U.S. 217 (1967); Brotherhood of R.R. Trainmen v. Virginia ex rel. Va. State Bar, 377 U.S. 1 (1964).
294. 401 U.S. at 585.
295. See generally Wolfram, Modern Legal Ethics §16.5.5, at 912.

ABA adopted amendments to the Model Code in 1974 and 1975, but even with these changes lawyer participation in group legal services plans was severely restricted.[296]

The Model Rules of Professional Conduct reflect a substantial shift in attitude toward group legal services plans from the bar's traditional hostility. The proposed final draft of Model Rule 5.4 included a provision allowing lawyers to participate with group legal services plans provided four relatively mild conditions were met. This section was deleted, however, from the final version of the Model Rules.[297] Given the historical controversy surrounding group legal services plans, it is surprising that such plans are barely mentioned in the Model Rules of Professional Conduct. (The one specific mention is in Rule 7.3(d).)

The absence of a Model Rule provision dealing with group legal services does not mean that lawyer participation in such plans is unrestricted. Lawyers participating in group legal services plans must still comply with all rules of professional conduct, including those dealing with confidentiality and conflicts of interest. In Formal Opinion 87-355, the ABA's Committee on Ethics and Professional Responsibility dealt with the status of for-profit group legal services plans under the Model Rules of Professional Conduct and issued an opinion broadly endorsing such plans, provided certain ethical requirements were met:

> The plan must allow the participating lawyer to exercise independent professional judgment on behalf of the client, to maintain client confidences, to avoid conflicts of interest, and to practice competently. The operation of the plan must not involve improper advertising or solicitation or improper fee sharing and must be in compliance with other applicable law. It is incumbent upon the lawyer to investigate and ensure that the arrangement under the plan fully complies with the Rules before the lawyer participates in the plan. Where the plan or the plan sponsor is in violation of the Rules, the lawyer who participates in the plan may violate Rule 8.4(a) by assisting the plan sponsor or by violating the Rules through the acts of the plan sponsor.[298]

296. See id. at 912-915.
297. See id. at 915-916.
298. ABA Comm. on Ethics and Prof. Resp., Formal Op. 87-355, at 2.

Lawyer participation in group legal services plans will, of course, depend on the rules of ethics and other law applicable in each state.

3. Restrictions on the Unauthorized Practice of Law

———————— **Problem 4-8** ————————

Regulation of the Unauthorized Practice of Law

You are a member of your state bar's unauthorized practice committee. Your committee has been asked to make recommendations on two issues: relaxation of restrictions on the unauthorized practice of law by nonlawyers and practice by out-of-state lawyers. (1) The ABA Commission on Nonlawyer Practice has recommended that states reconsider their restrictions on the unauthorized practice of law. Your committee has been asked to advise whether there are any areas of law in which it would be appropriate to remove or relax current restrictions on the unauthorized practice of law. (2) Under current court rules, out-of-state lawyers may appear in court if they are associated with a local lawyer and are admitted pro hac vice. Your committee has been asked to advise whether this rule is sufficient in light of the increasing national practice of many law firms.

Read Model Rule 5.5 and comments.

History and policy of restrictions on the unauthorized practice of law

Nonlawyers have not always been prohibited from practicing law. From the colonial period through the nineteenth century, many states allowed nonlawyers to represent clients, even in court.[299]

---

299. Wolfram, Modern Legal Ethics §15.1.1, at 824-825.

The modern concept of unauthorized practice did not develop until the early part of this century, particularly during the Depression. Beginning in the 1930s, the ABA and many state and local bar associations appointed unauthorized practice committees. These committees engaged in a variety of activities, including bringing lawsuits, to prevent the unauthorized practice of law. During this period, many states enacted or greatly expanded statutes prohibiting the unauthorized practice of law.[300] While bar officials claimed that their aggressive enforcement efforts originated because of public demand about improper activities by nonlawyers, evidence indicates that the bar was attempting to protect its economic position, which had deteriorated during the Depression.[301]

Rules prohibiting the unauthorized practice of law can be enforced in a variety of ways.[302] Traditionally, courts have held that they have the inherent power to determine who is admitted to practice law. Pursuant to this power courts have enjoined or held in contempt nonlawyers who practiced law.[303] Bar committees are typical plaintiffs in such proceedings. In the vast majority of states, legislatures have enacted statutes making the unauthorized practice of law a crime.[304] Finally, the Model Rules of Professional Conduct indirectly prohibit the unauthorized practice of law because the rules forbid lawyers from assisting nonlawyers in the unauthorized practice of law. Model Rule 5.5(b).[305]

300. See generally Barlow F. Christensen, The Unauthorized Practice of Law: Do Good Fences Really Make Good Neighbors — or Even Good Sense? 1980 Am. Bar Found. Res. J. 159, 161-197; Deborah L. Rhode, Policing the Professional Monopoly: A Constitutional and Empirical Analysis of Unauthorized Practice Prohibitions, 34 Stan. L. Rev. 1, 6-10 (1981).

301. Rhode, Policing the Professional Monopoly, 34 Stan. L. Rev. at 8-9.

302. For a comprehensive study of enforcement efforts, see id.

303. See Florida Bar v. Furman, 451 So. 2d 808 (Fla. 1984) (respondent held in criminal contempt for violating injunction against engaging in unauthorized practice of law in divorce cases); Florida Bar v. Brumbaugh, 355 So. 2d 1186 (Fla. 1978) (respondent, a nonlawyer operating as a secretarial service, was enjoined from preparing papers and giving advice to individuals in connection with divorce proceedings; court permitted respondent to publish divorce forms and to complete these forms using information supplied by clients).

304. Rhode, Policing the Professional Monopoly, 34 Stan. L. Rev. at 11-12.

305. See People v. Laden, 893 P.2d 771 (Colo. 1995) (en banc) (lawyer

While the doctrine of the unauthorized practice of law and the judicial power to enforce the doctrine are well established, controversy regarding the unauthorized practice of law has intensified in recent years. The fundamental issue is whether broad restrictions on the unauthorized practice of law serve the public interest.[306] The basic argument in favor of prohibitions on the unauthorized practice of law rests on protection of the public. The argument runs as follows: Legal services are complicated. Because of this complexity, lay people are unable to evaluate the competency of nonlawyers who might offer to render such services. Therefore, the state is justified in prohibiting nonlawyers from engaging in the practice of law.

This argument in favor of prohibitions on the unauthorized practice of law is suspect. First, although some legal services are complex, many types of legal services are relatively uncomplicated and are routinely performed by paralegals, almost all of whom are nonlawyers. The usual response to this argument is that paralegals operate under the supervision of lawyers. But this response begs the question: It admits that nonlawyers can perform legal services, but argues that the proper form of regulation for such services is by direct lawyer supervision. Whether direct lawyer supervision should be the only means for regulating nonlawyer practice is open to question. Moreover, experienced well-trained paralegals typically require little supervision, and at least some states authorize lawyers to employ independent paralegals whom they do not directly supervise.[307]

Second, while lay people may be unable to evaluate the

---

guilty of aiding in unauthorized practice of law by cooperating with nonlawyer who counseled and sold living trust packages).

306. For an empirical study of the unauthorized practice rules in the area of pro se divorce, see Project, The Unauthorized Practice of Law and Pro Se Divorce: An Empirical Analysis, 86 Yale L.J. 104 (1976) (study casts substantial doubt on wisdom of restrictions on unauthorized practice for nonlitigation matters, especially for indigents or individuals of modest means; benefits to clients of unauthorized practice restrictions have been exaggerated and costs are substantial).

307. In re Opinion No. 24 of Comm. on Unauthorized Practice of Law, 607 A.2d 962 (N.J. 1992). But see Carl M. Selinger, The Retention of Limitations on the Out-of-Court Practice of Law by Independent Paralegals, 9 Geo. J. Legal Ethics 879 (1996).

quality of legal services provided by nonlawyers, this does not justify the conclusion that such services should be prohibited. Lay people buy many products and services whose quality they lack the ability to evaluate. Automobiles and insurance are two examples. A variety of solutions to lack of consumer information is possible. The market will often provide a response to lack of information. *Consumer Reports* and other publications provide information to consumers about the quality of most consumer products. It is not difficult to imagine similar publications developing for legal services. Further, regulatory solutions short of prohibition, such as disclosure or limited licensing, can be considered.

Policy considerations and constitutional principles also raise questions about the wisdom of the prohibition on the unauthorized practice of law.[308] Low- and moderate-income individuals have a vast unmet need for legal services. A national sample of low-income households found that 43 percent of respondents experienced legal difficulties during the past year, but legal services were unavailable for about 50 percent of those problems.[309] Other national and state studies have reached similar conclusions. Indeed, one consequence of the continued application of rules on the unauthorized practice of law is that individuals of modest means may increasingly turn to pro se representation.[310]

The prohibitions on the unauthorized practice of law also raise constitutional issues. In Lassiter v. Department of Social Services[311] the Supreme Court held that indigents do not have an absolute right to appointed counsel in civil cases, but quite clearly access to counsel in civil cases has due process implications. Moreover, the Court has not yet addressed the question of the constitutionality under the First Amendment of prohibitions on advertising of legal services by nonlawyers. Under the *Central Hudson* test,[312] truthful advertising is subject to regulation if the state shows a substantial interest in the regulation and if the regulation

---

308. Deborah L. Rhode, The Delivery of Legal Services by Non-lawyers, 4 Geo. J. Legal Ethics 209, 228-233 (1990).

309. The Spangenberg Group, National Survey of the Civil Legal Needs of the Poor 3, 18 (May 1989) (Report sponsored by ABA Consortium on Legal Services and the Public).

310. For a study of this issue, see Bruce D. Sales et al., Self-Representation in Divorce Cases (ABA 1993).

311. 452 U.S. 18 (1981). See Problem 4-9.

312. See Problem 4-7.

is in proportion to the interest. States certainly have a substantial interest in regulation of legal services, but it is questionable whether prohibition of such services by nonlawyers is in proportion to that interest.

Approaches to regulation of nonlawyer practice

The ABA Commission on Nonlawyer Practice has issued reports and recommendations on the extent of nonlawyer practice in the United States. In 1994 the commission issued a discussion draft that contains a wealth of factual detail on the subject.[313] The report describes practice by "legal technicians" (nonlawyers providing legal services without supervision by lawyers) in the following areas: federal and state administrative agency practice, immigration practice, federal and state taxation, specially authorized practice in certain courts, housing disputes, family law, real estate, independent claim adjusters, debt collection, debt counseling, and general practice.[314] The report also includes a summary of the current rules on nonlawyer practice in many jurisdictions.

In August 1995 the commission issued a report, "Nonlawyer Activities in Law-Related Situations," finding that with adequate protection for the public, nonlawyers had an important role to play in delivery of legal services to the public. The commission recommended that the ABA reconsider its ethics rules and policies in a variety of areas, including those governing the unauthorized practice of law. The commission proposed an analytical framework that could be used by states to determine whether a particular activity should be regulated, unregulated, or prohibited:

- Does the activity if performed by nonlawyers present a serious risk to life, health, safety, or economic well-being of members of the public?
- Do potential consumers have sufficient knowledge to evaluate the qualifications of nonlawyers offering the services?
- Do the benefits to the public likely to accrue from regu-

---

313. ABA Commn. on Nonlawyer Practice, Nonlawyer Practice in the United States: Summary of the Factual Record (1994).
314. Id. at 17-22.

lation outweigh any likely negative consequences of regulation?

If the activity poses a serious risk of harm and consumers lack information to evaluate the quality of service, the commission indicated that the activity should be regulated; the form that the regulation takes would depend on a weighing of the costs and benefits of the regulation. The commission outlined a wide range of regulatory options that states might consider, including registration, licensing, or disclosure. The commission also summarized various areas in which states might consider regulation, including age, experience, education, training, recordkeeping, continuing education, and admission examinations.[315] Problem 5-3 considers various approaches to regulation of nonlawyer practice in real estate transactions.

A central issue in connection with reevaluation of restrictions on the unauthorized practice of law is bar control. The bar obviously has a financial interest in limiting competition by nonlawyers. To the extent that the bar controls such restrictions, reform is unlikely to be great. The experience in California is illustrative. In July 1990, a Commission on Legal Technicians created by the California Bar issued a report recommending that the state supreme court adopt a rule allowing nonlawyers to practice law, initially in the areas of bankruptcy, family, and landlord-tenant, under a licensing and regulatory system.[316] Unsurprisingly, the report caused considerable controversy within the bar. In August 1991 the Board of Governors of the California Bar defeated a more limited proposal for a bar-controlled board that would license legal technicians only in the area of landlord-tenant.[317] Meaningful reform of the rules on the unauthorized practice of law is likely to require reduction in bar control of the process.[318]

315. For criticism of the commission's proposals, see Deborah L. Rhode, Professionalism in Perspective: Alternative Approaches to Nonlawyer Practice, 22 N.Y.U. Rev. L. & Soc. Change 701 (1996).
316. See Kathleen E. Justice, Note, There Goes the Monopoly: The California Proposal to Allow Nonlawyers to Practice Law, 44 Vand. L. Rev. 179 (1991). See also Ryan J. Talamante, Note, We Can't All Be Lawyers . . . Or Can We? Regulating the Unauthorized Practice of Law in Arizona, 34 Ariz. L. Rev. 873 (1992).
317. Don J. DeBenedictis, California Bar Drops Technician Plan, 77-Nov. A.B.A. J. 36 (1991).
318. See Rhode, The Delivery of Legal Services by Non-lawyers, 4 Geo.

Application of restrictions on unauthorized practice to out-of-state lawyers

The practice of law is increasingly becoming national and even international. As a result lawyers admitted in one jurisdiction often must deal with legal problems in or the law of other jurisdictions where they are not admitted to practice. Such transactions pose unauthorized practice problems for lawyers.

One way in which such a problem can arise is if a lawyer represents a client in a legal matter that involves more than one jurisdiction. If the matter involves litigation, an out-of-state lawyer may associate local counsel and with court permission appear pro hac vice to represent the client in the matter. Often, however, an out-of-state lawyer may be called on to represent a client in connection with a matter that does not necessarily involve litigation, such as negotiating a dispute or drafting a contract.

Does a lawyer engage in the unauthorized practice of law if the lawyer handles a nonlitigation matter in a jurisdiction in which the lawyer is not admitted? The California Supreme Court addressed this issue in Birbrower, Montalbano, Condon & Frank, P.C. v. Superior Court (ESQ Business Services, Inc.).[319] Birbrower was a New York law firm without any members licensed to practice law in California. ESQ, a California corporation, retained Birbrower to represent it in a dispute with Tandem Computers regarding a software development and marketing contract. The contract stated that California law governed. Birbrower attorneys traveled to California on several occasions to meet with representatives of ESQ and its accountants, to interview potential arbitrators, and to negotiate with Tandem on ESQ's behalf. The parties ultimately agreed to a settlement of the matter before it went to arbitration. ESQ subsequently brought a legal malpractice claim against Birbrower, and the firm counterclaimed for unpaid legal fees.

The California Supreme Court held that the firm's fee agree-

J. Legal Ethics at 232-233. See also Alan Morrison, Defining the Unauthorized Practice of Law: Some New Ways of Looking at an Old Question, 4 Nova L.J. 363 (1980) (calling for creation of body consisting of lawyers, consumers, and competitors of lawyers to set standards for performance of legal services by non-lawyers).

319. 949 P.2d 1 (Cal. 1998).

ment was unenforceable as to work performed in California (but not necessarily for work performed in New York to the extent that it could be severed from the California work) because the firm had engaged in the unauthorized practice of law in violation of section 6125 of the California Business and Professional Code. The court stated that a lawyer admitted to practice in another state but not in California engages in the unauthorized practice of law "in California" when the lawyer has sufficient contacts with a California client to amount to a clear legal representation:

> In our view, the practice of law "in California" entails sufficient contact with the California client to render the nature of the legal service a clear legal representation. In addition to a quantitative analysis, we must consider the nature of the unlicensed lawyer's activities in the state. Mere fortuitous or attenuated contacts will not sustain a finding that the unlicensed lawyer practiced law "in California." The primary inquiry is whether the unlicensed lawyer engaged in sufficient activities in the state, or created a continuing relationship with the California client that included legal duties and obligations.[320]

Physical presence in California is a factor, but does not determine whether an out-of-state lawyer is practicing law in California. The court, however, rejected the notion a person automatically practices law in California by giving advice on California law or by entering the state virtually:

> Our definition does not necessarily depend on or require the unlicensed lawyer's physical presence in the state. Physical presence here is one factor we may consider in deciding whether the unlicensed lawyer has violated section 6125, but it is by no means exclusive. For example, one may practice law in the state in violation of section 6125 although not physically present here by advising a California client on California law in connection with a California legal dispute by telephone, fax, computer, or other modern technological means. Conversely, although we decline to provide a comprehensive list of what activities constitute sufficient contact with the state, we do reject the notion that a person automatically practices law "in California" whenever that person practices California law anywhere, or "virtually" enters the state by telephone, fax, e-mail, or satellite.[321]

320. Id. at 5.
321. Id. at 5-6.

The court rejected Birbrower's arguments that the California statute prohibiting the unauthorized practice of law was intended to apply only to nonlawyers, not to out-of-state lawyers, and that the statute did not apply to representation incident to arbitration proceedings.[322]

As the court in *Birbrower* indicates, unauthorized practice problems can arise even if the lawyer does not physically enter the jurisdiction. Sometimes a lawyer admitted in one jurisdiction is asked to advise a client or represent a client in a matter involving the law of another jurisdiction. Does a lawyer engage in the unauthorized practice of law by providing advice about the law of a jurisdiction in which the lawyer is not admitted? Cases subsequent to *Birbrower* indicate that the determination of whether a lawyer is engaged in the unauthorized practice of law depends on whether the client is a "California client." For example, in Estate of Condon (Condon v. McHenry)[323] the California Court of Appeals held that a Colorado lawyer did not engage in the unauthorized practice of law when the lawyer gave advice to a Colorado resident who was co-executor of the estate of a California decedent about the application of California law even though the lawyer entered the state physically or virtually because the client was not a "California client."[324]

4. Delivery of Legal Services to Indigents in Civil Cases

--------- **Problem 4-9** ---------

Mandatory Pro Bono and Delivery of Legal Services to Indigents

a. You have been chosen to participate in a debate on the following proposition:

322. Id. at 7-10.
323. 76 Cal. Rptr. 2d 922 (Ct. App. 1998) (on reconsideration after *Birbrower*).
324. See also Fought & Co. v. Steel Eng. & Erection, Inc., 951 P.2d 487 (Haw. 1998) (supplier's Oregon general counsel did not practice law "within the jurisdiction" of Hawaii when it rendered legal services in role of consultant to supplier and supplier's Hawaii counsel, and thus statutes did not bar supplier's recovery of appellate attorney fees for general counsel's services).

RESOLVED, that the State Bar of Your State should adopt a mandatory pro bono plan.

Be prepared to debate the affirmative or negative of that proposition at the next class.

b. Your instructor will assign members of the class to make short reports on ways in which delivery of legal services to indigents can be improved. For a bibliography of materials from which to choose a topic for a report, see Bibliography to the Conference on the Delivery of Legal Services to Low-Income Persons: Professional and Ethical Issues, 67 Fordham L. Rev. 2731 (1999). See also Roger C. Cramton, Delivery of Legal Services to Ordinary Americans, 44 Case W. Res. L. Rev. 531 (1994).

c. Be prepared to articulate and justify the portion of your philosophy of lawyering (recall Chapter 1 and Problem 1-5) regarding the nature and extent of your obligation to assist in providing pro bono legal services.

Read Model Rules 6.1, 6.2, 6.3, 6.4 and comments.

Constitutional right to appointed counsel in civil cases

While indigent criminal defendants have a broad constitutional right to appointed counsel under the Sixth and Fourteenth Amendments, the Supreme Court has refused to recognize a general right to appointed counsel in civil cases. The leading case is Lassiter v. Department of Social Services,[325] an action for termination of parental rights. In *Lassiter* the Supreme Court stated that a presumption exists that appointed counsel was constitutionally required only in cases involving a risk of incarceration.[326] The Court went on to decide, however, that due process may require appointment of counsel in cases in which the defendant does not face a deprivation of physical liberty:

325. 452 U.S. 18 (1981).
326. Id. at 26-27.

The case of Mathews v. Eldridge, 424 U.S. 319, 335 [(1976)], propounds three elements to be evaluated in deciding what due process requires, viz., the private interests at stake, the government's interest, and the risk that the procedures used will lead to erroneous decisions. We must balance these elements against each other, and then set their net weight in the scales against the presumption that there is a right to appointed counsel only where the indigent, if he is unsuccessful, may lose his personal freedom.[327]

The Court found that the private and governmental interests involved in cases seeking termination of parental rights were great and the risk of error in such cases significant. Nonetheless, the Court held that the application of the *Eldridge* factors was not rigid and would "be answered in the first instance by the trial court, subject . . . to appellate review."[328] The Court went on to hold that the trial court did not commit error in failing to appoint counsel for Ms. Lassiter because on the facts of the case these factors did not outweigh the presumption against appointed counsel.[329]

Justice Blackmun's dissenting opinion criticized the Court's case-by-case approach. He concluded that this framework undermines the concept of general fairness on which due process is based, makes it difficult for a reviewing court to determine from the record whether the proceedings were fair since the absence of evidence in the record may be the source of unfairness, and is cumbersome and costly.[330] In Justice Stevens's view, due process required appointed counsel in cases involving termination of parental rights, which he viewed as more serious than most criminal cases.[331]

The framework for analysis set by the Supreme Court in *Lassiter* continues to be the approach used by federal and state courts in deciding right-to-counsel issues in civil cases.[332]

---

327. Id. at 27.
328. Id. at 32.
329. Id. at 32-33.
330. Id. at 49-52.
331. Id. at 59-60.
332. See, e.g., Iraheta v. Superior Court, 83 Cal. Rptr. 2d 471 (Ct. App. 1999, *review denied*), (alleged street gang members named as defendants in action seeking injunction to abate public nuisance not entitled to counsel under *Lassiter*); Joni B. v. State, 549 N.W.2d 411 (Wis. 1996) (state statute erecting per se bar to appointment of counsel in protective services cases unconstitutional because it deprived courts of discretion under *Lassiter*).

Legal services programs

The Supreme Court in *Lassiter* noted that its decision was based on the minimal requirements of the Constitution: "A wise public policy, however, may require that higher standards be adopted than those minimally tolerable under the Constitution."[333] Both the federal and state governments have to varying degrees been willing to provide for appointed counsel in some civil cases as a matter of public policy; such programs are commonly referred to as *legal aid.*

The legal aid movement began in the latter part of the nineteenth and early twentieth centuries in New York, Chicago, and other large cities. Individuals and charities formed legal aid societies and other organizations to provide legal services to the poor, particularly to the large number of immigrants coming into the cities. The focus of legal aid at that time was charitable: to provide legal services to individuals who could not afford to hire lawyers.[334]

The legal aid movement showed little growth and change until the 1960s, when it underwent a fundamental transformation. One of the principal vehicles for change was the Ford Foundation, which began funding various experiments in providing legal services to the poor, including support for law reform efforts. The philosophy of law reform differs fundamentally from that of service. Under a law reform strategy, legal aid attorneys seek to use the legal system to make fundamental institutional and systemic changes that will remove discrimination against or provide benefits to the poor. Class actions and lobbying for legislative change became major tools of law reform efforts.[335]

In 1963 President Lyndon Johnson called for a "War on Poverty." Among the programs passed by Congress in response to this initiative was the Office of Economic Opportunity (OEO), which included the Legal Services Program. Thus, for the first time, the federal government became involved in the funding of legal services for the poor.[336] During the next 10 years, however, the Legal Services Program became embroiled in political controversy, particularly its funding of law reform activities. Federal funding for

333. 452 U.S. at 33.
334. Wolfram, Modern Legal Ethics §16.7.2, at 933.
335. Id. at 934-935.
336. Id. at 936-937.

legal services still continued to enjoy substantial support in the bar, particularly in the ABA.

In 1974, with the support of the president and the ABA, Congress created the Legal Services Corporation (LSC). The LSC represented a political compromise between the proponents and opponents of government-funded legal services. Its creation showed a continued commitment by the federal government to fund legal services. Indeed, legal services were now "upgraded" from a program to the status of a separate federal corporation. In addition, by creating a separate federal corporation with its own board of directors, supporters of the LSC hoped to take legal services "out of politics." At the same time, however, the statute creating the LSC put strict limits on various types of law reform activities.[337]

The hope that the creation of the LSC would remove federal funding of legal services from politics has not been realized. When the Reagan administration came to power in 1981, it targeted the LSC for abolition. Backers in Congress with the support of the ABA were able to save the LSC from extinction, but its appropriation lagged substantially behind inflation, and the number of attorneys funded by the LSC diminished.[338] In 1995 the Republican Congress again called for abolition of the LSC. In 1996 Congress reauthorized funding for legal services but placed substantial new restrictions on the activities of legal services lawyers, including limitations on the use of funds received from nonfederal sources.[339]

---

337. On the history of the LSC, see id. §16.7.3, at 937-939. For articles tracing the history of legal services and discussing many of the problems confronting the effort to provide legal representation to the poor, see Marc Feldman, Political Lessons: Legal Services for the Poor, 83 Geo. L.J. 1529 (1995). For commentary on Professor Feldman's article, see Gary Bellow & Jeanne Charn, Paths Not Yet Taken: Some Comments on Feldman's Critique of Legal Services Practice, 83 Geo. L.J. 1633 (1995); Alan W. Houseman, Political Lessons: Legal Services for the Poor — A Commentary, 83 Geo. L.J. 1669 (1995).

338. Wolfram, Modern Legal Ethics §16.7.3, at 938. For a description of the impact of cuts in federal funding on legal services programs, see David Barringer, Downsized Justice, 82-Jul. A.B.A. J. 60 (1996).

339. Omnibus Consolidated Rescissions and Appropriations Act of 1996, Pub. L. No. 104-134, §504, 110 Stat. 1321 (1996) (restricting right to use federal funds to engage in activities such as class actions, to initiate rulemaking proceedings, or to claim attorney fees; restrictions also prohibit recipients of federal funds from using private, state, or local donations for these purposes or from transferring nonfederal funds to anyone who does not follow same restrictions). On

Federal courts found most of these restrictions constitutional.[340]

Today most local legal services programs receive funding not only from the LSC but also from state and local sources as well. A major source of funding for legal services in many communities is IOLTA (Interest on Lawyer Trust Account) grants.[341] Various charities also provide support for legal services. Nonetheless, the bulk of financing for legal services programs still comes from the LSC.

Legal services programs have woefully inadequate resources to meet the needs of low- and moderate-income individuals. The LSC funds approximately one legal services lawyer for every 10,000 individuals below the poverty line.[342] Further, a number of studies have documented the existence of a vast unmet need for legal services. For example, a survey conducted for the ABA in 1992 showed that approximately 50 percent of both low- and moderate-income individuals had a new legal problem during 1992. Only 39 percent of moderate-income individuals and only 29 percent of low-income individuals took any action about their legal problems.[343] Because of these unmet needs, proposals for imposing an obligation on lawyers to assist in providing legal services have been made from a variety of quarters.

---

the ethical obligations of legal services lawyers in light of these restrictions, see ABA Comm. on Ethics and Prof. Resp., Formal Op. 96-399.

340. Velazquez v. Legal Servs. Corp., 164 F.3d 757 (2d Cir. 1999) (statute upheld except for provision prohibiting welfare suits that attempt to change or invalidate existing law); Legal Aid Socy. of Haw. v. Legal Servs. Corp., 145 F.3d 1017 (9th Cir.), *cert. denied*, 119 S. Ct. 539 (1998).

341. See Phillips v. Washington Legal Found., 524 U.S. 156 (1998) (holding that clients had constitutionally protected property interest in interest income generated by their funds held in trust under Texas IOLTA program and remanding for further proceedings to determine whether client's property had been "taken" constitutionally, and if so, amount of just compensation).

342. Based on the poverty population as reported by the Bureau of the Census and funded attorneys as reported by the LSC.

343. Institute for Survey Research at Temple University, Findings of the Comprehensive Legal Needs Study (1994). A summary of the principal findings of the survey can be found in Mark Hansen, A Shunned Justice System, 80-Apr A.B.A. J. 18 (1994).

The Marrero Committee Report

Since funded legal services programs do not have sufficient resources to come even close to satisfying the need for legal services of the poor, the bar has in recent years considered ways in which this need could be met, at least in part. One idea that has stirred considerable controversy within the profession is that lawyers be required to devote a certain amount of time periodically to providing legal services to persons of limited means.

Mandatory pro bono proposals must deal with a number of issues. Probably the most detailed mandatory pro bono proposal to date was offered in New York by the Marrero Committee;[344] the proposal has the following major elements:

1. *Quantity of required service:* 40 hours every two years.
2. *Coverage and exemptions:* All attorneys admitted to practice law in New York and currently practicing. The committee provided for exemptions for cause on a case-by-case basis. The committee also recognized that some practical difficulties could arise in applying the proposal to government lawyers and other classes of attorneys, but it concluded that universal coverage was extremely important.
3. *Qualifying services:* Services must be rendered to the poor or to organizations that serve the poor. The committee rejected two broader definitions of pro bono services — uncompensated legal service and public interest legal service — because the underlying rationale for its proposal was the special needs of the poor to have access to the legal system.
4. *Compliance:* Generally compliance must be personal, but the proposal recognizes two exceptions: First, attorneys who are members of groups such as law firms can satisfy their pro bono obligation collectively. This means that partners in firms can assign associates to handle pro bono work and obtain credit for their services. It also means that firms could hire full-time pro bono lawyers and re-

344. Committee to Improve the Availability of Legal Services, Final Report to the Chief Judge of the State of New York (April 1990), reprinted in 19 Hofstra L. Rev. 755 (1991).

ceive credit for their services. Second, the proposal provides for a financial contribution in lieu of service at the rate of $1,000 for 20 hours ($50 per hour). The buyout option only applies, however, to lawyers practicing in firms of 10 or fewer lawyers. The committee felt that the group practice concept gave larger firms sufficient flexibility, but that smaller firms needed the additional buyout option because the group alternative would not be as useful for smaller firms.

5.   *Excess time:* Excess time may be carried forward for no more than four years.

6.   *Disbursements:* Reasonable expenses incurred in handling pro bono matters are reimbursable. The proposal does not specify the source of reimbursement but suggests two possibilities: funds generated by contributions in lieu of service and IOLTA funds.

7.   *Professional liability insurance:* The committee concluded that no special provision for insurance was necessary because most lawyers would already have insurance that would apply or such insurance could be obtained by sponsoring organizations.

8.   *Incompetence:* The committee concluded that the flexibility built in to its proposal was adequate to deal with concerns about competency of representation.

Justifications and criticisms of mandatory pro bono

What are the arguments in favor of and in opposition to mandatory pro bono? The Marrero Committee focused on several points to justify its proposal. First, numerous studies show a vast, unmet need for legal services by low-income households. Second, the failure to receive adequate legal services has inflicted an "intolerable toll" on both the poor and society as a whole. Lack of representation in eviction proceedings increases homelessness; absence of representation in domestic matters leads to violence; want of legal assistance in federal benefit cases increases the burden on the states. Further, lack of counsel undermines the legitimacy of the legal system itself.[345] The committee considered the possibility

345. Id. at 774-775.

that various alternatives other than mandatory pro bono could solve or reduce the problem, but it concluded that this was unrealistic. The committee noted that the decline in federal funding for legal services and the increased economic pressures on law firms made it less likely that voluntary efforts would be successful.[346]

Given the documented need and the likelihood that the need would not be met through either federal funding or voluntary efforts, the committee turned to the role of the lawyer in providing legal services to the poor. While the committee agreed with the proposition that society as a whole bore responsibility for redressing the problem, it concluded that "lawyers, independent of their ordinary duty as citizens, have a professional responsibility to mobilize their own resources in order to meet these needs."[347] The special duty of lawyers to provide legal services to the poor flows from the unique training and skills of lawyers, their exclusive license to practice law, and the lawyers' responsibility to promote the legitimacy and proper functioning of the legal system.[348]

The principal arguments against mandatory pro bono fall into four categories: quality of service, unfairness to lawyers, administrative and practical difficulties, and lack of benefit to the poor. Some critics have questioned whether lawyers who are forced to provide legal services would do so competently. In addition, many legal problems facing the poor (over welfare, housing, and employment, for example) involve complicated bodies of law in which private practitioners may have little knowledge or experience.[349] Quality-of-service issues could be addressed in several ways. While some legal problems facing the poor involve specialized bodies of law, many legal problems (divorce, wills, transfer of real estate) are fairly routine. In addition, for areas that require specialized knowledge, back-up facilities could assist lawyers in providing these services.[350] In addition, the buyout provision

---

346. Id. at 776.

347. Id. at 780.

348. Id. For other arguments for pro bono service, see Robert A. Katzman ed., The Law Firm and the Public Good (1995) (essays on pro bono); Steven Lubet & Cathryn Stewart, A "Public Assets" Theory of Lawyers' Pro Bono Obligations, 145 U. Pa. L. Rev. 1245 (1997).

349. Roger C. Cramton, Mandatory Pro Bono, 19 Hofstra L. Rev. 1113, 1127 (1991).

350. See ABA, Standards for Programs Providing Civil Pro Bono Legal

found in the Marrero proposal could generate funds sufficient to hire lawyers with expertise to provide specialized services.

Some opponents of mandatory pro bono argue that such proposals are unconstitutional because they involve violations of individual liberty and taking of lawyers' property without just compensation. Such constitutional arguments have generally been rejected by the courts, however, on the ground that the legal profession is a regulated industry and requiring lawyers to devote a limited amount of time or money to provide legal services for the poor falls within the scope of reasonable regulation.[351] Even if mandatory pro bono is not unconstitutional, some adversaries argue that it is unfair to impose this burden on lawyers when society as a whole should provide for legal services to the poor. As noted above, the Marrero Report addressed this point; it concluded that lawyers have a special duty to provide legal services to the poor flowing from the unique training and skills of lawyers, their exclusive license to practice law, and the lawyers' responsibility to promote the legitimacy and proper functioning of the legal system. However, some critics, noting the increased competitiveness of the legal profession, question whether this justification is adequate.[352] Moreover, the program can generate other fairness issues. Mandatory pro bono tends to be regressive. The Marrero proposal suffers from this problem. Senior partners in large firms can satisfy

---

Services to Persons of Limited Means (1996); ABA Center for Pro Bono, Pro Bono Support and Delivery: A Directory of Statewide Models (1998).

351. Cramton, Mandatory Pro Bono, 19 Hofstra L. Rev. at 1131-1132.

352. Id. at 1134-1136. Professor Timothy Terrell and James Wildman also reject the monopoly argument for imposing a duty on lawyers to deliver legal services because they find that the existence of free entry, full competition, and lack of anticompetitive behavior in the legal profession means that lawyers no longer collect "monopoly rents." Timothy P. Terrell & James H. Wildman, Rethinking "Professionalism," 41 Emory L. J. 403, 421 (1992). Terrell and Wildman believe, however, that lawyers have a duty as professionals to enable those members of the profession who want to assist in delivering legal services to do so. Id. at 430. While rejecting any personal obligation to deliver legal services, Terrell and Wildman suggest that the bar could impose a tax on its members to assist other lawyers in their efforts. Id. at 431. For a contrary view arguing that a duty to provide public service is justified because lawyers receive the benefits of a state monopoly, see Tigran W. Eldred & Thomas Schoenherr, The Lawyer's Duty of Public Service: More Than Charity? 96 W. Va. L. Rev. 367 (1993-1994). See also Steven Lubet, Professionalism Revisited, 42 Emory L.J. 197 (1993) (arguing that personal involvement of prestigious members of the profession can have a transformative impact on ways in which courts handle cases).

their pro bono obligations by assigning associates to perform the work or by funding full-time poverty lawyers. These options are unavailable or less attractive for solo practitioners or lawyers in small firms. In addition, if the program has a fixed-dollar buyout provision, this option also operates regressively, falling more heavily on lawyers with lower incomes.[353] To the extent that the obligation is imposed only on the lawyers of certain states (New York, for example), it places those lawyers at a competitive disadvantage with lawyers in other states who do not bear this "tax."[354]

Critics of mandatory pro bono refer to significant practical and administrative difficulties with any such program. The program must address whether the requirement applies to lawyers engaged in teaching, politics, business, or government practice.[355] The definition of qualifying services must be carefully considered. If charitable or bar work counts, then the goal of delivering legal services to the poor will be eroded, but if bar and charitable work does not qualify, the availability and willingness of lawyers to perform these services will diminish. A question exists as to whether reduced-fee work will qualify in part as pro bono work. In addition, the range of service options must be broad to avoid forcing lawyers into service that conflicts with their political or religious values.[356] Additional administrative personnel will be required to review reports to determine whether lawyers are in compliance with their pro bono obligations and to institute proceedings against lawyers who fail to do so. Finally, increasing the supply of legal services for the poor may harm rather than help the poor because more litigation may increase the cost of basic services provided to the poor, such as housing.[357]

The concept of mandatory pro bono has not been received

353. Cramton, Mandatory Pro Bono, 19 Hofstra L. Rev. at 1133-1134.
354. Id. at 1130-1131.
355. Id. at 1128.
356. Id. at 1129-1130.
357. Jonathan R. Macey, Mandatory Pro Bono: Comfort for the Poor or Welfare for the Rich? 77 Cornell L. Rev. 1115 (1992). But see Ronald H. Silverman, Conceiving a Lawyer's Legal Duty to the Poor, 19 Hofstra L. Rev. 885 (1991). Professor Silverman's article is part of a symposium on mandatory pro bono, which includes the Marrero Report and the Cramton article cited earlier. See Symposium on Mandatory Pro Bono, 19 Hofstra L. Rev. No. 4 (1991). For other perspectives on the mandatory pro bono debate, see Symposium, Mandatory Pro Bono in Maryland, 49 Md. L. Rev. 1 (1990).

with much enthusiasm by the bar. No state has adopted a mandatory pro bono requirement, although there has been some movement to place greater emphasis on voluntary pro bono service. In 1993 the ABA amended Model Rule 6.1 to provide for a voluntary pro bono standard of 50 hours per year, a substantial majority of which should be directed to "persons of limited means." Prior to the amendment, the rule provided:

> A lawyer should render public interest legal service. A lawyer may discharge this responsibility by providing professional services at no fee or a reduced fee to persons of limited means or to public service or charitable groups or organizations, by service in activities for improving the law, the legal system or the legal profession, and by financial support for organizations that provide legal services to persons of limited means.

The older version of Rule 6.1 did not specify an hourly standard, nor did it direct lawyers to focus their pro bono efforts on the poor. Several states, including Arizona, Florida, and Kentucky, have changed their rules of professional conduct to include more substantial provisions on voluntary pro bono representation.[358] The Florida rule provides an aspirational standard of either 20 hours of pro bono service or a contribution of $350 to a legal services organization per year.[359] Under the Florida rule lawyers must report whether they have complied with the rule's aspirational standard:[360] "The reporting requirement is designed to provide a sound basis for evaluating the results achieved by this rule, reveal the strengths and weaknesses of the pro bono plan, and to remind lawyers of their professional responsibility under this rule."[361] The majority of states, however, continue to adhere to the ABA's older version of Rule 6.1.

358. Ariz. R. Prof. Conduct 6.1; Fla. R. Prof. Conduct 4-6.1; Kentucky Sup. Ct. R. 3.130 (6.1).
359. Fla. R. Prof. Conduct 4-6.1(b).
360. Id. 4-6.1(d).
361. Id. cmt.

Chapter 5

Ethical Issues in Office Practice

In previous chapters we have examined the application of fundamental ethical obligations, such as the duty of confidentiality, the obligation to avoid conflicts of interest, and limitations on zealous representation in the context of criminal practice and civil litigation. The world of office practitioners, whether they are involved in general business practice, securities, real estate, estate planning, tax, or other specialized fields, poses ethical problems that also require application of these fundamental ethical concepts. Indeed, in some respects the ethical and related legal issues facing office practitioners are more acute than in litigation practice because the amounts of money (and therefore the potential liability) involved in office practice can be staggering.

Section A of this chapter considers ethical problems of office practitioners engaged in business and securities practice. The problems focus on conflicts of interest in business formations and lawyers' obligations when they learn of fraud by their clients. Section B examines ethical issues in real estate, estate planning, and tax practice. These areas do not, of course, exhaust the specialized areas in which lawyers may practice. For example, bankruptcy practice involves a complex interrelationship between rules of professional conduct and provisions of the bankruptcy code.[1]

---

1. See generally 1 Norton Bankruptcy Law & Practice ch. 27 (2d ed.). See, e.g., In re Granite Partners, 219 B.R. 22 (Bankr. S.D.N.Y. 1998) (law firm

The practice areas covered in these materials do illustrate, however, the most common ethical dilemmas faced by office practitioners.

A.   Business and Securities Practice

Problem 5-1

Lawyers as Intermediaries, Investors, and Board Members

Nancy McDow, one of your long-time clients, has called you to arrange a meeting. McDow tells you that she and Vulkan Bronowski, a person whom you have never met, wish to establish a small business to develop and market computer programs that will assist American companies doing business in Eastern Europe. McDow, an entrepreneur, will supply the capital for the venture. Bronowski, an expert in computer programming who recently emigrated to the United States, will lead the development of software. McDow says that she and Bronowski will bring in a third individual in the near future to take charge of marketing. McDow wants you to handle the legal work for formation of the business. Given the uncertain prospects for the business, McDow wants to limit cash expenditures. She asks whether you would be willing to receive a 10 percent ownership interest in the business in payment for your services. She says that it might turn out to be "lucrative." McDow also wants you to serve on the new company's board of directors. How would you handle the initial meeting with McDow and Bronowski?

Read Model Rules 1.8(a), 2.2, and comments.

---

representing Chapter 11 trustee denied compensation of more than $2 million for failure to disclose conflict of interest).

Louis D. Brandeis: "lawyer for the situation"

In 1916 President Woodrow Wilson nominated a prominent Boston lawyer, Louis D. Brandeis, to the Supreme Court. Brandeis's distinguished career had involved him in many of the day's most important public issues.[2] The Brandeis nomination, however, was controversial for a number of reasons. Wilson had been elected as a minority president in a three-way election in 1912, and it was not at all clear that he would be reelected in a direct confrontation with a Republican. In addition, Brandeis had been a central figure in the downfall of the Taft administration though his representation of Louis Glavis, a subordinate in the Department of the Interior, who resigned in a conservation scandal involving the secretary of the interior. Brandeis had brought to light documents showing that the president and the attorney general had made public misrepresentations in an effort to protect the secretary of the interior. Taft opposed the Brandeis nomination not only because of this incident but also because he personally wanted an appointment to the Court. Moreover, some powerful business interests fought against the Brandeis appointment because he had opposed them in various legal matters. Finally, Brandeis was the first Jew nominated to the Court.[3]

Brandeis's opponents reviewed his entire legal career in an effort to find ammunition to scuttle the nomination. As a result, the Republican minority on the Senate Judiciary Committee issued a report charging Brandeis with 12 instances of ethical misconduct. In a study of these 12 cases, John Frank concluded that the charges against Brandeis were not meritorious and that "[o]ne's main impression is surprise that the powers of wealth and political position, which had been hitting at Brandeis for years and searching for every possible ground of complaint, should have

2. Biographies of Brandeis include Alpheus T. Mason, Brandeis, A Free Man's Life (1946); Philippa Strum, Brandeis: Beyond Progressivism (1993); and Philippa Strum, Louis D. Brandeis: Justice for the People (1984).

3. John P. Frank, The Legal Ethics of Louis D. Brandeis, 17 Stan. L. Rev. 683, 683-685 (1965).

found so little to work with."[4] One of the cases, the Lennox matter, is of particular interest to our study, because it relates to the issue of the propriety of lawyers' representing multiple clients in business transactions.

The Lennox matter involved a company that was in financial difficulty. The son of the owner of the company and an attorney for one of its creditors sought Brandeis's advice about the matter. Brandeis never specifically agreed to represent the company in the matter. Instead, he recommended an assignment for the benefit of creditors. A trust was established for the benefit of creditors, with one of Brandeis's partners as trustee. Ultimately, the company was forced into bankruptcy because the Lennox partners failed to convey assets to the trust. Brandeis represented petitioning creditors in the bankruptcy. The Lennox partners felt that Brandeis had turned against their interests, and they hired a lawyer to investigate Brandeis's conduct. Brandeis denied that he had ever agreed to represent the Lennoxes. He described his role as "counsel for the situation."[5]

Scholars have had mixed reactions to Brandeis's view of his role. Professor Thomas Shaffer praised Brandeis for a moral vision that recognizes groups as prior to individuals, and group harmony as a worthy moral goal.[6] John Frank, while vindicating Brandeis against charges of ethical misconduct, criticized his conception of the lawyer for the situation as "too vague to be intelligible."[7]

Representation of multiple parties in business transactions under the Code of Professional Responsibility and the Model Rules of Professional Conduct

Brandeis's view that a lawyer may act for multiple parties with potentially conflicting interests in an effort to produce a plan that serves all of their interests was problematic under the Code of Professional Responsibility. Disciplinary Rule 5-105(C) provided

4. Id. at 707.

5. Id. at 698-703. See also John S. Dzienkowski, Lawyers as Intermediaries: The Representation of Multiple Clients in the Modern Legal Profession, 1992 U. Ill. L. Rev. 741, 748-757.

6. Thomas L. Shaffer, The Legal Ethics of Radical Individualism, 65 Tex. L. Rev. 963, 981 (1987).

7. Frank, The Legal Ethics of Louis D. Brandeis, 17 Stan. L. Rev. at 702.

that "a lawyer may represent multiple clients if it is obvious that he can adequately represent the interest of each and if each consents to the representation after full disclosure of the possible effect of such representation on the exercise of his independent professional judgment on behalf of each." The use of the word "obvious" made it questionable whether a lawyer should represent multiple parties in a business transaction with potentially conflicting interests.[8]

The drafters of the Model Rules were well aware of Brandeis's concept of the "lawyer for the situation." Professor Geoffrey Hazard, the chief reporter for the Kutak Commission, devoted a chapter of his book *Ethics in the Practice of Law* to the concept. Hazard criticized the Code for recognizing only a "fragment of this kind of lawyering."[9] He suggested that it ought to be possible "to define the role of intercessor."[10]

Model Rule 2.2 takes up this task. Recall that we have already seen the application of Rule 2.2 in connection with domestic practice. See Problem 3-10. While the rule uses the term *intermediary*, this role differs from that of an arbitrator or a mediator. Arbitrators and mediators do not represent parties in a legal capacity. By contrast, a lawyer serving as an intermediary under Rule 2.2 represents all the parties. See Comment 2 to Model Rule 2.2.[11] Recall Problem 4-6 dealing with the role of lawyers as arbitrators and mediators. The drafters of Rule 2.2 considered it to be a specific application of general principles of loyalty and confidentiality found in Model Rules 1.6 and 1.7. They decided, however, to create a separate rule to emphasize and perhaps to validate the distinctive role of lawyers as counselors for clients who, "though adverse in their respective positions, share a more compelling interest in reaching agreement as a group."[12]

The rule imposes obligations on lawyers at three stages of the representation. Rule 2.2(a) deals with lawyers' obligations before undertaking representation. The rule parallels Rule 1.7; it requires lawyers to reasonably believe that they can undertake representa-

---

8. Legal Ethics Forum, Representation of Multiple Clients, 62 A.B.A. J. 648 (1976).

9. Geoffrey C. Hazard, Jr., Ethics in the Practice of Law 62 (1978).

10. Id. at 67.

11. See 1 Hazard & Hodes, The Law of Lawyering §2.2:101, at 511.

12. Id. at 512.

tion and to obtain the consent of their clients to such representation after consultation regarding the implications of common representation. Rule 2.2(a), however, is more specific than Rule 1.7 in several respects. It sets three requirements before the lawyer may serve as an intermediary:

1. consultation and consent (Model Rule 2.2(a)(1))
2. reasonableness of representation (Model Rule 2.2(a)(2))
3. impartiality (Model Rule 2.2(a)(3))

While the rule lists consultation and consent first, a lawyer must initially address the other two requirements to decide whether multiple representation is permissible. If these requirements are met, then the lawyer must consult with the potential clients and seek their consent under Rule 2.2(a)(1).

Under Rule 2.2(a)(2) the lawyer must reasonably believe that "each client will be able to make adequately informed decisions in the matter and that there is little risk of material prejudice to the interest of any of the clients if the contemplated resolution is unsuccessful." When a prospective client is unsophisticated, a lawyer's service as an intermediary is particularly likely to be dangerous. Under Rule 2.2(a)(3), the lawyer must reasonably believe that the representation can be undertaken impartially. When a lawyer has a long-standing relationship with one of the prospective clients, the risk of partiality is great.

Assuming a lawyer concludes that she can meet the requirements of Rule 2.2(a)(2) and (3), Model Rule 2.2(a)(1) requires the lawyer to consult with "each client concerning the implications of the common representation, including the advantages and risks involved, and the effect on the attorney-client privileges." Among the points to be addressed are the following:

- *Advantages of intermediation.* If one lawyer represents all of the parties, the lawyer has duties to all of them. The lawyer cannot favor one party at the expense of any other. The lawyer has a duty to raise any issue that may be material to any of the parties. Intermediation can save legal fees because the parties are only hiring one lawyer rather than multiple lawyers. In addition, the use of a single lawyer may increase the likelihood that any differences between the clients will be resolved because one lawyer can focus on common interests and agreement rather than on possible points of disagreement.

- *Disadvantages of intermediation.* If the clients fail to reach agreement or if a dispute develops that cannot be resolved, the lawyer will be forced to withdraw from representation of all the parties. Model Rule 2.2(c). The lawyer's withdrawal would force the parties to hire new counsel, unfamiliar with the matter, at added expense. The rule followed in most jurisdictions is that the attorney-client privilege does not apply to any dispute between jointly represented clients. See Comment 6 to Model Rule 2.2.[13] Thus, the lawyer may be required to testify as to any communications received from any other party. The lawyer's files would also be available to any party to the dispute. While a lawyer who represents multiple parties has a duty to treat all of them evenhandedly, the lawyer may intentionally or unconsciously favor one party over the others. This risk exists particularly when the lawyer has a long-standing relationship with one of the parties.

Rule 2.2(b) deals with a lawyer's obligations once the lawyer assumes the role of intermediary. The rule requires full consultation with each of the clients so that each client can make informed decisions. During mediation it is common practice to meet with each party privately and to maintain confidentiality of information received in these private sessions. May a lawyer serving as an intermediary also receive confidential information during private sessions? Comment 6 to Rule 2.2 points out a tension between the duty of confidentiality owed to each client and the obligation to keep each client informed, but it does not offer lawyers specific guidance on this issue.

Rule 2.2(c) deals with termination of intermediation. The lawyer must withdraw from representation at the request of any client or if the lawyer is no longer able to serve in the role of intermediary. On withdrawal, the lawyer may not represent any of the parties without the consent of all. This rule is a specific application of the former client rule, Model Rule 1.9.[14]

Professor John Dzienkowski has authored a comprehensive

---

13. See also 1 id. §2.2:202, at 515.
14. 1 id. §2.2:401, at 519-520.

study of the role of the lawyer as intermediary under Model Rule 2.2. While approving of the concept in principle, he argues that Rule 2.2 is defective and should be redrafted because it fails to answer a number of basic questions regarding the role of the lawyer as intermediary. Among his criticisms, Professor Dzienkowski faults the rule for failing to provide sufficient guidance to lawyers on how they should function as intermediaries and on the scope of the duty of confidentiality during intermediation.[15]

The Ethics 2000 Commission is recommending the deletion of Rule 2.2 because neither the concept of intermediation nor its relationship to the general conflict-of-interest provision, Model Rule 1.7, is well understood.[16] The commission has concluded that it would be preferable to deal with the ideas expressed in current Rule 2.2 through comments to Rule 1.7. The Restatement of the Law Governing Lawyers does not use the term *intermediation*; instead, the Restatement applies general conflict-of-interest principles to representation of clients in nonlitigated matters.[17] The Restatement recognizes that a lawyer may represent clients outside of litigation either to assist them achieve a common goal, such as forming a business, or to help them resolve a dispute prior to litigation.[18]

Conflicts of interest resulting from lawyers' ownership of interests in their clients' businesses

Ordinary commercial contracts may be rescinded because of fraud, duress, mistake, impossibility, unconscionability, illegality, and other invalidating events.[19] Contracts between fiduciaries and their principals, however, are subject to special restrictions in addition to those limitations that apply to ordinary business transactions. Principals may rescind contracts with their fiduciaries if the contract is unfair to the principal or if the fiduciary fails to

15. See Dzienkowski, Lawyers as Intermediaries, 1992 U. Ill. L. Rev. at 768-771.

16. See Ethics 2000 Commission, Memorandum on Proposed Deletion of Rule 2.2 (Mar. 23, 1999).

17. Restatement (Third) of the Law Governing Lawyers §211 and cmt. *a*.

18. Id. cmt. *a* and illus. 4 and 5.

19. See Charles L. Knapp, Nathan M. Crystal, and Harry G. Prince, Problems in Contract Law chs. 8 and 9 (4th ed. 1999).

disclose all material facts to the principal regarding the transaction. These special rules are justified because of the high degree of trust and confidence that principals repose in fiduciaries.[20]

Disciplinary Rule 5-104(A) of the Code of Professional Responsibility provided that a lawyer "shall not enter into a business transaction with a client if they have differing interests therein and if the client expects the lawyer to exercise his professional judgment therein for the protection of the client, unless the client has consented after full disclosure." While the rule did not refer to the obligation of fairness, decisional law had imposed this duty on lawyers when they engaged in business transactions with their clients. Model Rule 1.8(a) goes even further, requiring lawyers to disclose the terms of the transaction in writing. In addition, under Model Rule 1.8(a)(2), the client must be given a reasonable opportunity to seek advice of independent counsel regarding the transaction.[21]

Ordinary fee contracts between lawyers and clients are, of course, a type of business transaction. It appears, however, that the drafters of the Model Rules did not intend for the restrictions of Rule 1.8(a) to apply to standard fee agreements in which lawyers receive only money and not any form of ownership interest in their clients' property, probably because of the impracticality of clients' obtaining independent advice regarding standard fee agreements. Fee contracts are subject, however, to a "fairness" requirement by virtue of Rule 1.5(a), which provides that legal fees must be "reasonable." Comment 1 to Rule 1.8 also states that Rule 1.8(a) does not apply to "standard commercial transactions between the lawyer and the client for products or services that the client generally markets to others."

Application of the rules of ethics limiting business transactions between lawyer and client is illustrated by Committee on Professional Ethics & Conduct v. Mershon.[22] In Mershon the respondent attorney handled the formation of a land development corporation in which there were three stockholders. Miller contributed the land for development, while an engineer and Mershon each contributed promissory notes representing the value of their

20. See Restatement (Third) of the Law Governing Lawyers §207.
21. See, e.g., Underhill v. Kentucky Bar Assn., 937 S.W.2d 193 (Ky. 1997).
22. 316 N.W.2d 895 (Iowa 1982).

services. Miller and the engineer each received 40 percent of the stock while Mershon received 20 percent. Mershon understood that he and the engineer would release their shares if the land was not developed, but he did not put this provision in writing. In fact, the land was not developed. After Miller's death, Mershon renounced his interest in the corporation, but the engineer refused to do so. The dispute ultimately led to a grievance against Mershon filed by Miller's family. The court administered a public reprimand. While the court found that Mershon had acted in good faith, it concluded that he had failed to comply with the obligation of full disclosure required of lawyers who engage in business transactions with their clients. The court went on to hold that "full disclosure" requires a lawyer to advise the client of the need to seek independent counsel. If the lawyer does not do this, or if the client does not seek independent counsel, then the lawyer has a duty to give the client the kind of advice that independent counsel would give.

A number of other courts have also found that lawyers acted improperly in business transactions with their clients.[23] A common situation that has given rise to grievances against lawyers occurs when lawyers borrow money from their clients, typically after a client has received a substantial sum of money in settlement of a lawsuit or from the sale of property.[24]

Conflicts of interest resulting from service on the boards of directors of clients

The issue of whether lawyers should be allowed to serve as members of the boards of directors of their clients has been controversial in the profession for a number of years.[25] The Model Rules do

23. See, e.g., Miller v. Sears, 636 P.2d 1183 (Alaska 1981) (clients able to rescind contract for sale of property by lawyer to them because of lawyer's failure to disclose personal liability of clients on note); In re James, 452 A.2d 163 (D.C. 1982), cert. denied, 460 U.S. 1038 (1983) (lawyer disciplined for failure to make full disclosure to clients of risks and advantages of sale of building from clients to lawyer).

24. See In re Tolley, 975 P.2d 1115 (Colo. 1999)(en banc); In re Scott, 694 A.2d 732 (R.I. 1997).

25. Compare David S. Ruder, The Case Against the Lawyer-Director, 30

not prohibit lawyers from serving on the boards of directors of their clients, but Comment 14 to Rule 1.7 cautions lawyers about the possible conflicts of interest that can arise and advises lawyers that if "there is material risk that the dual role will compromise the lawyer's independence of professional judgment, the lawyer should not serve as a director."[26]

Why would a lawyer agree to serve on the board of directors of a client? Prestige is one reason; service on the board of a major corporate client brings a measure of prominence to the lawyer. Service on the board can also strengthen the business relationship between the lawyer's firm and the client. In addition, service on the board can facilitate the lawyer's role as counselor because the lawyer is more familiar with the activities of the client. At the same time, any lawyer who contemplates serving on the board of directors of a client should be aware of the substantial risks involved, including the following:[27]

- *Risk of loss of the attorney-client privilege.* The privilege applies only to communications between lawyer and client for the purpose of seeking legal advice. To the extent that communications were with the lawyer in the lawyer's capacity as director or to the extent they involved business rather than legal matters, the privilege is lost. In addition, the privilege applies only if the communications were

---

Bus. Law. 51 (Special Issue, March 1975) *with* Sam Harris, The Case for the Lawyer-Director, 30 Bus. Law. 58 (Special Issue, March 1975).

26. See ABA Comm. on Ethics and Prof. Resp., Formal Op. 98-410 (Model Rules do not prohibit lawyer from serving as director of corporation while simultaneously serving as its legal counsel, but there are ethical concerns that lawyer occupying dual role should consider); Restatement (Third) of the Law Governing Lawyers §216, cmt. *d* (duties of director and lawyer are generally consistent; when obligations as director are materially adverse to those of lawyer as corporate counsel, lawyer may not continue to serve as corporate counsel without informed consent of corporate client).

27. See Craig C. Albert, The Lawyer-Director: An Oxymoron? 9 Geo. J. Legal Ethics 413 (1996) (examining the benefits and risks of dual role and arguing against rule prohibiting lawyers from serving as directors). See also James H. Cheek, III & Howard H. Lamar, III, Lawyers as Directors of Clients: Conflicts of Interest, Potential Liability and Other Pitfalls, 712 PLI/Corp. 461 (1990) (on Westlaw).

made in confidence, a condition that may not be met when the communications occur in board meetings.

- *Disqualification of the lawyer's firm.* If the corporation is a party to litigation, the lawyer's firm may be disqualified from handling the matter because the lawyer may be a witness in the matter. Similarly, if the lawyer is a party to the litigation, the firm may be disqualified because of a conflict of interest between it and the client. If the corporation is forced into bankruptcy, the firm may be disqualified from representing the corporation in bankruptcy because of the lawyer's service on the board.
- *Increased exposure to liability.* Service on the board exposes the lawyer to increased liability. Not only is the lawyer subject to liability for malpractice, but the lawyer also becomes subject to liability as a director on various theories, including violation of federal and state securities laws. Law firms may also face increased liability when one of their members serves on the board of a client. The law firm could be held vicariously liable for the lawyer's conduct.
- *Inadequate insurance.* Many malpractice policies exclude from coverage service on a board of directors or other non-legal activities.

In Formal Opinion 98-410 the ABA Committee on Ethics and Professional Responsibility opined that lawyers may properly serve in the dual capacity of corporate director and counsel for the corporation, but the committee cautioned lawyers about the ethical difficulties involved. The committee offered lawyers a number of suggestions for performing these dual roles to avoid disciplinary violations.[28]

─────────────────── **Problem 5-2** ───────────────────

Fraud by Clients in Business Transactions

a.   Your firm represents National Computer, Inc., a large manufacturer of computer equipment. Ellen Lee

─────────────────────────

28. See ABA Section of Litigation, The Lawyer-Director: Implications for Independence (1998).

is National's vice president for procurement. Recently,
Lee called you about negotiating a renewal of a supply
contact between National and Microchip International.
Your firm prepared the original contract three years ago.
Lee has told you that the contract expires in six months
and that National wishes to renew the contract for as
long as possible. Lee also has informed you that micro-
chips have been in short supply and that renewal of the
contract is essential to National's business. During the
conversation Lee mentions that it was difficult to obtain
the first contract and that she found it necessary to give
Microchip's vice president of sales "something on the
side" to finalize the contract. How would you proceed?

   b.   The firm is also defending a breach of warranty
action brought by one of National's customers. As far
as Ms. Lee knows, there does not appear to be any relationship between this matter and the contract with Microchip, but it is a little hard to tell at this point because
the firm has just submitted an answer on National's behalf. Discovery has not begun.
   In addition, National Computer has a line of credit
with Interstate Bank. In connection with the line of
credit, your firm has given an opinion letter to Interstate
regarding the Microchip agreement. The letter included
the following opinions regarding the Microchip agreement:

   1. The agreement is legally enforceable against
       National.
   2. Execution, delivery, and performance by Na-
       tional of the provisions of the agreement do not
       breach or result in a default under any other
       agreements that are material to National's
       business.
   3. Execution, delivery, and performance by Na-
       tional of the provisions of the agreement do not
       violate applicable provisions of statutory law or
       regulations.
   4. There are no actions or proceedings against
       National, pending or overtly threatened in

writing, before any court, governmental agency or arbitrator, that seek to affect the enforceability of the agreement.

In light of what Ms. Lee has told you, what actions, if any, would you take regarding the breach of warranty action and the Interstate Bank loan?

   c.   You have been appointed by the president of your state bar to a committee formed to study and make recommendations for revisions of your state's rules of professional conduct. To what extent does your state's current rule on confidentiality permit or require disclosure of confidential information to prevent or rectify a client's fraud in a business transaction? What changes would you recommend making in your state's rule? Why? If you believe the current rule should not be changed, be prepared to explain why the current rule is sound as a matter of policy.

Read Model Rules 1.2(d), 1.6, 1.13, 1.16, and comments.

The tension between ethics and law on the issue of client fraud

The issue of how a lawyer should respond if the lawyer learns that a client plans to or has engaged in fraud on third persons in a business transaction has been marked by tension between views of the legal profession and federal administrative agencies that regulate corporations, particularly the Securities and Exchange Commission (SEC) and the Office of Thrift Supervision (OTS). While the dominant view in the legal profession strongly supports client confidentiality, the SEC and OTS have sometimes claimed that lawyers have a legal obligation to disclose confidential information to prevent or rectify serious client fraud.[29] Fraud by clients can, of course, arise in transactions that are not subject to federal administrative regulation. Indeed, some commentators have argued that

---

29. See Geoffrey C. Hazard, Jr., Lawyers and Client Fraud: They Still Don't Get It, 6 Geo. J. Legal Ethics 701 (1993).

different rules should apply to lawyers representing clients in regulated transactions on the ground that the context of a regulated transaction makes a difference in determining the lawyer's obligations.[30] Positions of federal administrative bodies, however, have still been influential on the general issue of client fraud. Unfortunately, the courts, which are the ultimate forum for deciding fundamental legal disputes such as this, have not always provided clear resolution of the controversy, leaving the profession and the regulators at odds.[31]

The material that follows focuses on three aspects of lawyers' legal and ethical obligations when confronted with client fraud: (1) the prohibition on consultation or assistance of fraud, (2) the duty to prevent fraud by action short of disclosure of the fraud to the victims, and (3) the extent of the obligation to disclose client fraud.

Ethical and legal obligations of lawyers not to counsel or assist clients in fraud

Ethically, lawyers have an obligation not to counsel or assist their clients in transactions that they know are fraudulent. The Code of Professional Responsibility stated in DR 7-102(A)(7) that a lawyer shall not "[c]ounsel or assist his client in conduct that the lawyer knows to be illegal or fraudulent." Model Rule 1.2(d) carries forward this prohibition.[32] Note that the obligation of lawyers not to counsel or assist their clients in fraudulent business transactions parallels the obligation of criminal defense lawyers not to assist their clients in criminal activity. Recall Problem 2-4 and in particular In re Ryder.[33]

While it is well established that lawyers may not ethically counsel or assist clients in illegal or fraudulent conduct, the scope of civil liability for such conduct is less clear. Beginning in the

---

30. See David B. Wilkins, Making Context Count: Regulating Lawyers after *Kaye Scholer*, 66 S. Cal. L. Rev. 1145 (1993).

31. Susan P. Koniak, When Courts Refuse to Frame the Law and Others Frame It to Their Will, 66 S. Cal. L. Rev. 1075, 1079-1091 (1993).

32. See Florida Bar v. Calvo, 630 So. 2d 548 (Fla. 1993) *cert. denied*, 513 U.S. 809 (1994) (lawyer disbarred for participation in fraudulent securities offering).

33. 263 F. Supp. 360 (E.D. Va.), *aff'd*, 381 F.2d 713 (4th Cir. 1967).

1970s a number of courts ruled that lawyers could be held legally liable for "aiding and abetting" violations of the federal securities laws. Probably the best known of these cases is SEC v. National Student Marketing Corp,[34] in which the court found that a prominent New York law firm was liable as an aider and abetter when it participated in the closing of a merger even though it knew that management had solicited proxies based on false financial statements. After *National Student Marketing,* many courts held lawyers civilly liable for aiding and abetting securities law violations. Another highly publicized situation in which lawyers were accused of aiding or abetting client fraud was the OPM leasing scandal. In that matter a law firm continued to close leasing transactions even after it had learned that its client was using phony leases as collateral for loans.[35]

In 1994 the Supreme Court, in Central Bank of Denver, N.A. v. First Interstate Bank of Denver, N.A.,[36] surprised many members of the securities bar. The Court overturned more than 20 years of case law and repudiated the decisions of all 11 circuit courts of appeal, holding in a 5-4 decision that "aider and abetter" liability did not exist under the federal securities laws. Reasoning from the plain text of the statute and from the scope of the statute's express causes of action, the Court concluded that Congress did not intend to create aider and abetter liability. The Court rejected arguments that Congress had adopted or acquiesced in judicial creation of aider and abetter liability.

While *Central Bank* appears to insulate lawyers and other professionals from secondary liability under the federal securities laws, this protection is not unlimited.[37] *Central Bank* recognized that if the professional's conduct went beyond aiding or abetting to the level of a primary securities violation, the professional could still be held legally liable. Thus, a lawyer who issues a false or mis-

34.   457 F. Supp. 682 (D.D.C. 1978).

35.   For a complete discussion of the OPM case, see Philip B. Heymann & Lance Liebman, The Social Responsibilities of Lawyers 184-197 (1988).

36.   511 U.S. 164 (1994).

37.   For articles analyzing the implications of the *Central Bank* decision, see Symposium on the *Central Bank* Decision: The Demise of Aiding and Abetting? 49 Bus. Law. 1429 (1994). See also Gareth T. Evans & Daniel S. Floyd, Secondary Liability Under Rule 10b-5: Still Alive and Well After *Central Bank?* 52 Bus. Law. 13 (1996); Ann Maxey, Competing Duties? Securities Lawyers' Liability After *Central Bank,* 64 Fordham L. Rev. 2185 (1996).

leading opinion, or who commits any other primary violation of the securities laws, could still be held liable.[38] In 1995 Congress passed the Private Securities Litigation Reform Act. The act provides that the SEC (as opposed to a private civil litigant) may bring an enforcement action against any person who knowingly provides substantial assistance to another person in the violation of the anti-fraud provisions of the securities laws.[39] Many jurisdictions recognize common law aider and abetter liability when a person knowingly provides substantial assistance or encouragement to another person's primary wrong.[40] Moreover, regardless of legal liability, lawyers still have an ethical obligation not to counsel or assist illegal or fraudulent conduct.

Although the principle that lawyers may not counsel or assist clients in illegal or fraudulent conduct is well established, the scope of this obligation is imprecise. First, it should be clear that a lawyer does not counsel or assist a client in committing a crime or fraud if the lawyer does nothing more than advise a client that the client's planned course of action would be illegal or fraudulent. Model Rule 1.2(d) states that a lawyer "may discuss the legal consequences of any proposed course of conduct with a client." See also Comment. 6.[41]

Second, a lawyer may not counsel or assist a client in conduct that the lawyer *knows* is illegal or fraudulent, but when does the

38. 511 U.S. at 191. See United States v. O'Hagan, 521 U.S. 642 (1997) (defendant who purchased stock in target corporation prior to its being purchased in tender offer, based on inside information acquired as member of law firm representing tender offeror, could be found guilty of securities fraud under misappropriation theory); In re American Continental Corp./Lincoln Sav. & Loan Sec. Litig., 794 F. Supp. 1424 (D. Ariz. 1992) (cause of action stated against law firm that represented Lincoln Savings and Loan for issuing misleading opinion in violation of §11 of Securities Act of 1933, which imposes liability on experts who make statements in connection with registration of securities).

39. Private Securities Litigation Reform Act of 1995, Pub. L. No. 104-67, §104, 109 Stat. 737.

40. See Restatement (Second) of Torts §876(b) (actor liable for tort of another if actor knows that other's conduct is breach of duty to third person and provides substantial assistance or encouragement); Granewich v. Harding, 985 P.2d 788 (Or. 1999) (complaint alleging that law firm assisted corporate directors in breach of fiduciary duty to minority shareholders stated cause of action under §876).

41. See also Geoffrey C. Hazard, Jr., Rectification of Client Fraud: Death and Revival of a Professional Norm, 33 Emory L. J. 271, 281-282 (1984).

lawyer know of a crime or fraud? We encountered this issue in Problem 2-5, which addressed the lawyer's ethical obligations when a client commits perjury in a criminal case. As we saw, courts and commentators have suggested several possible standards for knowledge, including a "firm factual basis" or "beyond a reasonable doubt." Other commentators have argued that "willful blindness" or "conscious avoidance" should be treated as the equivalent of knowledge.[42]

Third, as to the lawyer's ability to represent the client, what are the consequences of the duty not to counsel or assist a client in criminal or fraudulent conduct? The lawyer obviously cannot continue to handle legal aspects of illegal or fraudulent transactions (such as preparing opinions or other documents or participating in closings) since such conduct would amount to direct assistance of the client's wrongdoing. Must the lawyer formally resign from representation in connection with any wrongful transactions? For example, the client might retain other counsel, who is unaware of the wrongdoing, to handle the transaction, but might ask the first lawyer to refrain from formally resigning to avoid raising a "red flag." If the purpose of withholding the lawyer's resignation is to mislead new counsel into believing that the lawyer is still associated with the client and that the client is not engaged in misconduct, isn't the lawyer providing indirect assistance of fraud?

Is a lawyer who knows that a client is engaged in an illegal or fraudulent transaction prohibited from having any involvement whatsoever with the transaction? Suppose, for example, that a lawyer knows that a client is engaging in a fraudulent financial transaction, but the lawyer is not representing the client in the transaction. May the lawyer respond to a letter from the client's accountant asking the lawyer to state the amount of outstanding legal fees that the client owes to the lawyer, or does even providing factual information constitute assistance of the fraud? In aider and abetter liability cases, the courts have held that lawyers were liable only if they provided "substantial" assistance to client fraud.[43]

A related aspect of the question as to how far the prohibition

---

42. Cf. John P. Freeman & Nathan M. Crystal, Scienter in Professional Liability Cases, 42 S.C. L. Rev. 783, 833-838 (1991); Hazard, Rectification of Client Fraud, 33 Emory L. J. at 282-283.

43. See SEC v. National Student Mktg. Corp., 457 F. Supp. 682, 713-715 (D.D.C. 1978); see also Restatement (Second) of Torts §876(b).

on counseling or assisting a crime or fraud extends deals with representation in unrelated matters. Does the obligation mean that the lawyer can have no involvement in transactions that are unrelated to the crime or fraud? For example, suppose a law firm knows that a client is engaging in a fraudulent securities transaction. Must the firm refuse to represent the client in unrelated civil litigation? Must it refuse to represent the client in unrelated business matters? In essence, must the firm resign from all employment by the client?

In Formal Opinion 92-366, the ABA Committee on Ethics and Professional Responsibility examined the ethical aspects of a lawyer's continued representation of a client who was engaged in fraud in matters that were both related and unrelated to the fraud. The committee opined that a lawyer was ethically required to withdraw from representation in matters directly involving fraud. As to unrelated matters, the committee concluded that withdrawal was more likely to be permissive under Model Rule 1.16. The committee also advised, however, that "complete severance may be the preferred course in these circumstances, in order to avoid any possibility of the lawyer's continued association with the client's fraud."[44]

Ethical and legal obligations of lawyers to prevent fraud by actions other than disclosure of the fraud to third parties

Both rules of ethics and case law provide that a lawyer who knows that a client is engaged in a fraudulent transaction has additional duties beyond simply refusing to counsel or assist in the fraud. In the Model Rules, these additional duties flow from Model Rule 1.13, which defines a lawyer's ethical obligations when representing an entity. Rule 1.13(a) adopts an "entity representation" principle, providing that a lawyer retained by an organization represents the entity rather than any of its "constituents." The term *constituents* includes directors, officers, employees, members, and shareholders. Model Rule 1.13(d). (The Code of Professional

---

44. ABA Formal Op. 92-366, at 6. See also Hazard, Lawyers and Client Fraud, 6 Geo. J. Legal Ethics at 728-729 (arguing that duty not to counsel or assist in fraud does not preclude defense of litigation arising from fraud or representation in unrelated matters).

Responsibility also followed the entity representation principle in Ethical Consideration 5-18.) The principle means that a lawyer does not have a client-lawyer relationship with any of the constituents of an entity merely because the lawyer represents the entity.[45] Even though a lawyer does not represent a constituent of an entity, information received from any constituent of the entity may still be subject to the attorney-client evidentiary privilege, depending on how broadly a court interprets the privilege.[46]

The absence of a client-lawyer relationship with the constituents of an entity has important implications if a lawyer learns about wrongdoing by a constituent.[47] Suppose a lawyer for an entity learns about misconduct committed by one of the officers of the entity. How should the lawyer proceed? Because of the entity representation principle, the lawyer cannot simply follow instructions from the officer to keep the matter confidential. Further, the lawyer must advise the officer that the lawyer represents the entity, not the officer. See Model Rule 1.13(d). Normally, the lawyer should discuss the matter with the officer before consideration of any further action to give the officer an opportunity to take cor-

45. It is, of course, possible for a lawyer who represents an entity to also have a client-lawyer relationship with one of the entity's constituents. Such a relationship, however, arises expressly rather than by virtue of the lawyer's representation of the entity. For example, if the lawyer for a corporation performs estate planning or real estate services for an officer of the corporation, the lawyer has a client-lawyer relationship with both the corporation and the officer. In some cases, it is permissible for a lawyer to represent both the corporation and its officers in litigation. See Model Rule 1.13(e). But see Forrest v. Baeza, 67 Cal. Rptr. 2d 857 (Ct. App. 1997) (lawyer may not represent corporation and majority shareholders/directors in derivative action that accuses directors of fraud).

46. Compare Upjohn Co. v. United States, 449 U.S. 383 (1981) (under federal law attorney-client privilege extends to communications between lawyers and lower-level employees and is not limited to corporate officials in "control group") with Consolidation Coal Co. v. Bucyrus-Erie Co., 432 N.E.2d 250 (Ill. 1982) (control group test applies under Illinois law). See also the discussion in connection with Problem 3-3. For a criticism of the corporate attorney-client privilege, see Elizabeth G. Thornburg, Sanctifying Secrecy: The Mythology of the Corporate Attorney-Client Privilege, 69 Notre Dame L. Rev. 157 (1993). See also Garner v. Wolfinbarger, 430 F.2d 1093 (5th Cir. 1970), cert. denied, 401 U.S. 974 (1971) (in shareholder derivative litigation corporate attorney-client privilege does not apply if shareholders establish good cause).

47. See George C. Harris, Taking the Entity Theory Seriously: Lawyer Liability for Failure to Prevent Harm to Organizational Clients Through Disclosure of Constituent Wrongdoing, 11 Geo. J. Legal Ethics 597 (1998).

rective action. Model Rule 1.13(b) states: "Any measures taken shall be designed to minimize disruption of the organization and the risk of revealing information relating to the representation to persons outside the organization." Voluntary reporting by the officer to other officials in the organization is one possible option.

Suppose the officer refuses to take any action regarding the matter. The officer could offer various reasons for inaction: "it's common industry practice," or "it's too small to worry about," or "that would kill the company," or "you're fired." How should a lawyer proceed in that event? Model Rule 1.13(b) provides that a lawyer must take further action to protect the entity when a constituent is engaged in conduct that is a "violation of a legal obligation to the organization, or a violation of law which reasonably might be imputed to the organization, and is likely to result in substantial injury to the organization." The section apparently envisions two types of cases. In the first, the official is engaged in some type of breach of fiduciary duty, such as misappropriation of the entity's funds. In the second, the official is involved in illegal conduct as to third parties, such as securities fraud.

Assuming the lawyer has a duty to act under Rule 1.13(b), what must the lawyer do? The rule provides that the lawyer "shall proceed as is reasonably necessary in the best interest of the organization." Note that the focus of the rule is on protecting the interests of the organization, not third parties. The rule goes on to identify factors that the lawyer should take into account in deciding how to proceed, along with possible ways in which the lawyer could proceed. The ultimate step allowed by Rule 1.13(b) is "referring the matter . . . to the highest authority that can act in behalf of the organization as determined by applicable law." In the case of a corporation, this will typically be the board of directors. See Comment 5 to Rule 1.13.

Suppose the lawyer informs the board of directors, but the board decides not to take any action in the matter. Rule 1.13(c) allows but does not require the lawyer to withdraw; this provision, however, must be read in connection with other rules. See Comment 6, which provides as follows: "If the lawyer's services are being used by an organization to further a crime or fraud by the organization, Rule 1.2(d) can be applicable." As discussed above, under Rule 1.2(d) a lawyer would be required to withdraw from the matter if the lawyer's services would be used to perpetuate a fraud. The comment states that lawyers could disclose confidential information if permitted under Rule 1.6. Under the ABA's Model Rule 1.6, lawyers would rarely be able to do so. (See the discussion that follows on disclosure.)[48]

The preceding discussion assumes that the entity is fairly large. The lawyer's obligations are likely to be different if the entity is closely held. Unless the lawyer's engagement clearly specifies otherwise, in closely held entities it is likely that the attorney has a client-lawyer relationship with all the principals.[49] If such a relationship with the principals does exist, two courses of action seem available to the attorney. One is to make full disclosure to all clients; disclosure would be justified on the ground that there is no expectation of confidentiality nor does the attorney-client privilege apply to joint clients. Cf. Model Rule 2.2, cmt. 6. The other option is to withdraw from the matter, based on the principle that an irreconcilable conflict of interest exists between multiple clients. Cf. Model Rule 2.2(c).

Case law dealing with a lawyer's legal obligations when a corporate officer engages in fraud is consistent with Model Rule 1.13. The leading case is In re Carter & Johnson.[50] The case was a disciplinary proceeding brought against two lawyers claiming that they violated SEC Rule of Practice (2)(e)(1)(ii), which prohibits a practitioner from engaging in "unethical or improper professional conduct."[51]

Most administrative agencies, including the SEC, require at-

---

48. For criticisms of Model Rule 1.13, see Freedman, Understanding Lawyers' Ethics at 201-205 (arguing that it gives greater protection to corporations than to individuals); Stephen Gillers, Model Rule 1.13(c) Gives the Wrong Answer to the Question of Corporate Counsel Disclosure, 1 Geo. J. Legal Ethics 289 (1987) (arguing that lawyers should have discretion to reveal confidential information to prevent or rectify substantial injury resulting from conduct or inaction set forth in Rule 1.13(b)).

49. E.g., Rosman v. Shapiro, 653 F. Supp. 1441 (S.D.N.Y. 1987) (in two-person corporation, it is reasonable for each shareholder to view corporate counsel as his individual attorney); Meyer v. Mulligan, 889 P.2d 509 (Wyo. 1995) (facts-and-circumstances test used to determine whether lawyer for closely held corporation has client-lawyer relationship with shareholders).

50. Fed. Sec. L. Rep. (CCH) ¶82,847 (SEC 1981).

51. See generally Simon M. Lorne & W. Hardy Callcott, Administrative Actions Against Lawyers Before the SEC, 50 Bus. Law. 1293 (1995). Cf. Checkosky v. SEC, 139 F.3d 221 (D.C. Cir. 1998) (action against two accountants for improper professional conduct under Rule 2(e)(1)(ii) dismissed because SEC failed to articulate mental standard necessary for violation).

torneys to apply to appear before the agency and to comply with their rules of practice. Often rules of practice of administrative agencies incorporate general ethical obligations, although agencies may impose additional duties. Violation of a rule of practice subjects a practitioner to discipline by the agency. An attorney would also be subject to discipline for the same conduct by any court before which the attorney is admitted to practice.

Carter and Johnson represented National Telephone Company (National), which leased telephone equipment to commercial customers. The company ultimately filed for bankruptcy. During the period when the company's financial problems were escalating, the company issued a misleading press release and filed overstated financial information with the SEC. Carter and Johnson gave repeated warnings to National's chairman that the company was violating the securities laws, but they took no further action.

The case focused on the issue of when lawyers have an obligation under the securities laws to go beyond simply giving warnings to corporate officials that their conduct is a violation of the law. Without defining precisely a lawyer's obligations, the SEC ruled that at some point a lawyer must do more than simply give warnings:

> When a lawyer with significant responsibilities in the effectuation of a company's compliance with the disclosure requirements of the federal securities laws becomes aware that his client is engaged in a substantial and continuing failure to satisfy those disclosure requirements, his continued participation violates professional standards unless he takes prompt steps to end the client's noncompliance.[52]

The SEC offered some suggestions on how lawyers should proceed in such cases:

> Initially, counseling accurate disclosure is sufficient, even if his advice is not accepted. But there comes a point at which a reasonable lawyer must conclude that his advice is not being followed, or even sought in good faith, and that his client is involved in a

---

52. Fed. Sec. L. Rep. (CCH) ¶82,847, at 84,172. See also In re Gutfreund, Exchange Act Release No. 31,554, [1992 Transfer Binder] Fed. Sec. L. Rep. (CCH) ¶85,067 (Dec. 3, 1992) (responsibilities of compliance counsel for brokerage firm regarding wrongdoing by firm's employees and management).

continuing course of violating the securities laws. At this critical juncture, the lawyer must take further, more affirmative steps in order to avoid the inference that he has been co-opted, willingly or unwillingly, into the scheme of non-disclosure.

The lawyer is in the best position to choose his next step. Resignation is one option, although we recognize that other considerations, including the protection of the client against foreseeable prejudice, must be taken into account in the case of withdrawal. A direct approach to the board of directors or one or more individual directors or officers may be appropriate; or he may choose to try to enlist the aid of other members of the firm's management. . . .

[T]here may occur situations where the lawyer must conclude that the misconduct is so extreme or irretrievable, or the involvement of his client's management and board of directors in the misconduct is so thoroughgoing and pervasive that any action short of resignation would be futile. We would anticipate that cases where a lawyer has no choice but to resign would be rare and of an egregious nature.[53]

While the SEC concluded that lawyers have obligations beyond simply advising compliance with the law, the SEC did not impose a duty on lawyers to disclose confidential information to the agency or to third parties to prevent the client's wrongdoing. At most the lawyer's obligation was to withdraw from representation. The SEC's views of lawyers' obligations as expressed in *Carter & Johnson* are very similar to the professional obligations under Model Rule 1.13. The Restatement of the Law Governing Lawyers also largely follows Rule 1.13.[54] By contrast, a different federal administrative agency, the Office of Thrift Supervision (OTS), has taken the position that in some situations lawyers have a duty to disclose material facts when dealing with the agency. (See the discussion later in this problem.)

Controversy over whether lawyers should have an ethical obligation to disclose confidential information to prevent or rectify client fraud

Whether lawyers should have an ethical obligation to disclose confidential information to prevent or rectify client fraud has been the

53. Fed. Sec. L. Rep. ¶82,847, at 84,172-84,173.
54. Restatement (Third) of the Law Governing Lawyers §155.

subject of sharp division within the legal profession. The history of the issue under the Code of Professional Responsibility and the Model Rules provides insight into the disagreement within the profession.[55]

Disciplinary Rule 4-101 of the Code established a general duty of confidentiality, subject to certain exceptions, two of which could arguably apply in the case of client fraud. Disciplinary Rule 4-101(C)(3) provided that a lawyer may reveal the "intention of his client to commit a crime and the information necessary to prevent the crime." This rule granted lawyers discretion but did not require them to reveal confidential information to prevent future crimes. The rule allowed lawyers to reveal confidential information to prevent a future fraud only if the fraud was also a crime. The rule did not apply to completed crimes, but it arguably applied to continuing crimes.[56]

Disciplinary Rule 4-101(C)(4) provided that "a lawyer may reveal confidences or secrets . . . to defend himself or his employees or associates against an accusation of wrongful conduct." The leading decision dealing with the "self-defense" exception to the duty of confidentiality is Meyerhofer v. Empire Fire & Marine Insurance Co.[57] The case involved a securities fraud action alleging that Empire had marketed securities using a registration statement and prospectus that were materially false and misleading. The complaint named Empire's law firm and several of its partners as defendants. In addition, the complaint included as a defendant Stuart Goldberg, an attorney who had worked on the Empire matter but who had resigned from the firm in a dispute with the firm over the adequacy of disclosures being made in the Empire offering. On the same day that he resigned from the firm, Goldberg informed the SEC of his concerns about the offering; he subsequently filed an affidavit with the SEC about the matter. When Goldberg was named as a defendant in the securities fraud litigation, he contacted plaintiffs' counsel, informed them of his noninvolvement in the offering, and supplied them with a copy of the affidavit he filed with the SEC. As a result the plaintiffs dismissed

---

55. The following discussion of the history of the treatment of the issue of client fraud under the Code and the Model Rules is drawn from Hazard, Rectification of Client Fraud, 33 Emory L.J. at 292-304, and Kenneth J. Drexler, Note, Honest Attorneys, Crooked Clients and Innocent Third Parties: A Case for More Disclosure, 6 Geo. J. Legal Ethics 393, 396-400 (1992).

56. ABA Comm. on Prof. Ethics and Grievances, Formal Op. 156 (1936).

57. 497 F.2d 1190 (2d Cir.), *cert. denied,* 419 U.S. 998 (1974).

Goldberg from the suit. Defendants then moved to disqualify plaintiffs' counsel from continuing in the case on the ground that they had received confidential information from Goldberg. The district court granted the disqualification motion but the Second Circuit Court of Appeals reversed:

> DR 4-101(C) recognizes that a lawyer may reveal confidences or secrets necessary to defend himself against "an accusation of wrongful conduct." This is exactly what Goldberg had to face when, in their original complaint, plaintiffs named him as a defendant who wilfully violated the securities laws.
>
> The charge, of knowing participation in the filing of a false and misleading registration statement, was a serious one. The complaint alleged violation of criminal statutes and civil liability computable at over four million dollars. The cost in money of simply defending such an action might be very substantial. The damage to his professional reputation which might be occasioned by the mere pendency of such a charge was an even greater cause for concern.
>
> Under these circumstances Goldberg had the right to make an appropriate disclosure with respect to his role in the public offering. Concomitantly, he had the right to support his version of the facts with suitable evidence.[58]

Although the court expressed some concern with Goldberg's method of disclosure — turning over to plaintiffs' counsel a 30-page affidavit with 16 attached exhibits — the court concluded that his action was the "most effective way for him to substantiate his story."[59] In addition to the two exceptions found in DR 4-101, the Code contained another apparent exception to the duty of confidentiality in DR 7-102(B)(1) (1969 version):

> A lawyer who receives information clearly establishing that: (1) his client has, in the course of the representation, perpetrated a fraud upon a person or tribunal shall promptly call upon his client to rectify the same, and if his client refuses or is unable to do so, he shall reveal the fraud to the affected person or tribunal.

Interestingly, DR 7-102(B)(1) and DR 4-101 did not refer to each other. As a result, the Code was ambiguous regarding the rela-

---

58. 497 F.2d at 1194-1195.
59. Id. at 1195.

tionship between the fraud disclosure principle of DR 7-102(B)(1) and the confidentiality principle of DR 4-101.[60]

The draft of the Model Rules proposed by the Kutak Commission in 1982 would have given lawyers discretion to reveal confidential information either to prevent fraud by a client or to rectify client fraud when the lawyer's services had been used in connection with the fraud. At its February 1983 meeting, however, the ABA's House of Delegates rejected the proposed rule by a vote of 207 to 129. The final version of Rule 1.6 adopted by the ABA differed from the proposed rule in several respects. First, the rule limited disclosure of confidential information to prevent harm to those cases in which clients were planning to commit criminal acts that involved "imminent death or substantial bodily harm." The rule thus eliminated lawyers' discretion to reveal confidential information to prevent other criminal acts or to prevent fraud. Second, the rule adopted by the ABA eliminated lawyers' discretion to reveal confidential information to rectify the consequences of past criminal or fraudulent acts by clients. Third, the rule deleted the "required by law" exception. Proponents of the strict view of confidentiality adopted in Rule 1.6 apparently felt that withdrawal rather than disclosure was the only proper response to client fraud.[61]

Because the final version of Model Rule 1.6 adopted by the ABA differed substantially from the Kutak Commission's proposal, the original comments to Rule 1.6 needed revision as well. Representatives of the contending positions on confidentiality met to discuss modifications of the comments. During the negotiations over the comments, advocates of the Kutak Commission proposal pointed out that withdrawal was an ineffective solution when the client had already completed the fraud or when the parties affected by the fraud were too unsophisticated to understand the significance of the lawyer's withdrawal.[62] As a result of these negotiations the ABA ultimately approved Comments 14 and 15 to Rule 1.6, authorizing a "noisy notice of withdrawal":

> If the lawyer's services will be used by the client in materially furthering a course of criminal or fraudulent conduct, the lawyer must withdraw, as stated in Rule 1.16(a)(1).

60. John P. Freeman, Current Trends in Legal Opinion Liability, 1989 Colum. Bus. L. Rev. 235, 246 n.35.
61. Hazard, Rectification of Client Fraud, 33 Emory L.J. at 299-300.
62. Id. at 302-304.

>   After withdrawal the lawyer is required to refrain from making
>   disclosure of the clients' confidences, except as otherwise provided
>   in Rule 1.6. *Neither this Rule nor Rule 1.8(b) nor Rule 1.16(d) prevents*
>   *the lawyer from giving notice of the fact of withdrawal, and the lawyer*
>   *may also withdraw or disaffirm any opinion, document, affirmation, or*
>   *the like.* (Emphasis added.)

The comment thus allowed lawyers who were required to withdraw because of clients' criminal or fraudulent conduct to go beyond a simple withdrawal. It also authorized lawyers to withdraw
or to disaffirm opinions or documents. While such a disaffirmance
would constitute a clear signal that something was amiss, it would
not amount to a direct revelation of confidential information.

Questions remain, however, about the application of the
"noisy notice" comment. Paragraph 9 of the scope note to the
Model Rules states: "The Comments are intended as guides to
interpretation, but the text of each Rule is authoritative." Thus,
arguably the noisy notice comment should be given no effect since
it is not authorized by the text. In 1992 the ABA Committee on
Ethics and Professional Responsibility issued Formal Opinion 92-
366 dealing with the noisy notice of withdrawal. The committee
concluded that the comment was a proper interpretation of the
text but only in the situation in which the client was continuing to
use the lawyer's work product to commit a crime or fraud. In that
situation, according to the committee, the "representation" of the
client continued and the noisy notice might have been required to
effectuate a full withdrawal:

>   [W]here the client avowedly intends to continue to use the lawyer's
>   work product, this amounts to a de facto continuation of the rep-
>   resentation even if the lawyer has ceased to perform any additional
>   work. The representation is not completed, any more than the fraud
>   itself is completed. In order to fully effectuate the withdrawal man-
>   dated by Rule 1.16(a)(1), and to avoid assisting client fraud as man-
>   dated by Rule 1.2(d), the lawyer may have to repudiate her
>   preexisting work product in addition to refusing to perform any
>   further work for the client.[63]

In cases where the lawyer's work product was not being used, the
committee opined that application of the noisy notice was improper.[64]

---

63. ABA Comm. on Ethics and Prof. Resp., Formal Op. 92-366, at 12.
See also Formal Opinion 93-375 (disaffirmance mandatory).
64. Formal Opinion 92-366, at 9 n.10.

As a result of the committee's analysis, therefore, a lawyer could not use the noisy notice of withdrawal if the client had already completed the fraud or if the fraud was ongoing but the lawyer's work product would not be used. Three members of the ABA committee strongly dissented (historically dissents have been rare in ABA ethics opinions). The dissent argued that the proposition accepted by the majority — that a noisy notice of withdrawal might be required to effectuate a complete withdrawal when the client continues the "representation" by using a lawyer's preexisting opinion to commit a crime or fraud — is not supported by the text of the rules, uses an artificial and strained conception of what constitutes "representation," and goes beyond even the comment by indicating that a noisy notice may be mandatory.[65]

Controversy continues over the issue of disclosure of confidential information to prevent or rectify client fraud. The American Law Institute has adopted the following section on the issue:

§117B. Using or Disclosing Information to Prevent, Rectify, or Mitigate Substantial Financial Loss

(1) A lawyer may use or disclose confidential client information when and to the extent that the lawyer reasonably believes such use or disclosure is necessary to prevent a crime or fraud, and:

(a) the crime or fraud threatens substantial financial loss to a person;
(b) the loss has not yet occurred;
(c) the lawyer's client intends to commit the crime or fraud either directly or through a third person; and
(d) the client has employed or is employing the lawyer's services in committing the crime or fraud.

(2) In the situation of a loss otherwise described in Subsection (1) but that has already occurred, a lawyer may use or disclose confidential client information when and to the extent that the lawyer reasonably believes such use or disclosure is necessary to rectify or mitigate the loss.

(3) Before using or disclosing information pursuant to this Section, the lawyer must, if feasible, make a good faith effort to persuade the client either not to act or, if the client has already

---

65. Professor Hazard has also authored a stinging criticism of the committee's reasoning and conclusions, and even of the realism of the hypothetical that the committee considered. Hazard, Lawyers and Client Fraud, 6 Geo. J. Legal Ethics 701.

acted, to warn the victim or take other action to prevent, rectify, or mitigate the loss and, if relevant, to advise the client of the lawyer's ability to use or disclose pursuant to this Section and the consequences thereof.

(4) A lawyer who, in a situation described in this Section, takes action or decides not to take action permitted under this Section is not, solely by reason of such action or inaction, subject to professional discipline, liable for damages to the lawyer's client or any third person, or barred from recovery against a client or third person by an affirmative defense based solely thereon.

The Ethics 2000 Commission has proposed revisions to Rule 1.6 that are similar to Restatement §117B. The Commission's proposal is quoted in Problem 2-3.

Civil liability for failing to disclose client fraud

To what extent are lawyers legally liable for damages to third parties who are the victims of client fraud when lawyers have failed to disclose knowledge of the fraud gained in a professional capacity? (Recall our discussion of a lawyer's civil liability for failure to disclose a client's intention to commit a crime, Problem 2-3.) The question cannot be answered simply, because of the wide variety of legal theories, both statutory and common law, that can form the basis of lawyer liability to third parties.[66] It is important, however, to distinguish cases in which lawyers have issued legal opinions from those in which they have not. If a lawyer prepares a legal opinion in a transaction and the lawyer knowingly or recklessly omits material information from the opinion, the lawyer can be liable for such omissions under federal securities law and common law principles. Problem 5-5 examines legal and ethical obligations that apply to lawyers issuing opinions in tax matters and other transactions.

Lawyers who have not issued opinion letters in connection with a transaction but who have actively participated in the transaction have been subject to liability to third parties, sometimes as

---

66. See Robert J. Haft, Liability of Attorneys and Accountants for Securities Transactions (1999-2000 ed.), John P. Freeman, Current Trends in Legal Opinion Liability, 1989 Colum. Bus. L. Rev. 235. See generally Restatement (Third) of the Law Governing Lawyers ch. 4 (Lawyer Civil Liability).

principals in the transaction but more often for fraud, negligent misrepresentation, or aiding and abetting client wrongdoing.[67] As noted above, however, the Supreme Court in *Central Bank* held that the federal securities laws should not be interpreted to provide for aider and abetter liability.

If a lawyer does not actively participate in a fraudulent transaction, it is unlikely that the lawyer would be held liable to a third party simply for nondisclosure of the client's wrongdoing. For example, in Tew v. Arky, Freed, Stearns, Watson, Greer, Weaver & Harris, P.A.[68] the district court dismissed a legal malpractice complaint against a law firm alleging that the firm had failed to disclose its knowledge of the client's insolvency to its auditors. The firm had not issued an opinion letter or otherwise taken part in the transaction.

In 1992 the Office of Thrift Supervision (OTS) created quite a stir in the legal profession when it brought an administrative complaint against Kaye, Scholer, Fierman, Hays & Handler,[69] a prominent New York law firm, for its representation of Lincoln Savings & Loan. The complaint contained 10 charges against Kaye, Scholer, a number of which alleged that the firm had failed to disclose material facts to the Federal Home Loan Bank Board. The OTS claimed that in acting as Lincoln's agent under the governing statutory laws, Kaye, Scholer had a duty not to omit material facts. The OTS's action was controversial in another sense because it accompanied its complaint with an ''asset protection order'' that limited the firm's ability to transfer assets and required sequestration of 25 percent of the earnings of all partners with a higher percentage for certain named defendants. Under the pressure of the order, Kaye, Scholer promptly settled the case, paying $41 million in restitution — so the issue of whether the firm had a duty of disclosure as contended by the OTS was not resolved. Professor Hazard argues that the case should be understood not as a third-party liability case but rather as a case involving the

---

67. See McCamish, Martin, Brown & Loeffler v. F.E. Appling Interests, 991 S.W.2d 787 (Tex. 1999) (borrower states cause of action against lender's attorney for negligent misrepresentation under Restatement (Second) of Torts §552).

68. 655 F. Supp. 1571 (S.D. Fla. 1987), *aff'd*, 846 F.2d 753 (11th Cir.), *cert. denied*, 488 U.S. 854 (1988).

69. Reported as In re Fishbein, OTS AP-92-19, 1992 WL 560939 (March 1, 1992).

scope of a law firm's obligations to a regulatory agency that has jurisdiction over the lawyer's client.[70] Other commentators, however, see much broader implications in the case.[71]

B.   Specialized Areas of Office Practice

──────── **Problem 5-3** ────────
Real Estate Practice

a. Your firm has a substantial residential real estate practice. The typical transaction proceeds as follows: The purchaser signs a standard form contract completed by the broker who has been assisting the purchaser in finding a residence. The broker then submits the contract to the "listing" broker, the one who listed the seller's home for sale. If the parties are able to negotiate a final contract, the financing process then begins. Most contracts are subject to a "financing contingency." The purchaser, usually with the assistance of the broker, takes the contract and applies to one or more financial institutions for a mortgage loan. In connection with the loan application, the lender will ask the purchaser to identify the attorney who will be representing the purchaser in the transaction. Since many lenders require title insurance as a condition of their loans, the attorney selected by the buyer must be approved by a title insurance company to issue opinions on which it can rely. Your firm is an agent for a major title insurance company and receives a commission from the sale of title insurance. The terms of the loan require

70. Geoffrey C. Hazard, Jr., Lawyer Liability in Third Party Situations: The Meaning of the *Kaye Scholer* Case, 26 Akron L. Rev. 395 (1993).

71. See Symposium, From the Trenches and Towers: The *Kaye Scholer* Affair, 23 L. & Soc. Inquiry 237 (1998); Symposium, In the Matter of Kaye, Scholer, Fierman, Hays & Handler: A Symposium on Government Regulation, Lawyers' Ethics, and the Rule of Law, 66 S. Cal. L. Rev. 977 (1993); Symposium, The Attorney-Client Relationship in a Regulated Society, 35 S. Tex. L. Rev. 571 (1994).

the purchaser to pay the legal fees of the closing attorney. After the lender completes its credit examination and approves the loan, the lender sends to the attorney its standard package of closing documents for the transaction. Residential real estate transactions occur in high volume under time pressure. Lenders normally provide real estate attorneys with closing packages only a few days before the closing is to occur.

Your firm does the following in the typical transaction: (1) prepares the note, mortgage, and various disclosure documents using forms supplied by the lending institution; (2) arranges for title examination, usually by employing a title abstract company that examines the title and then gives the firm a report that it uses to prepare your title opinion; (3) obtains a title insurance policy for the lender, and for the owner if the owner desires to pay the additional premium required for an owner's policy, with a commission payable to your firm for selling the insurance; (4) prepares a general warranty deed for the seller to sign if the seller does not have an attorney at closing, which is often the case; (5) completes the closing statement showing the source and disbursement of all funds; (6) handles the closing, answering any questions that the parties may have; disburses funds, and records various documents; (7) institutes foreclosure actions on behalf of the lender in those cases in which borrowers default. The lender often asks the closing attorney to handle any foreclosure action because the attorney already has the file and is familiar with the transaction. To reduce the expense of real estate closings, your firm has several experienced paralegals who handle all aspects of the typical transaction, including the closing, although a lawyer is always available should any problems arise.

For the next firm meeting, you have been asked to review and comment on the ethical and malpractice issues involved in your firm's handling of the typical residential real estate transaction.

b.   You have been appointed by the president of your state bar to a special committee to examine whether the bar should recommend to the state supreme court that it make changes in the restrictions on unauthorized practice of law in order to improve delivery of legal services. You are a member of the subcommittee on residential real estate transactions. What questions do you think should be addressed in deciding whether nonlawyers should be allowed to provide legal services in connection with residential real estate transactions? Consider the general approach suggested by the ABA Commission on Nonlawyer Practice, discussed in Problem 4-8. What form of regulation, if any, would you recommend for nonlawyers who are authorized to provide legal services in connection with residential real estate transactions?

Read Model Rules 1.7, 1.8(a), 1.15, 2.2, 5.3, 5.4, 5.5, and comments.

The role of attorneys and conflicts of interest in real estate transactions

Real estate transactions vary considerably in their form and complexity, from large commercial transactions, in which all or almost all of the interested parties will be independently represented by counsel, to relatively routine residential sales, in which one attorney handles the closing on behalf of all the parties. Indeed, in most jurisdictions lawyers are becoming marginalized in residential real estate transactions, largely because of the development of title insurance.[72]

When all the parties in a real estate transaction are represented by counsel, uncertainties about the lawyer's role are largely eliminated, but problems of role can surface when a single lawyer handles the transaction. Unfortunately, lawyers often fail to reach a clear agreement about whom they represent with the parties to real estate transactions. Lawyers who allow such uncertainties to occur face an increased risk of disciplinary action or malpractice

---

72. Michael Braunstein, Structural Change and Inter-professional Competitive Advantage: An Example Drawn from Residential Real Estate Conveyancing, 62 Mo. L. Rev. 241 (1997).

liability.[73] In addition, as discussed below, lawyers who fail to clarify their role in real estate transactions are likely to encounter conflict-of-interest problems if they represent one of the parties to the transaction in a subsequent dispute arising out of the transaction.

How can lawyers avoid confusion about whom they represent in real estate transactions? In large commercial transactions, the possibility of confusion is reduced because each party is typically represented by counsel. Even in commercial transactions, however, if a lawyer is preparing documents that will be executed by other parties, it would be prudent for the lawyer to have the other parties sign statements acknowledging that the attorney does not represent them and that they will look to their own counsel for advice in the transaction. In fairly routine residential real estate transactions, the expense of separate counsel often renders this option infeasible.

If the parties to a real estate transaction are not separately represented, real estate attorneys have two models available to clarify their roles: the multiple-representation model and the single-client model. In the multiple-representation model, the lawyer has multiple clients: buyer and seller; buyer and lender; buyer, seller, and lender; or perhaps even buyer, seller, lender, and title company. As discussed in Problem 5-1, Model Rules 1.7 and 2.2 authorize lawyers to represent multiple clients in business transactions under some circumstances. To do so, lawyers must conclude that they can reasonably undertake the representation without adverse impact on any of the clients, and each client must consent after consultation with the lawyer about the advantages and risks of multiple representation.

Is a real estate transaction the type of matter in which a lawyer can reasonably undertake multiple representation without adverse impact on the representation of any of the clients? In some cases, courts have found that lawyers have acted improperly by representing multiple clients in real estate transactions. These cases, however, typically involved attorneys who failed to obtain the in-

---

73. E.g., Iowa Supreme Court Bd. of Prof. Ethics & Conduct v. Wagner, 599 N.W. 2d 721 (Iowa 1999) (lawyer suspended for misconduct arising from representation of buyer and seller in sale of commercial property); Stinson v. Brand, 738 S.W.2d 186 (Tenn. 1987) (question of fact whether attorney who handled real estate closing had client-lawyer relationship with sellers, exposing attorney to malpractice liability).

formed consent of their clients or who neglected to carry out their duties to one of the clients.[74] While such cases highlight the dangers of multiple representation, they do not go so far as to establish a per se bar to multiple representation in real estate transactions.[75] Attorneys should recognize, however, that multiple representation, even in fairly routine residential real estate transactions, has risks. Further, the climate of professional opinion may be shifting against the practice. For example, the leading treatise on legal malpractice states:

> Historically, the practice of an attorney representing both parties to a transaction in the transfer of a property interest was common and, seemingly, approved. Today such representation is doubtful, at best, and usually is improper.[76]

If a lawyer concludes that he can adequately represent multiple parties, the lawyer must also obtain the informed consent of the parties. Informed consent requires more than a statement that the lawyer does not have a conflict of interest.[77] Given the possibility for confusion regarding the lawyer's role, written disclosure of the advantages and disadvantages of the lawyer's role, and written consent if the attorney will be representing multiple parties, is highly desirable.

If an attorney decides to undertake multiple representation, the fundamental problem facing the attorney is how to advise and counsel the clients on solutions to issues that may benefit one party at the expense of another. The problem is especially acute if the

74. E.g., Florida Bar v. Teitelman, 261 So. 2d 140 (Fla. 1972) (failure to obtain informed consent to multiple representation); Attorney Grievance Comm. v. Lockhart, 403 A.2d 1241 (Md. 1979) (improper certification of title and release of funds). See generally Annotation, Attorney and Client: Conflict of Interest in Real Estate Closing Situations, 68 A.L.R.3d 967 (1976).

75. See Westport Bank & Trust Co. v. Corcoran, Mallin & Aresco, 605 A.2d 862 (Conn. 1992) (potential for conflict of interest does not preclude such representation). But see Baldasarre v. Butler, 625 A.2d 458 (N.J. 1993) (because of high likelihood of actual conflict of interest in complex commercial real estate transactions, multiple representation is improper even with consent of parties).

76. 4 Mallen & Smith, Legal Malpractice §30.6, at 20.

77. See In re Lanza, 322 A.2d 445 (N.J. 1974) (lawyer disciplined for representing buyer and seller without informed consent and for continuing representation of both once actual conflict developed over payment of portion of purchase price).

attorney is employed before the buyer and seller have executed a binding contract. Real estate contracts, like other agreements, can be drafted to favor either of the parties. Even if the attorney is not employed until after the parties sign a contract, as is usually the case in residential transactions, issues may still arise. For example, suppose the contract fails to specify which party bears the cost of a certain item, such as repairs resulting from a termite inspection. Or suppose at closing a question arises whether certain fixtures are included with the sale to the purchaser or may be taken by the seller. One way in which an attorney could respond to such issues is to act in essence as an arbitrator. The attorney informs the parties how the issue should be resolved, either based on the lawyer's opinion or based on what the lawyer believes is customarily done. While it is possible for the clients to agree for the lawyer to act as arbitrator of any disputes they may have, absent such an agreement the arbitration approach seems inconsistent with the lawyer's obligations as a representative of both parties.

How can lawyers act consistently with their obligations as representatives of both parties? Consider the possibility of acting as a "neutral information source." In this role, the lawyer identifies any issue that is likely to be of concern to either of the parties, whether raised by them or not. The lawyer provides information to the clients about how they could resolve the issue. This information includes the lawyer's understanding of how such matters are customarily resolved in the locality, but the method of presenting this information differs from the approach when the lawyer assumes the role of arbitrator. In the capacity of "neutral information source," the lawyer supplies this information but also advises the parties that the custom is not necessarily binding on them and that they can agree to a different resolution of the issue. The lawyer should also inform the parties that if the issue is significant to them, and if they are unable to reach agreement, the lawyer cannot proceed with the closing. See Model Rule 2.2(c).

Instead of undertaking multiple representation, lawyers handling real estate transactions could decide to adopt a single-client representation model. Under this approach, the lawyer represents only one party to the transaction. Whom does the lawyer represent? The natural answer is either the buyer or the lender, since they are the principal parties in the transaction. As between the buyer and the lender, the buyer is obviously more in need of legal advice and protection than a sophisticated lender. Further, stat-

utes in some jurisdictions grant borrowers in residential real estate
financing transactions the right to select counsel.[78] Some lenders
may insist, however, that lawyers represent their interests at closing. Lawyers who want to do business with such lenders must
accept a client-lawyer relationship with the lender as well as with
the buyer. The following discussion assumes that single-client representation is a feasible alternative for the lawyer.

The fact that the lawyer represents only the buyer does not
prevent the lawyer from preparing documents to be signed by
other parties to the transaction, nor does the fact that the lawyer
is preparing documents for the other parties necessarily result in
the formation of a client-lawyer relationship with those parties.[79]
The lawyer would be acting as agent for the buyer, preparing documents that must be signed by other parties for the buyer's benefit.

How are the lender's legal interests protected if the lawyer
represents only the buyer? Lenders' commitment letters will attach
various conditions to the closing of the loan to protect the lender.
These conditions typically include use of the lender's closing documents and issuance of a title insurance policy to protect the
lender. Many lenders have their own general or in-house counsel
who review the lender's standard form closing package and advise
them should any problems arise. The use of the lender's closing
package generally precludes the possibility of the lawyer negotiating changes in the forms on behalf of the buyer. Since the forms
are fairly standard in most jurisdictions, rarely would there be
much to negotiate in any event. The attorney would, of course,
have an obligation to advise the buyer generally as to the nature
of the documents the buyer is signing and to point out any unusual
provisions of which the buyer should be aware. Although the
lender requires the buyer's attorney to use its forms, this should
not be considered to be improper third-party interference with the
lawyer's relationship with the buyer. See Model Rule 5.4(c). The
use of the lender's forms is simply a condition to the loan, similar
to other conditions, such as the buyer's creditworthiness. Even
though the lender may be a sophisticated commercial party, a prudent closing attorney will clarify in writing that the attorney is
handling the closing as the attorney for the buyer, not the lender.

---

78. E.g., S.C. Code Ann. §37-10-102(a).
79. E.g., Dolan v. Hickey, 431 N.E.2d 229 (Mass. 1982) (drafting and
presentation of documents does not amount to legal advice).

Similarly, the fact that the attorney is representing the buyer should not preclude the attorney from preparing documents for the seller's signature that are necessary to close the transaction, such as the deed from the seller, affidavits from the seller regarding liens on the property, and the closing statement. The attorney should advise the seller that the attorney represents the buyer, that such documents are being prepared for the benefit of the buyer, and that the seller may wish to hire separate counsel for advice about these documents. Notification of the lawyer's role should be given to the seller in writing in advance of the closing so that the seller has sufficient time to retain counsel. This may not be easy given the time pressures under which many real estate closings occur.

Note that even if a real estate attorney makes it clear that she represents only one party in the transaction, in many jurisdictions the attorney may still be held liable to one of the other parties to the transaction, typically on a theory of negligent misrepresentation.[80]

May a lawyer who has handled the closing of a real estate transaction represent one of the parties in a subsequent legal dispute arising from the transaction, such as litigation between the buyer and seller or a mortgage foreclosure action brought by the lender? The answer depends largely on whom the attorney represented in the original transaction. If the lawyer represented multiple clients, the lawyer may not represent any of these clients in a subsequent dispute arising from the matter. This conclusion follows from a standard application of the subsequent representation rule. See Model Rules 1.9(a) and 2.2(c). If the lawyer represented only one client, the lawyer could handle a matter on behalf of that client against any of the other parties to the transaction. Thus, a lawyer who represented the buyer at the closing could represent the buyer in subsequent litigation with the seller or lender. The

---

80. See First Nat. Bank of Durant v. Trans Terra Corp. Intl., 142 F.3d 802 (5th Cir. 1998) (no client-lawyer relationship between lender and borrower's attorney, but lender may recover from attorney under theory of negligent misrepresentation for inaccurate title opinion); Seigle v. Jasper, 867 S.W.2d 476 (Ky. Ct. App. 1993) (attorney for lender could be liable to purchasers for negligent title examination under Restatement (Second) of Torts §552); Petrillo v. Bachenberg, 655 A.2d 1354 (N.J. 1995) (attorney for seller of real estate owed duty of care to buyer to avoid misleading buyer concerning suitability of land for septic system).

lawyer could not, however, accept such representation if the lawyer's representation in the original transaction would be an issue in the litigation. For example, the lawyer could not represent the buyer in a foreclosure action brought by the lender when an issue in the litigation would be whether the buyer had properly executed the mortgage. Such representation would involve an inherent conflict of interest because to succeed on behalf of the buyer the lawyer would need to establish his own malpractice. See Model Rule 1.7(b). In addition, it would probably be necessary for the lawyer to be a witness in the matter as to the validity of the mortgage. Model Rule 3.7.

May a lawyer who represented the buyer in a residential real estate transaction handle a subsequent mortgage foreclosure proceeding on behalf of the lender? On one hand, such representation appears to be a clear violation of the former client rule because the lawyer is undertaking representation against a former client in the very matter the lawyer previously handled. Model Rule 1.9(a). On the other hand, mortgage foreclosure proceedings are fairly routine, the risk of use of confidential information gained in the prior representation is practically nonexistent, and it would often be more efficient for the closing attorney to be able to handle the foreclosure since the attorney already has the file and is familiar with the transaction. Some courts have indicated that they saw no impropriety in a lawyer's handling a mortgage foreclosure proceeding on behalf of a lender when the lawyer represented the buyer at closing.[81] Nonetheless, if the closing attorney plans to be available to handle mortgage foreclosures on behalf of the lender, the attorney should disclose this fact to the buyer and obtain the buyer's consent when the buyer first retains the lawyer.

In residential real estate transactions, lawyers often have a financial interest in the transaction arising from their relationship with title insurance companies. Lawyers frequently act as agents for title insurance companies, receiving a commission from the sale of title insurance to owners and lenders. Further, some lawyers have an ownership interest in title insurance companies. In Formal

---

81. In re Anonymous Member of the S.C. Bar, 378 S.E.2d 821, 821 n.1 (S.C. 1989). See also Griffith v. Taylor, 937 P.2d 297 (Alaska 1997) (recognizing "scrivener's exception" to representation against former client, when attorney merely drafted statutory form of deed or performed clerical or ministerial tasks).

Opinions 304 (1962) and 331 (1972), the ABA Committee on Ethics and Professional Responsibility decided that lawyers could properly advise their clients about the availability of title insurance even though they received a commission or had a financial interest in a title insurance company, but such financial relationships should be fully disclosed and consented to by the client. These opinions seem consistent with Model Rule 1.8(a), which involves business transactions between lawyer and client.[82] In addition, the Real Estate Settlement Procedures Act (RESPA)[83] requires lawyers to disclose to buyers commissions received from selling title insurance.

In some commercial real estate transactions, lawyers may have a financial interest in the transaction or in one of the parties to the transaction. A lawyer who has a financial interest has a duty to comply with Model Rule 1.8(a) regarding the transaction. Note that the rule requires the client's written consent and an opportunity to seek the advice of independent counsel. Lawyers have been disciplined and held liable for damages to their clients for failing to disclose their financial interest in real estate transactions.[84] If the lawyer's financial interest in the transaction is substantial, prudence dictates that the lawyer decline representation in the matter.

Unauthorized practice of law issues in real estate transactions

Lawyers involved in real estate practice frequently deal with non-lawyers: real estate brokers, title insurance companies, title examiners or abstractors, and paralegals. Rules of professional conduct prohibit lawyers from assisting nonlawyers in the unau-

---

82. But see N.J. Adv. Comm. on Prof. Ethics, Op. No. 682 (1996), 1996 WL 74060 (inherent, nonwaivable conflict for lawyers to refer clients to title company for examination and insurance when they retain portion of premium as compensation, because lawyer's financial interest interferes with independent professional judgment).

83. 12 U.S.C. §2607(c).

84. See Iowa Supreme Court Board of Prof. Ethics & Conduct v. Wagner, 599 N.W. 2d 721 (Iowa 1999) (lawyer failed to disclose to buyer percentage commission to be paid by seller).

thorized practice of law. Model Rule 5.5(b). The definition of what constitutes the practice of law varies among the jurisdictions.[85] Traditionally, courts have broadly defined the practice of law to include not only appearances in court but also advice to clients about legal matters and preparation of documents having legal consequences.[86] Over the years, tensions and disputes have developed between lawyers and nonlawyers when nonlawyers have attempted to provide services in real estate transactions that lawyers have considered to be the practice of law.[87] Areas of controversy have revolved around completion of real estate forms, title examinations, and real estate closings.[88] In some states, real estate brokers or title companies have been able to convince state legislatures to enact statutes authorizing their activities, but courts have often invalidated such legislation on separation of powers grounds. The courts have reasoned that these statutes invade the province of the courts to regulate the practice of law.[89] In Arizona an association of realtors was able to obtain a constitutional amendment overturning a supreme court decision prohibiting them from completing real estate contracts and related documents.[90]

Some state supreme courts have adopted rules allowing exceptions to the traditional restrictions on the unauthorized practice of law. In 1983 Washington became the first state to provide for licensing of nonlawyers, but on an extremely limited basis. By rule the state supreme court created a Limited Practice Board, which has the authority to certify "closing officers." Closing officers must pass an examination, demonstrate financial responsibility, and

85. See Model Rule 5.5, cmt., and Wolfram, Modern Legal Ethics §15.1.3, at 835-836. See also In re First Escrow, Inc., 840 S.W.2d 839 (Mo. 1992) (en banc) (establishing unauthorized practice guidelines for escrow companies).

86. E.g., State v. Buyers Serv. Co., 357 S.E.2d 15 (S.C. 1987).

87. For a review of these developments, see Joyce Palomar, The War Between Attorneys and Lay Conveyancers — Empirical Evidence Says "Cease Fire!" 31 Conn. L. Rev. 423 (1999).

88. See, e.g., Perkins v. CTX Mortgage Co., 969 P.2d 93 (Wash. 1999) (en banc) (mortgage company did not engage in unauthorized practice when its lay employees filled in blanks in mortgage forms without exercising discretion).

89. E.g., Bennion, Van Camp, Hagen & Ruhl v. Kassler Escrow, Inc., 635 P.2d 730 (Wash. 1981) (en banc).

90. See Palomar, The War Between Attorneys and Lay Conveyancers, 31 Conn. L. Rev. at 470.

meet continuing education requirements. The rule allows closing officers to do the following:

> select, prepare and complete documents in a form previously approved by the Board for use in closing a loan, extension of credit, sale or other transfer of real or personal property. Such documents shall be limited to deeds, promissory notes, guaranties, deeds of trust, reconveyances, mortgages, satisfactions, security agreements, releases, Uniform Commercial Code documents, assignments, contracts, real estate excise tax affidavits, and bills of sale. Other documents may be from time to time approved by the Board.[91]

Closing officers cannot give legal advice and all parties to the transaction must consent to their participation.

New Jersey has adopted an even more open approach than Washington in real estate transactions. The New Jersey Supreme Court has held that activities of real estate brokers and title officers in preparing contracts and in closing real estate transactions constitute the practice of law, but that the public interest justifies allowing such practices provided the broker or title officer notifies the vendor and purchaser of their conflicting interest in such transactions and of the general risk involved in not being represented by an attorney.[92]

Virginia has taken a quite different approach to the issue of the unauthorized practice of law. That state's supreme court has adopted a set of rules defining what constitutes the unauthorized practice of law in the following areas: practice before tribunals, lay adjusters, collection agencies, estate planning and settlement, tax practice, real estate practice, title insurance, trade associations, and administrative agency practice.[93] Rather than providing for licensing, the Virginia rules attempt to define fairly precisely the kinds of activities that nonlawyers may perform incident to their business activities. While the Virginia rules allow nonlawyers to perform certain legal services, they also operate as a restriction on nonlawyer practice by prohibiting those activities that they do not

91. Wash. Ct. Rules, Admission to Practice Rule 12(d).
92. In re Opinion No. 26 of the Comm. on the Unauthorized Practice of Law, 654 A.2d 1344 (N.J. 1995).
93. Va. Sup. Ct., Unauthorized Practice Rules and Considerations.

specifically allow.[94] For example, Rule 6-103 deals with preparation of legal instruments incident to real estate transactions:

UPR 6-103. *Preparation of Legal Instruments*

(A) A non-lawyer shall not, with or without compensation, prepare for another legal instruments of any character affecting the title to or use of real estate, except:

(1) A non-lawyer may prepare a deed with respect to, or deed of trust secured by, real estate owned by him.

(2) A regular employee may prepare legal instruments for use by his employer, other than in aid of his employer's unauthorized practice of law, for which no separate charge shall be made.

(3) A real estate agent, or his regular employee, involved in the negotiation of a transaction and incident to the regular course of conducting his licensed business, may prepare a contract of sale, exchange, option or lease with respect to such transaction, for which no separate charge shall be made.

(4) A lending institution may in the regular course of conducting its business prepare a deed of trust or mortgage on real estate securing the payment of its loan, for which no separate charge shall be made.

Lawyers' use of paralegals in real estate transactions also involves unauthorized practice questions. The comment to Model Rule 5.5 provides that lawyers may properly delegate to nonlawyers a variety of legal tasks: "Paragraph (b) does not prohibit a lawyer from employing the services of paraprofessionals and delegating functions to them, so long as the lawyer supervises the delegated work and retains responsibility for their work." (See also Model Rule 5.3 on the supervisory responsibilities of lawyers for nonlawyers.) Under Model Rule 5.5, lawyers could delegate a wide variety of tasks to paralegals, including title examination, preparation of closing documents, and recording of instruments. How far may lawyers go in using paralegals? May lawyers allow

---

94. In 1997 the Virginia legislature limited the application of one of these rules by passing the Consumer Real Estate Settlement Protection Act. The act allows Virginia-licensed title insurance companies and agents, attorneys, real estate brokers, and financial institutions to provide residential real estate settlement services provided the transaction does not involve more than four residential units. See Va. Code Ann. §§ 6.1-2.19 to-2.29.

paralegals to deal personally with clients? May paralegals sign opinion letters? May they sign other correspondence that does not amount to a formal legal opinion? May paralegals handle closings without lawyers being present if lawyers are available should problems arise? May lawyers use independent paralegal firms or must paralegals be their employees? All these questions stem from the general issue of the adequacy of supervision. Ethics advisory opinions may provide some guidance on these issues, but most of these questions are left to the judgment of lawyers about what constitutes proper supervision of their nonlawyer employees. Some states have adopted rules dealing with the use of paralegals.[95] We will consider the issue of supervision of paralegals and nonlawyer personnel in Problem 7-1.

Trust account management and disbursement of funds at real estate closings

Real estate transactions, even relatively routine matters, involve substantial sums of money. Rules of professional conduct require lawyers to use trust or escrow accounts for depositing of client funds. See Model Rule 1.15. Recall Problem 2-2. Typically, lawyers have real estate escrow accounts that are separate from their firms' general trust accounts.

   A major issue that has troubled real estate attorneys deals with disbursement of funds at closing. The parties who receive money from the transaction, usually the seller and any real estate brokers, want to take their checks with them from the closing. The closing attorney typically receives funds at closing from the lender and the buyer. But even if the lawyer deposits these funds immediately, the lawyer's bank has not yet collected these funds. If the lawyer issues checks to the seller and broker at closing and later either the buyer's or the lender's check is not honored for some reason, then the lawyer has an escrow account problem. If the escrow account contains the funds of other clients, which is normally the case, the lawyer will have disbursed funds belonging to other clients. The lawyer could try to stop payment on checks issued to the seller or brokers, but it may be too late to do so.[96]

---

95. See Ky. Sup. Ct. R. Practice 3.700.
96. See Legacy Homes, Inc. v. Cole, 421 S.E.2d 127 (Ga. Ct. App. 1992).

Various ways exist for lawyers to avoid the problem of disbursement against uncollected funds. In Advisory Opinion 454 (1980), the New Jersey Supreme Court Advisory Committee on Professional Ethics suggested three possibilities:

(1) escrow closings in which no funds are disbursed and no closing completed until all funds have cleared;

(2) pre-arrangement by the attorneys involved so that the necessary closing figures are known far enough in advance for the parties to provide funds in such a manner as to obviate the necessity of using the trust account (undoubtedly this would require cooperation of the bank-mortgagee which may be asked to provide mortgage funds in several checks);

(3) establishment of an account by the attorney of his own funds which can be used to accommodate a client when there is no other solution.[97]

The committee understood, however, that these solutions might not be practical. It then addressed the question of whether it was ever proper for an attorney to disburse funds at a real estate closing from uncollected funds. Recognizing the practical reasons and customary practice of doing so among many attorneys, the committee ruled that an attorney could properly disburse at closing from uncollected funds if the funds consisted of a certified or cashier's check issued by a bank. The committee concluded that such disbursements involved almost nonexistent risk because the checks were the obligations of the bank rather than a private party. Later the committee extended this rule to cashier's and certified checks issued by savings and loan institutions. The committee went on to make clear that disbursement against the personal check of the buyer was improper.[98]

While receptive to the practicalities of real estate practice, the approach authorized by the New Jersey committee does expose attorneys and clients who have funds in escrow accounts to some degree of risk. Indeed, given the debacle in the savings and loan industry, the committee's assumption that checks issued by financial institutions bear almost no risk can be questioned. Most states

97. 1980 WL 78467, at 1.
98. See In re Moras, 619 A.2d 1007, 1011 (N.J. 1993).

do not follow the New Jersey approach and prohibit lawyers from making disbursements against uncollected funds.

——————— **Problem 5-4** ———————

Estate Planning and Probate Practice

a.   John and Ellen Bryson have come to you seeking advice regarding an estate plan. The couple has two minor children and total assets, including insurance, of approximately $3 million. Almost all of the assets are in John's name, although they own their home as tenants in common. Ellen's father is deceased and her mother is in poor health. On her mother's death, Ellen expects to inherit approximately $300,000. You have discussed with them a fairly typical estate plan for their situation. Under the plan each spouse would execute a will with two parts: a "credit shelter trust" (sometimes called a "bypass trust") and a "marital deduction" bequest.

The credit shelter portion is an amount equal to the maximum credit allowed for federal estate tax purposes; this figure is gradually rising from $600,000 to $1,000,000 over the next few years. The credit shelter share goes into trust for the benefit of the surviving spouse for life, with remainder to their children. Use of the bypass trust avoids taxation of the credit shelter amount on the death of both spouses. On the death of the first spouse, the credit shelter amount is not taxed in that spouse's estate because of the application of the federal estate tax credit. On the death of the second spouse, the credit shelter amount still escapes tax because the second spouse only has a life interest in the trust. The income and principal of the credit shelter trust are available for the surviving spouse if needed, although it is typically anticipated that the surviving spouse will have sufficient assets from the marital portion to avoid encroaching on the principal of the credit shelter trust.

The marital deduction bequest consists of the remainder of the first spouse's estate. On the death of the first spouse, this portion passes free of estate tax as a

result of the marital deduction. On the second spouse's
death, the marital deduction portion will be subject to
tax. The marital deduction portion can be left to the
surviving spouse outright, or it can be placed in what is
called a QTIP (Qualified Terminable Interest Property)
trust. The major difference between an outright bequest
and the QTIP trust deals with the degree of control that
the first spouse can exercise over the principal of the
bequest. With an outright bequest, the surviving spouse
enjoys the unfettered right to use the income and principal of the marital bequest. With a QTIP trust, the first
spouse can limit the surviving spouse to an income interest in the bequest and can control the ultimate disposition of the trust when the surviving spouse dies.

After you met with John and Ellen, they decided
that they wanted to think about your suggested plan for
a few days. About a week later, you receive a call from
John. He tells you that he and Ellen have decided to go
ahead with the plan. For his will, he says that he wants
Ellen's marital portion held in a QTIP trust. John says
that Ellen is a very attractive woman, and he knows that
she will remarry if something happens to him. He wants
to make sure that his estate goes to their children, and
not to a second husband. John says that in Ellen's will
the marital portion should go to him outright rather than
in trust; because she does not have a large estate, a trust
is unnecessary and too much paperwork for him. John
also asks you about an executor and trustee for his will.
He wants to know if you would be willing to serve because he really doesn't trust a bank to handle his estate.
Be prepared to continue the conversation with John
from that point.

b. Suppose John and Ellen have executed wills
following the general structure that you outlined. About
a year later, John calls and says that he has a "tax question," he needs to ask you. He says that he has a friend
to whom he has loaned about $100,000. He has decided
to forgive the loan and wants to know about the tax
consequences of doing so. You advise him that a gift
that exceeds $10,000 per year is subject to gift tax, but

that several options exist for avoiding the tax. First, he could give the friend $10,000 each year until the loan is forgiven. You tell him that the exact number of years that it will take to forgive the loan is a little complicated because of some tax rules dealing with interest-free loans. If he wants to accelerate the forgiveness, he and Ellen could agree to make a joint gift of $20,000. They would be required to file a gift tax return, but no tax would be due. He could also add a codicil to his will forgiving any amount still due at death. Second, he could forgive the entire amount immediately, but avoid tax by using a part of his unified credit for federal estate and gift tax purposes. Ellen would not need to join in this return. Partial use of the unified credit would reduce the amount that would go into the credit shelter trust under John's will and would increase the amount that would go to Ellen under the marital portion of John's will. John tells you that the loan is something private, and he really can't ask Ellen to get involved in the matter. He says that he wants to get this done now, and he asks you to prepare a gift tax return using a portion of his unified credit to eliminate any tax. Explain how you would proceed and why.

Fid duty to honesty [handwritten margin note]

   c.   You are attorney for the estate of Horace Bellrod. Bellrod died recently, leaving an estate of approximately $10 million. He is survived by his wife, Nancy, age 77, and three adult children. Bellrod's will leaves half of his estate outright to his children and half in trust for his wife, remainder to the children. Bellrod appointed his three children as personal representatives of his estate and as cotrustees of a marital deduction trust created under his will. Under the law of your jurisdiction, a surviving spouse can elect to receive a statutory share of one-third of the estate instead of taking under the will. You have advised the children of this. They have asked you whether it is necessary for their mother to take this amount because they question her ability to manage the money. They also say that her memory appears to be failing, and they are concerned that she may be suffering from early stages of Alzheimer's disease.

They believe that the trust arrangement is much better for her and that this arrangement is what their father wanted. You have advised them that Nancy has the right to elect a forced share, but that she does not have to exercise this right. The children tell you that they do not plan to inform their mother of her statutory right and simply hope that it lapses. Under local law the statutory right expires unless it is exercised within eight months after the date of death. A few days after meeting with the children to discuss the statutory forced share matter, you receive a telephone call from Nancy Bellrod. She says that she is calling to see what she needs to do about the estate. Be prepared to continue the conversation from that point.

Disclose
· is she a client?

Read Model Rules 1.7, 1.8(c), 1.14, 2.1, 2.2, 5.3, and comments.

The Model Rules and ethical issues facing lawyers engaged in estate planning and administration

The trust and estate bar has criticized the Model Rules for failing to provide adequate guidance regarding common ethical problems in this area of practice. A study by a committee of the Real Property, Probate, and Trust Law Section of the ABA concluded that "the Model Rules do not deal effectively with some of the most important and most difficult problems of professional conduct in the practice of estate planning."[99]

As a result of this criticism, the ABA Real Property, Probate, and Trust Law Section appointed a special committee to study ethical issues confronting trust and estate lawyers. In 1993 the special committee issued three reports that were approved by the council of the section:

---

99. Committee on Significant New Developments in Probate and Trust Law Practice, Developments Regarding the Professional Responsibility of the Estate Planning Lawyer: The Effect of the Model Rules of Professional Conduct, 22 Real Prop. Prob. & Tr. J. 1, 1-2 (1987). See also American College of Trust and Estate Counsel, Commentaries on the Model Rules of Professional Conduct, 28 Real Prop. Prob. & Tr. J. 865, 866 (1994).

- Comments and Recommendations on the Lawyer's Duties in Representing Husband and Wife (hereinafter Special Report — Representing Husband and Wife);
- Preparation of Wills and Trusts that Name Drafting Lawyer as Fiduciary (hereinafter Special Report — Drafting Lawyer as Fiduciary); and
- Counseling the Fiduciary (hereinafter Special Report — Counseling the Fiduciary).[100]

In addition, the American College of Trust and Estate Counsel has adopted Commentaries on the Model Rules of Professional Conduct.[101] The material that follows focuses on several of the most important ethical problems facing lawyers in trust and estate practice.

Conflicts of interest and confidentiality in estate planning

The Model Rules include two provisions dealing with conflicts of interest involved in representing multiple clients in a single matter: Rules 1.7(b) and 2.2. We have explored the application of these provisions in a number of areas of practice: criminal defense (Problem 2-7), joint representation of plaintiffs in tort matters (Problem 3-8), insurance defense practice (Problem 3-9), family practice (Problem 3-10), and business practice (Problem 5-1). Both rules contemplate that lawyers may represent clients with potentially conflicting interests provided the lawyer reasonably believes that multiple representation can be undertaken without adverse effect on the clients and provided both clients consent after consultation regarding the advantages and disadvantages of multiple representation. How do these rules apply to representation of spouses in estate planning?[102]

---

100. All three reports are published in 28 Real Prop. Prob. & Tr. J. 765, 803, 825 (1994).

101. 28 Real Prop. Prob. & Tr. J. 865 (1994) (hereinafter ACTEC Commentaries).

102. For a different approach, see Russell G. Pearce, Family Values and Legal Ethics: Competing Approaches to Conflicts in Representing Spouses, 62 Fordham L. Rev. 1253 (1994) (proposing modification of rules of ethics to allow lawyers to represent families as communities rather than collection of individu-

The Special Report — Representing Husband and Wife takes these general rules and attempts to provide interpretive guidance to estate planning practitioners. The report concludes that Rule 2.2 will rarely apply because the lawyer in estate planning is not seeking to assist the clients in achieving binding agreements with each other.[103] The report discusses two forms of representation that are permissible for estate planning lawyers: separate and joint representation.

What are the differences between separate and joint representation? In separate representation, the lawyer represents each spouse separately as to that spouse's rights and interests.[104] Further, in separate representation the lawyer must maintain the confidentiality of information received from either spouse, even if the information might affect the estate plan of the other spouse.[105] The lawyer, however, may have a duty to withdraw if the receipt of confidential information means that an actual conflict of interest exists between the spouses.[106] By contrast, in joint representation the lawyer represents both spouses "joined to accomplish a mutual goal."[107] If a lawyer who is engaged in joint representation receives confidential information from one spouse that has an impact on the estate plan of the other spouse, the lawyer must act as a fiduciary to both spouses and must choose to disclose, to maintain confidentiality, or to withdraw based on the lawyer's determination of which action does the least harm.[108]

The report also considers two methods by which a lawyer may undertake representation: either with or without an agreement regarding the nature of the lawyer's representation. The report adopts the view that a lawyer may ethically proceed with the representation of both spouses in estate planning without complying with the requirements of Rule 1.7(b) when the lawyer has no reason to believe that a potential conflict exists between the spouses. The report goes on to state that the mere fact of marriage is not in itself sufficient to trigger the requirements of Rule

---

als). See generally Symposium, Should the Family Be Represented as an Entity? 22 Seattle U. L. Rev. 1 (1998).

    103. 28 Real Prop. Prob. & Tr. J. at 782-783, 795.
    104. Id. at 772.
    105. Id. at 796.
    106. Id. at 794-795.
    107. Id. at 771.
    108. Id. at 787.

1.7(b).[109] If the lawyer proceeds in this manner, that is, without discussion of the lawyer's role, the report concludes that the representation should be deemed joint rather than separate.[110]

Alternatively, a lawyer could choose to undertake representation after full discussion with the clients about the differences between joint and separate representation. The report provides that a lawyer who does so has flexibility to set the terms of the engagement: "The lawyer may confirm the implicit disclosure rules discussed above; may define his or her duty to require immediate disclosure and withdrawal; or may agree to neither disclosure nor withdrawal."[111] Even with an engagement agreement, however, the report recognizes limits on the lawyer's conduct. For example, a lawyer could not participate in active deception of the other spouse.[112]

While the report concludes that engagement agreements are not required, it advises that discussion and agreement are the "better practice."[113] If the lawyer does use an engagement agreement, how does the lawyer choose between separate or joint representation?

> The lawyer may determine to use consistently either mode, or to adopt different modes of representation for different fact patterns. Some practitioners may offer both modes and allow the couple to choose, although this should be offered only by the lawyer who is confident he or she can perform competently in either mode. However, the method of representation must be constantly reconsidered by the lawyer as new facts and situations arise. The lawyer also must make a personal choice, individually developed, based on his or her perspective of the couple's planning needs, their sophistication, their responsibilities to each other, and his or her ability to remain independent and loyal as competing goals emerge.[114]

Some commentators have disagreed with the central ideas of the Special Report — Representing Husband and Wife. Professor

109. Id. at 779.
110. Id. at 778.
111. Id. at 793-794.
112. Id. at 794-795.
113. Id. at 801-802.
114. Id. at 796-797. For examples of engagement agreements for joint and separate representation, see Edward B. Benjamin, Jr., 15 Prob. Notes 125-126 (1989).

Jeffrey Pennell differs with the view that a lawyer may proceed with joint representation without disclosure and consent of the spouses, even when the lawyer has no reason to believe that a conflict of interest exists between the spouses. He argues that Model Rules 1.7(b) and 2.2 are clear: When a potential for conflict exists, the lawyer cannot proceed with representation of the spouses without full disclosure of the possible conflicts and consent of both spouses.[115] The Restatement of the Law Governing Lawyers, however, takes the position that in situations when lawyers know the spouses and no apparent differences exist, they may proceed to represent the spouses in estate planning without disclosure and consent.[116]

Professor Geoffrey Hazard has criticized probate and estate lawyers for claiming that their practice should be subject to special rules. He argues that while joint representation is consistent with the Model Rules, separate representation is "incorrect as a matter of law and therefore a legally dangerous mode of practice."[117] The Restatement of the Law Governing Lawyers, while not rejecting the concept of separate representation outright, refers to it as "novel" and cautions lawyers about the substantial risks involved in undertaking this form of representation.[118]

Professor Teresa Stanton Collett criticizes the report for concluding that lawyers engaged in joint representation are not necessarily required to reveal information received from one spouse to the other spouse when the information affects the other spouse's estate planning. Collett recognizes that the rules of ethics and agency law are unclear on the issue of disclosure. She argues, however, that absent a clear agreement providing for confidentiality, a lawyer should make "disclosure of unilateral confidences when the information contained within that confidence is relevant to the estate planning process, is unknown to the nonconfiding client,

---

115. See Jeffrey N. Pennell, Ethics, Professionalism, and Malpractice Issues in Estate Planning and Administration, SC75 ALI-ABA 67, at 76-83 (1998) (on Westlaw).

116. Restatement (Third) of the Law Governing Lawyers §211, cmt. c and illus. 1.

117. Geoffrey C. Hazard, Jr., Conflict of Interest in Estate Planning for Husband and Wife, 20 Prob. Law. 1, 6 (1994) (published by the Am. Coll. of Tr. & Estate Counsel).

118. Restatement (Third) of the Law Governing Lawyers §211, Reporter's Note to cmt. c.

and is adverse to the interests of the nonconfiding client."[119] Collett justifies this approach because (1) spouses reasonably expect that information will be shared; (2) the spouse who claims confidentiality is acting unfairly, seeking the benefit of complete information from the other spouse, while refusing to accept the burden of full disclosure; and (3) the lawyer is at fault in not obtaining a clear agreement with the clients at the inception of the relationship regarding confidentiality. In contrast to Professor Collett, the AC-TEC Commentaries support the view of the Special Report — Representing Husband and Wife, providing lawyers with discretion to reveal confidential information in cases of joint representation.[120]

Bequests to lawyers and wills that name the drafting lawyer as fiduciary

Occasions may arise in which a client would like to make a gift or bequest to a lawyer. The lawyer and client may be related or may have developed a close, personal relationship. Although the Code of Professional Responsibility did not contain a disciplinary rule making it improper for a lawyer to draft an instrument in which the lawyer was also a beneficiary, some courts disciplined lawyers who did so.[121]

Model Rule 1.8(c) now deals with this problem:

> A lawyer shall not prepare an instrument giving the lawyer or a person related to the lawyer as parent, child, sibling, or spouse any substantial gift from a client, including a testamentary gift, except where the client is related to the donee.[122]

Note that the rule does not preclude a lawyer from preparing a will for the lawyer's spouse or other relative when the lawyer will

---

119. Teresa S. Collett, Disclosure, Discretion, or Deception: The Estate Planner's Ethical Dilemma From a Unilateral Confidence, 28 Real Prop. Prob. & Tr. J. 683, 762 (1994).

120. See 28 Real Prop. Prob. & Tr. J. at 916-921 (commentary to Rule 1.6) and 932-933 (commentary to Rule 1.7).

121. See Committee on Professional Ethics & Conduct v. Behnke, 276 N.W.2d 838 (Iowa), appeal dismissed, 444 U.S. 805 (1979).

122. See In re Polevoy, 980 P.2d 985 (Colo. 1999) (en banc) (suspension for drafting will in which lawyer named as beneficiary).

be receiving a bequest under the will. If a client wishes to leave a bequest to a lawyer to whom the client is not related, the lawyer must advise the client that the lawyer cannot prepare the will and that the will must be drafted by independent counsel. Another lawyer in the lawyer-beneficiary's firm could not prepare the will because disqualification would be imputed to the other lawyer under Model Rule 1.10(a).[123]

Some states have statutory provisions invalidating gifts and bequests to the person who drafted the instrument. For example, California law invalidates certain donative transfers, including a transfer to any person who drafted the instrument.[124] An exception applies if an independent attorney counsels the transferor about the instrument, and completes and delivers to the drafter and to the transferor a statutory form stating that the instrument has not been the product of undue influence or other misconduct.[125]

The Restatement goes somewhat beyond the Model Rules with regard to client gifts. Under the Restatement, a lawyer may not draft an instrument making a gift or bequest to the lawyer even when the lawyer is related to the donor if the amount of the transfer is significantly disproportionate to those made to other similarly situated donees.[126] This prohibition would not prevent a lawyer from preparing a will in which the lawyer's spouse left the spouse's entire estate to the lawyer because it would not run afoul of the disproportionality rule, but it could apply if a lawyer drafted an instrument for a parent that gave the lawyer a greater share of the estate than other children.[127] The Restatement also prohibits lawyers from receiving substantial gifts from clients to whom they are not related, even if the lawyer does not prepare a document effectuating the gift, when the client has not had the opportunity to receive independent advice before making the gift.[128]

A more common situation in which a lawyer has a financial interest in the will occurs when a client asks if the lawyer would

---

123. Cf. People v. Berge, 620 P.2d 23 (Colo. 1980) (en banc) (lawyer-beneficiary who received bequest from client under will drafted by attorney who shared office space with lawyer-beneficiary was suspended for 90 days).

124. Cal. Prob. Code §21350(a)(1).

125. Id. §21351.

126. Restatement (Third) of the Law Governing Lawyers §208(1).

127. Id. illus. 1.

128. Id. §208(2).

be willing to serve as a fiduciary under the will.[129] Clients may make this request because of reasons such as trust in the lawyer, distrust of corporate fiduciaries, and a desire to save fees that would otherwise be payable to a corporate fiduciary. May a lawyer draft a will in which the lawyer will be named as a fiduciary? Lawyers are not prohibited from serving as fiduciaries on behalf of their clients and of drafting instruments in which they are so named. Model Rule 1.8(c) does not apply to this situation because the lawyer is not receiving a gift from the client. A variety of ethical duties are implicated, however, by a client's request to name the lawyer as fiduciary, including (1) the duty to provide a client with competent estate planning advice (Model Rules 1.1 and 2.1), (2) the duty to exercise independent judgment on behalf of a client (Model Rule 2.1), (3) the duty to provide competent fiduciary services (Model Rule 1.1), (4) the duty not to take advantage of a fiduciary relationship (Model Rule 1.8(h)), (5) the avoidance of conflicts of interest with other clients (Model Rule 1.7(b)), and (6) the duty not to charge unreasonable fees (Model Rule 1.5).[130]

The Special Report — Drafting Lawyer as Fiduciary found no per se prohibition against a lawyer drafting a will in which the lawyer is named as fiduciary, but it cautioned that "the rules regarding counseling, disclosure and consent all must be observed."[131] The ACTEC Commentaries agree.[132] The Special Report went on to provide specifics regarding counseling, disclosure, and consent:

> [B]efore the lawyer prepares a document in which he or she is designated as fiduciary, the client should be counseled, with disclosures by the lawyer, regarding: (1) the nature of the fiduciary office (the role and function of the fiduciary); (2) those persons and institutions available and suitable for appointment; (3) any potential conflicts of interest with other fiduciary relationships or with other

129. See generally Edward D. Spurgeon & Mary Jane Ciccarello, The Lawyer in Other Fiduciary Roles: Policy and Ethical Considerations, 62 Fordham L. Rev. 1357 (1994).

130. See Special Report — Drafting Lawyer as Fiduciary, 28 Real Prop. Prob. & Tr. J. at 805.

131. Id. at 815.

132. See 28 Real Prop. Prob. & Tr. J. at 935-936 (commentary to Model Rule 1.7).

clients, including the client's family members, which the fiduciary appointment might trigger; (4) compensation issues; and (5) the additional factors discussed . . . below.[133]

As to compensation issues, the Special Report outlined the following disclosures:

> (1) whether the lawyer or his or her firm may be retained by the fiduciary to provide legal services and the fees to which the lawyer would be entitled as lawyer and as fiduciary; (2) any understanding or practice the attorney has with the named fiduciary regarding hiring the drafting attorney; (3) the extent, if any, to which dual compensation for legal services and fiduciary services is allowed; (4) a comparison of fees if a fiduciary other than the lawyer is appointed; and (5) a comparison with other options, including any local practice that is common in the community of professional fiduciaries retaining the drafting lawyer for representation of the fiduciary.[134]

California law imposes limitations on an attorney's ability to receive compensation for serving as both attorney for an estate or trust and as the fiduciary.[135]

Finally, the Special Report indicated additional factors that the drafting lawyer should consider and discuss with the client before preparing a will in which the lawyer is named as a fiduciary, including the following: (1) increased risk of challenge to the will resulting from the drafting lawyer's being named as a fiduciary, (2) the lawyer's competency to perform the duties of fiduciary, (3) possible conflicts with other clients, and (4) whether the will may contain a provision exonerating the attorney from liability for negligence as a fiduciary in light of Model Rule 1.8(h).[136]

---

133. See Special Report — Drafting Lawyer as Fiduciary, 28 Real Prop. Prob. & Tr. J. at 818.

134. Id. at 819-820.

135. Cal. Prob. Code §§10804 (personal representative) and 15687 (trustee).

136. See Special Report — Drafting Lawyer as Fiduciary, 28 Real Prop. Prob. & Tr. J. at 820-822.

Ethical problems in estate administration: conflicts of interest, confidentiality, fees, and supervision of nonlawyers

The administration of many estates proceeds routinely without serious controversy regarding the estate or its distribution. Depending on the number of individuals involved, their personalities, and the complexity and size of the estate, however, disputes may arise among the parties, creating the possibility that the lawyer may face conflict-of-interest issues.[137]

An initial step for lawyers in recognizing and handling conflicts of interest in estate administration is identification of whom the lawyer represents when the lawyer is retained to handle the legal work for the estate. This situation should be distinguished from one in which a beneficiary retains a lawyer to advise the beneficiary regarding the estate, or a situation in which the fiduciary hires the lawyer personally rather than to represent the estate. In these cases the identity of the client is clear.[138]

Three possible answers to the question "Who is the client?" are apparent: the beneficiaries, the estate, or the fiduciary.[139] Since the estate is being administered in the interest of the beneficiaries, it is plausible to conclude that a lawyer handling the legal work involved in administering an estate represents the beneficiaries. This answer, however, presents some difficulties. First, the fiduciary rather than the beneficiaries has the legal authority to make a number of decisions regarding the estate. It seems odd to place the lawyer in the position of representing a group of individuals who do not have authority to act, while not representing the one person who legally has the power to act. Second, although it is true that the estate is being administered in the interest of the beneficiaries, that does not mean that the beneficiaries' desires or decisions should control. The testator appointed the fiduciary for the purpose of making decisions, in some cases because the testator did not fully trust the beneficiaries to make such decisions. The

---

137. See Special Report — Counseling the Fiduciary, 28 Real Prop. Prob. & Tr. J. 825 (1994).

138. See id. at 840-842 (duties when representing beneficiary) and 854-855 (fiduciary hiring separate counsel to protect its personal or corporate interests).

139. See generally Jeffrey N. Pennell, Representations Involving Fiduciary Entities: Who Is the Client? 62 Fordham L. Rev. 1319 (1994).

fiduciary should be entitled to retain independent counsel to receive advice about these matters.

The second possible answer to the client identification question is that the lawyer represents the "estate" rather than either the beneficiaries or the fiduciary.[140] This approach treats the estate as an entity, like a corporation. Under Model Rule 1.13(a) a lawyer retained by an organization is treated as representing the entity rather than any of its "constituents." Under the entity representation approach, a lawyer is generally required to follow the decisions of a duly appointed representative of the entity, even if the lawyer does not agree with the decision or thinks it to be unwise. Model Rule 1.13, cmt. 4. Model Rule 1.13(b) recognizes, however, that in some cases a lawyer must take steps to protect the entity from misconduct by a representative.

Thus, under the entity theory, if the fiduciary engaged in misappropriation of funds, the lawyer would be required to act "in the best interest" of the estate. Rule 1.13(b) specifies various steps that the lawyer could consider taking, including ultimately "referral to the highest authority that can act in behalf of the organization as determined by applicable law." In the case of an estate, who is the "highest authority"? Because an estate, unlike a corporation, does not have a board of directors, the highest authority would probably be the court that supervises the estate.

The third approach to defining the client of the lawyer handling estate matters is that the lawyer represents the fiduciary rather than either the beneficiaries or the estate as an entity. A possible objection to this approach is that it seems to ignore the fact that the fiduciary has duties to the beneficiaries for whom the estate is being administered. While this argument would have force if an estate lawyer had no obligations to the beneficiaries, it loses some of its power when it is recognized that lawyers have some duties to third parties, even if they are not treated as clients of the lawyer. Some of these duties are discussed more fully below.

Most courts have reached the conclusion that a lawyer represents the fiduciary, not the estate or its beneficiaries.[141] In some

140. See Pennell, Ethics, Professionalism, and Malpractice Issues in Estate Planning and Administration, SC75 ALI-ABA at 131-159 (arguing for adoption of entity theory).

141. See, e.g., Goldberg v. Frye, 266 Cal. Rptr. 483 (Ct. App. 1990) (no cause of action by beneficiaries against lawyer for administrator of estate because

jurisdictions, however, courts have held that a lawyer represents the estate, or, perhaps, even the beneficiaries.[142] The Special Report — Counseling the Fiduciary adopts the view that a lawyer retained to handle estate matters represents the fiduciary rather than the estate or its beneficiaries, although it does note that the entity theory "offers some interesting solutions where the fiduciary has engaged or is engaged in misconduct."[143] Given this uncertainty, Comment 13 to Model Rule 1.7 provides good advice:

> In estate administration the identity of the client may be unclear under the law of a particular jurisdiction. Under one view, the client is the fiduciary; under another view the client is the estate or trust, including its beneficiaries. The lawyer should make clear the relationship to the parties involved.[144]

Reaching the conclusion that the lawyer represents the fiduciary rather than the estate or its beneficiaries, does not, however, mean that the lawyer owes no duties to the beneficiaries. Lawyers for fiduciaries must take into account a number of duties to beneficiaries. First, beneficiaries may well misunderstand the role of the lawyer and may view the lawyer as protecting or representing their interests. Such misunderstanding is especially likely to occur when the lawyer has represented the beneficiary in the past or is currently handling an unrelated matter on behalf of the beneficiary. We have already studied on several occasions the application of Model Rule 4.3, which deals with communications with unrep-

---

attorney does not owe duty to beneficiaries); Ferguson v. Cramer, 709 A.2d 1279 (Md. 1998) (same); Spinner v. Nutt, 631 N.E.2d 542 (Mass. 1994) (attorney for testamentary trustee does not owe duty to beneficiaries because recognition of such a duty would create conflicting loyalties). See also S.C. Code Ann. §62-1-109 (lawyer retained by fiduciary represents fiduciary rather than beneficiaries). But see Leyba v. Whitley, 907 P.2d 172 (N.M. 1995) (attorney for personal representative handling wrongful death case has duty to beneficiaries to use due care in distribution of proceeds; duty of personal representative administering estate or trust distinguished because duty to disburse proceeds of wrongful death action does not involve discretion).

142. See Steinway v. Bolden, 460 N.W.2d 306 (Mich. Ct. App. 1990) (entity theory); Charleson v. Hardesty, 839 P.2d 1303 (Nev. 1992) (lawyer owes fiduciary duties to beneficiaries).

143. 28 Real Prop. Prob. & Tr. J. at 827.   .

144. See also id. at 860-863 (defining duties of lawyer by written agreement).

resented parties. Recall Problem 2-4 (dealing with tangible criminal material) and Problem 3-10 (family practice). Under Rule 4.3, when a lawyer "knows or reasonably should know that the unrepresented person misunderstands the lawyer's role in the matter, the lawyer shall make reasonable efforts to correct the misunderstanding."[145]

Second, a lawyer for a fiduciary may not counsel or assist the fiduciary in criminal or fraudulent conduct. See Model Rule 1.2(d). See also Model Rules 3.3(a)(1) and 4.1 (prohibiting lawyer from making false statements of law or fact to tribunal or third person). This prohibition would include participation in the preparation or filing of fraudulent tax returns or assisting the fiduciary in self-dealing.[146]

Third, under some circumstances a lawyer may have a duty to inform either the beneficiaries or the court of wrongdoing by a fiduciary. In Formal Opinion 94-380, the ABA Committee on Ethics and Professional Responsibility considered whether under the Model Rules an attorney for a fiduciary has an obligation to disclose wrongdoing by the fiduciary to either the beneficiaries or the court. The committee noted that Model Rule 1.6 provides three exceptions to confidentiality: impliedly authorized disclosures, disclosures to prevent criminal acts involving imminent death or substantial bodily harm, and disclosures related to controversies between lawyer and client. The committee decided that none of these exceptions would allow a lawyer to reveal confidential information establishing wrongdoing by a fiduciary to either the beneficiaries or a court. The committee did recognize, however, that a lawyer might be permitted or required to withdraw from representation of the fiduciary if the lawyer's continued representation would involve assistance of the fiduciary in fraud or would involve misrepresentation by the attorney to a court or to third parties.[147]

---

145. See also id. at 837-839; ACTEC Commentaries, 28 Real Prop. Prob. & Tr. J. at 980 (commentary to Rule 4.3).

146. Special Report — Counseling the Fiduciary, 28 Real Prop. Prob. & Tr. J. at 836-837. See Pierce v. Lyman, 3 Cal. Rptr. 2d 236 (Ct. App. 1991) (beneficiaries state cause of action against trustee's lawyer for participation in trustee's breach of fiduciary duty).

147. ABA Comm. on Ethics and Prof. Resp., Formal Op. 94-380, at 5. Professor Robert W. Tuttle has criticized the view expressed in Formal Opinion

In Formal Opinion 94-380, the ABA committee rejected the view that an attorney for a fiduciary is "impliedly authorized" to reveal confidential information establishing wrongdoing by a fiduciary either to the beneficiaries or to the court.[148] The Special Report, however, adopts a different view. The report notes that Comment 5 to Model Rule 1.6 provides that the basis for the duty of confidentiality is derived from agency law and the law of evidence. The report concludes that neither body of law prevents beneficiaries from obtaining information from fiduciaries. Thus, lawyers should be impliedly authorized to disclose to beneficiaries a breach of fiduciary duty.[149] The report goes on to outline how lawyers should proceed when they learn of a breach of fiduciary duty:

> Before a perceived breach of fiduciary duty is disclosed to a beneficiary, the lawyer should counsel the fiduciary to avoid the prospective breach of duty or to take corrective action with respect to a breach that already has occurred. If those efforts fail, the lawyer should consider a number of factors: (i) whether the information to be disclosed is substantial and important to the trust estate, (ii) whether disclosure is needed to protect the trust, (iii) whether the acts or omissions might continue or be repeated, (iv) whether the beneficiary is capable of acting on the information, and (v) whether the interests of the beneficiary might be harmed. If the beneficiary is a client of the lawyer, the lawyer's responsibilities to that client may weigh heavily in favor of disclosure. Disclosure of information to beneficiaries should occur only after a careful weighing of all these factors.[150]

94-380 that lawyers for fiduciaries should not have legal and ethical duties to beneficiaries. See Robert W. Tuttle, The Fiduciary's Fiduciary: Legal Ethics in Fiduciary Representation, 1994 U. Ill. L. Rev. 889. Professor Tuttle also analyzes and rejects Professor Geoffrey Hazard's view that a fiduciary and the beneficiaries should be considered joint clients. See Geoffrey C. Hazard, Jr., Triangular Lawyer Relationships: An Exploratory Analysis, 1 Geo. J. Legal Ethics 15 (1987). While agreeing that the fiduciary should be considered the lawyer's client, Tuttle calls for amendments to Model Rules 1.2(d) and 1.6 to express specific duties for lawyers to protect beneficiaries from harm by fiduciaries. 1994 U. Ill. L. Rev. at 954.

148. ABA Formal Op. 94-380 at 4.

149. Special Report — Counseling the Fiduciary, 28 Real Prop. Prob. & Tr. J. at 850-851.

150. Id. at 852.

While the ABA committee adhered to a strict view of confidentiality in Formal Opinion 94-380, the committee noted that a number of states have adopted variations of the Model Rules. Under these modifications, a lawyer might be required or authorized to reveal confidential information to protect the beneficiaries from wrongdoing by the fiduciary.[151] For example, Rule 1.6(c) of the Washington Rules of Professional Conduct provides that "a lawyer may reveal to the tribunal confidences or secrets which disclose any breach of fiduciary responsibility by a client who is a guardian, personal representative, receiver, or other court appointed fiduciary."

The previous discussion has focused on the issue of who is the client. In some estates a lawyer may be asked to undertake multiple representation: for example, a beneficiary and a fiduciary, or multiple beneficiaries, or multiple fiduciaries. The Special Report — Counseling the Fiduciary advises that lawyers are generally permitted to engage in multiple representation of a beneficiary and the fiduciary because in the typical case a harmony of interests exists between the beneficiary and the fiduciary.[152] The lawyer must, however, be alert to potential conflicts of interest, and if they exist, the lawyer should proceed only after full disclosure and consent by both the clients, as required by Model Rule 1.7(b).[153] If an actual conflict develops between clients, the lawyer should not continue the multiple representation.[154] The lawyer will be required to withdraw from representation of both clients unless one of the clients is willing to consent under Model Rule 1.9.[155]

For some time in many jurisdictions, based either on custom or on statute, lawyers charged fees for estate administration based on a percentage of the estate. In a number of jurisdictions, however, fees based on a percentage of the estate have been declared improper either by legislation or court decision on the ground that

151. ABA Formal Op. 94-380, at 4 n.7.

152. See also ACTEC Commentaries, 28 Real Prop. Prob. & Tr. J. at 934 (commentary to Model Rule 1.7, example 1.7-3) (permissible for lawyer to represent both bank and wife with full disclosure and consent). On multiple representation of fiduciaries, see Special Report — Counseling the Fiduciary, 28 Real Prop. Prob. & Tr. J. at 855-858.

153. Special Report — Counseling the Fiduciary, 28 Real Prop. Prob. & Tr. J. at 842-846.

154. Id. at 847.

155. Id. at 848.

a fee based on a percentage of the estate, regardless of the difficulty of the work, is unreasonable.[156]

Estate administration is an area in which lawyers often make extensive use of paralegals and other nonlawyers. Lawyers must be aware of and careful to adhere to the obligations regarding supervision of nonlawyers. See Model Rule 5.3. Problem 7-1 examines lawyers' supervisory obligations in more detail. In Office of Disciplinary Counsel v. Ball[157] the attorney's long-time secretary and paralegal became delinquent in filing various documents and papers in probate proceedings, and she misappropriated more than $200,000 from estate and guardianship accounts. This misconduct had taken place over a 10-year period. The attorney learned about his secretary's misconduct when he was contacted about a delinquent probate matter. He immediately reviewed his accounts, discovered what had taken place, fired the secretary, and paid all misappropriated funds with interest. The attorney denied any knowledge of his secretary's actions, and his secretary fully exonerated him from any participation in her wrongdoing. Nonetheless, the Ohio Supreme Court found the attorney guilty of misconduct because of his failure to supervise his secretary, and the court administered a six-month suspension. The court rejected the attorney's argument that he was not responsible for his secretary's actions under Model Rule 5.3(c) unless he had knowledge of her misconduct. The court ruled that an attorney has a duty under Rule 5.3(a) to adopt proper supervisory practices.

---

156. See, e.g., In re Estate of Painter, 567 P.2d 820 (Colo. Ct. App. 1977) (Colorado legislature has repealed authorization for percentage fees and adopted reasonable fee standard); Estate of Davis, 509 A.2d 1175 (Me. 1986) (abuse of discretion for probate court to rely on local custom of using percentage method in setting attorney fee); In re Estate of Rolfe, 615 A.2d 625 (N.H. 1992) (disapproval of fee guidelines based on size of estate). But see Fla. Stat. Ann. §733.6171 (attorneys are entitled to compensation at flat rate for estates under $100,000 and on percentage basis for larger estates for ordinary services; attorneys may seek additional compensation for extraordinary services).

157. 618 N.E.2d 159 (Ohio 1993).

——————————— **Problem 5-5** ———————————

Tax Practice

a.   You represent Johnson Supply Company, a privately held corporation that provides plumbing materials to contractors for commercial and residential construction.[158] The company has elected Subchapter S status under the Internal Revenue Code.[159] Subchapter S status means that a corporation is taxed like a partnership. Generally, a Subchapter S corporation pays no tax at the corporate level.[160] Instead, the shareholders report their pro rata share of income and losses of the company on their individual returns.[161] A Subchapter S election thus avoids "double taxation": taxation to the corporation on its income and taxation to the shareholders of distributions received from the corporation. To qualify as a Subchapter S corporation, the corporation must meet various requirements, one of which is that the corporation cannot have more than one class of stock.[162]

You have just received a call from Johnson Supply's accountant. He explains to you that the corporation has substantial income for the current calendar year. He also informs you that one of the shareholders made a substantial working capital loan to the corporation. The loan is in writing and bears interest, but is convertible into common stock. The shareholder also has certain additional voting rights if the loan is not repaid within a certain time period. The accountant is concerned that the convertible loan constitutes a second class of stock, invalidating the Subchapter S election. He has asked you to provide him with an opinion that this loan does not amount to a second class of stock and does not disqualify the corporation from Subchapter S status.

———

158. This hypothetical, and *b* below, are based on the article by Deborah H. Schenk, Conflicts Between the Tax Lawyer and the Client: Vignettes in the Law Office, 20 Cap. U. L. Rev. 387 (1991).

159. I.R.C. §§1361, 1362.

160. I.R.C. §1363(a).

161. I.R.C. §1366(a).

162. I.R.C. §1361(b)(1)(D).

You have researched the matter. Under IRS regulations, "straight debt" is not treated as a second class of stock, but this loan does not qualify as straight debt because of its convertibility feature.[163] When a loan does not qualify as straight debt, it will be treated as a second class of stock when the loan amounts to "equity" rather than "debt" for tax purposes.[164] Whether a loan amounts to debt or equity is a question of fact. Section 385 of the Internal Revenue Code and relevant case law set out a variety of factors to determine whether a loan amounts to debt or equity. Based on your analysis of section 385 and the case law, you have concluded that only a weak argument could be made that the loan qualifies as debt rather than equity. How would you respond to the accountant's request? What obligations, if any, do you have regarding tax returns that were filed for prior years when the loan was also outstanding?

b. Repayment of Johnson Supply's loan to its shareholder would not eliminate the Subchapter S problem because the existence of the loan has already jeopardized Subchapter S status. However, repayment of the loan might make it less likely that the IRS would discover the problem if the corporation were audited. For example, repayment of the loan would remove the loan from the corporation's year-end balance sheet. Would it be proper for you to advise Johnson to consider repaying the loan for this reason?

Suppose Johnson does repay the loan. Subsequently, the IRS audits Johnson for the year in which the loan was repaid. During the audit, the agent asks: "Did the corporation have any other classes of stock outstanding during the year?" How would you respond?

c. Johnson Supply has negotiated a loan from Central Bank & Trust Company. In connection with the loan, the bank has asked Johnson to supply an opinion of counsel stating that Johnson is in compliance with all applicable laws and is not in breach or default of

163. Treas. Reg. §1.1361-1(*l*)(5).
164. Treas. Reg. §1.1361-1(*l*)(4)(ii)(A)(1),(iv).

any agreements to which it is a party and the firm is unaware of any pending or threatened litigation that would have a material affect on Johnson's operations.

Your firm has a committee on opinion letters. Any opinion by the firm must have the approval of the committee before it can be issued. You have discussed the opinion request with the committee and have learned that the Committee on Legal Opinions of the ABA Section of Business Law has issued a report on third-party opinions, commonly called the "Silverado Report," after the California town where the committee first met. The central part of the report is 22 black letter rules (the "Legal Opinion Accord") that lawyers can use in preparing legal opinions.[165] The report provides that it is generally improper for a third party to demand a comprehensive legal opinion, like the one requested by Central Bank.[166] The committee has suggested that you issue an opinion that adopts and follows the standards of the Legal Opinion Accord. Instead of the comprehensive opinion requested by the bank, you would supply an opinion stating that (1) the proposed loan agreement is enforceable against Johnson, (2) execution, delivery, and performance of the loan agreement will not result in a default under any other agreements or obligations to which Johnson is a party, (3) execution, delivery, and performance of the loan agreement will not violate any applicable provisions of statutory law or regulation, and (4) no actions or proceedings against Johnson are pending or overtly threatened in writing before any court, governmental agency, or arbitrator, which would affect the enforceability of the agreement or would be material to Johnson's operations. In addition, the opinion would state that the opinion is being provided by your firm to Johnson Supply and may not be used or relied on by any third person without your firm's written consent. Would it be proper for the firm

---

165. See Third-Party Legal Opinion Report, 47-Nov Bus. Law. 167 (1991).

166. Id. at 228.

to issue this limited opinion based on the Legal Opinion
Accord? Would it make any difference if the IRS had
formally notified the corporation that it was denying
Subchapter S status and assessing taxes, penalties, and
interest against the corporation for current and prior
years?

Read Model Rules 1.2(d), 2.3, 3.1, and comments.

Advising clients with regard to tax return positions

One of the most significant responsibilities of tax lawyers is providing advice to clients regarding issues involved in filing tax returns. While lawyers may also prepare returns for clients, it is
probably more common for accountants to prepare the returns,
with lawyers providing advice about significant issues.

What are tax lawyers' ethical and legal responsibilities in providing advice to clients in connection with their tax returns? In
Formal Opinion 85-352 the ABA Committee on Ethics and Professional Responsibility noted that in matters before the IRS an
attorney was acting as both an advocate and an advisor.[167] As an
advocate, under Model Rules 1.2(d) and 3.1, a lawyer could assert
any position so long as the lawyer had a good faith belief that the
position was not frivolous and so long as the lawyer was not counseling or assisting the client in fraud. While a lawyer could have a
good faith belief that the client's position was not frivolous even
though the attorney believed that the client would lose, there must
be "some realistic possibility of success if the matter is litigated."[168] If a realistic possibility of success existed, the lawyer was
not ethically required to insist that the client attach a rider to the
return fully disclosing the client's position.[169] In discussing the
"realistic possibility" standard, the committee noted that it was
possible for a client's position to meet this standard, even though
no "substantial authority" in support of the client's position ex-

---

167. For an earlier statement of the lawyer's ethical obligations in tax practice, see Formal Opinion 314 (1965). For a critique of this view of the lawyer's
role, see Loren D. Prescott, Jr., Challenging the Adversarial Approach to Taxpayer Representation, 30 Loy. L.A. L. Rev. 693 (1997).

168. ABA Comm. on Ethics and Prof. Resp., Formal Op. 85-352, at 3.

169. Id.

isted. The lawyer's role as advisor meant that the lawyer should discuss with the client the likelihood of success of the client's proposed position, the penalties that would apply if the position was not sustained, and the advantages and disadvantages of disclosing the position by rider.[170] The committee warned tax lawyers not to deliberately mislead the IRS "either by misstatements or by silence or by permitting the client to mislead."[171] The committee summarized the lawyer's obligations as follows:

> [A] lawyer may advise reporting a position on a return even where the lawyer believes the position probably will not prevail, there is no "substantial authority" in support of the position, and there will be no disclosure of the position in the return. However, the position to be asserted must be one which the lawyer in good faith believes is warranted in existing law or can be supported by good faith argument for an extension, modification or reversal of existing law. This requires that there is some realistic possibility of success if the matter is litigated. In addition, in his role as advisor, the lawyer should refer to potential penalties and other legal consequences should the client take the position advised.[172]

The IRS, like most federal agencies, has published standards of conduct for lawyers and other practitioners admitted to practice before the agency. These standards are commonly referred to as "Treasury Circular 230" and are codified in the Code of Federal Regulations.[173] In June 1994 the Treasury Department adopted the following new regulation dealing with tax return positions and preparation of returns:

§10.34. *Standards for advising with respect to tax return positions and for preparing or signing returns*

(a) Standards of conduct —

170. Id. at 4.

171. Id.

172. Id. For criticisms of the ABA's position in Formal Opinion 85-352, see Theodore C. Falk, Tax Ethics, Legal Ethics, and Real Ethics: A Critique of ABA Formal Opinion 85-352, 39 Tax Law. 643 (1986); Matthew C. Ames, Note, Formal Opinion 352: Professional Integrity and the Tax Audit Lottery, 1 Geo. J. Legal Ethics 411 (1987).

173. 31 C.F.R. §§10.0 et seq. See Steven C. Salch, Tax Practice Ethics: Practitioner Discipline and Sanctions, SD29 ALI-ABA 367 (1998) (on Westlaw); Camilla E. Watson, Tax Lawyers, Ethical Obligations, and the Duty to the System, 47 U. Kan. L. Rev. 847 (1999).

(1) Realistic possibility standard. A practitioner may not sign a return as a preparer if the practitioner determines that the return contains a position that does not have a realistic possibility of being sustained on its merits (the realistic possibility standard) unless the position is not frivolous and is adequately disclosed to the Service. A practitioner may not advise a client to take a position on a return, or prepare the portion of a return on which a position is taken, unless —

(i) The practitioner determines that the position satisfies the realistic possibility standard; or

(ii) The position is not frivolous and the practitioner advises the client of any opportunity to avoid the accuracy-related penalty in section 6662 of the Internal Revenue Code of 1986 by adequately disclosing the position and of the requirements for adequate disclosure.

(2) Advising clients on potential penalties. A practitioner advising a client to take a position on a return, or preparing or signing a return as a preparer, must inform the client of the penalties reasonably likely to apply to the client with respect to the position advised, prepared, or reported. The practitioner also must inform the client of any opportunity to avoid any such penalty by disclosure, if relevant, and of the requirements for adequate disclosure. This paragraph (a)(2) applies even if the practitioner is not subject to a penalty with respect to the position.

(3) Relying on information furnished by clients. A practitioner advising a client to take a position on a return, or preparing or signing a return as a preparer, generally may rely in good faith without verification upon information furnished by the client. However, the practitioner may not ignore the implications of information furnished to, or actually known by, the practitioner, and must make reasonable inquiries if the information as furnished appears to be incorrect, inconsistent, or incomplete.

(4) Definitions. For purposes of this section:

(i) Realistic possibility. A position is considered to have a realistic possibility of being sustained on its merits if a reasonable and well-informed analysis by a person knowledgeable in the tax law would lead such a person to conclude that the position has approximately a one in three, or greater, likelihood of being sustained on its merits. The authorities described in 26 CFR 1.6662-4(d)(3)(iii), or any successor provision, of the substantial understatement penalty regulations may be taken into account for purposes of this analysis. [This regulation lists various authorities that can be taken into account in determining whether a position has a realistic possibility of success. It includes proposed regulations but excludes treatises, law review articles, and opinions of tax experts.] The possibility that a position will not be challenged by the Service (e.g., because the taxpayer's return may not be audited or because the issue may not be raised on audit) may not be taken into account.

   (ii) Frivolous. A position is frivolous if it is patently improper.

   (b) Standard of discipline. As provided in §10.52, only violations of this section that are willful, reckless, or a result of gross incompetence will subject a practitioner to suspension or disbarment from practice before the Service.[174]

   Several points about the IRS standards of conduct in comparison to the position of the ABA committee in Formal Opinion 85-352 are worth noting. First, unlike the ABA opinion, which is merely persuasive, IRS standards have the force of law; violation of these standards could result in proceedings to disbar a lawyer from appearing before the IRS, although the standard for discipline as reflected in 31 C.F.R. §10.34(b) is quite high. Second, in Opinion 85-352 the committee defined frivolous to mean not having a "realistic possibility of success." The IRS standards draw a sharper distinction between the realistic possibility of success standard and frivolousness. A position is frivolous if it is "patently improper," while a realistic possibility of success requires a one in three chance of success. Thus, the IRS standard is substantially tougher than the standard set forth in Opinion 85-352. Third, the IRS standards apply not only to return preparers but also to practitioners who "advise a client to take a position on a return," even if the practitioner will not be signing the return. This is the most common role for tax lawyers.

   The IRS standards for practitioners regarding advising and preparing tax returns provide that a practitioner must advise the client of "the penalties reasonably likely to apply to the client with respect to the position advised, prepared, or reported" and also must "inform the client of any opportunity to avoid any such penalty by disclosure, if relevant, and of the requirements for adequate disclosure."[175] What are these penalties?

   Section 6662 of the Internal Revenue Code provides a penalty in the amount of 20 percent of the portion of any underpayment of tax under certain circumstances, which include the

174. 31 C.F.R. §10.34.
175. 31 C.F.R. §10.34(a)(2).

following: (1) negligence or disregard of rules or regulations or (2) any substantial understatement of income tax. The section provides the following definition:

> [T]he term "negligence" includes any failure to make a reasonable attempt to comply with the provisions of this title, and the term "disregard" includes any careless, reckless, or intentional disregard.[176]

The section provides that a taxpayer makes a substantial understatement if the amount of the understated tax exceeds the greater of $5,000 ($10,000 in the case of a corporation) or 10 percent of the tax due.[177] In determining whether a substantial understatement occurs, however, the amount of any understatement is excluded if there is or was "substantial authority" for the taxpayer's position, or if "the relevant facts affecting the item's tax treatment are adequately disclosed in the return or in a statement attached to the return, and there is a reasonable basis for the tax treatment of such item by the taxpayer."[178] The section goes on to provide that the secretary of the treasury is required to publish annually in the Federal Register a list of positions for which "the Secretary believes there is not substantial authority."[179] Section 6662, however, must be read in light of section 6664(c), which provides that the IRS may not impose a penalty "with respect to any portion of an underpayment if it is shown that there was a reasonable cause for such portion and the taxpayer acted in good faith with respect to such portion." Thus, a taxpayer is liable for a penalty only if the IRS establishes "fault" by the taxpayer. In addition to the negligence and substantial understatement penalties of section 6662, section 6663 provides for a penalty of 75 percent of the amount of any understatement of tax due to fraud.

The penalties set forth in sections 6662 and 6663 apply to taxpayers. Section 6694 of the Code imposes a penalty in the amount of $250 per return on a tax return preparer who prepares a return with understated tax liability if (1) the understatement results from a position "for which there was not a realistic possi-

---

176. I.R.C. §6662(c).
177. I.R.C. §6662(d).
178. I.R.C. §6662(d)(2)(B).
179. I.R.C. §6662(d)(2)(D).

bility of being sustained on its merits," (2) the preparer knew or should have known of the position, and (3) the position was not fully disclosed on the return or was frivolous. If the understatement results from a willful attempt to understate tax liability or a reckless or intentional disregard of rules or regulations, the penalty is $1,000 per return. In addition, section 6701 provides a penalty of $1,000 in the case of individual returns and $10,000 in the case of corporate returns against any person who knowingly aids and abets an understatement of tax liability by another person. Since aiding and abetting includes providing advice about the preparation of a return, it clearly covers lawyers in their normal role as tax counselors. The Internal Revenue Code also has some penalties specially applicable to "abusive tax shelters."[180]

Third-party opinions regarding tax matters and other issues

Another major activity for tax lawyers is providing opinions in connection with transactions in which their clients seek financing of their business operations. The Model Rules of Professional Conduct do not specifically address the standards applicable to lawyers in preparing opinions that involve third parties. The rules, however, do consider circumstances under which a lawyer may not undertake such an evaluation. Under Model Rule 2.3 a lawyer may prepare an evaluation for a third party at the request of the client provided the lawyer reasonably believes that "making the evaluation is compatible with other aspects of the lawyer's relationship with the client" and "the client consents after consultation." Comment 4 elaborates on this standard:

> The lawyer must be satisfied as a matter of professional judgment that making the evaluation is compatible with other functions undertaken in behalf of the client. For example, if the lawyer is acting as advocate in defending the client against charges of fraud, it would normally be incompatible with that responsibility for the lawyer to perform an evaluation for others concerning the same or a related transaction. Assuming no such impediment is apparent, however, the lawyer should advise the client of the implications of the eval-

180. See I.R.C. §6700.

uation, particularly the lawyer's responsibilities to third persons and the duty to disseminate the findings.

While the Model Rules do not establish standards for issuance of third-party opinions, the IRS and the ABA Committee on Ethics and Professional Responsibility have developed guidelines for such opinions. During the 1970s the IRS began investigating abusive tax shelters and the role of lawyers and accountants in connection with such offerings. The IRS found that some tax shelters were being marketed based on opinions from lawyers that, among other defects, ignored material facts or failed to address material issues. Such partial or incomplete opinions had the potential to mislead investors. As a result the Treasury Department published standards for lawyers to follow when issuing opinions in connection with tax shelters.[181] The regulation requires lawyers to comply with specific requirements in the following areas:

(1)   factual matters
(2)   the relation of law to facts
(3)   identification of material issues
(4)   opinion on each material issue
(5)   overall evaluation
(6)   description of opinion

The IRS's regulation on tax shelter opinions applies to lawyers admitted to practice before the IRS. The ABA Committee on Ethics and Professional Responsibility has issued Formal Opinion 346 (1982) setting forth ethical obligations for lawyers in connection with tax shelter opinions. Opinion 346 is similar in most important respects to the IRS's regulation. The committee summarized the ethical obligations of lawyers regarding tax shelter opinions as follows:

1.   Establish in the beginning the lawyer's relationship with the offeror-client, making clear that in order to issue the opinion, the lawyer requires from that client a full disclosure of the structure and intended operations of the venture and complete access to all relevant information.
2.   Make inquiry as to the relevant facts and, consistent with the standards developed in ABA Formal Opinion 335, be

181. See 31 C.F.R. §10.33.

satisfied that the material facts are accurately and completely stated in the offering materials, and that the representations as to intended future activities are clearly identified, reasonable and complete.

3. Relate the law to the actual facts to the extent ascertainable and, when addressing issues based on future activities, clearly identify what facts are assumed.

4. Make inquiries to ascertain that a good faith effort has been made to address legal issues other than those to be addressed in the tax shelter opinion.

5. Take reasonable steps to assure that all material federal income and excise tax issues have been considered and that all of those issues which involve the reasonable possibility of a challenge by the Internal Revenue Service have been fully and fairly addressed in the offering materials.

6. Where possible, provide an opinion as to the likely outcome on the merits of the material tax issues addressed in the offering materials.

7. Where possible, provide an overall evaluation of the extent to which the tax benefits in the aggregate are likely to be realized.

8. Assure that the offering materials correctly represent the nature and extent of the tax shelter opinion.[182]

Tax shelter opinions are not the only form of opinions that lawyers issue. In Formal Opinion 335 the ABA committee addressed the lawyer's ethical obligations in connection with opinions in securities offerings. The committee focused in particular on whether lawyers had an obligation to inquire into facts provided by their clients or could instead accept those facts as given. The committee rejected the notion that lawyers had a general obligation to audit or to investigate their clients' affairs, but it also ruled

---

182. ABA Comm. on Ethics and Prof. Resp., Formal Op. 346, at 9 (1982). For a discussion of lawyers' ethical obligations in preparing opinions in connection with tax shelter transactions, see William A. Falik, Standards for Professionals Providing Tax Opinions in Tax Shelter Offerings, 37 Tax Law. 701 (1984); Joseph J. Portuondo, Abusive Tax Shelters, Legal Malpractice, and Revised Formal Ethics Opinion 346: Does Revised 346 Enable Third Party Investors to Recover from Tax Attorneys Who Violate Its Standards? 61 Notre Dame L. Rev. 220 (1986).

that under some circumstances lawyers were ethically and legally required to make further inquiry regarding the facts on which their opinions are based:

> [T]he lawyer should, in the first instance, make inquiry of his client as to the relevant facts and receive answers. If any of the alleged facts, or the alleged facts taken as a whole, are incomplete in a material respect; or are suspect; or are inconsistent; or either on their face or on the basis of other known facts are open to question, the lawyer should make further inquiry. The extent of this inquiry will depend in each case upon the circumstances; for example, it would be less where the lawyer's past relationship with the client is sufficient to give him a basis for trusting the client's probity than where the client has recently engaged the lawyer, and less where the lawyer's inquiries are answered fully than when there appears a reluctance to disclose information.
>
> Where the lawyer concludes that further inquiry of a reasonable nature would not give him sufficient confidence as to all the relevant facts, or for any other reason he does not make the appropriate further inquiries, he should refuse to give an opinion. However, assuming that the alleged facts are not incomplete in a material respect, or suspect, or in any way inherently inconsistent, or on their face or on the basis of other known facts open to question, the lawyer may properly assume that the facts as related to him by his client, and checked by him by reviewing such appropriate documents as are available, are accurate.[183]

Another form of opinion that lawyers are often asked to render involves responses to accountants' requests for information about clients' loss contingencies. Accountants use this information in preparing clients' financial statements. For many years such requests were a source of tension between lawyers and accountants. Accountants naturally wanted to receive complete information from lawyers because they were concerned about their legal liability for preparing misleading financial statements. Lawyers were wary about revealing confidential information that could generate claims that otherwise might not have been brought. In 1975 the ABA and the American Institute of Certified Public Accountants reached an accord to resolve the question how lawyers could

---

183. ABA Comm. on Ethics and Prof. Resp., Formal Op. 335, at 3 (1974).

respond to auditors' requests for information consistently with their ethical obligations.[184] See also Model Rule 2.3 and cmt. 6.

As Problem 5-5 mentions, the Committee on Legal Opinions of the ABA Section of Business Law has issued a set of standards (the Legal Opinion Accord) that lawyers can adopt in issuing general third-party opinions as opposed to specialized opinions relating to tax or securities matters.[185] Other bar association committees have issued reports dealing with legal opinions.[186]

In addition to these standards, lawyers who issue opinions in transactions involving third parties also face the possibility of legal liability to third parties. The traditional rule has been that lawyers are liable only to their clients and not to third parties with whom there is no privity of contract.[187] In a number of jurisdictions, however, the privity barrier has been eroded. Depending on the jurisdiction, lawyers who fraudulently[188] or negligently[189] issue false opinions can be held liable to third parties. Opinion letters typically state that they are intended for the use of the client only and should not be relied on by third parties. Such statements, however,

184. See ABA Statement of Policy Regarding Lawyers' Responses to Auditors' Requests for Information, 31 Bus. Law. 1709 (1976). See also Ad Hoc Committee on OTS Attorney Inquiry Letters, Guidance for Lawyers Responding to the OTS Revised Attorney Letter, 50-Feb Bus. Law. 607 (1995).

185. 47-Nov Bus. Law. 167 (1991).

186. See citation to reports and bibliography included in Association of the Bar of the City of New York et al., Mortgage Loan Opinion Report, 54-Nov Bus. Law. 119, 132 (1998).

187. Savings Bank v. Ward, 100 U.S. 195 (1879).

188. See, e.g., Rubin v. Schottenstein, Zox & Dunn, 143 F.3d 263 (6th Cir. 1998).

189. See Roberts v. Ball, Hunt, Hart, Brown & Baerwitz, 128 Cal. Rptr. 901 (Ct. App. 1976) (law firm may be liable for negligent misrepresentation in issuing opinion letters under California law); Mehaffy, Rider, Windholz & Wilson v. Central Bank Denver, N.A., 892 P.2d 230 (Colo. 1995) (en banc) (law firm retained by borrower may be liable for negligent misrepresentation to lender); Prudential Ins. Co. v. Dewey, Ballantine, Bushby, Palmer & Wood, 605 N.E.2d 318 (N.Y. 1992) (recognizing cause of action under New York law against law firm for negligent misrepresentation). See also Restatement (Second) of Torts §552(1) (1977) (liability for information negligently supplied for guidance of others in business transaction). But see Krawczyk v. Bank of Sun Prairie, 496 N.W.2d 218 (Wis. Ct. App.), review denied, 501 N.W.2d 458 (Wis. 1993) (lawyers subject to liability to third parties only for fraud, not for negligent misrepresentation).

will not necessarily protect a law firm from liability if it is aware that its opinion letter is being used to obtain investors.[190] If the lawyer has not issued an opinion letter, however, liability of the lawyer to third parties, especially under the federal securities laws, may be difficult to establish.[191]

Other ethical obligations in tax practice

The preceding discussion has focused on some of the most important legal and ethical obligations of lawyers in connection with tax matters. Internal Revenue Service regulations establishing standards of conduct for practitioners cover a number of other topics, including conflicts of interest, contingent fees, and solicitation of business.[192]

Lawyers who engage in tax practice are, of course, subject to malpractice liability.[193] In addition, it is likely that general practitioners who undertake to handle tax matters will be held to the standard of conduct expected of a specialist in tax law.[194]

190. See Kline v. First W. Govt. Sec., Inc., 24 F.3d 480 (3d Cir.), *cert. denied*, 513 U.S. 1092 (1994).

191. See Central Bank of Denver, N.A. v. First Interstate Bank of Denver, N.A., 511 U.S. 164 (1994), discussed in connection with Problem 5-2 above (no aider and abetter liability under federal securities laws); Fortson v. Winstead, McGuire, Sechrest & Minick, 961 F.2d 469 (4th Cir. 1992) (law firm not liable under federal securities laws for failure to disclose material information in connection with real estate limited partnership offering; duty to disclose under securities laws is determined by state law, and Texas law does not recognize exceptions to requirement of privity; no cause of action for violation of ABA opinions and IRS regulations governing issuance of tax shelter opinions).

192. Practice before the Internal Revenue Service, 31 C.F.R. pt. 10. For a general discussion of the ethical obligations of tax practitioners, see Bernard Wolfman et al., James P. Holden, Ethical Problems in Federal Tax Practice (3d ed. 1995).

193. See Jacob L. Todres, Malpractice and the Tax Practitioner: An Analysis of the Areas in Which Malpractice Occurs, 48 Emory L.J. 547 (1999).

194. See Horne v. Peckham, 158 Cal. Rptr. 714 (Ct. App. 1979).

Chapter 6

Lawyers in Public Service: Judges, Government Attorneys, and Public Interest Lawyers

The preceding four chapters have examined ethical problems facing lawyers in private practice: criminal defense and prosecution, civil litigation, and business practice. The Statistical Abstract of the United States reports 805,872 lawyers practiced in the United States in 1991. Of this number, 87,763, or approximately 10.9 percent, were engaged in some form of public legal service rather than private practice. This number consisted of the following:

Federal government	27,985
State government	38,242
Federal judicial	3,119
State and county judicial	18,417[1]

1. United States Bureau of the Census, Statistical Abstract of the United States 210, chart no. 327 (1994).

Lawyers engaged in public rather than private practice face special ethical problems because their roles and the governing standards differ from those of private counsel. Federal and state judges perform their duties subject to the Code of Judicial Conduct and to various special statutory provisions. Federal and state prosecutors act pursuant to a wide range of statutory provisions, and they are required to adhere to ethical standards that differ from those applicable to private counsel.

This chapter examines the ethical issues facing lawyers in public service. Section A considers issues of judicial ethics, focusing principally on two questions: When are judges disqualified from hearing cases? What are the limitations on judges' extrajudicial activities? Section A touches on other topics: ex parte communications between lawyers and judges, methods of judicial selection, and restrictions on campaign activities of judges.[2] Section B examines the ethical obligations of government lawyers, and considers a phenomenon that straddles the public/private distinction: the development of the public interest law movement.

A. Judicial Ethics

—————— Problem 6-1 ——————
Judges in Their Official Capacities

a. You are a clerk for a newly appointed state supreme court justice. The justice and her husband have substantial investments in common stock and real estate. The real estate investments are principally limited partnerships in which she or her husband or both are limited partners. In every case the property is subject to a mortgage to a financial institution, typically a bank. She asks you whether their present investments will cause any disqualification problems for her, and if so,

_____

2. On judicial ethics generally, see The Responsible Judge: Readings in Judicial Ethics (John T. Noonan, Jr. & Kenneth I. Winston eds. 1993). See also Cynthia Gray, Key Issues in Judicial Ethics (1996) (series of background papers available from the American Judicature Society, ⟨http://www.ajs.org⟩).

how her investments could be restructured to avoid those problems.

   b. The wife of a recently appointed federal district court judge is a partner in a major law firm. That firm frequently handles cases before her husband's court. Under what circumstances will the judge be required to recuse himself when his wife's firm appears in cases before him? Under what circumstances will the judge be required to recuse himself when his former firm appears before him?

   c. A class action claiming that conditions in the state's prisons violate the prisoners' constitutional rights is pending in federal court. You are counsel for the plaintiffs. In several conferences about the case, the judge has expressed hostility to your position. At one conference he referred to you as "one of those liberal lawyers who doesn't care anything about cleaning up crime, only making a reputation in big cases." The judge initially denied the state's motion to dismiss, but otherwise has consistently ruled against you on discovery motions. In particular, the judge has granted numerous requests and motions of the defense to delay discovery. You have also learned that the judge has made telephone calls to both prison officials and expert witnesses in the case asking them various questions. How would you evaluate the likelihood of success of a disqualification motion?

Read Canon 3 of the Code of Judicial Conduct and 28 U.S.C. §455.

Regulation of judicial conduct: standards and procedure

Regulation of the behavior of judges both in their official and in their unofficial capacities rests on important policies. First, the adversarial system is founded on a principle of judicial impartiality. As a matter of fairness, litigants are entitled to have judges who are not swayed by bias, prejudice, or favoritism. Second, the primary function of our judicial system is to provide a mechanism for resolving disputes nonviolently. Public use of and acceptance of the results of the judicial system depend in part on the public's respect for judicial integrity.

The ABA has been active in establishing standards of conduct for judges, just as it has been for lawyers. The ABA first adopted Canons of Judicial Ethics in 1924. In 1972 the ABA approved the Code of Judicial Conduct to replace the Canons of Ethics. Almost every state adopted the Code or used it as the model for standards of judicial conduct.[3]

In 1990 the ABA issued a major revision of the Code of Judicial Conduct. The 1990 Code is divided into five articles. Canons 1 and 2 are relatively short. Canon 1 provides that judges "shall uphold the integrity and independence of the judiciary." Canon 2 directs judges to "avoid impropriety and the appearance of impropriety in all of the judge's activities." An important addition to the 1990 Code, not found in the 1972 Code, is Canon 2(C), which prohibits judges from holding membership in any organization that practices invidious discrimination on the basis of race, sex, religion, or national origin. Canons 3, 4, and 5 contain the bulk of the substantive provisions of the Code. Canon 3 deals with a judge's adjudicative responsibilities, while Canon 4 regulates nonjudicial conduct. Canon 5 controls a judge's political activities. The 1990 Code also requires judges not to manifest bias or prejudice in the performance of judicial duties, to prevent such conduct by court personnel, and to require lawyers appearing before them to refrain from such conduct. Canon 3(B)(5), (6). The discussion that follows is based on the 1990 Code unless otherwise indicated.

All states and the District of Columbia have judicial conduct commissions or organizations that have the power to investigate, prosecute, and adjudicate allegations of judicial misconduct. The structure and method of appointment of these organizations vary from state to state.[4] In August 1994 the ABA adopted Model Rules for Judicial Disciplinary Enforcement.[5] The ABA rules call for the

---

3. Jeffrey M. Shaman et al., Judicial Conduct and Ethics §1.02 (2d ed. 1995).

4. For a directory of these organizations, see the website of the American Judicature Society, ⟨http://www.ajs.org⟩.

5. See Law. Man. on Prof. Conduct (ABA/BNA) §§01:3101 et seq.

creation of a 12-member Commission on Judicial Conduct, consisting of four judges of the intermediate or appellate courts of the state, appointed by the highest court in the state; four lawyers appointed by the bar association; and four members of the public appointed by the governor. Rule 2(C). The commission has responsibility for investigating charges of misconduct against judges, conducting hearings into such charges, and making recommendations to the highest court of the state. The ABA rules provide that the highest court of the state has the power to discipline judges found guilty of misconduct, including the power to remove a judge from office. Rule 6(B)(1).

The Judicial Conference of the United States adopted the Code of Judicial Conduct to apply to federal judges in 1973.[6] The Code of Conduct for federal judges has been amended to include some of the provisions from the ABA's 1990 Code, but it is still based largely on the 1972 Code.[7]

Federal judges serve for life tenure and may be removed from office only through the impeachment process.[8] In 1980 Congress passed the Judicial Councils Reform and Judicial Conduct and Disability Act.[9] The law creates a process for discipline of federal judges short of removal and provides for referral of impeachable offenses to the House of Representatives.[10] Because of questions about the operation and constitutionality of the system for disciplining federal judges, in 1990 Congress passed the National Commission on Judicial Discipline and Removal Act.[11] The legislation created a national commission charged with studying the problems involved in discipline and removal of Article III judges, evaluating possible alternatives to the present system, and preparing a report of its work. The commission's exhaustive study examines a number of constitutional issues and makes recommendations to the legislative, executive, and judicial branches. While

6. Judicial Conf. of United States, Rep. of Proc. at 9-11 (1973).

7. For the current text of the Code of Judicial Conduct applicable to United States judges, see 175 F.R.D. 363 (1998).

8. U.S. Const. art. II, §4.

9. Pub. L. No. 96-458, 94 Stat. 2035 (codified in various sections in 28 U.S.C). See generally Symposium, Disciplining the Federal Judiciary, 142 U. Pa. L. Rev. 1 (1993).

10. 28 U.S.C. §372(c)(7), (8).

11. Pub. L. No. 101-650, §408 et seq., 104 Stat. 5089.

the commission's report includes numerous thoughtful proposals, it does not suggest a fundamental overhaul of the present system.[12]

Disqualification of judges because of personal involvement or interest in matters

One of the most important aspects of judicial conduct involves disqualification of judges from hearing cases.[13] Canon 3(E) of the Code of Judicial Conduct deals with disqualification of judges. The Code begins with a general principle of disqualification: whenever the judge's "impartiality might reasonably be questioned." The Code contains, however, a number of specific rules of disqualification, and because of the vagueness of the general standard, it is useful to begin with the specific rules. The disqualification rules distinguish circumstances affecting the judge personally from situations in which a judge is disqualified because of a relationship with another person who has an interest in the matter.

Four situations requiring disqualification of judges based on personal involvement in the matter are fairly straightforward. A judge is disqualified when the judge

(1)   has personal knowledge of disputed evidentiary facts, Canon 3(E)(1)(a)
(2)   served as a lawyer in the matter in controversy before assuming the bench, Canon 3(E)(1)(b)
(3)   has been a material witness to the matter in controversy, Canon 3(E)(1)(b)
(4)   is a party to the proceeding, or an officer, director, or trustee of a party, Canon 3(E)(1)(d)(i)

While these disqualification rules are relatively easy to apply, two further disqualification provisions are more difficult. The Code of Judicial Conduct requires disqualification when a judge

12. Report of the National Commn. on Judicial Discipline & Removal, 152 F.R.D. 265 (1993). For criticism of the report, see generally Victor Williams, Third Branch Independence and Integrity Threatened by Political Branch Irresponsibility: Reviewing the Report of the National Commission on Judicial Discipline and Removal, 5 Seton Hall Const. L.J. 851 (1995).

13. See Richard E. Flamm, Judicial Disqualification (1996).

has "personal bias or prejudice concerning a party." Canon
3(E)(1)(a). The meaning of this provision and its interrelationship
with the general standard that requires disqualification when a
judge's "impartiality might reasonably be questioned" has been
the subject of several Supreme Court decisions. These cases are
discussed in the section below that examines disqualification of
federal judges.

Under the 1990 Code, a judge is subject to disqualification
when the judge either personally or as a fiduciary has an economic
interest in the subject matter in controversy or in a party to the
proceeding. Canon 3(E)(1)(c). The 1990 Code of Judicial Conduct made a substantial change from the 1972 Code regarding
disqualification because of economic interest. (The 1972 Code
used the term "financial interest.") Under the 1972 Code, a
judge's financial interest in a party or in the subject matter of a
proceeding, *no matter how small*, required disqualification. Thus,
under the 1972 Code, if a judge held one share of stock in a party,
the judge was disqualified. By contrast to the 1972 Code, the 1990
Code provides that "economic interest" means "ownership of a
more than de minimis legal or equitable interest, or a relationship
as officer, director, advisor or other active participant in the affairs
of a party," subject to certain exceptions. (See Terminology section of 1990 Code, definition of "economic interest.") The Code
goes on to define a de minimis interest as "an insignificant interest
that could not raise reasonable question as to a judge's impartiality." (See Terminology section of 1990 Code, definition of "De
minimis.")

The Code of Judicial Conduct lists certain exceptions to what
constitutes an economic interest:

(1)   ownership of a mutual fund does not amount to own-
      ership of securities owned by the fund unless the judge
      participates in the management of the fund or unless
      the case could substantially affect the value of the fund
      shares
(2)   service by the judge or a member of the judge's family
      in an active role in a charitable or similar organization
      does not create an economic interest in securities owned
      by the organization
(3)   deposits in financial institutions, ownership of insur-
      ance policies, and similar propriety interests do not con-

stitute economic interests in those institutions unless
the proceeding could substantially affect the value of the
judge's interest

(4)   ownership of government securities is not an economic
interest in the issuer unless the proceeding could substantially affect the value of the judge's interest

(See Terminology section, definition of "Economic interest.")
These exceptions are sensibly designed to allow judges to continue
to have routine financial interests without forcing their disqualification.

Disqualification of judges based on relationships with persons interested in the matter

Judges are subject to disqualification not only because of personal
involvement or interest in a matter but also because of certain
relationships with persons interested in a matter. Canon
3(E)(1)(b) provides that a judge is disqualified if "a lawyer with
whom the judge previously practiced law served during such association as a lawyer concerning the matter." Note that the mere
fact that the judge's former law partner appears in a case is not
disqualifying under this rule; the case must be one that was "in
the office" when the judge was practicing. Should judges recuse
themselves from cases involving their former firms on the ground
that the judge's "impartiality might reasonably be questioned"? In
Informal Opinion 87-1524, the ABA Committee on Ethics and
Professional Responsibility ruled that a judge was not required to
disqualify himself simply because the judge had been associated
with counsel for one of the parties two years earlier. The committee indicated that a period of one or two years after termination of
professional association was appropriate, depending on factors
such as the closeness of the relationship and the amount of continued contact.[14]

As noted earlier, a judge is disqualified if the judge personally

14. See Kinard v. Kinard, 986 S.W.2d 220 (Tenn. Ct. App. 1998, *appeal
denied*) (trial judge's two-year office-sharing arrangement with husband's attorney
eight years before filing of divorce suit did not require recusal). See generally
Anne M. Payne, Annotation, Judge's Previous Legal Association with Attorney
Connected to Current Case as Warranting Disqualification, 85 A.L.R.4th 700
(1991).

has an economic interest in the subject matter in controversy or in a party to the proceeding. The judge is also disqualified if close family members — the judge's spouse, the judge's parent or child wherever residing, or any other member of the judge's family residing in the judge's household — have an economic interest in the subject matter or a party to the proceeding. Canon 3(E)(1)(c). Thus, if the judge's grandchild residing in the judge's house has more than a de minimis financial interest in a party to a proceeding, the judge is disqualified.

Finally, Canon 3(E)(1)(d) requires disqualification when the judge's spouse or a person within the third degree of relationship to either of them, or the spouse of such a person,

(1)   is a party to the proceeding, or an officer, director, or trustee of a party
(2)   is acting as a lawyer in the proceeding
(3)   is known by the judge to have a more than de minimis interest that could be substantially affected by the proceeding
(4)   is to the judge's knowledge likely to be a material witness in the proceeding

The following relatives are included within the third degree of relationship: great-grandparent, grandparent, parent, uncle, aunt, brother, sister, child, grandchild, great-grandchild, nephew, or niece. (See Terminology section of 1990 Code, definition of "third degree of relationship.") Cousins are not included. Under this rule, a judge is disqualified if one of the listed relatives is a lawyer in the proceeding, but would not be disqualified simply because the relative is a member of a firm that is handling a case, unless the relative has an interest that could be substantially affected by the case. (See the commentary to Canon 3(E)(1)(d).) This could occur, for example, if the firm was handling a major class action and the relative's potential compensation from the case was substantial.

Disqualification of federal judges

Two statutes, 28 U.S.C. §§144 and 455, govern disqualification of federal judges. Section 455 is the broader of the two statutes. It applies to all federal judges, whether trial or appellate, and specifies numerous grounds for disqualification. Section 144, enacted much earlier, deals only with disqualification of district court judges because of bias or prejudice. Most cases will be governed by section 455 because of its broader scope. The only aspect of section 144 that is not covered by section 455 is the requirement of filing a timely affidavit of disqualification.

Section 455 was based on the ABA's 1972 Code of Judicial Conduct. Because the ABA's 1990 Code incorporates many principles from the 1972 Code, the 1990 Code and section 455 remain very similar in many respects. Section 455, like the Code of Judicial Conduct, has two broad disqualification provisions. Section 455(a) provides that a judge is disqualified if the judge's "impartiality might reasonably be questioned." See also Canon 3(E)(1). Section 455(b)(1) provides that a judge is disqualified if the judge "has a personal bias or prejudice concerning a party." See also Canon 3(E)(1)(a) (which adds "or a party's lawyer").

Disqualification based on "personal bias or prejudice" is the older of the provisions. In United States v. Grinnell Corp.[15] the Court considered a motion by the defendants to disqualify the district judge in an antitrust case under 28 U.S.C. §144 on the ground that the judge had expressed views regarding the merits of the government's case. Ironically, it was the defendants who had sought the judge's expression of his position on the government's case. In affirming the denial of the disqualification motion, the Court stated: "The alleged bias and prejudice to be disqualifying must stem from an extrajudicial source and result in an opinion on the merits on some basis other than what the judge learned from his participation in the case."[16] Over the years, Grinnell came to stand for an "extrajudicial source doctrine." Under this doctrine, disqualification was not appropriate unless the basis for disqualification arose from an extrajudicial source. Thus, anger or irritation expressed by a judge during a case,[17] consistent rulings by the judge against a party,[18] and participation in previous proceedings involving a party[19] were all insufficient to warrant disqualification.

15. 384 U.S. 563 (1966).
16. Id. at 583.
17. E.g., Souder v. Owens-Corning Fiberglas Corp., 939 F.2d 647 (8th Cir. 1991).
18. E.g., Nilsson, Robbins, Dalgarn, Berliner, Carson & Wurst v. Louisiana Hydrolec, 854 F.2d 1538 (9th Cir. 1988).
19. E.g., United States v. Bond, 847 F.2d 1233 (7th Cir. 1988).

In Liteky v. United States[20] the Court again addressed the application of the extrajudicial source doctrine. *Liteky* was a criminal prosecution for a political protest at a military installation. The judge hearing the case had presided over a prior case involving one of the defendants. During the case, the judge admonished and limited defense counsel's representation in several respects. The Court in *Liteky* decided that the extrajudicial source doctrine should not be used as a litmus test to decide disqualification based on bias or prejudice. Instead, extrajudicial source was only a factor in deciding whether bias or prejudice existed. Nonetheless, the Court reaffirmed the results of decisions that had used the extrajudicial source doctrine:

> As we have described it, however, there is not much doctrine to the doctrine. The fact that an opinion held by a judge derives from a source outside judicial proceedings is not a *necessary* condition for "bias or prejudice" recusal, since predispositions developed during the course of a trial will sometimes (albeit rarely) suffice. Nor is it a *sufficient* condition for "bias or prejudice" recusal, since *some* opinions acquired outside the context of judicial proceedings (for example, the judge's view of the law acquired in scholarly reading) will *not* suffice. Since neither the presence of an extrajudicial source necessarily establishes bias, nor the absence of an extrajudicial source necessarily precludes bias, it would be better to speak of the existence of a significant (and often determinative) "extrajudicial source" *factor*, than of an "extrajudicial source" *doctrine*, in recusal jurisprudence.
>
> The facts of the present case do not require us to describe the consequences of that factor in complete detail. It is enough for present purposes to say the following: First, judicial rulings alone almost never constitute a valid basis for a bias or partiality motion. See United States v. Grinnell Corp., 384 U.S. at 583. In and of themselves (i.e., apart from surrounding comments or accompanying opinion), they cannot possibly show reliance upon an extrajudicial source; and can only in the rarest circumstances evidence the degree of favoritism or antagonism required (as discussed below) when no extrajudicial source is involved. Almost invariably, they are proper

---

20. 510 U.S. 540 (1994). *Liteky* actually involved the scope and meaning of §455(a), which deals with disqualification because a judge's impartiality might reasonably be questioned. The Court considered the meaning of §455(b)(1), which deals with disqualification because of bias or prejudice, because it was examining the relationship between §455(a) and 455(b)(1).

grounds for appeal, not for recusal. Second, opinions formed by the judge on the basis of facts introduced or events occurring in the course of the current proceedings, or of prior proceedings, do not constitute a basis for a bias or partiality motion unless they display a deep-seated favoritism or antagonism that would make fair judgment impossible. Thus, judicial remarks during the course of a trial that are critical or disapproving of, or even hostile to, counsel, the parties, or their cases, ordinarily do not support a bias or partiality challenge. They *may* do so if they reveal an opinion that derives from an extrajudicial source; and they *will* do so if they reveal such a high degree of favoritism or antagonism as to make fair judgment impossible. An example of the latter (and perhaps of the former as well) is the statement that was alleged to have been made by the District Judge in Berger v. United States, 255 U.S. 22 (1921), a World War I espionage case against German-American defendants:

> "One must have a very judicial mind, indeed, not [to be] prejudiced against the German Americans" because their "hearts are reeking with disloyalty." Id., at 28.

Not establishing bias or partiality, however, are expressions of impatience, dissatisfaction, annoyance, and even anger, that are within the bounds of what imperfect men and women, even after having been confirmed as federal judges, sometimes display. A judge's ordinary efforts at courtroom administration — even a stern and short-tempered judge's ordinary efforts at courtroom administration — remain immune.[21]

As the Court indicated in *Liteky,* extrajudicial source is no longer a requirement for disqualification, but it remains an important factor.[22] A judge's race, religion, gender, and political affiliation are, of course, extrajudicial but do not constitute a basis for disqualification.[23]

Disqualification because a judge's impartiality might reasonably be questioned under section 455(a) was added to the statute in 1974. The Court first addressed the meaning of this provision in Liljeberg v. Health Services Acquisition Corp.,[24] an action by

21. 510 U.S. at 554-556.
22. See Hathcock v. Navistar Int. Transp. Corp., 53 F.3d 36 (4th Cir. 1995) (district judge disqualified in part for remarks made about defense counsel at continuing legal education program).
23. See MacDraw, Inc. v. CIT Group Equip. Fin., Inc., 138 F.3d 33 (2d Cir.), *cert. denied,* 119 S. Ct. 175 (1998).
24. 486 U.S. 847 (1988).

Health Services seeking a declaration of ownership of a hospital corporation. The district court found for Liljeberg. Ten months after the decision, Health Services learned that at the time the district judge rendered his decision he was a member of the board of trustees of Loyola University and that Liljeberg had been negotiating with Loyola to purchase a parcel of land on which to construct a hospital. The success and benefit of these negotiations turned in part on Liljeberg's prevailing in the litigation with Health Services.

Health Services moved to vacate the judgment under Federal Rule of Civil Procedure 60(b)(6) on the ground that the judge was disqualified under 28 U.S.C. §455. Section 455(b)(4) provides that a judge shall disqualify himself when he "knows that he, individually or as a fiduciary, . . . has . . . any other interest that could be substantially affected by the outcome of the proceeding." The Supreme Court found that the judge was not disqualified under that section because the evidence showed that the judge did not "know" of Loyola's interest when he decided the case. Nonetheless, the Court held that the judge was disqualified under section 455(a) because a reasonable person would conclude that the judge's impartiality might be questioned. The Court reasoned that knowledge was irrelevant to determining whether a violation of section 455(a) had occurred because the purpose of the section was "to promote public confidence in the integrity of the judicial process."[25] The Court recognized that it was absurd to require judges to disqualify themselves based on facts of which they are unaware, but when the matter was brought to the judge's attention, the judge could then have taken appropriate action to recuse himself.[26]

The Court also discussed the relationship between the specific disqualification provisions of section 455(b) and section 455(a). Liljeberg contended that section 455(a) was limited by section 455(b)(4), and accordingly the judge was not disqualified absent actual knowledge of the disqualifying circumstances. The Court rejected this argument. Noting several differences between section 455(b) and section 455(a), the Court found that the sections were independent, that is, a judge is disqualified if any of the provisions of section 455(b) apply, but in addition the judge's par-

25. Id. at 860.
26. Id. at 861.

ticipation in the case is also subject to the general standard of whether the judge's impartiality might reasonably be questioned.[27]

The Court also addressed the remedy appropriate for violation of section 455(a). The statute itself does not specify a remedy, and the Court declined to adopt a per se rule that required vacating the judgment simply because the judge was disqualified from hearing the case. Instead, the Court stated:

> We conclude that in determining whether a judgment should be vacated for a violation of §455(a), it is appropriate to consider the risk of injustice to the parties in the particular case, the risk that the denial of relief will produce injustice in other cases, and the risk of undermining the public's confidence in the judicial process.[28]

On the facts of the case, the Court found the "violation is neither insubstantial nor excusable," and agreed with the court of appeals that the judgment should be vacated and a new trial ordered.[29]

Three dissenting Justices argued that an actual rather than a constructive knowledge standard should apply under section 455(a) as well as under section 455(b). Given the trial judge's lack of knowledge, they also questioned the propriety of the remedy of vacating the judgment.

The Court's opinion in *Liteky,* however, decided six years after *Liljeberg,* raises questions about the standard that applies in cases governed by section 455(a). In *Liljeberg* the Court held that a judge was disqualified under section 455(a) if a reasonable person would conclude that the judge should be disqualified. The Court also reasoned that section 455(a) established a standard for disqualification that was separate from and not limited by section 455(b). By contrast, in *Liteky* the Court held that under section 455(a) the standard for disqualification was whether "fair judgment was impossible" and that section 455(a) was limited by the specific standards of section 455(b).

One important difference between the ABA's 1990 Code and the federal disqualification statute deals with disqualification because of financial interest. Compare Canon 3(E)(1)(c) with 28 U.S.C. §455(b)(4). The federal statute is based on the 1972 Code

27. Id. at 860 n.8.
28. Id. at 864.
29. Id. at 867.

of Judicial Conduct, which provides that a judge is disqualified from hearing a matter if the judge has a financial interest in the subject matter of a proceeding or in a party to the proceeding. Unlike the 1990 Code of Judicial Conduct, however, the statute goes on to define "financial interest" to mean "ownership of a legal or equitable interest, however small."[30] Thus, if a federal judge owns one share of stock in a party to the proceeding, the judge is disqualified from hearing the matter. Note that federal judges are also disqualified if their spouses or minor children residing in their household have even a small financial interest in a party.[31] In In re Cement Antitrust Litigation[32] a federal judge who had been handling a class action antitrust case for more than five years was required to disqualify himself because his wife owned stock in seven of the 210,235 members of the plaintiff class worth less than $30. The Court of Appeals for the Ninth Circuit bemoaned the strictness of the statute and called for legislative evaluation of the reasonableness and consequences of the per se rule.[33]

In 1988 Congress took action to ameliorate the harshness of the "however small" rule, adding 28 U.S.C. §455(f), which allows judges to avoid disqualification by divestiture of financial interests in a party when the disqualifying interest appears or is discovered after substantial judicial time has been devoted to the matter. The divestiture rule also applies to financial interests held by a judge's spouse and minor children. The section does not apply, however, if the interest could be substantially affected by the outcome of the case. The Code of Judicial Conduct does not have a rule on divestiture equivalent to the federal statute.

If the judge has an interest other than a financial interest, the impact on the judge must be substantial to warrant disqualification. For example, in In re New Mexico Natural Gas Antitrust Litigation,[34] the Tenth Circuit held that the district judge's status as natural gas consumer did not warrant disqualification because the judge would not be substantially affected by the outcome of the proceeding.

---

30. 28 U.S.C. §455(d)(4).
31. 28 U.S.C. §455(b)(4).
32. 688 F.2d 1297 (9th Cir. 1982), *aff'd by absence of a quorum*, 459 U.S. 1191 (1983).
33. 688 F.2d at 1315.
34. 620 F.2d 794 (10th Cir. 1980).

Waiver or remittal of disqualification

Both the Code of Judicial Conduct and the federal statute provide
for *remittal* (the term used by the Code) or *waiver* (the term used
by the federal statute) of disqualification, but they differ dramatically in the situations in which waiver is allowed. Under the Code,
disqualification may be remitted in all cases except ones in which
the judge is disqualified because of personal bias or prejudice concerning a party. The Code allows remittal in situations in which
the judge was disqualified because of economic interest. Canon
3(F). The procedure for remittal is as follows: The judge discloses
the basis for disqualification on the record and asks the parties and
their lawyers to consider, out of the presence of the judge, whether
to waive disqualification. If all parties and the judge agree to waive
disqualification, the judge may continue in the case. The agreement waiving disqualification should be made part of the record
in the case. Canon 3(F).

   Under the federal statute, waiver of disqualification is allowed
only in cases involving the general standard of when the judge's
impartiality might reasonably be questioned. Waiver is not allowed
for any cases in which rules specifically provide for disqualification,
including cases of disqualification because of financial interest.[35]

Ex parte contacts

Another important provision of the Code of Judicial Conduct dealing with judges' official functions is the rule prohibiting judges
from initiating, permitting, or considering ex parte communications. Canon 3(B)(7). Model Rule 3.5(b) prohibits lawyers from
engaging in ex parte communications except when authorized by
law. The Restatement of the Law Governing Lawyers contains
similar restrictions.[36] An ex parte communication is any communication between the judge and any other person regarding the
case except a communication in the course of official proceedings.
The prohibition applies to parties, their lawyers, witnesses, and

---

35. 28 U.S.C. §455(e).

36. Restatement (Third) of the Law Governing Lawyers §173(1) (prohibition on ex parte communication with judge or official before whom case is
pending). See also id. §175(1), (2) (prohibition on communication with prospective and sitting jurors).

even third persons unconnected with the litigation. The purpose of the rule is to protect the integrity of the adversarial process, which assumes that each party has the opportunity to respond to contentions and facts presented by an adversary.

The Code of Judicial Conduct provides several practical exceptions to the prohibition on ex parte communications to judges. See Canon 3(B)(7)(a)-(e). For example, the Code allows ex parte communications "for scheduling, administrative purposes or emergencies that do not deal with substantive matters or issues on the merits." Canon 3(B)(7)(a).[37] Even in these situations, however, the judge must reasonably believe that no party will gain a procedural or tactical advantage because of the ex parte communication, and the judge must promptly notify all parties of the ex parte communication and give them an opportunity to respond. Canon 3(B)(7)(a)(i), (ii). In some cases ex parte communications are permissible, for example, when a party is seeking a temporary restraining order to prevent irreparable harm.[38] Ex parte communications are permitted in this situation because the communication is "authorized by law." Canon 3(B)(7)(e). See also Model Rule 3.3(d), which requires lawyers in an ex parte proceeding to inform the tribunal of all material facts to enable the tribunal to make an informed decision, even when the facts are adverse.

The rule prohibiting judges from engaging in ex parte communications is long standing. Canon 3 of the ABA's 1908 Canons of Ethics prohibited ex parte communications. Nonetheless, it is surprising how many judges seem to freely seek advice and information about cases in violation of the rule against ex parte communication. Such ex parte initiatives by judges can put lawyers in very awkward situations. Most courts have held, however, that ex parte communications do not warrant reversal of a case absent a showing of prejudice.[39]

---

37. See also id. §173, cmt. c.
38. See Fed. R. Civ. P. 65(b).
39. *Compare* Ex parte Masonite Corp., 681 So. 2d 1068 (Ala. 1996) (refusing to set aside class certification order drafted by plaintiffs' counsel at court's request where court had already reached decision and subsequently gave opposing party opportunity to argue prejudice); Burgess v. Stern, 428 S.E.2d 880 (S.C.), *cert. denied*, 510 U.S. 865 (1993) (reversal not warranted because no showing of prejudice) *with* Strothers v. Strothers, 567 N.E.2d 222 (Mass. Ct. App. 1991) (reversal warranted when ex parte communication had effect on judge's decision in divorce case).

--------------- **Problem 6-2** ---------------

Extrajudicial Conduct and Judicial Selection

a. You are a law clerk for Justice Gates, an associate justice on your state supreme court. Before appointment to the bench Justice Gates had a distinguished legal career. She served as president of the state
bar association, had an active litigation practice, and was
a member of the state legislature for a number of years.
Justice Gates was also very involved in civic and charitable organizations and often spoke before legal and
nonlegal groups. Justice Gates has asked you to give her
advice about the propriety of the following situations
now that she has been appointed to the bench:

(1) Justice Gates is a member of a task force appointed by the state legislature to study and make recommendations regarding control of violence in the
public schools. Justice Gates believes that she will receive invitations to serve on similar task forces and commissions in the future.

(2) Justice Gates is a member of the board of visi-
tors of the state university where she attended both un-
dergraduate and law school. The board comes to the
university annually, meets with the president and the
various deans, discusses problems facing the university,
and makes recommendations for the administration to
consider.

(3) While in practice Justice Gates handled a number of employment discrimination cases. She has been
asked to write an introductory essay to a symposium on
"Emerging Issues in Employment Discrimination Litigation."

(4) Justice Gates has been asked to deliver a speech
to the Defense Lawyers Association at its annual meeting. She will not receive a fee for her speech, but the
association will pay all expenses for her and her husband
for the weekend.

(5) Justice Gates and her husband are close friends
with Tom and Eleanor Landing, both attorneys who
were in the same class with Justice Gates in law school.

Eleanor is a trial attorney and from time to time has cases in the supreme court. The Gates and the Landings frequently have dinner together, and Justice Gates and Ms. Landing have a regular once-a-month golf game. In addition, they jointly own a beach house.

b. You have been asked to speak to a meeting of a statewide organization devoted to political reform. Your topic is "Judicial Selection." The organization has asked you to address the following questions, as well as others that you consider important: What is the method of judicial selection in your state for judges of trial courts of general jurisdiction and for state supreme court justices? What are the advantages and disadvantages of this method compared to selection methods used in other states? What suggestions for reform or improvement of the current system do you have?

Read Canons 4 and 5 of the Code of Judicial Conduct.

Limitations on judges' extrajudicial activities

Canon 4 of the Code of Judicial Conduct deals with limitations on judges' nonjudicial activities. The Canon reflects a balance between contending policies. On one hand, judges should avoid any conduct that casts doubt on their impartiality, demeans their office, or interferes with their judicial duties. Canon 4(A). On the other hand, judges should not be isolated from the people and activities of the communities in which they live. See commentary to Canon 4(A).

The Code prohibits extrajudicial activities that clearly violate one or more of the policies expressed in Canon 4(A). Thus, judges may not practice law (except that they may act pro se, and they may draft or review legal documents and give legal advice to family members without compensation). Canon 4(G). Similarly, judges may not appear as private arbitrators or mediators unless authorized by law. Canon 4(F). The Code also prohibits judges from serving in a fiduciary capacity (for example, as a personal representative, a trustee, or a guardian), except for family members, and even then the judge cannot appear if it is likely that the judge as fiduciary would handle a matter that would come before the judge. Canon 4(E). Note that some provisions of the Code (including the prohibitions against practicing law, serving as arbitrators or mediators, and acting as fiduciaries) do not apply to part-time judges. See Application of the Code of Judicial Conduct sections C and E.

By contrast to these prohibited activities, the Code broadly authorizes judges to "speak, write, lecture, teach and participate in other extrajudicial activities concerning the law, the legal system, the administration of justice and non-legal subjects, subject to the requirements of this Code." Canon 4(B). Under this section, a judge may speak or write on controversial topics of policy as well as ones that involve technical improvements of the legal system, and may advocate change in the law. The limitation expressed in Canon 4(B) — "subject to the requirements of this Code" — is intended to remind judges that even in connection with educational activities, judges are still subject to other Canons of the Code. For example, a judge should not engage in public comment about a proceeding that "might reasonably be expected to affect its outcome or impair its fairness." Canon 3(B)(9).[40] Judges are always subject to the dictates of Canon 1, which requires them to maintain high standards of integrity and independence.

The Code allows judges to receive compensation and expense reimbursement for speaking and writing, subject to the financial reporting requirements of Canon 4(H). Thus, within the guidelines of Canon 4(H)(1), a judge could receive a salary for teaching part time at a law school and could accept an honorarium and expense reimbursement for delivering a speech. Canon 4(H)(1) provides that compensation and expense reimbursement must be reasonable and the source of payments must not "give the appearance of influencing the judge's performance of judicial duties or otherwise give the appearance of impropriety."

The difficulty of striking a balance between social involvement and regulation of nonjudicial conduct appears quite clearly in connection with governmental, civic, and charitable activities. Canon 4(C). The Canon provides that judges may not appear at public hearings or consult with legislative or executive bodies or officials except on matters concerning "the law, the legal system or the administration of justice," or except when the judge appears

---

40. See generally Symposium, The Sound of the Gavel: Perspectives on Judicial Speech, 28 Loy. L.A. Law Rev. 795 (1995).

pro se in a matter affecting the judge's own interest. Although the Canon is written as a prohibition, it could be construed as a rather broad authorization for judicial participation in governmental and civic activities, because such participation will often involve issues of law. Indeed, even some of the most controversial political topics of our day — abortion, health care reform, government spending — arguably involve "the law, the legal system or the administration of justice." But perhaps a fair reading of the intent of the Canon is that judges should not become involved with other branches of government in issues of public policy or politics. Viewed in that light, an appearance by a judge at a legislative hearing on health care reform would probably be improper. This distinction finds support in the wording of Canon 4(C)(2), which states that a "judge shall not accept appointment to a governmental committee or commission or other governmental position that is concerned with issues of fact or policy on matters other than the improvement of the law, the legal system or the administration of justice [subject to exceptions for ceremonial occasions]." It should be noted that this provision prohibiting judges from serving on governmental committees and commissions constitutes a departure from the historical practice of many respected judges. Probably the most famous example of judicial service that would now be a violation of this canon was Chief Justice Earl Warren's acceptance of an appointment to serve as chair of the commission investigating the assassination of President John F. Kennedy.

Canon 4 allows a judge to serve as an official (officer, director, trustee) or nonlegal advisor of an organization or governmental agency devoted to the improvement of law, the legal system, or the administration of justice or of "an educational, religious, charitable, fraternal or civic organization not conducted for profit," subject to "other requirements of this Code." Canon 4(C)(3). A judge may not engage in such service if the organization is likely to be involved in proceedings before the judge or in any court subject to the appellate jurisdiction of the court of which the judge is a member. Canon 4(C)(3)(a).

The Code limits judges' involvement in fund-raising activities and membership solicitation on behalf of such organizations. A judge may help in planning fund raising and may give advice regarding fund raising and investments, but may not participate personally in fund raising (except that a judge may solicit contributions from other judges over whom the judge does not have appellate jurisdiction or supervisory authority), nor may a judge lend the prestige of the judge's office to fund raising or membership solicitation (for example, by permitting a quotation or statement that the judge endorses the activities of the organization). Canon 4(C)(3)(b). The commentary to Canon 4(C)(3)(b) draws some precise distinctions. For example, a judge may attend but may not speak at a fund-raising dinner. A judge may be listed on the letterhead of an organization's fund-raising letter, provided comparable listings are made for other persons. Note also that under the 1990 Code, a judge may not hold membership (much less serve in a leadership capacity) in any organization that practices "invidious discrimination" on the basis of race, sex, religion, or national origin. Canon 2(C).

Business and financial activities by judges pose two potential problems. First, judges can exploit their public position for private gain. Second, judges can be placed in a position where they must disqualify themselves because of financial interest in a party or proceeding. See Canon 4(D)(1). Recall the discussion in Problem 6-1. The Code generally allows judges to hold and manage their own investments and those of their family members and to engage in remunerative activity, but this authorization is subject to other provisions of the Code. Canon 4(D)(2). The Code requires judges to manage their investments "to minimize the number of cases in which the judge is disqualified," and judges are directed to divest themselves of financial interests that might require frequent disqualification. Canon 4(D)(4). Judges may not serve in a managerial capacity in a business, with two exceptions: a business closely held by the judge or members of the judge's family and a business entity operated primarily to manage the investments of the judge or members of the judge's family. Participation in even these entities would still be improper if the entity were to regularly appear before the judge. Commentary to Canon 4(D)(3).

Acceptance by judges of gifts, bequests, loans, and favors poses obvious problems of improper influence. Canon 4(D)(5) states a broad general rule prohibiting judges from accepting a gift, bequest, favor, or loan from anyone, subject to certain exceptions. The canon requires judges to urge family members residing in the judge's household to comply with the rule. The broadest exception is found in Canon 4(D)(5)(h), which allows the judge to accept a gift, bequest, favor, or loan from any person so long as the transaction does not involve a person or interest that has appeared or is likely to appear before the judge and provided the judge reports any such transaction that exceeds $150.

A number of the other exceptions to the general prohibition on gifts, loans, bequests, and favors recognize that judges should not be required to act as hermits and are allowed to engage in many activities in which other citizens can engage. Thus, Canon 4(D)(5)(f) permits judges to receive loans from lending institutions in the regular course of business of the institution on the same general terms available to others. Similarly, Canon 4(D)(5)(g) permits the receipt of scholarships or fellowships awarded on the same general terms and criteria applied to other applicants. Canon 4(D)(5)(d) permits gifts from relatives or friends on special occasions (weddings and birthdays), provided the gift is commensurate with the occasion and the relationship. Canon 4(D)(5)(e) allows judges to receive gifts, bequests, and loans from a relative or close friend "whose appearance or interest in a case would in any event require disqualification under Section 3E." Canon 4(D)(5)(b) allows the spouse of a judge or a family member residing in the judge's household to accept gifts, awards, or other benefits "incident to the business, profession or other separate activity" of such person, even if the judge receives an incidental benefit, provided the transaction "could not reasonably be perceived as intended to influence the judge in the performance of judicial duties."

One potentially troublesome exception is Canon 4(D)(5)(c), which permits judges to accept "ordinary social hospitality." The section allows judges to have social contacts with anyone, including lawyers who regularly appear before them. The Reporter's Notes to the 1972 Code of Judicial Conduct, which also included a "social hospitality" exception to the prohibition on gifts, stated that a "judge should not be excluded from all social relationships with lawyers or persons who are likely to be litigants in his court."[41] The Code does not, however, define what is meant by "ordinary social hospitality." De minimis matters such as infrequent lunch or dinner engagements with lawyers or others should clearly be proper under the exception. Suppose, however, the judge has regular and substantial contacts with either a lawyer or another person

---

41. E. Wayne Thode, Reporter's Notes to Code of Judicial Conduct 84 (1973).

who may appear regularly before the judge. The Reporter's Notes
give the following example of conduct that exceeds the ordinary
social hospitality exception:

> The Committee felt that there are common sense limits and that
> the standard is understandable and defensible; for example, the of-
> fer to a judge of a month at the mountain cabin of a lawyer friend
> who practices in the judge's court is clearly not ordinary social hos-
> pitality, and acceptance is prohibited.[42]

   Canon 4(D)(5)(a) allows judges to accept gifts incident to
public testimonials and to accept materials from publishers on a
complimentary basis for official use. That canon also allows judges
to accept gifts (expense payments, for example) incident to bar-
related functions or to activities devoted to the improvement of
the law, the legal system, or the administration of justice. The
comment to that section states, however, that the canon does not
allow such gifts from individual lawyers or groups of lawyers. Such
gifts would be subject to Canon 4(D)(5)(h), which prohibits
judges from accepting gifts from any person whose interests have
or are likely to come before the judge. Thus, it appears to be improper for a judge to receive an expense-paid weekend at a convention sponsored by a specialized bar group, for example, one
representing either the plaintiffs' bar or the defense bar, but it
would be proper for a judge to receive an expense-paid weekend
at a convention sponsored by the bar association representing the
entire bar membership of the state. Could a judge make a speech
before a specialized bar group and receive as compensation for the
speech (rather than a gift) an honorarium plus expenses? As discussed above, Canon 4(H) allows judges to receive compensation
and expense reimbursement for activities permitted by the Code
(note that Canon 4(B) authorizes judges to speak, write, or lecture
on legal topics), provided the compensation and expense reimbursement are reasonable and provided that the source of payment
"does not give the appearance of influencing the judge's performance of judicial duties or otherwise give the appearance of impropriety." Canon 4(H)(1). Expense reimbursement may include
that of the judge's spouse or guest, "where appropriate to the occasion." Canon 4(H)(1)(b).

42. Id. at 84-85.

Methods of judicial selection and the problem of judicial independence

The choice of method of judicial selection involves a tension between the goals of independence and accountability. The rule of law, one of the core principles of our society, requires an independent judiciary in which judges render decisions based on the law rather than on political considerations or favoritism to one of the litigants. Yet at the same time, the rule of law demands that judges, like other public officials, be accountable for their conduct.

The Constitution adopts a system of judicial selection that emphasizes independence over accountability. Federal judges are nominated by the president, subject to confirmation by the Senate.[43] Once appointed, federal judges serve for life tenure and may be removed from office only through the impeachment process.[44]

During the past 60 years, the federal judiciary has come to exercise significant power over important social issues both through constitutional decisions and cases involving statutory interpretation. As a result of this expansion of judicial power, the accountability of federal judges has become an increasingly important issue. In Problem 6-1 we discussed the creation of judicial councils in each federal circuit to take disciplinary action against federal judges, short of removal from office. The Senate has been active in seeking to increase the accountability of federal judges. Beginning with the confirmation hearings of Robert Bork in 1987, the Senate Judiciary Committee has conducted searching inquiries into the constitutional and judicial philosophies of nominees.[45] The Senate has also streamlined the impeachment process.[46]

Most states originally struck the balance between indepen-

----

43. U.S. Const. art. II, §2, cl. 2 ("[The President] shall nominate, and by and with the Advice and Consent of the Senate, shall appoint Ambassadors, other public Ministers and Consuls, Judges of the Supreme Court, and all other Officers of the United States, whose Appointments are not herein otherwise provided for, and which shall be established by Law. . . .").

44. U.S. Const. art. II, §4.

45. Stephen J. Wermiel, Confirming the Constitution: The Role of the Senate Judiciary Committee, 56 Law & Contemp. Probs. 121 (autumn 1993) (part of Symposium: Elected Branch Influences in Constitutional Decisionmaking).

46. See Nixon v. United States, 506 U.S. 224 (1993) (Senate rule allowing committee rather than full Senate to hear testimony and gather evidence nonjusticiable political question).

dence and accountability more toward the accountability side than was the case at the federal level, but the general trend among the states has been toward greater judicial independence. During the colonial era, judges were appointed by the king. After the Revolution, distaste for the arbitrary exercise of royal power led many states to place the authority to appoint judges with one or both houses of the legislature. In the "democratic period" in American history, the vast majority of states moved to popular elections to select judges. Dissatisfaction with some of the political excesses resulting from popular elections (particularly control of judges by political machines) produced a late nineteenth-century movement for reform of judicial selection. Some states changed to "nonpartisan" elections, but this system also had its critics because it failed to take politics out of the election process and because it deprived voters of information about the party affiliation of candidates.[47] During the early twentieth century, reformers presented various proposals for judicial nominating commissions. In 1940 Missouri became the first state to adopt a nominating commission. (Today, a plan to use a judicial nominating commission, regardless of form, to select judges is often referred to as a "Missouri Plan.")[48]

A study of methods of judicial selection currently used throughout the country comments on the lack of uniformity among the states:

> One of the first things to strike one who looks at judicial selection in the states is the amazing variability not only between states, but within the individual states. Almost no two states choose all their judges the same way. Very few states use the same selection method for all levels of court.[49]

States generally follow, however, one of four models of judicial selection,[50] although a state may choose to use different methods for different courts:

47. For a criticism of the legitimacy of an elective judiciary, see Steven P. Croley, The Majoritarian Difficulty: Elective Judiciaries and the Rule of Law, 62 U. Chi. L. Rev. 689 (1995).

48. On the history of judicial selection, see American Judicature Socy., Judicial Selection in the United States: A Compendium of Provisions 3-6 (Lyle Warrick ed., 2d ed. 1993).

49. Id. at v.

50. For a detailed discussion of the various methods of selection and retention of judges in each state, see id.

Appointive systems — the governor or the legislature appoints and/or reappoints judges;

Partisan elective systems — voters select and/or retain judges
from among competing candidates identified by political party label;

Nonpartisan elective systems — voters select and/or retain
judges through elections where competing candidates are not identified by party label; and

"Merit selection" systems — the governor initially appoints
judges from a short list of candidates evaluated and recommended
by a nominating committee and voters decide periodically whether
to keep judges in office by voting "yes" or "no" on their retention.[51]

More than 30 states now use some form of nominating commission for selection of judges. The details of nominating commissions vary from state to state, but some features are common
to commission plans. Typically, the legislature creates a permanent nominating commission consisting of both lawyers and nonlawyers. Various public and private officials (as set forth in the
enabling legislation) appoint members of the commission. The
commission has the task of identifying, investigating, and evaluating candidates for judicial office. Typically, it will hold public
hearings on candidates. When a judicial vacancy occurs, the commission, after investigation and deliberation, forwards to the governor a list of nominees (three to five is a common number). The
governor appoints judges from the list for a probationary period
of one to three years. At the end of the probationary period, the
judge runs unopposed on the question of whether the judge should
be retained in office for a full term. Periodically, the judge must
stand for unopposed reelection in which the public votes whether
to retain or to remove the judge from office.

Recent developments indicate that the public may believe
that the movement toward greater independence of state judges
has gone too far. Retention elections for judges were low profile
until 1986, when a coalition of groups defeated the reelection of
Chief Justice Rose Bird and two associate justices of the California
Supreme Court.[52] Later in Texas, a coalition of medical, business,

51. Sara Mathias, Electing Justice: A Handbook of Judicial Election Reforms 5 (1990). See also Peter D. Webster, Selection and Retention of Judges:
Is There One "Best" Method? 23 Fla. St. U. L. Rev. 1 (1995).

52. Paul D. Carrington, Judicial Independence and Democratic Accountability in Highest State Courts, 61 Law & Contemp. Probs. 79, 81-87 (summer
1998).

and insurance interests ousted a number of state supreme court justices who were viewed as proplaintiff.[53] In the 1996 election, grass roots political campaigns removed a number of judges from state appellate courts.[54]

The appropriate balance between judicial independence and accountability is controversial, and opinions vary on where the line should be drawn.[55] Nonetheless, indications exist that the movement toward increased accountability may now have gone too far. During the 1996 presidential election, Republican candidate Robert Dole criticized federal district judge Harold Baer for issuing a ruling suppressing evidence of seizure of cocaine and heroin by New York City police officers. Dole called for Judge Baer's impeachment. In response to Dole's charge, the White House suggested that President Clinton would ask for Judge Baer's resignation unless he changed his decision. Judge Baer did in fact reverse his ruling.[56] Because of this and other perceived threats to judicial independence, the president of the ABA appointed a special commission to conduct hearings and make recommendations on the issue of judicial independence. The commission has released its report.[57] Among its findings and recommendations are the following: disagreement with a judge's decision is not an appropriate basis for threatening or initiating impeachment proceedings; state and local bar associations should develop procedures for evaluating criticisms against federal judges and for responding when appropriate; and Congress should resist efforts to restrict the authority of federal courts to vindicate constitutional rights.[58] Oth-

53. See Rogers v. Bradley, 909 S.W.2d 872 (Tex. 1995) (with appendix containing "Court Wars" report from the television show *60 Minutes*).

54. West Legal News, 1996 WL 652140, 652141 (Nov. 12, 1996). On the increasing importance of money in state judicial elections, see Mark Hansen, Run for the Bench, 84-Oct A.B.A. J. 68 (1998).

55. See generally Symposium on Judicial Independence, 25 Hofstra L. Rev. 703 (1997); Symposium, Judicial Independence and Accountability, 72 S. Cal. L. Rev. 311 (1999).

56. Stephen B. Bright, Casualties of the War on Crime: Fairness, Reliability and the Credibility of Criminal Justice Systems, 51 U. Miami L. Rev. 413, 415-416 (1997).

57. ABA, An Independent Judiciary: Report of the Commission on Separation of Powers and Judicial Independence (1997).

58. John Gibeaut, Mending Judicial Fences: Commission Suggests Ways to Dodge Politics, Bolster Public Support, 83-Aug A.B.A. J. 92 (1997).

ers have made recommendations for protecting judicial independence in the state courts.[59]

Judges and political activity

The relationship between judging and political activity poses both interesting questions about legal theory as well as practical questions regarding permissible nonjudicial activities. A widely accepted ideal for judges is one of political neutrality. Under this view, law and politics are separate activities. Judges should decide cases in accordance with the law; issues of politics should be left to the legislative and executive branches. A substantial body of scholarly literature challenges the view that judges can be politically neutral. Under this view, all law is to some extent vague or "open textured." Because law has this characteristic, judges must develop approaches or theories to a wide range of legal questions, many of which involve controversial questions of morals, values, and politics.[60]

Even if one accepts the view that the judicial process inherently involves questions of politics or values, it does not follow that judges should participate in other political activities, particularly the work of political parties and organizations. Such participation undermines public confidence in the independence of judges and exposes them to situations in which they may be forced to disqualify themselves. The Code of Judicial Conduct establishes some restrictions on political activity by judges. Canon 5(A)(1) imposes broad restrictions on participation in political activities by all judges and candidates for judicial office, including prohibitions on participation in political gatherings and fund-raising activities. Canon 5(A)(3) directs candidates for judicial office to "maintain the dignity appropriate to judicial office." The Code then defines this limitation more specifically to include, among other restrictions, prohibitions on campaign pledges and public statements on pending controversies. Canon 5(A)(3)(d). Canon 5(B) sets forth restrictions on political activity applicable to judges seeking judicial appointments; Canon 5(C) limits political activity by judges

59. See Carrington, Judicial Independence and Democratic Accountability in Highest State Courts, 61 Law & Contemp. Probs. 79 (summer 1998).
60. See generally Ronald M. Dworkin, Taking Rights Seriously (1977).

subject to public election. These canons reflect obvious differences between these selection methods. For example, when judges are appointed to the bench, candidates can engage in only very limited political activity, but when judges are selected or retained by public election, candidates are permitted greater political participation. Thus, a candidate for an appointive position may not solicit campaign funds, Canon 5(B)(1), while a candidate for an elected position may solicit funds through a campaign committee, Canon 5(C)(2). Model Rule 8.2(b) requires lawyers who are candidates for judicial office to comply with the Code of Judicial Conduct. In addition, Model Rule 8.2(a) prohibits lawyers from making statements that the lawyer knows to be false and from making statements with reckless disregard of the truth about the qualifications or integrity of judges, candidates for judicial office, or other public legal officers. Section 174 of the Restatement of the Law Governing Lawyers adopts similar standards.

B.   Representation of the Public Interest

——————— Problem 6-3 ———————
Government Attorneys[61]

You are an assistant state attorney general. Your boss, the deputy attorney general, has been asked to speak to a convention of attorneys employed by the state and federal government; the lecture is titled "The Ethical Obligations of Lawyers Employed by the Federal and State

---

61. Federal and state governments employ attorneys in a wide variety of capacities: for example, as prosecutors, agency counsel, members of legislative staffs, judges, and law clerks. See generally Symposium, Government Lawyering, 61 Law & Contemp. Probs. Nos. 1 & 2 (1998). The duties and ethical obligations of these attorneys are obviously not the same. Problems 6-1 and 6-2 dealt with the ethical obligations of judges. The material that follows deals principally with the ethical issues facing executive or legislative branch attorneys, such as attorneys employed by the Justice Department, by the office of a state attorney general, by a federal or state regulatory agency or department, by a member of Congress, or by a state legislator. Prosecutors face some additional special ethical problems; see Problem 2-10.

Governments." Several lawyers who will be attending the lecture have written to your boss with questions that they would like her to address. These questions include the following:

(1) "To preserve confidentiality I am asking this question generally and omitting reference to my state. The office of the attorney general in my state, as in most states, defends cases brought against the state. Our office is defending the state retirement system in a class action alleging that the system has improperly computed retirement benefits for state employees. We have received an offer of settlement from the plaintiffs. Our office has recommended rejection of the offer. The board of the state retirement system, however, has voted to accept the offer. The AG strongly disagrees with this decision and believes that the proposed settlement is not in the state's interest. What are our ethical obligations?"

(2) "What should an attorney who works for a state agency do if the attorney becomes aware of serious improprieties by agency officials? I'm talking about use of agency equipment and personnel for personal purposes."

(3)"Suppose a lawyer with a federal agency has been involved in the agency's investigation into the health hazards associated with a certain product. The attorney is planning on leaving the agency and has made overtures to a number of firms about the possibility of joining those firms. One of the firms that the lawyer has contacted represents a company that markets the product that the lawyer's agency is investigating. What ethical and legal restrictions apply to the lawyer's possible employment by the firm?"

Read Model Rules 1.11, 1.12, 1.13, and comments.

The role of the government lawyer and the duty to seek justice

The prevailing ethic of the profession is that lawyers representing private clients do not have a professional obligation to strive for a fair outcome or to seek justice in cases they handle. Thus, a private lawyer may assert a defense such as the statute of limitations even if the defense would bar a claim that the lawyer knows to be otherwise valid. This position flows from the role of lawyers in an adversarial system. The adversarial system is process oriented rather than substantively based. The system assumes that so long as the process is fair, the outcome that occurs is fair. Indeed, for lawyers to undertake obligations to produce substantively fair outcomes would itself be procedurally unfair since it would undermine the adversarial process.[62]

To say that lawyers in private practice do not have a professional obligation to seek a fair outcome in cases they handle does not mean that lawyers should be indifferent to fairness. Under the current model of lawyers' professional obligations, lawyers should counsel their clients regarding both legal and nonlegal aspects of their cases, including the fairness of any action that the client intends to take. Code of Professional Responsibility EC 7-8; Model Rule 2.1.[63] The client retains, however, the right to reject the advice of the lawyer, and the lawyer does not bear any responsibility if the client chooses to act in a way that is unfair. Model Rule 1.2(b). Some commentators have questioned this view of lawyers' ethical obligations and have argued that lawyers should, at least in some circumstances, have obligations regarding the fairness of the outcomes of matters in which they are involved.[64]

Do government lawyers have different obligations from lawyers in private practice regarding the fairness of the outcomes of cases they handle?

The conventional wisdom . . . suggests that zealous representation of clients is inappropriate for government lawyers. Most lawyers and judges who have considered the ethical responsibilities of the government lawyer have assumed that government counsel should temper their advocacy in the interests of "justice." This notion has been expressed by judges both on and off the bench, by

---

62. See, e.g., Catherine J. Lanctot, The Duty of Zealous Advocacy and the Ethics of the Federal Government Lawyer: The Three Hardest Questions, 64 S. Cal. L. Rev. 951, 958-964 (1991).

63. See also Restatement (Third) of the Law Governing Lawyers §151(3).

64. See the materials in connection with Problem 1-2.

the American Bar Association, by former government attorneys, by scholars, and by other commentators generally.[65]

Various justifications have been offered for the view that the government lawyer has an ethical obligation to seek justice. It has been argued that government lawyers represent the public interest rather than particular individuals or agencies. Since the public interest favors just resolution of cases, imposing an obligation on government lawyers to seek just outcomes does nothing more than require government lawyers to carry out the goals of their "clients." Further, since the government usually has substantially greater resources than private litigants, imposing an obligation of fairness on government lawyers helps prevent governmental oppression of private citizens.[66]

As noted above, one of the principal arguments in support of imposing a duty to seek fairness or justice on government lawyers is that the government lawyer's client is the public interest rather than an agency or official of the government. Professor Geoffrey Miller has vigorously attacked this view:

> Despite its surface plausibility, the notion that government attorneys represent some transcendental "public interest" is, I believe, incoherent. It is commonplace that there are as many ideas of the "public interest" as there are people who think about the subject. . . . If attorneys could freely sabotage the actions of their agencies out of a subjective sense of the public interest, the result would be a disorganized, inefficient bureaucracy, and a public distrustful of its own government. More fundamentally, the idea that government attorneys serve some higher purpose fails to place the attorney within a structure of democratic government. Although the public interest as a reified concept may not be ascertainable, the Constitution establishes procedures for approximating that ideal through election, appointment, confirmation, and legislation. Nothing systemic empowers government lawyers to substitute their individual conceptions of the good for the priorities and objectives established through these governmental processes. Accordingly, the

---

65. Lanctot, The Duty of Zealous Advocacy and the Ethics of the Federal Government Lawyer, 64 S. Cal. L. Rev. at 955-957.

66. See generally id. at 981-982; Jack B. Weinstein & Gay A. Crosthwait, Some Reflections on Conflicts Between Government Attorneys and Clients, 1 Touro L. Rev. 1, 11-12 (1985).

initial intuition, which suggested that sabotage might be justified as a means of combating a bad policy, seems seriously misguided.[67]

Professor Miller goes on to argue that because an agency lawyer operates within a constitutional system, the agency lawyer's client is the executive branch. This means that the attorney's duties run to the official who has legal authority to decide a matter. Normally, that will be an official within the agency, although circumstances may exist in which the president has delegated authority to decide a matter to a person outside the agency.[68]

What is the position of the Code of Professional Responsibility and the Model Rules on the issue? Ethical Consideration 7-14 of the Code of Professional Responsibility seems to accept the position that government lawyers have special responsibilities to justice:

> A government lawyer who has discretionary power relative to litigation should refrain from instituting or continuing litigation that is obviously unfair. A government lawyer not having such discretionary power who believes there is lack of merit in a controversy submitted to him should so advise his superiors and recommend the avoidance of unfair litigation. A government lawyer in a civil action or administrative proceeding has the responsibility to seek justice and to develop a full and fair record, and he should not use his position or the economic power of the government to harass parties or to bring about unjust settlements or results.

The Model Rules do not include a provision similar to EC 7-14. In Formal Opinion 94-387, the ABA Committee on Ethics and Professional Responsibility concluded that the Model Rules impose no greater obligation on government attorneys than on private lawyers to achieve just outcomes. Yet Comment 4 of the Scope section of the Model Rules recognizes the possibility that "other law" may grant government lawyers greater authority than private counsel over the outcome of litigation:

67. Geoffrey P. Miller, Government Lawyers' Ethics in a System of Checks and Balances, 54 U. Chi. L. Rev. 1293, 1294-1295 (1987).
68. Id. at 1298. See also Lanctot, The Duty of Zealous Advocacy and the Ethics of the Federal Government Lawyer, 64 S. Cal. L. Rev. at 1012-1017 (also rejecting view that government lawyers have obligation to do justice or to produce fair outcomes, resting conclusion on benefits of adversarial system in addition to constitutional principles).

Under various legal provisions, including constitutional, statutory and common law, *the responsibilities of government lawyers may include authority concerning legal matters that ordinarily reposes in the client in private client-lawyer relationships.* For example, a lawyer for a government agency may have authority on behalf of the government to decide upon settlement or whether to appeal from an adverse judgment. Such authority in various respects is generally vested in the attorney general and the state's attorney in state government, and their federal counterparts, and the same may be true of other government law officers. Also, lawyers under the supervision of these officers may be authorized to represent several government agencies in intragovernmental legal controversies in circumstances where a private lawyer could not represent multiple private clients. They also may have authority to represent the "public interest" in circumstances where a private lawyer would not be authorized to do so. These Rules do not abrogate any such authority. [Emphasis added.]

A government lawyer possessing authority that "ordinarily reposes in the client" presumably could exercise this power in the interests of justice or fairness. As the Model Rules indicate, when this authority exists, it is based on constitutional, statutory, and common law principles.

The Restatement of the Law Governing Lawyers largely agrees with the approach of the Model Rules.[69] Under the Restatement, government lawyers, like private attorneys, do not have a general obligation to represent the public interest or to promote justice. Instead, government lawyers are required to follow the directions of their clients, which are normally the agencies by which they are employed.[70] The Restatement, like the Model Rules, recognizes that applicable law sometimes grants governmental lawyers (prosecutors, for example) discretionary authority, which they should exercise to advance the governmental and public objectives of the lawyer's client as defined by law.[71]

When do constitutional, statutory, or common law principles provide a government attorney with "client authority" over a matter? Suppose, for example, that the Justice Department is representing a federal agency in litigation. Who has the authority to

---

69. Restatement (Third) of the Law Governing Lawyers §156.
70. Id. cmts. *c, f.*
71. Id. cmt. *g.*

decide what the government's position will be if the Justice Department and the agency have different views on the issue?[72] The highest legal official in the federal government is the attorney general. Federal law provides that the attorney general has the power to control litigation in which the United States is involved:

> Except as otherwise authorized by law, the conduct of litigation in which the United States, an agency, or officer thereof is a party, or is interested, and securing evidence therefor, is reserved to officers of the Department of Justice, under the direction of the Attorney General.[73]

This authority is exclusive and plenary, so long as the attorney general acts within the law.[74] Thus, the attorney general has the authority to determine the legal position of the United States and to authorize settlement, subject to legal restrictions.[75] If an agency disagrees with the position the Justice Department plans to take in litigation, the agency can attempt to convince the Justice Department to change its position. If this is unsuccessful, the agency's only resort would be to the president, who has authority over the executive branch, including the attorney general. If the president agrees with the position of the agency rather than the attorney general, the president can order the attorney general to adopt the agency's view as the official position of the United States in litigation. Since the attorney general serves at the pleasure of the president, the president could discharge an attorney general who refused to follow the president's policy.[76] In summary, in the federal system, Justice Department lawyers, acting pursuant to the authority of the attorney general, rather than agency officials, have

72. See generally James R. Harvey III, Note, Loyalty in Government Litigation: Department of Justice Representation of Agency Clients, 37 Wm. & Mary L. Rev. 1569 (1996) (discussing various models of Justice Department representation).

73. 28 U.S.C. §516. See also 28 U.S.C. §§518, 519 (argument of cases and supervision of litigation).

74. See, e.g., Executive Business Media, Inc. v. United States Dept. of Defense, 3 F.3d 759 (4th Cir. 1993).

75. Id. at 762.

76. See 28 U.S.C. §503.

the right to control litigation, unless authority is specifically given by statute to the agency rather than to the attorney general.[77]

The authority of the attorneys general in the states depends on the particular constitutional, statutory, and common law framework of each state. Some states are much like the federal system, with the attorney general having the power to control litigation involving the state, subject to the authority of the governor. For example, in People ex rel. Deukmejian v. Brown[78] the California Supreme Court held that the attorney general of California did not have authority to seek a writ of mandamus to stop the governor from enforcing an allegedly unconstitutional statute because the authority of the attorney general was subject to that of the governor, who was entrusted with executive power of state. In other states, the attorney general may be the final legal authority. In Feeney v. Commonwealth[79] the Supreme Judicial Court of Massachusetts decided that the attorney general had authority to seek judicial review of a lower court decision holding that a civil service preference for veterans unconstitutionally discriminated against women, despite objections of the agency and the governor. In still other jurisdictions the attorney general is treated much like private counsel whose client is the agency that the attorney general represents pursuant to statute. Thus, in Chun v. Board of Trustees of the Employees' Retirement System[80] the Hawaii Supreme Court held that the state attorney general did not have authority to file an appeal that the attorney general believed was in the state's interest in a class action involving computation of retirement benefits when the retirement system in a divided vote had refused to authorize the appeal.

Suppose an attorney in the Justice Department or in the office of the attorney general in a state disagrees with the policy position taken by that attorney's superiors. The attorney can, and should, argue for the position that the attorney believes is correct. If the attorney's superiors reject those arguments, the attorney is bound

---

77. See, e.g., FDIC v. Irwin, 727 F. Supp. 1073 (N.D. Tex. 1989), aff'd, 916 F.2d 1051 (5th Cir. 1990) (FDIC has statutory authority under "sue and be sued" clause to litigate without approval of attorney general).

78. 624 P.2d 1206 (Cal. 1981) (en banc).

79. 366 N.E.2d 1262 (Mass. 1977).

80. 952 P.2d 1215 (Haw. 1998).

to follow the decision of the superiors since they have the legal authority to make the decision. If the attorney in good conscience cannot accept the decision, the attorney should ask to be relieved from participation in the matter or resign. To the extent that the decision of the superior involves ethical rather than policy issues, the subordinate lawyer may still follow the senior attorney's decision if it is a "reasonable resolution of an arguable question of professional duty." See Model Rule 5.2(b).

Attorneys who are employed by agencies rather than by the Justice Department or the office of a state attorney general do not have "client authority." That authority is vested in the officials of the agency. Thus, agency attorneys normally should follow the decision of the official of the agency authorized to make decisions in the matter. In some cases, agency attorneys may be justified in taking a matter higher in the government. See Model Rule 1.13 and cmt. 7. In situations that involve illegal conduct by officials, agency attorneys may be justified in revealing the matter beyond the agency. The next section discusses the scope of the government attorney's duty of confidentiality.

Confidentiality of information: government attorneys and wrongdoing by government officials

Earlier we considered the issue of the scope of the lawyer's duty of confidentiality when the client has engaged or intends to engage in wrongdoing. Recall Problem 2-5 (perjury in criminal cases) and Problem 5-2 (fraud by clients in business transactions). As we saw in these problems, lawyers in private practice may not counsel or assist their clients in conduct that is illegal or fraudulent. Lawyers must generally maintain the confidentiality of information that they received regarding client wrongdoing, but they have a limited area of discretion to reveal confidential information to prevent clients from committing future crimes. Lawyers employed by organizations have a duty to protect the organization from harm caused to the organization by its constituents. In fulfilling this duty, lawyers have discretion to reveal information about wrongdoing by constituents to higher authority in the organization. See Model Rule 1.13(b).

Do government lawyers have any special legal or ethical obligations when they learn of wrongdoing by employees of an agency that they represent? The Code of Professional Responsibility and the Model Rules of Professional Conduct do not contain any specific provisions regarding the scope of the duty of confidentiality as applied to government lawyers. Comment 7 to Model Rule 1.13, which deals with an organization as client, states that the rule also applies to governmental organizations. The comment goes on to refer to the complexity of the matter when the client is a governmental entity and to the possible applicability of statutes and regulations. The Restatement takes the position that a government lawyer should follow the principles applicable to entity clients when dealing with wrongdoing by a constituent, unless applicable law provides otherwise.[81]

Statutory or regulatory provisions at the federal, state, or local level, however, regulate the disclosure or release of government information and the scope of the government lawyer's duty of confidentiality.[82] Federal law provides that the head of an agency or department shall report violations of federal criminal law to the attorney general.[83] In In re Lindsey (Grand Jury Testimony),[84] one of the legal proceedings in connection with the investigation by the Office of Independent Counsel of the Monica Lewinsky matter, the independent counsel subpoenaed Deputy White House Counsel Bruce Lindsey to testify before a federal grand jury. While the court recognized that the attorney-client privilege applies to government entities, the court held that the privilege must yield in the context of criminal investigations:

> The public interest in honest government and in exposing wrongdoing by government officials, as well as the tradition and practice, acknowledged by the Office of the President and by former White House Counsel, of government lawyers reporting evidence of federal criminal offenses whenever such evidence comes to them, lead to the conclusion that a government attorney may not invoke the attorney-client privilege in response to grand jury questions seeking information relating to the possible commission of a federal crime.[85]

---

81. Restatement (Third) of the Law Governing Lawyers §156(2) and cmt. *j.*

82. Roger C. Cramton, The Lawyer as Whistleblower: Confidentiality and the Government Lawyer, 5 Geo. J. Legal Ethics 291, 294-295 (1991).

83. 28 U.S.C. §535(b).

84. 158 F.3d 1263 (D.C. Cir.), *cert. denied,* 119 S. Ct. 466 (1998).

85. 158 F.3d at 1266.

In its opinion the court stated that tradition and practice show government lawyers, including White House counsel, have an obligation to report criminal conduct.[86] Initially, the government lawyer should report the matter to the head of the lawyer's agency or department. If the head officer is involved, the attorney may report directly to the attorney general or other appropriate Justice Department official.[87] Such disclosure does not involve a breach of confidentiality if the client of the government attorney is considered to be the executive branch of the government since the agency head and the attorney general are both part of that branch.[88]

Congress has also enacted "whistleblower" legislation to protect government employees who disclose information from retaliation for their disclosures, particularly from losing their jobs.[89] The act makes its unlawful for the government to take a personnel action against a governmental employee who discloses information that the employee "reasonably believes evidences" either (1) "a violation of any law, rule, or regulation" or (2) "gross mismanagement, a gross waste of funds, an abuse of authority, or a substantial and specific danger to public health or safety." The act allows an employee to make disclosure within the government either to a designated official in the agency or to the Office of Special Counsel of the Merit Systems Protection Board.[90] Further, the act authorizes employees to disclose information outside the government provided "such disclosure is not specifically prohibited by law and if such information is not specifically required by Executive order to be kept secret in the interest of national defense or

86. Id. at 1274-1276. See also In re Grand Jury Subpoena Duces Tecum (Hillary Rodham Clinton), 112 F.3d 910 (8th Cir.), *cert. denied*, 521 U.S. 1105 (1997) (government attorney-client privilege does not apply to grand jury proceedings).

87. See Fed. Bar Assn. Op. 73-1, 32 Fed. Bar J. 71, 73-74 (1973) (cited with approval in *Lindsey;* federal government lawyer may report "corrupt conduct and other illegal conduct of a criminal character, that is, the willful or knowing disregard of or breach of law, in either the legislative or executive branch" to head of department or agency).

88. Cramton, The Lawyer as Whistleblower, 5 Geo. J. Legal Ethics at 303.

89. Civil Service Reform Act of 1978, as amended by the Whistleblower Protection Act of 1989, 5 U.S.C. §2302(b)(8), (b)(9).

90. 5 U.S.C. §2302(b)(8)(B).

the conduct of foreign affairs."[91] Disclosure outside the government could be made to a reporter, congressional staffer, or interest-group representative.[92]

The whistleblower provision does not expressly apply to government attorneys, nor does it expressly exclude government attorneys from its application. While it is possible that courts would construe the act not to override an attorney's duty of confidentiality, given the strong public policies behind the act and the absence of any specific exclusion for attorneys, it is unlikely that they will do so.[93] In an analysis of the act, Professor Roger Cramton argues that the general professional obligation of confidentiality is "overridden by the more specific permission of disclosure afforded by the whistleblower enactments."[94] Professor Cramton finds this to be a desirable result to the extent that a lawyer is reporting government corruption, but he questions the wisdom of the act to the extent it would give protection to lawyers for reporting what are in essence policy disagreements.[95] Note, however, that the whistleblower act does not require government attorneys to disclose confidential information. Assuming the legislation applies to attorneys, the act would simply protect them from various personnel actions, including discharge, if they did blow the whistle.

In Crandon v. State[96] the general counsel for the office of the Kansas banking commissioner was discharged after she reported alleged misconduct by the deputy commissioner to the Federal Deposit Insurance Corporation. She sued, claiming that her discharge violated the Kansas whistleblower statute. The Kansas Supreme Court affirmed summary judgment for the state, however, finding that the general counsel had acted improperly by failing to present the matter to the banking commissioner before reporting it outside the agency.[97] The court also found that the attorney

---

91. 5 U.S.C. §2302(b)(8)(A).

92. Cramton, The Lawyer as Whistleblower, 5 Geo. J. Legal Ethics at 308.

93. See Jacobs v. Schiffer, 47 F. Supp. 2d 16 (D.D.C. 1999) (Justice Department attorney allowed to reveal confidential government information to his privately retained counsel to determine whether attorney may have claim under whistleblower statute).

94. Cramton, The Lawyer as Whistleblower, 5 Geo. J. Legal Ethics at 313.

95. Id.

96. 897 P.2d 92 (Kan. 1995), cert. denied, 516 U.S. 1113 (1996).

97. 897 P.2d at 103.

acted recklessly in reporting the matter because she relied on sec-
ondhand information without conducting an adequate investigation to verify the allegations of misconduct.[98]

The "revolving door": movement of lawyers into and out of government practice

The "revolving door" refers to "the phenomenon of individuals
who move between government and the private sector and who
are often regulators one day, regulated the next, and regulators
again the day after."[99] While the term is often used in a derogatory
manner, the revolving door offers both public benefits as well as
problems. A Harvard Developments Note identifies the following
benefits and problems:

Benefits of the Revolving Door

The first and most fundamental benefit of the revolving door
is avoidance of the likely alternative: a permanent legal bureaucracy.
. . . [The] professionalism of government service is in direct conflict
with the model of citizen participation in government. . . .
The revolving door also enhances the quality of official decisionmaking. Policymakers must always strike a careful balance between independence and accountability, and an official will be
better able to maintain his independence if he is relatively free to
leave the government. . . .
Finally, the revolving door is an important aid to government
recruitment of attorneys with talent and imagination. The main
advantages that government agencies have to offer young attorneys
are training and experience, both of which can be turned into financial gain when and if the attorney chooses to leave the government. . . .

Problems of the Revolving Door

Perhaps the most frequently voiced fear concerning the revolving door is that the government attorney might abuse his position to benefit his future career in the private sector. . . .
A second danger of the revolving door involves one of the

98. Id. at 103-104.
99. Developments in the Law — Conflicts of Interest in the Legal Profession, 94 Harv. L. Rev. 1244, 1428 (1981).

principal bases for conflict of interest regulation in all types of legal practice: protection of client confidences. . . . This danger is real, but its significance should not be exaggerated [because of the presence of various statutes that make a wide variety of government information public].

A third problem with the revolving door is the unfair advantage that it might give private parties who are able to hire former agency attorneys having special contacts and expertise. . . .

A fourth abuse attributed to the revolving door is that it encourages favoritism to former government attorneys by their former colleagues in the agency or department in which they worked. . . .

Finally, there is a basic objection to the fact that the revolving door continually permits the fundamental impropriety of "switching sides."[100]

Regulation of the revolving door occurs through a complex array of rules of ethics, statutes, and regulations. Model Rule 1.11 deals with ethical limitations on successive governmental and private employment. (See also Model Rule 1.12 dealing with former judges and arbitrators.) Rules 1.11(a), (b), and (c)(2) apply to movement from government service into private practice, while Rule 1.11(c)(1) applies to movement from private practice to government service.

Rule 1.11(a) prohibits a lawyer who leaves government service from representing a "private client" in a "matter in which the lawyer participated personally and substantially as a public officer or employee, unless the appropriate government agency consents after consultation." The term "private client" as used in the rule is broadly construed. See Rule 1.11, cmt. 4.[101] An example of the application of Rule 1.11(a) is In re Sofaer,[102] where the respondent received an informal admonition for undertaking representation of the government of Libya in connection with various legal matters arising from the 1988 bombing of Pan American Flight 103 over Lockerbie, Scotland, after the respondent, while serving as legal advisor to the State Department, took part personally and sub-

---

100. Id. at 1428-1433.

101. See also General Motors Corp. v. City of New York, 501 F.2d 639 (2d Cir. 1974) (attorney disqualified from representing city in antitrust action when attorney had participated in same matter while Justice Department attorney; attorney was engaged in private employment because of contingent fee agreement with city).

102. 728 A.2d 625 (D.C. 1999).

stantially in the government's investigation of the bombing and in related diplomatic and legal activities.

Several aspects of the scope and limitations of Rule 1.11 are particularly significant. First, the rule bars representation of all private clients as to matters in which the attorney was personally and substantially involved while in government employment. It is not necessary that the former government client be involved in the matter or have an adverse interest to the lawyer's private client.[103] While the rule protects the government from disloyalty and misuse of confidential information, it has a broader goal. The rule prevents the prospect of private employment from tainting the lawyer's judgment while in public service.[104] See also Rule 1.11, cmt. 3.

Second, Rule 1.11(a) restricts the activities of a former government lawyer only as to a "matter" in which the lawyer participated personally and substantially. Under Rule 1.11(d), a matter generally is limited to a proceeding involving specific parties, as distinguished from rulemaking and issues of general policy, although conflict-of-interest rules of an agency may define a matter more broadly.[105] Thus, a former agency lawyer who was directly involved in drafting regulations for a governmental agency is not precluded from advising a private client about those regulations after leaving government service, unless the agency's conflict-of-interest rules provide otherwise.[106]

Third, Rule 1.11(a) provides that with the consent of the agency, a lawyer may handle a matter in which the lawyer was personally and substantially involved. If the agency refuses to consent, the lawyer is personally disqualified from handling the matter, but other members of the firm are not disqualified from handling the matter if the disqualified lawyer is screened from any

103. 1 Hazard & Hodes, The Law of Lawyering §1.11:201, at 354.1.

104. Id. For a discussion of the policies behind the rule, see ABA Comm. on Ethics and Prof. Resp., Formal Op. 97-409.

105. At one time rules of the Environmental Protection Agency defined "matter" to include participation in rulemaking, but that restriction has been repealed. See 50 Fed. Reg 39,622-01 (1985).

106. See ABA Comm. on Ethics and Prof. Resp., Formal Op. 97-409 (former agency attorney may represent private party in challenge to agency rules even though lawyer was personally involved in development and implementation of those rules, unless lawyer has confidential information under Rule 1.9(c); even if lawyer is personally disqualified because of possession of confidential information, firm is not if it implements appropriate screening procedures pursuant to Rule 1.11(a)).

participation in the matter, receives no part of the fee from the matter, and the agency receives notice so that it can monitor compliance with the rule.[107] Note that the Model Rules have different provisions on screening of former government lawyers and screening when private lawyers switch firms. See Rule 1.10, cmt. 5. Section 214 of the Restatement follows Rule 1.11 in most material respects.

Professor Monroe Freedman has criticized the screening and waiver provisions of Rule 1.11(a) on three grounds. First, "no workable standards for the screening have ever been suggested." Second, "it is virtually impossible to police violations of screening once a waiver has been given." Third, "waiver by a government agency compounds the initial conflict of interest. Agency lawyers who are called upon to grant or deny a waiver on behalf of a former colleague's law firm have a substantial personal incentive to be generous in granting the waiver, because they will themselves be making similar requests within a short time when they leave government service." Freedman also argues that the rationale for the provision — the government's need to be able to attract competent lawyers — is totally speculative.[108]

As discussed above, Rule 1.11 applies even if the government is not a party to the proceeding. Suppose, however, the government is an adverse party. Rule 1.9 generally governs representation against former clients. Does Rule 1.9, or Rule 1.11, or both apply when the former government client is an adverse party? Hazard and Hodes argue that Rule 1.9 applies in the case of side-switching, when the former government client is now an adverse party. They reason that government clients should be entitled to at least the same protection as private clients.[109] Under this analysis, when the former government attorney is disqualified under Rule 1.9(a) or (b), the lawyer's entire firm is disqualified under Rule 1.10. Screening is not permitted. In Formal Opinion 97-409, the ABA Committee on Ethics and Professional Responsibility concluded that Rule 1.11 applies to representation against former government clients. While the committee decided that a govern-

---

107. See Armstrong v. McAlpin, 625 F.2d 433 (2d Cir. 1980) (en banc), (denying motion to disqualify firm when former government lawyer who joined firm had been screened from participation in matter) *vacated on other grounds,* 449 U.S. 1106 (1981).

108. Freedman, Understanding Lawyers' Ethics at 208-209.

109. 1 Hazard & Hodes, The Law of Lawyering §1.11:101, at 352.

ment attorney has a duty to protect the confidentiality of information received from a former government client under Rule 1.9(c), the committee concluded that Rule 1.11 was intended to supplant Rules 1.9(a) and (b). Under the committee's analysis, even if the former government attorney is personally disqualified because of either Rule 1.11 or Rule 1.9(c), the lawyer's firm can avoid disqualification by complying with the screening procedures of Rule 1.11(a).

Rule 1.11 applies to all government lawyers, whether federal, state, or local. The rule must be read, however, in conjunction with federal and state statutory and regulatory provisions. This body of law imposes restrictions on former government lawyers in addition to those found in Rule 1.11. Unlike Rule 1.11, the statutory provisions are not limited to lawyers but apply to other government officials and employees. Moreover, violation of these statutory provisions may subject government officials to criminal penalties. State statutes and regulations dealing with former governmental employees vary considerably, so attorneys leaving state governmental employment must consult these provisions. For federal governmental employees, the most important provision is 18 U.S.C. §207. That statute contains two provisions somewhat similar to Rule 1.11, although these provisions are narrower in scope than the rule. Section (a)(1) provides as follows:

(a) Restrictions on all officers and employees of the executive branch and certain other agencies. —

(1) Permanent restrictions on representation on particular matters. — Any person who is an officer or employee (including any special Government employee) of the executive branch of the United States (including any independent agency of the United States), or of the District of Columbia, and who, after the termination of his or her service or employment with the United States or the District of Columbia, knowingly makes, with the intent to influence, any communication to or appearance before any officer or employee of any department, agency, court, or court-martial of the United States or the District of Columbia, on behalf of any other person (except the United States or the District of Columbia) in connection with a particular matter —

(A) in which the United States or the District of Columbia is a party or has a direct and substantial interest,

(B) in which the person participated personally and substantially as such officer or employee, and

(C) which involved a specific party or specific parties at
the time of such participation,
shall be punished as provided in section 216 of this title.

The section is narrower than Rule 1.11(a) in at least two
respects. First, it applies only to communications or appearances
before the federal government or the District of Columbia, while
Rule 1.11 applies to any private representation. Second, the statute applies only if the United States or the District of Columbia
is a party or has a direct or substantial interest; Rule 1.11 applies
even if the government is not directly involved.

Federal statute 18 U.S.C. §207(a)(2) is similar to section
(a)(1) except that it applies only to matters that the former employee reasonably should know were "under his or her official responsibility." In this case, the restriction is effective for two years
rather than permanently.

Remaining subsections of 18 U.S.C. §207 are quite different
in scope from Rule 1.11. These sections establish one-year "cool-
ing off" periods for certain executive and legislative officials and
employees, prohibiting various appearances or contacts. For example, certain former employees of the executive branch and of
independent federal agencies are prohibited for one year from
making any appearances or communications with employees of
their former departments or agencies with an intention to influence a decision.[110] Similarly, any employee of a senator or representative is prohibited for one year after termination of
employment from communicating with the senator or representative for whom the former employee worked or with any employee
of that senator or representative with the intent to influence an
official decision.[111]

In 1993 President Clinton issued an executive order requiring high-level executive branch appointees to agree to an ethics
pledge as a condition of employment. The pledge prohibits various
activities, including lobbying any officer or employee of an agency
in which the appointee served for a period of five years.[112] The
executive order applies in addition to other legal restrictions.[113]

The Model Rules contain one provision dealing with lawyers

110. 18 U.S.C. §207(c).
111. 18 U.S.C. §207(e)(2).
112. Exec. Order No. 12,834, 58 Fed. Reg. 5911 (1993).
113. Id. §1(a)(5).

joining government service. Rule 1.11(c)(1) prohibits a government lawyer from participating in a matter in which the lawyer participated "personally and substantially" while in private practice, unless no one else is legally authorized to act in the matter. The rule is the converse of Rule 1.11(a).

Much more important for lawyers who join federal government service is the vast array of statutory and regulatory provisions governing their conduct, which have been codified by the government.[114] Each state will have its own statutory and regulatory scheme for government attorneys.[115]

The preceding material has focused on ethical problems facing lawyers employed by the government. A related area involves ethical issues facing lawyers who are elected to serve in state legislatures. In most states, service in the state legislature is a part-time job. As a result lawyer-legislators must deal with a variety of conflicts of interest between their official duties and their private interests.[116]

Problem 6-4

Public Interest Practice

Plaintiff approaches Enviro-PILF (Public Interest Law Firm) and asks if Enviro-PILF would be interested in taking on a case against Polluter. Plaintiff alleges that Polluter has violated public policy and federal law by releasing toxic material into the water system that serves Plaintiff's neighborhood. Plaintiff wants to bring suit against Polluter but does not have the economic means

114. See generally 5 C.F.R. pt. 2600, subch. B et seq. (Government Ethics). See Crandon v. United States, 494 U.S. 152 (1990) (separation payment by company to official leaving company to accept government position did not violate statutory provision prohibiting dual compensation for government employees).

115. For a critical evaluation of such restrictions, see W. J. Michael Cody & Richardson R. Lynn, Honest Government: An Ethics Guide for Public Service (1992).

116. See George F. Carpinello, Should Practicing Lawyers Be Legislators? 41 Hastings L.J. 87 (1989); Dennis M. Henry, Commentary, Lawyer-Legislator Conflicts of Interest, 17 J. Legal Prof. 261 (1992); Thomas M. Kellenberg, When Lawyers Become Legislators: An Essay and a Proposal, 76 Marq. L. Rev. 343 (1993).

to bring the suit on her own. So she wants Enviro-PILF to take the case.

After considering Plaintiff's allegations, Enviro-PILF decides that exposing Polluter's misdeeds will be in the public interest, and so Enviro-PILF takes the case. Before signing a retainer agreement with Plaintiff, however, Enviro-PILF is careful to explain the PILF's objectives thoroughly to Plaintiff. Ms. PILF Attorney, the lawyer assigned to the case, makes sure that Plaintiff understands Enviro-PILF's policies and goals. Plaintiff seems to agree that the goal of exposing Polluter should be paramount.

Later in the litigation, however, circumstances look different to Plaintiff. After months of preparation for litigation, Plaintiff is tired of waiting for relief. The water system is still polluted, and Plaintiff is frustrated. At this point in the litigation, counsel for Polluter approaches Ms. PILF Attorney and offers a settlement that will satisfy Plaintiff's new short-term goals. The proposed settlement will give Plaintiff special access to a separate (uncontaminated) water supply and will give Plaintiff a generous cash settlement. Under the ethics rules, Ms. PILF Attorney thinks that she should counsel Plaintiff to accept the settlement because it is in Plaintiff's best interest to do so.

Several aspects of the settlement trouble Ms. PILF Attorney, however. First, the settlement benefits only Plaintiff. Her neighbors who have also suffered as a result of the toxic spill will get nothing. Second, in order for Plaintiff to receive the benefits of the settlement, both Plaintiff and Ms. PILF Attorney must agree never to disclose the information they have gathered about Polluter's environmentally damaging misdeeds. Ms. PILF Attorney wonders whether she can accept the settlement given these concerns.[117]

Read Model Rules 1.2, 2.1, and comments.

117. Nicole T. Chapin, Note, Regulation of Public Interest Law Firms by the IRS and the Bar: Making It Hard to Serve the Public Good, 7 Geo. J. Legal Ethics 437, 439-440 (1993).

The history and meaning of public interest law

Oliver A. Houck, With Charity for All

93 Yale L.J. 1415, 1439-1443 (1984)

The concept of providing disadvantaged people with legal representation — as opposed to hot meals, hospital care, and a variety of other charitable services — arose in this country at least as early as 1876, when the German Society of New York established a legal aid office in New York City to assist newly arrived immigrants. By 1917, forty-one cities had established legal aid programs for the poor, and the numbers have risen and fallen since then with the revenue available from local governments, community drives, and the private bar. In the early 1960s, the Federal Office of Economic Opportunity began funding independent legal services; the funding grew to over $71 million in the next five years, and in 1974, Congress created the independent Legal Services Corporation. The original legal aid programs dealt with arbitrary landlords, impounded property, and the day-to-day problems of the poor, as they walked in the door, in the after-the-injury manner of a traditional law practice. The legal services programs, representing the same poverty-level clients, began to draw some conclusions about the causes of these problems from their recurring problems and began to seek larger remedies: They not only asked for the apartment back, they wanted to change the rules for eviction. In arriving at this law reform approach, which came to be known as "impact litigation," they were not alone.

A second root of public interest practice grew from the American Civil Liberties Union (ACLU), created in 1916 as the American Union Against Militarism to protect the rights of pacifists when much of America was calling for war. Led from this beginning into the defense of labor organizers and deportees, the organization broadened its name and scope to include the rights of agnostics, Nazis, and an almost unlimited spectrum of political and social minorities. With this growth came a change in style. A handful of prestigious, volunteer attorneys in the early years, filing selective briefs of amicus curiae, became by 1974 an organization of 275,000 members with 34 full-time lawyers in local offices and another 18 staff attorneys at national headquarters. These numbers were multiplied through volunteer counsel in every state, enlisted for specific cases on a low-fee and even no-fee basis. With this growth came a shift in tactics, from amicus to direct representation, and to the offense. Of the eighteen attorneys at ACLU headquarters in 1974, fourteen were addressing not the problems of individual clients but rather, in more general actions, the rights of juveniles, treatment of prisoners, and military justice. The ACLU was catching the same "impact litigation" breeze.

The National Association for the Advancement of Colored People (NAACP), founded in 1909, entered litigation on behalf of black Americans as early as 1914 and has been involved in suits against individual acts of discrimination ever since. In 1930, however, having received a major foundation grant, the NAACP launched a long-term litigation strategy to eliminate discrimination in housing, education, and employment. Its 1934 Annual Report described the strategy as follows: "It should be made clear that the campaign is a carefully planned one to secure decisions, rulings, and public opinion on the broad principle instead of being devoted to merely miscellaneous cases." In 1939, this campaign was assumed by the newly-created NAACP Legal Defense and Educational Fund (NAACP/LDF) which ran a string of successes through *Brown v. Board of Education* in 1954. By 1975, NAACP/ LDF maintained a staff of twenty-five attorneys and a network of volunteer cooperating lawyers in every state. The caseload was enormous, and bottomed heavily on the defense of individuals as demonstrators, draft resisters, freedom riders, and a dozen similar postures, defending the accused. Concurrently, however, the NAACP/LDF was mounting initiatives to eliminate the death penalty, de facto segregation, voting inequalities, and discrimination in the real estate market. It, too, was in the business of law reform.

These three large movements in poverty, civil liberties, and civil rights practice changed more than the law of their respective fields. As they evolved, particularly into the 1960s, these organizations changed the way lawyers approached the law. Their lawyers had clients and the clients were injured, but so also was a larger sense of justice which is as difficult to define precisely as it would be to deny. Most importantly, they did not simply seek compensation for their clients; increasingly they sought to change the law.

There are no "three sources" of anything, neither the Fall of the Roman Empire nor the rise of public interest law. The strategy and success of these three organizations were propelled by other movements of the times, each contributing to the character of public interest law. Prominent among them was the attitude of the organized bar. As recently as 1951, the President of the American Bar Association was writing that the greatest threat to America, apart from Communism, was "the propaganda campaign for a federal subsidy to finance a nation-wide plan for legal aid and low-cost legal service." Within the next twenty years, the Bar came to full support not only of federal assistance to legal aid programs, but also to Bar involvement in a far broader range of unrepresented or underrepresented interests. The Lawyer's Committee for Civil Rights Under Law was formed, and sent hundreds of lawyers into the South to come up against "the system" and to come away dedicated to changing the system through the use of law.

At the same time, thousands of middle-class urban residents, solid citizens who led lives no closer to protest than the headlines of their evening newspapers, were suddenly confronting intractable government programs like the federal Interstate Highway System and the destruction, as they saw it, of downtown Chicago, Boston, Baltimore, New York, Atlanta, San Francisco, San Antonio, New Orleans, Nashville, Memphis, Washington . . . and were taking their cases to court. Moreover, for the first time, under the impetus of the Administrative Procedure Act, the courts were overcoming their traditional difficulties with sovereign immunity, standing, law to apply, ripeness, mootness and private rights of action . . . and listening. . . . Scientist Rachel Carson published *Silent Spring*. Consumer advocate Ralph Nader published *Unsafe at Any Speed*. Americans read them. Foundations read them, and increased their funding not only for the ACLU and NAACP's law programs but for new ones directed to consumer protection and the environment. The Environmental Defense Fund was formed in 1968. The Center for Law and Social Policy, a catalyst for public interest law in Washington, D.C., began in 1969.[118]

---

118. On the history of public interest law, see also Robert L. Rabin, Lawyers for Social Change: Perspectives on Public Interest Law, 28 Stan. L. Rev. 207 (1976).

What is *public interest law?* The term is not easy to define, but some distinctions may be helpful in clarifying the concept. First, public interest law is not the same as *pro bono* representation. Pro bono cases normally involve the representation of individuals in typical legal problems, such as divorce or landlord/tenant. Such cases usually do not involve broad issues of public interest, other than the public interest in the fair and just resolution of all disputes. This is not to say that pro bono cases cannot involve public interest issues, only that the terms *pro bono* and *public interest law* are not coextensive. Pro bono and public interest representation differ in another respect. Lawyers typically provide pro bono representation without compensation. Indeed, the term *pro bono* has come to mean without charge, although the Latin phrase *pro bono publico* means for the public good. In public interest cases, lawyers usually seek payment of their fees from the opposing party pursuant to a fee-shifting statute.

Public interest law is not linked to any particular area of substantive law, to any specific form of litigation, or with any political movement. For example, public interest law is not limited to consumer cases; public interest issues range across the entire spectrum of law, from voting rights to employment discrimination. While it is certainly true that many public interest cases involve class actions or other "big" litigation, that is not always the case. A lawsuit on behalf of an individual that seeks to establish important principles of law qualifies as a public interest case. While the public interest law movement originally had strong liberal leanings, conservatives responded in the 1970s by establishing their own public interest law organizations. Today it would be inaccurate to characterize public interest law as either liberal or conservative.[119]

Professor Robert Rabin argues that the key factor in distinguishing public interest practice from ordinary private practice is the criteria lawyers use to select cases. In public interest practice, lawyers select cases because they are "socially desirable." By contrast, in traditional private practice, cases are chosen on the basis of the market — the demand for legal services and the availability of lawyers to provide those services.[120]

119. See Houck, With Charity for All, 93 Yale L.J. at 1454-1514.
120. Rabin, Lawyers for Social Change, 28 Stan. L. Rev. at 209 n.8. For a description of the realities of public interest practice, see Anita P. Arriola &

A more detailed definition of public interest law comes from the Internal Revenue Service, which has issued a Revenue Procedure that defines when a public interest law firm qualifies for tax-exempt treatment.[121] The Revenue Procedure outlines general requirements that a public interest law firm must satisfy (section 3) and then establishes specific requirements regarding attorney fees (sections 4, 5). Under IRS rules, the basic requirement that a public interest law firm must meet to qualify for tax-exempt status is that the firm must engage in "representation of a broad public interest rather than a private interest."

> Litigation will be considered to be in representation of a broad public interest if it is designed to present a position on behalf of the public at large on matters of public interest. Typical of such litigation may be class actions in which the resolution of the dispute is in the public interest; suits for injunction against action by government or private interests broadly affecting the public; similar representation before administrative boards and agencies; test suits where the private interest is small; and the like.[122]

By contrast, the IRS's guidelines characterize private representation as "actions between private persons where the financial interests at stake would warrant representation from private legal sources."[123] (A public interest law firm may, however, participate as amicus curiae in private litigation even though it would be precluded from direct representation because of the financial interests at stake.)[124]

Sidney M. Wolinsky, Public Interest Practice in Practice: The Law and Reality, 34 Hastings L.J. 1207 (1983); Debra S. Katz & Lynne Bernabei, Practicing Public Interest Law in a Private Public Interest Law Firm: The Ideal Setting to Challenge the Power, 96 W. Va. L. Rev. 293 (1993/1994); Patricia M. Wald, Whose Public Interest Is It Anyway? Advice for Altruistic Young Lawyers, 47 Me. L. Rev. 3 (1995). See also Nan Aron, Liberty and Justice for All: Public Interest Law in the 1980s and Beyond (1989). For a discussion of the current state of public interest law, see David R. Esquivel, Note, The Identity Crisis in Public Interest Law, 46 Duke L.J. 327 (1996). For a defense on moral grounds against various criticisms of public interest practice, see David Luban, Lawyers and Justice 293-391 (1988).

121. Rev. Proc. 92-59, 1992-2 C.B. 411.
122. Id. §3.01.
123. Id. §3.02.
124. Id.

To ensure that public interest law firms are operated in the public interest, the guidelines establish the following requirement for organizational policies:

> The policies and programs of the organization (including compensation arrangements) are the responsibility of a board or committee representative of the public interest, which is not controlled by employees or persons who litigate on behalf of the organization nor by any organization that is not itself an organization described in section 501(c)(3) of the Code.[125]

The IRS rules also provide that a public interest law firm may not engage in political campaigns and "no substantial part of its activities may consist of carrying on propaganda or otherwise attempting to influence legislation."[126]

Under IRS rules a public interest law firm may accept reimbursement from clients or opposing parties for direct out-of-pocket expenses incurred in litigation.[127] Public interest law firms may charge fees to their clients (although they rarely do so) only if the fee does not exceed the "actual cost" incurred in such case, including salaries, overhead, and other costs fairly attributable to the case.[128] Public interest law firms may also receive fees awarded or approved by a court or administrative body, provided such fees do not exceed 50 percent of the total operating cost of the organization's legal functions.[129]

Ethical problems facing public interest lawyers

The most difficult ethical problems facing public interest lawyers involve conflicts of interest. Public interest representation takes several forms: representation of an individual whose claim reflects a broader public interest, representation of a group of individuals who are not formally organized but who have a common interest in pursuing a public interest claim, representation of an entity that

125. Id. §3.05.
126. Id. §3.09.
127. Id. §3.10.
128. Id. §5.01.
129. Id. §§4.01, 4.05. See generally Chapin, Note, Regulation of Public Interest Law Firms by the IRS and the Bar, 7 Geo. J. Legal Ethics 437.

wishes to pursue a public interest claim, or representation of a class of plaintiffs.[130] Each of these forms of representation poses conflict-of-interest issues.[131]

For example, if a public interest law firm is representing an individual plaintiff, a conflict between the policies of the public interest firm and the desires of the client can develop. Such conflicts could arise at any stage of the case, but they become particularly acute when the opposing party offers a settlement. A defendant may find it advantageous to settle an individual claim to avoid adverse publicity, to reduce the possibility of being subject to an avalanche of similar suits, or to avoid an adverse precedent. Because of such factors, defendants are often willing to pay a premium to settle an individual case. In addition, in connection with such settlements, defendants typically demand confidentiality agreements. Confidentiality agreements take various forms, from private agreements to court orders sealing discovery and other records in a case.[132] Some jurisdictions, such as Texas[133] and Florida,[134] have court rules or statutes that prohibit or limit confidentiality agreements. In most jurisdictions, however, confidentiality agreements are valid.[135] A confidentiality agreement may not, however, restrict the lawyer's ability to represent future clients. See Model Rule 5.6(b). A client may be willing to settle a public interest case for a payment that seems advantageous to the client, subject to confidentiality provisions, but the public interest lawyer may believe that the settlement, particularly its confidentiality provisions, is not in the public interest.

How should public interest lawyers deal with such conflicts? Under a traditional client-lawyer model, the lawyer could advise

130. See Stephen Ellmann, Client-Centeredness Multiplied: Individual Autonomy and Collective Mobilization in Public Interest Lawyers' Representation of Groups, 78 Va. L. Rev. 1103 (1992).

131. See Ann Southworth, Collective Representation for the Disadvantaged: Variations in Problems of Accountability, 67 Fordham L. Rev. 2449 (1999) (based on interviews with public interest lawyers, conflicts of interest are less difficult when lawyers represent organizations with established decisionmaking procedures).

132. See generally Richard Zitrin & Carol M. Langford, The Moral Compass of the American Lawyer ch. 9 (1999).

133. Tex. R. Civ. P. 76a.

134. Fla. Stat. Ann. §69.081.

135. See Arthur R. Miller, Confidentiality, Protective Orders, and Public Access to the Courts, 105 Harv. L. Rev. 427 (1991).

the client of the advantages and disadvantages of the settlement, including any moral, economic, social, or political factors. See Model Rule 2.1. The right to accept or reject the settlement, however, rests with the client. Model Rule 1.2(a). If the client decides to accept a settlement offer against the lawyer's advice, the lawyer has a choice: carry out the client's wishes or move to withdraw. See Model Rule 1.16(b) (lawyer may withdraw if withdrawal "can be accomplished without material adverse effect on the interests of the client" or because the client "insists upon pursuing an objective that the lawyer considers repugnant or imprudent"). Neither option is attractive to the public interest lawyer. If the lawyer carries out the client's wishes, the lawyer is acting contrary to the policies of his firm and to his own strongly held views. Further, the lawyer's actions could conceivably jeopardize the tax-exempt status of the organization. Withdrawal is not a satisfactory solution, either. First, a court will probably deny a motion to withdraw either because of the stage of the case, because substitute counsel is not available, or because the client has the right to decide whether to accept or reject a settlement. Second, withdrawal means that the firm has devoted its limited resources to the case without producing results that advance its goals.[136]

One technique that public interest law firms can consider to deal with such potential conflicts is the use of *limited engagement agreements*. Under such an agreement the client concurs to be bound by the policies of the organization in the conduct and settlement of the litigation, in exchange for the organization's agreement to provide legal representation without charge to the client. A limited engagement agreement could specify that the client agrees not to accept any settlement with confidentiality provisions that would keep from disclosure evidence of danger of substantial physical harm to members of the public.[137] The Model Rules authorize the use of limited engagement agreements. See Model Rule 1.2(c). The comment to the rule, however, imposes limitations on their use:

> An agreement concerning the scope of representation must accord with the Rules of Professional Conduct and other law. Thus,

---

136. See Chapin, Note, Regulation of Public Interest Law Firms by the IRS and the Bar, 7 Geo. J. Legal Ethics at 459-460.

137. See Zitrin & Langford, The Moral Compass of the American Lawyer at 207 (suggesting such a provision).

the client may not be asked to agree to representation so limited in scope as to violate Rule 1.1, or to surrender the right to terminate the lawyer's services or the right to settle litigation that the lawyer might wish to continue.

Model Rule 1.2, cmt. 5.[138] The Restatement of the Law Governing Lawyers is somewhat more tolerant of limited engagement agreements than the Model Rules.[139] One commentator has argued that the rules of ethics do not provide adequate guidance for public interest lawyers and has called on the bar to draft a specific rule dealing with their problems.[140]

When a public interest case is brought as a class action, conflicts of interest can become even more difficult, particularly if the class involves minors or individuals with disabilities.[141] In class actions, conflicts can develop not only between the wishes of the clients and the policies of the public interest firm, but between groups of clients. David Luban gives the following example:

> In one of its class-action suits . . . Public Interest Law Center attempted to force the construction of a housing project in a racially mixed neighborhood that already had one project. The residents of that development opposed the action because they feared (correctly) that the second project would "tip" the neighborhood and turn it into a ghetto. The center purported to be representing the interests of public housing residents, but in formulating its strategy it chose to disregard the preferences of some of these residents. What gave the lawyers the right to act in opposition to the wishes of some of the very people whose interests they claim to represent?

---

138. See Marshall J. Breger, Accountability and the Adjudication of the Public Interest, 8 Harv. J.L. & Pub. Poly. 349, 350-351 (1985) (questioning validity of limited engagement agreements). But see Joel S. Newman, Gagging on the Public Interest, 4 Geo. J. Legal Ethics 371 (1990) (arguing that provisions in engagement agreements in which clients of public interest lawyers agree not to settle cases subject to confidentiality agreements should be valid).

139. See Restatement (Third) of the Law Governing Lawyers §30, cmt. c (quoted in Problem 3-2).

140. Chapin, Note, Regulation of Public Interest Law Firms by the IRS and the Bar, 7 Geo. J. Legal Ethics at 467-471.

141. See, e.g., Martha Matthews, Ten Thousand Tiny Clients: The Ethical Duty of Representation in Children's Class-Action Cases, 64 Fordham L. Rev. 1435 (1996).

What if those people had been in the majority? This is the problem of class conflicts in class actions. It arises often.[142]

How class counsel should deal with class conflicts is controversial. Professor Luban rejects the claim that lawyers should simply attempt to determine the wishes of the class members because it is often impractical to identify their desires and because class members may not fully represent the interests of the entire class, particularly when the case can affect future generations. Instead, he argues that lawyers should be as "responsibly representative of the client class as a whole" as it is possible to be.[143] Other scholars argue that public interest lawyers have gone too far in asserting their views of the public interest in opposition to their clients' interests.[144] Scholars developing *critical lawyering theory* and ideas of *progressive lawyering* have called on lawyers to help to empower rather than to control their clients.[145] Problems of lawyer control of clients are not unique to public interest practice.[146]

Recovery of legal fees can also pose ethical problems in public interest representation. In Evans v. Jeff D.[147] the Supreme Court ruled that statutes providing for recovery of attorney fees did not confer any rights on attorneys; clients, therefore, had the right to

142. Luban, Lawyers and Justice at 341.

143. Id. at 356. For further treatment of the ethical and legal problems facing lawyers in class actions, see Deborah L. Rhode, Class Conflicts in Class Actions, 34 Stan. L. Rev. 1183 (1982).

144. See Derrick A. Bell, Jr., Serving Two Masters: Integration Ideals and Client Interests in School Desegregation Litigation, 85 Yale L.J. 470 (1976) (questioning propriety of civil rights lawyers' commitment to integration when many of their clients favored educational improvement). See also William B. Rubenstein, Divided We Litigate: Addressing Disputes Among Group Members and Lawyers in Civil Rights Campaigns, 106 Yale L.J. 1623 (1997) (considering ways in which traditional individualistic method of litigation could be modified to take into account democratic values and to provide greater emphasis on expertise).

145. See, e.g, Gerald P. Lopez, Rebellious Lawyering: One Chicano's Vision of Progressive Law Practice (1992); Lucie E. White, To Learn and Teach: Lessons from Driefontein on Lawyering and Power, 1988 Wis. L. Rev. 699. For a criticism of this approach, see Ann Southworth, Taking the Lawyer out of Progressive Lawyering, 46 Stan. L. Rev. 213 (1993) (reviewing Lopez, above).

146. See Douglas E. Rosenthal, Lawyer and Client: Who's in Charge? (1974).

147. 475 U.S. 717 (1986).

waive recovery of legal fees without the consent of their attorneys. As a result of this decision, a potential conflict exists between public interest lawyers and their clients when defendants make settlement proposals that seek waiver of fees. A carefully drafted engagement agreement that addresses the client's obligation to pay the fees of the public interest lawyer out of any settlement that the plaintiff receives is one way of dealing with this problem. (*Evans* held that the plaintiff could agree to waive its claim to fees against the defendant, but the plaintiff's obligation to pay fees to the plaintiff's lawyer is a matter of contract between them.)[148]

In some situations, public interest lawyers may conclude that it is necessary for them to reach out to educate and even to enlist clients to bring litigation. The Supreme Court has given a measure of constitutional protection to such efforts. Recall In re Primus, discussed in connection with Problem 4-7. The precise contours of that protection, however, are uncertain.

---

148. For a discussion of these fee issues, see Stephen Yelenosky & Charles Silver, A Model Retainer Agreement for Legal Services Programs: Mandatory Attorney Fee Provisions, 28 Clearinghouse Rev. 114 (1994).

Chapter 7

Special Ethical Problems of Law Firms

In previous chapters we have focused on ethical problems lawyers face in specific areas of practice. Regardless of the type of practice, most lawyers work in private law firms. The law firm method of organization, however, creates a number of ethical problems. In this chapter we examine issues involving supervision of lawyers and nonlawyers, departures of lawyers from firms, expansion of law firms beyond legal services into ancillary businesses, and quality of life for lawyers practicing in firms.

A. Regulation Within Firms

Problem 7-1

The Duty to Supervise

a. At a recent partnership retreat, members of your firm attended a continuing legal education program in which the presenter warned members of the firm of their obligation to supervise paralegals, office personnel, investigators, associates, and even other partners. The presentation included citations to cases in which lawyers had been disciplined or sanctioned for failure to supervise. With regard to nonlawyers, the presenter recommended that at a minimum the firm prepare a memorandum that all nonlawyers are required to read and sign when they are hired, providing them with information about their obligations as nonlawyers working in a law firm. You have been asked to prepare a draft of this memorandum. The presenter also advised the firm to have in place procedures for supervision of lawyers, including both senior partners as well as associates. You have been asked to make recommendations for the types of procedures that would be appropriate for supervision of lawyers, including senior lawyers.

b. Another issue that the firm is considering is whether to adopt a policy on romantic relationships between members of the firm and individual clients, representatives of entity clients, other members of the firm, and nonlawyer members of the firm. What policy if any would you recommend? Why?

Read Model Rules 5.1, 5.2, 5.3, and comments.

Supervisory principles

The Model Rules set forth three principles that apply to supervision of partners, associates, and nonlawyers. First, partners in a firm have a duty to make reasonable efforts to ensure that the firm has in place "measures giving reasonable assurance" that the conduct of other partners, associates, and nonlawyers employed or retained by the firm conforms to the rules of professional conduct. See Model Rules 5.1(a), 5.3(a). Second, a lawyer having direct supervisory responsibility over another lawyer or a nonlawyer has a duty to use reasonable efforts to ensure that the conduct of the other lawyer or nonlawyer conforms to the rules of professional conduct. Model Rules 5.1(b), 5.3(b). Finally, a lawyer is subject to discipline for the conduct of another lawyer or a nonlawyer if the lawyer (1) orders the lawyer or nonlawyer to engage in conduct that violates the rules of professional conduct or ratifies such conduct, or (2) is partner or supervising lawyer who knows of misconduct by the other lawyer or nonlawyer and fails to take corrective action when the consequences of misconduct could be avoided or mitigated. Model Rules 5.1(c), 5.3(c). The Restatement contains similar principles.[1]

There are, of course, differences between supervision of lawyers and nonlawyers. As the Restatement states:

> Supervision of a non-lawyer must often be more extensive and detailed than of a supervised lawyer because of the presumed lack of training of many non-lawyers on legal matters generally and on such important duties as those on dealing properly with confidential client information . . . and with client funds and other property . . . , which may be different from duties generally imposed in non-law practices and businesses.[2]

Supervision of nonlawyers generally requires at least an informal program of instruction in which nonlawyers are educated about basic ethical principles.[3] In addition, lawyers must monitor the activities of nonlawyers working under their supervision to assure compliance with standards of professional conduct.[4]

While lawyers may generally delegate legal work to nonlawyers provided the nonlawyers are properly supervised, nonlawyers may not perform certain legal activities. Court rules or state ethics advisory opinions often provide guidance on these prohibited activities. For example, the ABA Standing Committee on Legal Assistants has established Model Guidelines for the Utilization of Legal Assistant Services (1991).[5] The ABA guidelines provide that a lawyer may not delegate to a nonlawyer responsibility for establishing a client-lawyer relationship, the amount of a fee to be charged for legal services, or a legal opinion for a client. The ABA

1. Restatement (Third) of the Law Governing Lawyers §12.
2. Id. cmt. *f.*
3. Id. cmt. *c.*
4. See Spencer v. Steinman, 179 F.R.D. 484 (E.D. Pa. 1998) (lawyer sanctioned for failure to supervise paralegal who issued subpoena to nonparty without notice to parties); Mays v. Neal, 938 S.W.2d 830 (Ark. 1997) (lawyer disciplined for improper delegation and supervision of nonlawyers).
5. Quoted in Laws. Man. on Prof. Conduct (ABA/BNA) 91:201. See also ABA, The Legal Assistant's Practical Guide to Professional Responsibility (1998).

guidelines do not mention, but probably assume, that nonlawyers cannot appear in court on behalf of clients.[6]

The duty to supervise nonlawyers also applies to independent contractors, such as investigators employed by a firm. See Comment to Model Rule 5.3, which specifically refers to investigators and independent contractors. In Formal Opinion 95-396, the ABA Committee on Ethics and Professional Responsibility addressed the applicability of Rule 4.2, which prohibits lawyers from communicating with represented parties, to the conduct of investigators employed by lawyers. The committee stated that lawyers have ethical responsibility for the conduct of investigators they employ both under Rule 5.3 and under Model Rule 8.4(a), which prohibits lawyers from knowingly violating a rule of professional conduct "through the acts of another":

> Since a lawyer is barred under Rule 4.2 from communicating with a represented party about the subject matter of the representation, she may not circumvent the Rule by sending an investigator to do on her behalf that which she is herself forbidden to do. Whether in a civil or a criminal matter, if the investigator acts as the lawyer's "alter-ego," the lawyer is ethically responsible for the investigator's conduct.

Similarly, in Upjohn Co. v. Aetna Casualty & Surety Co.[7] Aetna's lawyers hired an investigation firm to interview former employees of Upjohn about the environmental damages that were the subject matter of the litigation. The investigators did not determine whether the former employees were represented by counsel, did not identify themselves as working for attorneys representing a client in litigation, and did not state the purpose of the interview. The court found that the investigators had misled Upjohn's former employees and had violated Rule 4.3. The court's order included suppression of evidence obtained through improper interviews.[8]

Supervision of lawyers is both easier and more difficult than supervision of nonlawyers. Supervision of lawyers is easier because

---

6. See Pa. Bar Assn. Comm. on Legal Ethics and Prof. Resp., Ethical Considerations in the Use of Nonlawyer Assistants, Formal Op. 98-75 (nonlawyer assistants may not appear in court, conduct depositions, conduct real estate closings, or impersonate lawyers).

7. 768 F. Supp. 1186 (W.D. Mich. 1990).

8. Id. at 1212-1217.

they have received instruction in the rules of professional conduct
while in law school. But supervision of lawyers, particularly senior
attorneys, is difficult because of the status and power they possess.
Nonetheless, partners in a firm must establish methods of supervision of all lawyers, including the most senior lawyers in the firm,
both because it is an ethical obligation to have such procedures
and because of the risks that members of the firm face if senior
lawyers are allowed to practice without any degree of supervision.[9]
For example, in Home Insurance Co. v. Dunn[10] the senior partner
in a firm applied for renewal of the firm's malpractice coverage.
The senior partner had embezzled client funds. His failure to reveal this information to the insurer entitled the insurer to void the
entire malpractice policy, even against innocent members of the
firm. Similarly, in Weeks v. Baker & McKenzie[11] the firm was held
liable for $3.5 million in punitive damages in a sexual harassment
case because the managing agents of the firm ignored for more
than four years evidence that the partner had a propensity to engage in sexual harassment.[12] The court stated that when such conduct becomes known the firm may not continue to "employ the
abusive employee without taking reasonable steps to prevent him
or her from being or continuing to be abusive."[13]

While partners in a firm have an obligation to make sure that
the firm has in place measures designed to give reasonable assurance that the conduct of lawyers and nonlawyers complies with
the rules of professional conduct, partners may delegate aspects of
this duty to other members of the firm, such as a managing partner
or an executive committee.[14] However, a delegating partner remains responsible to take corrective action if the partner reasonably should know that the person or body to whom delegation has
been made is not providing or implementing proper supervisory
practices.[15]

9. See Susan Saab Fortney, Are Law Firm Partners Islands unto Themselves? An Empirical Study of Law Firm Peer Review and Culture, 10 Geo. J.
Legal Ethics 271 (1997).
10. 963 F.2d 1023 (7th Cir. 1992).
11. 74 Cal. Rptr. 2d 510 (Ct. App. 1998, *review denied*).
12. Id. at 529.
13. Id. at 528.
14. Restatement (Third) of the Law Governing Lawyers §12, cmt. *d.*
15. Id.

Regulation of sexual relationships between lawyers and clients, other lawyers, and nonlawyers

Weeks v. Baker & McKenzie holds that a law firm has an obligation to take steps to prevent a partner from continuing to engage in sexual harassment of a secretary. Sexual relationships can develop between lawyers and clients and between lawyers and other lawyers. In addition, unlike *Weeks*, such relationships can be voluntary rather than coercive, although the possibility exists that a relationship that was at one time voluntary can become coercive. Should the bar or law firms attempt to regulate this broad range of possible sexual relationships in whole or in part? If so, how?

In 1992 the ABA Committee on Ethics and Professional Responsibility made the following observation about sexual relationships between lawyers and clients: "Although no detailed statistics are presently available to document the incidence of sexual relations between clients and their lawyers, there is information enough to substantiate both the existence and the seriousness of problems in this area."[16] The committee went on to conclude that while no specific Model Rule prohibited sexual relations between lawyers and clients, such relationships could lead to abuse of fiduciary obligations, impairment of independent judgment, involvement in conflicts of interest, and exposure of confidential information. Because of these risks, the committee warned that the "lawyer would be well advised to refrain from such a relationship." If such a relationship occurs and the client-lawyer relationship has been impaired, the lawyer will have violated the rules of ethics.[17]

A California statute provides that an attorney engages in misconduct if the attorney (1) expressly or impliedly conditions performance of legal services on the client's willingness to engage in sexual relations, (2) employs coercion or undue influence in entering into sexual relations, or (3) continues representation of the client if the sexual relationship would cause the lawyer to act incompetently or to otherwise prejudice the client's case.[18] The statute provides several exceptions, one of which is for sexual-relationships that predate the formation of the client-lawyer relationship.[19]

---

16. ABA Comm. on Ethics and Prof. Resp., Formal Op. 92-364, at 1-2.
17. Id. at 9.
18. Cal. Bus. & Prof. Code §6106.9(a).
19. Cal. Bus. & Prof. Code §6106.9(b).

Some state supreme courts have adopted rules defining when sexual relationships between lawyers and their clients are improper.[20] These rules typically provide that such relationships are improper unless the relationship was in existence before the attorney began representing the client. For example, Minnesota Rule 1.8(k) provides as follows:

A lawyer shall not have sexual relations with a current client unless a consensual sexual relationship existed between them when the lawyer-client relationship commenced. For purposes of this paragraph:

(1) "Sexual relations" means sexual intercourse or any other intentional touching of the intimate parts of a person or causing the person to touch the intimate parts of the lawyer.

(2) If the client is an organization, any individual who oversees the representation and gives instructions to the lawyer on behalf of the organization shall be deemed to be the client. In-house attorneys while representing governmental or corporate entities are governed by Rule 1.7(b) rather than by this rule with respect to sexual relations with other employees of the entity they represent.

(3) This paragraph does not prohibit a lawyer from engaging in sexual relations with a client of the lawyer's firm provided that the lawyer has no involvement in the performance of the legal work for the client. . . .

B. Organizational Form, Departing Lawyers, and Sale of a Practice

1. Legal Structures

Traditionally, law firms have been organized as general partnerships. It was considered improper for lawyers to practice in corporations because law was a profession rather than a business. In addition, the corporate form of organization interfered with the

---

20. See Abed Awad, Attorney-Client Sexual Relations, 22 J. Legal Prof. 131 (1998).

personal nature of the client-lawyer relationship and improperly
limited lawyers' liability to their clients.

Beginning in the 1960s state legislatures passed statutes making new forms of business organization available to professionals.
The first wave of legislation involved adoption of professional corporation or association statutes, which were designed to give professionals the same tax benefits of corporate organization as were
available to ordinary businesses. Many of the tax advantages of
corporate organization for professionals, however, no longer exist.[21]

In the 1980s and 1990s, many state legislatures passed limited liability company (LLC) and limited liability partnership
(LLP) statutes. Both LLCs and LLPs are taxed as partnerships
rather than corporations, so their owners avoid double taxation of
income.[22] LLP statutes allow existing general partnerships to convert into LLPs. LLC statutes require the creation of a new legal
entity. LLCs can have centralized management like a corporation,
but most LLCs involving professionals will have decentralized
management, like a general partnership.[23]

The most controversial aspect of LLCs and LLPs when used
by lawyers is limitation of liability. State statutes vary in the degree
to which they provide for limited liability. In assessing the scope
of protection provided by a statute, it is useful to distinguish four
forms of liability that lawyers may face: (1) personal liability for
professional malpractice or for failure to supervise; (2) vicarious
liability for malpractice or other wrongful acts committed by lawyers or nonlawyers with whom the lawyer practices; (3) personal
liability for general business debts of the firm, such as leases or
other contractual obligations; and (4) personal liability for torts
unrelated to the practice of law.[24]

State supreme courts have the inherent power to regulate the
practice of law.[25] They could refuse to allow lawyers to practice
as LLCs or LLPs, although it appears unlikely that many courts

21. Robert W. Hillman, The Impact of Partnership Law on the Legal Profession, 67 Fordham L. Rev. 393, 393 n.1 (1998).

22. See Rev. Rul. 88-76, 1988-2 C.B. 360 (taxation of LLCs).

23. See Jennifer J. Johnson, Limited Liability for Lawyers: General Partners Need Not Apply, 51 Bus. Law. 85 (1995).

24. Id. at 91.

25. See Charles W. Wolfram, Inherent Powers in the Crucible of Lawyer
Self-Protection: Reflections on the LLP Campaign, 39 S. Tex. L. Rev. 359
(1998).

will take this extreme step. Instead, courts could restrict the degree to which lawyers are entitled to limited liability or perhaps require lawyers to have adequate malpractice insurance coverage.[26] In all states lawyers remain liable for their personal malpractice, regardless of the form in which they practice.[27] A lawyer's attempt to limit liability for personal malpractice is unethical. See Model Rule 1.8(h). Jurisdictions vary on the extent to which lawyers may receive the protections of limited liability for vicarious malpractice liability, for nonmalpractice torts, and for business debts.[28]

While not binding on state supreme courts, the ABA Committee on Ethics and Professional Responsibility has supported the use of limited liability forms of business organization by lawyers. In Formal Opinion 303 (1961), the committee ruled that lawyers could ethically practice in professional corporations or associations so long as (1) the lawyers rendering legal services to the client remained personally responsible to the client, (2) limitations on liability of other lawyers in the firm were made apparent to the client, and (3) prohibitions on the financial or managerial involvement of nonlawyers were maintained. In Formal Opinion 96-401, the committee extended the same analysis to LLPs. The committee advised that lawyers may ethically practice in LLPs provided the lawyer who renders services is personally responsible to the client and any restrictions on liability of other lawyers in LLPs are made apparent to clients. A majority of the committee decided that the use of the initials "LLP" is sufficient to put clients on notice of limitations of liability. The committee noted that while lawyers practicing in LLPs may take advantage of statutory provisions limiting their liability for conduct of others, they continue to have an ethical duty to supervise.[29] Despite support from the

26. Id. at 397-398.
27. Johnson, Limited Liability for Lawyers, 51 Bus. Law. at 104, 107.
28. See Henderson v. HSI Financial Servs., Inc., 471 S.E.2d 885 (Ga. 1996) (while court reserves right to regulate practice of law, lawyers may practice in professional corporations and receive same statutory benefits as other professionals, including limited liability for misconduct committed by other lawyers in firm in which lawyer was not personally involved), *overruling* First Bank & Trust Co. v. Zagoria, 302 S.E.2d 674 (Ga. 1983) (attorneys may practice in professional corporations, but they remain vicariously liable for misconduct of other lawyers practicing in firm).
29. For a criticism of Formal Opinion 96-401, see Susan Saab Fortney, Professional Responsibility and Liability Issues Related to Limited Liability Law Partnerships, 39 S. Tex. L. Rev. 399 (1998).

ABA and many courts of the use of limited liability forms of organization, a number of scholars have questioned the wisdom of the trend.[30]

2.   *Covenants Not to Compete and Other Restrictions on Departures from Firms*

━━━━━━━━━━━━ **Problem 7-2** ━━━━━━━━━━━━

Law Firm Organization and Breakups

   a.   You and two other classmates have decided to form a limited liability company (LLC) when you leave law school. You have been discussing various provisions to include in the operating agreement. One issue deals with compensation if one of you decides to withdraw from the firm. What provision would you recommend to deal with this issue? Why? Be prepared to participate in a meeting in which you discuss the issue with your classmates.

   b.   A lawyer who is a partner in a local firm has sought your advice about her plans to leave the firm and open her own practice. What issues would you raise with her and what advice would you give?

───

Read Rule 5.6 and comments.

In recent years the legal profession has witnessed a growth in lawyer turnover. Lawyers leave their old firms, join new firms, and open their own practices.[31] Departures of lawyers from their

---

   30. See generally Symposium, Ethical Obligations and Liabilities Arising from Lawyers' Professional Associations, 39 S. Tex. L. Rev. 205 (1998). See also Susan Saab Fortney, Seeking Shelter in the Minefield of Unintended Consequences — The Traps of Limited Liability Law Firms, 54 Wash. & Lee L. Rev. 717 (1997); Martin C. McWilliams, Jr., Limited Liability Law Practice, 49 S.C. L. Rev. 359 (1998).
   31. See generally Robert W. Hillman, Hillman on Lawyer Mobility (2d ed. 1998).

firms[32] raise some difficult legal and ethical issues. Three issues have been of particular significance: First, to what extent may departing lawyers notify firm clients of their departure? Second, for those clients who decide to employ the departing lawyers, how are fees received in those cases allocated between the departing lawyers and the old firm? Finally, may firms impose restrictions through covenants not to compete or other agreements on the practice of departing lawyers?

First, with regard to the issue of notification of clients, both the departing lawyer and the firm must recognize that clients do not "belong" to either of them. Clients have the right to choose to have either the departing lawyer or the firm represent their interests.[33] Thus, both the firm and the departing lawyers have the right and the obligation to notify clients of their departure so that clients can decide whether the firm, the departing lawyer, or some other attorney will handle the case.[34] In Formal Opinion 99-414 the ABA committee advised that joint notification by the departing lawyer and the firm was the preferred approach. Recognizing that joint notice was infeasible if the departure was not amicable,[35] the committee concluded that departing lawyers could properly provide either in-person or written notice to their current clients — those clients for whom the lawyer was responsible or for whom the lawyer played a principal role in the firm's delivery of legal services — but not clients with whom the lawyer had little or no personal involvement.[36] The committee advised that the initial notice of the lawyer's anticipated departure to clients should conform to the following requirements:

1. The notice should be limited to current clients.
2. The departing lawyer should not ask the client to end its

---

32. The discussion that follows focuses on partners withdrawing from partnerships, but similar rules should apply to withdrawals by associates, see In re Smith, 843 P.2d 449 (Or. 1992) (en banc) (associate disciplined for breach of fiduciary duty in connection with departure from firm), and to withdrawals from PCs, LLCs, or LLPs, see Fox v. Abrams, 210 Cal. Rptr. 260 (Ct. App. 1985) (partnership principles apply to dissolution of professional corporation).

33. 2 Hazard & Hodes, The Law of Lawyering §5.6:202. See also ABA Comm. on Ethics and Prof. Resp., Formal Op. 99-414.

34. See ABA Comm. on Ethics and Prof. Resp., Formal Opinion Op. 99-414.

35. Id. at 6-7.

36. Id. at 2-4.

relationship with the firm but the notice could state the
departing lawyer's availability to provide services.
3. The notice must make clear that the client has the ultimate right to decide who will handle the client's matter.
4. The departing lawyer must not disparage the former
firm.[37]

The committee stated that the departing lawyer could provide the
client with additional information, including a statement of
whether the lawyer will be able to continue to represent the client
at her new firm.[38] A departing lawyer may also ethically respond
to requests for information from clients to assist them in making
informed decisions about the handling of their cases.[39] Notification to clients, while important, is only one of many issues that
arise when lawyers depart from their firms. Professor Robert Hillman, the leading authority on lawyer mobility, has offered a set of
principles, drawn from decided cases and ethics opinions, to guide
departing lawyers and their firms on these issues.[40]

While departing lawyers have a right and duty to inform current clients of their departure, these lawyers owe fiduciary duties
to their former firms. A wide range of conduct can constitute a
breach of fiduciary duty or violate other legal standards, such as
unfair competition. Breach of fiduciary duty can lead to disciplinary action or civil liability. For example, in In re Smith,[41] during
the two and one-half months prior to his departure from his firm
Smith met secretly with 31 clients and had them sign individual
retainer agreements. He did not open firm files for these cases
while he was planning his departure. When he left the firm, he
took with him the information relating to these cases as well as the
files in other cases that he was handling. Smith immediately wrote
to these clients informing them that they should contact his new
office regarding their cases. The Oregon Supreme Court imposed
a four-month suspension on the attorney for misconduct. The
court pointed out that his conduct involved potential harm to cli-

37. Id. at 5.
38. Id. at 6.
39. Id.
40. See Robert W. Hillman, Loyalty in the Firm: A Statement of General
Principles on the Duties of Partners Withdrawing from Law Firms, 55 Wash. &
Lee L. Rev. 997 (1998).
41. 843 P.2d 449 (Or. 1992) (en banc).

ents because of his failure to open files. In addition, the court found that the attorney's conduct violated his fiduciary duties to his firm:

> Although there is no explicit rule requiring lawyers to be candid and fair with their partners or employers, such an obligation is implicit in the prohibition of DR 1-102(A)(3) [see Model Rule 8.4(c)] against dishonesty, fraud, deceit, or misrepresentation. Moreover, such conduct is a violation of the duty of loyalty owed by a lawyer to his or her firm based on their contractual or agency relationship.[42]

Departing lawyers who violate fiduciary obligations to their former firms can also be subject to civil liability to their firms.[43] In the leading case of Meehan v. Shaughnessy[44] the Supreme Judicial Court of Massachusetts held that departing partners owed fiduciary obligations to their remaining partners and that they could be held civilly liable for breach of those obligations. The court decided that the withdrawing partners did not breach their fiduciary obligations by making "logistical arrangements" (executing a lease, preparing a list of clients they expected to retain after their departure, and arranging for financing based on their expected clientele) for their new firm because fiduciaries may "plan to compete with the entity to which they owe allegiance," provided that they do not otherwise breach their fiduciary obligations.[45] The court found, however, that the withdrawing partners did breach their fiduciary duties by seeking and obtaining prior to their departure secret consents from clients to retain their services after they left the firm.[46] The court remanded for a determination of

---

42. Id. at 452. See also In re Cupples, 952 S.W.2d 226 (Mo. 1997) (en banc) (attorney secreted client files prior to his withdrawal, removed files without appropriate consent from clients, and concealed from clients change in nature of representation).

43. Conversely, law firms can also be liable to partners for wrongful expulsion. See, e.g., Cadwalader, Wickersham & Taft v. Beasley, 728 So. 2d 253 (Fla. Dist. Ct. App. 1998).

44. 535 N.E.2d 1255 (Mass. 1989).

45. Id. at 1264.

46. Id. See Dowd & Dowd, Ltd. v. Gleason, 693 N.E.2d 358 (Ill. 1998) (firm states causes of action against departing lawyers for breach of fiduciary duty, tortious interference with prospective economic advantage, and civil conspiracy for allegedly soliciting clients prior to departure); Graubard Mollen Dannett &

whether there was a causal connection between the departing lawyers' breach of fiduciary duty and damage to the partnership. It
imposed the burden of proving lack of causation on the departing
lawyers because of their breach of duty.[47]

Second, for those clients who decide to retain the services of
the departing lawyer rather than the old firm, how are the fees
from these cases allocated between the departing lawyer and her
old firm? Traditionally, the withdrawal of a partner constituted a
dissolution of the partnership.[48] Further, during the period in
which a partnership's affairs were being wound up following a
partner's withdrawal, the *no-additional-compensation rule* applied.
This rule of partnership law meant that withdrawing partners were
not entitled to additional compensation for services rendered in
winding up partnership business.[49] Thus, under the no-additional-
compensation rule, if a lawyer leaves a firm and a client that the
lawyer was representing while a member of the firm elects to have
the lawyer complete the client's case, the lawyer is *not* entitled to
the full fee from that matter. Under partnership law, the fee would
be paid to the old firm, and the lawyer would receive the lawyer's
share pursuant to the partnership agreement or pro rata based on

Horowitz v. Moskovitz, 653 N.E.2d 1179 (N.Y. 1995) (summary judgment denied in breach of fiduciary duty claim against departing lawyer who sought and
received assurances from long-term client that client would continue to retain
lawyer after lawyer left firm; court outlines poles of permitted and improper conduct).

47. 535 N.E.2d at 1267.

48. Under the Uniform Partnership Act, the withdrawal of a partner
amounts to a dissolution of the partnership. Unif. Partnership Act §29, 6 U.L.A.
752 (1995). The partnership continues, however, during the period necessary to
wind up partnership business. Id. §30. The Revised Uniform Partnership Act
makes some fundamental changes in partnership law, one of which is that the
"dissociation" of a partner does not necessarily result in the dissolution of a
partnership. Unif. Partnership Act §801 and comment 1 (1997), 6 U.L.A. 97
(Supp. 1999). The Revised Uniform Partnership Act has been modified on a
number of occasions. See 6 U.L.A. 2 (Supp. 1999).

49. Unif. Partnership Act §18(f), 6 U.L.A. 526 (1995); Jewel v. Boxer,
203 Cal. Rptr. 13 (Ct. App. 1984) (postdissolution fees should be allocated to
partners based on their respective partnership interests without any additional
compensation for work done to complete cases); Fox v. Abrams, 210 Cal. Rptr.
260 (Ct. App. 1985) (rule of Jewel v. Boxer applies to professional corporations).
The Revised Uniform Partnership Act reverses this rule, §401(h), 6 U.L.A. 70
(Supp. 1999).

the lawyer's interest in the partnership in the absence of an agreement.[50] Note that departing partners also receive benefits from the no-additional-compensation rule because they are paid their partnership percentage in any cases that remain with the firm, even though they will not be performing any services on those cases.

Lawyers practicing in partnerships, LLCs, or LLPs are free to modify the no-additional-compensation rule by agreement.[51] Provided the agreement is reasonable and does not amount to an indirect attempt to restrict the departing lawyer's ability to practice law, the agreement should be enforceable.[52] In the absence of an agreement, a court has a choice on how to allocate fees between the departing lawyer and the old firm. The court could apply the no-additional-compensation rule or it could allocate the fees between the departing lawyer and the old firm on a quantum meruit basis.[53]

Third, to what extent may firms impose restrictions on the practice of law by departing lawyers? In the business world, covenants not to compete are quite common and are legally enforceable provided the covenant protects a legitimate interest of the covenantee and provided the covenant is reasonable in its restrictions. Thus, a reasonable covenant by a seller of a business not to compete with the purchaser, or by an employee not to compete with his employer, is valid.[54]

---

50. For a case that follows a different approach, awarding the firm from which the lawyers departed compensation on a quantum meruit basis, see In re L-Tryptophan Cases, 518 N.W.2d 616 (Minn. Ct. App. 1994).

51. Unif. Partnership Act §18, 6 U.L.A. 526 (1995) (rules are subject to any agreement between parties); Unif. Partnership Act §103 (1997), 6 U.L.A. 40 (Supp. 1999). See Kelly v. Smith, 611 N.E.2d 118 (Ind. 1993) (recognizing no-additional-compensation rule but interpreting partnership agreement to provide that firm would be paid on quantum meruit basis for work done on cases where clients elected to retain departing lawyer).

52. See Barna, Guzy & Steffen, Ltd. v. Beens, 541 N.W.2d 354 (Minn. Ct. App. 1995), *review denied* (1996) (shareholder agreement requiring departing lawyer to turn over 50 percent of contingent fees received upheld). See also Miller v. Jacobs & Goodman, P.A., 699 So. 2d 729 (Fla. Dist. Ct. App. 1997), *review denied*, 717 So. 2d 533 (Fla. 1998) (employment agreement with associates that required them to pay 75 percent of fees that they receive after their departure upheld as valid).

53. See Hurwitz v. Padden, 581 N.W.2d 359 (Minn. Ct. App. 1998) (in absence of agreement, no-additional-compensation rule should be applied to LLC).

54. See Restatement (Second) of Contracts §188 (1979).

By contrast to the "rule of reason" that governs covenants in
general, covenants by lawyers not to compete are per se invalid.
See Model Rule 5.6(a) and DR 2-108(A). The rationale for this
prohibition rests on the interests of clients. The client-lawyer relationship is personal and fiduciary in character. It is against public
policy to deprive a client of the right to employ the lawyer of the
client's choosing.[55] The rule also protects young lawyers from bargaining away their future employment prospects.[56]

The rule applies not only to direct restrictions on a lawyer's
right to practice law but also to indirect restrictions as well. Partnership agreements typically provide for payments to a departing
partner of that partner's share of the capital of the partnership and
of any earned but uncollected fees. If a partnership agreement
provides that a departing lawyer forfeits that partner's share of
termination payments when the partner continues practice in competition with the partner's former firm, courts are likely to find
such a provision invalid as an indirect restriction on the departing
lawyer's right to practice law. In Cohen v. Lord, Day & Lord[57] the
New York Court of Appeals ruled that a partnership agreement
that conditioned payment of a departing partner's share of earned
but uncollected revenues on noncompetition by the departing
partner was unenforceable because of the ethical prohibition on
restriction of practice by lawyers.[58] Other courts have agreed with
this approach.[59]

<hr />

55. See Dwyer v. Jung, 336 A.2d 498, (N.J. Super. Ct. Ch. Div.) *aff'd*,
348 A.2d 208 (N.J. Super. Ct. App. Div. 1975). Note that in contrast to covenants not to compete between lawyers, covenants not to compete by other professionals are enforceable provided that they satisfy the reasonableness
requirement. See, e.g., Karlin v. Weinberg, 390 A.2d 1161 (N.J. 1978).
56. See 2 Hazard & Hodes, The Law of Lawyering §5.6:201, at 824.
57. 550 N.E.2d 410 (N.Y. 1989).
58. See also Denburg v. Parker Chapin Flattau & Klimpl, 624 N.E.2d 995
(N.Y. 1993) (financial disincentives objectionable on public policy grounds because they interfere with client's choice of counsel). But see Hackett v. Milbank,
Tweed, Hadley & McCloy, 654 N.E.2d 95 (N.Y. 1995) (arbitrator's determination that clause requiring reduction of departing partner's payments to extent
compensation from other sources exceeds $100,000 does not violate public policy
because clause was "competition neutral").
59. See Jacob v. Norris, McLaughlin & Marcus, Inc., 607 A.2d 142 (N.J.
1992) (service termination agreement providing that departing partners could
receive compensation only if they did not render services to clients of firm during
one year following termination was unenforceable); Spiegel v. Thomas, Mann &

In cases like *Cohen* the departing lawyers forfeited all payments from their former firms if they continued to practice law. Less restrictive provisions may be upheld. For example, clauses may be valid if they reasonably reduce the amount that a departing lawyer receives to reflect the financial impact on the firm of the lawyer's departure, or if they attempt to measure compensation due the firm for its quantum meruit contribution to cases in which clients elect to retain the departing lawyer rather than continue to have the firm represent them.[60]

In Howard v. Babcock[61] the California Supreme Court rejected decisions from other states and held that a contractual provision imposing a reasonable cost on departing partners to compensate their former firm for their loss was enforceable. The court noted the change in economic climate in which law firms now operate. It expressed the view that such provisions could benefit clients by reducing the "culture of mistrust" among partners that can damage law firm stability.[62]

Model Rule 5.6 does contain an exception to the general prohibition against covenants not to compete among lawyers: Covenants not to compete are permissible when the lawyer is receiving "benefits upon retirement."[63] In that case, the public interest in unfettered selection of counsel is not involved since the lawyer has agreed to retire to receive the benefits.[64] Comment 3 to Rule 5.6 states that the prohibition against covenants not to compete does

---

Smith, P.C., 811 S.W.2d 528 (Tenn. 1991) (agreement that denied deferred compensation to withdrawing stockholder who continued to practice law was void as against public policy set forth in rules governing attorney ethics).

60. See Barna, Guzy & Steffen, Ltd. v. Beens, 541 N.W.2d 354 (Minn. Ct. App. 1995), *review denied* (1996) (shareholder agreement that required departing lawyer to turn over 50 percent of contingent fees received upheld; since lawyer would have received less than 50 percent of fee if lawyer remained with firm, agreement does not operate as financial restriction on practice). See generally Laws. Man. on Prof. Conduct (ABA/BNA), 10 Current Rep. 392 (1994).

61. 863 P.2d 150 (Cal. 1993).

62. Id. at 159.

63. On the meaning of the exception, see Neuman v. Akman, 715 A.2d 127 (D.C. 1998).

64. See Miller v. Foulston, Siefkin, Powers & Eberhardt, 790 P.2d 404 (Kan. 1990) (provision that prevented departing partner who practiced law from receiving retirement benefits was enforceable because of specific exception for retirement benefits found in ethics rule).

not apply to the sale of a practice under Rule 1.17. One of the conditions of Rule 1.17 is that the selling lawyer must cease to engage in the practice of law (either in the geographical area or in the jurisdiction, as elected by the jurisdiction). See Model Rule 1.17(a).

3.   Sale of a Law Practice

Traditionally, the profession has viewed the sale of "good will" of a law practice as unethical. ("Good will" refers to the value of the list of clients as opposed to the tangible assets of the practice.) In Formal Opinion 266 (1945), the ABA Committee on Professional Ethics and Grievances dealt with the issue as follows:

> A law firm has asked the opinion of the committee as to the ethical propriety of the purchase from the heirs or personal representatives of a deceased lawyer who had no partner, of his good will and practice, whether by payment of a lump sum or by an agreement to pay a stated percentage of the future receipts, gross or net, from his clients. . . .
>
> The good will of the practice of a lawyer is not, however, of itself an asset, which either he or his estate can sell. As said by the Committee on Professional Ethics of the New York County Lawyers' Association in its Opinion 109 (October 6, 1943):
>
> > Clients are not merchandise. Lawyers are not tradesmen. They have nothing to sell but personal service. An attempt, therefore, to barter in clients, would appear to be inconsistent with the best concepts of our professional status.

Aside from professionalism concerns, sale of good will of a practice raises various ethical problems. Professor Leslie Minkus summarizes these as follows:

> (1) To turn over the selling lawyer's files to the purchasing lawyer would, in virtually all cases, constitute a violation of the selling lawyer's duty of confidentiality.
>
> (2) To the extent that the purchase price is a function of fees earned by the purchasing lawyer, the agreement violates the proscription of sharing fees without sharing the effort and/or responsibility.
>
> (3) To the extent that some or all of the purchase price is

paid, not to the selling lawyer, but to his estate, the
agreement violates the proscription against sharing of
fees with laypersons.

(4)   The fact that the value of the lawyer's practice will depend largely on the number of clients who follow his
recommendation and retain the purchasing lawyer puts
the selling lawyer in a position of direct conflict with his
clients.

(5)   The sale would almost inevitably involve the recommendation of employment of the purchaser in violation of
the prohibition against the payment of money by a lawyer for the recommendation of him by another. Such
recommendation might also be considered improper solicitation.

(6)   Because most sales will include a covenant not to compete with the purchasing lawyer, the agreement arguably
violates the prohibition against such covenants except as
a condition to payment of retirement benefits by a lawyer's former firm.[65]

Some commentators argued, however, that the ethical concerns outlined above did not justify a total ban on the sale of the
good will of law practices.[66] In addition, proponents of allowing
sales of law practices made two arguments in favor of their position. First, they made a "consumer protection" case for permitting
sales of practices. By allowing such sales, sole practitioners would
have a financial incentive to provide for the orderly transition of
their cases in the event of their illness, retirement, or death. The
present prohibition on sales removes that incentive. Second, proponents made a fairness case for allowing sales. They argued that
the rules of ethics discriminated in favor of partners over sole practitioners.[67] Under the Code of Professional Responsibility and the

65. Leslie A. Minkus, The Sale of a Law Practice: Toward a Professionally
Responsible Approach, 12 Golden Gate U. L. Rev. 353, 356-357 (1982).

66. See Stephen E. Kalish, The Sale of a Law Practice: The Model Rules
of Professional Conduct Point in a New Direction, 39 U. Miami L. Rev. 471
(1985); Minkus, The Sale of a Law Practice, 12 Golden Gate U. L. Rev. at 357-
377.

67. But see James K. Sterrett II, The Sale of a Law Practice, 121 U. Pa.
L. Rev. 306 (1972) (arguing that different treatment for sole practitioners, who
were prohibited from selling their practices, and partners, who were permitted to
receive retirement payments based on their partnership interests, was justified
because the quality of legal service that clients may expect to receive from partners

original Model Rules of Professional Conduct, partners and their beneficiaries could receive retirement payments that included compensation for the good will value of their partnerships interests. See DR 2-107(B), 3-102(A), and Model Rule 5.4(a). Sole practitioners, however, could not capitalize on their good will by selling their interests.[68]

Note, however, that the traditional prohibition on the sale of a law practice did not actually prevent many sole practitioners from receiving compensation for their good will. Sole practitioners could ethically provide for the orderly transition of their practices after their retirement or death by entering into a partnership agreement in which the new partner could continue the practice while paying death or retirement benefits to the former partner.

In 1989 the California Supreme Court amended its Rules of Professional Conduct to allow lawyers to sell their practices, including good will, provided certain conditions for the protection of clients were met.[69] Following the lead of the California Supreme Court, the ABA amended the Model Rules of Professional Conduct at its February 1990 meeting to include Model Rule 1.17, permitting the sale of law practices.[70]

A number of states have adopted rules like ABA Model Rule 1.17 providing for sale of law practices.[71] In states that have not adopted such a rule, sale of the good will of a law practice is still unethical. Further, any resulting contract may be unenforceable because it violates public policy. For example, in O'Hara v. Ahlgren, Blumenfeld & Kempster[72] the Illinois Supreme Court held that the widow of a deceased attorney could not enforce a contract for the sale of her husband's law practice because the agreement violated the ethical prohibition on fee splitting.

---

is higher than the quality that they can expect to receive from purchasers of practices). See also ABA Comm. on Prof. Ethics and Grievances, Formal Op. 266 (1945) (permissible to make arrangements for handling cases in event of emergency).

68. See generally Laurel S. Terry, Law Firms for Sale . . . The Rules Are Changing, 12 Pa. Law. 7 (June 1990) (on Westlaw).

69. Cal. R. Prof. Conduct 2-300.

70. For a criticism of various aspects of Model Rule 1.17, see Scott M. Schoenwald, Model Rule 1.17 and the Ethical Sale of Law Practices: A Critical Analysis, 7 Geo. J. Legal Ethics 395 (1993).

71. See, e.g. N.Y. Code Prof. Resp. DR 2-111.

72. 537 N.E.2d 730 (Ill. 1989).

C. Ancillary Businesses and Multidisciplinary Practice

1. Ancillary Businesses

Rules of ethics have traditionally prevented lawyers from entering into partnerships (or corporations) with nonlawyers, including other professionals, when the activities of the entity will involve the practice of law. Canon 33 of ABA's 1908 Canons of Ethics provided as follows: "Partnerships between lawyers and members of other professions or nonprofessional persons should not be formed or permitted where any part of the partnership's employment consists of the practice of law." This prohibition was carried forward in DR 3-103(A) (partnerships) and DR 5-107(C) (corporations or associations) of the Code of Professional Responsibility and in Model Rules 5.4(b), (d). This restriction rested on two rationales: prevention of interference by nonlawyers with lawyers' independent professional judgment on behalf of their clients and concern about the unauthorized practice of law. See EC 3-8, EC 5-24, and Model Rule 5.4(b), cmt.[73]

In the 1980s some prominent law firms began offering to their clients a variety of nonlegal services. A 1991 survey[74] identified the following "ancillary business" activities by law firms:

15 engaged in lobbying, legislative services, or government relations

13 tax, investment, and financial consulting

13 international trade

4 environmental consulting

4 real estate brokerage and development

4 labor relations

3 economic research

3 public affairs

2 media relations

73. See Wolfram, Modern Legal Ethics §16.2.1 at 879.

74. Stephanie B. Goldberg, More Than the Law: Ancillary Business Growth Continues, 78-Mar A.B.A. J. 54 (1992) (citing a study done by Phyllis W. Haserot).

Some law firms provided these services directly by lawyers or non-lawyer employees of the firm. For example, many law firms have lawyers who engage in lobbying or other legislative activities. More typically, however, a firm creates a corporate or partnership subsidiary or affiliate to furnish ancillary services. The subsidiary form was particularly appealing when other professionals would be providing the ancillary services. Such professionals often demanded an ownership interest in any ventures in which they engaged. The rules of ethics, however, prohibited nonlawyers from owning an interest in a partnership or professional corporation that involved the practice of law. Thus, nonlawyer professionals could not own an interest in the law firm itself. The subsidiary form avoided this ethical problem because the subsidiary engaged only in nonlegal services.

Spurred by concerns expressed by Chief Justice Warren Burger about trends in the profession, in 1984 the ABA created a Commission on Professionalism (the Stanley Commission). The commission issued a report in 1986 finding the development of ancillary businesses by law firms "disturbing" and calling for further study of the trend.[75] Over the next eight years the ABA debated and oscillated on the regulation of ancillary business services by law firms. In 1991 the ABA House of Delegates in a narrow vote of 197 to 186 adopted a proposal from the ABA Section of Litigation's Task Force on Ancillary Business Activities. The proposal would have eliminated many of the nonlegal service activities that law firms had developed during the 1980s, even ones conducted through subsidiaries or affiliates, because of professionalism concerns.[76] In 1992 and then in 1994, the House of Delegates reversed itself and adopted current Rule 5.7, which allows ancillary business activities subject to certain requirements.[77]

75. ABA Commission on Professionalism, ". . . In the Spirit of Public Service": A Blueprint for the Rekindling of Lawyer Professionalism, 112 F.R.D. 243, 281 (1986).

76. See Dennis J. Block et al., Model Rule of Professional Conduct 5.7: Its Origin and Interpretation, 5 Geo. J. Legal Ethics 739, 764-777, 816 (1992) (Block was chair of the Litigation Section's task force).

77. Laws. Man. on Prof. Conduct (ABA/BNA), 10 Current Rep. 13 (1994). For a review and criticism of the ABA's original decision to prohibit ancillary business activities, see Ted Schneyer, Policymaking and the Perils of Professionalism: The ABA's Ancillary Business Debate as a Case Study, 35 Ariz. L. Rev. 363 (1993). Professor Gary Munneke offers a different perspective on

State supreme courts are, of course, free to adopt their own rules on the issue of ancillary businesses. (If a court does nothing, ancillary business activities would be largely unregulated when conducted through subsidiaries or affiliates. The Rules of Professional Conduct prohibit partnerships and fee splitting involving the practice of law with nonlawyers, but these have little impact on ancillary business activities conducted through related entities.)

2. Multidisciplinary Practice

Multidisciplinary practice (MDP) refers to a partnership, corporation, or other legal entity that includes lawyers and has as one of its purposes the providing of legal services to clients other than the MDP itself.[78] While lawyers cannot practice in MDPs in the United States under current rules of ethics, the Big Five accounting firms and other entities have formed MDPs in other countries where the rules are not as strict or as strictly enforced.[79]

In 1998 the president of the ABA created the Commission on Multidisciplinary Practice to make recommendations to the ABA on whether to relax the rules of professional conduct dealing with practice and fee splitting with nonlawyers so as to permit MDPs to develop in the United States. In 1999 the commission issued its report in which it recommended "a limited relaxation of the prohibitions against sharing legal fees and forming a partnership or other association with a nonlawyer when one of the activities is the practice of law."[80] Central to its recommendations was a proposed rule of professional conduct in which an MDP would be required to provide assurances that it would respect the pro-

---

the issue. He argues that rules of ethics prohibiting law firm diversification impede the ability of lawyers to compete in the market for professional services. Professor Munneke also claims that the rules may not withstand antitrust and First Amendment scrutiny. See Gary A. Munneke, Dances with Nonlawyers: A New Perspective on Law Firm Diversification, 61 Fordham L. Rev. 559 (1992). For a contrary view on the constitutionality of restrictions on ancillary business activities, see Block et al., Model Rule of Professional Conduct 5.7, 5 Geo. J. Legal Ethics at 811-814.

78. ABA Commn. on Multidisciplinary Practice, Report to House of Delegates app. A (1999).

79. Id. app. C, notes 8, 9.

80. Id. app. C.

fessional obligations of lawyers. (The commission's proposed rule is quoted below in Problem 7-3.) At its August 1999 meeting, the ABA House of Delegates voted not to allow lawyers to practice and share fees with other professionals "unless and until additional study demonstrates that such changes will further the public interest without sacrificing or compromising lawyer independence and the legal profession's tradition of loyalty to clients."[81] Prior to the ABA's action, the New York State Bar Association voted against allowing lawyers to form partnerships with accountants and other professionals without proof that such arrangements would not undermine the delivery of legal services to the public. The New York bar has, however, formed a special committee for further study of the issue.[82] Despite the actions of the ABA and the New York bar, the issue of MDPs is likely to remain a major subject of debate within the profession for several years.

Problem 7-3

Practicing with Nonlawyers

You are a member of the professional responsibility committee of your state bar association. Your committee has been asked to investigate and to make recommendations to the house of delegates of the state bar regarding modification of the rules of professional conduct that restrict lawyers from practicing law and dividing fees with nonlawyers, such as accountants, investment advisors, and engineers, in professional organizations. Your committee has before it two rules: District of Columbia Rule 5.4 and Rule 5.8 proposed by the ABA Commission on Multidisciplinary Practice:

Rule 5.4 Professional Independence of a Lawyer

(a) A lawyer or law firm shall not share legal fees with a nonlawyer, except that: . . .

---

81. 85-Sept A.B.A. J. 23 (1999).
82. See N.Y. State Bar Assn. News Rel., Aug. 2, 1999.

(4) Sharing of fees is permitted in a partnership or other form of organization which meets the requirements of paragraph (b).

(b) A lawyer may practice law in a partnership or other form of organization in which a financial interest is held or managerial authority is exercised by an individual nonlawyer who performs professional services which assist the organization in providing legal services to clients, but only if:

(1) The partnership or organization has as its sole purpose providing legal services to clients;

(2) All persons having such managerial authority or holding a financial interest undertake to abide by these Rules of Professional Conduct;

(3) The lawyers who have a financial interest or managerial authority in the partnership or organization undertake to be responsible for the nonlawyer participants to the same extent as if nonlawyer participants were lawyers under Rule 5.1;

(4) The foregoing conditions are set forth in writing.

ABA Proposed Rule 5.8   Responsibilities of a Lawyer in a Multidisciplinary Practice Firm

(a) A lawyer shall not share legal fees with a nonlawyer or form a partnership or other entity with a nonlawyer if any of the activities of the partnership or other entity consist of the practice of law except that a lawyer in an MDP controlled by lawyers may do so, subject to the present provisions limiting the holding of equity investments in any entity or organization providing legal services. A lawyer in an MDP not controlled by lawyers may do so, subject to the conditions set forth in paragraphs (c)(1)-(5), and subject to the present provisions limiting the holding of equity investments in any entity or organization providing legal services.

(b) A lawyer in an MDP remains subject to all the Model Rules of Professional Conduct, unless this Rule provides otherwise.

(c) A lawyer may practice in an MDP in which lawyers do not own a controlling interest only if the MDP provides the highest court with the authority to regulate the legal profession in each jurisdiction in which the MDP is engaged in the delivery of legal services written undertakings signed by the chief executive officer (or similar official) and the board of directors (or similar body) that:

(1) it will not directly or indirectly interfere with a lawyer's exercise of independent professional judgment on behalf of a client;

(2) it will establish, maintain and enforce procedures designed to protect a lawyer's exercise of independent professional judgment on behalf of a client from interference by the MDP, any member of the MDP, or any person or entity associated with the MDP;

(3) it will establish, maintain and enforce procedures to protect a lawyer's professional obligation to segregate client funds;

(4) its members will abide by the rules of professional conduct when they are engaged in the delivery of legal services to a client of the MDP;

(5) it will respect the unique role of the lawyer in society as an officer of the legal system, a representative of clients and a public citizen having special responsibility for the administration of justice. This statement should acknowledge that lawyers in an MDP have the same special obligation to render voluntary *pro bono publico* legal service as lawyers practicing solo or in law firms;

(6) it will annually review the procedures established in subsection (2) and amend them as needed to ensure their effectiveness; and annually certify its compliance with subsections (1)-(6) and provide a copy of the certification to each lawyer in the MDP;

(7) it will annually file a signed and verified copy of the certificate described in subsection (6) with the highest court with the authority to regulate the legal profession in each jurisdiction in which the MDP is engaged in the delivery of legal services, along with information identifying each lawyer who has been a member of the MDP during the reporting period, the jurisdiction in which the principal office of each such lawyer is located, and the jurisdiction(s) in which those lawyers are licensed to practice law;

(8) it will permit the highest court with the authority to regulate the professional conduct of lawyers

in each jurisdiction in which the MDP is engaged in the delivery of legal services to review and conduct an administrative audit of the MDP, as each such authority deems appropriate, to determine and assure compliance with subsections (1)-(7); and

(9) it will bear the cost of the administrative audit of MDPs described in subparagraph (8) through the payment of a reasonable annual certification fee.

(d) An MDP that fails to comply with its written undertaking shall be subject to withdrawal of its permission to deliver legal services or to other appropriate remedial measures ordered by the court.

In preparation for the next committee meeting, you are considering the following questions: What issues do these proposed rules raise? What are the differences in approach between these rules? Do you favor either or some other proposal? Why?

D.   Quality of Life in Law Firms

In a 1999 article, Professor Patrick Schiltz presented a disturbing portrait of the quality of life in American law firms.[83] Lawyers suffer from depression, anxiety, alcoholism, drug abuse, divorce, and suicide at rates significantly greater than the population as a whole.[84] Job dissatisfaction among lawyers is substantial and growing worse.[85] A RAND study of California lawyers found that only half of the members of the bar would become lawyers if they had to do it over again.[86] ABA surveys of lawyers conducted in 1984 and 1990 showed significant declines in job satisfaction:

83. Patrick J. Schiltz, On Being a Happy, Healthy, and Ethical Member of an Unhappy, Unhealthy, and Unethical Profession, 52 Vand. L. Rev. 871 (1999).

84. Id. at 874-881.

85. Id. at 881 n. 68. For a study showing different results, at least among Chicago lawyers, see John P. Heinz et al., Lawyers and Their Discontents: Findings from a Survey of the Chicago Bar, 74 Ind. L.J. 735 (1999).

86. 52 Vand. L. Rev. at 881 n. 69.

In the past six years, the extent of lawyer dissatisfaction has increased throughout the profession. It is now reported in significant numbers by lawyers in all positions — partners as well as junior associates. It is now present in significant numbers in firms of all sizes, not just the largest and the smallest firms.[87]

Job dissatisfaction varies depending on practice setting and is particularly acute in large firms.[88]

Professor Schiltz argues that overwork is the major cause of these problems. Various studies show substantial increases in the number of billable hours expected of attorneys. Thirty years ago associates typically billed 1,400 to 1,600 hours per year. In the mid-1980s, the norm for New York firms had increased to 1,800 hours per year. Today, most associates are expected to bill a minimum of 2,000 hours per year.[89] Professor Schiltz attributes the increase in the amount of work that lawyers do to the pervasive influence of money on the practice of law. Clients, senior partners, junior partners, and senior associates all have financial interests in seeing that those below them work "inhumane hours, year after year."[90]

The impact of excessive work loads has a disproportionately negative impact on women. At a time in their lives when many women wish to consider starting a family, they are also faced with career demands of increasingly high levels of work and responsibility.[91]

African-Americans, Latinos, gays and lesbians continue to face discrimination.[92] While the ABA has not adopted an antidiscrimination rule, a number of states have done so. For example, Rule 2-400 of the California Rules of Professional Conduct provides that

87. Id at 883-884, quoting ABA, Young Lawyers Div., The State of the Legal Profession 1990 at 81 (1991).
88. 52 Vand. L. Rev. at 886.
89. Id. at 891.
90. Id. at 902. For criticism of Schiltz's views, see Kathleen E. Hull, Cross-Examining the Myth of Lawyers' Misery, 52 Vand. L. Rev. 971 (1999); Mary A. McLaughlin, Beyond the Caricature: The Benefits and Challenges of Large-Firm Practice, 52 Vand. L. Rev. 1003 (1999).
91. 52 Vand. L. Rev. 915-916, n. 267.
92. David B. Wilkins & G. Mitu Gulati, Why Are There So Few Black Lawyers in Corporate Law Firms? An Institutional Analysis, 84 Cal. L. Rev. 493 (1996).

In the management or operation of a law practice, a member shall not unlawfully discriminate or knowingly permit unlawful discrimination on the basis of race, national origin, sex, sexual orientation, religion, age or disability in:

>   (1) hiring, promoting, discharging or otherwise determining the conditions of employment of any person; or
>   (2) accepting or terminating representation of any client.

DR 1-102(A)(6) of the New York Code of Professional Responsibility is similar.[93]

Note that attorneys are entitled to legal protection against some forms of discrimination in employment. In Hishon v. King & Spalding[94] the Supreme Court held that a female associate who had been passed over for partnership stated a cause of action for sex discrimination against her firm under Title VII of the Civil Rights Act of 1964.

--- **Problem 7-4** ---

Discrimination and Related Issues

Your instructor will show a videotape or lead a panel discussion of a group of lawyers who practice in various types of law firms. The tape or the panel will focus on issues involving the quality of life in firms. Prepare a list of questions that you have about the quality of life in law firms.

---

93. For discussions of the issue of discrimination in the profession, see Susan D. Gilbert & Michael P. Allen, Overcoming Discrimination in the Legal Profession: Should the Model Rules be Changed? 6 Geo. J. Legal Ethics 933 (1993) (proposing rule that would prohibit discrimination by lawyers in employment practices and in course of representation); Ronald D. Rotunda, Racist Speech and Lawyer Discipline, 6 Prof. Law. 1 (Feb. 1995) (arguing against disciplinary rules prohibiting racist speech on First Amendment grounds). See generally Brenda J. Quick, Ethical Rules Prohibiting Discrimination by Lawyers: The Legal Profession's Response to Discrimination on the Rise, 7 Notre Dame J.L. Ethics & Pub. Poly. 5 (1993).

94.   467 U.S. 69 (1984).

Table of Cases

Table of Model Rules and Other Standards

OTHER STANDARDS OF CONDUCT

ABA, Criminal Justice Mental Health Standards

ABA, Lawyer's Creed of Professionalism

ABA, Model Rules for Lawyer Disciplinary Enforcement

[1] Numbering based on proposed drafts. For conversion table to final published version of the Restatement, see page xxxvii.

Table of Articles, Books and Reports[1]

---

[1] For additional entries, see the Bibliography at end of Chapter 1.

Index